P9-ECZ-716

Jesus: One and Many

The
Christological Concept
of
New Testament Authors

Jesus: One and Many

The Christological Concept of New Testament Authors

by

Earl Richard

 Michael Glazier
Wilmington, Delaware

About the Author

Earl Richard pursued his graduate studies at the University of Ottawa in Canada, John Hopkins University, Baltimore, and The Catholic University, Washington. Currently, he is on the faculty of Loyola University, New Orleans, and is director of the graduate program. Among his many publications is *Acts 6:1-8:4: The Author's Method of Composition* (Scholars Press).

First published in 1988 by Michael Glazier, Inc.,
1935 West Fourth Street, Wilmington, Delaware 19805.

Library of Congress Catalog Card Number: 87-82346
International Standard Book Number: 0-89453-641-9

Typography by Angela Meades.

Printed in the United States of America.   EB

For the Richard and Boudreaux,
Miller and Dugas families
of Acadiana
and
in memory of
Donna, Dixie, and Rody

Contents

7

PART II: JESUS ACCORDING TO MARK, MATTHEW, LUKE,
AND THE JOHANNINE WRITINGS

Prologue and Epilogue

Following the advice of the famous 17th-century French thinker and writer Blaise Pascal that an introduction should be composed after both analysis and conclusions have been formalized, we have decided to address the readers of this work with book in hand and conclusions drawn before attempting to act as their guide to the long series of portraits of Jesus inherited from the early church. The work has been in progress for sometime and represents a long journey or a series of journeys through the New Testament and its cast of actors, writers, and readers. What the reader of this volume then will find is the result of several years of reading, dialogue, and confrontation both with the ancient texts of the New Testament and with a variety of biblical students in classroom, seminar, and pastoral situations.

The person of Jesus, the focus of Christian thought and devotion, provides the dynamism of this long search. Thus, the project begins with the realization that there was one Jesus but many perceptions of him. The New Tesament in the variety of literary compositions (gospels, historical narrative, letters, theological tracts, and apocalypse) presents the Lord of the early Christians' faith and praxis not the Jesus of history sought by some contemporary scholars. Each early strand of the Jesus tradition as well as each NT community and writer had their peculiar portrait of the founder. Jesus the Nazarene is the foundation of or basis for these various portraits and stories. Jesus, his teaching, exemplary life, and salvific death and resurrection provide either the content of these new religious texts (as story) or their religious and behavioral motivation (as pastoral advice).

The reader is invited to take a journey through the New Testament and to join the original hearers and readers by listening to the authors and by participating in the initial dialogue which led them to compose these literary documents. Not only will the reader realize that the Christ was many things to many people but also that the very nature of language and culture requires the conclusion that christology is the result less of the retelling of a historical event (the one Jesus) than of the manifold claims

13

made on Jesus' behalf by generations of believers (the many images or portraits of the Lord of faith). The New Testament contains a multitude of mediated and complex images which grew out of or resulted from the early communities' life, teaching, and practice. There emerged after the death of Jesus living communities for which the teacher from Nazareth provided the key to God's plan and kingdom. These also developed out of a wide variety of groups with different ethnic, social, economic, geographical, and religious backgrounds. For these communities the prophet from Palestine provided the challenge and supplied a variety of visions either for a new world order or a transformation of the old. Jesus' teaching about God, the kingdom, and the human community, and the new movement's very claims about its master inspired a new literature which eventually was collected and endowed with canonical status as the movement sought to establish stable and uniform structures.

Even if, several centuries later, the movement's thinkers will focus more upon Jesus' identity and relationship to God the Father than upon his role as God's agent in history, the witness of the first Christian century is believed to be the normative, though polyvalent, expression of the meaning of the Christ-event. In the books of the New Testament the reader will find various perceptions, from the early enigmatic representations of Jesus returning as judge, Son, or Son of Man (1 Thess. 1:9-10; the Q-Source; Mark 8:38) to the refined theological expressions of Jesus' role in God's plan (e.g., those of Paul and the writer of Hebrews), and the even better known, detailed portraits offered by the gospel writers. In this volume I have taken seriously the literary character of these early Christian documents in order to discern each author's perception of who Jesus was, what he accomplished, and how he related both to the author and community of that specific text. I hope that the many portraits which emerge in the Christian anthology which is the New Testament will be a constant reminder that genuine faith and due consideration of language and culture point to the dialectic which did and still must exist between the one Jesus and the many perceptions his followers have or have had of him. If this volume has focused upon the latter, i.e., the many portraits rather than the historical Jesus, it is because it takes seriously what the NT writers themselves did, namely, accept the fact that the Christ figure is the basis of each particular perception of the Christian reality. Christology in a doctrinal and devotional sense, therefore, is the symbiotic or mutual relationship of the one and the many.

The intended readers of this study are either interested bible students who wish to advance beyond the rudimentary concerns of NT reading and interpretation or other bible teachers who are compelled daily to dialogue with student and text to discern the varity of NT perceptions of the man from Nazareth. The shape of this work has been determined and the method of analysis chosen with this readership in mind. In the first case, particular attention is given both in the beginning chapters and in the introduction to each NT work to the major concerns of biblical scholarship either as they pertain to the development of the Jesus movement and a particular author's or work's connection to that development or as they focus on the issues relating to a given NT book. The interested bible student, therefore, will find in each instance a fairly extensive introduction to each NT book and its particular problems. In the second case, the method of analysis has been to address the depth structure of each NT work to discern both its perception of Jesus and to appreciate how that image functions in the work's overall perspective. It is hoped that both theologian and bible teacher will find ideas for further dialogue.

While this book intends to serve as an introduction to the NT books, it does not raise all issues nor argue all points of view. Instead, it presents what its author considers to be the consensus on most issues and offers new proposals on others. Also, owing to the focus of the entire project, i.e., discerning in the NT anthology the many perceptions of Jesus the Christ, and taking the intended readership into consideration, footnotes have been kept to a minimum as has reference to non-English bibliography. The interested reader is supplied with "suggested readings" and scholarly resources for further consideration.

Finally, I must thank a number of students of the bible, whether colleagues, students at Loyola University, or various members of the New Orleans community, who, though they will remain unnamed, have participated with me in this long dialogue with the writers and audiences of the NT writings. A very special word of thanks to Professor Stephen Duffy, a colleague here at Loyola, for his perceptive contribution in the christology of the post-NT period (chapter 12). I also express my appreciation to Loyola's Dean of Arts and Sciences for financial assistance in attending to editorial matters. Lastly, gratitude is owed to Mary Ann, Daniel, and Michael.

Abbreviations

BJRL	Bulletin of the John Rylands University Library of Manchester
BTB	Biblical Theology Bulletin
CBQ	Catholic Biblical Quarterly
ETL	Ephemerides theologicae lovanienses
HeyJ	Heythrop Journal
HTR	Harvard Theological Review
IB	Interpreter's Bible
IDB	Interpreter's Dictionary of the Bible
IDBSup	Interpreter's Dictionary of the Bible, Supplementary Volume
Int	Interpretation
JBC	The Jerome Biblical Commentary
JBL	Journal of Biblical Literature
JJS	Journal of Jewish Studies
JSJ	Journal for the Study of Judaism in the Persian, Hellenistic and Roman Period
MQR	Michigan Quarterly Review
NovT	Novum Testamentum
NTS	New Testament Studies
PCB	Peake's Commentary on the Bible
PRS	Perspectives in Religious Studies
RB	Revue biblique
RSR	Review for Religious
RSV	Revised Standard Version
SE	Studia Evangelica
TD	Theology Digest
TDNT	Theological Dictionary of the New Testament
TS	Theological Studies
ZTK	Zeitschrift für Theologie und Kirche

Part I
Introduction

1

Jesus in the New Testament

The central figure of Christianity is a person named Jesus Christ, a man who lived centuries ago in Palestine and who, Christians insist, was God's Son. From the beginning, according to the sources, perceptions of him differed from community to community. Even within orthodox Christianity that perception has varied considerably from generation to generation. Furthermore, since the rise of critical scholarship during the last two and a half centuries, theories about him, images of him, and claims concerning him have proliferated. Now, nearly twenty centuries after the fact, the Christian believer must still read the New Testament to find out who Jesus of Nazareth was, what he was like, what he did and taught, and what happened to him.

Jesus of Nazareth

To the Christian, exposed annually to the liturgical cycle and its dramatic enactment of Jesus' life, it may come as a surprise that there is controversy concerning *what happened to Jesus*. Instructed about these matters as a child and having recited passages from the ancient creeds ("suffered under Pontius Pilate, was crucified, died and was buried"), the believer takes it for granted that the Jews, or, more specifically, the Jewish authorities, were responsible, with the assistance of the Roman governor, for the trial and death of Jesus

If it is an established fact that Jesus was executed during the procuratorship of Pilate (c. 25-35), the circumstances, motivation, and varying degrees of participation and responsibility of actors in the drama are unclear. Who condemned Jesus to death; was it Pilate or the Jewish authorities? During Roman rule did the religious leaders of Jerusalem or Sanhedrin have jurisdiction over cases involving capital punishment? Furthermore, what role did Pilate play in the whole affair? The relatively sympathetic portrait given of him in the gospels has always puzzled scholars, for Pilate did not have good press among ancient historians, particularly the Jewish writer Josephus, who is certainly not anti-Roman in his sympathies. Perhaps NT authors tipped the scale toward Rome at the expense of Jerusalem. Also one finds in individual gospels varying treatments of both Jewish and Roman authorities, whether in terms of content (episodes underscoring plot, complicity, or the reticence of different characters of the story) and of attitude (sympathy, antipathy, polemics, or patronage). Thus, at the very least, one is forced to distinguish between the attitudes and views of members of the early church and those manifested by Jesus himself, if one reads different gospel accounts with a degree of seriousness.[1]

Besides one might ask: why was he executed? Was it because of blasphemy (was this sufficient cause for capital punishment in Jewish law?), because of seditious royal, messianic claims (the gospels offer conflicting evidence), or because of some power play involving a miscarriage of justice (armed resistance, religio-political acts such as driving out of merchants in the temple area, or abrogation of due process by some of the actors involved)?[2] Should we accept these factors as the motivation for the trial, we would be forced to adjust our image of Jesus accordingly—a misunderstood, unlucky man or a mistaken dreamer—in any event one deserving not respect but sympathy or pity.

---

[1]See J.A. Fitzmyer, *A Christological Catechism: New Testament Answers* (NY: Paulist, 1982), for an easy-to-read and balanced treatment of such "historical issues" as "who was responsible for the death of Jesus?" (58-62), "do the gospel stories present an accurate factual account of the teaching and deeds of Jesus of Nazareth?" (7-10), "how are we to understand the reference to the brothers and sisters of Jesus in the New Testament?" (71-73), or "after the resurrection was Jesus proclaimed unambiguously from the start as Son of God, equal to the Father?" (89-91).

[2]Among the many works on this topic, one might consult E. Rivkin, *What Crucified Jesus? The Political Execution of a Charismatic* (Nashville: Abingdon, 1984) or the more technical *Jesus and the Politics of His Day*, eds, E. Bammel and C.F.D. Moule (London: Cambridge University, 1985) and *The Trial of Jesus: Cambridge Studies*, ed., E. Bammel (London: Cambridge University, 1970).

What happened to bring about his death? If we admit that the whole episode of Jesus of Nazareth was fully human in its dimensions then we are led to seek the cause for his death in the circumstances of first-century Palestine and in his life and teaching. To view his death as the mechanical working out of a divine plan is to belie the intrinsic human character of the drama. The ambiguity of the evidence leads modern scholars and believers to diverse interpretations of Jesus' life and therefore to a large variety of images of him. The understanding and focusing of these images of Jesus of Nazareth will occupy us throughout this volume.

Anyone who inquires in some detail concerning *what Jesus did and taught* is in for a surprise, for the matter is neither simple nor the solution ready at hand. The complexity of the issue is to a great extent due to the diversity of the sources. The hallmark of Jesus' teaching according to the Synoptics (Matthew, Mark, and Luke) is the parable and aphoristic saying;[3] however, the Gospel of John presents no parables and portrays Jesus as one who teaches in long, repetitious discourses.[4] Furthermore, Paul, the earliest and most prolific writer of the New Testament, betrays no knowledge of Jesus' parables and relatively little of his other teachings.[5]

What was the content of his teaching? If the central concern of his message was "the kingdom of God" why is this expression rarely found outside the Synoptics and hardly ever in the literature of the early Church? Did Jesus preach a future or present, a spiritual or social, a human or heavenly kingdom?[6] How much did his message differ from the best that Judaism had to offer? Did Jesus come to abolish, to fulfill, or to replace Judaism and its Torah? Did Jesus offer a new vision of the

---

[3]Consult Fitzmyer's answers to two basic questions concerning Jesus' preaching: "what themes in the gospels are accepted as representing the teaching of Jesus himself?" and "what did Jesus teach about the kingdom of God?" *A Christological Catechism*, 23-29; see also J. Fenton, *What Was Jesus' Message?* (London: SPCK, 1971) and R.H. Stein, *The Method and Message of Jesus' Teaching* (Philadelphia: Westminster, 1978).

[4]D.M. Smith, *John* (Philadelphia: Fortress, 1976) 2-18.

[5]L.E. Keck, *Paul and His Letters* (Philadelphia: Fortress, 1980) 37-42 and J. Murphy-O'Connor, *Becoming Human Together: The Pastoral Anthropology of St. Paul* (Wilmington: Glazier, 1982) 19-32.

[6]M. Hengel, *Was Jesus a Revolutionist?* (Philadelphia: Fortress, 1971) and B.D. Chilton, ed., *The Kingdom of God in the Teaching of Jesus* (Philadelphia: Fortress, 1984).

world and its social order? Was he a prophet, a lawgiver, a revolutionary? What did he offer his audience: a fresh understanding of life, society, and God, a new vision of history, of religion, or of human responsibility?[7] Of the various concepts found in the New Testament, which are owing to Jesus of Nazareth, to various early Christian communities, or to the writers themselves?[8]

There is similar ambiguity concerning Jesus' activity. For example, the length of his public ministry is unknown. If one were to follow the Synoptics or John one could conclude that his public activity lasted a few months (Mark) or three years (John). Did his ministry include the Gentiles or Jews only?—either response causes difficulty to the NT reader. Did Jesus baptize; did he found or intend to found a new community, one distinct from historical Israel?[9] Did Jesus predict, stage, or resist his death? Did he drive out the merchants from the temple at the beginning of his ministry (John) or just prior to his arrest (Synoptics)? Did this episode bring about his death, as implied by the Synoptics (*contra* John)?

Students of the New Testament agree that the unifying subject of these writings is Jesus the Christ and what he means to or demands from his followers. But precisely *what he was like* or what his background was is not easily discerned. It is unclear whether Jesus had any education although there are hints of surprise at his knowledge. To what class or social group did his family belong? Was Jesus of royal or priestly lineage? Did he belong to or was he influenced by any of the religious or political groups of the time? Was he Galilean or Judaean in outlook and in sympathy? Was he influenced by the apocalyptic, the political, or the Hellenizing (Greek) tendencies of first-century Palestine? How similar or different was Jesus from contemporary Jewish teachers? Was he primarily a rabbi, a teacher, a wonder worker, a charismatic

---

[7]E.P. Sanders, *Jesus and Judaism* (Philadelphia: Fortress, 1986).

[8]For a short discussion of the three types of materials contained in the gospels and the corresponding stages in the development of the Jesus tradition (the Jesus, oral, and gospel levels), see our discussion in chapter 3, as well as Fitzmyer, *A Christological Catechism*, 18-23.

[9]G. Lohfink, *Jesus and Community: The Social Dimension of Christian Faith* (Philadelphia: Fortress, 1984).

holy man (a *Hasid*), or a member of the Dead Sea community, all of which had prototypes in contemporary Judaism?[10]

Was Jesus a man limited in power and knowledge (Mark 6:5 and 13:32) or one who avoided public disclosure of his messianic role (e.g., Mark 3:12)? Did he claim to be a new Moses or "God with us" (Matthew)? Was he severe and demanding (Matthew) or kind and gentle with the poor and lowly (Luke)? Was his power such that at the sound of his voice opponents were struck down (John 18:6)? Was he antagonistic toward or friendly with the Sadducee and Pharisee authorities (Mark 2:1f. and Luke 14:1f.)? Was he a religious Jew or a less than observant Galilean?

If we were able to answer all of the above queries with satisfaction, we would still have to grapple with the question: *who was he*; what claims were made in his name; what did he claim to be? Undoubtedly, Jesus was a man, despite repeated claims through the centuries to the contrary. But was he God's Son? If he was, in what sense must this term be understood? This expression is predicated of Jesus on numerous occasions in the New Testament. But what did the readers of these works understand by that term or other titles (Son of Man, Christ, Lord, Savior, Son of David, etc.) used by or about Jesus?[11] Would Jewish and Gentile Christian readers interpret titles or sayings of Jesus in the same way?

Our understanding of who Jesus was is complicated both by the process which produced the early communities and their literature and by centuries of evolving christological tradition. Jesus was a Jew who lived in a Palestinian milieu, used Jewish concepts and modes of expression, and preached to Jewish audiences. A century later, however, the Jesus movement had spread beyond Palestine; its members consisted

---

[10]See G.S. Sloyan, *Jesus in Focus: A Life in Its Setting* (Mystic: Twenty-Third Publications, 1983) or the more technical *Ideal Figures in Ancient Judaism: Profiles and Paradigms*, eds. J.J. Collins and G.W.E. Nickelsburg (Chico: Scholars, 1980) and G. Vermes, *Jesus the Jew: A Historian's Reading of the Gospels* (NY: Macmillan, 1974).

[11]See A.E. Harvey, *Jesus and the Constraints of History* (Philadelphia: Westminster, 1982), especially chaps 6 and 7 on "Christ" and "Son of God," 120-73; also Fitzmyer, *A Christological Catechism*, 82-91. One might still consult the older but insightful work of O. Cullmann, *The Christology of the New Testament* (Philadelphia: Westminster, 1963).

primarily of Gentile Christians; and its language and culture were those of the Greco-Roman rather than of the Semitic world. Sayings and stories once at home in Palestine and communicated in Aramaic to Jewish audiences were now transposed into a new language and addressed to unfamiliar hearers. With the destruction of Jerusalem by the Roman army in 70, there disappeared the original ideational and geographic center of both Judaism and of the fledgling Jesus movement.

Modern Scholarship and Our Knowledge of Jesus

While one can isolate occasional remarks regarding the ambiguous historical character of the NT books (e.g., Celsus on the virgin birth, Origen concerning textual problems, Clement of Alexandria on the nature of John's Gospel, Dionysius of Alexandria on the authorship of the Book of Revelation, or Julian the Apostate on inconsistencies in the scriptures),[12] one must wait for the eighteenth century before critical attention is directed to the study of the gospels. The intellectual revolution of the Enlightenment saw the flourishing of scientific research. Since all areas of human endeavor were being submitted to critical investigation, it was to be expected that the bible and the gospels in particular should receive their share of attention. The writings of John Locke in England (1632-1704), Richard Simon in France (1638-1712), and Hermann Reimarus in German (1694-1768), initiated the critical approach to the bible. Basic questions, initially concerning miracles, inerrancy of the biblical record, and historical accuracy, caused interest and anxiety in scholarly and ecclesiastical circles. The study of mythology, ancient Semitic languages, and Classical culture and literature intensified the investigation of the NT books as literature of their time. The development of scientific inquiry also influenced the critical study of Jesus of Nazareth.[13]

[12]The opinions of these various authors are discussed in chaps 7, 11, and especially 13.

[13]For brief surveys of this topic, see H.C. Kee, *Jesus in History: An Approach to the Study of the Gospels* (NY: Harcourt Brace Jovanovich, 1977), chap 1: "The Rise of Historical Criticism in the Study of the Gospels," pp. 9-39 and J.H. Neyrey, *Christ Is Community: The Christologies of the New Testament* (Wilmington: Glazier, 1985), 7-26. For a different perspective on the rise of modern criticism, see H.G. Reventlow, *The Authority of the Bible and the Rise of the Modern World* (Philadelphia: Fortress, 1985), who maintains that Deism rather than the Enlightenment was at the core of this development.

Earlier, theologians had been content, following the second-century Diatessaron of Tatian, to produce harmonies of the life of Jesus by interweaving gospel episodes within the Johannine framework. This presumably achieved both a unified picture of Jesus' life and ministry for the believer and countered doubts raised by skeptics concerning inconsistences and contradictions in the gospel record.

Critical scholarship, however, began to distinguish between the Synoptic gospels and John and to base its inquiries concerning Jesus upon the former since the latter was obviously more theological than historical. It became increasingly clear that the first three gospels were not independent versions of the life of Jesus but instead that there was a literary relationship between them. Eventually this led to the generally accepted theory that Mark was the first written gospel and that Matthew and Luke borrowed freely from it to compose their own texts.[14]

Because of critical inquiry Jesus was situated in his Palestinian context and cause and effect relations were sought between his life and the socio-political currents of that time. Explanations of gospel sayings were sought in Jesus' Jewish background, whether messianic, apocalyptic, or Pharisaic. Such concerns marked the beginnings of modern critical research and contributed to the development of biblical scholarship. Another legacy of the Enlightenment was an increased awareness of science and order in the universe, an attitude labeled rationalism. Scholars as a result adopted a skeptical attitude toward an uncritical past for which miracles and the intermingling of the natural with the supernatural was commonplace. Instead, researchers sought a type of religion, therefore a Jesus, compatible with the dictates of reason.

A last, crucial development should be mentioned, namely, the distinguishing by scholars between the facts about Jesus (what he taught and did during his lifetime) and the beliefs of his early followers (what they taught about him in their preaching and writings). This insight, usually attributed to the eighteenth-century scholar H. Reimarus, led to the classic formulation of the problem at the end of the nineteenth century by M. Kähler as "the Jesus of history and the Christ of faith." On the one hand, scholars inferred from this distinction that the goal of

---

[14]Biblical methods are discussed briefly in the following chapter.

research was to unravel the actual plot of Jesus' life using clues derived from the data of the gospel narratives. On the other hand, many, concluding that the gospel texts were entirely the product of the believing community, either despaired of reaching the historical Jesus and settled for the teaching of the early church or sought in this distinction a basis for explaining the human and divine elements of the early credal formulas.

The late eighteenth, the nineteenth, and now the twentieth centuries have seen numerous attempts to reconstruct the life of Jesus, each as much the product of its author's presuppositions and imagination as a genuine look at the data. Albert Schweitzer, in his classic work, *The Quest of the Historical Jesus*, noted that each generation found in the biblical text or created from its clues a Jesus according to its own image and need (although he himself did not heed his own advice). Rationalists (Thomas Jefferson included) had been busy excising the miraculous from the gospel story so as to produce a natural, but noble religious ideal, one which recent liberal theologians would qualify as "the quintessential religion" (e.g., A. Harnack or P. Tillich). Authors of varying intellectual backgrounds began to seek in the biblical text the scenario for countless romaticized lives of Jesus: of a loving but misunderstood man (E. Renan), of a mistaken, apocalyptic visionary (A. Schweitzer), of a revolutionary earthly messiah (S.G.F. Brandon or A.B. Cleage), or a messianic schemer (H.J. Schonfield). Others treated the biblical text as a challenging puzzle from which to draw clues for understanding Jesus' life. As a result fictionalized lives were published claiming that Jesus had been a member of an Essene community (from K.F. Bahrdt in the eighteenth century to wild speculations after the discovery of the Dead Sea Scrolls in the 1950s), the founder of a secret society (M. Smith), or a law-abiding married Jew (W.F. Phipps). Still others, either because their outlook could not countenance the miraculous or because they viewed the Jesus of the gospels as a creation of the early church, sought to portray him as a great moral teacher whose followers soon came to regard as more than human, but whose teaching was of a natural, spiritual character.

This list is incomplete both because it is schematic and because such attempts to portray Jesus persist. Just as revolutionary lives of Jesus were common in the past, so one continues to find Marxist and liberation portraits in the present. There seems to be no limit to imagination or need. Believers and theologians continue to view Jesus of Nazareth in a variety of ways, from one extreme to another, from "Son of God to Super Star."[15]

Quest for the Historical Jesus

As a result of his extensive survey of 19th-century lives of Jesus and their philosophical underpinnings, Schweitzer concluded that each modern writer created a Jesus according to that writer's expectations, and further insisted that it was impossible to discover with any assurance the Jesus of history. Early 20th-century German biblical scholars, Rudolf Bultmann in particular, added their considerable weight to Schweitzer's negative evaluation of the data. Little could be known about Jesus; instead attention could be more profitably directed to the Christ of faith, that is, the content of the kerygma or preaching of the early church. The results of form-critical work,[16] seemed to confirm Schweitzer's conclusion since the gospels were thought to be composed almost entirely from traditions of the early church's preaching.

Bultmann has often insisted that faith then and now is based on the commitment of Jesus' followers, not upon the facts of the master's life. The gospels and Christian faith itself were fundamentally kerygmatic and not historical. The task of the biblical scholar, as Bultmann saw it, was to investigate the preaching of the early community and its development in the NT writings. While it should be noted that such skepticism with regard to the quest was not shared by French and English-speaking scholars, the issue came to a head in the post-war years when a student of Bultmann, E. Käsemann, issued a call in 1954 for a new quest for the historical Jesus, a quest which dominated 1960s' scholarship. Numerous books and articles were produced to examine the philosophical and theological basis for such an endeavor and to formulate criteria to discern within the biblical literature elements relating to Jesus of Nazareth.

A variety of criteria for authenticity have been proposed. Since it is readily agreed that none of the gospels, even Mark the oldest, is *prima*

---

[15]J.H. Hayes, *Son of God to Super Star: Twentieth-Century Interpretations of Jesus* (Nashville: Abingdon, 1976), devotes entire chapters to the various theories (mainly sensational ones) noted above.

[16]See a discussion of this method in the following chapter.

facie a document of historical intent, scholars endeavor to work with evidence which has multiple attestations. Sayings or events which seem to occur in different strands of the tradition (e.g., Mark, Matthean-Lukan source, John) gain a greater degree of probability, although even at this level the tradition could reflect early Christian concerns rather than facts from the life of Jesus. The criterion of uniqueness or discontiuity is often proposed. If, for example, some element in the gospel record cannot be attributed to either contemporary Judaism or to the interests of the early church then it must relate to the Jesus level. There is an obvious weakness in this kind of criterion since Jesus would have assimilated elements from his Jewish background and have had a profound influence on his followers. Another criterion stresses the influence of eschatological and apocalyptic views on the sayings and thinking of Jesus. As a result of the research particularly of J. Weiss., A. Schweitzer, and Dead Sea Scrolls scholars, it is commonly recognized that Jesus' sayings are embued with apocalyptic eschatology. Constant tension is felt between the present and the future, the divine acting within the human sphere, and the "already and not-yet" character of Jesus' ministry. Along with these criteria scholars apply a variety of literary methods to investigate the Jesus tradition in the quest for the historical figure behind the NT writings.

The results of the quest (old or new) have been variously assessed. Recently book-length portraits of Jesus have been produced (e.g., G. Bornkamm[17]), re-creations of his teaching attempted (e.g., N. Perrin[18]), and gospel portraits proposed (e.g., H.C. Kee and J.D. Kingsbury[19]). The picture of Jesus of Nazareth can be expansively drawn as Bornkamm does, or it can be as tersely, and reductively given as in the following:[20]

[17] *Jesus of Nazareth* (NY: Harper & Row, 1961).

[18] *Rediscovering the Teaching of Jesus* (NY: Harper & Row, 1967).

[19] *Jesus in History* and *Jesus Christ in Matthew, Mark, and Luke* (Philadelphia: Fortress, 1981), respectively. We should also note here a "story of Jesus" series by Fortress Press: of Matthew (R.A. Edwards, 1985), of Mark (W. Kelber, 1979), of Luke (O.C. Edwards, 1981), and of John (R. Kysar, 1984).

[20] See Kee, *Jesus in History*, 298-99 and Fitzmyer, *A Christological Cathechism*, 16-17, for different summaries.

His name was Jesus (*Yeshu*); he was the son of Mary and his putative father was Joseph. He was probably born in Bethlehem during the reign of Herod the Great (therefore before 4 B.C.). He grew up in Nazareth as a carpenter, was a Galilean who presumably had little education, and had brothers and sisters (Mark 6:3).

He exercised a brief, itinerant Galilean ministry of preaching and healing—Jewish sources accuse him of sorcery. He used parables and eschatological pronouncements in his preaching, concentrated on the imminent coming of God's kingdom, enjoyed a certain popularity, and created an inner group of followers. He offered a severe critique of the Law and preached repentance as a means to covenant fellowship for rich and poor alike.

He traveled to Jerusalem, where, after a brief ministry (involving a meal with his followers and confrontation with the religious authorities), he was brought to trial at the instigation of the Jewish leaders and executed by the Roman authorities during the procuratorship of Pontius Pilate. In the face of death he showed real anxiety (Mark 14:33f; 15:34).

After his death, some of his followers claimed he had been raised from the dead and had been seen by some (gospels and 1 Cor. 15:3-7).

The quest has provoked a serious ideological battle. Some theologians opt for a less critical approach to the question. By minimizing the role played by the early community in the formation of the tradition, this option sees little difference between the Jesus of history and the Christ preached by the early Christian missionaries. One does not expect serious theological activity from such a stance, since it does not acknowledge the existence of the problem. Another option is to pursue the quest in all earnestness and to posit its historical reconstruction as the basis for christology. Opposed to this position is the choice to abandon the quest and to opt for some formulation of the earliest Christ-Kerygma, i.e., the fundamental belief of the first Christian followers of Jesus. This then becomes the foundation for christological speculation. The last two options present serious challenges to theological inquiry. On the one hand, the latter opts for a theology of the word which confronts the hearer but which also deemphasizes the historical Jesus. There seems to be concern that faith may be compromised by overly historical considerations, a posture which L.E.

Keck advisedly calls "a Protestant understanding of faith."[21] Granted that faith should not seek its object in the reconstructed life of Jesus by the biblical scholar, one must still seek the relationship of the person presented in the gospels to the faith claims made in his name by early followers. On the other hand, the option for the quest betrays an excessive concern for history and historicity. Faith and history are by no means the same and often make strange bed-fellows. Frequently implied in such an historical approach is that the Jesus of history, if known correctly, will reveal the fullness of christological development. Such an option reads too much into the historical level and tends to rob faith of its dynamics. In response to both positions, we might cite Keck's conclusion: "though the historical Jesus is but a part of the whole of Christology, it is the crucial part without which nothing else has validity or significance in the long run."[22]

"Historical Jesus" or "Jesus in the New Testament"?

The quest is a thing of the past, a popular topic of the 1960s. While some scholars were formulating criteria for discerning the authentic sayings of Jesus (*ipsissima verba*), others were studying the evangelists as writers on their own terms. Less attention was given to the pre-gospel level of the material and more to the gospels themselves. Instead of seeking the Jesus behind the NT documents, these scholars directed their attention to the image of Jesus which the evangelists presented in their works.

The quest for the historical Jesus is a legitimate endeavor. It is an area which should receive the attention of critical scholarship, but whether it should be, negatively or positively, as central to scholarly endeavor as it was a generation ago is questionable.[23] Theologians have come to realize that the New Testament presents not one but rather a diversity of

---

[21]*A Future for the Historical Jesus: The Place of Jesus in Preaching and Theology* (Philadelphia: Fortress, 1981) 37.

[22]*Ibid.*, 38.

[23]The current scholarly and pastoral project known as the "Jesus Seminar" headed by R. Funk, a project attempting to classify sayings of Jesus according to probable historicity, is a good example of the continuing interest of many in the quest for the historical Jesus.

theologies and christologies, all within the NT canon or official list. Attention should be given to these responses occasioned by the life and teaching of Jesus of Nazareth. Who he was, what he was like, what he did and taught, and what happened to him are important items both for the scholar's agenda and the believer's overall perspective. This, however, constitutes only the background for christology, since christology, properly speaking, begins with the diverse responses of Jesus' followers in light of his death and resurrection.[24]

The goal of this study, therefore, will be to survey the variety of images which NT writers present of Jesus of Nazareth. He was many things to many communities. What twentieth-century Christians have at their disposal in the New Testament are many "mediated images" of the one who is the object of faith. Since, as is generally agreed, a balanced christology and spirituality should be based on that person and what he means, biblical scholarship holds out a challenge to the modern reader to be aware of the rich diversity which the believing community's books present, whether overtly or between the lines.

The quest of this book is not the historical Jesus but the pictures or images of Jesus which exist in the New Testament. After a brief introduction to the issues (part I), attention will be given to Jesus as presented in the gospels and Acts (part II), as perceived by Paul and his disciples (part III), and as viewed in the remaining books of the New Testament (part IV). The study will conclude with observations on Jesus in early post-NT times (part V).

As diverse forces within the early communities vied with one another for allegiance, credibility, and authority, the variety of interpretations of Jesus succumbed to the historical process. Some became normative; others were forgotten; and still others were modified in subsequent theological development. Realizing that the historical process, as it affects the developing tradition, tends to synthesize differences and to impose uniformity on the whole, it is important that, in examining the development of the Jesus tradition, one consider the diversity which the

---

[24]Some scholars propose the expression "incipient or implicit christology" to describe what is presumed to have been Jesus' critical stance *vis-à-vis God,* the Law, and the kingdom. See for example, I.H. Marshall, *The Origins of New Testament Christology* (Leicester: InterVarsity, 1977), who, after asking: "Did Jesus have a Christology?" responds in the affirmative, namely, that "the origins of the church's Christology lie in the use of Jesus' own Christology" (57).

ages either forgot or judged nonmainstream. The insights of early believers, the images of Jesus from different communities, and the many responses elicited by the man from Nazareth merit our attention for they are both the witnesses on which faith is based and the path (*via* the NT writings) to Jesus of Nazareth, "the paradigm for man and the parable of God."[25] We turn our attention, therefore, to the early church's books since they enshrine the movement's earliest images of the master and contain the clues which we need to understand and appreciate this precious legacy.

[25]*Future for the Historical Jesus*, 265.

2

Brief Introduction to
the New Testament

Before initiating a study of individual NT authors and their respective images of Jesus, it is helpful to consider the rudiments of NT study. Since this "book" is in reality an anthology of early Christian works, i.e., ancient, religious, Christian literature of the first century, it is necessary to dwell on each of these facets. The writings are the product of creative voices within the early communities and of the interaction of these leaders with the social and cultural forces in their society. We address first the historical-cultural matrix of the beginnings of the Jesus movement in order to see the movement's self-understanding. Secondly we will consider the principal literary methods which biblical scholars employ to discern the communities' varying portraits of their founder.

Since biblical studies developed as a result of the intellectual revolution set in motion by the Enlightenment and more recently by the astounding rediscovery of the Near Eastern and Hellenistic cultures that produced both the Old and New Testaments, the modern reader is confronted by the fundamental problem of the nature of the methods and the wisdom of employing these relatively new approaches to the study of Jesus and of NT literature.[1] On the one hand, scholars attempt to rediscover the historical and cultural matrix of the literary produc-

---

[1]See Fitzmyer, *A Christological Catechism*, 18-23, who responds to the following question: "Is not such an approach to the historical Jesus and to the canonical gospels tantamount to an implicit reduction in Christian faith and contrary to centuries-long tradition of gospel-interpretation?"

tions under discussion and have increasingly more data and sophisticated tools at their disposal to pursue this goal. The first part of this chapter will focus upon this cultural matrix. On the other hand, the large quantity and variety of ancient literary texts discovered throughout what are called the "bible lands," the increasing sophistication of modern theories of literary (biblical) interpretation, and the vast collections of materials and the reconstructions of these ancient cultures in political, cultural, and sociological terms have forced current readers to take seriously the axiom that ancient texts should not be isolated from their cultural and literary milieu. They are compelled to examine literary conventions, forms, and narratives comparable to those encountered in the biblical text, to reconstruct the historical and cultural forces that were brought to bear on these authors and audiences, and to employ the insights of literary critics to delve into the structure and meaning of these writings. The second part of the chapter will address these literary concerns.

Before proceeding to the principal topics of this chapter a final problem requires attention. While many routinely refer to the approach described above as the "historical-critical method" and thus find therein much to criticize,[2] it is this writer's contention that the label itself is a misnomer. Instead one should speak of the "literary-critical method," since one is dealing first of all with texts, conventions and forms of verbal expression, and various literary genres. Even historical works are by definition literature and participate in varying degrees in the conventional modes of literary expression. Biblical methods are not essentially, nor primarily, historical in perspective or goal. Instead they are defined by the objects to be studied, namely ancient, religious, literary texts from a variety of backgrounds and with considerable range of complexity in literary, historical, and religious terms. The goal of NT study is not the rediscovery and recreation of what happened in Jesus' life, though this can be a consideration, but rather the explication and appreciation of literary works which present specific perspectives on Jesus of Nazareth and are the products of the creative voices within the early communities which professed him to be God's agent and Son.

---

[2]Confer N.R. Petersen, *Literary Criticism for New Testament Critics* (Philadelphia: Fortress, 1978), especially chapter 1: "Literary Problems in the Historical-Critical Paradigm," 9-23.

Social, Historical, and Cultural Milieu

The New Testament reflects the period in which its writers formulated their images of Jesus and their advice to communities throughout the Greco-Roman world. The authors were concerned about a Palestinian Jewish preacher who had lived a few decades earlier and whose life, teachings, and faith claims formed the basis of their way of thinking and living. Their communities, whether Jewish, Gentile, or mixed, were spread throughout the Roman empire, particularly among its Greek-speaking citizens. The social and cultural heritage of these early Christians, especially that of the writers, was indeed a rather complex one.

> The proclamation of Jesus as the Christ did influence the way [they] envisioned their world, but that world itself gave the church its own language and literary forms for expressing that belief. Its scriptures were Jewish; its language, Greek; its urban setting, hellenistic; its political and legal forum, Roman—and its mythology of evil a curious blend of each. Thus all were integral parts of the world that influenced these writers and their audience.[3]

In social and cultural terms one must conclude that the NT books are at once Jewish, Greek, Roman, and Christian.

To understand properly the social, historical, and cultural milieu of the NT books one must again reflect upon the nature of the inquiry. Since these books, particularly the gospels, represent the end-product of a lengthy process of oral transmission of stories about Jesus and his disciples, one should distinguish methodologically between the several levels of the material, namely the original movement, event, or speech, then the transmission of that "historical" item, and finally its recording in a document available to posterity. In the case of the first level one can speak of the historical Jesus, Pilate, Pharisees, etc. In each instance one must interrogate the sources available to catch a glimpse of that person, event, or movement. In general terms one speaks of the historical, cultural, and social background into which these persons or events fit and thereby gains a better perspective of these. The process, however, is more complex still since scholars are forced to be both literary historians

---

[3]C.J. Roetzel, *The World That Shaped the New Testament* (Atlanta: John Knox, 1985) viii.

and critics. The quest for the historical Jesus is one of many challenges to NT scholars since, along with Judaic and Classical researchers, they must, for example, seek to understand the nature of the role played by the Pharisee movement in the first centuries B.C. and A.D., and the character and quality of Pilate's procuratorship. As literary historians and critics they are forced to come to grips with the NT documents, the Mishnah, and other contemporary works as historical resources. Only by understanding the evolution these documents have undergone and by evaluating the data they contain can they be properly employed as historical resources.[4] Not only do NT critics need to know what the gospels say about Jesus but how the early church formulated its beliefs concerning him and how and why eventually the gospel writers put together lives of the founder. The social, historical, and cultural milieu of these books, therefore, requires a historical panorama of the period in which Jesus and his contemporaries lived, a reconstruction of early Christian history (especially its varied relationships with Judaism and Greco-Roman culture), and an analysis of the pastoral and literary relationship between the authors and audiences of the various NT books.

With this in mind we offer the following historical outline to assist the reader in understanding the historical and cultural background of the New Testament.

BC	587	Fall of Jerusalem and Babylonian Exile
	539	Fall of Babylon, Persian Rule & Edict of Cyrus
	333	Alexander's Conquests
	300	Ptolemaic (Egyptian) Control of Palestine
	198	Seleucid (Syrian) Control of Palestine
	167	Maccabean Revolt against Antiochus IV
	63	Roman intervention
	37	Rule of Herod the Great
	4	Death of Herod
		4 BC-39 AD Antipas: Galilee

---

[4]See for example, D.J. Harrington, *Interpreting the New Testament: A Practical Guide* (Wilmington: Glazier, 1980), 85-95 and 108-23, as well as the more technical discussions of A.R.C. Leaney, *The Jewish and Christian World 200 BC to AD 200* (London: Cambridge University, 1984) and "Sources" with contributions by S. Safrai, M. Stern, M. de Jonge, and M. Avi-Yonah, 1:1-77 in *The Jewish People in the First Century*, eds, S. Safrai et al (Philadelphia: Fortress, 1974).

4 BC-34 AD Philip: Transjordan
4 BC- 6 AD Archelaus: Judaea
AD   6 Roman Procurators in Judaea
         30 Death of Jesus (approx.)
         66 First Jewish Revolt
         70 Fall of Jerusalem
        132 Second Jewish Revolt

JEWISH BACKGROUND AND CHARACTER

The New Testament, while Christian in content, is a collection of Jewish works and commands a place in the history of Jewish literature and culture, since its principal hero is a Jew of first-century Palestine and since many of its authors are Jewish. Some of its authors (Paul surely) did not view the Jesus movement as separate from Judaism; others (at least some members of the Matthean and Johannine communities) probably considered themselves as belonging to an estranged subgroup; while still others (James and Hebrews) clung vigorously to their Judaeo-Christian culture. Judaism furnishes the cultural, historical, and religious background of the New Testament and the thought world of its authors and first readers. Hence we explore three areas in the development and character of Judaism in order to gain a better perspective about Christian origins: the political and historical evolution of Israel, the diversity of first-century Judaism, and its relationship to the early Jesus movement.

1) Following upon the momentous events of the Babylonian exile, which provoked both a religious and a political crisis, there began to develop within Judaism the institutions and scriptures of the pre-NT period. Owing to the idealism and enthusiasm of the returnees ("men of the exile"), recounted in the books of Ezra and Nehemiah, a small, viable Jewish territory was established around Jerusalem, an area which for the next six centuries was to serve as the religious and political center of Judaism. Under the watchful eye of its Persian overlords, the territory of Judah remained a quiet backwater limited in power and resources and governed by aristocratic high priests. It was at this time that Aramaic, a Semitic sister-language of Hebrew and the *lingua franca* of the Persian rulers, became the language of Judah as well.

In 332, however, the political make-up of the area changed drastically following Alexander's whirlwind military campaign against the Persians, Greece's bitter enemies. The importance of these events for world and

Palestinian history should not be underestimated, since Asia Minor, Syria, Palestine, and Egypt entered the Classical world, first of Greece and several centuries later of Rome. This change became evident in political and cultural terms, for these areas passed from Persian domination to some form of Greek rule and became increasingly subject to Hellenization in cultural as well as in religious and linguistic matters.

Palestine welcomed the young liberator but later, because of its geographical position, became once more an area contested by the two neighboring superpowers, the Ptolemies of Egypt and the Seleucids of Syria, the two major heirs to Alexander's non-Greek, conquered territories. During the first two centuries of Greek rule, Judaism underwent a period of consolidation and diversification. After the peaceful and tolerant rule of the Ptolemies (c. 300-200), Hellenization became a burning issue for the Jews when the Seleucid ruler, Antiochus IV Epiphanes, resolved to abolish tolerance of non-Greek cultural and religious groups among his subjects. There resulted the well-known Maccabean revolt in 167, as a result of which the Jews under the Maccabean revolutionaries and later the Hasmonaean rulers gained political independence. Ironically, what began as an anti-Hellenistic movement became a stronghold and patron of Greek culture and influence, thereby provoking further opposition among Jewish thinkers.

In 63 B.C. as a result of civil strife between two Hasmonaean princes, Rome under the leadership of Pompey the Great, intervened in Jewish affairs, thereby establishing control over the once independent territory. A few decades later (37 B.C.) a local Judaeo-Idumaean politician, Herod, was appointed as vassal king over the whole of Palestine.[5]

2) As a result of the exilic experience pronounced differences within Judaism arose in regard to one's adherence to the God of Israel. Following upon the unambiguous affirmations of monotheism by the exilic prophets (see Isaiah 40f) and upon the conviction that Yahweh was the lord of history, the energies of Judaism were channeled in many directions. If it is true that "any group that holds unusual views [such as exclusive monotheism] is inevitably under pressure to establish their plausibility, not only to win the respect of outsiders, but primarily to

---

[5]For short overviews of Palestinian history, with special attention given to the Hellenistic and Roman periods, see E. Lohse, *The New Testament Environment* (Nashville: Abingdon, 1974) 15-54 and Roetzel, *The World That Shaped the New Testament*, 1-23.

maintain the allegiance of its own members,"⁶ then one can appreciate the variety of literature generated in Palestine and the Diaspora, i.e., the Hellenistic Jewish communites of the empire. This literature, particularly that generated outside of Palestine, had an apologetic quality "directed simultaneously to those within and to those outside."⁷ The concept of one God became a binding force within Judaism itself and a bridge to the surrounding non-Jewish cultures.

Some saw the belief in the one God as a precious possession which, along with the great revelation expressed in the Law (Torah), the privileged holy place (temple), and kosher or purity laws, must be fostered and protected that a holy people might be produced. Attention focused on the role which Jerusalem, the temple there, and its priesthood played in Jewish religion. Others instead became convinced that monotheism led to a universal outlook which encompassed all knowledge and wisdom. The same God was the source both of the wisdom of the Torah and that of the philosophers and pagan religions. The influence of Hellenism was felt as Jewish writers viewed the Torah as universal law and divine wisdom. Still others professed a more practical piety which saw its duty to be worship of the Lord in the temple or synagogue and humane treatment of fellow believers. The little book of Tobit is an admirable example of such a spirituality, where prayer, fasting, and almsgiving were the cornerstone on which many centered their response to the God of Israel. There also developed an important spiritual movement which saw Judaism's ideal in the just sufferer. For many, Job the innocent became the model of religious conduct. They held that doing God's will, whether in martyrdom or persecution, was possible since God provided for the elect (throne mysticism). Other groups "set up the sage, the wise teacher and expounder of the Torah, as the ideal pattern" of Jewish life.⁸ Also popular during this period was a mentality

---

⁶J.J. Collins, *Between Athens and Jerusalem: Jewish Identity in the Hellenistic Diaspora* (NY: Crossroad, 1983) 2.

⁷*Ibid.*, 9.

⁸G.W.E. Nickelsburg and M.E. Stone, *Faith and Piety in Early Judaism: Texts and Documents* (Philadelphia: Fortress, 1983) 3. For surveys and collections of the literature see: Collins, *Between Athens and Jerusalem*; Nickelsburg and Stone, *Faith and Piety*; L. Rost, *Judaism Outside the Hebrew Canon* (Nashville: Abingdon, 1976); M.E. Stone, ed., *Jewish Writings of the Second Temple Period: Apocrypha, Pseudepigrapha, Qumran Sectarian Writings, Philo, Josephus* (Philadelphia: Fortress, 1984); J.H. Charlesworth, ed., *The Old Testament Pseudepigrapha* (NY: Doubleday, 1983-85); and H.E.D. Sparks, *The Apocryphal Old Testament* (Oxford: Clarendon, 1984).

and a literature which we today classify as apocalyptic. Convinced that God is lord of history and source of knowledge and of victory and that the world is totally beyond human help, the apocalypticist believed that God would intervene on behalf of the righteous chosen ones to give them ultimate victory, a victory that would come as a result of a cataclysmic battle between the forces of God and those of evil. It is in such a context that the concept of afterlife and reward after death was introduced into Jewish literature. The intertestamental period (c. 200 B.C. and following) abounded in this type of religious and pious literature. These approaches to belief in God contributed greatly to the diversity of religious and political thought which existed in first-century Palestine.

At this point we are confronted with a methodological impasse, namely, the quest for an assessment of the situation in Palestine prior to 70 A.D.

> This period is crucial for an understanding of the history of Judaism and the rise and development of Christianity, for at this time the types of Jewish religion were many, and the social settings in which they developed and received formulation were complex. The literature of this period allows us to perceive this richness and diversity. The subsequent course of political events led to the destruction of the temple (70 C.E.), with the loss of national independence and the exile of many Jews. This in turn brought about a certain withdrawal, consolidation, and conscious delimitation of variety, and as a result, many of the types of Jewish thought and piety that were earlier vital and living disappeared.[9]

Thus, since both Judaism and the young Jesus movement underwent radical changes due to that catastrophic episode and since most of our literature on the Judaism of that period comes either from the New Testament or later Jewish works, such as the Mishnah and Talmud, the view that we have, particularly of the Pharisees, is very suspect.

Because of Josephus' descriptions of the three major Jewish groups of the time,[10] and relying on the extensive research of recent years, we are

[9]Nickelsburg and Stone, *Faith and Piety*, 5.

[10]Josephus treats the Sadducees, Pharisees, and Essenes in three places: The Jewish Wars 2:119-66; Jewish Antiquities 13:171-73; and 18:11-25. In the last passage (23-25) he adds a fourth group, the "Pharisee-like" revolutionaries; see *Josephus*, eds, H.St.J. Thackeray et al (Cambridge: Harvard University, 1965-67).

in a good position to appreciate the dynamic, diverse character of Jewish thought and life then current.[11] There were the politically liberal but conservatively religious Sadducees whose outlook fostered cooperation with the Greco-Roman rulers and established control of the temple and priestly-oriented cult. Along with this priestly aristocracy, there existed the important Pharisee movement whose approach to the Torah and oral tradition was considerably more liberal. As reputed interpreters of the Law (especially their scribes), the Pharisees, under the influence of Hillel, became a major force for renewal, which stressed the application of the Law to daily life and the practice of piety.

Here one enters the current debate concerning the Pharisees. The issue might be summarized thus:

> While Neusner believes that Pharisaism in Jesus' day was quietistic and apolitical, concerned primarily with matters of ritual, Rivkin takes the opposite view—that Pharisaism was revolutionary and concerned with a wide range of issues beyond ritual purity. The Pharisaic concern for the rites of cleanliness, Rivkin claims, was subordinated to Pharisaic concern for the two-fold law (i.e., oral and written) and a strenuous political effort to impose that law on society. Rivkin maintains that ... the Pharisees were popular with the masses, served as a scholar class interpreting both oral and written traditions, believed in individual immortality, and promulgated new law.[12]

Whether one agrees with Neusner or Rivkin, the picture that emerges from the NT books is quite different from the above. Further, it is the Pharisaic group which survived the catastrophic destruction of Jerusalem, became the foundation of Rabbinic Judaism, and left its mark on the polemical NT descriptions of the Judaism of the period.

While these were the two dominant groups in the power structure of first-century Palestinian Judaism, there existed other groups whose existence and influence are vaguely or indirectly attested. Herodians

[11]See the brief treatments of Lohse, *The New Testament Environment*, 55-145; Roetzel, *The World That Shaped the New Testament*, 24-45; S. Freyne, *The World of the New Testament* (Wilmington: Glazier, 1980) 81-128.

[12]Roetzel, *The World That Shaped the New Testament*, 27-28; see J. Neusner, *From Politics to Piety: The Emergence of Pharisaic Judaism* (Englewood Cliffs: Prentice-Hall, 1973) and E. Rivkin, *A Hidden Revolution: The Pharisees' Search for the Kingdom Within* (Nashville: Abingdon, 1978).

and God-fearers are mentioned in our sources and presumably represented, political and religious stances vis-à-vis Judaism. We also hear of revolutionaries both in the New Testament and at length in Josephus. These were called Zealots, Sicarii, or messianic pretenders (see Acts 5:35f). A growing number of armed bandits and revolutionary groups arose during the time of Herod the Great, under the Roman procurators, and later under the leadership of Bar Kochba.[13]

Finally we are led to discuss more heterodox forms of Judaism. While various groups continued to produce works of piety inspired by traditional forms of thought (such as wisdom speculation, mysticism, and halakic/haggadic concerns), there flourished in Judaism such movements as the apocalyptic covenanters of Qumran, also known as Essenes, whose library was discovered in the 1940s along the Dead Sea,[14] as well as others which generated the vast literature of the intertestamental period: apocalypses, testaments, messianic oracles, reinterpretations of the Torah, and biblical narratives. The abundance of apocalyptic literature and other writings of the intertestamental period alerts us to the diversity of first-century Judaism, the period contemporary with the life of Jesus and with the production of the New Testament.

3) Under the rubric of "the relationship of Judaism to the early Jesus movement" one could consider a wide array of issues, such as the Jewish culture of Jesus and his early followers, their dependence on the religion of Israel for ideas and language, the role played by the Jewish leaders in the trial and death of Jesus, or the social and religious intercourse between Christians and Jews. While all of these topics claim our attention it is the last which will be developed briefly. The Jesus movement began as an outgrowth of Jewish messianism. Its earliest members were Jewish followers of the man from Galilee, whom they professed to be the fulfilment of God's promises to Israel. As we survey the NT books in the following chapters, it will become clear that the new

---

[13]R.A. Horsley and J.S. Hanson, *Bandits, Prophets, and Messiahs: Popular Movements at the Time of Jesus* (Minneapolis: Winston-Seabury, 1986).

[14]G. Vermes, *The Dead Sea Scrolls: Qumran in Perspective* (Philadelphia: Fortress, 1981); J.T. Milik, *Ten Years in the Wilderness of Judaea* (Naperville: Allenson, 1959); R. de Vaux, *Archaeology and the Dead Sea Scrolls* (NY: Oxford University, 1973); J.A. Fitzmyer, "The Dead Sea Scrolls and the New Testament after Thirty Years," *TD* 29 (1981) 351-67; and D. Dimant, "Qumran Sectarian Literature," 483-550 in Stone, *Jewish Writings of the Second Temple Period.*

movement's relationship to its parent varied greatly from community to community and from period to period. In some cases the interchange seems to have been pacific while in others polemics and mutual recrimination were common. The relationship of pre-and-post-70 Judaism to the budding Jesus movement, whether to individual communities or to the movement in general, is not an easy one to discern owing to the nature of the resources at our disposal and to the complexity and diversity within Judaism and early Christianity. This is further complicated by the limits of our knowledge of Judaeo-Christianity. Thus each NT work must be examined to discern what in it is tradition, rhetoric, or the attitude of its author and community toward Judaism. It is important, in methodological terms, for the modern reader to realize that the attitudes and judgments conveyed in the Christian scriptures are those of a later period, when the two movements were beginning to diverge structurally and theologically, when the religio-political situation of the early years was a faint memory, and when Jewish and Christian authorities and missionaries were vying with one another for adherents, for tolerance from the Roman populace, and for the right to claim for themselves the perduring traditions of Israel.

GREEK MILIEU OF THE NEW TESTAMENT

The legacy of Alexander was far-reaching, not the least being the influence which Greek language and culture had on Judaism and on early Christianity.[15] As the Near East was brought under Greek domination, it adopted the conqueror's language which, in its Hellenistic form (often called *koine*), became the *lingua franca* of the new territories. Thus, a standardized form of Greek, greatly influenced by local speech, became the language of commerce and cultural pursuits. Soon the Jews of Egypt felt the need to translate their scriptures into Greek, a translation known as the Septuagint (LXX)[16] and began to compose

[15]J.A. Fitzmyer, "The Languages of Palestine in the First Century A.D.," *CBQ* 32 (1970) 501-31 and G. Massies, "Greek in Palestine and the Diaspora," 2:1040-64 in Safrai, *The Jewish People in the First Century*; see also C. Rabin, "Hebrew and Aramaic in the First Century," 2:1007-39 in *ibid.*

[16]The name "Septuagint" or "seventy" (thus LXX) derives from an old story purporting to be from a Ptolemaic Jewish scholar (Letter of Aristeas) to the effect that 72 Jewish wise men (6 from each of the 12 tribes) translated the Hebrew scriptures into Greek for the great Alexandrian library in the second century BC. See J.R. Bartlett, *Jews in the Hellenistic World: Josephus, Aristeas, the Sibylline Oracles, Eupolemus* (London: Cambridge University, 1985) 11-34.

works in Greek, some of which today are incorporated within the Catholic and Orthodox canons of the Old Testament.[17] It is also a consequence of these conquests that NT authors, adjusting to the language and culture of their readers, employed the Septuagint version of the Jewish scriptures as their bible and composed their works in Greek, a language which was to remain the dominant means of communication of the early Christian movement for two more centuries, until indigenous languages (e.g., Syriac and Coptic) and Latin (in the western part of the Roman empire) emerged as the idiom of most Christian communities.

Greek influence upon Judaism and Christianity extended far beyond the use of language, for during the Ptolemaic and Seleucid as well as during the Hasmonaean and Herodian periods Greek culture and religion or Hellenism, deeply affected the entire Near East. The language and culture of the upper classes of the Mediterranean world became increasingly Hellenistic as these were adopted as the medium of diplomacy, commerce, travel, and education. Under the aegis of Greek rulers who fostered a common language and standard political structures, there developed a universal, hybrid culture in the Mediterranean area. Similar systems of taxation and commerce, styles in art and architecture, and philosophical and religious outlooks became widespread as Greek culture affected all areas of life.[18]

In Egypt, Ptolemy, inspired by Alexander's brilliant cultural accommodation, created an impressive administrative system out of indigenous and Hellenistic elements.

> Throughout the Greek world the word went out: Ptolemy needed Greeks of every sort—clerks, accountants, masons, engineers, artists, doctors, actors, scholars, and of course, able-bodied men to serve in his army. Ptolemy intended that the Egyptian economic system should continue as before, staffed at the lowest bureaucratic levels by the Egyptians, but at a certain point, every channel of authority, every chain of command should become Greek, or Macedonian, and

[17]For literature on the LXX see E. Tov and R.A. Kraft, "Septuagint," 807-15 in *IDBSup* and P.W. Skehan, "Texts and Versions," 2:561-74 in *JBC*.

[18]V. Tcherikover, *Hellenistic Civilization and the Jews* (NY: Atheneum, 1979); M. Hengel, *Judaism and Hellenism: Studies in Their Encounter in Palestine during the Early Hellenistic Period* (Philadelphia: Fortress, 1974); A.H.M. Jones, *The Cities of the Eastern Roman Provinces* (Oxford: Clarendon, 1971).

continue to the upper levels where an entirely Graeco-Macedonian
elite would exist and operate in an artifically created Greek world, a
thin veneer riding upon and wholly insulated from the great mass of
Egyptian peasants.[19]

To the Egyptian capital came vast numbers of Jews who found there
occupational opportunity and cultural challenge. So successful was this
venture that by the time of Philo (c. 40 A.D.), two-fifths of Alexandria
was Jewish. Just as successful was the Jewish participation in the
Ptolemaic educational culture of Greek gymnasia, theaters, and the
famous Museum of Alexandria. If in that city, "the more pious Jews
founded a quarter and stayed in it, keeping their faith and their customs,
... the young and adventurous joined youth from a hundred other
races in taking Greek names and mastering the Greek language, for this
way lay advancement."[20] Egypt by its cosmopolitan approach to culture
and economy, provided an ideal situation for the preservation and
enhancement of Jewish culture and for the great Hellenizing adventure.
Philo of Alexandria, philosopher, writer, and statesman, represents a
fine example of mediation betweeen the two cultures.[21]

There also arose in other parts of the Greek world "Hellenistic Greek
megalopoleis" such as Antioch on the Orontes, Seleuceia, and Perga-
mon. To these "Hellenistic super-cities" flocked large numbers from the
newly conquered areas, populations that gradually underwent Hellenizing assimilation. "That such blending of populations did nothing to
hinder continuing intellectual development was conclusively demonstrated by such Graeco-Syran literary figures as the philosopher-
polymath Posidonius, the poet Meleager of Gadara, St. Paul, the
authors of the Gospels, and that most stylish humorist of the Roman
period, Lucian of Samosata."[22] Jewish communities arose throughout
the Greek-speaking areas and, owing to Judaism's strong religious and
ethnic character, fared well as they set up cohesive mechanisms and

---

[19]F.J. Frost, *Greek Society* (Lexington: Heath, 1980) 145.

[20]*Ibid*, 150.

[21]For an excellent, brief discussion of Philo, see P. Borgen, "Philo of Alexandria,"
233-82 in Stone, *Jewish Writings of the Second Temple Period*.

[22]Frost, *Greek Society*, 155; see also H. Stern, "The Jewish Diaspora," 1:117-83 in
Safrai, *The Jewish People in the First Century*.

acquired imperial privileges to foster external advancement and internal solidarity.[23]

Contrary to earlier assumptions that Palestine was isolated from the Hellenistic world, it is now commonly held that there also the process of Hellenization was widespread. Even before the time of Alexander contacts with the Greek world were not infrequent. After the Macedonians' conquests Palestine joined others in welcoming the cosmopolitan culture of the new rulers.

> In all some thirty towns of the area have been counted that were either Greek foundations or transformed *poleis*. These Hellenistic cities dotted the countryside of Palestine for several centuries prior to the first Christian century and were clearly centers from which the Greek language spread to less formally Hellenistic towns, such as Jerusalem, Jericho, or Nazareth.[24]

However, Palestinian Judaism, never the enthusiastic proponent of foreign cultures, reacted in varying ways to the influx of Hellenistic influence, from outright hostility and rebellion (during the Maccabean revolt and later), to peaceful coexistence, and even to considerable Hellenization under the Hasmonaeans and Herodians.

Christianity in its turn adopted concepts from Platonic, Stoic, and Cynic thought and from the popular mystery cults (e.g., the Greek Eleusian and Dionysiac mysteries) as its preachers and writers conveyed the meaning of the Christ-event to their disparate audiences throughout the Greco-Roman world. It was to that cosmopolitan world that early missionaries addressed their message of salvation through the prophet from Nazareth. Initially Semitic in character the young movement found its home in the Hellenistic domain, first of Judaism and then of the Gentile world. Thus the Christian scriptures must be considered, in varying degrees, the product of Hellenistic Judaism, but a literature that increasingly addressed the problems and concerns of the Gentile Greek population of the empire.

---

[23]Tcherikover, *Hellenistic Civilization and the Jews*, 296-333 and S. Applebaum, "The Organization of the Jewish Communities in the Diaspora," 1:464-503 in Safrai, *The Jewish People in the First Century*.

[24]Fitzmyer, "Languages of Palestine," 508; see also Tcherikover, *Hellenistic Civilization and the Jews*, 90-116; and Jones, *The Cities of the Eastern Roman Provinces*, especially chap. 10, pp. 226-94 and 446-69, revised by M. Avi-Yonah and H. Seyrig.

ROMAN POLITICAL CONTEXT

If Greece provided the cultural and linguistic background of early Christianity and Judaism its religious matrix, it was Rome that furnished the historical, political, and structural foundation. With expansion of the Roman republic to the west and east and especially its intervention in Jewish internal affairs in 63 B.C., the history of Judaism and its Christian offspring became inextricably linked with the vicissitudes of Roman politics. As it became ruler of the Mediterranean basin, Rome provided it with political, mililtary, legal, and cultural unity. For Palestine this meant the stable rule of the Herodian family in the political sphere and of Sadducean aristocrats in the religious domain. Herod the Great, the wily vassal king of Palestine, while despised by many of his subjects for his cruelty and foreign origin (an Idumaean whose Judaism was rather superficial), was nonetheless an energetic builder and competent ruler. Under his administration the city of Jerusalem underwent a Hellenistic and religious renaissance. At his death the kingdom was divided among his sons: Herod Antipas as tetrarch of Galilee and Peraea (4 B.C.-39 A.D.), Herod Philip as that of Ituraea, Trachonitis, and Paneas (4 B.C.-34 A.D.), and Herod Archelaus as ethnarch of Judaea, Samaria, and Idumaea (4 B.C.-6 A.D.).[25] Only the last mentioned proved troublesome and so the Judaean area was provided with a series of surprisingly incompetent Roman prefects, one of whom was responsible for the death sentence carried out against Jesus. It was due in large measure to such government agents that Palestine during the 50s and 60s was in constant turmoil resulting in the futile revolt against Rome and destruction of Jerusalem and its temple in 70.[26] Thus, these events were significant for the history both of Judaism and of the budding Jesus movement.

Events of the Roman period are relatively well-known due to the writings of an important participant, Josephus, the statesman and historian (c. 37-100 A.D.). After having led the Jewish forces in Galilee against Vespasian's troops, Josephus was compelled in defeat (67) to

---

[25]For a brief survey of the Herodian period see Leaney, *The Jewish and Christian World*, 99-120 and M. Stern, "The Reign of Herod and the Herodian Dynasty," 1:216-307 in Safrai, *The Jewish People in the First Century.*

[26]M. Stern, "The Province of Judaea," 1:308-76 in Safrai, *The Jewish People in the First Century.*

become an interpreter for the Romans. After the war he returned to Rome with Titus, the conqueror of Jerusalem and son of the newly acclaimed emperor Vespasian. There Josephus recieved citizenship, a generous pension, and an estate, circumstances which provided him leisure to compose a work on the Jewish war as well as a history of his people, titled "The Jewish Antiquities." These and his other works are crucial for an understanding of this period.[27]

While most of the NT writers were Hellenistic in language and cuture, or greatly influenced by it, they were either citizens or wards of the Roman empire whose benefits they enjoyed. Christian missionaries traveled with relative ease and safety (see Luke's accounts in Acts). The laws of Rome improved the lot of all, as did its commercial, military, and governmental structures. It was within such a universal community that Christianity spread through the Roman empire and produced the books of the New Testament.

However, Roman citizens and non-citizens, men and women of diverse ethnic, cultural, and religious background, and peoples of all classes, were alienated as a result of immense cultural turmoil of empire building and the disintegration of old world views. This process began during the Hellenistic and greatly accelerated during the Roman periods. Thus people sought meaning and goals for their lives in the many philosophical and theological movements of the period. Arrival of the Jesus movement upon the scene must have provoked curiosity and interest as well as opposition, ostracization, and in some cases persecution.[28] Of importance to us is that the movement both survived and succeeded and that it produced an anthology of works which allows us to examine the communities' many perceptions of their founder.

CHRISTIAN CHARACTER

To say that the New Testament is a collection of early Christian works is to underscore the importance of understanding the historical and cultural dynamics of the period during which these works were

---

[27]See D.M. Rhoads, *Israel in Revolution: 6-74 C.E.: A Political History Based on the Writings of Josephus* (Philadelphia: Fortress, 1976); T. Rajak, *Josephus: The Historian and His Society* (Philadelphia: Fortress, 1984); H.W. Attridge, "Josephus and His Works," 185-232 in Stone, *Jewish Writings of the Second Temple Period*; and Bartlett, *Jews in the Hellenistic World*, 72-191.

[28]We will have several occasions to discuss the Jesus movement's Roman setting; see especially chapter 13.

written. The sequence of events and their bearing upon these writers are crucial to our analysis of the literature.

Jesus was born some time before 4 B.C. and died around 30 A.D.[29] This is as precise as the sources will allow us to be. Another consideration is the conclusion of scholars that Mark, the first gospel, was not composed until c. 65-70; Matthew and Luke are dated somewhat later, c. 80-90. Within this long gap, between 30 and 70, only the letters of Paul of Tarsus can be situated with any confidence.[30] How the teaching of Jesus and the stories about him survived is the subject of discussion, since there was a lengthy period during which nothing was recorded. This material is presumed to have been handed down by word of mouth from believer to believer and from preacher to convert.

During this period one must also envision the spread of the Jesus movement beginning from Jerusalem. The passion narratives show that Jesus died alone and abandoned.[31] His immediate followers were without exception Palestinian Jews from Galilee and Judaea, whose language, like that of Jesus, was Aramaic.[32] It is around this nucleus that the early community evolved, having Jerusalem as its center. At the beginning it must have appeared as no more than a Jewish subgroup whose allegiance was to the teacher from Nazareth. The sources imply that the movement soon spread to the Greek-speaking Jews of Palestine and the Diaspora. These new members were called Hellenists (Greek in language and culture—Acts 6:1) and were more open to non-Jewish influences.[33] The movement appears to have spread rapidly among these outward-looking Greek-speaking Jews who had already become accustomed to the religious thinking of their Greco-Roman neighbors. It is among Hellenistic Christians, since there existed an intensive

[29] For a discussion of this chronology see J.L. McKenzie, *Dictionary of the Bible* (Milwaukee: Bruce, 1965) 132-33 and 432-36 and J . Finegan, *Handbook of Biblical Chronology* (Princeton: Princeton University, 1964) 215-59 and 285-98.

[30] For a brief, overall discussion of the relative dating of the NT books, see Harrington, *Interpreting the New Testament*, 146-47.

[31] On the importance of this fact for the relation of faith to the resurrection experience, see Harvey, *Jesus and the Constraints of History*, 166-73.

[32] On the language of Jesus and the early Christian community, confer Fitzmyer, "Languages of Palestine;" J.N. Sevenster, *Do You Know Greek? How Much Greek Could the First Jewish Christians Have Known?* (Leiden: Brill, 1969).

[33] E. Richard, *Acts 6:1-8:4: The Author's Method of Composition* (Missoula: Scholars, 1978) 338-46.

Jewish missionary movement in the Diaspora, that the admission of Greek-speaking Gentiles into the movement became widespread. By the time of Paul of Tarsus (late 40s and 50s) the mission to the non-Jews (whether Law-observant or Law-free) was extensive and a cause of tension within the early communities.

Expansion of the movement in terms of time and geography was considerable and rapid. This meant increased membership, greater diversity of cultural and ethnic background, and a multiplicity of stances vis-à-vis Greco-Roman culture and religion. As communities grew, so did the need for organization, unity, and information. Among their pagan and Jewish neighbors Christians experienced peaceful coexistence and successful proselytism, as well as social and religious ostracization, persecution, and cultural adaptation. These experiences produced much diversity. Early Christians, in various parts of the Roman empire, adjusted to contemporary culture in a rich variety of ways—both as internal and external strategy. These communities and the Jesus movement itself survived and prospered in terms of membership and ideological continuity (christology and ecclesiology).[34] Thus, one of the principal goals of this study is the examination of the NT works to discern the manner in which different writers, in their portraits of Jesus, adapted the Christ-event to contemporary culture in their efforts to communicate to and dialogue with believers and non-believers.

In the final analysis, this NT anthology is Christian by virtue of its central concern, Jesus of Nazareth. The role he plays in God's grand design, belief in him as God's agent and Son, and the hope placed in his community of fellowship are at the core of these writings.

Literary Approach to the Christian Anthology

Since the books of the New Testament are products of their time, they need to be examined in the light of what scholars know about the literature of that period. The student of the New Testament should employ the insights of literary criticism and theory to situate these early Christian works in their religious and literary context, to inquire about

---

[34]Among others, see B.J. Malina, "Normative Dissonance and Christian Origins," 35-59 in J.H. Elliott, ed., *Social-Scientific Criticism of the New Testament and Its Social World* (Decatur: Scholars, 1986).

their author and audience, and to investigate the structure and message of these documents. The New Testament consists of 27 literary works, some of which are related to one another in some way (common authorship, same subject) but most of which are independent creations by authors whose theological backgrounds and literary abilities were diverse. They are works of literature whose goal is the communication of a message, obviously inspired by the Christ-event, to an audience in need of their advice and information. The reader, separated from these by centuries of historical and theological evolution and by a different language and culture, is obliged to employ a combination of artistic sense and the tools of literary criticism to understand the New Testament since its works are ancient, religious, canonical literary texts. So one should inquire about these significant factors if one wishes to gain a sound interpretation of these works.[35]

Methodological considerations, however, take us further. Since the proper approach to these books is a literary-critical rather than a historical-critical one, the focus of the reader and scholar's effort should not be the quest of a historical event or authentic saying but rather appreciation of early Christian works and comprehension of their message. Whatever authors say about past events or however exact they are in recording a saying or episode, these are secondary considerations in the analysis of literature. Of primary concern is the work's narrative world or rhetorical construct. An author's point of view, purpose, and strategy along with the reader's perception of these are crucial in textual analysis. The literary work, author, and audience are at the core of the process called biblical criticism or interpretation. Beyond general literary considerations, however, there exist a number of important methods which scholars over the years have developed to assist the reader with these ancient religious texts. The remainder of this chapter, therefore, will introduce the reader to the basics of biblical criticism.

LITERARY-CRITICAL METHODOLOGY

Picking up the New Testament is like reading a newspaper or an anthology of 20th-century literature. One must be aware of the variety

---

[35]J. Barr, "Reading the Bible as Literature," *BJRL* 56 (1973) 10-33; Harrington, *Interpreting the New Testament*; Petersen, *Literary Criticism for New Testament Critics.*

of literary items and of the proper questions to be addressed to each. Reading is an art or a learned ability, an ability acquired over years of repeated and corrective action. The normal reader has learned to ask appropriate questions of specific types of reading materials and has acquired the give-and-take of reader response to most texts encountered.[36] Thus, one does not expect a cartoon to be as factual as a headline story or a sports column to be as thought-provoking as an editorial, nor does one read a short story or play with the same intensity and purpose as one does a five-line poem. A discriminating sense operates when one reads a newspaper, textbook, or bulletin board; it should be likewise when one reads various NT books. So one does not read an incidental note to a friend (Paul's letter to Philemon) with the same intensity or purpose as a foundational document (John or Matthew).

Furthermore, reading requires that the audience enter another's world, that originally of an author (who produced a text) and now, from the reader's perspective, that of the text being read. Distance, objectivity, and respect for the integrity of the text are necessary. So the methods examined in this chapter focus on the text, its world, structure, and strategy. Also, there is an effect on the consciousness of the reader as the text and its content are engaged; thus "the incorporation of the new requires a re-formation of the old."[37] Hence we consider such issues of modern literary theory as reader response and author/text interaction with reader/audience. In this last category we will speak of strategy, rhetoric, and author/audience horizons.

In terms of genre or literary type there is much variety within the NT canon. There are four gospels or biographies which present the Christ-event as narrative, i.e., stories about Jesus constructed on a time-line. These documents are stories and need to be read as such, since they have beginnings and endings, climaxes, a cast of characters, and other typical literary conventions. There is another type of narrative, like the Classical monograph, which relates the spread of Christianity from Jerusalem to Rome, namely the Acts of the Apostles. Here too one encounters a narrative world with a logic and strategy of its own. Further, this text is related to the Gospel of Luke and should be read in conjunction with it

---

[36]W. Iser, *The Act of Reading: A Theory of Aesthetic Response* (Baltimore: Johns Hopkins University, 1978).

[37]*Ibid*, 159.

if one is to do justice to the author's strategy and understand the audience's response. One also finds 21 letters and pastoral documents by Paul and others on a variety of subjects, many of which follow closely the epistolary genre of the period. Study of Hellenistic letters sheds light upon these early Christian creations and allows one to delve into the authors' purpose and message and to comprehend the original readers' horizon and the interaction between author and audience. Additionally, letters have specific issues and readers in view while other pastoral documents may envision more general life-situations and ideal audiences. Lastly, there is a visionary document called an apocalypse, the Book of Revelation. Much work, of late, has been devoted to this type of literature which is concerned with the end of the world and the plight of small but righteous communities of believers. It too presents its challenge to the reader who has virtually no acquaintance with this ancient genre. Each type described here, therefore, has its own literary conventions and requires of the reader a minimal familiarity with the peculiarities of that type of text. Genre criticism, a much neglected area of study until recently and one still in flux, is fundamental to biblical interpretation.[38]

Literary criticism prompts the reader to inquire not only about a book's genre but also about the ability and background of its author and about its structure, purpose, and message. It leads the interested student to seek information concerning the author's style and artistry, about the events narrated, about its author's and audience's cultural and religious milieu, and about a host of other pertinent issues. These questions, then, should be asked of any literary text if one wishes to obtain a better understanding and appreciation of its artistry and message.

Such considerations lead the reader to examine each of the NT books as separate entities produced by authors who lived in concrete situations during the first century and who wrote to specific audiences whose needs they addressed. By approaching each work on its own terms it becomes possible to understand what the author wished to communicate (to an intended reader) and from this to benefit from the writer's wisdom, a wisdom which the church (the extended audience) judged to

---

[38]The issue of genre will be addressed in the following chapters as each new work or group of works is introduced: gospel (chap. 4), acta (chap. 6); letters (chap. 8; also 7); pastoral documents (chap. 10; also 7); and apocalypse (chap. 11).

be normative of its beliefs. Thus, one becomes increasingly aware of the individuality of each author and of the uniqueness of each portrait of Jesus.

Following upon initial pointed criticism of NT methodology,[39] recent trends in literary analysis have supplemented more traditional approaches. More attention is given to rhetorical matters and therefore to the author's strategy and the audience's interaction with the text. Analyses of ancient rhetorical handbooks and practice have provided greater appreciation of early writers' ability and success in persuading readers and influencing their thought and behavior. Study of Classical norms for composing speeches, scenes, and narrative links, presenting characters, and developing time and space considerations have made modern readers more conscious of the art of narration or story-telling. Rhetorical analysis has also lent its attention to the peculiar conventions of poetry, the rhetoric of persuasion (the art of composing defense speeches, use of traditional arguments and commonplaces or *topoi*, etc.), and in general the writer's strategy.[40]

Related also to biblical criticism's interest in an author's strategy and its concern for the nature and use of language are two other methods, reader-response criticism and structuralism.[41] The first focuses upon the audience's interaction with the text. Relying upon reader-response and narrative theory, scholars examine the characteristics of successful strategy (closure, character portrayal, setting, point of view), the relation of narrative and rhetorical prose to real and ideal readers, and in general subscribe to the Greek rhetorical axiom that a text has "the ability to influence human behavior in a direct and practical manner."[42] This

---

[39]Among others, consult E. Güttgemanns, *Candid Questions Concerning Gospel Form Criticism: A Methodological Sketch of the Fundamental Problematics of Form and Redaction Criticism* (Pittsburgh: Pickwick, 1979).

[40]A.N. Wilder, *The Language of the Gospel: Early Christian Rhetoric* (NY: Harper and Row, 1971); G.A. Kennedy, *New Testament Interpretation through Rhetorical Criticism* (Chapel Hill: University of North Carolina, 1984).

[41]For a convenient introduction to both, see T.J. Keegan, *Interpreting the Bible: A Popular Introduction to Biblical Hermeneutics* (NY: Paulist, 1985).

[42]J.P. Tompkins, "An Introduction to Reader-Response Criticism," xxv in *Reader-Response Criticism: From Formalism to Post-Structuralism* (Baltimore: Johns Hopkins University, 1980); see also G. Genette, *Narrative Discourse: An Essay in Method* (Ithaca: Cornell University, 1980).

method, therefore, focuses upon the reader's response and the author's ability to influence thought and behavior by literary means.[43]

The second method pays greater attention to the nature of language, the processes of human communication, and the participation of specific texts in this intelligibility-enabling process. Lending attention to the minute symbols and structures of speech, scholars maintain that language and anthropology are intimately linked and so all texts participate in specific patterns: time-space complexes, communicative system or semiotics (and thus its decoding), and surface and depth structures. These scholars, therefore, relying upon theories of opposites (and the inversion of functions) or actantial and functional constants (and the relation of actor to receiver) propose to analyze author and reader relationships to text, the ultimate means of human communication.[44]

PRINCIPAL LITERARY METHODS

Over the years scholars have developed several important methods for the elucidation of scriptural texts.[45] 1) The first important one is source criticism, which elucidates a biblical work by examining its use of traditions, quotations, and its relation to other contemporary works— did an author borrow some facts, ideas, or traditions from other documents? Scholars propose that Matthew and Luke made generous use of the Gospel of Mark and a now lost, written sayings collection

---

[43] As related to Mark, see for example, F. Kermode, *The Genesis of Secrecy: On the Interpretation of Narrative* (Cambridge: Harvard University, 1979); N. Petersen, "When Is an End Not the End?" *Int* 34 (1980) 151-66; and D. Rhoads and D. Michie, *Mark as Story: An Introduction to the Narrative of a Gospel* (Philadelphia: Fortress, 1982); for Matthew, see R.A. Edwards, "Uncertain Faith: Matthew's Portrait of the Disciples," 47-61 in F.F. Segovia, *Discipleship in the New Testament* (Philadelphia: Fortress, 1985); and for John, confer R.A. Culpepper, *Anatomy of the Fourth Gospel: A Study in Literary Design* (Philadelphia: Fortress, 1983).

[44] D. Patte, *What Is Structural Exegesis?* (Philadelphia: Fortress, 1978). For a discussion of "surface and deep structures," see R.C. Tannehill, *The Sword of His Mouth* (Philadelphia: Fortress, 1975) 31-36.

[45] For a relatively short presentation, explanation, and examples of these methods see Harrington, *Interpreting the New Testament*; also confer W.A. Beardslee, *Literary Criticism of the New Testament* (Philadelphia: Fortress, 1970); E.V. McKnight, *What Is Form Criticism?* (Philadelphia: Fortress, 1969); and N. Perrin, *What Is Redaction Criticism?* (Philadelphia: Fortress, 1969).

usually referred to as the Q-Source (for German *Quelle*).[46] Source critics also discuss the relationship of John to the Synoptic gospels or to oral Jesus tradition, the dependence of 2 Peter 2 upon Jude 3-16, and the relationship of Colossians and Ephesians. They also investigate the extent to which an author like Paul or that of Hebrews made use of contemporary philosophical thought. The isolation of such influences are of concern to the source critic who also inquires about Luke's sources for the composition of Acts and about the origin of the esoteric images and world view of the Book of Revelation. For most NT writers one is obliged to inquire about their use of the Jesus tradition. One often detects early kerygmatic (preaching) formulas and liturgical fragments in various NT passages. The source critic is interested in isolating OT citations, themes, and vocabulary, as well as contemporary Jewish tradition, since most of these writers were either Jewish or familiar with Jewish Christian materials. Besides, the Jewish scriptures were the basis for early Christian theology and Judaism the matrix of both the life of Jesus and the early attempts at formulating and explaining the Christ-event. Source criticism then, in seeking to discover a particular author's resources, is invariably drawn into an examination of the thought world of the New Testament, its communities, and its writers.

If at the turn of the century the almost exclusive concern of source critics had been to discern written documents behind NT works, particularly the Synoptic gospels and Acts (for the former: Aramaic Matthew, Urmarkus, Proto-Luke, or Q and for the latter: Aramaic Acts, Jerusalem and Antiochene sources), more recent scholars, while still inquiring about sources, are more concerned about the entire range of influences which were brought to bear upon specific authors. More attention is given to NT authors' use of the Jewish scriptures and methods of biblical interpretation then current,[47] their knowledge and use of contemporary history, mythology, literature, and philosophy, and especially their use of the Jesus tradition.

2) Another method which contributes to our understanding of NT authors has received the name "form criticism" (*Formgeschichte*) since

---

[46]We will have occasion to discuss what is traditionally called the two-source hypothesis (i.e., the two sources of Matthew and Luke) in chap. 4 and the Q-Document in chap. 3.

[47]See Roetzel, *The World That Shaped the New Testament*, chap. 4: "Scripture and Interpretation," 77-94.

it attempts to isolate, examine, and classify the narrative and dicourse units which the evangelists and other writers employed in composing their works: e.g., miracles, parables, doxologies, hymns, etc.[48] Within the gospel narratives, for example, a writer may use speeches, tell stories, use other types of narrative, or make general summary or explanatory statements for the reader. Within a letter an author may use moral examples from various sources, employ invective or praise, or enunciate theological principles. Noting the existence of many such literary units or forms within the New Testament, scholars began to isolate and classify them according to literary characteristics to which they had been alerted by earlier studies of folkloric and oral literature. Since oral tradition and folk literature, to a far greater degree than conscious literary writing, tend to exhibit predictable patterns, to employ standard conventions, and to manifest regular laws of development, and since it became obvious that the decades which separated the death of Jesus from the emergence of the New Testament constituted an oral period, it was natural that the results of this discipline should be applied to the gospel narratives. By studying the standard features of various types of literary units, e.g., the parable and its development during oral transmission (increased allegorizing and moralizing characteristics),[49] it became possible to examine with some assurance the evolution of pre-NT traditions and of the Jesus movement. As a result of such study by scholars early in the century,[50] it became clear that the gospel and other tradition resulted from a complex, oral development within communities and not from the verbatim recording of the events of Jesus' life or the evolution of a unified point of view concerning the Christ-event. Stories were remembered, retold, applied, and eventually written down by authors, who, as members of worshiping communities, wished to counter internal and external problems and crises by appealing to the communities' traditions and wisdom.

Thus form criticism in its original usage refers to the study of oral pre-literary sense units which scholarship distingushed and identified in

---

[48]See chap. 3 for a more complete list of these.

[49]J. Jeremias, *The Parables of Jesus* (NY: Scribner's, 1972) 23-114; see especially 113-14.

[50]M. Dibelius, *From Tradition to Gospel* (NY: Scribner's, 1971) and R. Bultmann, *History of the Synoptic Tradition* (NY: Harper and Row, 1968); originally 1919 and 1921 respectively.

typological terms. As a result scholars became keenly aware of the importance of the oral period in the development of Jesus tradition and ecclesial lore, prior to and contemporary to the composition of the New Testament. If originally form criticism was focused upon the analysis of Synoptic tradition as the product almost exclusively of the community, more recently scholars have broadened the scope of this method in theoretical and practical terms. No longer viewing the gospels as anonymous productions of specific communities (owing to the insights of redaction criticism), scholars admit to a great complexity for both oral tradition and literary creativity. The term "form" is now employed to include literarily conscious structures and defensive strategies of these writers. Thus form criticism, in its more sophisticated and recent practice, is often hard to distinguish from rhetorical analysis and redaction criticism. Finally, it should be pointed out that form criticism, whether in its older sense or more recent practice, underscores the importance of literary rather than historical methods for the analysis of ancient literature.

3) While earlier studies emphasized the pre-gospel and early Christian tradition embedded in various NT works and focused upon the quest for the historical Jesus, it has become increasingly clear to later scholars that appreciation of the role played by the writers themselves is of equal importance for understanding this literature. Since the authors in question had a number of sources at their disposal and a variety of traditional units to draw upon, it seemed appropriate to investigate their choice of episodes, sayings, and traditions, their organization of these, their presuppositions, and their theology. So there developed a new discipline called "redaction criticism,"[51] i.e., a method whose goal is the study of the writers as authors, authors with diverse backgrounds, abilities, resources, goals, and points of view. Initially, the new method gave particular attention to an author's use of sources, peculiar vocabulary and idioms (use of word counts), and sought structural indicators and characteristics. For example, scholars noted that Matthew regularly modified the expression "kingdom of God" from Mark (1:15) and Q

---

[51]See the important contributions of W. Marxsen, *Mark the Evangelist: Studies on the Redaction History of the Gospel* (Nashville: Abingdon, 1969); G. Bornkamm, et al, *Tradition and Interpretation in Matthew* (Philadelphia: Westminster, 1963); and H. Conzelmann, *The Theology of St. Luke* (NY: Harper and Row, 1961); originally 1954, 1948, and 1954 respectively.

(Luke 6:20) to "kingdom of the heavens" (Matt. 4:17 and 5:3 respectively), or that Luke preferred "lake"(8:22f) to the Markan "sea"(4:39f).
Thus, repetition of themes, organization of episodes or arguments,
redactional additions to traditional elements, and omissions provided
clues to the writer's point of view (e.g., Matthew's grouping of similar
forms or Luke's addition to and insistence on the motifs of prayer and
journey). Unfortunately the results were far from unanimous in discerning individual authors' theologies.[52]

More recently the discipline has concentrated not only upon the
redactional features of the gospels and other works but also upon the
internal structure of these compositions, upon their theological interests,
and upon these works as overall stories or unities. At this juncture the
method becomes closely allied with composition analysis and rhetorical
criticism in its focus upon the overall structure of the composition and
upon its inner dynamics.

To illustrate in greater detail the methods just described, we offer in
parallel columns ("synopsis") the following brief passage, using the RSV
or Revised Standard Version, to facilitate our comparative analysis.

Matt 13:1-3	Mark 4:1-2	Luke 8:4
That same day	Again	
Jesus went out	he began to teach	
of the house		
and sat		
beside the sea.	beside the sea.	
And	And	And
great crowds	a very large crowd	when a great crowd
gathered	gathered	came together
		and people from
		town after town
about him,	about him,	came to him
so that he got	so that he got	
into a boat	into a boat	
and sat there	and sat in it	
	on the sea;	

[52]See J. Rohde, *Rediscovering the Teaching of the Evangelists* (Philadelphia:
Westminster, 1968), for an extensive survey of such studies from German scholarship.

and the whole crowd	and the whole crowd	
stood	was beside the sea	
on the beach.	on the land.	
And he taught them	And he taught them	
many things	many things	
in parables	in parables,	he said
	and in his teaching	
saying:	he said to them:	in a parable:

Considering the literary interrelationship of such passages as well as the sequence of events in all three gospels, most scholars conclude that Matthew and Luke made independent use of Mark to compose their narratives (the two-source hypothesis). From this example one sees that Matthew is more faithful to the Markan text than is Luke. Further, Matthew reproduces almost entirely Mark's subsequent parable chapter and expands it with material drawn from other sources, while Luke reduces the parable section and transfers much of it to a later chapter.

The verses are transitional in form and function and owe to Markan redaction; that is, they are composed by Mark to introduce a traditional parable collection (4:3f). This brief passage, while reflecting Markan style and themes, nonetheless, adopts the form and function of what form critics call an "editorial formulation" to make the broader narrative "coherent geographically, chronologically, and in part also materially."[53] Matthew and Luke, even while imposing changes upon these verses, also see them as a convenient transition from narrative to discourse.

Matthean and Lukan editorial activity calls for added attention. The former enhances both the temporal introduction ("again" becomes "that same day") and spatial element of the passage ("Jesus went out of the house"—a link is established with the preceding episode). Other features of Matthean editing are the simplification of the Markan text (reduction of the seemingly redundant stress given to the motif of teaching) and the improvement of its style ("sat in it on the sea" becomes "sat there" and "was beside the sea on the land" is reduced to "stood on the beach"). Luke, as usual, imposes greater changes upon the Markan source. The passage is simplified and reformulated into a complex sentence. Both the temporal and spatial settings are eliminated: the temporal owing to changes in the order of episodes before and following

---

[53]Bultmann, *History of the Synoptic Tradition*, 340-41.

the passage (see 8:1-3 and 8:19-21) and the spatial because of Luke's refusal to use the term "sea" for the "Lake [of Galilee]." Also since Luke only employs one parable at this point, the Markan "in parables" is modified to "in a parable." Since there is no surviving Markan source for comparison, it is more tenuous to estimate that author's redactional activity. Nonetheless, after surveying the entire gospel, it becomes clear that 4:1-2 are Markan in style and theme. We would note especially the author's stress upon the theme of teaching and liking of "began to teach," and lake settings. For Matthew we should note the emphasis upon Jesus' "sitting" position (see the setting of the sermon on the mount—5:1 and contrast with Luke 6:17 where Jesus "stands" instead) and for Luke we would point out the note of universalism ("people from town after town").

4) While most scholars describe themselves as practioners of redaction criticism or of its more evolved form, composition analysis, few limit themselves to any one method in analyzing NT literature. Instead, the scholar employs a variety of literary, historical, sociological, and theological methods to arrive at a better understanding of this literature. The complete student of the New Testament should be acquainted with linguistic and textual issues, since it is an anthology of literature written in an ancient language (Greek of the post-Classical era) long before the invention of the printing press. Thus, proper translation (reliable, modern editions) and integrity of text are essential to proper interpretation.[54] Further, informative introductions and footnotes as well as critical tools (handbooks and dictionaries) greatly assist the interested reader. The production of such tools constitutes another facet of biblical scholarship.

5) Finally, we might discuss a relatively recent method which is gaining respectability in NT circles, namely, the anthropological or sociological approach to the world and literature of the New Testament.

---

[54]For a discussion of the relative merits of recent translations, one might consult J.J. Pilch, "Selecting a Bible Translation," *BTB* 10 (1980) 71-77 and Harrington, *Interpreting the New Testament*, 25-41. As regards textual criticism, the modern reader might pay particular attention to the footnotes of recent, critical translations; see for example the textual notes in the Revised Standard Version for Mark 16:8 and John 7:52. More generally see J. Finegan, *Encountering New Testament Manuscripts: A Working Introduction to Textual Criticism* (Grand Rapids: Eerdmans, 1974) and L.R. Bailey, ed, *The Word of God: A Guide to English Versions of the Bible* (Atlanta: John Knox, 1982).

At first glance one might presume that it should have been considered in the first part of the chapter along with historical issues. One should distinguish, however, between a method which has as its goal "social description and analysis" (historical method) and one which attempts "the application of social theory to New Testament texts"[55] (literary approach). Employing sociological models scholars attempt to discern leadership roles, community structures, social dynamics, pivotal values, social groupings, and other processes of interaction or restraint discernible within NT literature.[56] Such methodology shows promise on several levels. It provides additional instruments to verify conclusions obtained from purely literary criteria. Its structural models, if employed judiciously, can fill in lacunae in the biblical data. Finally, such an approach offers assistance for pursuing the hermeneutical task of conveying the meaning of ancient texts to extended readers.

Having surveyed the historical and literary concerns of NT study, the reader is set to embark upon a journey through that literature in search of the many images the early communities had of their founder. It has become clear that, in addition to a social and historical description of the NT world, one should employ all suitable methods in the study of this anthology so that it might reveal its meaning to a new audience and thereby continue to have significance for new generations of believers who desire to be serious students of the bible.[57] Before moving on to an examination of the first gospel, however, one last issue, that of the pre-gospel development of the Jesus tradition, will be addressed in the following chapter.

---

[55]C. Osiek, *What Are They Saying about the Social Setting of the New Testament?* (NY: Paulist, 1984) 4-6.

[56]*Ibid.*; B.J. Malina, *The New Testament World: Insights from Cultural Anthropology* (Atlanta: John Knox, 1981); H.C. Kee, *Christian Origins in Sociological Perspective: Methods and Resources* (Philadelphia: Westminster, 1980); and G. Theissen, *The Sociology of Early Palestinian Christianity* (Philadelphia: Fortress, 1978).

[57]The reader might again consult Fitzmyer's discussion of the relationship of critical methodology to Christian faith, *A Christological Catechism*, 18-23.

3

Development of
the Jesus Tradition

A fascinating and crucial stage in the development of many world religions was the early struggle within these traditions to formulate an adequate view of the founder. The founder's uniqueness is a given, though the extent and nature of the claims made by believers is the result of a process whereby the self-identity of the movement becomes focused. So it was with the early church.

> Some movements have no dominant figure in the beginning; but Christianity began with Jesus. And it was *the meaning of Jesus*, of what he had said and done, together with what the first Christians understood him to be and to have been, to be doing and to have done, which was the most significant factor in the new sect's own developing self-understanding and developing sense of distinctiveness over against the other religions, sects, and philosophies of the time. Hence the need to focus particular attention on this area of Christianity's beginnings.[1]

The New Testament offers much data for tracing such a process. In this chapter, therefore, we will explore the pre-NT development of the community's views of its founder as a prelude for studying the NT writings.

In approaching this task one is again confronted by methodological issues. Until recently the standard procedure was to use the titles given Jesus in different strata of NT literature as the key to discern early

---

[1]J.D.G. Dunn, *Christology in the Making: A New Testament Inquiry into the Origins of the Doctrine of the Incarnation* (Philadelphia: Westminster, 1980) ix.

christologies. While an earlier generation of scholars presumed "that Jesus deliberately and consistently reinterpreted existing titles such as Son of God, Son of Man, Messiah, Lord, and so forth," some more recent authors insist that these "were shattered and remolded by what he was and by what he had achieved."[2] The procedure then has been to trace the pre-Christian meaning of these titles, to examine their NT usage, and to discern a chronological and typological schema for this development.[3] It is in this context that studies concerned either with Jesus' usage of various titles (e.g., the Son of Man)[4] or the problem of his self-consciousness and claims should be situated.

This approach has not gone unchallenged, since the scholar is obliged "to ask whether, when we have finished asking about the '*titles*' of Jesus, there is not something even more basic, of which any description of the genesis of Christology must take account, namely the *experience* of him reflected in the New Testament."[5] Whether one insists that the Jewish heritage of the early Jesus movement provided the grounds for or a restraint to the development of christology,[6] or whether one maintains that the experience and memory of Jesus of Nazareth and faith in him constitute the beginnings of that reflection,[7] one would have to conclude with C.F.D. Moule that "a 'developmental' account of the genesis of

---

[2]R.H. Fuller, "Christology: Its Nature and Methods," 5 in R.H. Fuller and P. Perkins, *Who Is This Christ? Gospel Christology and Contemporary Faith* (Philadelphia: Fortress, 1983).

[3]For example, F. Hahn, *The Titles of Jesus in Christology* (London: Lutterworth, 1969); Cullmann, *The Christology of the New Testament*; R.H. Fuller, *The Foundations of New Testament Christology* (NY: Charles Scribner's, 1965); and W. Kramer, *Christ, Lord, Son of God* (London: SCM, 1966).

[4]See especially the classical work of H.E. Tödt, *The Son of Man in the Synoptic Tradition* (Philadelphia: Westminster, 1965) and more recently the surveys of the issue by Dunn, *Christology in the Making*, 65-97 and B. Lindars, *Jesus Son of Man: A Fresh Examination of the Son of Man Sayings in the Gospels in the Light of Recent Research* (London: SPCK, 1983).

[5]C.F.D. Moule, *The Origin of Christology* (London: Cambridge University, 1977) 9; see also the critiques of Marshall, *The Origins of New Testament Christology*; W. Marxsen, *The Beginnings of Christology, Together with the Lord's Supper as a Christological Problem* (Philadelphia: Fortress, 1979); and M. Hengel, *The Son of God: The Origin of Christology and the History of Jewish-Hellenistic Religion* (Philadelphia: Fortress, 1976).

[6]Hengel, *The Son of God* and Harvey, *Jesus and the Constraints of History*.

[7]Moule, *The Origin of Christology*; Marshall, *The Origins of New Testament Christology*; and Marxsen, *The Beginnings of Christology*.

Christology does ... better justice to the evidence than an 'evolutionary' account."[8] Our approach, therefore, will be both developmental and literary, developmental since we view it not as uniform or successive stages of an evolutionary process but as an outgrowth of early followers' experience as expressed in credal formulas and literary since our exposition will be based upon a study of these credal formulas.

Discerning the Earliest Christologies

Between the Jesus level and that of the NT writers there was continuous intellectual activity within the community regarding the Christ-event. Knowledge of this activity, however, is available only from the writings of believers who composed their works at a later date. Between the time of Jesus' death and that of the first Christian writings there is a significant gap. Since Paul's first letters were penned in the 40s and Mark was probably written around 65-70, one must reckon with a sizeable lapse of time between the life of Jesus and the emergence of most NT literature between 80 and 100.

Another factor to consider is the nature of the literature and the character of the sources of our knowledge. These texts are closely associated with specific problems and their resolutions. Thus the NT letters are "occasional" documents written with audiences and problems in mind and not christological treatises or early Christian histories. The letters and tracts of our Christian anthology rarely indulge in extended christological discussions; instead they prefer to establish a doctrinal basis for their moral concerns and problem-solving. The letters tell us little about the events following the death of Jesus; the gospels concentrate upon his life; and only the Acts of the Apostles relates sequentially the events following the death and resurrection. But since Acts was written much later than the events discussed (c. 80-90) and since its writer presents a theological version of the Christian experience[9] and not, like a modern historian, a blow-by-blow account of the events,

---

[8]Moule, *The Origin of Christology*, 9.

[9]Luke, in the prologue of the gospel, speaks of "compiling a narrative of the things which have been accomplished among us" (Luke 1:1), i.e., which God has brought to fulfilment (use of divine passive—see I.H. Marshall, *The Gospel of Luke* [Grand Rapids: Eerdmans. 1979] 41).

we must use this information with caution when reconstructing the history and thought of that period. Further, these documents reveal Christian communities and theologies at different stages of development. In other words, they are diverse and complex and one finds in them multiple and variously evolved christologies. In the gospels especially one discovers developed and complex portraits of Jesus which presuppose years of community reflection, preaching, and worship.

From the post-resurrection perspective of these writers and their later, advanced christological stance, we are forced to glean clues to the early communities' thinking. As a result of literary analysis we are able to isolate traditional units and fragments (embedded as unsuspecting quotations) which these writers borrowed from their common store of tradition. One is able to isolate christological formulas and hymns by noting the peculiarity of language, style, vocabulary, thought, and poetic or other types of structure which a textual unity may manifest. An example is found in Paul's Letter to the Thessalonians, where he uses a traditional Hellenistic fragment in describing the conversion of this community:

a   you turned to God from idols
b   to serve the living and real God
c   (and) to wait for his Son from the heavens
a'   whom he raised from the dead
b'   Jesus who delivers us
c'   from the wrath to come

(1 Thess. 1:9-10—RSVmod)[10]

Owing to the non-Pauline expressions used: "turn to" for "believe," "real" only here in Paul, "deliver" never in an eschatological context, not the usual word for "wait," and "heavens" for "heaven," we conclude that these verses are pre-Pauline. The last mentioned, "heavens" in the plural, is Jewish rather than idiomatic Greek; the latter is usual in Paul. Further, the text is poetic in rhythm and structure. One notes that parts *a* and *a'* are in the past, *b* and *b'* in the present, and *c* and *c'* in the future, that the first stanza centers on God and the second on Jesus, and that

---

[10]The RSV (Revised Standard Version) will be employed throughout this study and will on occasion be slightly modified (indicated as *RSVmod*) in order to facilitate analysis and comparision.

"deliver" (*b*) is a pun on the Aramaic name "Jesus," i.e., "God saves or delivers" (also Matt. 1:21). Finally, there is a delicate balance between theology (centered on God), christology (Jesus as agent), and eschatology (resurrection, return, and judgment). Already in the pre-Pauline confessions the Christ-event is central to Christian belief; namely, by his resurrection Jesus is united to his Father and is the believer's means of deliverance from this age and from the wrath of the next.

It is from such fragments and more developed christological hymns that one perceives the great concern followers had about the founder of their movement. In all likelihood, early preaching centered on the binary profession of faith or kerygmatic formula (*kerygma* being Greek for "what is preached") concerning Jesus' death and resurrection or, as Paul would have it, "Christ crucified" (the term "Christ" being a proclamation of faith in Jesus as messiah or lord). Early kerygmatic units or credal formulas and early belief itself were binary in expression and in character since they were centered on the pre- and post-resurrection realities of the Christ-event. This basic core was expressed in formulas such as "Jesus is Lord" or "Jesus is the Christ" (see Rom. 10:9; 1 Cor. 12:3; Phil. 2:11). There was a focus on the earthly existence or death of Jesus and on his subsequent resurrection or glory. This is well expressed in a pre-Pauline formula found in Rom. 1:3-4:

> his Son, who was descended from David
> according to the flesh
> and designated Son of God in power
> according to the Spirit of holiness by his
> resurrection from the dead.

Since the language of this text (Davidic descent, "Spirit of holiness") is not particularly Pauline, we conclude that the formula expresses earlier Christian beliefs, which Paul and his Roman audience could accept. From it we see that Christians perceived in Jesus one approved by God, one whose death was intimately related to his resurrection (theme of sonship), and to their deliverance.

Another example is found in 1 Peter 1:21 (RSV mod), where the author employs a hymnic fragment:

a	he raised	he gave	a'
b	him	to him	b'
c	from the dead	glory	c'

We find here a verse-like passage which consists of parallel participial constructions ("who raised" and "who gave" of the RSV represent participles in Greek) and result in a chiastic structure, i.e., an abc-c′b′a′ pattern. Theologically, the passage dwells not on the death/ resurrection antithesis but focuses on post-resurrection realities, namely, Christ's glorification. Additionally, we perceive here an early, low christology wherein God is the agent and Jesus the servant.

With time and reflection communities pursued the christological tendencies and hints found in the tradition. It was the death and resurrection which claimed attention since these realities were central to the Christian's faith and interpretation of the Christ-event. However, speculation about Jesus' post-resurrection and pre-death existence bore fruit in hymnic and liturgical lore and oral tradition, fragments of which are found in many NT books: Phil. 2:6-11; Heb. 1:2-4; Col. 1:15-20; 1 Tim. 3:16; John 1:1-18; and fragments in 1 Peter. The importance of such hymns is underscored by Paul (1 Cor. 14:26), post-Pauline writers (Col. 3:16-17; Eph. 5:15), and Pliny the governor who, in 112 A.D., writes to the emperor Trajan that his Christian subjects "were in the habit of meeting on a certain fixed day before it was light, when they sang in alternate verses a hymn to Christ, as to a god" (Eph. 10:96).[11]

Early Christological Development

From an examination of traditional fragments and hymnic passages we are led to see early christological development as an expansion forward and backward of the early kerygma,[12] as in the following diagram:

Agency ◄──Life
              ►◄──Death/ Resurrection ──►Heavenly Abode
Pre-Existence ◄

The forward movement involved interest in the Christ's post-resurrection activity while the backward dynamics focused either upon

[11]See W. Melmoth and W.M.L. Hutchinson, eds, *Pliny: Letters* (Cambridge: Harvard University, 1947) 2:403.

[12]See also Marxsen, *The Beginnings of Christology* and "Christology in the NT," 146-56 in *IDBSup*

the life and ministry of Jesus or upon his cosmic activity and pre-existence. The two movements reveal varying interests in the Christ-event, interests expressed in hymnic formulations about the Christ's role as agent of God, about his destiny and eventually his origin, and also tantalizing hints about his work as God's servant. At the same time, apparently, there developed interest in the "mighty works and wonders and signs which God did through him" (Acts 2:22). This interest contributed immensely to the preservation, formulation, and development of the Jesus tradition as expressed orally and then, via narrative conventions, in a variety of gospels.

CHRISTOLOGICAL TITLES

At this juncture, we should consider the function of the "titles of majesty" conferred on Jesus. As Marxsen has insisted, they are not "statements *about* Jesus' history," but instead, presuming this history and the central elements of the kerygma (death and resurrection), they are statements about Christ's role or function vis-à-vis God and God's work for humanity.[13] The early christologies, whether expressed in hymnic liturgical fragments or by exalted titles, were functional in nature. If one must agree with Hengel that

> these forms of Jewish thought and language concerned with a mediator of revelation and salvation at the beginning and the end of time almost forced earliest Christianity to interpret Jesus' preaching and actions, his claim to be God's eschatological messianic ambassador, his unique connection with the Father, the imminence of whose salvation he announced, his shameful death and his resurrection, which was interpreted as exaltation, in a concentrated form as a *unique, 'eschatological' saving event*,[14]

then one must also insist that the titles which both the Jewish and Jesus traditions offered early believers also forced themselves upon their christological thought and language, allowing them to confess Jesus in roles worthy of his soteriological function or as "unique, eschatological saving event." The titles served the community both

---

[13]"Christology in the NT," 148.
[14]*The Son of God*, 90.

as bearers of the content of early tradition and as convenient vehicles for developing christology.[15]

KERYGMA: FORWARD AND BACKWARD DYNAMICS

Returning to the diagram noted above, we begin by considering the forward dynamics and its numerous vestiges detectable in the NT writings. Despite the frequent, negative statements of a generation ago that some NT authors betrayed the early kerygma by capitulating to "early catholicism" (i.e., turning away from the core of the kerygma to historical, structural, and moral concerns),[16] there is a definite tendency in the traditional and hymnic fragments to move beyond the perimeters of the binary formula of the kerygma. This tendency is evident in 1 Cor. 15:1-7. There Paul states that he is using traditional material concerning the Christ's death, burial, and resurrection (vv. 3-4) and then gives a list of resurrection appearances (vv. 5-7).[17] In defense of the key role which the theme of resurrection plays in Christian belief ("if Christ has not been raised then our preaching is in vain and your faith is in vain," v. 14), Paul appeals to the post-resurrection activity of the Christ, that is, to his appearances to members of the community. This same dynamic, it seems, will contribute to the development of resurrection lore and narratives. Thus, although Paul is addressing community problems, he none-theless participates in the process responsible for the production and preservation of lore about the Christ's post-resurrection activity.

The NT books contain many hints about such activity. In relation to his being raised by God from the dead, Jesus is said to be the one who "has been given glory," "designated Son of God," and the one who will return as "Son from the heavens" (1 Peter 1:21; Rom. 1:4; 1 Thess. 1:10). He is enthroned in heaven and sits at God's right hand,

---

[15]On the "titles of majesty" (*Hoheitstitel*) as vehicles of tradition in the development of christology, see Dunn, *Christology in the Making* and Harvey, *Jesus and the Constraints of History*.

[16]See particularly the discussion of E. Käsemann's views by D.J. Harrington, "Ernst Käsemann on the Church in the New Testament," 15-45 and "The 'Early Catholic' Writings of the New Testament: The Church Adjusting to World History," 61-78 in *Light of All Nations: Essays on the Church in New Testament Research* (Wilmington: Glazier, 1982).

[17]See J. Kloppenborg, "An Analysis of the Pre-Pauline Formula in 1 Cor. 15:3b-5 in Light of Some Recent Literature," *CBQ* 40 (1978) 351-67.

from where he will return as judge in the final days. The following fragment (1 Tim. 3:16) illustrates an early formulation of these post-resurrection themes:

he was manifested in the flesh,	a
vindicated in the spirit,	b
seen by angels,	b
preached among the nations,	a
believed on in the world,	a
taken up in glory.	b

The letters *a* and *b* refer to earthly and heavenly realities respectively; i.e., "flesh," "nations," and "world" address the lower realm while "spirit," "angels," and "glory" deal with the upper realm.[18] The fragment is divided into two stanzas, each of which is binary in form. In the first, one line deals with the first part of the kerygmatic formula and two with the second, while in the second, all three lines deal with Christ's post-resurrection role, two referring to his earthly (through the work of ministers) and heavenly activity. Indeed, comparison of this fragment with a passage in 1 Peter 3:18-19 confirms this interpretation.[19] The text, after an initial statement about Jesus' life and death, eulogizes his post-resurrection role. Examination of 1 Peter 3 and other hymns reveals traces of still more post-resurrection activities: the "descent into hell" (release of imprisoned spirits—1 Peter 3:19), the subjection of all the powers (reconciliation), and the enthronement (right hand, bestowing of glory, exaltation, conferring of lordship or preeminence). Mention should be made here of the importance of Psalm 110 (its emphasis on lordship, right hand, and scepter) in this early christological development.[20]

---

[18]See the analysis of J.T. Sanders, *The New Testament Christological Hymns: Their Historical Religious Background* (Cambridge: UP, 1971) 15-17 and 94-95.

[19]In partial agreement with Sanders, *ibid.*, 17-18; for a fuller discussion of the hymnic material of 1 Peter, see chapter 10.

[20]Among others see D.M. Hay, *Glory at the Right Hand: Psalm 110 in Early Christianity* (Nashville: Abingdon, 1973) and M. Gourgues, *A la droite de Dieu: résurrection de Jésus et actualisation du Psaume 110:1 dans le Nouveau Testament* (Paris: Gabalda, 1978).

A final note should be made regarding the Christ's post-resurrection activity, namely, the reading back into the ministry of post-resurrection themes.[21] For example, the concept of sonship, associated in the early tradition with resurrection (Rom. 1:4 and 1 Thess. 1:10), becomes in Mark 1:11 a means to establish Jesus' divinely sanctioned identity, while the theme of glory, also related to resurrection or enthronement (1 Peter 1:20), is associated in Mark 9:2-8 with his earthly activity.

We turn next to the backward dynamics and its hymnic vestiges (again see diagram above). Some traditional fragments indicate that there was, early in the churches' consciousness, a concern for Jesus' salvific role (Col. 1:20; Heb. 1:3) as well as for his earthly activity and background (emphasis upon his humanity as in Phil. 2:7-8 or upon his Davidic descent as in Rom. 1:3). This interest in the life and ministry of the master was to find its impetus in the fascination for storytelling and will be treated below.

A similar dynamic is the tradition's desire to attribute cosmic activity to the Christ and to dwell on the nature of his relationship to God; thus he is seen as having lordship over all creation ("heir of all things," Heb. 1:2 and "first born from the dead" and "preeminent," Col. 1:18; see also John 1:3). One also finds tentative ventures into pre-existence christology. In temporal terms the Christ is said to be one who "is before all things" (Col. 1:17) or who existed before time was (John 1:1). But more significantly Colossians calls him "image of the invisible God" or one in whom "all fulness was pleased to dwell" (1:15, 19). The Johannine hymn, while never explicitly identifying Jesus with the Logos, attributes divinity to the eternal Word (John 1:1-2, 18).

Lastly, we examine a hymnic fragment (Heb. 1) which clearly illustrates this backward dynamics:

2	a Son, whom he appointed the heir of all things through whom also he created the world,	
3	who, being the reflection of (his) glory	a
	and the stamp of his nature,	
	bearing all things	b
	by the word of his power,	
	having made purification for sins,	c

---

[21]Fuller, "The Titles of Jesus in Early Christology," in *Who Is This Christ?*, deals at length with what he calls "the retrojection of the titles of Jesus" (43-49).

sat down at the right of the majesty on high,   d
4   having become so much superior to angels as the name
he has obtained is more excellent than theirs.

Only verse 3 (RSVmod) is considered part of the hymn, though vv. 2
and 4 contain hymnic themes. "Being," "bearing," and "having made" of
v. 3 are participles, a feature of early hymns by which a series of
qualifying phrases is attributed to the subject. The rhythmic pattern and
theological concepts also argue for a hymnic source. Verse 3a implies
divine pre-existence; 3b a role in governance of the universe; 3c salvific
work on humanity's behalf; and 3d enthronement at God's right hand.
Parts 3c and 3d reflect the earlier binary form of traditional, kerygmatic
formulas.

It is the theme of pre-existence, however, which is of concern to us at
this point. 3a and 3b (also v. 2) concentrate upon two pre-earthly
aspects, the Son's pre-existence and role vis-à-vis creation. Both are
expressed in Hellenistic terms, reminiscent of Jewish wisdom speculation. The following passage (Wisdom 7:25-8:1) is crucial for understanding the intellectual context out of which a pre-existence christology
developed:

7:25   For she is a breath of *the power* of God,
and a pure emanation of *the glory* of the Almighty;
therefore nothing defiled gains entrance into her.
26   For she is *a reflection* of eternal light,
a spotless mirror of the working of God,
and an image of his goodness.
27   Though she is but one, she can do all things,
and while remaining in herself,
she renews all things;
in every generation she passes into holy souls
and makes them friends of God, and prophets;
28   for God loves nothing so much
as the man who lives with wisdom.
29   For she is more beautiful than the sun,
and excels every constellation of the stars.
Compared with the light she is found to be superior,
30   for it is succeeded by the night,
but against wisdom evil does not prevail.

8:1   She reaches mightily from one end of the earth
        to the other,
        and she orders all things well.[22]

This is a fine example of Hellenistic Jewish thought so evident in the Alexandrian writer Philo and intertestamental Enoch literature. Wisdom, in "Platonic terms," becomes an emanation of God (note the metaphorical synonyms of breath, reflection, mirror, and image):[23] like in nature, separate in essence, and self-abiding yet one with the source of its being. Description of the Son as "reflection of [God's] glory" is identical to that of Wisdom (italicized words above indicate identical Greek terms in the two texts). Further, the phrase "the stamp (*charaktēr*) of his nature" is probably synonymous to "image" (*eikon*) of the same verse (see also Col. 1:15). While Wisdom's activity is manifold, its role in relation to the universe is of interest here. It is all powerful, world renewing, and source of order. In like manner the Christ is given a role in the creation, ordering, and sustaining of the universe (Heb. 1:2, 3b; see also Col. 1:15-17 and John 1:3-4).[24]

We conclude that believers professed Jesus first of all to be an agent of God, whose death was regarded by that same God as expiation for human wrongdoing and who consequently was raised to a glorious status by God. Just as Christians reflected on the role of their Lord they also speculated about his destiny and origin. If reflection about his post-resurrection activity or destiny led to speculation about his relationship to God or origin, it is nonetheless preoccupation with his salvific role as expressed in the theme of exaltation which one finds in NT writers. The mythic or structural pattern associated with such a view is usually called an "exaltation or enthronement christology" and might be shown as follows:

                                              Enthronement As Son

        Death/ Resurrection

Such a diagram represents an extension forward of the kerygmatic

---

[22] Author's own literal translation from the Greek.

[23] Even Philo, when describing the Divine Logos, does not employ such bold terminology; see D. Winston, *The Wisdom of Solomon* (NY: Doubleday, 1979) 184-90.

[24] Further contacts might be noted between this passage from Wisdom and other christological hymns concerning the invincibility of light/ Wisdom, the relation between "image" and "stamp," creation "by his word," and superiority of Son/ Wisdom.

formula and illustrates the type of low christology commonly encountered in the New Testament. Even the christological hymn of Phil. 2:6-11 can plausibly be thus interpreted. Paul, relying upon an early hymn, believed, along with that source, that Jesus, though made according to God's likeness and image like Adam, unlike him did not grasp at equality with the Divine.[25] Paul was not interested in Jesus' origin but in his role (humble obedience) vis-à-vis the Father and humanity. It was Jewish and Hellenistic thinking as represented by the suffering servant (Isaiah 40:1f), the old and new Adam (Genesis 1-3), the primal man (contemporary thought), the revealing word of God, and pre-existent Wisdom which fueled speculation concerning Jesus' role in the history of salvation and also his destiny and origin.

Beyond this pattern there developed a concept of agency, not only of one who did the will of God but also of one who was sent by God to carry out the divine plan. This "agency christology" was particularly conducive to the narrative genre where the concept serves to establish Jesus' divine power and authority (see Mark 9:37).

It was the paradigm of wisdom and the influence of wisdom speculation which contributed greatly to the christologies of the late New Testament and subsequent church councils. In many cases, what had been stated concerning Jesus' role and relationship to the Father (obedient servant, one foretold and manifested as part of God's plan, the one who orders and even creates and recreates the universe), soon, in an increasingly more Hellenized world, took on the perspective of origin and status. A passage such as Wisdom 7:25-8:1 contributed to the development of a pre-existence christology as Christians attempted to define the Son's relationship to the Father. The mythic structure, however, owes to other influences. The following passage from the intertestamental work 1 Enoch 42 is of interest here:

1. Wisdom could not find a place in which she could dwell;
   but a place was found (for her) in the heavens.
2. Then Wisdom went out to dwell with the children of the
   people,

---

[25]Murphy-O'Connor, *Becoming Human Together*, 46-48; idem, "Christological Anthropology in Phil 2:6-11," *RB* 83 (1976) 25-50; Dunn, *Christology in the Making*, 114-21; Neyrey, *Christ Is Community*, 218-27; and J. Ziesler, *Pauline Christianity* (NY: Oxford University, 1983) 41-44.

but she found no dwelling place.
(So) Wisdom returned to her place
and she settled permanently among the angels.[26]

Wisdom has a home only in the heavens; so while visiting humanity and finding no lasting, earthly home, she returns to her seat among the angels. Similarity to the christological hymns is obvious. The Christ leaves heaven, visits humanity, and returns to his heavenly abode. The author of the Fourth Gospel makes extensive use of this heavenly-abode imagery with its implications of human rejection, while some of the hymns employ explicitly this mythic structure. We might diagram this "pre-existence christology" as follows:

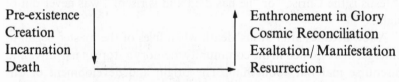

Pre-existence	Enthronement in Glory
Creation	Cosmic Reconciliation
Incarnation	Exaltation/ Manifestation
Death	Resurrection

As Wisdom began in heaven, came to visit humanity, and returned to her rightful place with God, so did the Christ; the wisdom model existed for the borrowing.

While one might be tempted in the development from low to high christologies, involving pre-existence, to see the main line of the development of NT tradition, it is reflection on the founder's role which predominates. The authors are concerned with the Christ-event and consequently with the role which Jesus played in the eternal plan. They are interested in how and why Jesus acted more than in who he was, i.e., an agency or functional rather than an incarnational christology.[27] The christological titles too denote function, whether obedient service, establishment of God's rule, or rendering of eschatological judgment (Son of God, Christ, and Son of Man respectively), rather than identity. The gospels, to which we direct our attention next, dwell upon the unique period when the Jewish Messiah put into effect the Father's plan for him. They too employ traditional titles, for they are interested in his role as Lord, Messiah, Son of Man, and Son of God. The evanglists and other writers see Jesus as paradigmatic of God's concern for humanity

---

[26]Translation by E. Isaac in Charlesworth, *The Old Testament Pseudepigrapha*, 1:33.

[27]See the convenient and classic discussion of early christological schemata in Fuller, *The Foundations of New Testament Christology*, 243-49.

and his life both as salvific and normative for his followers.[28]

Development of the Jesus Material

While worship tended to foster christological speculation, preaching (*kerygma*), teaching (*didache*), and moral exhortation (*paraenesis*) seem to have spurred the development of the Jesus material. The former favored the hymnic or poetic, the latter prefered the narrative or story form. But in both instances the credal formulas retained their structural and dynamic force as preachers, teachers, and writers set about the task of theologizing, for the binary kerygmatic affirmation "Jesus is Lord" ("Jesus is the Christ," or "he has died and is risen") was never out of sight.

A few decades after Jesus' death when lives of the master began to emerge, there existed in the community memory a store of narrative and discourse material about him. The origin and development of this material will always be of interest to us, though the process and details of this development are shrouded in mystery. Nonetheless, scholarship by employing literary methods can provide the reader with interesting and helpful insights. It is to the results of these various types of criticism, as applied to the development of early Christian tradition, that we now turn our attention.

Along with the early community's focus upon the kerygma or death and resurrection of Jesus, already in these formulas we see the community's interest in Jesus' life, ministry, and background. Paul in Rom. 1:3-4 employs a fragment whose formulation of the binary formula is of interest, especially that the Christ "was descended from David according to the flesh." While such a passage in its Pauline formulation focuses upon the continuity in salvation history (prophets in v. 2, Jesus as son of David in v. 3, son of God as the one raised from the dead in v. 4, and the roles of his followers in ministry and conversion in v. 5), that of the

---

[28]From the above discussion it should be clear that the expressions "high" and "low" (or " higher" and "lower"), as employed in this study, are relational terms. Their use represents an attempt to situate a particular christological formulation or portrait relative to claims of pre-existence or unique, divine sonship and does not recall the terminology of late 19th-century theologians, for whom Jesus was either God in the flesh ("high") or a noble religious ideal ("low"). For further discussion see chapter 12, n. 19.

pre-Pauline text betrays an interest in the founder's background and in the movement's Jewish roots. If most early formulas dwell upon the central theme of death, the frequent contrast between "flesh" and "spirit" to designate the binary elements of the kerygma are sure signs of interest in the life and ministry of the master (1 Tim. 3:16; Rom. 1:3-4; 1 Peter 3:18; see also Phil. 2:7-8).

THREE DEVELOPMENTAL LEVELS

Biblical criticism has clarified, methodologically, our understanding of the Jesus material's development. Influenced by W. Marxsen,[29] scholars routinely speak of a three-level process.[30] 1) Initially, there is the historical level. A man, called Jesus, lived in first-century Palestine where he exercised a ministry of uncertain length, preaching to the crowds of Palestine, in Galilee especially, and gathering disciples who accompanied and assisted him. During this ministry and the final days in Jerusalem he was observed performing various deeds and teaching the crowds, the Jewish authorities, and his own followers. This activity, characterized simply as the historical level, constitutes the beginnings and the foundation of the Jesus tradition.

In light of what was said in chapter one about the complexity of the Jesus material and in chapter two about the contributions of literary methods for studying this material, it should come as no surprise that two extremes should be avoided in assessing the Jesus level. On the one hand, the literalist approach to the gospels is inexcusable for it does not do justice to the complexity of the material, to the process of transmission, and to the creativity of the early community and its evangelists. On the other hand, extreme skepticism, which sees most of the Jesus material as a creation of the early church is not supported by modern scholarship. Studies in the development of oral and folk literature as well as in the dynamics of the transmission of traditions have demonstrated keen interest by those who transmit these traditions in retaining the wisdom of the materials being handed down and a certain creativity on the part of the communities and writers involved as the material is reappropriated by successive generations. It is in discourse material that

---

[29] *Mark the Evangelist*, 15-29.

[30] See Fitzmyer's discussion of the Biblical Commission's acceptance of such a schema in the 1964 Vatican document entitled "An Instruction about the Historical Truth of the Gospels," *A Christological Catechism*, 97-142.

one finds the greatest constancy and therefore basis for reaching the Jesus level, particularly the parables, which often allow the modern reader to strip away later layers of interpretation.[31] Nonetheless, caution mixed with a certain optimism is in order.[32]

2) the second level is that of the community or early church, a period of oral development particularly studied by form criticism and more recently by sociological methods, a time when the Jesus material was remembered, recited, and reappropriated as it was applied to the community's needs. Sayings of the Lord were put at the service of the church's needs, often with mixed results as the poor and less poor in the community acted according to their social perceptions, for example, in regard to meat offered to idols or behavior at the Lord's supper.[33] Traditions thus appropriated either made their way into early texts, as was the case for Paul's Corinthian correspondence, or else was passed on to other members of the community who in their turn left their imprint upon the material. As materials were handed on orally, the stories and sayings tended to adopt stereotyped structures or forms. This was a period of great creativity and we will return below to examine further this process.

3) The third and final level, that examined by redaction criticism and composition analysis, is that represented by the gospel writers. These authors, who themselves were members of the community, inherited oral and written sources and community traditions and proceeded to compose lives of the master. They imposed upon the material their own and their communities' points of view and theologies. Most of this book will be devoted to a study of this level, i.e., the NT writings.

FOCUS UPON THE ORAL LEVEL

There are therefore three levels in the development of the Jesus tradition: the Jesus, oral, and written levels. We return to the second of

---

[31]See C.H. Dodd, *The Parables of the Kingdom* (London: Collins, 1965); Jeremias, *The Parables of Jesus*; M.I. Boucher, *The Parables* (Wilmington: Glazier, 1983); and J. Lambrecht, *Once More Astonished: The Parables of Jesus* (NY: Crossroad, 1981).

[32]S.B. Marrow, *The Words of Jesus in Our Gospels: A Catholic Response to Fundamentalism* (NY: Paulist, 1979); Barr, "Reading the Bible as Literature," 10-33.

[33]See especially G. Theissen, *The Social Setting of Pauline Christianity: Essays on Corinth* (Philadelphia: Fortress, 1982), 121-43 on meat offered to idols and 145-74 on the Lord's supper. On a more literary note for the latter, see J. Jeremias, *The Eucharistic Words of Jesus* (Philadelphia: Fortress, 1977).

these, since it requires further attention. The period of development between the death of Jesus and the putting down in writing of the traditions about him is a fascinating and mysterious one for the 20th-century reader. It is a time when Jesus' followers handed on the stories and sayings of the master in an effort to understand the role which God's envoy played in the divine plan and was to play in their lives. As the material took shape through constant repetition and use within the community, a grouping of traditional units into larger collections of sayings, parables, or episodes occurred.[34] One suspects that Mark's parable, miracle, and conflict-story sections owe in large measure to the oral recitation of the Jesus material prior to the composition of the gospel (see Mark 2:1-3:6; 4:1-34; 4:35f and 11:27f).

The process which led to such grouping of materials seems to have been twofold. The first galvanized around the pattern of the kerygmatic formula and focused on the passion and resurrection. As the story was told in the community, in the style of the recitation of ancient epics in oral cultures,[35] the central episodes of Jesus' final days in Jerusalem took shape and, because of the different communities reciting such tales during the commemorations of Jesus' salvific death, there resulted a variety of passion "narratives" or oral stories.

A major impulse to this process was the Christians' reading and use of the Jewish scriptures, initially in a Semitic (Hebrew or Aramaic) and then in its Greek form. Seemingly, one of the early elements of the kerygma was the fulfilment by Jesus of the Jewish scriptures. Rom. 1:2 implies that not only the prophetic voices but also "the gospel concerning God's Son" was foretold "in the holy scriptures." 1 Cor. 15:3-4 is of interest here since Paul explicitly tells the audience that he is employing the received tradition

> that Christ died for our sins
>   in accordance with the scriptures
> that he was buried
> that he was raised on the third day
>   in accordance with the scriptures.

---

[34]Bultmann, *History of the Synoptic Tradition*, 322-67.

[35]W.H. Kelber, *The Oral and Written Gospel: The Hermeneutics of Speaking and Writing in the Synoptic Tradition, Mark, Paul, and Q* (Philadelphia: Fortress, 1983) 44-89.

Appeal to the scriptures is not only Paul's idea, as it is often in his letters, but that of the formula cited.

Additionally, a strong case can be made for viewing the Jewish scriptures as the quarry from which Christian believers drew the building blocks for their theological and christological formulations and constructs.[36] Two passages come to mind as probable influences upon the formulation of the passion stories: Isaiah 53 and Psalm 22. The former speaks of one who "had no form or comeliness," "despised and rejected by men," "a man of sorrows," "bearer of our griefs and . . . sorrows . . . wounded for our transgressions . . . bruised for our iniquities" (vv. 2-5). One suspects that passages such as "he opened not his mouth" and "like a sheep that before its shearers is dumb" (v. 7) as well as "they made his grave with the wicked and with a rich man in his death" (v.9) contributed to the evolution of the story since Jesus is silent before Pilate (Mark 15:5), crucified with robbers (Mark 15:27-32; see Luke's development of this theme: 23:39-43), and buried by Joseph of Arimathea (Mark 15:43f; Matt. 27:57 adds: "a rich man").

The early tradition's use of Psalm 22 calls for more extended treatment, since from its opening verse the Markan passion narrative draws the last words of Jesus: "My God, my God, why hast thou forsaken me?" The following list suggests points of contact and possible influence of the Psalm on the developing tradition in terms of formulation, fulfiling reinforcement, and creative theologizing.

Ps 22	*Mark (et al)*
1 "forsake"	15:34 citation
2 cry by day—no answer	15:34 cry on cross
cry by night—no rest	14:34 prayed at Gethsemane
4 & 8 trust in God—deliver	[Matt. 27:43]
6 scorned by men	passion generally

---

[36]B. Lindars, *New Testament Apologetic: The Doctrinal Significance of Old Testament Quotations* (London: SCM, 1961). On Mark's use of the Old Testament to compose the passion narrative, see H.C. Kee, "The Function of Scriptural Quotations and Allusions in Mark 11-16," 165-88 in E.E. Ellis and E. Grässer, eds, *Jesus und Paulus* (Göttingen: Vandenhoeck & Ruprecht, 1975). In more general terms, for Luke's use of the Old Testament to compose Acts 7 or Paul to compose 2 Cor. 3:1f, see the present writer's *Acts 6:1-8:4* and "Polemics, Old Testament, and Theology. A Study of II Cor., III, 1-IV, 6," *RB 88* (1981) 340-67.

7 mocking, making mouths at, wagging heads	15:29-31 deriding, wagging heads, mocking
11 there is none to help	15:31
14 bones out of joint	[John 19:32-33]
15 tongue cleaves to jaws	15:23 and 36 gave to drink
16 encircled by company of evildoers	death scene generally
piercing	crucifixion
18 dividing garments	15:24 dividing garments [John 19:24 cites text]
casting lots	15:24 casting lots
20 the sword	[John 19:34 piercing-spear]

So many thematic and stylistic contacts argue strongly that extensive use of the Jewish scriptures was made by the early communities as they attempted to relive and reflect upon the core elements of their faith.[37]

A second area of development involved materials dealing with the actions and sayings of the master. Form critics have classified these into three general categories:

> *Deed/ Narratives*:
>> Miracles (also called tales, Novellen)
>>> cures, exorcisms, nature miracles
>> Stories (also Muthen, Legende)
>>> cultic legends, biographical legends, special stories
>
> *Sayings/ Logia*:
>> Discourse and Dialogues
>> Sapiential Sayings
>>> exhortations, questions, proverbs, statements (maxims, macarisms, arguments *a minore ad maius*)
>> Prophetic Sayings
>>> predictions of messianic salvation, dire warnings, admonitions,

[37]For further treatment of this subject, see Lindars, *New Testament Apologetic*; as well as Lindars, "The Place of the Old Testament in the Formation of New Testament Theology: Prolegomena" and P. Borgen, "Response," in *NTS* 23 (1976) 59-75.

apocalyptic sayings
Legal Sayings
 laws, rules for the community,
 sentences of holy law
I Sayings
Parables
 similies or metaphors, similitudes or
 comparisons, parables (strictly),
 exemplary stories, allegories
Pronouncement Stories (also paradigms, apothegms,
 aphoristic narratives)

The variety of forms involving narrative and speech demonstrates the complex development of the Jesus material and also the vastness of its concerns. The community appealed to the authority of Jesus in many areas and ways. We are able to detect the influence of the Old Testament upon the formulation, development, and creation of narratives and discourses. It is probable that the nature miracle, the "stilling of the storm"(Mark 4:35-41), was inspired by a passage such as Psalm 107:23-30 and that the Lukan parallel (8:22-25) makes further use of the Greek text in its formulation. Other influences of the Old Testament on the Jesus material are classified as prophecy-fulfilment, others as typological (especially concerning Elijah the miracle worker), and still others as providing suitable language and tone. Finally, one detects in this stage of development the grouping of similar forms and themes into miracle, parable, and controversy-story cycles as preachers and teachers used the Jesus material.

MIRACLE TRADITION AS A TEST-CASE

To conclude our discussion of the Jesus material's passage through three stages of development we might briefly consider the issue of miracle stories and their relationship to this developmental process. The gospels present a number of miracles which Jesus allegedly performed during his ministry. While unreflective readers tend to view these as one group, the form critic divides them into several categories, such as nature miracles, healings, exorcisms, and resuscitations. Examination of these shows that some exhibit folkloric characteristics; others seem more symbolic and didactic than standard narration would warrant; while still others are told with striking moderation. Some miracle stories manifest "clear instances of protological thinking. Persons afflicted with what we would call today mental disturbances were regarded as possessed because observers were unable to analyze properly the causes of the maladies in question, and consequently ascribed them to a demon."[38] Such literary and historical considerations warrant caution in analyzing the miracle traditions.

The threefold process identified earlier assists the reader of the miracle stories. At the Jesus level, scholars recognize that his contemporaries had no problem accepting his extraordinary powers (the biblical texts speak not of *miracles* but of *dynameis* or acts of power). Even Jesus' Jewish opponents admit that he performs extraordinary acts although they attribute these to sorcery or demonic power. Other figures in the Semitic and Hellenistic world are assumed to have unusual powers, e.g., Rabbi Hanina ben Dosa and the religious figure Apollonius of Tyana.[39] Whether one wishes, on philosophical grounds, to admit or reject the possibility of miracles is a question well beyond our concern. What seems clear from the gospels is that Jesus' contemporaries accepted the fact that he performed mighty deeds and they reacted in varying ways to that belief.

When one proceeds to the second, oral level, an even more complex situation is found. Form critics have attempted to clarify this level and to assist the reader in discerning the types of miracle narratives, their constitutive parts, and their function within the community's life and teaching. Invariably the tradition and the gospel writers present "Jesus' miracles as an essential part of a larger undertaking: the defeat of the evil powers in preparation for the coming of God's kingdom."[40] At this level the stories on the one hand became standardized and on the other served as vehicles of the community's thought and as handy tools for

[38]Fitzmyer, *A Christological Catechism*, 36. More generally see his answer to the question: "How do contemporary New Testament interpreters understand the miracle stories?"; confer also Harvey, *Jesus and the Constraints of History*, 98-119.

[39]G. Vermes, "Hanina ben Dosa," *JJS* 23 (1972) 28-50 and 24 (1973) 51-64 and E.L. Bowie, "Apollonius of Tyana: Tradition and Reality," 2:16:2:1652-99 in H. Temporini and W. Hasse, eds, *Aufstieg und Niedergang der römischer Welt* (Berlin: de Gruyter, 1979). In more general terms, see J. M. Hull, *Hellenistic Magic and the Synoptic Tradition* (Naperville: Allenson, 1974); G. Theissen, *The Miracle Stories of the Early Christian Tradition* (Philadelphia: Fortress, 1983); and H.C. Kee, *Miracle in the Early Christian World: A Study in Sociohistorical Method* (New Haven: Yale University, 1983).

[40]H.C. Kee, "Miracle Workers," 599 in *IDBSup*.

preaching and teaching. The modern reader is alerted to pay close attention to the form and function of the miracle stories and less to alleged historical detail.[41]

The third level, which constitutes the end point of oral development, represents the only firm basis of knowledge. Two important methods assist the reader in appreciating the miracle stories. First, the redaction critic pays special attention to an author's use of the miracle stories to recite the story of Jesus to a believing community. Each evangelist has a particular portrait of Jesus, a portrait in which the miracle stories have a role to play. Secondly, the social sciences assist the reader in appreciating the part which the miracle stories played in the gospel writers' presentation of Jesus' soteriological role. By understanding body symbolism or purity and boundary mechanisms, the modern reader is better able to discern the NT writers' concern not about the curing of deseases but about the healing of personal and social illness and subjugation brought about by disease and its cultural and religious disruption.[42]

The miracle stories, as part of the developing Jesus tradition, underwent a process of change and use, a process which has left many traces in the biblical narrative. The modern reader must meet this challenge head on with the tools and knowledge offered by biblical scholarship along with literary and theological common sense.

Excursus on the Q-Source

One final topic must be treated before addressing the concerns of the individual writers of the New Testament. On the cutting edge of the oral and written levels of this developmental process one finds an enigmatic document which scholars, following German usage, call the Q-Source (usually related to *Quelle* meaning "source"). Since it is not an existing or extant NT work, it seems logical to treat it here as we conclude our chapter on the pre-gospel development of the Jesus tradition.

---

[41]See Theissen, *The Miracle Stories of the Early Christian Tradition*, especially 231f on "the miracle stories as symbolic actions."

[42]See for example, J.J. Pilch, "Biblical Leprosy and Body Symbolism" *BTB* 11 (1981) 108-113.

NATURE AND CHARACTERISTICS OF THE SOURCE

Once scholars were convinced of the priority of Markan composition, greater attention was given to a proposal that the later Synoptics had an additional common source at their disposal.[43] Were one to eliminate from Matthew and Luke the passages borrowed from Mark, they would still have about 235 verses in common. In Matthew most of this Q-material or double tradition is found in thematic groupings in major discourses (chapters 5-7, 10, 13, 18, 23, and 24-25), while in Luke, although scattered throughout the gospel, there are concentrations in two redactional sections: Luke's sermon (6:20-7:35) and the journey narrative (9:51-18:14). The Q-passages constitute a sayings source consisting of prophetic, eschatological, sapiential (wisdom), and oracular sayings with little narrative. We use the following convenient form-critical classification:[44] parables (well over a dozen, among others: the marriage feast/great supper, the stray/lost sheep, and talents/pounds), oracles (against the Galilean cities or woes against the Pharisees and scribes/lawyers), beatitudes, prophetic pronouncements (promises, present/future correlatives, and sentences of holy law), wisdom words (on love of enemies, on judgment), exhortations (Lord's prayer, advice on forgiveness and final judgment), and lastly narratives. The last category is poorly represented, namely, the temptations and the healing of the centurion's slave; but we also add to this category a dialogue between John's disciples and Jesus as well as the Beelzebub controversy.

Scholarship agrees that the double tradition was a written source. Verbal agreement between the two is estimated at 71% for the entire Q-material,[45] since many passages offer verbatim correspondence. The following (RSVmod) is paradigmatic of Matthean and Lukan usage.

---

[43]For an overall, brief treatment of the Q-Source, see H.C. Kee, *Jesus in History*, 76-120; Kingsbury, *Jesus Christ in Matthew, Mark, and Luke*, 1-27; and J.A. Fitzmyer, *The Gospel According to Luke* (NY: Doubleday, 1981-85) 75-81; and for discussion of the methodological issues involved in the investigation of this non-extant source, see J.S. Kloppenborg, "Tradition and Redaction in the Synoptic Sayings Source," *CBQ* 46 (1984) 34-62 and I. Havener, *Q: The Sayings of Jesus* (Wilmington: Glazier, 1987).

[44]Kee, *Jesus in History*, 84-89; see Havener, *Q*, 111-46, for a tentative reconstruction of Q.

[45]Kingsbury, *Jesus Christ in Matthew, Mark, and Luke*, 3; see also the statistics given by Fitzmyer, *Luke*, 76.

Matt. 8:19-22	Luke 9:57-60
And	*And* as they were going along the road,
a scribe came up and *said* to *him,* "Teacher,	a man *said* to *him,*
I will follow you wherever you go."	*I will follow you wherever you go.*"
And Jesus says *to him, Foxes have holes, and birds of the air have nests; but the Son of Man has nowhere to lay his head. Another* of the disciples *said* to him,	*And Jesus* said *to him, Foxes have holes, and birds of the air have nests; but the Son of Man has nowhere to lay his head.* To *another* he *said,* "*Follow me.*" But he said,
"*Lord, allow me first* to go and *bury my father.*" *But* Jesus says *to him,* "*Follow me,* and *leave the dead to bury their own dead.*	"*Lord, allow me first,* going, to *bury my father.*" *But* he said *to him,* "*Leave the dead to bury their own dead;* but as for you, going, proclaim the kingdom of God. [vv. 61-62]

Neither evangelist offers clues as to the original setting of the Q-material. Luke simply situates the material at the beginning of the journey to Jerusalem ("they were going along the road"), while the Gospel of Matthew inserts these sayings within its threefold miracles/discipleship sequence (chapters 8-9).[46] The Q-Source probably had no narrative setting. There are signs of minor editing by both authors. Luke seems to have eliminated the inelegant "historical present" of the source ("he says," Matt. 8:20, 22) and to have replaced these by "he said," the

---

[46]J. Meier, *Matthew* (Wilmington: Glazier, 1980) 79-101.

form consistently used in vv. 57-62 (7 times). Luke is also probably responsible for transfering "follow me" from Jesus' response (v. 60, as in Matt. 8:22) to the beginning of the discipleship saying. In this way all three Lukan passages on would-be followers (57-58, 59-60, 61-62) open with the theme of "following." Further, one suspects that the Matthean statements: "a scribe came up and said to him, 'Teacher,I will follow you'" and "Another of the disciple said to him," were composed by that evangelist under the influence of the "rich young man" episode (Matt. 19:16 and 21) and that of the "great commandment." From the latter the evangelist seems to have borrowed the favorable view of the Markan scribe who was "not far from the kingdom of God" (Mark 12:28-34). To compose a new version of the "great commandment" Matthew would have followed the lead of Q which speaks of a lawyer who, after calling Jesus "Teacher," would put him to a test (compare Matt. 22:35-36 and Luke 10:25). Therefore, while one is led to agree with the consensus of scholarship that the order of the Q-Document and the form of the sayings are closer to the Lukan form, one must be leary, in light of analyses such as the above, of too simply considering the Lukan passages original.

There is uncertainty concerning many issues relating to the Q-Source. For one thing we are not sure about its length. By definition the source is identified as Matthew and Luke's non-Markan material. Such a definition is problematic since it is inconceivable both that the two evangelists felt compelled to employ the whole of the Q-Document (they felt no such obligation to exhaust Mark) and that they independently chose the same passages to supplement their Markan source. For example, it is possible that Luke 9:60b-62 belonged to Q. The additional saying is a complement to the first two, in thought and structure, and so Luke would have preserved them. Matthew on the contrary would have eliminated the two "kingdom of God" sayings (Luke 9:60b, 62b) and have found the burying of a dead father and a leave-taking redundant. Besides, the Matthean Gospel's identification of the speaker of 8:21 as "another of the disciples" and its threefold treatment of discipleship, ending with the missionary discourse in chapter 10, would have made less urgent an additional saying about following Jesus and proclaiming the kingdom.

Another point of concern is the document's possible overlap with Markan episodes. It was suggested above that the great commandment is derived both from Mark and Q. Scholars agree that the same would apply for the mustard seed parable, where the elements of "the smallest of all seeds," the mustard plant as a "shrub," the image of "shade" and the double question at the beginning of the parable are derived from Mark while those of the mustard plant as a "tree," the nesting "in the branches," and the single question owe to the Q-Source (Mark 4:30-32 and parallels). In some cases, it is probable that some agreements between Matthew and Luke against Mark in regard to the triple tradition (passages shared by all the Synoptics) would also be due to overlap between Mark and Q.[47]

Examination of the materials ascribed to the Q-Source reveals much interest in the themes of the kingdom of God, the imminent expectation of the end-times, an uncompromising call to leave all to follow Jesus and continue his ministry, a challenge to radical observance of the Law (according to Jesus' interpretation), and warnings of impending judgment against Israel. Because of this concern for eschatological themes scholars describe this source as apocalyptic in character. The document's stress is not on the cross and resurrection as we might expect from our analysis of the early kerygmatic formulas, nor as one finds in Paul and in Mark, but instead there is emphasis upon the imminent return of Jesus as the Son of Man for judgment, that is, Jesus as the one vindicated by God, whose return as the glorious Son of Man would justify both his and the community's experience of suffering (see Dan. 7:13-14; 12:1-4).[48] Thus the document's view of the Christ-event and of salvation history is determined by an apocalyptic perspective. Before discussing this claim, however, it should be pointed out that most of the hymnic fragments examined stress the Christ's cosmic lordship, whereby he is either seated at God's right hand in glory or will receive the subjection of the cosmic powers and the hommage of the nations (Col. 1:16; 1 Peter 3:22; 1 Tim. 3:16; Phil. 2:9-11; Heb. 1:3; also Rom. 1:4). Even more important is the fragment cited by Paul in his early correspondence, 1 Thess. 1:9-10, where we see clearly the themes which predominate in the Q-Source, namely, Jesus (God's Son) as the eschatological agent, the nearness of the end, and deliverance from the

---

[47]For further discussion and examples, see Fitzmyer, *Luke*, 81-82, F. Neirynck, *The Minor Agreements of Matthew and Luke against Mark with a Cumulative List* (Gembloux: Duculot, 1974), and Havener, *Q*, 153-61.

[48]J.R. Donahue, "Recent Studies on the Origin of 'Son of Man' in the Gospels," *CBQ* 48 (1986) 497.

approaching judgment. The Pauline citation mentions the death and resurrection but stresses Christ's followers and their service of "the living and real God" while awaiting "his Son from the heavens," for it is this Jesus "who delivers [them] from the wrath to come." We should note, however, both the strange absence in these fragments of the expression "Son of Man"and its occurrence virtually only in the gospel tradition, that is, the Q, Markan, and Johannine versions.[49]

The Q-Source, therefore, represents the views, not unique in this early period, of an apocalyptic group whose sense of the Christ-event was deeply affected by its experience of the vicissitudes of discipleship within the Roman empire. While we will have occasion in our treatment of the Book of Revelation to examine the background and nature of apocalyptic thought and literature, it would be helpful at this point to anticipate that discussion.

> Fundamental to all apocalypticism is the self-consciousness of a community that is experiencing rejection and persecution from its contemporaries, but is sustained by its sense of God's favor, both now and in the age to come, when he will act in their behalf to judge the wicked and vindicate them. It is precisely this view of life that is embodied in the Q document.[50]

The views of the community that produced this source are similar to those of other apocalyptic documents of the intertestamental period (1 Enoch, Daniel 7-12, the Qumran community). Examination of their social and religious settings, their ideology, and theological concerns assists us in understanding the background of the Q-Source.

The community has its own view of history. It sees the prophets of old along with John, Jesus, and the disciples as God's messengers who call for repentance. Indicative of their apocalypticism is the negative tone of the document for it sees continuity between the past and its own present not in the theme of acceptance of the good news but in that of rejection. They are to rejoice at being rejected, for there is both reward in heaven

---

[49]Donahue, "Recent Studies on the Origin of 'Son of Man' in the Gospels," 498, suggests that the use of the "Son of Man" phrase to integrate "the earthly ministry, the suffering, and the return of Jesus . . . may be connected with the origin of the Gospel form itself."

[50]Kee, *Jesus in History*, 81.

and knowledge that the prophets suffered in like manner (Matt. 5:11-12; Luke 6:22-23). Both John and the Son of Man were repudiated, one as an ascetic and the other as a bon-vivant (Matt. 11:18-19; Luke 7:33-35). The destiny of Jesus' followers is thus compared to that of the prophets which Wisdom sent to Israel. The thrust of these comparisons is final judgment (Matt. 23:34-36; Luke 11:49-51).

The time is running out; the New Age has begun; and the moment must be seized (Matt. 11:12; Luke 16:16). There is hope and urgency since "the harvest is plentiful, but the laborers are few" (Matt. 9:37; Luke 10:2). John came to prepare for the eschatological event and the challenge has been launched, since Jesus' coming has ushered in the New Age (Matt. 3:12; 11:18-19; Luke 3:17; 7:33-35). Salvation is now; the end is coming soon. Thus, the themes of judgment, suddenness (delayed or not, the end will be sudden: Matt. 24:48; Luke 12:45), cosmic signs, and the centrality of the Son of Man receive much attention.

Before discussing the document's portrait of Jesus, it is necessary, in light of its apocalyptic character, to consider the issues of provenance, date, and community. Recently, a scholar has seized upon the passage discussed above ("foxes have holes") to characterize the milieu of this community as one of "itinerant radicalism." Taking the sociological model of the wandering philosopher-teachers of the Cynic movement, he has suggested that the community that produced the Q-Document was one that gloried in its lack of security and itinerant character. In this way he explains the preservation of much of the Jesus material on radical discipleship, the negative attitude toward wealth and family, and the sayings of Jesus on crisis, judgment, and reward.[51]

It seems to me, however, that an apocalyptic model explains more satisfactorily the data concerning the community and its theological perspective. The reason radical statements are preserved is related to the community's apocalypticism. The world is seen in an adversarial role since it is corrupt and deserves condemnation for its persecution of God's envoys. The community, in dire straits, appeals to God's forthcoming judgment in the person of the returning Son of Man. It sees itself as a community of righteous followers, which, while awaiting its master's return, has a mission vis-à-vis Israel. It is a Jewish Christian

---

[51]G. Theissen, *The Sociology of Early Palestinian Christianity.*

community of Greek language which sees itself, at least initially, as sent not to the Gentiles but to the various groups within Judaism (Matt. 22:2-10; Luke 14:16-24). Q is a prophetic document whose concern for the Gentiles must be set in relation to Israel's constant rejection of God's messengers. The community uses Jesus' sayings about Gentiles as prophetic taunts to Israel's intransigence (Matt. 8:10; Luke 7:9). At the same time it holds out the traditional Jewish hope to the Gentiles that in the end-days they will be gathered along with Israel into God's kingdom, for they too will "sit at table in the kingdom"(Matt. 8:11; Luke 13:29).[52]

Finally, we can surmise that it comes from a Near Eastern area, probably Asia Minor, Syria, or Palestine where Greek would have had much currency. As to time of composition, a date prior to the composition of Mark (c. 65-70) is indicated. Its emphasis on the imminence of the end and the urgency of the mission to unbelievers within the house of Israel suggests such a conclusion.

JESUS IN THE Q-DOCUMENT

The principal title for Jesus is that of Son of Man, that heavenly figure that will come at the end-time as judge (Dan. 7:13; Mark 13:26; 14:61-62; Rev. 14:14-20). Jesus is the coming Son of Man—the *parousia* or return of Jesus—looms large for this author and community (Matt. 24:37-39; Luke 17:26-30). As John had stated (Matt. 3:12; Luke 3:17-18) Jesus had come for judgment and so life was to be a preparation for that event (Matt. 5:25-26; Luke 12:57-59). Israel is called to repentance lest, like the reckless servant, it undergoes severe punishment (Matt. 24:48-51; Luke 12:45-46). Both Israel and Jesus' followers, therefore, must be ready (Matt. 24:44; Luke 12:40). By confessing Jesus in the world they might in their turn be acknowledged by the Son of Man in the heavenly realm (Matt. 10:32-33; Luke 12:8-9).[53]

If the key to this eschatological document is the returning Son of Man as judge, its preoccupation and primary focus, in true Christian fashion, is the life and ministry of the Son, i.e., Jesus as God's eschatological agent. It is through the Son's words and deeds that one

---

[52]See also Kingsbury, *Jesus Christ in Matthew, Mark, and Luke*, 23-24 and Havener, *Q*, 91-104.

[53]This is another case, among several, of an overlap between Q and Mark (8:38); see M. Devisch, "La relation entre l' évangile de Marc et le document Q," 59-91 in M. Sabbe, ed., *L'éangile selon Marc: tradition et rédaction* (Gembloux: Duculot, 1974).

witnesses God's power and learns God's secrets. He is the revealer of "hidden things," that is, knowledge of the Father (see Matt. 11:25-27 and Luke 10:21-22). Furthermore, these secrets are made known not to the wise, not even to prophets and the righteous/kings (Matt. 13:17; Luke 10:24), but to the little ones, the disciples who, in the ministry of Jesus, have been privileged to see and hear this revelation. Jesus is the otherworldly mediator of God's secrets and purposes.

The Son knows God's will and is faithful to that plan. Service of God, bowing to the divine will, and proper knowledge of these are the ingredients of servanthood (Matt. 4:3-10; Luke 4:3-12). Jesus' ministry was one of salvation (Matt. 11:4-5; Luke 7:22), a call to repentance (Matt. 11:21-23; Luke 10:13-15), and so a time of challenge that calls for wisdom. Jesus' contemporaries are chided for their lack of discernment; they are able to read the signs of the sky but not "the signs of the times" (Matt. 16:2-3; Luke 12:54-56). The inbreaking of God's kingdom will be preceded by many signs, not the least being deep familial and social division. Jesus' ministry and mission of necessity were to bring in the turmoils of the end-time before he would usher in the peace of the kingdom (Matt. 10:34-36: Luke 12:51-53).

Jesus' call to repentance, to faith, and to radical discipleship ("foxes have holes") must be seen in light of his preaching of the kingdom. It belongs to the poor, to those who are oppressed on account of the Son of Man (Matt. 5:3-12; Luke 6:20-23). While it is a future reality ("may your kingdom come"—see Matt. 6:10 and Luke 11:2), it begins in the ministry of Jesus which promises sure results (see the parables of the mustard seed and leaven—Matt. 13:31-33 and Luke 13:18-21). Further, Jesus' healing powers are a sure sign that God is at work in him and that the kingdom of God has already begun (Matt. 12:28; Luke 11:20).

The corollary to Jesus' preaching of the kingdom in the Q-Source is his fierce condemnation and radical challenge to Israel. It has rejected God's eschatological agent, has rejected Wisdom and its envoys (Matt. 23:34-35; Luke 11:49-51), and did not recognize the sign of Jonah or the greatness of the messenger (Matt. 12:38-42; Luke 11:29-32). Against Israel, therefore, the Q-Source launches its most severe criticism in the form of warnings, whether "woes" against the nation's leaders, condemnations against the privileged cities of Galilee, invective toward the present, evil generation, or lament over Jerusalem.[54]

[54]See Kee, *Jesus in History*, 92-98, for an excellent treatment of this topic.

Jesus is the locus of salvation. When he returns at the end, human activity will be the gauge of the Son of Man's judgment. Jesus' words leave no room for doubt: "And I tell you, every one who acknowledges me before men, the Son of Man also will acknowledge before the angels of God, but he who denies me before men will be denied before the angels of God" (Luke 12:8-9; see also Matt. 10:32-33). Acceptance of Jesus and reception of his followers (Matt. 10:40; Luke 10:16) will determine the verdict of the returning Son of Man. Jesus, for this author and community, therefore, is the agent of present crisis in view of fellowship in the future kingdom (Matt. 8:11; Luke 13:29). It is not the cross of Jesus which is central, since only the saying of Matt. 10:38 and Luke 14:27 addresses that theme. Instead, the focus is upon God's plan as it operates through the person of the heavenly and earthly Son of Man. The community, in the midst of what it perceives to be the end-time tribulations, longs for the return of the Son of Man, accompanied by "lightning flashes and lights from one side of the sky to the other" (Luke 17:24 and Matt. 24:27), when its tribulations will cease and the promised kingdom will become a reality.

Note on Non-Canonical Jesus Tradition

It is logical to assume and scholarship confirms that oral Jesus traditions persisted throughout the formative period of the New Testament. As source criticism makes clear, Matthew and Luke made generous use of their respective communities' oral tradition when they formulated their lives of the master. More recent redactional studies have become far more sensitive to this influence. Stories about Jesus and his sayings continued to be heard in the communities that had no evangelists and even in those that produced the canonical and other gospels.

For our purpose we might use H. Koester's convenient summary of such traditional materials:

> Words of Jesus and traditions about Jesus which are comparable to the Synoptic tradition are found in special writings belonging to the genre of the gospels and in quotations in other literature. There is no literary dependence upon the canonical Gospels in many instances. Rather, the source of such traditions is either oral transmission or

independent written tradition. *1 Clement* quotes two small collections of sayings ... A similar collection has been inserted into the first chapter of the *Didache*, and *2 Clement* apparently used a collection of Jesus' sayings ... An independent tradition of Jesus' sayings has recently come to light in the newly discovered (Coptic) *Gospel of Thomas* ... The fragment of an *Unknown Gospel* ... and the gospel fragment *Papyrus Egerton 2* present sayings that have been set into scenes resembling the Synoptic apophthegms [pronouncement stories], but are somewhat more elaborate.[55]

The same summary lists collections of Jesus sayings by Papias of Hierapolis, and *agrapha* or written sayings quoted by Church Fathers and discusses the flourishing of miracle, childhood, and revelatory or epiphany traditions in various apocryphal texts. The majority of NT scholars are far less sanguine than Koester about maintaining the independence from the canonical gospels of many of these late traditions, particularly as concerns the Gospel of Thomas. Nonetheless, more work needs to be done to understand the period and literature in question.

As the early church increasingly focused its attention on written texts or collections of the Jesus material and as it became embroiled in doctrinal controversy, oral tradition receded into the background and disappeared with the passing generations. This tradition, however, has left a few traces in post-NT Christian literature. On a popular level, oral tradition generated much interest in the lore about the miracles of the master, his hidden life, and his post-resurrection activity. These two important post-NT developments, the evolution of the thought and literature of the official church and the literary output of popular spirituality, will be discussed in chapters 12 and 13.

---

[55] *Introduction to the New Testament* (Philadelphia: Fortress: 1982) 2:67-68 and D. Wenham, ed., *The Jesus Tradition Outside the Gospels* (Sheffield: JSOT, 1985).

Part II
Jesus According To
Mark, Matthew, Luke and
the Johannine Writings

4

The Gospel of Mark

The story of Jesus is known to student and scholar, its sequence of events learned from the continuous readings of the liturgical cycle. In a similar way early Christians learned the drama of the life of the preacher from Nazareth. As missionaries traveled far and wide they repeatedly told the story of the founder. In an oral culture where writing was rare, especially among the lower classes of urban and rural areas, the recitation of stories and the answering of questions formed the basis of both missionary activity and religious instruction. To those who did not yet know it, the story of Jesus was proclaimed; for those who were his followers the story was celebrated in word and action within the community's liturgy. At some crucial point within the community's history some of its leaders were moved to put into writing the story which formed the basis of their lives. It is to this process that we now turn.[1]

General Considerations

If communities thrived for decades without written foundational documents, such as the story of their founding or a treatise about their beliefs, some time after the death of Paul, however, stories learned from the elders began to be recorded. During the period between Jesus' death and the initial writing of the stories and sayings of his ministry, there occured the frequent telling and retelling, application and reinterpretation of the tradition which form criticism has assisted us in

---

[1]See P.J. Achtemeier, *Mark* (Philadelphia: Fortress, 1975), 1-21.

undertanding. Following this formative era of oral activity, "lives of the founder" began to appear, a process which biblical scholars in the past have viewed as a natural step or logical outcome in the development of the tradition. The writing down of the traditions may indeed have been the next step chronologically but it was not the logical one. To view the transformation thus is to oversimplify oral development and to underestimate the role played by the authors.[2]

The passage from oral tradition to written gospel was a momentous and innovative development. Rather than the natural outgrowth of the oral process, the putting of the sayings and stories about Jesus into narrative form was a notable modification. Oral development, while manifesting a tendency to gather stories into small collections of similar content and forms (groups of miracles, parables, conflict stories) is essentially fragmentary in its dynamics—note the fundamental differences between the Synoptic, Johannine, and Pauline uses of the Jesus material. The tradition about Jesus, in other words, was becoming more diffused as successive generations employed it in their missionary and communal activities. The writing of the gospels was a bold attempt to reverse this process. Whether a desperate maneuver to counter disruptive forces within the community or to preserve the primitive traditions as the first generation of believers was passing away, the evangelists imposed upon the materials their literary artistry and theological perspective.

Scholars readily conclude that Mark composed the first gospel. This fact establishes that composition as Christianity's most important book, since the sequence of events and the structure and interpretation of Jesus' life and ministry have been forever marked by the first evangelist's literary activity. Even Matthew and Luke owe their narrative framework to Mark. The role of the author of Mark, therefore, can hardly be overestimated.

Mark composed what we today call a "gospel." This term, however, is not self-explanatory, since in popular usage it refers both to the canonical gospels and later apocryphal works, many of which contain no narrative materials and since such a literary category would have no contemporary parallel. This observation implies that Mark, the first evangelist, created a new literary genre. While this opinion is usually

[2]Kelber, *The Oral and the Written Gospel.*

found in NT introductions, many scholars are not convinced since it presumes an unusual degree of creativity on the part of the author and isolates Christian writers from their literary and cultural milieu. It is far more reasonable to inquire about the model which Mark employed or was acquainted with when writing this work. Deciding the genre of Mark is crucial to proper interpretation of the work.[3]

Despite the pioneering work of C.W. Votaw who in 1915 made a strong case for seeing the gospels as parallel to popular ancient Greek biographies, it is the view of R. Bultmann which has dominated scholars' efforts to define the literary genre of the gospels. As a result of his extensive form-critical work, Bultmann insisted that the gospels were not biographies but credal, literary outgrowths of the apostolic kerygma or "cult legends." Ever since, introductions and commentaries have routinely insisted that Mark's work is not a chronicle or that none of the evangelists were writing biographies of Jesus in the modern sense of the word. Because of recent textual discoveries and renewed interest in the subject, scholars have looked to a variety of literary categories to explain the genre of the gospels, which are variously described as aretalogies (miracle collections), tragedies, comedies, foundational documents, apocalyptic texts or parables. Some of these apply specifically to Mark's Gospel.

However, studies of Greco-Roman narrative literature and the foundational work of C.H. Talbert on the genre of the gospels lead us to the Hellenistic biography as the most convincing literary parallel for Mark and other NT gospels. Examination of the biographical genre of that period and the functions, organizational structures, and attitudes toward the world which it reveals (*contra* Bultmann) casts the gospels in a different light. The gospels are not haphazard, mechanical products of the laws of oral literature. Instead they are well-constructed stories whose intricate details show considerable sophistication. The gospels, Mark included, are structurally complex; so are their purpose, setting in life (*Sitz im Leben*), and theology. Reading the gospels and other NT

---

[3]For the necessary background to the question of genre, see C.W. Votaw, *The Gospels and Contemporary Biographies in the Greco-Roman World* (Philadelphia: Fortress, 1970), first published in *American Journal of Theology* (1915); Bultmann, *The History of the Synoptic Tradition*; and C.H. Talbert, *What Is a Gospel? The Genre of the Canonical Gospels* (Philadelphia: Fortress, 1977); confer also P.L. Shuler, *A Genre for the Gospels: The Biographical Character of Matthew* (Philadelphia: Fortress, 1982).

books without some knowledge of Greco-Roman literature is comparable to trying to understand Jesus' teaching without a minimal acquaintance with contemporary Jewish thought and culture.

Works devoted to the life and career of individuals were a common phenomenon in the ancient world (one might consult Talbert's list of biographies). When Mark and the other evangelists took pen in hand they were not inventing a literary genre out of thin air. Acquainted, however superficially, with the literary customs of their time, they decided in their turn to organize the Jesus tradition for their communities. As in the case of other biographers they were limited by their sources, governed by their purpose for writing, and subject to their peculiar literary talents.[4] Choice of the biographical genre suited their purpose for it provided an outline for organizing the Jesus traditions inherited from Christian predecessors. Mark, the unmatched storyteller, instinctively opted for a genre which provided scope for narrative talent. Besides, the data seemed ready made for the genre; Jesus was the focus of the material and other characters natural foils for revealing who Jesus was. The gospels, therefore, are ancient, not modern, biographies which share the literary conventions and historical subjectivity of writings of that period. Like other ancient biographers, the evangelist was consumed neither by interest in detail nor sequential accuracy as is the modern historian, but rather was concerned with the meaning of events, the moral of episodes, and the challenge of speech and action.[5]

Finally, the issue of authorship should be treated briefly before we turn our attention to Mark's Gospel.[6] 2nd and 3rd-century tradition, from Papias to the Canon of Muratori, drew connections between the canonical gospels and figures of apostolic time. Thus Matthew is presumed to have been written by Matthew Levi the tax collector and the Fourth Gospel by John the son of Zebedee, both therefore by immediate followers of Jesus. The Gospel of Mark is attributed to John Mark who was an associate of Paul and an assistant of Peter, while the Gospel of Luke is presumed to have been written by someone referred

---

[4]Rhoads and Michie, *Mark as Story.*

[5]In this regard the reader might consult the instructive work of the Greek writer Lucian of Samosata, "How to Write History" in *Lucian*, ed., K. Kilburn (Cambridge: Harvard University, 1959).

[6]Achtemeier, *Mark*, 111-17 and G. Kümmel, *Introduction to the New Testament* (Nashville: Abingdon, 1975) 95-98.

to by Paul as "Luke our beloved physician." While these names are provided as introductions to the gospels by modern translations, they were clearly not part of the earliest Greek manuscripts. Since scholarship does not substantiate these alleged connections, we conclude that such identifications were early attempts to establish the authority and orthodoxy of the gospels. A similar process was at work in important Christian centers which also sought apostolic connections. Mark and the other gospels are anonymous documents by creative leaders of the community whose identity, racial or sexual background, and cultural or social milieu are unknown to us (beyond what can be deduced from the texts themselves) but whose legacy is invaluable to later generations.

Literary Introduction to Mark

This gospel's contribution to the development of the Jesus tradition is far-reaching since its author molded it into a sequential narrative.[7] So it is to Mark's literary activity that we turn first. In terms of style it is by far the simplest. One finds an excessive use of "and" (kai-style) to introduce not only phrases and terms but also clauses and narrative units. Mark favors "and again," "and then," and "now after." Contrary to the rules of standard Greek, Mark regularly lacks transitional terms and employs excessively the harsh historical present (151 times as compared to 4 in Luke)—a feature which reveals poor style but underscores a storyteller's craft. The author loves the term "immediately," expressions of astonishment, superlatives, and other means of heightening the dramatic effect of episodes, such as the frequent use of "begin" as a helping verb (26 times). Since these stylistic and lexical features are frequent in Hellenistic Greek, one must conclude that they indicate not stylistic aberration or literary ineptness but instead underscore Mark's ability as storyteller for whom vividness, colloquialisms, diminutives, historical presents, multiplication of participles, and simple, direct speech, are preferred tools. Nonetheless, the gospel's Greek lacks elegance and its vocabulary tends toward the vulgar and uneducated.

[7]More generally on Mark as writer and narrator, see N. Petersen, "'Point of View' in Mark's Narrative," *Semeia* 12 (1978) 97-121; R. Tannehill, "The Gospel of Mark as Narrative Christology," *Semeia* 16 (1979) 57-92; and A. Stock, *Call to Discipleship: A Literary Study of Mark's Gospel* (Wilmington: Glazier, 1982)

Important editorial features assist us in understanding Markan composition, whether distinguishing redaction from tradition or perceiveing the text's structure. Mark has a fondness for the expression "he began to," for the themes of "teaching" and privacy ("alone," "by themselves," "call aside") for stereotyped expressions to introduce direct discourse ("and he says, said, was saying ... to them"), for the telescoping or preparation for events, for what is called a "sandwich or interpolation technique," for the astute use of climaxes, and the frequent recourse to summary and transitional statements. The last mentioned are numerous and so constitute an *embarras de richesses*, since such passages are usually excellent structural indicators. So they are for Mark, though their frequency and function present difficulties. Some introduce textual divisions (1:14-15 and 3:7-12); others conclude series of episodes (1:32-34 and 3:6); nonetheless, most are redactional or heavily edited. These have become a favorite organizational tool for a biographical treatment of the Jesus tradition as Mark attempts to impose sequential unity upon the overall narrative. These literary devices are Mark's principal means of arranging the episodes and giving them continuity, rhythm, and context.

The gospel, however, was not written from scratch and one presumes the author made use of sources. In fact, a number of pre-Markan complexes have been proposed by scholars, proposals which vary in probability: "the day of Capharnaum" (1:21-35f); 5 controversy stories (2:1-3:6); a series of 5 parables (4:1-34); a double miracle cycle with a conclusion (4:35-8:21); 5 controversy stories with a parable (11:27-12:40); an apocalyptic discourse (chap. 13); and a passion narrative (chaps. 14-15).

With recent scholars we reject the suggestion that Mark employed an extended, written passion narrative; too many Markan themes and redactional elements are interwoven into the text's fabric to make such a theory credible. What did develop before Mark wrote was a group of stories relating to Jesus' passion and its salvific character, particularly as fulfilment of the Jewish scriptures.[8] Mark 13 is recognized as based on a pre-Markan oral or written source, although analyses vary greatly, since

---

[8]J.R. Donahue, "Introduction: From Passion Traditions to Passion Narrative," 1-20 in W.H. Kelber, ed., *The Passion in Mark: Studies on Mark 14-16* (Philadelphia: Fortress, 1976) and H.C. Kee, "The Function of Scriptural Quotations and Allusions in Mark 11-16," 165-88.

Markan redaction was extensive.[9] The parable chapter, once editorial links and additions are removed, seems to rely upon a pre-Markan source also. The setting (4:1-2), discussion of parables (vv. 10-12 and 33-34), allegory on the sower (vv. 13-21), and the introductory formulas are redactional. A five parable collection remains. One should note that the controversy series of chapters 2 and 11 also consist of five episodes.

Following the suggestions of P.J. Achtemeier's recent study, we propose the following pre-Markan schema:

Stilling of storm 4:35-41	Jesus walks on sea 6:45-51
Gerasene demoniac 5:1-20	Blind man at Bethsaida 8:22-26
Woman with haemorrhage 5:25-43	Syro-Phoenician woman 7:24-30
Jairus' daughter 5:21-23/35-43	Deaf mute 7:32-37
Feeding of 5000 6:34-44/53	Feeding of 4000 8:1-10

In this study, Markan redactional characteristics are considered, non-Markan clues are evaluated, and other features of the dual cycle are analyzed. Thus, it is concluded that the first series deals with Jewish subjects and themes while the second occurs in Gentile territory and lacks the Jewish features of the first, e.g., feeding in the wilderness.[10] Further, Mark rearranged the episodes and added a concluding section, 8:11-21. It seems likely, therefore, that Mark utilized several short collections, although most of this material consisted of isolated or short items of tradition and community lore. One might wonder, however, if the sources employed were written or oral in character.

As studies have shown, the basic feature of this gospel is the figure of Jesus. Whether this concern be called christological (a *vita*), soteriological (relation of disciple to master) or kerygmatic, the organizing principle is Jesus of Nazareth. Mark has inherited traditional complexes

[9]By far the best analysis of Mark 13 is that of J. Lamprecht, *Die Redaktion der Markus-Apokalypse* (Rome: Biblical Institute, 1967); for a more accessible presentation of his conclusions, see F. Neirynck, "Le discours anti-apocalyptique de Mc., XIII," *ETL* 45 (1969) 154-64; see also H.C. Kee, *Community of the New Age: Studies in Mark's Gospel* (Philadelphia: Westminster, 1977) 43-45.

[10]"Toward the Isolation of Pre-Markan Miracle Catenae," *JBL* 89 (1970) 265-91. I find questionable R.M. Fowler's conclusion: "one story is traditional (8:1-10) and the other a Markan composition (6:30-44). The evangelist has composed his own story as a backdrop for the traditional story, thereby controlling how the reader perceives the traditional story," *Loaves and Fishes: The Function of the Feeding Stories in the Gospel of Mark* (Chico: Scholars, 1981), 181. On the contrary, the entire narrative is the author's composition.

and fragments of narrative and discourse material and has assembled these around that focal point. The author composed summaries and transitional verses to provide narrative glue and to lend breadth and vigor to the story. Mark, we conclude, gathered disparate material and arranged it according to the needs and demands of both the narrative genre and the tradition itself.

So Mark's choice of this genre was dictated by several factors, among others, by a penchant for story rather than discourse and by the nature of the Jesus tradition which consisted of stories and sayings. A biographical pattern or time-line provided an organizational mechanism by which to reverse the dispersing tendency of the oral process. Further, choice of genre would have had a bearing upon Mark's purpose for writing in the first place. Votaw, after comparing the writings of Plato and Xenophon about Socrates with those of the evangelists about Jesus, insists:

> The purpose of the two groups of biographical writings ... was in general the same: to restore the reputation of a great and good man who had been publicly executed and defamed by the state, to re-establish his influence as a supreme teacher in respect to right living and thinking, and to render available to all the message of truth and duty which each had made it his life-work to promulgate.[11]

If this early, insightful proposal exaggerates in ascribing such didactic consciousness to an author like Mark, it nonetheless suggests interesting avenues of research.

Structural and Thematic Analysis

A literary text reveals structural organization at two levels, the first related to the literary conventions employed within a genre and the second based upon the dynamics or internal movement of the work. As previously noted, structural indicators abound in Mark. These features relate to the biographical conventions employed and so point to surface structure: transitional passages, narrative and temporal sequence of events, topical groupings, and geographical organization. Some of these

---

[11]Votaw, *Gospels and Contemporary Biographies*, 58.

derive from the tradition used, particularly the geographical and temporal factors: the beginning at the Jordan River (1:1f), the early Galilean ministry (1:14f), the journey to Judaea (10:1f), and the final days and episodes in Jerusalem (11:1f). Note that the independent Johannine tradition witnesses to a similar geographical and time-line structure (John 1:19f; 2:1f; 10:40f; and 12:12f). This geographical/ temporal schema seems therefore to have exercised an organizational function within the oral tradition and to have served as the skeletal outline for oral recitation.

Most Markan outlines, however, attempt to combine thematic and narrative factors. This approach generally respects geographical indicators but seeks to deal with the dynamics of the text, although this is done on a level close to the story-line. The themes, though indicated in theological terms (preparation for the ministry, prologue, kingdom announced by speech and action, etc.), are fundamentally biographical in nature. As one expects in a chronological presentation, preparation for the ministry comes at the beginning of a vita, while events leading to the end occur late in the story; the middle sections of such proposals are obvious attempts to delve more deeply into the Markan structure. Such outlines offer plot analyses and function as reading guides, since Mark is a story with a beginning and an ending, story about a Jesus who travels, acts, and speaks.

Two such outlines will be examined before our own analysis. The first is by H.C. Kee who sees author and community as subscribing to an apocalyptic point of view. After employing Jewish sectarian models to describe the social dynamics of an apocalyptic community, Kee presents the following aims of the Markan author:

1. Assert the Triumph of the Rule of God.
2. Assert the Defeat of the Hostile Powers.
3. Redefine the Community of Faith.
4. Demonstrate the Certainty of the Outcome.
5. Present the Message to the Community: Stand Firm![12]

These, he maintains, represent not divisions of Mark's text but constituent goals of the apocalypticist. According to Kee, Mark's agenda is the realization of these aims and so Jesus is the agent through whom these are achieved. Mark then is an apocalyptic interpretation

---

[12]Kee, *Community of the New Age*, 64-97, especially 70.

and proclamation of the Christ-event to an embattled Christian community. The dynamic nature of this structure is to be recommended, for Mark certainly views Jesus' activity as the triumph of God's rule, the defeat of Satan, and the ushering in of a new community of faith as the basis for hope and perseverance. What is not fully convincing, however, is the alleged apocalyptic agenda of Mark's Gospel. While there are many apocalyptic features in Mark, they can hardly be said to permeate the gospel. There is a virtual absence here of cosmic dualism, historical pessimism, and heavenly conflicts and battles, features so prominent in apocalyptic literature (see chapter 11). Mark, while imbued with apocalyptic thought and, like most NT writers, expecting the imminent return of the Lord, takes an anti-apocalyptic stance (see Mark 13) vis-à-vis the pressing concerns of the Christian community. We view Mark as anxious to counter the exaggerated apocalyptic tendencies of some within the community.[13] More attention to eschatology, mission, and the author's strategy and less to apocalypticism seems warranted. Kee's sense of the Markan community's reappropriation of the Jesus tradition, however, will contribute to our own study of the Markan portrait of Jesus.

A second proposal is that of N. Perrin who also sees Mark as apocalyptic in nature. While Kee, following a sociological approach, begins from a presumed community model to arrive at Mark's christological agenda, Perrin adopts a christological approach whereby the revelation of Jesus becomes central.[14] Relying upon summary passages as clues to structure, he sees the work as a progressive revelation whose principal concern is "the apocalyptic parousia of Jesus as Son of Man." The theme of progressive revelation will be retained in our analysis as will an emphasis upon Jesus as the Son of Man. Also to be underscored here is Perrin's insistence upon the structural significance of the two giving-of-sight stories (8:22-26 and 10:46-52). The too great concern for apocalyptic, the interpretation of Mark 13, the alleged centrality of Galilee, and the presumed polemic against a divine-man christology

---

[13]See Neirynck, "Le discours anti-apocalyptique de Mc., XIII," 154-64.

[14]N. Perrin, The New Testament: An Introduction (NY: Harcourt Brace Jovanovich, 1974) 147 (see his Markan outline); confer also his essay, "Toward an Interpretation of the Gospel of Mark,"1-78 in H.D. Betz, ed., Christology and a Modern Pilgrimage: A Discussion with Norman Perrin (Claremont: NT Coloquium, 1971).

(extensively developed by his students), are rightly contested by recent scholarship.[15]

Depth Structure and Markan Purpose

Since the end of the 19th century, Jesus' commands of silence, commonly called the "messianic secret," have featured prominently in analyses of Mark's christology.[16] The discussion centers on 10 instances where silence is commanded. Three passages (1:25, 34; 3:12) report commands to demons who know his identity. Also there are futile commands of silence (1:44; 7:36) and an unsuccessful attempt on Jesus' part to conceal himself (7:24). Other prohibitions occur at 5:43; 8:26; and finally at 9:9. In the last instance silence is imposed until the resurrection. For some reason, Jesus, in the first part of Mark's Gospel, does not want to be made known. The messianic secret then is a structural feature of the first part of the gospel, the section ending with Peter's confession (8:26-30).

Several themes are often brought into the discussion of the secrecy motif: the non-understanding of the disciples, their non-perseverance, and the private teaching of Jesus to them. This secret teaching, however, is related to Mark's concept of discipleship and faith. Associated with the notion of faith are the non-perseverance passages of chapter 14. These allusions to lack of understanding are either related to the predictions of the passion or to the double miracle cycle of 4:35-8:21. Interestingly, of the three occurrences, two terminate the initial scenes of the cycles, 4:40 and 6:51-52, the stilling of the storm and the walking on the water respectively, and the third is found in the last episode of the conclusion, 8:11-21. These themes, on the one hand, are related to important structural episodes (the granting of sight to the blind in chapters 8 and 10) and, on the other, serve as significant links between the two principal parts of the gospel.

Also of structural significance are several titles Mark confers upon Jesus. Mark employs the expression, Son of Man, 14 times, 12 of which occur after Peter's confession, 8:26-30. The other two (2:11, 28)

[15]J.D. Kingsbury, "The 'Divine Man' as the Key to Mark's Christology—The End of an Era?" *Int* 35 (1981) 243-57 and Achtemeier, *Mark*, 71-81.

[16]C. Tuckett, ed., *The Messianic Secret* (Philadelphia: Fortress, 1983).

seemingly appear too early in the gospel. Indeed they occur within a series of conflict stories (2:1-3:6), which probably constitutes a pre-Markan cluster, a fact which would account for their early appearance within the gospel. These are the only two instances where the Son of Man is one who acts on earth in the present. The other uses, all within the second part of Mark, either speak of the Son of Man as suffering (8:31; 9:9, 12, 31; 10:33, 45; 14:21 twice, 41; influence of the suffering servant of Yahweh: Isa. 52:13-53:12) or eschatologically as the one to come (8:38; 12:26; 14:62; as depicted in Daniel 7 and the Book of Enoch). The title, therefore, provides additional structural clues, since it relates to the second part of the gospel and since so many occurrences of the title cluster around the triple predictions of the passion. Finally, its eschatological use, particularly in the apocalyptic discourse (13:26), indicates another structural element.

The theme of sonship adds to our perception of the gospel's structure, since the title, Son or Son of God, appears strategically situated seven times in Mark. While one might be tempted to accept the long reading of 1:1 ("Jesus Christ *the Son of God*") and see the occurrence of the title there as introducing Mark's plan, it seems best textually and structurally to conclude that it appears for the first time at the baptism scene (1:11) where it involves a revelation to Jesus only.[17] In two cases where demons call Jesus Son of God (3:11; 5:7), he is quick to silence them. The next occurrence is situated within the central section (9:7), where the revelation at the transfiguration is a public one ("*this* is my beloved Son"). Further, the title is employed during Jesus' trial and immediately after his death (14:61 and 15:39). In all these instances it relates to the identity of Jesus and its human recognition; progressive disclosure of who Jesus is is a major Markan theme. One should note that exposition, even gradual manifestation of the hero, is a major feature of Greco-Roman biography.

The term "Christ" (Greek for "Messiah") is another Markan title whose distribution is structurally enlightening. It serves as a constituent part of the work's title, of Peter's confession, and of the High Priest's

[17]The absence of the phrase "the Son of God" in some important early manuscripts (e.g., 4th century Sinaiticus) and some early Church Fathers (Irenaeus and Origen)—see the discussion of B.M. Metzger, *A Textual Commentary on the Greek New Testament* (London: UBS, 1971) 73—leads us to reject the longer reading (*contra* RSV and NAB). Besides, this particular reading lends too much weight to the title "Son of God' which is *a* major not *the* central title of Mark's christology.

question (1:1; 8:29; 14:61). Also notable is its occurrence in the apocalyptic chapter (13:21) and at the cross (15:32). In the latter, though used in mockery, it is clearly ironic in meaning: "let the Christ, the King of Israel, come down now from the cross." This last text leads us to still another title of significance, that of "king." Of its twelve occurrences only six apply to Jesus and are situated within the trial and crucifixion scenes (15:2, 9, 12, 18, 26, 32, "King of the Jews/Israel"). Once again, we encounter a theme which is limited to one half of the gospel. In addition, the related image of "kingdom" (usually "kingdom of God," 14 of 20 occurrences) is also heavily concentrated in the second part of the gospel. A similar observation can be made concerning the title of "teacher" since 10 of its 12 occurrences are found after Peter's confession—the first two instances it should be noted are again found within the dual miracle cycle (4:35-8:21). Jesus' role as teacher vis-à-vis his disciples is stressed in the second part of the gospel while the more general theme of teaching is found throughout.

From these structural indicators we are led to see two important parts to Mark's narrative: 1:1-8:30 from the beginning to Peter's confession and 8:31-16:8 from the first prediction of the passion to the close of the gospel.[18] The messianic-secret motif unifies the first half of the work which we can qualify as the hidden gospel since Mark is intent on hiding the identity of Jesus from all but those who have faith lest his messiahship be misunderstood. On the level of the story-line Mark is concerned about misrepresentations of the messiahship which might have kingly, priestly or other social interpretations. But built into the structure of the narrative is an attempt to clarify the identity of Jesus, (what kind of Messiah he was) and the nature and object of faith in that Messiah. The first part of the gospel with its overall theme of secrecy, however, has for its object the progressive revelation of its hero, the one whom Peter, in the name of the disciples, confesses to be the Messiah or Christ (8:29). The second part of the gospel puts aside the secrecy motif and presents Jesus first as teacher who, by means of the passion predictions (chaps. 8, 9, 10), clarifies for the believer what his life-story means and then as the one who does the will of the Father (14:36) through the events of the Jerusalem ministry, supper, passion, death, and resurrection (chaps. 11-16). On the level of the story-line, Mark pursues the messianic theme by showing that once the nature of Jesus'

---

[18]E.J. Mally, "The Gospel according to Mark," 2:21-24 in *JBC*.

ministry is properly understood (i.e., in relation to the cross, 8:31), there is no longer need for secrecy (8:32) as Jesus now marches on his way to fulfill God's plan. At a deeper level Mark, by combining the themes of suffering and Son of Man, addresses fundamental community concerns. On the one hand, the issue of Jesus' rejection by his own people and his disgraceful death as a criminal at the hands of the Romans is subsumed under the rubric of gradual revelation whereby Mark discourses on the character of Jesus' suffering, on faith as related to the resurrection (9:9), and on the nature of Christian discipleship. The cross was both a scandal in historical and apologetic terms and a constituent of Christian existence. Accepting Jesus on any other terms, in Mark's view, was to denature Christian faith. Indeed, the figure of Jesus, in terms of faith and in the midst of explicit confession, is always shrouded in secrecy as "an elusive presence [which believers] cannot control."[19] On the other hand, Christian suffering and persecution were but one aspect of the Christ-event, a fact which Mark underscores by stressing Jesus' role as Son of Man. It is not so much the theme of resurrection as it is that of the parousia or return of Jesus as the Son of Man which furnishes the Markan Gospel and community with the grounds for hope and perseverance in the face of the apostolic mission and witness and their resultant hardship and suffering. Jesus is the suffering Son of Man.

Mark the storyteller inherited from tradition narratives and sayings out of which to construct the story of Jesus. The author traces the story's hero from the early days of John's ministry along the Jordan to the culminating event of his life, the death by crucifixion and does not fail to add the dimension which is the very basis for writing the gospel, namely, belief in the resurrection. Possessing the storyteller's keen sense of climax (see diagram), Mark imposes upon this material an impressive structure whereby the dramatic character of the narrative is highlighted and the identity of Jesus established.

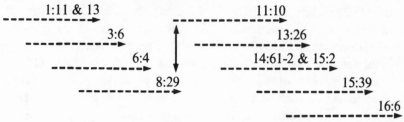

[19]H. Fleddermann, "'And He Wanted to Pass by Them' (Mark 6:48c)," *CBQ* 45 (1983) 395.

In each case Mark builds the narrative to a climax and then transposes the action to a new level. After the speaking of the heavenly voice and the climatic service of beast and angel (1:13), Jesus proceeds to Galilee to begin his ministry. There, as a result of a dramatic series of encounters with Jewish authorities concerning his exercise of God's power (2:7f), there occurs the first indication of a plot against Jesus (3:6) who then withdraws to another area. Further activity culminates in the rejection scene at Nazareth, since "a prophet is not without honor except in his own country, and among his own kin, and in his own house" (6:4). The story of Jesus' ministry proceeds episode by episode until, after a miracle on the gaining of sight (8:22-26), there occurs the first important confession of Jesus' identity as Messiah (8:29).

Signaling a new approach (8:32) to the presentation of the main character, the author inserts the threefold predictions of the passion of the Son of Man, a section which terminates, after another miracle on the granting of sight to a blind man, with the enthusiastic acclamation of Jesus as God's agent (11:9-10). It seems that Mark has taken pains to connect the two parts of the gospel to impress upon the reader that the quest for Jesus' identity which begins in the first part continues in the second and only there is fully resolved. In fact to introduce and conclude the core section of this quest, 8:27-10:42, Mark has provided an interesting duo of granting-sight-to-the-blind miracles, a pair which constitutes a striking inclusio (8:22-26 and 10:46-52).[20]

The Jerusalem ministry (11:11f) offers a variety of episodes and teaching and is "interrupted" by a farewell discourse, a forward-looking speech whose climax is the promise that all will see the Son of Man when he returns (13:26). Following this, the passion again gains center stage and reaches an obvious climax in the high priest's question ("Are you the Christ, the Son of the Blessed?") and Jesus' unqualified response ("I am, and you will see the Son of Man sitting at the right hand of Power, and coming with the clouds of heaven"—14:61-2). This is immediately followed by a complementary question by Pilate ("Are you the King of the Jews?") and answer ("You have said so"—15:2).

Mark, however, has not yet brought the story to a close, because the

---

[20]On the use of inclusio and other such devices by the author of this gospel, see J. Dewey, *Markan Public Debate: Literary Technique, Concentric Structure, and Theology in Mark 2:1-3:6* (Chico: Scholars, 1980) 131-80.

death of Jesus, accompanied by apocalyptic motifs, elicits the climactic confession of the centurion, who after witnessing Jesus' death, says: "Truly this man was the Son of God" (15:39). The gospel, after relating its author's tomb traditions, concludes on a note of awe and hope, but only after reiterating the basic tenets of its christology: "you seek Jesus of Nazareth, who was crucified. He has risen, he is not here" (16:6).

Markan Perspective: Who Was Jesus?

The overall schema of the gospel, therefore, is concentrated upon the revelation of Jesus' identity. From the title of the gospel through its revelatory episodes, acts of power, blocks of teaching material, and especially the crucial events in Jerusalem, Mark clarifies for the reader who Jesus is and what he means for faith. The construction of this gospel, therefore, reveals both the author's purpose in writing and conception of who Jesus was.

"DIVINE MAN" CHRISTOLOGY

Recently it became fashionable to describe the christology of Mark in relation to what historians of religion describe as a "divine man" (*theios anēr*) concept. It is maintained that Mark's traditions or opponents in the community advocated a perilous theology of glory which the evangelist counteracts by means of "a corrective Christology."[21] In this approach the title "Son of God" is seen as expressive of a false portrait of Jesus, while that of "Son of Man," associated with Mark's theology of the cross, serves as its corrective. Originally viewed as a miracle worker whose story took on the form of an aretalogy or miracle gospel, the Markan Jesus is a supernatural being similar to the demi-gods of the Hellenistic world. More recently, however, this approach has taken a more negative turn. Its proponents maintain that the title "Son of God" represents the christology of Mark's opponents and that Mark inserted the suffering Son of Man component to remedy such a defective portrait of Jesus.

---

[21]J.D. Kingsbury, *The Christology of Mark's Gospel* (Philadelphia: Fortress, 1983) 25-45.

This once popular "divine man" christology, however, has become the subject of heated criticism. Studies have demonstrated the conjectural nature of the concept and a growing number of literary analyses has found this approach to Mark unsatisfactory and even contradictory to the author's structure and purpose. The scholarly view is such that J.D. Kingsbury has characterized the present situation as the "end of an era" of Markan research.[22]

Kingsbury follows this judgment by a new proposal. Mark, he concludes, presents Jesus "as the royal Son of God" since the principal titles: Messiah, Son of David, and King of the Jews/Israel, relate to and further identify Jesus according to God's "evaluative point of view"(the voice from heaven on two occasions calls Jesus "Son," 1:11 and 9:7). The messianic secret, he maintains, is related to this theme and is resolved only at the cross. Further, he insists that the title "Son of Man" as opposed to "Son of God" has an "outward orientation"; that is, it describes Jesus' contacts with his enemies and the public, and "is without content as far as the identity of Jesus as such is concerned." While one might understand why he insists, contrary to those who hold a "corrective Christology," that the "Son-of-Man sayings...*complement*—not 'correct'—each other within the plot of Mark's story,"[23] one cannot but be surprised both at this insistence upon royal messianism and at his negative assessment of the Son-of-Man sayings in Mark. We agree with his analysis of the present state of research, namely, that the "divine man" concept is counterproductive to further Markan studies. Also one applauds his insistence that the title "Son of God" is both central to Mark's christology and that it is to be understood as a positive designation of Jesus. We cannot accept the false dichotomy which he posits between the two principal titles of the gospel nor his facile identification of the title "Son of God" with royal messianism.

We begin our search for the Markan Jesus by noting what Kingsbury says about the baptism scene, namely, that sonship is central for Mark since it is "God himself who sets forth the understanding of Jesus which

---

[22]"The 'Divine Man' as the Key to Mark's Christology;" confer also H.C. Kee, "Mark's Gospel in Recent Research," *Int* 32 (1978) 323-68, and D.L. Tiede, *The Charismatic Figure as Miracle Worker* (Missoula: Scholars, 1972).

[23]*The Christology of Mark's Gospel*, 174; see pp. 173-76 for the author's overall summary.

is normative for Mark's story."[24] A difficulty arises in interpreting the meaning of the heavenly statement: "you are my Son, the Beloved, in you I am well pleased"(RSVmod). Scholars routinely refer to Psalm 2:7 as the source for the citation. Examination, however, shows that the statement is not a quotation of this text. If the idea of a heavenly voice declaring Jesus " Son" is derived from Psalm 2:7 even though the wording is not exact, its significance in the baptism scene is not then obvious, especially since the author eliminates or ignores the messianic context which some scholars take for granted.[25] Nothing in the Markan context requires a kingly interpretation since the remainder of the statement leads one away from or at least makes ambiguous such a precise reading. While the evangelist's use of the term "beloved" might suggest the story of Isaac (Gen. 22), there are good reasons to believe that Mark or its tradition is dependent upon Isaiah 42:1 for the formulation of the heavenly statement. Evidence for this is forthcoming from the Matthean (12:18) as opposed to the standard Greek reading of the prophetic text.[26] The Matthean vesion of this OT verse

> (Behold my servant whom I have chosen
> my *beloved* with whom my soul is *well pleased*
> I will put my Spirit upon him
> and he shall proclaim justice to the Gentiles.
> Matt. 12:18 [= Isa. 42:1])

suggests the form and provides a clue to the meaning of the Markan passage. Both the terms "beloved" and "well pleased" are found in the Matthean citation[27] and the context of the Isaiah passage is instructive for Jesus is chosen by a heavenly voice whose spirit in the form of a dove, descends upon him. Significant of course is the preference for the term "son" (note "servant/ child" of the Isaiah citation). We are, therefore, led to accept the following explanation of the heavenly voice:

---

[24]*Ibid.*, 68.

[25]*Ibid.*, 65-66.

[26]The Septuagint varies considerably from the Hebrew at this point, while the Matthean citation of the prophetic text, supported in part by later Greek revisors of the LXX, is closer to the original Hebrew and Mark 1:11.

[27]The Greek revisors (Symmachus and Theodotion) both employ "well pleased" (*eudokeō*) and "chosen one" (*eklektos*) rather than "beloved."

... a more fitting analogy is to the Old Testament tradition of theophanies and divine auditions by which chosen persons received their commission from God, as in the case of Moses at Sinai (Exod. 3:4ff), Elijah on Horeb (1 Kings 19:12ff), or Daniel on the bank of the Tigris (Dan. 10:2ff). In Jewish usage of the time, the term Son of God designated a man who had been chosen and empowered by God to do his will, and especially to exercise authority in God's stead. Hence, it was a familiar way of referring to the king, both the historical kings of Israel (Ps. 2, 45, and especially 72), and the idealized ruler whose coming was to usher in the new age (Isa. 9:6, 7).[28]

The title "Son of God" then is both central to Mark's christology and ambiguously presented at the beginning so as to allow the story to reveal its meaning.

STRUCTURAL CONSIDERATIONS

Our quest for Mark's christology then will focus both upon the titles given to Jesus and upon the structural use which the author makes of these. Special attention will be given to the depth structure described earlier. It is correct to underscore the significance of the heavenly voice and to characterize the two statements (1:11 and 9:7) as expressing God's evaluative point of view; this analysis, however, does not do justice to the structural use which Mark makes of these heavenly statements. It is important to note that these divine declarations are situated at the beginning of the two principal parts of the story, where they serve parallel yet unique functions. In the first case, the statement is made to Jesus alone and thereby introduces the section on the messianic secret. Throughout this part of the story Mark demonstrates by means of words and deeds that Jesus, the hero, is indeed God's beloved one for he does God's will. On the one hand, people follow him because of his deeds (1:18, 20, 45; 2:14), praise his teaching (1:27), and wonder at his power (1:27; 2:12; 4:41; 5:20, 42; 7:37), a power which Mark implies is from God (2:7; see also 2:28 and 3:4). On the other hand, Mark refuses to divulge the true identity of the hero for that is the real issue of the story. Ironically only the followers of the prince of this world penetrate the messianic secret (1:24, 34; 5:7).

The second heavenly statement (9:7), addressed to those accom-

[28]H.C. Kee, *Understanding the New Testament* (Englewood Cliffs: Prentice-Hall, 1983) 102.

panying Jesus, introduces a new section of the story, the manifestation of the suffering and rising Son of Man. After identifying Jesus as "beloved Son," the voice issues a momentous command: the characters in the plot as well as the intended audience are to listen to Jesus' teaching. Thus, 8:31-10:52 is centered upon the threefold teaching about the suffering and rising of the Son of Man (8:31; 9:31; 10:33). We conclude (contrary to Kingsbury) that the Son's teaching about the suffering Son of Man forms part of the divine evaluative point of view. The divine voice, in this part of the story, both reiterates the sonship theme of the baptism scene and provides divine authority for the suffering Son of Man sayings. The first saying, indeed, clearly states: "It is necessary [divine necessity] that the Son of Man suffer many things" (8:31 RSVmod).

Important for our discussion of the Markan Jesus are some structural observations which have a bearing on the author's use of titles. In 6:6b-8:30 one finds a section of Mark's narrative which is set off by questions about Jesus' identity. After the initial statement of John concerning the "mightier one" (1:7) and frequent hints and questions about who Jesus is (1:24, 34, 2:6-8, etc.), about his reputation (1:27-28, 37, 45, etc.), and statements of amazement concerning his acts and sayings (1:27; 2:12; 4:41; 5:20, 42), Mark sets the stage for a more direct consideration of the story's principal topic, the identity of Jesus. In the context of Jesus' popularity (6:14b: his "name had become known") a threefold identification is made: he is John the Baptist, Elijah, or a prophet according to different elements of the population. The titles obviously overlap in Mark since John is presented earlier as a prophetic, Elijah-like figure (1:2, 6), since Elijah the wonder-worker is just as much an apocalytic character as is John (1:4-8 and 9:9-13), and since both John and Jesus are accepted by some of the population as prophets (6:15; 8:28; and 11:32). While the prophetic figure is left undeveloped by Mark, it should be noted that Jesus in the previous episode has been rejected by the Nazarene population precisely in his role as prophet and finally that , while the expression "a prophet like one of the prophets of old" (6:15) might signal Jesus' relation to Israel's classical prophetic tradition, Mark's associating Elijah with Moses at the transfiguration (9:4-5) and the long discourse on Mosaic kosher laws (chap. 7) point to the tradition of a "prophet like Moses" (Deut. 18:15). These titles, therefore, are introduced into the narrative to allow Mark to comment on Jesus' role. Narratively,the author pays immediate attention to the story of John's death and burial—John has been introduced in 6:14 as one who had allegedly "been raised from the dead." The rest of the section (6:30f) dwells upon various acts of power which Jesus in Elijah-like fashion performs and upon his relation to Jewish or Mosaic tradition. Mark terminates the section by repeating the threefold popular identification of Jesus as John the Baptist, Elijah, or one of the prophets. Presumably, Mark is saying, Jesus is all three and more, for he, beyond that, is the Christ or Messiah. After seeing his acts of power, knowing his reputation, and hearing his teaching, his followers are able to recognize him as the one promised in the Jewish scriptures, the Messiah (8:29).

Structurally, 8:27-10:45, along with the introductory (8:22-26) and concluding episodes (10:46-52) about restoring sight to blind individuals, is crucial for discerning Mark's use of titles and presentation of the story's principal character. On three occasions (chaps. 8, 9, 10) Mark presents a similar pattern for the passages traditionally referred to as the passion predictions: place, prediction of passion, lack of understanding, and Jesus' teaching on discipleship. The section is constructed so as to highlight the threefold teaching on the necessity of the suffering of the Son of Man and the bearing this has on discipleship. Mark focuses on Jesus the teacher[29] and his message concerning the suffering Son of Man (7 of the 14 occurrences of the title are found in this section). Further, on 5 occasions (one related to each passion-prediction section: 9:17, 38; 10:35) Jesus is addressed as teacher. Finally, the two sight-to-the-blind miracles are strategically situated to stress the nature of faith, namely, the recognition of Jesus' real identity. In the first case recognition of reality comes in stages (8:24-25) and in the second restoration of sight leads to discipleship (10:52).

PRINCIPAL CHRISTOLOGICAL TITLES

With these passages in mind we turn to Mark's use of the three principal titles for Jesus: Son of God, Son of Man, and Christ. Scholars agree that the first two titles, in the usage of the early community, referred to Jesus' resurrection (exaltation) and return (eschatology); and by extention Son of God in Mark becomes associated with Jesus' ministry. Thus, in early formulas such as Rom. 1:4 one hears that Jesus

---

[29]See especially the interesting work of V.K. Robbins, *Jesus the Teacher: A Socio-Rhetorical Interpretation of Mark* (Philadelphia: Fortress, 1984).

"is designated Son of God . . . by his resurrection." Presumably, Mark or pre-Synoptic tradition extended the title to the period of Jesus' ministry, since the unclean spirits as a result of Jesus' mighty works readily recognize him as God's Son (3:11; 5:7). Further, the heavenly voice declares him Son, ostensibly because he pleases the Father by his words and deeds (1:11). The title, Son of God, in Mark, therefore, is associated with the ministry and, as a presupposition, with the resurrection (see 14:61-62; 15:39; 16:6).[30] The second title, Son of Man, whatever its usage on the Jesus level, had an apocalyptic meaning in the thinking of the early community. This is the usage one finds in Mark 8:38; 13:26; and 14:62, particularly in the last two where the eschatological imagery of Daniel 7 is prominent. To this extent we agree with Kingsbury's contention that the two titles have different functions in Mark's Gospel. The situation, however, is more complex.

If Son of God and Son of Man refer to the ministry/resurrection and parousia respectively, they nonetheless, in Mark, extend beyond their traditional perimeters and interface with one another. Mark clearly employs the title Son of Man to refer to Jesus' ministry at 2:10, 28 and more frequently in relation to the suffering and resurrection (especially the passion predictions). The title, therefore, extends far beyond its traditional apocalyptic connotation. The other title, Son of God, also receives new content. The Son does not know the time of the parousia; only the Father does (13:32). Further, the concept of sonship is explicitly associated with the Son of Man; see 8:38 where the latter is said to return "in the glory of *his* Father" and 14:36, 41 where the one who addresses God as Father virtually identifies himself as the Son of Man who is about to be betrayed.

The third central title, Christ, also occurs principally in the second part at strategic points in the narrative. If we are correct in accepting the short reading of 1:1 then "Christ" alone serves as the title of Mark's Gospel and constitutes the author's initial statement about Jesus' identity. Investigation of the remaining occurrences of the title reveals that it functions as a bridge to other christological concepts. In 8:29 it serves as Peter's confession, but is immediately followed by teaching on the suffering Son of Man (8:31) and the declaration of the heavenly

[30]Mark 16:6 should read "he was raised" by God (*contra* RSV: "he has risen"); see R.G. Bratcher and E.A. Nida, *A Translator's Handbook on the Gospel of Mark* (Leiden: Brill, 1961) 504.

voice that Jesus is God's Beloved Son (9:7). Of course it is preceded by the threefold identification of Jesus as John the Baptist, Elijah, or one of the prophets (8:28). Its occurrence in 9:41 (receiving water to drink because one belongs to Christ) is preceded by the second prediction of the Son of Man's passion and death (9:31) and by the important statement that Jesus is one sent by God (9:37). At 12:35 Mark employs the title to clarify Jesus' relationship to David (see 10:47-48): how can the Christ be David's son when "David himself calls him Lord?" The answer is that he is of the Davidic line and therefore a son, but as Christ or Messiah is David's master for he is the one who brings in the kingdom of "our father David" (11:9-10). On three occasions earlier in chapter 12 (14, 19, 32) Jesus is addressed as teacher. The verse introducing the text in question states emphaticaly that "Jesus was teaching in the temple" (12:35). In the eschatological chapter Mark begins by having Jesus addressed as "teacher" (13:1), warns the reader that messianic claims are only signs of the final struggles (21-22), then expands the discussion of the parousia to include the titles of Son of Man (26) and Son of God (32). The following, 14:61-62, is the principal text where Mark joins together the major titles of Jesus: the Christ, the Son of the Blessed One, the Son of Man. The term "Christ" obviously appears here as a bridge between the other two. When asked if he is the Christ, i.e., described in terms of sonship, Jesus answers in the affirmative, all the while expanding the concept of messiahship to include his function as Son of Man "sitting at the right hand of Power and coming with the clouds of heaven."

The final occurrence of the title "Christ" (15:32) requires extended treatment because of the complexity of chapter 15. We are probably correct in accepting a recent study which sees the appearance of this title along with that of "King of the Jews/ Israel" (vv. 2, 9, 12, 18, 26, 32), and Son of God (15:39) as forming part of a complex series of messianic rejection/ mockery scenes;[31] that is, after Jesus admits that he is "King of the Jews" (v. 2) there follow alternating scenes of rejection and mockery. First Jesus is submitted to a mock coronation and hailed as "King of the Jews" (18), then during the crucifixion, he is addressed mockingly as a pathetic would-be Savior: "let the Christ, the King of Israel, come down now from the cross that we may see and believe" (32). The christological

---

[31] F.J. Matera, *The Kingship of Jesus: Composition and Theology in Mark 15* (Chico: Scholars, 1982), especially 136.

progression is obvious; Jesus is being rejected not as a royal pretender but as Messiah. Mark then reports a final, intriguing scene where Jesus in a loud voice is made to utter the opening line of Psalm 22 in Aramaic and provides the translation: "My God, my God, why hast thou forsaken me?" (34). The bystanders, on hearing this, mock Jesus by referring to Elijah, for "in their eyes there is no possibility that Elijah will come because Jesus is a false Messiah King,"[32] a messianic pretender. We might note that Mark had already addressed Jesus' relation to Elijah not only in 6:15 and 8:28 but also in 9:11-13 where Elijah, in the divine scheme of things ("must" of v. 11), was to have preceded the messianic restoration and, in effect, is said to have come and already been rejected in the person of John the Baptist. Chapter 15, however, continues by presenting the death of Jesus, the tearing of the temple curtain in two (vv. 37-38), and the confession of the centurion ("Son of God," v. 39), who standing there both saw and believed (*contra* the mockers of v. 32 who promised that upon seeing they would believe). Once again, Mark uses this title as a bridge concept to bring together several important facets of Jesus' identity; Jesus is the Messiah, a title to be understood in relation to the royal promises to the line of David, to the role of Elijah/John the Baptist, and to the important title "Son of God." Finally, the concept of "Son of Man" lurks behind the whole of chapter 15 as Mark rewrites the passion predictions about the Son of Man, especially the third one (10:33-34).

> By intertwining prediction and passion Mark has reminded the reader that his humiliation and rejection does not occur by chance. The only Son, the King of the Jews, suffers in his divinely appointed capacity as the Son of Man according to the scriptures[33]
> [see 9:12 and 14:21: "as it is written of him"].

If we consider Mark as narrative or story, we are obliged to take more seriously the declarations made from beginning to end about Jesus' identity. The story begins by telling the reader that the whole is good news which Jesus and others (1:1—"good news *of* Jesus Christ": subjective and objective genitives) have declared concerning the Christ/ Messiah. The story of Jesus, then, begins with John and with OT prophecy ("prepare the way of the Lord"—1:3). As the Dead Sea Scrolls

[32]*Ibid.*, 124.
[33]*Ibid.*, 97.

community before them had done, so the early Christians appealed to and applied to themselves the words of Isaiah 40. John the Baptist, in Elijah-like fashion, is cast in the role of preparing for the coming Messiah who is mightier than he and who is to baptize with the Spirit. The whole life of Jesus is situated within the messianic expectation of the time. OT themes and titles are deliberately incorporated into the story's presentation of the hero, who is first of all the Christ (1:1). Jesus gathers disciples, heals, teachers, wins the crowds, encounters opposition, sends the twelve on mission. Mark presents these episodes to guide the reader into a polyvalent discussion of Jesus' identity.

THREE HEAVENLY MESSAGES: GOD'S POINT OF VIEW

On three occasions a heavenly message is given concerning Jesus' identity. The first half of the gospel is introduced by a heavenly voice declaring Jesus the Beloved Son who has God's favor (1:11). The narrative then proceeds to show by acts of power and words of wisdom, all the while commanding silence, that Jesus indeed has God's favor. Only otherworldly figures penetrate the secret of Jesus' identity (1:24, 34; 3:11; 5:6), i.e., the Son of God who has eschatological power (a Son-of-Man-like figure). The reaction to these divinely based acts, as we saw was the case in chapter 15, is twofold. Mark in 6:14-8:30 contrasts the reaction of the general populace (Jesus is John, Elijah, or a prophet) with that of Jesus' followers (he is the Christ). Thus, like Mark (1:1), the whole community is able to subscribe to Peter's confession that Jesus is the one promised in the Jewish scriptures (8:29). So with this goal achieved and the principle established that commitment to the master is the prerequisite for discipleship, Mark has reached a climax in the story, corresponding to the commands of silence, and is able narratively to address more fundamental issues regarding Jesus' identity.

The second part of the gospel is also introduced by a heavenly message. Again Jesus is declared God's Beloved Son, but this time the voice adds a crucial command: "listen to him" (9:7). Indeed, this part of Mark's narrative is given to Jesus' teaching about himself as the Son of Man who must suffer, die, and be raised from the dead (8:31; 9:31; 10:33).[34] God's evaluative point of view is focused upon Jesus' teaching

---

[34]Indeed, one might wish in agreement with Robbins, *Jesus the Teacher*, to see all of Mark's story as a relationship between Jesus the teacher and his disciples: introduction (1:1-3:6), teaching and learning phase (3:7-12:44), and farewell/death (13:1-16:8).

concerning the Son of Man. Jesus the Christ is the Son of God, the one who has suffered and died, and now risen, awaits the time of his return as Son of Man.

Once Jesus' teaching about the suffering Son of Man begins, the commands of silence cease. In fact, Mark underscores this immediately after the first passion prediction: "he said this plainly" (8:32a). Jesus on three occasions says very plainly what must happen. Further, the heavenly voice reveals to the public (9:7) that Jesus is God's Son and that his teaching is to be received as divinely inspired. While there has been some discussion about when the messianic secret terminates in Mark,[35] it seems clear that the theme of secrecy takes on a dramatic change after Peter's confession. It is proposed here that the narrative from 8:31 to 15:39 constitutes a special teaching section about Jesus' identity—a hiatus between the messianic confession of Peter/the community and that of Mark's ideal reader/believer (the centurion—15:39). Between these two points Mark studiously avoids human confessions about Jesus' identity. Instead the author focuses attention upon the heavenly voice's insistence that the Son's raison d'etre is to reveal and to act out the role of the suffering/rising Son of Man. In fact, the section reaches its climax only after the Christ, identified, hailed, and rejected as a royal figure (11:9-10; 12:10-11; 15:32), has suffered and died as the Son of Man (15:37; also passion predictions) and is finally confessed, once the veil of the temple/secrecy has been torn, as the Son of God (15:39). The reader can then feel confident that this is "the side of God and not of men" (8:33c). Indeed, the final command of silence (9:9) pointed to this very episode, namely, that nothing was to be said about the heavenly voice until the Son of Man should rise from the dead.[36]

Narratively the author prepares the reader for the revelation of Jesus' identity by the two miracles of giving sight to the blind and arranges Jesus' entry and activity in Jerusalem to underscore his acclamation as "the one who comes in the name of the Lord" (11:9-10) and as "the very stone which the builders rejected" (12:10). This teaching section (frequent use of "teacher," "teaching," and conflict stories) has made extensive use

---

[35]See Kingsbury's discussion, *The Christology of Mark's Gospel*, 1-23.

[36]In lieu of resurrection appearances (absent in Mark) we find eschatological signs of divine approval: "darkness over the whole land until the ninth hour" (15:35) and the renting of the temple curtain "in two from top to bottom" (v. 38).

of Psalm 118 (especially vv. 22-26) to discuss Jesus' acclamation and rejection.[37]

After a farewell speech which warns the audience about exaggerated apocalyptic expectations,[38] Mark presents Jesus as eating the passover with his disciples, an event which the author suggests has soteriological and eschatological meaning ("blood of the covenant poured out for many" and a cup taken in view of "the kingdom of God"—14:24-25). There follows the dramatic garden scene where Jesus prays to God as "Abba, Father" (14:36) and the subsequent prediction of the Son of Man's betrayal (v. 41). During the succeeding trial and death scenes the reader encounters two important passages, first the crucial statement about the Son of Man who will return vindicated (14:62) and that about the Son of God, who is recognized in an act of faith as the dying Son of Man (15:39).

The third heavenly message is found at the end of the gospel.[39] A young man dressed in a white robe gives the reader a final otherworldly message about the bringer of good news; he is Jesus of Nazareth, the crucified one, whom God raised from the dead, the one who goes to Galilee ahead of the community (16:6-7). The suffering human figure who was raised from the dead, is the suffering Son of Man (passion predictions), the same Jesus of Nazareth who had come from Galilee to be baptized and had been declared Son of God by the heavenly voice (1:9-11). This crucified one is the Son of Man who, as he was dying, was confessed by the centurion to be Son of God. Finally, he is the one who precedes the community to Galilee.

With this last identification we reach a problematic area: does 16:7 anticipate a non-recorded resurrection appearance or does it refer to apocalyptic expectation?[40] The text of Mark seems to demand that one

[37]Kee, "The Function of Scriptural Quotations and Allusions in Mark 11-16," 167-79.

[38]Neirynck, "Le Discours anti-apocalyptique de Mc., XIII," 154-64.

[39]Matera's statement, *The Kingship of Jesus*, 140: "Inasmuch as this confession [15:39] is the final identification of Jesus' person, its importance cannot be overestimated for the passion narrative or for the gospel," is a good example of overlooking a crucial element in Mark's narrative and thereby overstressing one title at the expense of others; the same critique can be made of Kingsbury's entire study in *The Christology of Mark's Gospel*, 133-37.

[40]See R.H. Stein's discussion of the debate, "A Short Note on Mark xiv. 28 and xvi. 7," *NTS* 20 (1974) 445-52. For example, Kingsbury, *The Christology of Mark's Gospel*, 135-37, opts for resurrection appearances while T.J. Weeden, *Mark—Traditions in Conflict* (Philadelphia: Fortress, 1971) 111-17, defends a parousia hypothesis.

understand the promise in the latter, though modified, sense, i.e., Jesus is expected to return in the near future, but beyond the throes of the Judaeo-Roman war ("the end is not yet," 13:7). Mark no less than the author of 2 Thessalonians is concerned about exaggerated apocalyptic notions and so warns the community that "this is but the beginning of the sufferings [of the end-time]" and that it must preach the gospel to all nations, and not be deceived by false messiahs (13:5-10, 21-23). Though subscribing to the notion that the end is near, Mark holds that much remains to be done. The gospel ends on the same note on which it began; in 1:38-39 Jesus tells his disciples: "'let us go on to the next towns, that I may preach there also; for that is why I came out.' And he went throughout all Galilee, preaching in their synagogues and casting out demons." As he had promised at the end of the supper ("after I am raised up, I will go before you to Galilee," 14:28), so after the resurrection (16:6) he leads his community, in view of the coming end and hardship (13:9-13), in the mission launched to the nations, a mission crystallized in Galilee of the Gentiles.[41]

The good news recorded in Mark's narrative, therefore, is the story of Jesus the Christ, a man sent by God (9:37) as a ransom for many (10:45), one in whom God found delight (1:11) because he submitted to the divine plan as a suffering man for others (8:31), one whose goal and achievement was that "whoever receives me, receives not me but him who sent me" (9:37).[42] For Mark Jesus is first of all the Christ, promised in the Jewish scriptures, the one who as Son of God/Son of Man suffered, died, was raised, and awaits the final restoration of God's kingdom. In the meantime those who follow him on the way (10:52) he leads in their missionary task among the nations until all "see the Son of Man coming in the clouds with great power and glory" (14:62 RSVmod). Mark is a witness to the beginning and continuation of the good news of Jesus the Christ.

Mark's Jesus is a human character on a human stage, but as was common in Semitic and Classical worldviews, it is a stage where otherworldly characters figure prominently, whether the divinity, angels or other messengers, and satanic or unclean figures of the underworld. If the story narrates communications between these worlds, it is

---

[41]On the missionary thrust of Mark, see J.R. Donahue, "A Neglected Factor in the Theology of Mark," *JBL* 101 (1982) 592-94.

[42]*Ibid.*, 587-89.

nonetheless primarily about a human hero and his divine mission, written in an inimitable story-like fashion. Jesus is God's Beloved Son (1:11, a man for others; see 10:45), but, as he teaches (9:7, one who suffers and rises), he is both God's eschatological messenger/Son of Man who will return at the end-time and Son who, risen from the dead and established in glory and power (proleptically as Son of Man), leads his community. Mark, anxious for the end-days, but wise enough to know that only the Father was privy to that knowledge (13:32), advises the community to believe in God's messenger, to be wise in reading the signs of the times (13:4f), to be watchful (13:33-37), and to see to it that the good news is preached to all nations (13:10). The community, professing Jesus to be Christ, all the while, must act in his name and follow his example (the pattern of Christian life: the death and resurrection, 8:34-35), while waiting to "see the kingdom of God come with power" (9:1).

Mark's purpose for writing concerns first of all the exposition and development of a christology (Jesus' identity according to God's point of view) whose proper understanding has a bearing on the community's mission (10:52; 13:10; 16:7). Whether there were some in the community who advocated a faulty christology is far from certain, but what does seem evident is that Mark sees the role of Jesus as related to a proper interpretation of the kerygma, namely, the cross and resurrection.

The three heavenly messages, therefore, underscore what the author perceives to be God's point of view and thus the authentic Markan view, that of both author and reader. Each message introduces a part of the gospel whose point is crucial to the author. In the first the theme of secrecy defines the nature of belief in Jesus; it is only in observing what he does and hearing what he says that one is able to confess with the disciples that Jesus is the Christ. In the second it is the crucial teaching of the kerygma which defines what Jesus' role in God's plan is. The voice declares that Jesus is God's Son in his role as the dying and rising Son of Man. Faith in Jesus requires that both his death (as Son of Man) and resurrection (as Son of God) be confessed by his followers. The third heavenly message brings the story to closure by introducing an open-ended section of the gospel where the followers, with the risen Jesus in the lead or "on the way," are introduced to their missionary task.[43] Far

---

[43]E.S. Malbon, "Galilee and Jerusalem: History and Literature in Marcan interpretation," *CBQ* 44 (1982) 242-55 and E. Best, *Following Jesus: Discipleship in the Gospel of Mark* (Sheffield: JSOT, 1981) 208-50.

from being a "failed message" or indictment of contemporary leaders, Mark is a story of optimism which ends with a message to a growing community about the world mission.[44] Mark, read as a story, albeit an ancient popular narrative, reaches out to its intended reader and offers a version of the master's story which presents, in view of that author's vision and strategy, God's perspective upon Jesus' identity and salvific role.

---

[44]T.E. Boomershine, "Mark 16:8 and the Apostolic Commission," *JBL* 100 (1981) 225-39 and N.R. Petersen, "When Is an End not the End?" 97-121; see also the latter's comments in *Literary Criticism for New Testament Critics*, 73-80. For a similar conclusion regarding the theme of mission in Mark, see D. Senior, "The Struggle to be Universal: Mission as Vantage Point for New Testament Investigation," *CBQ* 46 (1984) 66-81.

5

The Gospel of Matthew

The composition of Mark, the first gospel, was an event of momentous consequences, for it established an organizational sequence and a measure of standardization for the Jesus tradition. Mark set in motion a development which greatly modified the nature of this tradition. Prior to Mark's composition Christian culture was essentially oral in character but following this initiative there began to appear other similar works (see Luke 1:1-4). This chapter, therefore, will be devoted to one of Mark's first successors.

Why a New Gospel?

It is important to inquire, in general terms, about Matthew's reason for writing. Scholars concede that Mark's Gospel was a prized possession of the Matthean community, for it was this document which its leaders and teachers employed in their ministry and which its members relished as part of their liturgy. Mark then would have attained a respectable status in some Christian communities of the eastern part of the Roman empire.

Why then a new gospel? A satisfactory response must of necessity remain conjectural and, in part, paradoxical. On the one hand, Mark was held in such esteem by Matthew's church, that one of its leaders employed it as the basis of a new composition. Then, as now, imitation is an impressive witness of esteem. On the other hand, Matthew felt no inhibition in modifying and expanding the work of an esteemed predecessor. Some in the community then no longer considered Mark adequate for their needs, even while respecting that author's accomplishment.

By contrasting Matthew with Mark, particularly the former's redactional passages, we are able to discern an author and a community's concern about new problems, new issues, and a contrasting interpretation of who Jesus was. A community, living in a different part of the empire, consisting of a heterogeneous membership, and at a further remove from the time of Jesus and the Palestinian milieu of the beginnings, confronted a new situation requiring reinterpretation of the Jesus tradition. The gospel exhibits a Jewish community, at least in its point of view, whose concern for the Gentile mission is paramount. The composition of Matthew, no doubt, was the culmination of a lengthy process of teaching, of Judaeo-Christian exchange, and of a successful Gentile mission, a process which accounts for the gospel's mixture of Jewish and Gentile elements. The evangelist offers a new appropriation of the tradition, now applied specifically to the community's situation. A bold example is Matthew's application of the parable of the stray sheep, not in relation to Jesus' ministry, as in Luke 15:3-7, but to community leaders' responsibility toward wayward fellow Christians (18:12-14). In this way the tradition acquired a more ecclesiastical character, much as Pharisaic oral interpretation made "the tradition of the Fathers" more actual for later generations. Both the Matthean community and its evangelist needed the Jesus tradition applied to their situation.[1]

While Mark by the act of writing had imposed some restraints and order upon the Jesus material, oral tradition persisted within the communities alongside Mark's Gospel. Far from exhausting the traditions concerning Jesus, the author of the first gospel had made a judicious choice of episodes and sayings to compose a life of the master. Members of the communities continued to recite stories and sayings of the Lord, even though with the appearance of Mark the tradition began to be standardized. Oral materials continued to exist alongside written texts, but gradually ceded ground to the latter.[2] In this chapter then we turn to one of Mark's successors, Matthew, a gospel which is the

---

[1]On the church of Matthew see E. Schweizer, "Matthew's Church," 129-55 in G. Stanton, ed., *The Interpretion of Matthew* (Philadelphia: Fortress, 1983); J.D. Kingsbury, *Matthew* (Philadelphia: Fortress, 1977) 78-106; J.P. Meier, *The Vision of Matthew: Christ, Church, and Morality in the First Gospel* (NY: Paulist, 1979) 26-39; and Neyrey, *Christ Is Community*, 81-104.

[2]Kelber, *The Oral and the Written Gospel.*

product of a discerning use of oral and written sources and of its author's literary talent and theological vision.

Matthean Redaction

The first book of the New Testament has been popular within the Christian community throughout the centuries. Its position at the beginning of the NT corpus owes probably to its length, extensive teaching and ethical materials, and superb craftsmanship. Matthew treats Jesus' life more extensively than Mark; a genealogy, annunciation and birth narratives, several extended speeches by Jesus, and resurrection appearances are added. These new materials are interwoven with the story known from Mark to form the author's new biography of Jesus.[3]

USE OF SOURCES

It is generally agreed that Matthew employed three distinct sources: the Gospel of Mark, the Q-Document, and an amorphous group of traditions usually labeled "M." Desite 19th-century attempts and some recent interest[4] to justify the priority of Matthew, it is readily admitted that the narrative structure of the gospel is Markan for, the birth and resurrection aside, Matthew's story-line is derived, even though its plot is further developed. Differences between the two in sequence and style are explained by Matthew's redactional activity. Further, Matthew has reproduced fully 90% of the first gospel in its text. Beyond this one concludes that Matthew offers a later ecclesiological and christological perspective than does Mark; for example, Jewish-Christian relations are more focused as are speculations concerning Jesus' lordship.

The second source employed is the well-known Q-Document, a written source with which Matthew and Luke supplemented their Markan outline. This document and its eschatological content had profound effects upon Matthew's perception of the Christ-event.[5] Lastly, Matthew used traditions stemming from the author's own

---

[3] *Shuler, A Genre for the Gospels*; see also Talbert, *What Is a Gospel?*

[4] C.M. Tuckett, *The Revival of the Griesbach Hypothesis: An Analysis and Appraisal* (London: Cambridge University, 1982).

[5] Neyrey, *Christ Is Community*, 67-81.

community. Analysis of this unique material indicates that it was oral in nature, representative of the community's concerns, and conducive to the author's purposes. In these passages one finds many of Matthew's major characteristics: Jewish background of the Jesus movement, urgency of the Gentile mission, and the challenging, moral and judgmental character of the evangelist's message.

If these sources contributed the gospel's content, the resulting composition with its intricate patterns and unique perspective is the work of the later writer whom, following later tradition, we call Matthew. Both story-line and content were borrowed from Mark and edited to achieve specific goals. This basic story was supplemented with materials from Q and oral tradition, materials which were inserted within the Markan outline to form a series of major speeches for Jesus, the narrative's principal character. In typical editorial fashion episodes are rewritten to underscore the author's point of view, as for example in the healing of Simon's mother-in-law.

Matt. 8	Mark 1
14 And Jesus, having gone into the house of Peter,	29 And immediately having gone out from the synagogue he went into the house of Simon and Andrew with James and John.
saw his mother-in-law laying down and sick with a fever	30 Now Simon's mother-in-law lay sick with a fever and immediately they told him of her.
15 And he touched her hand and the fever left her and she rose and served him.	31 And having come he lifted her, having taken her hand; and the fever left her; and she served them.

Matthew eliminates extraneous details (locale, list of apostles, repetitions) to focus upon the central character's activity. As a result only Jesus and the woman appear in the Matthean text. This and other such editorial activity give this gospel a solemn and severe tone.[6]

[6]For a classical study of Matthean redaction, see H.J. Held, "Matthew as Interpreter of the Miracle Stories," 165-299 in Bornkamm, *Tradition and Interpretation in Matthew*; for Matthew's rewriting of the passion narrative, see D.P. Senior, *The*

Matthew adds freely to the Markan outline materials acquired from other sources. The teaching of John the Baptist found in Mark is expanded by adding Q material (3:7f); the same occurs in the temptation narrative (4:1f). Matthew expands the eschatological discourse of Mark 13 by rewriting it, amplifying it with Q material, and then adding an entire chapter consisting of M and Q parables concerning the last days (chaps. 24-25). Beyond this the author judiciously chooses materials from available sources: shortening, expanding, modifying, clarifying, omitting, and at times exchanging one episode for another.[7] Matthew interweaves these sources to produce a continuous life of the master, one which provides the narrative's hero ample scope for the major speeches which the author wishes to communicate to the community.

CREATIVITY

Since each text has a style, vocabulary, and point of view of its own, Matthew is no exception, for by its author's literary choices and habits a unique personality and theology are revealed to the reader. From the brief episode reproduced above, some understanding of the author's stylistic tendencies is gained. In this episode, as usual, Matthew follows Mark's story-line faithfully but eliminates the ubiquitous "and" (*kai*) and employs a more complex sentence structure. Further, while Matthew's favorite connective is "then," a term employed 90 times versus Mark 6 and Luke 15, many others are used and thereby give this gospel variety and natural flow. Among these connectives, for example: " in that/ those day(s)," "at that time," participial constructions with postpositive "and" (*de*, especially "and seeing") and genitive absolutes, few have parallels in Mark and Luke. On the whole, one can say that Matthew's style and command of Greek is superior to that of Mark and John but inferior to Luke's. Improvement over Mark's unpolished style is reflected in a larger vocabulary, modification of poor grammatical constructions (especially the historical present) and tautology, and greater variety and complexity of sentence structure.

Grouping of Jesus material from various sources according to topics and types is clear evidence of Matthean editing. For example, the author has gathered in two chapters (8-9) ten miracles and in one (13) a

Passion Narrative According to Matthew: A Redactional Study (Leuven: Leuven University, 1975).

[7]Kingsbury, *Matthew*, 14-21.

number of parables. In both cases the cue was provided by Mark (chaps. 1-2 and 4 respectively). Later in the gospel closely following the Markan sequence, Matthew treats the parable of the wicked tenants. Since in the Markan sequence it is oddly sandwiched between a series of controversy stories and since it deals with a favorite theme, Matthew adds to it two parables also dealing with Jesus' call to and rejection by Israel, namely, the two sons and the marriage feast (21:28-22:14). In deference to contemporary Jewish piety, Matthew gathers sayings of Jesus on the three exemplary works: almsgiving, prayer, and fasting, each of which is introduced by "when you (neg.) . . . but when you (pos.) . . . " (6:2-18). After a short introduction on the validity of the Law or Torah, the author in six successive paragraphs writes about some of the principal issues of that Law: murder, adultery, divorce, swearing, retaliation, and love of one's enemies. A formulaic construction introduces each, "you have heard it was said . . . but I say to you . . . " (5:21-48). Interestingly, a seventh (the perfect number) is not given for the passage ends with the admonition: "You, therefore, must be perfect, as your heavenly Father is perfect" (5:48—note that the Lukan parallel, 6:36, uses the term "merciful"). Other examples of Matthean grouping involve the great thematic discourses, the logical placing of the infancy and resurrection stories at the beginning and end of the Markan sequence, and the accumulation of eschatological materials around Mark 13 (Matt. 23-25).

Also interesting in Matthew's method of composition is the concern for the development of ideas or themes. Formulas and themes are repeated and contrasted: "brood of vipers" (3:7; 12:34; 23:33), "suffer for Christ's sake" (5:11; 10:18; 13:21; 24:9), beatitudes and woes (5:3f and 23:13f), gospel of the kingdom (4:23; 9:35; 24:14; 26:13), receiving Jesus (10:40; 19:5; also 25:40).[8] This technique adds cohesion to the narrative, consistency to its themes, and depth to its author's perspective. An extended example, the author's theme of mission, will illustrate the importance of this technique for Matthew. The gospel ends with a command to make disciples of all nations, a theme which extends throughout the narrative. Indeed, the first chapters underscore the promise of a Jewish mission in the person of Jesus who will save his people (1:21, a pun on his name) and who will be the ruler and king of

---

[8]See D.L. Barr, "The Drama of Matthew's Gospel: A Reconsideration of Its Structure and Purpose," *TD* 24 (1976) 349-59.

the Jews and in anticipation that of Gentiles (coming of the wise men, 2:1f). After the preparation by John the Baptist, Jesus begins the mission in earnest, when he preaches the "gospel of the kingdom" (4:23 and 9:35) and sends his disciples on a mission to the Jews (10:6). The central chapter (13) is focused on the nature of the kingdom and those who "hear the word of the kingdom" (13:19). Further there is preparation for the world mission in chapters 18 (on community) and 22 (the wedding feast), when the disciples will preach "the gospel of the kingdom" (24:14). Remembering that they have one Father and one teacher and master (23:8-10), they will set out with "all authority" to "make disciples of all nations," baptizing and teaching as the Lord had commanded them (28:18-20). The theme of mission, therefore, is carefully developed from beginning to end of the gospel. Its Jewish and Gentile character as well as the related themes of authority, teaching, and community are finely interwoven to underscore the importance of mission and its relation to other aspects of Matthew's message.

A fondness for balance can be seen in the author's juxtaposition of negative and positive elements, narratives and discourses, theoretical with practical statements, and narratives with statements of OT fulfilment. As an example of this phenomenon, especially the alternating of positive and negative statements (also a case of theory followed by examples), we cite 18:5-14. Vv 5 and 6 state the positive and negative principles of community life; there then follow examples of negative (7-9) and positive (10-14) practice.[9] The alternation of narrative and discourse will be examined below, but the author's use of the Old Testament merits more attention at this point. If Matthew, like the other gospels, employs freely the Jewish scriptures to interpret the Christian reality, its use of formula citations underscores its uniqueness. No fewer than 12 times Matthew introduces quotations with a stereotyped formula such as "then was fulfilled what had been spoken by the prophet ..., saying" (1:22-23; 2:5-6, 15, 17-18, 23; 4:14-16; 8:17; 12:17-21; 13:14-15, 35; 21:4-5; and 27:9-10). These citations do not follow the usual promise-fulfilment pattern, where the citation comes first and its realization follows, but usually follow a Matthean narrative for which they provide documentation. Whatever their origin it is clear that Matthew employs these formula citations throughout to emphasize

---

[9]For an examination of this Matthean chapter, confer W.G. Thompson, *Matthew's Advise to a Divided Community: Mt. 17, 22-18, 35* (Rome: Biblical Institute, 1970).

the continuity in sacred history from Israel to the new Israel. The extended use of typology will be examined later in regard to Matthew's presentation of Jesus and the Christian community.

An important feature of Matthean composition is a love for architectonic features such as symmetry (chiasmus, inclusio, alternation, and balance), summaries, numbers, repetition, and formulas of various kinds. Their function in the gospel's structure should be stressed for they provide an aesthetic quality, a structured cohesion, and a depth of perception on Matthew's part which is sometimes overlooked.[10] The chiasmus (a-b-c-b'-a' or the like) provides an artistic touch as well as focuses attention upon the central element of the structure. Matthean examples are often related to OT citations (4:10 = Deut. 6:13 and 13:15 = Isa. 6:10); some scholars even view the whole gospel as forming a chiasmus around chapter 13.[11] The use of numbers is also of interest since Matthew often arranges episodes or blocks of material in twos, threes, fives, and sevens; in some cases these numbers seem to have symbolic value, as in the genealogy where Jesus' ancestry is presented in three groups of fourteen, 2 x 7, where Jesus is the final and perfect component of the end-time (1:17).

Structure and Matthean Purpose

Our study shows that the Matthean narrative gives the reader numerous architectonic, thematic, and linguistic indicators of its plan and purpose. Remembering that a literary text reveals its organization on at least two levels, we begin our investigation of Matthew's plan by considering the diversity of its structural indicators. By examining Matthew's plan we will discern its purpose and its particular perspective on the community (ecclesiology) and its Lord (christology).

STRUCTURE OF MATTHEW

Since the pioneer study of B.W. Bacon in 1930 scholars have become accustomed to defending a fivefold structure for Matthew. The theory is

---

[10]K.F. Nickle, *The Synoptic Gospels: An Introduction* (Atlanta: John Knox, 1980) 102-12, gives a good, brief survey of Matthew's literary and structural characteristics.

[11]J. Fenton, *The Gospel of St. Matthew* (Baltimore: Penguin, 1963) 14-17; Barr, "The Drama of Matthew's Gospel," 351; P.F. Ellis, *Matthew: His Mind and His Message* (Collegeville: Liturgical, 1974) 8-25.

based upon the fivefold use of the formula, "and when Jesus had finished . . . "(7:28; 11:1; 13:53; 19:1; 26:1) to mark the ending of major discourses. Further, each speech is preceded by a narrative section. The overall pattern then consists of an introductory birth account, a concluding death-resurrection narrative, and in between these five alternating narrative-discourse sections:

A. Arrival of the Messiah (1-2)
B. The Messiah and His Kingdom (3-25)
   1. Proclamation of the Kingdom
      narrative: Beginnings in Galilee (3-4)
      discourse: Sermon on the Mount (5-7)
   2. Spreading of the Kingdom
      narrative: Authority of Jesus (8-9)
      discourse: Missionary Discourse (10)
   3. Mystery/Nature of the Kingdom
      narrative: Rejection and Acceptance (11-12)
      discourse: Parabolic Discourse (13:1-52)
   4. Life within the Kingdom
      narrative: Life of the New Community (13:53-17:27)
      discourse: Discourse on Community Life (18)
   5. Establishment of the Kingdom
      narrative: conflict and Consumation (19-23)
      discourse: Eschatological Discourse (24-25)
C. Death/Passion/Resurrection of the Messiah (26-28).[12]

Following Bacon's suggestion, some see the five discourses as corresponding to the five books of Moses and, therefore, hint at a Moses-Jesus typology.

Building on this proposal some suggest that the whole is constructed in a chiastic pattern either as alternating narratives and discourses or as parallel blocks of material with the parabolic discourse as the central element.[13] Thus, there are correspondences between blocks of material which suggest a chiastic structure: the beatitudes and woes in sections 1 and 5, birth and death in parts A and C, mission/reception (10:40) and

---

[12]Meier, *Matthew*, 5 and D.J. Harrington, *The Gospel According to Matthew* (Collegeville: Liturgical, 1983) 8-9.

[13]Barr, "The Drama of Matthew's Gospel" and Fenton, *Matthew*, respectively. Confer also H.B. Green, "The structure of St. Matthew's Gospel," *SE* 102 (1968) 47-59, who finds a parabolic or chiastic structure in Matthew with chapter 11 as the central point.

community/reception (18:5) in the second and fourth discourses, and the crisis point in the third speech (13:36) marking private as opposed to public instruction.[14]

Some scholars object to this fivefold pattern because they reject a Moses-Jesus typology and since such a theory would relegate Jesus' passion, death, and resurrrection to the status of an appendix or epilogue to the great speeches.[15] Instead, they appeal to the twofold formula "from the time Jesus began to ... " at 4:17 and 16:21, and propose the following structure:

A. Coming of the Messiah: the beginnings 1:1-4:16
   (Old and New; God with us; person of Jesus)

B. Public Ministry of the Messiah 4:17-16:20
   (preaching, teaching, and healing—divine power;
   also climax of ministry in chapter 13)

C. Passion and Death of the Messiah 16:21-28:20
   (salvation to all: risen Jesus = God with us).[16]

The above presents an interesting developmental scheme, for its three parts underscore the essential components of Classical biography: the presentation, work or achievements, and destiny of the hero. Thus, each formula would introduce a new stage in the development of Jesus' life: the beginning of his preaching ("the kingdom of heaven is at hand," 4:17) and the first announcement of the passion (16:21). One could complement this outline by appealing to the formula citations since they also contribute to Matthew's evolving portrait of Jesus as God's envoy.[17]

The major difficulty I see in this approach is the dismissal by its advocates of the obvious discourse structure of chapters 5-25. The introduction and conclusion of these speeches are clearly discernible;[18] their structural and thematic prominence in the central section of the

---

[14]Fenton, *Matthew*, 14-17

[15]D.J. Harrington, "Matthean Studies since Joachim Rohde," 95-98 in *Light of All Nations.*

[16]Kümmel, *Introduction to the New Testament*, 105-6 and J.D. Kingsbury, *Matthew: Structure, Christology, Kingdom* (Philadelphia: Fortress, 1975) 1-39; idem, *Matthew*, 24-28.

[17]Kingsbury, *ibid.*, 36.

[18]T.J. Keegan, "Introductory Formulae for Matthean Discourses," *CBQ* 44 (1982) 415-30; confer also F.V. Filson, "Broken Patterns in the Gospel of Matthew," *JBL* 75 (1956) 227-31.

gospel underscores their importance in the author's plan. If one examines the summaries, 4:23; 9:35; 11:1; 16:21; 17:22-23; and 20:17-19, which appear in the gospel, one discovers interesting structural data. The first three are closely related to the fivefold discourse structure, while the second three are not. Instead the latter introduce the three traditional passion predictions. Matthew adds a fourth prediction of the passion (26:2), which, in association with the previous verse, forms both the conclusion of the final great discourse and the introduction of the passion narrative. If the summary of 16:21 seems to support the threefold structure, that of 4:23, coming so soon after the introduction of the ministry, does not. Finally, the author's penchant for structural connectives should give reason for pause, since Matthew contrasts Jesus' power in words and deeds (speech of part 1 and narrative of part 2), concludes narratives and introduces speeches with identical summaries (4:23-25; 9:35-37) and retells the history of Israel as the life of Jesus in chapters 2-9, thereby linking what most outlines propose as distinct parts of the story. Matthew's multifaceted techniques of composition should make us wary of settling for too simple an outline to explain this intricate narrative. Instead all pertinent structural indicators should be taken seriously and their function sought in relation to the author's plan.

The two schemes examined above, we believe, are based on structural features stemming from the author's redaction. Instead of choosing between them we seek in Matthew's Gospel a justification for both since one is related to the genre of the work (biography, the threefold structure) and the other to the author's purpose (the teaching of the risen Lord, the fivefold discourses). That justification is found in the dynamic structure indicated by the inclusio of 1:23 and 28:20. At the beginning of the gospel, following on a heavenly messenger's announcement of Jesus' divine conception and mission, one finds the first formula citation in support of the angel's message concerning the birth and naming (1:22-23). Parallel to the explanation of the name of Jesus (God "saves") is that of the messianic name, "Emmanuel" or "God with us." Jesus, therefore, is considered God's very presence and his ministry the work of God. It is with this key theme that Matthew ends: "and lo, I am with you always, to the close of the age" (28:20b). The risen Lord will abide with the community as mediator between heaven and earth, a theme which Matthew narratively stresses at the finale by leaving Jesus in the midst of his followers (also see John 20:29). Matthew has structured the story to focus upon the pre- and post-resurrection activity of Jesus as God's abiding presence in the world. The author, between the structural components of the opening and closing elements of the "inclusio," treats the various facets of this divine presence. Reception of Jesus means reception of the Father who sent him (10). There is eschatological blessedness for those who witness the divine presence and attend to its heavenly message (13:16-17). In the communion of believers (18:20) and in the reception and care of the lowly and needy (18:5 and 25:40, 45) Jesus, the divine envoy, continues to be present.

Why, therefore, does Matthew present several structural schemes? These we believe should be explained in relation to Matthew's choice of genre and purpose for writing on the one hand and perception of who Jesus was, what he did, and what his life meant for believers on the other. Thus, choice of the biography to address the community's needs, a choice influenced by reverence for, and yet need to revise, Mark, goes a long way in explaining Matthew's insistence upon the narrative of Jesus' life. It is the life and teaching of the master which personify the promise of 1:23 that he would be Emmanuel. The whole gospel is a progressive and developing portrait of Jesus not only as Messiah but as God's only Son. This picture Matthew etches by employing the developmental pattern of the biography.

Matthew was interested not primarily in past events, but in the post-resurrection situation of the community. The final verse of the gospel promises Jesus' continuing presence among his followers (28:20b). The master will be present in the community's life (18:20) and its attention to the needy (25:35f), and especially through its hearing, guarding, and doing all that Jesus said (28:20a). It is correct to envision this gospel as "a *collection* of sermons" spoken by the risen Lord to his own,[19] since Matthew has collected Jesus' teachings into five major (and some minor) discourses and, by situating them within the ministry and by subsuming them under the final command of the risen Lord, has blurred the distinction between the pre- and post-resurrection activity of Jesus. The community, as had the original disciples, listens to and observes all that the master commands. Matthew's choice of the biographical genre and concern for the community's situation have deeply affected the structure of the composition.

---

[19]Marxsen, *Mark the Evangelist*, 205-6.

THE CHURCH AS THE TRUE ISRAEL

Matthew's Gospel as opposed to Mark and Luke underscores Jesus' Jewish backgound, authority, and teaching. Thus the Matthean community represents a milieu, history, and theology distinct from those of the other Synoptics. It seems necessary as preliminary to our study of Matthew's christology, to submit that community and its self perception to an ecclesiological and sociological examination.[20]

20th-century scholarship has rarely failed to note the Jewish character of Matthew and to contrast this with its refreshing interest in the Gentile mission. In fact, many other data (e.g., attitude toward the Law, the Jewish authorities, and Jewish themes and heroes) render uncertain the identity and makeup of this community. Was it Jewish Christian in whole or in part, or was it Gentile primarily? Although some have suggested that the latter is true, on the whole scholars accept the following assessment: "The Matthean community was a mixed group, but the majority apparently was Jewish Christian."[21] Further, there is debate concerning its relation to the synagogue. Some insist, basing their argument upon texts which speak of "their scribes and their synagogues" (7:29; 9:35, etc.) as opposed to ours, that the Matthean community still situated itself within Judaism; others argue for a complete separation between the two; while still others, espousing some form of either thesis, propose that the Matthean community was geographically and theologically close to the synagogue, either in open animosity with the emerging Rabbinic movement or in some type of symbiotic relationship. Presently, scholarship prefers the separation between Matthew's community and the synagogue.[22]

Related to this issue is the background of the author, traditionally called Matthew—see 9:9 where the author modifies Mark's call of Levi (Mark 2:14) to that of Matthew. Was the author Jewish, as most

[20]Harrington, "Matthean Studies since Joachim Rohde," 98-104.

[21]D.J. Harrington, "Jesus as the Focus of the Conflict with the Synagogue," 96 in *God's People in Christ: New Testament Perspectives on the Church and Judaism* (Philadelphia: Fortress, 1979); for discussion of the issue see: Kümmel, *Introduction to the New Testament*, 114-19; Harrington "Matthean Studies since Joachim Rohde," 93-109; Kingsbury, *Matthew*, 78-106; and Meier, *The Vision of Matthew*, 6-25.

[22]See Meier, *The Vision of Matthew*, 15-17 and Kingsbury, *Matthew*, 98-101, and the earlier works of D.R.A. Hare, *The Theme of Jewish Persecution of Christians in the Gospel according to St. Matthew* (Cambridge: UP, 1967) and D.W. Davies, *The Sermon on the Mount* (Cambridge: UP, 1966).

scholars insist, or Gentile instead (perhaps a non-Jewish Semite)?[23] The arguments revolve around the author's acquaintance with the Jewish scriptures (and the complex issue of the origin of the formula citations), knowledge of customs and themes, and attitude both toward Judaism and the Gentile mission. While we lean to the first option, we think that detailed examination of the ecclesiological data in Matthew's Gospel calls for a nuanced perspective and reduces the either/or character of the issue.

First we will examine the community's stance with regard to Jewish and Gentile traditions to gain historical perspective. After that we will consider the community's self perception. There are statements in the gospel which indicate that the community, at least in the initial stages of its evolution, was Jewish. When the Matthean Jesus is confronted by the persistence of the Gentile Canaanite woman, he states (addition to the Markan source): "I was sent only to the lost sheep of the house of Israel" (15:24). Such statements and Matthew's attitude, in many passages, toward the Law (Jesus has come not to abolish but to fulfill it—5:17), Jewish piety (which he calls "righteousness"), Jewish typology and history, point to an author and a community deeply immersed in things Jewish. The Matthean parables acquire historicizing features whereby servants become Jewish prophets and other characters become transparent Jewish and Christian types; see especially the series of parables: the two sons, the wicked tenants, and the marriage feast: 21:28-22:10. Further, there is in Matthew a concerted effort to combine the old and the new: as fulfilment or return to the original sense of the Torah (antitheses of 5:21f), the new imitating the old (the community's rules of conduct are based upon regulations found in the Torah and contemporary Judaism, 18:15-17), or a combination of the two (the scribe who employs both new and old—13:52). There are, then, many indications that the Matthean community was of Jewish origin.

Matthean traditions, however, are not simply Jewish and certainly not pro-Jewish. Perhaps with the exception of John, Matthew qualifies as the most anti-Jewish of the gospels.[24] The Jewish leaders are rarely spared and the woes of chapter 23 reach a high level of polemics. Pharisees, Sadducees, and elders receive damaging criticism from Jesus, whether for empty gestures and prayer, ostentatious and self-serving

[23]Meier, The Vision of Matthew, 17-25.
[24]See C. Klein, Anti-Judaism in Christian Theology (Philadelphia: Fortress, 1978).

acts of piety or for "neglecting the weightier matters of the law" (23:23). They are accused of killing the prophets and building their tombs yet since they occupy the seat of Moses, they are to be obeyed (23:1-2). Their own practice, however, is severely condemned—they are even called "children of hell" (23:15). The Jews generally are blamed for Jesus' death and the gospel adds a telling sentence to the parable of the invited guests: "The king was angry, and he sent his troops and destroyed those murderers and burned their city" (22:7). The destruction of Jerusalem is seen as punishment for Israel's refusal to accept the Messiah. Perhaps the worst condemnation leveled against Judaism is found in an exchange between Pilate and the Jewish populace (a passage unique to Matthew), when the people answer: "His blood be on us and on our children" (27:25).[25]

Additionally, the gospel reveals an overarching concern for the Gentile mission. From the start one reads of Gentile ancestry for Jesus and of wise Gentiles who come from the East to do homage to the king of the Jews. Many non-Jews are favorably portrayed in this gospel, and so its author finds congenial the saying about the centurion: "not even in Israel have I found such faith" (8:10). Further, the Matthean parables foresee the inclusion of Gentiles into the "kingdom of the heavens," seen as a present reality (the wicked tenants and the marriage feast). The book ends with a mandate for universal mission to the nations (not just Gentiles).[26]

We conclude that the mixture of Jewish and Gentile elements in Matthew owes to the historical development of the community. What began as a Jewish community, with time and segregation from the synagogue, became a mixed group of believers for whom the Jewish past, both positive and negative, was a constitutive part of the story of Jesus and his followers. Indeed, in presenting an exclusive mission to Israel during Jesus' ministry (chap. 10) and then a universal mission on the authority of the risen Jesus (chap. 28), Matthew remained faithful to tradition.

---

[25]For a discussion of this passage, confer Senior, *The Passion Narrative According to Matthew*, 256-61, also 338; and J.A. Fitzmyer, "Anti-Semitism and the Cry of 'All the People' (Mt. 27:26)," *TS* 26 (1965) 667-71.

[26]With J.P. Meier, "Nations or Gentiles in Matthew 28:19?" *CBQ* 39 (1977) 94-102 *contra* D.R.A. Hare and D.J. Harrington, "'Make Disciples of All the Gentiles' (Matthew 28:19)," 110-23 in *Light of All Nations*.

It was a gradual drifting away from the controlling influence of the synagogue and the increasing impact of the Hellenistic culture of the Diaspora rather than a rhetorical plea for openness to the Gentile mission,[27] which led the author to view the community thus. Matthew is a product of its time, a period we might describe as follows:

> For fifteen years or so the religious and political center of Judaism had been destroyed. The heart of Jewish piety—the temple—had ceased to function, and all Judaism had to answer the question, Who is the true Israel? Apocalyptists like the authors of 4 Ezra and 2 Baruch clung to the hope that those who remain faithful in the present tribulation will finally be rewarded when God's kingdom comes. Political revolutionaries like the Zealots continued the armed struggle for a while only to go down to defeat at Masada. Law-oriented Jews like the scribes and Pharisees joined Yohanan ben Zakkai in his rabbinical academy at Yavneh (Jamnia) by the Mediterranean coast and devoted themselves to the understanding and observance of the biblical statutes and the traditions surrounding them. Christians like Matthew answered that the Church is now "the true Israel" in that Jesus of Nazareth is the Messiah of Jewish expectation and the fulfillment of the Old Testament promises.[28]

Matthew's Gospel should then be situated historically and theologically in the aftermath of the Judaeo-Roman war when different groups in Palestine and the Diaspora were competing to see who would become the heirs of Israel's traditions. The open conflict with the emerging Rabbinic movement (heirs of the Pharisaic group of the Second Temple period) would have left its mark in the form of the polemical elements of the gospel, while the ideals of Israel would have found rhetorical expression in this community's self-perception. Following W. Trilling,[29] recent scholars view Matthew as claiming that the Christian community had become the heir of the promise made to

---

[27] *Contra* Hare and Harrington, "'Make Disciples of All the Nations.'"

[28] Harrington, "Jesus as the Focus of the Conflict with the Synagogue," 96-97; see also J. Neusner, "Judaism in a Time of Crisis: Four Responses to the Destruction of the Second Temple," *Judaism* 21 (1972) 313-27.

[29] *Das wahre Israel. Studien zu einer Theologie des Matthäusevangeliums* (Munich: Kösel, 1964). One would do well to note Meier's caution (*The Vision of Matthew*, 55, n. 19) that for Matthew Jesus is the New Israel, though Matt. 2:6 gives some justification for calling the church the "true" Israel; see also Kümmel, *Introduction to the New Testament*, 116.

Israel, for its members had recognized and accepted the ruler who was to shepherd God's people (2:6 = Micah 5:2). Israel, as tenants of the vineyard, had refused to offer produce to God, so the kingdom was taken away from it "and given to a nation producing . . . fruit" (21:43). In the eyes of Matthew Israel ceased to be God's chosen people (contrary to Paul in Romans 9-11) though the mission to its members did not cease (23:34). In its stead came those who, like little children, welcomed the Messiah as Son of David, i.e., the ones who bring forth perfect praise (21:15-16), the ones whose righteousness exceeds that of the scribes and Pharisees (5:20), the ones who receive Jesus and thereby receive the one who sent him (10:40). Related to the gospel's ecclesiology, indeed its foundation, is its christology, for not only is God's people identified with the community, but also God's reign or lordship is exercised by the risen Jesus as Son of God and Son of Man.

The Matthean Jesus: "God with Us"

Matthew, in choosing to revise Mark's narrative, opted for the vita or gospel genre. Paramount for understanding this narrative's message is the appreciation of its portrait of Jesus, the story's main character. From Mark, Matthew drew the central elements of the life of Jesus: numerous episodes dealing with the master, the sequence of these events, and a variety of christological titles and concepts. No longer does the story of the Messiah commence with the preaching of the forerunner, John the Baptist, but it begins, as in ancient historiography, with a statement in the form of birth stories of the hero's relationship to the supernatural world and of his role in the divine plan.

PRESENTATION OF JESUS

Before picking up the Markan narrative in chapter 3, Matthew presents two chapters which consist of a genealogy, birth story, and early threats to the child's life. From the outset the author states that the work is about a man named Jesus. Clearly this personal name is of importance to author and community since in the narrative it has a heavenly origin (first use of command and achievement pattern, 1:21 and 25), since it anchors Jesus into the Jewish community via a genealogy (1:16), and since his name, as the result of a pun, manifests advanced christological speculation ("he will save his people from their sins," 1:21). It is important to note how the hero is introduced in the narrative. Matthew ends the genealogy by mentioning "Joseph the husband of Mary, of whom Jesus was born, who is called Christ"(1:16). From the start the gospel draws an important distinction and therefore connection between the character of its story (Jesus) and the faith proclamation claiming that this individual fulfils all Jewish expectations concerning the Messiah. After this initial presentation of the story's principal character, Matthew repeatedly refers to him simply as Jesus— only at 1:1 and 18 is he called "Jesus Christ."

In presenting Jesus to the reader, Matthew takes pains to underscore his Jewishness. In the first verse one learns that he is a descendant of David and Abraham, two great figures of Jewish tradition. Both reappear in Jesus' genealogy (1:2 and 6) where they serve as anchor points in the author's sweeping schema of salvation history (1:17). Thus, the genealogy situates Jesus within the culture that expected and received the long promised Messiah. Jesus, Matthew insists, is that Jewish Messiah, for he is the adopted son of Joseph, himself a son of David (1:20).

Matthew presents Jesus as "teacher" or "rabbi"[30] and provides him with rabbinic learning and rhetoric. Thus Matthew wishes to defend "the thesis that Jesus Messiah is the new Moses and the new Israel, and the fulfillment of the Law and the Prophets. This thesis which could only be directed to a Jewish audience, is supported by the type of argument accepted in Jewish learning."[31] Some have objected to the idea that Matthew intended a Moses-Jesus typology but, I believe, on insufficient grounds. Jesus' attitude, in Matthew, toward the Law is evidence of this, for the Torah is presented as eternally valid and Jesus has the wisdom and authority to interpret that Law according to God's intention.[32] He has come to fulfil the Law, to seek obedience to its weightier matters (justice, mercy, and faith, 23:23), and to teach the commandments upon which "all the law and the prophets depend" (22:40; note the special emphasis in vv. 36 and 40 upon the Law, both additions to Mark 12:28f). Even the six antitheses of Matt. 5:21-48, (on murder, adultery, divorce, vows and oaths, retaliation, and hatred of

---

[30]Matthew, however, is wary of the title "rabbi;" see 23:7-8 for the author's view, especially the switch in v. 8, from "rabbi" to "teacher."

[31]J.L. McKenzie, "The Gospel according to Matthew," 2:64 in *JBC*.

[32]Kee, *Jesus in History*, 168-80.

enemies) are based on a contrast between the Torah as mediated by Moses and the new Law proposed by Jesus; "his mission has rather the positive scope of giving the Laws and the Prophets their eschatological fulfilment, a prophetic fullness which rescinds the letter of the Law even as it completes its meaning."[33] The expression "it was said to the men of old" refers to divine speech, that is, the words of God as contained in the books of Moses. Further, the fivefold structure of the great speeches has usually been related in some way to the five books of Moses, thereby signaling further connection with the great lawgiver of Judaism. Many point out, correctly, that there are no correspondences between the speeches and the individual books of the Torah. Instead, one should see here a general comparison between Moses and Jesus both of whom are situated on a mountain (Sinai versus the mount of beatitudes) for their great "legislative" endeavors.[34] A general contrast seems intended; the stress upon the Law and its proper interpretaion by Jesus throughout the sermon (chaps. 5-7) would support such a conclusion. The ending of the last book of the Torah and therefore of Moses' life forms an interesting parallel to the end of Matthew's Gospel. In Deut. 34, after a farewell speech in view of his departure, Moses goes up Mount Nebo where he commissions Joshua for his task. At the end of Matthew, Jesus, once more on a mountain (28:14), commissions his disciples for the world mission. Matthew also retains from Mark the Moses/Elijah theme of the transfiguration (again on a mountain). Like Moses Jesus is a lawgiver, teacher, and preacher, for he teaches and interprets with authority.

Beyond that, Jesus is presented by Matthew as the New Israel. Narratively the author has drawn an extensive parallel between the early part of Jesus' life and the history of the chosen people. As Israel had arrived in Egypt under the direction of Joseph, sojourned there, suffered the slaughter of its male children under the Pharaoh, but nonetheless witnessed the salvation of Moses and the numerous episodes associated with the Exodus-event (water, sonship [Exod. 4:22-23], desert sojourn, temptations, 40-days of fasting, the stay on Mount Sinai, and the ten plagues),[35] so Matthew attempts a "rerun" of Israel's

[33]Meier, *The Vision of Matthew*, 240-64, citation 262.

[34]See Matt. 5:1 ("he went up on the mountain") as opposed to Luke 6:17 ("he came down with them and stood on a level place").

[35]The OT history referred to is found in the final chapters of Genesis and the first part of the book of Exodus.

history in the childhood and early ministry of the gospel's hero. Jesus is led into Egypt by one named Joseph (2:13), where he dwells for a while (14). There is a slaughter of male Jewish children, this time by Herod (16). In a parallel manner the object of the slaughter finds safety (13-15). The early ministry of Jesus, if one were to see the theme of salvation as a Christian exodus (first personally for Jesus and then for the community soon to be founded), then the themes of water, sonship, desert sojourn, temptations, 40-day fast, the mount of beatitudes, and the 10 miracles (chaps. 3-9) form fitting parallels for the new Israel. According to Matthew Jesus not only fulfils the OT prophecies but relives its history.

Equally, Jesus is the fulfilment of the Law and the Prophets. A dominant feature of this gospel is its frequent and astute use of formula or fulfilment quotations.[36] Despite their complex character and origin, it is reasonable to conclude that they represent a conscious, lengthy, and scholastic attempt to relate the Jesus tradition, via Rabbinic and other midrashic techniques, to the world of Judaism and its "eternally valid" Torah.[37] Practically everything that Jesus does or says is subsumed under the rubric of prophecy and fulfilment: the miracles of healing (8:17 = Isa. 53:4), the parables (13:35 = Ps. 78:2), the royal entry into Jerusalem (21:5 = Isa. 62:11 and Zech. 9:9). Crucial to the author's use of this device is the conviction that Jesus' life and ministry constitutes the time of fulfilment for all of Israel's hopes and dreams.

Messianic expectation then is crucial for understanding Matthew's presentation of Jesus, especially the use of the title "Christ." We have already noted Matthew's insistence that Jesus is the one whom believers call the Christ (1:16; also 22:17, 22). On several occasions the title is used in discussions about the Jewish Messiah: where he is to be born (2:4), what kinds of deeds he is to perform (11:2), or what his relation to David is (22:42). In each case the implication is that Jesus fulfils these requirements. Sometimes the title "Christ" functions within confessional scenes involving other important titles (16:16-20; 26:63-64) and will require further examination. Its use at 1:17 merits further attention owing to the author's temporal scheme. Jesus as Messiah closed out the Old Age and begins the New. By the use of multiple sevens (the perfect number), Matthew insists that "the Messiah closes out the sixth and final period of the old Israel [6x7 or 3x14] and introduces the seventh

---

[36]See the discussion of Kümmel, *Introduction to the New Testament*, 110-14.
[37]Kee, *Jesus in History*, 168.

period, the period of fulfilment, the period of the Messiah."[38]

Finally on two occasions, Matthew employs the appellation "Jesus Christ." The first (1:1) introduces the entire book and identifies Jesus as the Messiah in the line of David and Abraham. He is the royal Messiah expected by the Jews and indeed enters the city to be greeted twice as "Son of David" (21:9, 15), only to be rejected officially as "King of Israel" (27:11f). Besides, Jesus sends his disciples (10:6) and states that he is "sent only to the lost sheep of the house of Israel" (15:23). He is the Jewish Messiah, the one foreannounced as "Son of David," and is also the universal Messiah, as suggested by the title "Son of Abraham," who in Genesis was promised a progeny as numerous as the stars and called source of blessings for all (Gen. 12:3; see Matt. 8:11 where Gentile believers replace faithless Jews). The second use of the appellation "Jesus Christ" serves to introduce an important pericope on the origin of Jesus, a passage to which we return below.

TOWARD A HIGHER CHRISTOLOGY

Matthew makes significant use of the titles "Son of God" and "Son of Man." There has been debate concerning the role these play and the relative importance they have for understanding Matthew's christology. The discussion begins with the views of Kingsbury who insists that the central title for appreciating Matthew's portrait of Jesus is "Son of God" understood as royal appellation. According to him "Son of God" provides the key for appreciating the other Matthean titles for it is a confessional appellation. Further, "in consequence of the unique relationship that exists between Jesus Messiah, the Son of God, and God his Father, the Father entrusts the Son with divine authority (*exousia*)."[39] It is as Son of God that Jesus teaches, preaches, and gives his life in obedience to the Father. Son of Man then is a public, judgmental title and "is only marginally significant . . . as a vehicle for setting forth the earthly activity of Jesus (it does not occur until 8:20)."[40] J.P. Meier, however, has taken issue with this analysis in a reexamination of the function which "Son of Man" plays in Matthew's Gospel. Statistically, it plays a more important role than does "Son of God" (30

---

[38] Meier, *Matthew*, 5.

[39] Kingsbury, *Matthew*, 41.

[40] *Ibid.*, 56; see also his discussion in *Jesus Christ in Matthew, Mark, and Luke*, 64-73. As we saw in chap. 4, Kingsbury later advanced a very similar analysis of Markan thought in *The Christology of Mark's Gospel*.

versus 9 or 12 occurrences). Besides, its use by Matthew merits more careful attention since, as was seen in Mark, the two titles and their meanings interrelate on numerous occasions and, as Meier points out, "Son of Man has the widest conceivable span of meanings," which "form a continuum of meaning, an arch of tension spanning public ministry, passion and exaltation, rule of the world, the final judgment."[41]

On the one hand, the title "Son of Man" is more important in Matthew's redaction of the Jesus tradition than in Mark. Matthew retains the variety which the title had acquired in its Markan redaction and further emphasizes Jesus' role as Son of Man both as a future, eschatological figure and as one who acts with power in the present among believers, i.e., the time of the story's characters and that of the ideal audience. On the other hand, the expression "Son of God" or "Son" (said of Jesus) receives increased attention in Matthew's composition, particularly in the infancy narratives, temptations, and confessional and mockery scenes.

Nonetheless, it seems to me that neither title provides the key to Matthean christology. Both play vital and complementary roles in Matthew's presentation of Jesus. Regardless of how one interprets Matthew chapter 3 and following, perhaps imposing Mark's low christology upon the text, one must seriously attend to Matthew's treatment of the sonship theme in chapters 1-2. It seems clear that the author advocates a higher christology than do the Gospel of Mark and the Q-Source. A careful reading of 1:18-25, devoted to the origin of Jesus Christ, shows a consistent attempt on Matthew's part to stress Jesus' divine sonship. By means of passive expressions ("that which is conceived in her," 1:20, "she was found to be with child," 1:18, and "Mary of whom Jesus was born," 1:16), an impersonal construction ("a virgin shall conceive," 1:23), divine intervention ("of the Holy Spirit," 1:18, 20), and the repeated insistence either upon Mary's virginity or Joseph's non-involvement in the conception (1:18, 20, 23, 25), Matthew insists that Jesus has God for Father. Indeed this is the function of the virginal conception in the story.

The author continues the theme of divine sonship in chapter 2. After an introductory narrative concerning Jesus' identity as "King of the Jews," "Christ," and "ruler or shepherd" (2:2, 4, 6), Matthew studiously employs the terms "child" and "mother" (avoiding any hint that Joseph

[41] *The Vision of Matthew,* 217 and 118.

might be his real father),[42] thereby extending the notion of Jesus' divine sonship and relating it to the "rerun" of Jewish history. Thus the climax of the chapter is the divine statement: "Out of Egypt have I called my son" (2:15). God is the first to give Jesus this title.

Among other indications that Matthew espouses a higher christology we might briefly discuss two: Jesus' frequent references to God as his Father and wisdom motifs. On sixteen occasions Jesus refers to God as "my Father" and, on another, the Son of Man, it is said, will come "in the glory of his Father" (16:27). All excepting two of these are unique to Matthew and so require more attention, especially since most come from the author's special sources or owe to the editing of Mark or Q. Where a) Mark and Luke have "will of God," b) Luke "before the angels of God," c) Mark "kingdom of God," or d) "Abba, Father," Matthew offers a) "will of my Father in heaven" (12:50), b) "before my Father who is in heaven" (10:32 twice), c) "my Father's kingdom" (26:29), and d) "my Father" (26:39). While borrowing one occurrence from Mark (8:38 = Matt. 16:27) and one from Q (Luke 10:22 = Matt. 11:27), it seems that Matthew has seized upon this expression to depict the unique relationship which exists between God and Jesus, a relationship which could be predicated of no other human.[43]

Also of importance in understanding Matthew's presentation of Jesus are the beginnings of a wisdom christology which we detect in various passages of the narrative. It is especially 11:25-27 (also v. 19); 23:34f.; and the eschatological discourse (chaps. 24-25) which show the clearest traces of such thinking. Jesus like Wisdom is the revealer of the apocalyptic secrets of the Father (11:25-27).[44] Further, Jesus seen as Son of Man and as Wisdom (Matthew applies the Q saying to Jesus—see Luke 11:49) is the one who sends God's messengers to Israel. The change which Matthew has imposed upon the Q saying is a good indication of the movement from a lower to a slightly higher christology: "In Q Jesus is one, or perhaps even the last, of Wisdom's ambassadors, but in Matthew Jesus is more than the last messenger before the

---

[42]Kingsbury, *Matthew*, 38.

[43]See Meier, *The Vision of Matthew*, 56 and Kingsbury, *Matthew*, 41.

[44]For a survey of the theme and literature, see F.W. Burnett, *The Testament of Jesus-Sophia: A Redaction-Critical Study of the Eschatological Discourse in Matthew* (Lanham: University, 1981) and Meier, *The Vision of Matthew*, 76-83. On the background of the Q saying, confer Marshall, *Luke*, 430-38.

Eschaton. He *is* the personage who sent all of the messengers."[45] Meier is correct when he says: "The fusion of apocalyptic and sapiential themes in the service of a high christology could not be clearer."[46] The agency christology of Mark (Jesus is sent—9:37), while not rejected by Matthew (see 10:40), undergoes development whereby Jesus himself becomes the "sender" of messengers. Matthew, however, seems not to have related such thinking to pre-existence.[47]

PRESENCE FORMULAS: GOD WITH US

We now direct our attention to an overview of the author's christology. Matthew is both a story which tells the life of the Jewish Messiah and an ecclesiological and moral tract or collection of speeches for the community which the Messiah has founded. The author has chosen as strategy two basic structures: a biography by which to retell the life of Jesus and a narrative within which to situate speeches and commission, i.e., the threefold and fivefold outlines. Related to these is the inclusio of 1:23 and 28:20, "God with us." It is to a discussion of this depth structure and its relation to Matthew's christology that we direct our attention.

Revising the Markan story which the community revered, Matthew exploits the potential of this narrative genre. The threefold structure (1:1-4:16; 4:17-16:20; and 16:21-28:20) introduces and reveals the identity, develops the character, and reflects on the destiny of the story's hero. Recent studies are correct in seeing in the threefold structure the gradual and full revelation of Jesus' identity as the Christ, who as Son of God and Son of Man, is God's presence in the world.

The first statement about God's presence among humans (1:23) stresses Matthew's biographical character. It is within a discussion of Jesus' origin and identity (1:18-25) that this author first chooses to state the thesis of the story: Jesus, as God's unique or beloved Son, is God's presence in the world. It is to this function that Matthew dedicates the first formula citation:

> all this [story of Jesus' divine origin and birth] took place to fulfil what the Lord had spoken by the prophet: "Behold a virgin shall conceive

---

[45] Burnett, *The Testament of Jesus-Sophia*, 165.
[46] Meier, *The Vision of Matthew*, 80.
[47] See Burnett, *The Testament of Jesus-Sophia*, 169-71.

and bear a son, and his name shall be called Emmanuel" (which means, God with us) (1:23).

The throne name of the one who is a member of the house of David is Emmanuel and as such he, as God's divine Son, is God's presence among humans. This particular occurrence of the presence formula underscores Matthew's high christology. This section, after an initial declaration by God of Jesus' sonship (2:15), terminates with the public revelation from the heavenly voice: "this is my Beloved Son" (3:17).[48] The next section also presents a dual declaration, in this case a confession on the part of Jesus' disciples. After Jesus walks on the water and calms the sea, the disciples worship him and declare: "truly you are the Son of God" (14:33). The section concludes with Matthew's version of Peter's confession: "you are the Christ, the Son of the living God" (16:16). Of special note is v. 17 which declares that God ("my Father who is in heaven") is the source of this revelation. The third section takes further the identification of and witness to Jesus. In 26:63-64 the high priest pressures Jesus to state clearly whether he claims to be "the Christ, the Son of God." Jesus answers unequivocally: "you have said so. But I tell you, hereafter you will see the Son of man seated at the right hand of Power, and coming on the clouds of heaven." While several titles are brought together as they had been previously by Mark (14:61-62), it is the Son of God title which interests us here, a title which Matthew will highlight through editing the mockery scenes of the crucifixion (27:40, 43). The special sonship is accepted by Jesus and confessed by the centurion and others ("truly this was the Son of God," 27:54c) but only after Matthew has presented apocalyptic or divinely sanctioned signs (27:51-54).[49]

The first presence formula, therefore, confirms for Matthew's audience that first of all God was present in the life of Jesus. The ministry, suffering, death, and resurrection of the beloved Son (to whom Matthew and earlier traditions attribute many of the characteristics and functions of the Son of Man) are declared by Matthew to

[48]One should note the change from the second person in Mark 1:11 to the third person in Matthew.

[49]D. Senior, "The Death of Jesus and the Resurrection of the Holy Ones," *CBQ* 38 (1976) 312-29; on the relationship of 27:54 (the centurion and companions' confession) to 14:33 (the disciples' confession), see Senior, *The Passion Narrative According to Matthew*, 327-28.

be a "lived presence," the actual presence of God in the Son. The Jewish Messiah, God's Son, the figure of the end-days, has come and his story is being told for all to hear.

At the end of the narrative Matthew again employs a presence formula when promising that Jesus will always be with his community (28:20b). The author returns to this device to dwell upon the principal theme of the narrative, namely, an ecclesiology and morality based upon a solidly founded christology. Expressed succinctly:

> Matthew's two major convictions, both of which are made explicit in his gospel, are (1) that the Law of God, as given to ancient Israel, is eternally valid and (2) that Jesus is the final agent and plenipotentiary through whom God's purpose in the world is being consummated (Matt. 15:17-18). Putting the two beliefs together, one can say that for Matthew, Jesus is the inaugurator of the true Israel, the people through and among whom God's ultimate purpose for man is to be achieved.[50]

The risen Jesus, in a final speech to the assembled community, recapitulates the gospel story (particularly the speeches, the confession and worship),[51] the founding of the community, the insistence on righteousness, and the proper interpretation of the divine Torah. He orders the disciples that all be taught "to observe all that [he has] commanded [them]" (28:20). The whole life of Jesus—indeed the import of the fivefold structure as new Torah as well as the threefold schema as the biographically established presence of God take on new light—becomes the content of the new teaching. Every time the gospel is preached, it is the risen Jesus, who, remaining theologically and narratively among the believers, speaks to the community. The second presence formula, therefore, stresses that God was present among humans not only in the past through the life of Jesus but that as this life is retold, as the risen Jesus speaks again, and as the disciples reenact the Christ-event (18:20), God continues in the present, even "to the close of the age," to be with the community of believers. It is in the person of the Jewish Messiah that God then (in Jesus' earthly ministry) and now (within the Matthean

---

[50]Kee, *Jesus in History*, 168-69.

[51]See 28:9 and 17 for the author's stress upon the theme of worship. It should be noted that the theme of worship contributes to the gospel's closure while that of confession provides momentum to the overall story.

community) dwells among the people.

The final commission gives a striking description of the risen Lord who lives within the community and leads it in its task. He is unmistakably presented with the traits of the Son of Man (with "all authority in heaven and on earth") and yet he is called Son (juxtaposed with the title "Father"). Thus, one gets the impression that the frequent close use of the titles "Son of Man" and "Son of God" by the author is intentional and that the latter relates especially to Matthew's biographical interests and that the former emphasizes particularly Mathew's attempt to show that Jesus as final agent of God (Son of Man) leads his people in perfect praise to the Father.

Which title then is the key to Matthew's christology? In answer we begin by citing an interesting sentence of Meier: "A first, rather embarrassing result [of the study] is that Matthew is quite capable of making important Christological statements without titles—witness the sermon on the mount or the predominance of the simple name Jesus in chapter 28."[52] So we propose that it is the name of "Jesus" which, along with the frequent title "the Christ," unites the christology and its various formulations throughout the Matthean narrative. The gospel begins by speaking of Jesus the Christ (1:1) and, while it ends by referring simply to Jesus' commission, it is the same Jesus who has frequently been identified as "the one who is called the Christ" (1:16; 27:17, 22; also 1:1, 18; 16:20; and 26:63-64). The major confessions in Matthew involve the names of Jesus and a related proclamation of him as Christ; see Peter's confession which ends simply: "then he strictly charged the disciples to tell no one that he was the Christ" (16:20) or the centurion's confession (27:54) which follows upon the identification twice of Jesus as "the one who is called Christ" (27:17 and 22). Even God's declaration in 2:15 of Jesus as Son, is enveloped in a narrative where the title appears frequently: 1:1, 16, 17, 18, and 2:4. Also Jesus' admission to the high priest involves the three titles: Christ, Son of God, and Son of Man. So it is the name of Jesus which unites the story from opening to closure and which appears at the end of each major speech.

Matthew chose to write a life of Jesus, as earlier Mark had done, and amplified its biographical characteristics. The gospel, however, goes further in developing this narrative structure. Employing the hint provided by Mark that Jesus would see his disciples in Galilee (14:28;

52 The Vision of Matthew, 217.

16:7), Matthew creates a scene where Jesus does appear to his disciples and stresses, though without Mark's urgency, the passage's missionary thrust. Matthew brings the story to a close with Jesus on the mountain, like Moses, initiating a New Age. This the author does by drawing on the fountain of Jesus tradition so well incorporated in the vita and its great thematic speeches. In these speeches and in the life of Jesus are contained the wisdom of God made known and proclaimed by the beloved Son. In the final commission lies the authority (actually reiterated here since it is submerged throughout the vita) of the Son of Man, whose future, heavenly activity impinges on the present activity of the community. Matthew assures the community that with Jesus the Christ as its teacher and master (23:8, 10), the church (16:18; 18:17) now seen as the true Israel must produce the fruits of righteousness (21:43), because its Father (23:9) desires perfect praise from its little ones (21:16; see 18:1f). Matthew's portrait of Jesus, therefore, is a christology in search of an authentic ecclesiology.

6

The Gospel of Luke and the Acts of the Apostles

Apparently communities other than that of Matthew both employed Mark's composition and felt the need to revise this early gospel and to reinterpret the Jesus tradition with a view to new and more pressing problems. As the Jesus movement ventured out of its original habitat geographically and culturally, its missionaries found a measure of success among the Greek-speaking Jews of the Diaspora. They encountered many who recognized in Jesus the fulfilment of messianic and prophetic expectations. In this milieu they encountered Greeks of non-Jewish culture for whom the Nazarene was a challenge and an enigma. This chapter will examine one of the authors who addressed the Jesus tradition specifically to a Greco-Roman audience.

Christianity in the Hellenistic World

The roots of the Jesus movement go back to first-century Palestine, where Jesus preached and taught in Aramaic to the crowds and religious authorities of his homeland. While it is true that Hellenistic influences had been active in his country for several centuries, the differences between Palestine and the Diaspora were extensive. In Palestine the upper classes and merchant groups were relatively open to Greek cultural trends, but various religious factions (including the lower level functionaries of the synagogues and the Pharisees who, though liberal in religious terms, were conservative culturally) and the common-folk were less affected by Hellenism. Their language was Semitic, their

157

religious outlook derived from the piety of the intertestamental period, and their culture was rural or related to traditional occupations. The Hellenism which did affect these groups, as attested in the literature of Qumran, was readily incorporated into older patterns of Semitic thought and culture. Authors such as Mark and Matthew, and perhaps John, provide good examples of deeply Semitic perspectives in which traces of Hellenistic influence are clearly discerned. The use of the biography as genre for the composition of the Jesus tradition argues for cultural awareness of Hellenism on the part of early Christian writers. Matthew's sense of symmetry and balance and concern for the world mission of the church also argue for Greek influences within the early Christian communities. Most obvious of all, the use of Greek underscores the authors' acquaintance with Greco-Roman culture.[1]

HELLENIZATION OF THE JESUS MOVEMENT

If Hellenization moved at a snail's pace in Palestine, in other Semitic areas such as Syria, the process was more rapid and revolutionary. When the Jesus movement spread beyond Palestine it became increasingly Hellenized. This evolution required a change from Aramaic to Greek and involved a profound cultural shift. Missionaries and their audiences faced vastly different problems than had earlier preachers. Greek-speaking Jewish audiences varied widely in their responses to this new movement as they struggled to incorporate Jewish expectations, Hellenistic universalism, and the challenge of the preacher from Nazareth. Preachers such as Paul, the author of Hebrews, and probably those of First Peter and James exemplify this momentous shift in the development of the Jesus movement.

The work of Paul and of other Hellenized Jewish Christian missionaries had far-reaching consequences for the early church, because it soon began to evolve from being almost exclusively Jewish to becoming principally Gentile in membership. Few NT writers were unaffected by the crises engendered by this change in membership. From the outset the doctrine of the Nazarene and the movement associated with his name had seemed no different from the mystery cults of the period and

---

[1]On Jewish culture of New Testament times see J. Jeremias, *Jerusalem in the Time of Jesus* (Philadelphia: Fortress, 1981); Fitzmyer, "The Languages of Palestine"; Freyne, *The World of the New Testament*; and Leaney, *The Jewish and Christian World 200 BC and AD 200.*

many inhabitants of the Roman empire found it appealing. Thus, believers of Gentile origin increased rapidly and began to dominate the communities.

In the early stages of the movement there was much conflict between Jewish and Gentile Christians. Although we discussed this topic briefly in the chapter on Matthew, we return to it here since such problems were general and pervasive. There were issues of culture, language, theology, organization, and doctrinal fidelity. Paul frequently encountered Jewish Christians, whom we today, from Paul's perspective, call Judaizers, missionaries who insisted that Gentile converts be introduced to Jewish Christian belief and custom. At issue was the nature of the Jesus movement—at least in the eyes of Paul who resisted any attempt to make commitment to Christ Jesus contingent upon circumcision or obedience to the Law. Others, it should be noted, did not adopt such an extreme stance. Thus, we are led to speak of a variety of Jewish Christian and Gentile Christian groups within the early church.

Scholars have directed their attention to the early movement's diversity, especially its relation to Judaism. R.E. Brown discerns the following groups:

> a) "Group one, consisting of Jewish Christians and their Gentile converts, who insisted on *full observance of the Mosaic Law, including circumcision,* for those who believed in Jesus. In short, these ultraconservatives insisted that Gentiles had to become Jews to receive the Messianic blessings brought by Jesus."
> b) "Group two, consisting of Jewish Christians and their Gentile converts, who did *not* insist on circumcision but did require converted Gentiles to keep *some Jewish observances.* One may speak of this as a moderately conservative Jewish/Gentile Christanity."
> c) "Group three, consisting of Jewish Christians and their Gentile converts, who did *not* insist on circumcision and did *not* require observance of the Jewish ('kosher') food laws."
> d) "Group four, consisting of Jewish Christians and their Gentile converts, who did not insist on circumcision or observance of the Jewish food laws and who *saw no abiding significance in Jewish cult and feasts.*"[2]

---

[2] R.E. Brown and J.P. Meier, *Antioch and Rome: New Testament Cradles of Catholic Christianity* (NY: Paulist, 1983) 1-9; see also J.D.G. Dunn, *Unity and*

Additionally, Brown gives the following as examples of the four positions: a. the Judaizers of Galatia, b. James, c. Paul, and d. Stephen the Hellenist (Acts 6-7). Such a list of positions easily demonstrates the complexity of the issues confronting the Jesus movement as it reached out into the Gentile world of the Roman empire. The author we are now concerned with apparently was of such a background, i.e., Hellenistic and Gentile.

LUKE THE HELLENISTIC WRITER

With literary and cultural sophistication Luke, the author of the Third Gospel and the Acts of the Apostles, composes the story of Jesus and recounts the spread of the Jesus movement throughout the Roman empire. When one picks up these works one discerns a more elegant style, a greater consciousness of historical and geographical factors, and a broader perspective upon the Christ-event and its consequent Jesus movement. Further, Luke's work weds the Jewish and the Hellenistic components of the early tradition into an interesting and challenging perspective on the new movement.

Following contemporary literary custom, the author employs inter-locking prologues for Luke and Acts, prologues whose style and content reveal a literarily and historically self-conscious author. Luke knows that others have preceded as ministers of the word and as narrators of the events surrounding the life of Jesus. Thus the Gospel of Luke begins by telling the reader that it will, in its turn, be a narrative which will reflect the accurate research, the logic or sequence of interpretation, and the truthfulness of its author's message (1:1-4).[3] When we are told, with skillful hyperbole, that the beginnings of the movement did not occur in a hidden corner of the world (Acts 26:26), we know that the composition of Luke-Acts was a historically conscious activity. Providing a series of synchronisms to situate the reader into the story's crucial time setting, the author relates the events of Jesus' life to the reigns of emperors, kings, governors, and Jewish authorities (Luke 1:5; 2:1-2; 3:1-2; also 3:32). The Jesus movement, the author insists, has

Diversity in the New Testament: An Inquiry into the Character of Earliest Christianity (Philadelphia: Westminster, 1977).

[3]*Diēgēsis, akribōs, kathexēs*, and *asphaleia* respectively. More generally, see V.K. Robbins, "Prefaces in Greco-Roman Biography and Luke-Acts," *PRS* 6 (1979) 94-108 and R.J. Dillon, "Previewing Luke's Project from the Prologue (Luke 1:1-4)," *CBQ* 43 (1981) 205-27.

taken its place on the stage of world history. It is a universal movement whose founder, through narrative anticipation, initiated the Jewish and Gentile missions (sending of the twelve and seventy, Luke 9:1f and 10:1f). This theme of mission is often alluded to in Luke-Acts, as in Simeon's words ("a light for revelation to the Gentiles and for glory to thy people Israel," Luke 2:32), as in the message of the great banquet (14:15f), and as issue of debate at the Jerusalem meeting (Acts 15). This theme also forms an inclusio for the two volumes, since the unusual expresssion "the salvation of God" near the beginning of Luke (3:6) and at the end of Acts (28:28) underscores the centrality of the universalist motif in the author's thought (see also the Nazareth episode, Luke 4:16f).

Another feature of Luke-Acts which highlights the author's Hellenistic background is its apologetic theme. Luke is interested in presenting the Christ-event and the spread of the Jesus movement in a light favorable to Hellenistic contemporaries. Luke presents Jesus and his followers as innocent for they are above all political suspicion; Jesus is declared innocent by Pilate and the centurion underneath the cross (Luke 23:4f and 47), and Paul by Festus and Agrippa (Acts 26:31-32).[4] Besides, Roman and other government officials are presented in relatively sympathetic light in both Luke and Acts, whether centurions, Pilate, Cornelius, Gallio, or Agrippa. The theme of innocence, however, is secondary and probably motivated more by religious than by political concerns; note that the term translated as "innocent" at Luke 23:47 could more properly be rendered as "righteous," i.e., one who has a right relationship before God.[5] Luke's treatment of both Jewish and Roman authorities owes less to historical reminiscences or overt apologetics than to the author's perception of social, political structures and

---

[4]See P.W. Walaskay, "The Trial and Death of Jesus in the Gospel of Luke," *JBL* 94 (1975) 81-93; J. Kodell, "Luke's Theology of the Death of Jesus," 221-30 in D. Durken, ed., *Sin, Salvation, and the Spirit* (Collegeville: Liturgical, 1979); R.J. Karris, *Luke: Artist and Theologian: Luke's Passion Account as Literature* (NY: Paulist, 1985); R.L. Browley, "Paul in Acts: Lucan Apology and Conciliation," 129-47 in C.H. Talbert, ed., *Luke-Acts: New Perspectives from the Society of Biblical Literature Seminar* (NY: Crossroad, 1984); and several essays in R.J. Cassidy and P.J. Scharper, eds, *Political Issues in Luke-Acts* (Maryknoll: Orbis, 1983).

[5]One might consult the discussions of D. Schmidt, "Luke's 'Innocent' Jesus: A Scriptural Apologetic," 111-21 in Cassidy and Scharper, *Political Issues in Luke-Acts* and Karris, *Luke: Artist and Theologian*, 95-113.

concern for effective narrative continuity.[6]

Luke borrowed the gospel genre as well as its content from Mark and extended the time-line in both directions thereby enhancing the work's similarity to the Hellenistic biography. Jesus' post-resurrection activity is expanded to include resurrection appearances, Jesus' earthly departure, and, on into Acts, his intercession for his followers, either directly or through intermediaries. Luke has also extended the story backward to add annunciation and birth stories which stress the growth of the story's hero (Luke 2:40, 52). The unusual or virginal conception of Jesus in Luke indicates not a higher christology (as in Matthew) but meets the requirements of Hellenistic biography where heroes are routinely attributed divine origins or unusual births announced by prophetic omens.[7]

Like Matthew, Luke modifies the story to make it a more pliable instrument for a new perspective on Jesus. Scenes from Mark are recast and materials added to emphasize the journey to Jerusalem (Luke 9:51f), or Jesus' challenge to Jew and Gentile (5:17f). In the latter Luke recasts Markan controversy stories, by rewriting the introductory verse (17), to present Jesus as successfully performing before a jury of his contemporaries (6:11; see also 14:6). In still other instances Luke, following current literary conventions and employing traditional sayings, structures the last-supper episode into a farewell address for Jesus' instructions in view of his impending death (22:14-38)[8] or has made "redactional use of the Hellenistic symposium *genus litterarium* to organize and transmit traditional material" (Luke 7:36-50; 11:37-54; 14:1-24).[9]

---

[6]See for example, F.D. Weinert, "Luke, the Temple, and Jesus' Saying about Jerusalem's Abandoned House (Luke 13:34-35)," *CBQ* 44 (1982) 68-76.

[7]C.H. Talbert, "Prophecies of Future Greatness: The Contribution of Greco-Roman Biographies to an Understanding of Luke 1:5-4:15," 129-41 in J.L. Crenshaw and S. Sandmel, *The Divine Helmsman: Studies on God's Control of Human Events* (NY: Ktav. 1980); see also Fitzmyer, *Luke*, 192-219.

[8]W. Kurz, "Luke 22:14-38 and Greco-Roman and Biblical Farewell Addresses," *JBL* 104 (1985) 251-68.

[9]E.S. Steele, "Luke 11:37-54—A Modified Hellenistic Symposium?" *JBL* 103 (1984) 394.

Luke modifies episodes and adds new ones in favor of balance: alternation of stories about men and women, rich and poor, John and Jesus, word and deed (speeches and miracles).[10] Such modifications, however, are done from a universalist perspective, for the author contrasts high and low (1:51-52; 14:7-11), proud and humble (18:9-14), rich and poor (4:18; 6:20, 24; 16:19-31). The good news is intended for the dispossessed, particularly "the poor, maimed, lame, blind" (14:13, 21); salvation is for "all flesh" (3:6). Finally, Luke's story stretches from Adam in temporal terms to "the end of the earth" in geographical terms (Luke 3:38; Acts 1:8).[11]

The second volume, the Acts of the Apostles, is a work whose closest analogue in ancient literature is the historical monograph. It has all the qualities of ancient history writing, for it makes effective use of dramatic and rhetorical techniques. The work is replete with stock scenes. Since Classical monographs treat political and military matters one is accustomed to accept the battle scene as stock. In Acts the stock scenes are the trials and jail episodes, the missionary encounters, the farewell speech, and the sea voyage with its shipwreck scene.[12] There is abundant use of speeches (about one third of Acts) throughout the work. There are character-sketches, prefaces, appeal to omens or visions, and the conscious use of parallelism. The student of Greco-Roman literature is familiar with these conventions. Plutarch's lives are examples of the period's love for symmetry and parallels; Sallust's monographs illustrate the literary conventions one finds in Acts—the author even affects an archaizing manner as does Sallust.[13] Luke's practice matches the advice which a near-contemporary Lucian of Somosata gives to would-be

[10]P.J. Achtemeier, "The Lukan Perspective on the Miracles of Jesus: A Preliminary Sketch," 153-68 in C.H. Talbert, ed., *Perspectives on Luke-Acts* (Danville: ABPR, 1978).

[11]On Luke's use of sources see Fitzmyer, *Luke*, 63-106.

[12]Despite earlier puzzlement over the nature and function of Acts 27-28, this passage is now better understood in its Greco-Roman context; see S.M. Prader, "Acts 27:1-28:16: Sea Voyages in Ancient Literature and the Theology of Luke- Acts," *CBQ* 46 (1984) 683-706.

[13]E. Richard, "Luke—Writer, Theologian, Historian: Research and Orientation of the 1970's," *BTB* 13 (1983) 10-12. For a more general discussion of the genre of Luke-Acts see D.L. Barr and J.L. Wentling, "The Conventions of Classical Biography and the Genre of Luke-Acts: A Preliminary Study," 63-88 in Talbert, *Luke-Acts: New Perspectives* and Talbert, *What Is a Gospel?* and finally, for a more extended discussion of the Classical conventions of Acts, see Richard, *Acts 6:1-8:4*, 254-311 and W.C. van

historians of his day in terms of research and use of literary conventions (How to Write History 33-63).

We insist that Luke wrote the gospel and Acts in the spirit of Hellenistic historiography but we also need to repeat that ancient and modern conceptions of history vary greatly. The latter concentrates upon facts, chronology, cause and effect, and upon context. Its concerns differ from those of the ancient historian who was more subjective in approach and therefore emphasized the interpretation of the past and the lessons to be learned from it. From the perspective of an ancient writer, a story is told for a purpose; facts must contribute to the goal; and available literary conventions are tools at the writer's disposal to convey a message to the story's intended readers.

Luke, for whom fact and story along with literary conventions were at the service of the writer's view of reality, was very much a writer of the Hellenistic period. In composing the first volume, the author was less free since both the Jesus material and gospel genre had received their shape to a large extent from Mark and since these in their turn had become part of the tradition. Still, Luke felt free to restructure the story and to employ Hellenistic literary conventions to compose a new life of Jesus. The gospel introduces speeches, effectively uses dramatic techniques, and constructs parallels and thematic sequences as its hero is led to Jerusalem for the climax of the story. In Acts the author is freer in literary and theological terms to pursue the themes of the first volume and to make fuller use of current literary techniques. Luke, the Hellenistic Gentile, possibly proselyte or "God-fearer,"[14] addresses the reader fully aware of the Jesus movement's debt to Israel and of its socio-political and religious milieu within the Roman empire.

Content and Surface Structure

The plot of the Third Gospel is rather familiar since it is closely related to that encountered in Mark. The beginning and ending of the

Unnik, "Luke's Second Book and the Rules of Hellenistic Historiography," 37-60 in J. Kremer, ed., *Les Actes des Apôtres: tradition, rédaction, théologie* (Gembloux: Duculot, 1979).

[14]See T.M. Finn, " The God-fearers Reconsidered," *CBQ* 47 (1985) 75-84, for discussion of this issue.

work, however, are far less familiar as are many of the episodes, tone, and themes of the gospel. Just as in Matthew, the reader encounters old and new, for Luke has, with great fidelity, employed the community's tradition, which included the Gospel of Mark, the Q-Source, and a substantial amount of new materials, and has imposed a new perspective upon the tradition. With great innovation, the author focused on the community's early years and the lore which had developed about the beginnings.

SOURCES AND PLAN OF THE GOSPEL

Luke's dependence on Mark is not to be doubted since both the sequence of events and content of Jesus' life are borrowed from that source. Luke modifies Mark's poor grammar and style but, contrary to Matthew who tends to compress source materials, remains faithful to its content and vocabulary. An excellent example of this is the baptism of Jesus (RSVmod):

Mark 1	Luke 3
9 In those days Jesus came from Nazareth of Galilee and was baptized by John in the Jordan.	21 Now it happened that when all the people had been baptized, when Jesus had also been baptized and was praying,
10 And immediately coming up from the water, he saw the heavens torn open and the Spirit like a dove descending upon him;	22 that heaven was opened, then the Holy Spirit descended upon him in bodily form, as a dove,
11 And a voice came from the heavens: "You are my beloved Son, with you I am well pleased."	and a voice came from heaven: "You are my beloved Son, with you I am well pleased."

Luke borrows the elements of the episode: the baptism, the opening of heaven, the descent of the Spirit in the form of a dove, the voice, and the exact citation. Nonetheless, the text is greatly altered in detail and style. While the Markan episode is told in three independent statements connected by the ubiquitous "and" (*kai*), that of Luke consists of one compound-complex sentence. Luke has eliminated John from the picture (the story about John is rounded off by having Herod put him in prison), has omitted geographical references (Luke has a distinct theology of place), and presents Jesus at prayer (a frequent occurrence in the gospel). Instead of the Semitic plural ("heavens") the author employs the Greek singular ("heaven or sky") twice in v. 22. To replace the graphic Markan image of "tearing open the heavens," the author has recourse to an OT passage (Isa. 63:19 LXX—"if you should open heaven") to reformulate this clause (Matt. 3:16 also to some extent). Luke stresses the physical nature ("bodily form") of the phenomenon, a common characteristic of Luke-Acts.

Since the gospel follows closely the order of its Markan source departures from this sequence are explained in terms of Lukan redaction.[15] Luke has added a prologue and birth stories at the beginning (chaps. 1-2) and resurrection appearances at the end (chap. 24). The basic outline of Jesus' life follows that of Mark, for, apart from the occasional transposition of episodes, Luke imposed on it three major modifications: one omisson (elimination of Mark 6:45-8:26) and two interpolations (addition of 6:20-8:3 and 9:51-18:14 to the Markan sequence).

The transpositions of the source are variously achieved. In some instances Luke expands the narrative by supplementing it with Q or oral tradition; in others the writer adds new blocks of narrative and discourse material. By isolating these and by examining thematic and structural indicators, such as time/place factors and contrasting elements, one arrives at the following surface outline:

1:1-4	Prologue
1:5-4:13	John and Jesus
1:5-2:52	Dual Annunciation and Birth Stories
3:1-4:13	Public Introduction of John and Jesus
4:14-9:50	The Galilean Ministry
9:51-19:27	Journey to Jerusalem
19:28-21:38	The Jerusalem Ministry
22:1-24:53	Supper, Trial, Death, Resurrection

[15]J.A. Fitzmyer, "The Priority of Mark and the 'Q' Source in Luke," 3-40 in *To Advance the Gospel: New Testament Studies* (NY: Crossroad, 1981).

After a stylized prologue, there is a lengthy narrative about John the Baptist and Jesus. The first part of this narrative, spanning the first two chapters and consisting of two annunciation stories (one about John's father and the other concerning Jesus' mother), the meeting of the two mothers, dual birth narratives, and the temple scene, derives from Luke's own traditions.

The next part (3:1f), which pursues the contrast made between John and Jesus in the infancy stories,[16] follows the Markan schema to which Q and L material has been added to underscore the role and teaching of John, Jesus' genealogy, and his temptations. In the case of the last mentioned, Luke finds a simple statement that Jesus was "tempted by Satan" in the wilderness (Mark 1:13) and supplements this by adding a threefold narrative of Jesus' encounter with his eschatological rival (4:1-13).[17]

The Galilean ministry follows the Markan source although there are many traces of Lukan reorganization and rewriting. The most blatant modification is the moving forward of the Nazareth episode (Mark 6:1-6), which Luke expands and rewrites to serve as a programmatic statement of Jesus' ministry. Within this section occurs one of Luke's major additions, 6:20-8:3, consisting primarily of the sermon on the plain, a few miracles, and the delegation from John the Baptist. The last mentioned, 7:18-35. is related to the Nazareth episode and the program mapped out there for God's envoy. Lastly, one should note how, through omission of Markan material and the subtle rewriting of the episodes, Luke has structured chapter 9 to give a sequence of responses to the question assigned Herod: "who is this about whom I hear such things?" (9:9b). The chapter then functions as a christological inquiry for Luke.[18]

The journey to Jerusalem (9:51f), as a construct, is a Lukan creation. Taking a cue from Mark 10:1f, which notes that Jesus left Galilee and made his way to Judaea, Luke brings together a large amount of Q and L material and organizes this into a long journey from Galilee through

---

[16]On the unity of chapters 1-4 see Talbert, "Prophecies of Future Greatness."

[17]Matthew and Luke present the temptations in a different order; the latter seemingly has modified the order (bread, kingdoms, and temple) to underscore the importance of Jerusalem in God's plan.

[18]J.A. Fitzmyer, "The Compostition of Luke, Chapter 9," 135-53 in Talbert, *Perspectives on Luke-Acts.*

Jericho to the Judaean capital. The section opens with a Jesus who is fully conscious of his destiny and who resolutely heads toward the city of fulfilment: "and it happened that when the days were fulfiled for him to be received up, he set his face to go to Jerusalem" (9:51—RSVmod). During this journey Jesus speaks of many key themes (discipleship, love of God and neighbor, prayer, eschatological warning, mercy, forgiveness, perseverance) and confronts the Jewish authorities. The reader is often reminded that Jesus is making his way to the holy city: 13:22, 33; 17:11; 18:31 (already at 9:31). Also, some of Jesus' most beautiful parables, found only in Luke, are located here: the good Samaritan (10:29-37), the rich fool (12:13-21), the great banquet (14:16-24), the prodigal son (15:11-32), the rich man and Lazarus (16:19-31), the Pharisee and tax collector (18:9-14).

The Jerusalem ministry (19:28f) follows closely the Markan outline although the author indulges in some minor editorial work, especially the addition of sayings concerning the city and its fate and about the end-times.

The final section is also dependent on Mark for its basic sequence and the majority of its episodes; Luke, however, shows independence by omitting some episodes or details, by adding or expanding others, by occasionally displacing elements of the sequence, and by attending to small touches which underscore a new perspective. The anointing at Bethany (Mark 14:3-9) is omitted because Luke has a parallel tradition (the woman with the ointment, 7:36-50), which is placed earlier in the narrative to emphasize the crucial theme of forgiveness. Luke eliminates one of two multiplication stories and one of two mockery scenes found in Mark, *6:30-44* versus 8:1-10 and *14:65* versus 15:16-20 (the italicized passages are retained). Some details of Jesus' trial before the Jewish authorities are either eliminated, because Luke insists on a religious rather than a political cause for the death of Jesus, or transferred to the trials of Stephen or Paul in Acts.[19] Twice Luke eliminates the promise of Galilean appearances (22:39 and 24:6 versus Mark 14:28 and 16:7) because of the role assigned to Jerusalem, the locale of all Lukan resurrection appearances. The Lukan modifications lessen the accountability of Pilate (Jesus is declared innocent three times 23:4f) and state the responsibility of the Jewish authorities for the death

---

[19]E.J. Via, "According to Luke, Who Put Jesus to Death?" 122-45 in Cassidy and Scharper, *Political Issues in Luke-Acts.*

of Jesus (23:23, 25).[20] The resurrection narratives, apart from the empty tomb episode, have no Markan parallel and so derive solely from special Lukan material; these include the Emmaus story, the appearance in Jerusalem to the assembled believers, the final commission of the risen Lord, and his ascension.

PLAN OF ACTS

From the start Luke leaves no doubt what the scope of this volume will be, for in 1:8b there is a sketch of the new narrative's plot-line: "you will be my witnesses not only in Jerusalem but also in all Judaea and Samaria even to the end of the earth" (RSVmod). The narrative leads its characters and allows them to express their witness to the risen Lord throughout the Roman provinces of the East, Greece, and finally to Rome, i.e., "the end of the earth" or, in western imagery, to the center of the cultural and political world. Further, since Paul and companions set out on several ever-expanding missionary journeys, interrupted by a meeting of leaders in Jerusalem, and since several cities become the focal point of the remainder of the story, we propose the following surface structure for Acts:

1:1-26	Introduction
2:1-8:4	Mission to Jerusalem
8:5-12:25	Mission to Samaria and Judaea
13:1-28-31	Mission even to the End of the Earth
13:1-14:28	First Missionary Journey
15:1-35	Jerusalem Council
15:36-18:21	Second Missionary Journey
18:22-19:20	Third Missionary Journey
19:21-23-10	Jerusalem
23:11-26:32	Caesarea
27:1-28:31	Rome.[21]

Beginning with a few preliminaries (a prologue, a certain amount of narrative overlap with the ending of the previous volume, and the reconstitution of the eschatological, never-to-be-repeated group of

---

[20]See the various articles in Cassidy and Scharper, *ibid.*

[21]Such a structure results from a careful time-space analysis of the entire narrative.

twelve), Luke records at length and in physical terms the coming of the Spirit (the Father's promise). For fully six chapters Luke chronicles the beginnings in Jerusalem of the growing mission, the community and its life, and the worsening series of trials (warnings, beatings, and death of a Christian leader, chaps. 3-4, 5, 7). As a result of Stephen's death or, in Lukan terms, owing to God's hidden purpose (see 5:38-39), the mission spreads from Jerusalem to Judaea, Samaria, and further north into Antioch. The role of Peter is central until the arrival of Luke's hero, Paul of Tarsus, who is the principal character of the remainder of the story. Through successive journeys, after several ineffectual trials, and in spite of a dramatic shipwreck off the cost of Malta, Paul arrives finally in Rome. There Luke, with Paul as spokesman, comments upon the contemporary situation of the church; Israel is divided in its assessment of the Jesus movement (28:24), while the Gentile world gives much promise for missionary activity (28:28).[22] Nonetheless, Luke the inspired optimist, brings the curtain down on an open-ended mission. Paul "welcomed all who came to him, preaching the kingdom of God and teaching about the Lord Jesus Christ quite openly and unhindered" (28:30-31).

What sources did Luke employ to compose Acts? It was customary some decades ago to isolate the strands of material found in Acts and to assign blocks of tradition to various individuals or locales known from Acts or other sources. So scholars postulated Jerusalemite and Antiochene collections of traditions, or Hellenistic and Hebrew sources (Acts 6:1), or accounts associated with Peter, Paul, Philip, etc. Redaction and composition analysis, however, has not borne out such conjectures.[23] Further, it was and still is popularly affirmed a) that Luke was a companion of Paul (Phlm. 24; Col. 4:14; 2 Tim. 4:11—referred to in the second as "our beloved physician") and b) that the author discretely indicated this fact by the use of "we" in the latter part of the Acts (16:10-17; 20:5-21:18; 27:1-28:16). Or less conservative scholars sometimes insist c) that the writer of Acts, a Christian of a later generation, employed the diary of an eyewitness for the last third of the narrative. This last proposal, while attractive, fails to convince since there is no perceptible difference in style between the so-called "we sections" and

---

[22]E. Richard, "The Divine Purpose: The Jews and the Gentile Mission (Acts 15)," 188-209 in Talbert, *Luke-Acts: New Perspectives.*
[23]J. Dupont, *The Sources of the Acts* (NY: Herder & Herder, 1964).

the rest of the book. As to the first two affirmations there are insurmountable objections to their plausibility. The name Luke is traditional, dating back to the second century during the time of Marcion. That a person by that name was a fellow worker of Paul is clear from Philemon 24; but that such a person would have been, at the same time, a traveler with Paul, the author of Acts, and, therefore, the one responsible for the speeches in Acts said to be by Paul, is hard to believe. The author of Acts has seemingly no first hand knowledge of Pauline thought nor of Paul's correspondence. The simplest solution, the one which explains the anomalies of this work, is that its author is an anonymous post-apostolic Christian, who, like the authors of the Paulinist letters, was acquainted with the stories or legends circulating about the great apostle to the Gentiles.[24] The "we-sections," I believe, result from a literary convention sometimes employed in sea voyages and not the account or diary of an eyewitness.[25] The sources of Acts are unknown to us, though we surmise the use of a growing community lore about the "old days," particularly legends about Paul, by an author who did considerable personal research while traveling about and questioning the remaining "eyewitnesses and ministers of the word" (see Luke 1:1-4).

Developmental Character of Luke's Work

Redaction criticism has made scholars increasingly aware of the mistake of studying Acts and Luke in isolation from each other. They are related in style, thematic perspective, and in planning. The two works begin with elegant prologues, both of which are addressed to an otherwise unknown official or person of social standing (*kratistos*), Theophilus. The second prologue refers back to the earlier one and seeks to present a short résumé of the gospel: "in the first [i.e., 'earlier'] book, O Theophilus, I have dealt with all that Jesus began to do and teach, until the day when he was taken up ..." (Acts 1:1-2).

---

[24]M.C. de Boer, "Images of Paul in the Post-Apostolic Period," *CBQ* 42 (1980) 359-80; Richard, "Luke—Writer, Theologian, Historian," 6-8; and Brawley, "Paul in Acts: Lucan Apology and Conciliation."

[25]V.K. Robbins, "By Land and by Sea: The We-Passages and Ancient Sea Voyages," 215-42 in Talbert, *Perspectives in Luke-Acts.*

LUKE-ACTS AS A TWO-VOLUME WORK

Numerous parallels exist between these two Lukan works. Leaving aside for now the birth narratives (1-2), one notes their strikingly similar beginnings: dominant role of the Spirit, key initial speeches, and parallel programmatic episodes (Luke 3-4 and Acts 1-2). We observe that the part played by John the Baptist at the beginning of the gospel (3:1f), a theme inherited from the tradition, has its balanced references in the first chapter of Acts (vv. 5 and 22). As the Spirit descends upon Jesus at the baptism scene, leads him into the wilderness where he is tempted, empowers him, and dwells in him during the ministry (Luke 3:22; 4:1, 14, 18), so that same Spirit, often promised (24:49; Acts 1:4-5, 8), descends upon the assembled community at Pentecost accompanied by signs of the end-days (Acts 2). As the Spirit acted in Jesus' ministry so now it acts in that of Jesus' followers (2:38). Both works contain key beginning speeches which the author enshrines within key narratives (Luke 4 and Acts 2).

After describing the relationship between John and Jesus, the gospel focuses on its central character. To set the stage for the ministry Luke borrows from the Markan outline (6:1-6) a narrative about the rejection of Jesus by his townspeople. Luke rewrites and expands this episode to express "in a nutshell" the good news which Jesus preaches and is.[26] By means of an OT citation, Isa. 61:1-2 supplemented by 58:6, Luke lays out the messianic program which Jesus' life is to exemplify in his concern for the "poor, maimed, blind, and lame" (see 7:21-22; 14:13-14). Further, the author appeals to Elijah and Elisha eipsodes (4:24-27) from 1 and 2 Kings to comment upon Judaeo-Christian relations. The Nazareth episode with its speech encapsulates the promise and foreboding (rejection of 4:30) of the life of God's Messiah (9:20).

The parallel episode which launches the Acts of the Apostles is the pentecost narrative with its kerygmatic speech by Peter. Here too Luke sets the program for the second volume; among the central themes are the universal mission, the eschatological character of the Christian experience, salvation in the Name, and the risen Lord who pours out the Spirit as the Father had promised. The key to both the gospel and Acts, Luke tells us, is "Jesus of Nazareth, a man attested to [us] by God," who was delivered up, crucified, killed and raised "according to the definite

---

[26]J. Kodell, "Luke's Gospel in a Nutshell (Lk. 4:16-20)," *BTB* 13 (1983) 16-18.

plan and foreknowledge of God" (Acts 2:22-24), the one in whose name all must be saved (4:12).

Another structural and thematic parallel between the two Lukan works involves Luke 24:36-53 and Acts 1:3-13. Luke concludes the first volume with Jesus speaking about the mission which is to begin in Jerusalem, where the disciples, after receiving the promise of the Father ("clothed with power from on high"), become his witnesses. The disciples observe the Lord ascend into heaven and return to Jerusalem where they worship in the temple. The author, to situate the audience of the second work into the proper context, restates with some variation the themes and episodes of the concluding verses of the gospel. There are some changes, however. Luke now adds the theme of John's water baptism as contrasted to baptism with the Holy Spirit (Acts 1:5), a theme to be developed later (18:24-19:7). No longer will the mission simply begin from Jerusalem as in Luke 24:47, instead the author gives the itinerary for the second volume (Acts 1:8b).

Further, there is an important shift in the last item of the parallel, a shift which probably accounts for the added note about the 40-day period between the resurrection and ascension (Acts 1:3). The gospel ends with the disciples "continually in the temple blessing God," but Acts 1:13 has them going "up to the upper room." The modification signals Luke's decision to continue the story of Jesus, now absent but very much present among his followers. Luke is interested in narrating not only the promise with which the gospel had terminated but also the actualization of that promise. Since the second volume dwells on the Lord's work as done through his intermediaries, Luke takes pains to prepare the disciples for their part in the messianic age. The earliest period of the community owes its special character to its close and unique association with the risen Lord before his ascension, an experience never to be repeated. The risen Jesus spoke to them of the kingdom; he ate with them, training them, and preparing them for forty days—an obvious parallel to Jesus' own forty days (Luke 4:1f) and the ideal time of preparation for disciples according to Rabbinic tradition. The eating of Acts 1:4 probably alludes to the breaking of bread at Emmaus and the eating passages of Acts 2:42f. This decision by Luke to have the upper room rather than the temple as the locale for launching the mission is an important christological statement.

Other indications of unified purpose are the parallels which Luke draws between Jesus and important personalities in Acts. As the master raises men (son of the widow of Nain, 7:11-17 = L) and women (Jairus' little daughter, 8:40f = Mark 5:21f) from the dead so do his disciples; Peter raises Tabitha (Acts 9:36f) and Paul, Eutychus (20:7f). As Jesus has an introductory discourse (Luke 4) so do Peter (Acts 2) and Paul (Acts 13). Paralleling Jesus' farewell speech (Luke 21 = Mark 13) is that of Paul at Miletus to the Ephesian elders (Acts 20:18-35). Many episodes in Acts are composed with an eye to parallels in the gospel, e.g., the trials of Jesus and those of Stephen and Paul; Luke 9:5 and 10:11 versus Acts 13:51 and 18:6 (promise and fulfilment); Luke 4:38f and Acts 28:7f (Jesus and Peter's mother-in-law versus Paul and Publius' father).[27]

ACTS AS A CONTINUATION OF THE GOSPEL

For Luke the two works are parallel and continuous because of their subject matter, for the gospel tells the life of Jesus, while Acts dwells upon the activity of the "absent" Lord and that of his followers. Jesus is center stage in the gospel, while in Acts he is not far off in the wings. He acts through intermediaries and directly in the vision of Stephen or in the call and instruction of Paul (Acts 7 and 9). Acts is also centered upon the Christ-event, but because of a change in subject matter (post-resurrection period) and genre (monograph about Jesus' followers and the divinely sanctioned witnessing to the ends of the earth), the master's role is reduced only in appearance. Acts is the logical sequel to the master's life.[28]

If, therefore, the composition of Acts is a continuation of Luke's original project, an inquiry about the overall temporal schema of Luke-Acts is in order. This is particularly important since, until recently, Luke was routinely accused of having betrayed the early kerygma by the decision to compose the Acts of the Apostles. Luke was accused of being "early catholic," i.e., more interested in history, church organization, and doctrine than in Jesus and faith in him as the Christ. Much of the work done on Luke in the 60s took its cue from the otherwise crucial work of H. Conzelmann, who proposed a threefold time scheme for Luke-Acts: the time of Israel (including John the Baptist), the time

---

[27]Richard, "Luke—Writer, Theologian, Historian," 8-9.

[28]W.C. van Unnik, "The 'Book of Acts' the Confirmation of the Gospel," *NovT* 4 (1960) 26-59; see also F. Bovon, "L'importance des médiations dans le projet théologique de Luc," *NTS* 21 (1974) 23-39.

of Jesus (the middle or perfect time—but in the past nonetheless), and the time of the church. Wisely, recent scholarship has rejected this schema and proposes a standard twofold temporal outline: the Old Age (the time of Israel as preparation, prophecy, and promise) and the New Age (inaugurated by the Christ-event and awaiting the final consumation). Luke having inherited the apocalyptic scheme of contemporary Judaism and of the early Jesus movement, situated within it and reinterpreted in light of that scheme the Christ-event for a new generation of believers.[29]

Early tradition, followed by Luke, saw the coming of the Christ as the dawning of the New Age, for it was believed that God, through Jesus, had intervened in human history to set in motion the age of salvation. That is not where Luke's originality lies and certainly not where one might rightly accuse this author of betrayal. Instead, the Lukan community and its evangelist were concerned about continuity between Israel and Christianity and about the relationship between the period of Jesus' life and that of the community. The gospel was to be the story of the master's life among his disciples and Acts was to show how the now-departed Lord was present within the community of Luke's time. Though absent (the ascension accounts) Jesus was lord of the community and present to its members.[30]

The period of OT promise does not constitute a part of Luke's work in a structural sense since the gospel begins with the life of Jesus. Instead the Old Age permeates the entire work of Luke who wishes to show how that part of God's plan prepared for "the last days" (Acts 2:17). Phrases such as "it is written" (Luke 3:4; 4:8, 10, etc.), "this is he of whom it is written" (7:27), "Lord . . . who by the mouth of our father David . . . said" (Acts 4:25), "as the prophet says" (7:40), or "with this the words of the prophets are in harmony, as it is written" (15:15, RSVmod) underline the continuity in God's design for humanity between the time of Israel and the new and final epoch of salvation. In fact Luke ends the gospel narrative with a twofold insistence that the life, passion, and

[29]Richard, "Luke—Writer, Theologian, Historian," 3-15; see also J. Kodell, "The Theology of Luke in Recent Study," *BTB* 1 (1971) 115-44; C.H. Talbert, "Shifting Sands: The Recent Study of the Gospel of Luke," *Int* 30 (1976) 381-95; N.A. Dahl, "The Purpose of Luke-Acts," 87-98 in *Jesus in the Memory of the Early Church* (Minneapolis: Augsburg, 1976); and R.F. O'Toole, "Why Did Luke Write Acts (Lk-Acts)?" *BTB* 7 (1977) 66-76.

[30]R.F. O'Toole, "Activity of the Risen Jesus in Luke-Acts," *Bib* 62 (1981) 71-98.

resurrection of the Christ was part of God's plan as foretold by the scriptures (24:26-27, 44-46). Indeed, everything written about the Christ "in the law of Moses and the prophets and the psalms [had to] be fulfilled" (24:44). This argument then becomes a major motif of the kerygmatic speeches of Acts where Luke's principal characters announce the good news of the resurrected Lord who lives with the community.

If the time of Israel is in the background, that of Jesus (life, death, resurrection, and activity as "absent" Lord) is the content of Luke-Acts. Luke's presentation of the Christ-event (from birth through death to return) is offered in stages, first the special time of Jesus' ministry when he performs the mighty works of God and reveals the Father, secondly the central section which is devoted to the core of Christian teaching, the passion, death, and resurrection of Jesus, and thirdly, the time when Jesus, though absent, operates within the community. Luke opens the gospel narrative with an OT-like introduction to the public ministry of Jesus; the figures of Zechariah, Simeon, and Anna are intentionally given prophetic qualities, as is John the Baptist. The ministry of Jesus is a perfect time when the activity of Satan is reduced to a minimum (see 4:13 and 22:3) and "glorious things" (13:17) are done by Jesus that the people might "glorify God" (5:26). The public ministry presents Jesus as the righteous servant who does God's deeds before a jury of experts (5:17) which is unable to convict him (6:11; 14:6; 20:26, 40). It is the time of ministry to the poor and outcast, "the acceptable year of the Lord" (4:19), the year of reprieve (13:6-9).

The central period (Luke 22 through Acts 2) is devoted to the nucleus of the Christian message: the death and resurrection of Jesus the Christ. Since there has been much controversy concerning Luke's treatment of Jesus' death,[31] we will return to this topic at the end of this chapter. Nonetheless, this segment of Luke's work consists of the passion and death (22-23), the resurrection (24) and the departure of Jesus and the consequent resolution of his absence in the pentecost narrative.

The final stage of Luke's work, the period of Jesus' direct activity within the community of believers and that through his intermediaries, is presented throughtout Acts. There Luke employs three ecclesial models: a) that of the idealized Jerusalem community of the early chapters, b) that centered around Antioch and its missionary activity,

---

[31]See A. George, "Le sens de la mort de Jésus," 185-212 in *Etudes sur l'oeuvre de Luc* (Paris: Gabalda, 1978) and confer note 4 above.

and c) that reflected in the Miletus speech to the Ephesian elders consisting of a farewell address which both terminates the missionary journeys of Paul and looks forward beyond the apostolic period to Luke's time.[32] These models are skillfully interconnected as one period leads into another, as themes are pursued from episode to episode, and as the community increases and multiplies (Acts 2:47; 6:7; 9:31; 12:24; 28:31). By far the most striking and effective technique employed by Luke to interrelate the different stages of Luke and Acts is the frequent appropriation of the dictum: like master like disciples; that is, as Jesus prayed, preached, suffered, so the disciples are portrayed as doing the same.[33]

Luke and Acts are to be read in sequence. Current scholars tend to agree with H.J. Cadbury that Acts is not an "afterthought" or simply another work by the author of the gospel.[34] Luke and Acts then are companion volumes whose relationship results both from similarity of content and style and from conscious literary and theological creation. Indeed, I maintain that the author of the Third Gospel, whose original text would have been far closer to Mark than at present, at a later date, convinced that a companion volume would be helpful, began to compose a sequel (with revision of the former) as a continuation of the gospel which had presented God's gracious visitation in the works and teachings of God's obedient servant (Luke 7:16).

The Lukan Jesus: God's Messiah

There is a keen awareness from the beginning of the gospel to the end of Acts that the plan of God is at work in the world for the salvation of all who call upon the name (Acts 2:21, 38) of God's Christ (Luke 9:20). Luke's vision of the Christian reality is one which has a definite historical setting: origin and matrix in Judaism and its scriptures, embedded within the story of Jesus and his disciples, and at work throughout the Roman empire;[35] it has a philosophical-theological

[32]Richard, "Luke—Writer, Theologian, Historian," 6.

[33]C.H. Talbert, "Discipleship in Luke-Acts," 68-75 in Segovia, *Discipleship in the New Testament.*

[34]*The Making of Luke-Acts* (NY: Macmillan, 1927) 8-9.

[35]H.J. Cadbury's book, *The Book of Acts in History* (NY: Harper, 1955), is particularly illuminating in this regard.

framework: "the definite plan and foreknowledge of God," (Acts 2:23); and offers an unrelenting christological focus: a finely articulated agency christology. It is to these themes, as they shed light upon Jesus' role in Luke-Acts, that we turn our attention.

PORTRAIT OF JESUS

In the first speech of Acts Peter describes the narrative's hero to the audience as "Jesus of Nazareth, a man attested to you by God with mighty works and wonders and signs which God did through him in your midst" (2:22). Jesus for Luke is first and foremost a man who has won God's approval, i.e., God's Messiah. He is that envoy, promised in the Jewish scriptures, situated within that Semitic culture, yet destined to be the vehicle of universal salvation. At the outset Luke places Jesus within the cultural ambiance of Palestinian village life. Along with the poetic language and exalted promises of the infancy narratives, themselves couched in Hebraic or rather Septuagintal language and thought (chaps. 1-2), Luke takes pains to stress Jesus' Jewish background: genealogy, synchronisms, familiarity with the scriptures, Nazarene upbringing, and customary association with the synagogue (Luke 4:16). The author retains from Mark the blind man's address of Jesus as "Son of David" and adds two stories where first a woman and then a man are referred to, approvingly in the context of forgiveness, as children ("daughter" and "son") of Abraham (13:16 and 19:9).

While Jesus has obvious Jewish characteristics in Luke, he is nonetheless situated upon a Hellenistic stage. Jesus can trace his roots back both to noteworthy Jewish ancestors and to the father of the human race, Adam (3:38). He has come to seek not only the lost sheep of Israel but has also come that "all flesh might see the salvation of God" (3:6, addition to Mark). One should note throughout the ministry the many intimations of the Gentile mission: Simeon's statement concerning the child Jesus (2:32), the exemplary miracles of Elijah and Elisha on behalf of non-Jews as foreshadowing Jesus' own mission (4:25-27), the worthy centurion about whom Jesus says: "not even in Israel have I found such faith" (7:9), the mission of the seventy (10:1f), or Jesus' great banquet parable (14:16-24).

As readers readily recognize, Luke's Jesus is the most human of the gospel portraits, so much so that 19th-century romanticists had a special liking for Luke's Gospel. Jesus' fondness or "preferential option," in Luke, for the poor and the outcast is well known. He has been sent "to preach good news to the poor ... to set at liberty those who are oppressed"(4:18). Jesus is made to say: "blessed are you poor"and also "woe to you that are rich"(6:20 and 24). A favorite theme of the Lukan Jesus is his care for "the poor, maimed, lame, blind" (14:31; cf. 4:18). Jesus is accused of "receiving sinners and eating with them"(15:1; 5:30; 7:34), of paying special attention to sinners (7:36-50), to outcasts (lepers, 5:12-16 or Samaritans, 10:25-37; 17:11-19), and to other disadvantaged people. In regard to the last, one would have to discuss the role of women in the ministry of Jesus and life of the community.[36] Luke's Jesus takes seriously the task of universal salvation. It is principally Luke who attributes to Jesus such humanistic traits as forgiveness, mercy, love of enemy, stress upon doing rather than saying, upon giving, joy, and frequent prayer. It is Luke who, in the scene at Nain, says that Jesus "gave him back to his mother"(7:15), of Jairus' daughter that "he directed that something should be given her to eat" (8:55— addition to Mark), or about the epileptic boy that "he gave him back to his father" (9:42).[37]

Beyond the portrait of Jesus as a man for others we find in Luke an array of christological titles to describe who Jesus is and what he means to the reader. Luke employs the traditional titles: "Son of God,""Son of Man," "Lord," "Christ," and unusual ones such as "Servant" (*pais*) and "Savior." In a few instances Luke added the title "Son of God" to the Markan narrative: twice in the temptation story (4:3, 9—Q material), and once at the end of a Markan summary (4:41), but on the whole Luke follows Mark and imposes minor modifications. The title "Son of God" is extended to Jesus' childhood (1:32 and 35) and employed only twice in Acts (9:20 and 13:33). The title "Son of Man" though more frequent in Luke than in Mark nonetheless is applied by the former in a way consistent with the latter's usage. In other words, it is applied by Luke to Jesus' ministry, death and resurrection, and eschatological role; new examples are added for each from the Q-Source.

The other titles also merit attention. "Lord" is a favorite of Luke's

[36]E.S. Fiorenza, *In Memory of Her: A Feminist Theological Reconstruction of Christian Origins* (NY: Crossroad, 1983) and B. Witherington, *Women in the Ministry of Jesus: A Study of Jesus' Attitudes To Women and Their Roles as Reflected in His Earthly Life* (NY: Cambridge University, 1984).

[37]On the humanism of the Lukan Jesus, see R.F. O'Toole, *The Unity of Luke's Theology: An Analysis of Luke-Acts* (Wilmington: Glazier, 1984) 109-48 and various articles in Cassidy and Scharper, *Political Issues in Luke-Acts*.

throughout the gospel, where it is "an address of subordination to the earthly Jesus." In fact we would agree with D.L. Jones' conclusion:

> for him there is no distinction between the earthly and the exalted Lord. Not only is the predicate applied to the historical as well as the resurrected Jesus; he is Lord even before his birth. Since Jesus is already *kyrios* on earth, Luke, both in his gospel and in Acts, can use the title freely, unconsciously, and indiscriminately.[38]

The same author has done extended research on the variety of "Christological titles in Lk.-Acts, including Servant of God, the Holy One, the Righteous One, Lord, Author of life (Leader), Savior and Son of God" and has

> concluded that all of these titles were current in Lk.'s day, and that his utilization of them presupposed a certain amount of reflection upon Jesus' messianic mission. By and large, the designations had long and diverse histories, but by the time Lk. took them over they were merely different ways of calling Jesus 'the Christ.'[39]

This is the usage one finds in the kerygmatic speeches of Acts (2:22-24; 3:13-15; 4:10; 5:30-31; 10:36-41; 13:23-25, 28-31). Titles are used in close proximity and, it seems, indiscriminately. See for example 3:13-15 where the titles "servant Jesus," "Holy and Righteous One," and "Author of life" are used in a kerygmatic text about Jesus' trial before Pilate, and about his death and resurrection.

We would have to agree with Jones that christological titles in Luke-Acts play a different role than they do in Mark. In the former they are often used interchangeably while in the latter they usually retain their specific meanings. In fact, what we saw as occurring in Mark in regard to the title "Christ," where it was maintained that it served as a bridge between the various christological appellations, we now see on a far larger scale; in the words of Jones, "they are merely different ways of calling Jesus 'the Christ.'" Even the title "savior" (used only 4 times by Luke—three of which refer to Jesus) is thus used. In Luke 2:11 Jesus as

---

[38]"The Title *KYRIOS* in Luke-Acts," 96 in *Society of Biblical Literature Seminar Papers* (Missoula: Scholars, 1974).

[39]"The Title *Christos* in Luke-Acts," *CBQ* 32 (1970) 76; see also "The Title 'Servant' in Luke-Acts," 146-65 in Talbert, *Luke-Acts: New Perspectives.*

Savior is identified as "Christ the Lord;" in Acts 5:3 as the exalted one he is called "Leader and Savior"; and in 13:23, as David's descendant, he is "Savior, Jesus as [God] promised." From this we conclude that it is not the original meaning of the titles that is important but their use in Luke's overall christological scheme. The title "Savior" would be a good example. While the title is infrequent and lacks specificity, the related concept of "salvation" is a major theme from the beginning of Luke to the end of Acts.[40]

While it is misleading to single out one appellation as the central Lukan christological title, it is safe to say that Christ or Messiah plays the most significant role as it continues to serve as a bridge (as it had in Mark) for Luke's descriptions of Jesus and because of the importance such phrases as "the Christ of God" and "Jesus is the Christ" have for Luke. Indeed, the expression "the Christ of God," which serves as Peter's confession (9:20), provides a major clue to understanding the author's overall schema, namely, Luke's notion of the divine purpose or plan.

JESUS' ROLE IN THE DIVINE PLAN

The true historian according to Lucian of Samosata (*fl.* 165 A.D.) is endowed with two unmatched qualities: "political understanding and power of expression," i.e., the ability to comprehend events and to communicate these. He also maintains that the former is "a gift of nature" but the latter is the product of "much work, discipline, and imitation of the ancients" (How to Write History, 34). The two qualities, labeled thought and art or theology and style, are much in evidence in Luke's work. So we turn our attention to the first, namely, Luke's perception of the Christian experience.

We agree with Lucian that this quality is not one that is learned but one related to insight or genius. We conclude further that this author's perception of the history of salvation was no less than inspired, for Luke saw that God's plan for humanity was foretold by the prophets of old (Acts 26:22-23), was realized by the divine visitation of God's Son (Luke 7:16),and was being actualized through select intermediaries in the last days (Acts 1:8; 2:17). The theme of the divine purpose is pervasive in Luke-Acts and in its perception of the Christ-event; indeed, the concept

---

[40]On the general sense of "Jesus as Savior," see O'Toole, *The Unity of Luke's Theology*, 33-61.

embues Luke's entire perception of the Christ-event. The author misses few opportunities, whether in general concepts or details, to reflect upon God's design for humanity. Luke introduces this overarching theme in a variety of ways: terms and episodes that express divine agency or necessity are employed; and various types of supernatural intervention are emphasized (God acts; there are voices from heaven; the Spirit is omnipresent; there are angels, demons, appearances of the risen Lord, as well as dreams and visions). Luke also favors a variety of temporal expressions to stress the divine plan and appeals to the actualization of the Old Testament.[41]

Central to this concept of the divine plan is the Lukan stress on divine activity. It is God who controls human events, who directs, who leads, who plans. All aspects of the plan of salvation are viewed theologically. Jesus is God's agent; he is the one sent by God, the prophet of the Most High, the Son of God, the one obedient to the Divine, the one who does the "mighty works of God" (Acts 2:22). In fact all of salvation history can be defined as the mighty works of God and Jesus is the one par excellence who accomplishes (past and present) these acts. OT prophecy and the books of Moses are viewed by Luke as speech of God, who spoke through ("by the mouth of," "by the hand of") these about the "now" of salvation. The community, its witnesses, disciples, and even the Spirit who operates freely within that community, are God's intermediaries. God is in control and Luke takes pains to emphasize this. Statistically, for example, the occurrence of the word "God" (*theos*) is much higher for Luke than for the other evangelists.[42] Divine agency and control are everywhere evident; see the author's use of circumlocutions: Spirit, necessity, angels (these are agents also of the "absent" Lord). We give two examples of Luke's use of divine compulsion. In Acts 16:6-10 the Holy Spirit forbids Paul to speak in Asia. A Macedonian in a vision beckons Paul to come to the Greek mainland. Luke ends the story by saying: "we sought to go on into Macedonia concluding that God had called us to preach the gospel to them." The second example concerns the command in Acts 1:8 to spread the good news beyond Jerusalem. For eight chapters the community and its

[41]Richard, "Divine Purpose," 192-97.

[42]In terms of columns of occurrences in a concordance the evidence is overwhelming: Matthew 1½, Mark 1, Luke 2½, John 1¾, and Acts 4. One might say that God is the principal actor in the Lukan narratives.

leaders remain in the city, but as a result of events beyond its control, i.e., the great persecution that resulted from Stephen's death (8:1; 11:19), the community is forced out into Judaea and Samaria, thereby accomplishing the divine command of 1:8.

Luke's favorite term for expressing divine necessity is *dei*, translated as "it is necessary that " or "must, should, ought," a term which occurs no fewer than 41 times in Luke-Acts as compared to 61 times in the remainder of the New Testament. If the word is borrowed from Mark 8:31 for the first prediction of the passion (Luke 9:22), it then becomes a favorite Lukan expression. The term comes from ordinary speech and expresses the neutral necessity of the Hellenistic concept of fate. In the hands of biblical writers of an earlier period the term encompassed the concept of the personal will of a living God, i.e., a God who is in control of life, cosmic affairs, and human history and who gives them direction and purpose. This is Luke's idea of God, a Deity who intervenes in human affairs to achieve salvation for humanity. Luke, then, uses the term *dei* to underscore the wide variety of elements which make up the divine plan.[43] This is Luke's theology.

Luke, having borrowed this term from Mark, expanded its use in the gospel narrative to speak of Jesus doing God's work (2:49, even the child Jesus), of his ministry (4:43, addition to Mark), of the passion (9:22; 17:25; the first from Mark, the second added to Q material), to express the role of Judaism and the Law (11:42, etc.), of the Spirit (12:12), of Jerusalem (13:33), and to describe God's joy when confronted by human repentance. For this last usage one should consider 15:32, the conclusion of the parable of the two sons (prodigal son), where Luke presents the father as saying: "it was fitting [i.e., 'necessary,' *dei*] to make merry and be glad, for this your brother was dead, and is alive; he was lost, and is found." It is God's nature to rejoice in such circumstances. In Acts too the term is employed to relate a variety of persons and themes to the divine plan: fulfilment of scripture (1:16), eschatological aspect of Luke's christology (3:21), soteriology (4:12), and Paul's role in God's plan (9:6, 16; 19:21; 27:24).

Along with *dei* Luke employs other expressions for this concept: "necessary," "determined," "plan," "foreknowledge," "will," and "unless . . . you cannot." Luke also alludes to God's plan in the following ways:

---

[43]W. Grundmann, "*dei*," 2:22-24 in *TDNT*; see also Richard, "Divine Purpose: The Jews and the Gentile Mission," 192-94.

"it seemed good to the Holy Spirit and to us" (Acts 15:28), "he set his face to go to Jerusalem" (Luke 9:51) or "it cannot be that a prophet should perish away from Jerusalem" (13:33).

Luke sees the whole design of salvation history determined by "the definite plan and foreknowledge of God"(Acts 2:23), particularly by the role which Jesus plays on the human stage. God controls human events, directs their course, and sends agents to accomplish this plan. All facets of God's design Luke relates to divine necessity, a concept incorporating the Stoic idea of fate and the biblical notion of divine kingship. Luke saw God as the mover and the divine plan as the ultimate blueprint for human action. With the special hindsight of Christian faith and the natural gift of understanding the author of Luke-Acts envisioned the whole Christian experience as the working out of God's purpose with Jesus as agent, i.e., God's prophet and Son bringing God's salvation (in the gospel) and the risen, "absent" Lord continuing this task through his representatives (in Acts).

The dynamic structure of Luke's work is the unfolding and the working out of God's plan in an ambiguous human situation. Following the formative period of Israel's relationship with God, Luke saw the New Age dawning with the arrival of God's special envoy. The author has an all-encompassing view of the events or, as Luke puts it, "the things brought to fulfilment among us" (Luke 1:1—RSVmod). Luke interprets for a new generation God the Benefactor's eternal design for the salvation of the lowly, the children of faith.[44] But God, who does not operate alone, makes use of intermediaries[45] and Jesus is the agent par excellence, the one who performs God's mighty works. Thus, Luke's work finds its unity and dynamism in its presentation of the person and activity of Jesus Christ as the keystone of the divine plan for human salvation.

Luke has recounted the life of a marvelous individual, Jesus of Nazareth, and beyond this has related this unique episode of human history to a cosmic and indeed a divine scope. In the last days, in the person of the obedient servant Jesus, God has intervened in human history or "made a visitation." The verb "to visit" (*episkeptomai*), a rare Septuagint term which refers to the solemn Day of the Lord, is used on four occasions by Luke. It is used of John's role in Luke 1:68, of that of

[44]Kodell, "Luke's Theology of the Death of Jesus."
[45]Bovon, "L'importance des médiations dans le projet théologique de Luc."

Jesus' ministry in 7:16, of Jerusalem's destiny in 19:44, and of the divinely sanctioned Gentile mission in Acts 15:14. Of importance to us here is Luke's qualification of Jesus' actions among the chosen people by having them exclaim: "God has visited his people" (7:16). Jesus is God's gracious visitation to lay claim to what was lost. Likewise in 7:16 the people acclaim Jesus as prophet (also 9:8, 19; 24:19). The title of prophet takes on added importance for Luke who considers Jesus as the prophet who stands in the long succession of messengers of God. Jesus is the fulfilment of OT promises, greater than all the prophets, one who does God's will, revealer of God through preaching and power, one who brings salvation. His entire life, from birth to ascension, is the fulfilment of God's purpose, for his life is conditioned by the journey to Jerusalem (9:31, 51; 13:22, 33; 17:11; 18:31), where, after his death or "exodus" (9:31), he is to be received (9:51) at the right hand of God (Acts 2:33 and 7:55-56).[46] Further, Jesus is the righteous one who does God's will (2:49; 23:47), the one whose life and death is soteriologically conditioned, i.e., he has come to save what was lost (Luke 15 and 19:10). The Christ-event is framed by the concept of "the salvation of God" (from Luke 3:6 to Acts 28:28). Indeed, Jesus' whole life is considered redemptive by Luke, for it is this agent of God who has made possible universal salvation in the community of believers through the power of the Spirit.[47]

Theologically, it is the concept of divine visitation of and care for humanity through Jesus, God's intermediary, which provides the unity of Luke's vision and the basis for the continuity of salvation history (promise, fulfilment, actualization). Jesus is the Christ of God. When Peter responds to Jesus' question: "who do you say that I am?" it is important to note that Peter, in Luke, responds not simply "you are the Christ," as in Mark, but "the Christ of God" (9:20). This is not surprising since in the infancy narratives Luke has the Holy Spirit promise Simeon that he will "not see death before he had seen the Lord's Christ" (2:26). Other passages make the same claim (23:35; Acts 3:13, 18; 4:26, among others), namely, that Jesus' role is that of being God's promised agent. In fact repeatedly in Acts (5:42; 9:22; 17:3; 18:5, 28, especially in the kerygmatic speeches) the object of preaching and confession is the realization that "Jesus was the Christ" (9:22).

---

[46]Richard, "Luke—Writer, Theologian, Historian," 9.
[47]For a review of scholarship on Lukan christology, see Fitzmyer, *Luke*, 92-127.

With the first ascension story at the end of the gospel (24:50-53) the author, in the context of the resurrection appearances, brings to an end the earthly life of God's Christ. By means of the resurrection encounters the Lukan Jesus strengthens the faith of his followers and establishes them as witnesses and ministers of the universal mission.[48] The second ascension story in Acts,

> followed by the Pentecost episode, establishes Jesus in his heavenly abode and underscores the continuity between the time of Jesus and that of the church ... Jesus is Lord of heaven, where he will remain until his return, and Lord of the church ... From his abode at the right hand of the Father he acts on behalf of his people directly ... and especially through his word and the Holy Spirit ... The Spirit in turn empowers human mediators to act in Jesus' behalf ... [49]

Luke's portrait of Jesus is a unique and appealing one. If Lukan christology is central to the message of Luke-Acts, that same christology (the person, activity, and role of Jesus the Christ) is subsumed by Luke under the more fundamental rubric of theology. God's plan is the center and at the core of this plan is God's agent, the perfect human instrument whom God calls "my Beloved Son" (3:22), "my Son, my chosen One" (9:35). But most of all, for the author of Luke-Acts Jesus is "the Christ or Messiah of God."

---

[48]R.J. Dillon, "Easter Revelation and Mission Program in Luke 24:46-48," 240-70 in Durken, *Sin, Salvation, and the Spirit.*
[49]Richard, "Luke—Writer, Theologian, Historian," 9.

7

The Johannine Writings

This chapter focuses on several NT works classified as "Johannine." From early in Christian history four works, the Gospel of John, First, Second, and Third John, have been associated with an early disciple named John. Also sometimes linked with these in the past was the Book of Revelation, which scholars either dissociate from the Johannine corpus or postulate some remote connection with the Johannine community.

The Johannine Community and Its Literature

Study of the Johannine corpus affords us the opportunity to understand another major facet of NT theology. We will elucidate this particular community's founding, development, theology, and eventual disintegration, or in the words of R.E. Brown: "the life, loves, and hates of an individual church in New Testament times."[1] Central to this community's development were, on the one hand, its conception of who Jesus was, what he did, and what this meant for humanity and, on the other, the vicissitudes of its intellectual and cultural milieu and historical development. Both factors contributed significantly to that community's distinctive theological achievements and sociological/ideological disarray. Our study therefore will focus on its literature to gain a better understanding of the Johannine component of Christian history and theology, particularly its christology.

[1] *The Community of the Beloved Disciple: The Life, Loves, and Hates of an Individual Church in New Testament Times* (NY: Paulist, 1979).

Study reveals much theological diversity within the early church. Rather than speak of a NT theology, as was once fashionable, one does better to recognize a multiplicity of views concerning the Christ-event. Plurality not unity was the rule, since Jesus' acts and words meant different things to different groups of believers and since adherents to the Jesus movement represented much social, cultural, and ethnic diversity. Thus one can speak of many theologies: Synoptic thought consisting of the wide range of Markan, Matthean, and Lukan perspectives; Pauline theology represented by Paul's creative perspective and the later developments of his disciples (Colossians, Ephesians, and the Pastorals); and the theologies found in the disparate writings referred to as the catholic epistle (Hebrews, James, 1 Peter). Also one should speak of the apocalypticist strand of thought represented by the Q-Document, by the Paulinist 2 Thessalonians, by Jude, and by the final NT book, the Apocalypse. Beyond these, there were other communities which had their own theologies but left few written traces: communities mentioned in the New Testament, Syrian churches (later Syriac literature), Egyptian communities (second-century Greek and Coptic texts), and Judaeo-Christian and Samaritan groups that survived the catastrophic events of 70 A.D. The Johannine writings are basically the product of such a community and reflect that community's understanding of the Christ-event.

The community which produced and cherished the Fourth Gospel lived in a world all its own. It was a community whose history left profound traces upon the development of the Jesus tradition it used, upon the documents which it produced, and upon its interpretation of the Christ-event. Various currents of thought, social-political forces and events, as well as individuals had profound influence upon the Johannine corpus. At this point, we mention three factors which played a crucial role in the formation of the community's development: the traumatic expulsion of the Judaeo-Christian group from the synagogue, the seminal influence of wisdom speculation and Hellenistic thought upon the community, and the creative, formative role of the great Johannine theologian, preacher, writer.

This collection of Johannine works constitutes a body of literature whose affinities are discernible to the non-specialist. Their vocabulary, theology, and concerns are similar enough for them to be considered representative of a school of thought and the product of a distinct body of Christian believers in the years 80-120 A.D. These similarities constitute both the link which leads scholars to consider them a corpus and the distinctiveness which also compels them to contrast this group to other NT works. In effect, the Johannine writings contain a gospel, two genuine letters, and a theological treatise or pastoral document, genres which represent most NT literary types.

General Considerations
Concerning the Johannine Corpus

GENRE

The first work of the Johannine corpus to be considered, both in terms of time and importance, is the gospel. It is obviously related to the genre commonly called gospel, for it is a kind of life or biography of Jesus which tells about his deeds and words as well as the faith which these brought forth. Again we insist that John and the three Synoptics should be classified as biographical literature, since their closest literary analogues are the biographies of Greco-Roman literature.[2] Study of this vast narrative literature is enlightening for our understanding of the rhetoric and strategy both of the Synoptics and of John, since as first-century documents they subscribe to ancient historiographical conventions and goals. Interestingly, someone in the Johannine community selected a narrative with a time-line as genre to present the community's ideas and concerns; the writer might have chosen another literary form, such as the homily, the letter, or the theological tract. Regardless, the correct genre classification for the central Johannine document is the gospel since it shares the general narrative and compositional features of the Synoptics.

The second group of documents, First, Second, and Third John, is traditionally classified under the epistolary genre, a type of literature familiar to us both in every day life and from the New Testament. The letter is a document which a person writes to someone to convey a message; epistolary writers introduce themselves, state or defend their views in the body of the document, and send greetings. Letters, ancient

---

[2]On the genre of the gospels, see earlier the introduction to the Gospel of Mark, chapter 4.

or modern, therefore, usually contain three major divisions: greeting or introduction (salutation, identity, credentials, addressee), body carrying a message, and farewell or conclusion.[3] Second and Third John clearly belong to the epistolary genre.

First John is more problematic. Its genre has been described as an ethical letter, homily, religious tract, and catholic or pastoral epistle. Since it lacks an epistolary introduction and conclusion it should not be classified as a letter; and since it is addressed to a specific audience with defined purpose and problem in view, it does not fit the other categories. First John, some recent scholars suggest, might for want of a better classification be called a pastoral document written to Johannine communities concerning an ideological split and the ensuing controversy between the opposing factions. We conclude, therefore, that while First John has homiletic traits and sounds like a religious tract, it is a document written to a specific audience to address major pastoral and doctrinal problems.

JOHN AND THE OTHER GOSPELS

Since it is organized along a time-line, the Fourth Gospel demands comparison with the Synoptics. However, since the Synoptics are so close in order, episode, and style as opposed to John, attention must be given to the relationship of these documents. There are both significant resemblances and glaring differences between these two bodies of literature.[4] Since all four works are biographical in nature, we are not surprised to find similarities in their overall schema. 1) Like the Synoptics, John begins Jesus' public life with an encounter with John. Here in John there are references to Jesus' baptism (1:32) as well as to angels ministering to Jesus (1:51; see Mark 1:13). 2) John then introduces a scene wherein Jesus calls disciples to follow him and 3) presents Jesus' public ministry as beginning in Galilee. It might be noted that Jesus' home for the Synoptics is Nazareth, where reference is made to his mother, brothers, and sisters (Mark 6); for John it is Cana, where the reader meets his mother and brothers (2:1-12). The ministry in both consists of miraculous deeds (mostly healings), teaching, and conversations. In this part of the story there is a parallel series of Galilean

---

[3]For a more extensive discussion of the epistolary genre, see the introduction to the Pauline writings, chapter 8.

[4]Smith, *John*, 2-18, offers a short, informative discussion of this topic.

episodes: feeding of the crowd, stilling of the storm, and Peter's confession (John 6 and Mark 6 and 8). John also notes the opposition engendered by the Galilean ministry. 4) There follows a series of events in Jerusalem: arrest, trial, and death. In the city there occurs a last supper, whose Johannine version is very different and which is followed by unique farewell discourses. 5) There follows the resurrection narrative which begins with the discovery of the empty tomb and is supplemented by appearances to disciples in Jerusalem and Galilee. These structural similarities are both striking and extensive.

There are also episodes with parallels in the Synoptic tradition: the driving out of the money changers (2:13f), the healing of the official's son (4:43f), the loaves and storm sequence, the anointing of Jesus' feet (12:1f), and the triumphal entry (12:12f) leading to a series of Jerusalem ministry, arrest, passion, and death parallels. There are other less obvious comparisons, especially in the sayings material. These last, though not lengthy, are numerous and will require attention when we examine the composition of the gospel.

Comparisons between these texts also lead us to speak of differences, which are far greater than the similarities. While it may be difficult for the uninitiated to distinguish between passages from one of the Synoptics, it is usually simple to recognize a Johannine text, especially in relation to the Synoptics. The reason owes to the unique style of John. While in Mark there is considerable difference between Jesus' sayings and the gospel's narrative style, in John it is often difficult to distinguish the two. The Johannine author has greatly modified the materials employed. Further, the style of Jesus' sayings is similar in the three Synoptics but notably different from that of the Johannine Jesus. For example, Jesus speaks often of the kingdom of God in the first three gospels (the core of his message) but only twice in John. A major feature of the latter's composition is the "I Am" saying (Jesus calls himself: the way, the truth, and the life, the bread of life, the gate, the true vine), yet none of these occurs in the Synoptic gospels.

The Synoptics often speak of the Son of Man as a future apocalyptic figure; John rarely speaks of him as coming or as apocalyptic in a traditional sense. Nonetheless, the Son of Man plays a central role in John's christology. In the former, Jesus teaches in parables, the hallmark of his ministry; he speaks in short epigrammatic sayings ("give to Caesar," "the Son of Man did not come to serve"); he uses sharp, pithy language. None of these features are found in the latter. Instead, in John

Jesus speaks in elevated, poetic, sacred, and at times polemical tones. Familiar Synoptic stories about Jesus are not found in John, while the best-known Johannine narratives are missing in the Synoptics: the Cana (2:1f), Nicodemus (3:1f), and Samaritan (4:1f) stories; the long conversation with Pilate at the trial (18-19); and the Lazarus episode (11:1f).

There are major differences between these in regard to locale and chronology. In the Synoptics Jesus' ministry takes place in Galilee until the end when he goes up to the holy city to meet his death. In the Fourth Gospel he begins in Galilee but repeatedly goes to Jerusalem; in fact most of the gospel takes place in the city. In Mark Jesus takes one trip from Galilee to Jerusalem (10:1f); but in John he makes three journeys (2:13; 5:1; 7:10; see also 11:55). These geographical and chronological indicators point to a ministry of less than a year in Mark and of slightly longer duration in the Matthean and Lukan versions but of three years or more in the Fourth Gospel. Further, in the Synoptics Jesus cleanses the temple toward the end of his life, just prior to his arrest and death. In John the event is situated at the beginning of Jesus' ministry (2:13f). In the former, this religio-political act seems related to the death sentence, while in the latter the event has purely theological significance. In John it is the raising of Lazarus from the dead (11:1f) which serves a purpose and claims a place similar to that of the temple cleansing in the Synoptics. One last item of chronology should be noted; in Mark and parallels Jesus takes his last meal with his disciples on Friday, thus at a Passover meal, yet in John the meal occurs on Thursday, and instead Jesus dies in relation to the Passover, i.e., at the time when the lambs are sacrificed. Of importance here are the theological and not the historical implications of the gospel writers' chronology.[5]

Serious also are the different perspectives which the two bodies of literature present of the Jesus movement, of Jesus himself, of Judaism, of faith, and of the Christian message. The Synoptics present Jesus as a Palestinian Jew who is the fulfilment of the Jewish and Christian concept of the Messiah, while in John he is usually in opposition to the Jews. He is more Christian than Jewish and is quite distinct from "the Jews." In fact, in the first three gospels Jesus' dealings with the Jewish people and leaders are far less violent then in John where the religious authorities are his bitter and irreconcilable opponents. This writer then

[5]For chronological issues confer Finegan, *Handbook of Biblical Chronology*, 285-98.

is considerably more influenced by the community's situation, especially the Jewish-Christian conflict, when writing about Jesus than are Matthew, Mark, and Luke. Also, in the latter the disciple is pictured as following Jesus during the days remaining in this age while waiting for the imminent arrival of God's kingdom; in the former, the kingdom is no longer central nor at hand. Instead, the disciple is presented as one who enters eternal life now through union with Jesus.

PROBLEMS OF AUTHORSHIP

These dissimilarities underscore the differences in theological perspective between the Johannine and other Christian communities. The Fourth Gospel and its uniqueness are a reflection of a community that was also different and unique. While the Gospel of John is a mirror in which one can see the Johannine church, it is also a complex document whose background requires much attention, particularly in regard to the problem of authorship. It will be our goal to consider the factors which point to a school or community of authors,[6] factors which will then serve as the basis for a developmental theory of composition involving all the documents of the Johannine corpus.

The Fourth Gospel, like the Synoptics, makes no claim of authorship. Of interest in this regard is the mysterious figure known as "the beloved disciple" or "the disciple whom Jesus loved" (John 13:23; 19:26; 20:2; 21:7, 20; see also 1:40 and 18:15f). While on two occasions, 19:35 and 21:24, one might raise the question of authorship, it seems best to see these passages as stressing the authority of apostolic witness for the story of Jesus. First John has no superscription and nowhere mentions an author, so John and First John are anonymous. Lastly, Second and Third John identify "the elder" (*presbyteros*) as their author.

From such data later tradition, beginning explicitly with Irenaeus of Lyons (c. 180 A.D.), initiated a series of identifications: "Then John, the disciple of the Lord, who had even rested on his breast, himself also gave forth ['published'] the gospel, while he was living at Ephesus in Asia" (Against Heresies 3:1:1). Elsewhere Irenaeus also says that when he was a boy he had seen Polycarp (c. 69-155 A.D.), who had talked about his conversations "with John and with the others who had seen the Lord"

---

[6]R.A. Culpepper, *The Johannine School: An Evaluation of the Johannine School Hypothesis Based on an Investigation of the Nature of Ancient Schools* (Missoula: Scholars, 1976).

(Irenaeus' letter to Florinus).[7] We therefore arrive at the following schema:

    c. 100 John and Polycarp

    c. 145 Polycarp (c. 76) and Irenaeus (c. 15)—35 years earlier

    180 Irenaeus (c. 50)—writing of Against Heresies.

Later tradition added to the above identifications; based on Papias' work or a related tradition, writers spoke of an elder named John and presumed he was John the Apostle.[8] Further, since the Book of Revelation identifies its author as John, it was an easy correlation to make; John, the son of Zebedee, the apostle, the one whom Jesus loved, also known as the elder, wrote the whole Johannine corpus, including the last book of the New Testament.

While the above correlations could be discussed in detail, it suffices to offer a few critical observations. Irenaeus has been proven wrong on the topic of Papias being "a hearer of John," for Papias bishop of Hieropolis (c. 140 A.D.), himself never says he was "a hearer of John" and further distinguishes between the Apostle and an elder named John, neither of whom he seems to have known personally. Thus, on the basis of Irenaeus' witness it is impossible to maintain that the authors of the gospel and of Second and Third John are one individual named John, the apostle and elder. Further, while there is no reason to doubt that the author of Revelation was named John, we must also note that the author did not claim to be an apostle, i.e., one of the twelve (see 18:20; 21:14). Finally, a series of considerations (the seemingly non-historical character of the "disciple whom Jesus loved," the fourth evangelist's lack of interest in the sons of Zebedee, and the lack of corroboration from NT and other early writers for an Ephesian residence for John) leads us to conclude that the attempt to relate the entire Johannine corpus and the Book of Revelation to John the Apostle represents fanciful defense of apostolic witness rather than historical reminiscence. From the Johannine writings themselves we can discern the community's stress upon eyewitness testimony (John and 1 John), the symbolic role played by the beloved disciple, the editorial and developmental nature

---

[7] Both citations are supplied by Eusebius, Eccles. History 5:8:4 and 5:20:6 respectively; confer K. Lake et al, eds, *Eusebius: The Ecclesiastical History* (Cambridge: Harvard University, 1965).

[8] See Eusebius, Eccles. History 3:37:1-17 for the Papias traditions and Kümmel, *Introduction to the New Testament*, 239-46, for an estimate of ecclesiastical tradition regarding Johannine authorship.

of the gospel as well as First John's dialogical relationship to it, the multiplicity of authorship and style of these books, and the community of ideas between these writings. Thus, in our effort to gain a better understanding of the entire corpus, we will examine recent scholarship on the problems of authorship and composition, with special attention given to the gospel.

Composition of the Fourth Gospel

JOHN'S USE OF SOURCES

There exist in John data which scholars routinely subject to source and redaction analysis. Among these we note the following. 1) 2:11 and 4:54 mention the first and second signs performed by Jesus. Presumably John used a source that once enumerated Jesus' signs. 2) The similarities with the Synoptics will need further attention. 3) Since the first part of the gospel (chaps. 1-12) and the final discourse section (13-17) are arranged in relation to Jewish feasts and since these are related to long speeches, one might postulate a discourse source. 4) There are in John several textual displacements or *aporias* which suggest either accidental mix-up of manuscript pages or clumsy, later editing.

A few examples of the last mentioned are in order. a) 3:22-30 (about John's baptism) seems out of place since it interrupts the Nicodemus discourse. If placed between 2:12 and 13 the itinerary would be improved: Capharnaum (2:12), Judaea (3:22), and Jerusalem (2:13). b) A similar situation occurs in regard to chapter 6 since one goes from Jerusalem at the end of chapter 5 to an unmotivated crossing of the Sea of Galilee in the first verse of chapter 6. Again, transfer of a block of material (chap. 6 placed between chaps. 4 and 5) improves the geographical sequence. c) We note a final example concerning texts related in topic and argument but separated in a seemingly awkward fashion, e.g., 7:15-24 which might be situated after 5:47.

We turn to some of the issues raised above, the first of which concerns John's relation to the Synoptics. In explaining the similarities between John and the other gospels, it was standard procedure in the past to assume the author's use of Mark. In 1938, however, the work of P. Gardner-Smith turned the tide so that the independence of the fourth evangelist became almost universally accepted.[9] The similarities between these writers were explained in terms of oral tradition. However, C.K. Barrett, among major Johannine scholars, continues to defend John's use of the Synoptics.[10] His extensive discussion of the similarities between the Fourth Gospel and the Synoptics though falling short of proving literary dependence does stress a common base for them in early Jesus tradition. It is particularly the examination of the pre-literary stage of the tradition which attracts the attention of scholars, for it is at that level that contacts between John and the Synoptic materials seem most likely. One can presume that prior to the composition of the Fourth Gospel, the community employed an oral or written version of the Jesus tradition.

Convinced that John was independent of the Synoptics, R. Bultmann proposed in 1941 that the fourth evangelist employed three sources in composing the gospel: a sign source (*Semeia-Quelle*) consisting of miracle stories, a revelatory or discourse source (*Offenbarungsreden Quelle*) concerning a Gnostic redeemer, and a special passion-resurrection narrative. The last continues to be the object of much study since it bears many similarities and dissimilarities to Synoptic parallels. Conclusions in this regard, however, are determined by the posture scholars take vis-à-vis composition of the gospel generally. Bultmann's revelatory discourse source, the linchpin of his Gnostic interpretation of John, has generated much debate which led to the rejection of his source and theory. It should be noted that discussion of Gnosticism in Johannine studies is usually related to Bultmann's proposal.

It is particularly the sign source which has received attention and scholarly elaboration. Owing to its prominence in the scholarly literature and its acceptance among some Johannine scholars it merits further treatment. Several scholars, noting the importance signs have for John 2-12, proceed through literary and form analysis to isolate what they consider a pre-Johannine miracle source in terms of content and theology, and attempt through redactional study to examine the

---

[9]*John and the Synoptic Gospels* (London: Cambridge University, 1938).

[10]C.K. Barrett, *The Gospel According to St. John* (Philadelphia: Westminster, 1978; already in 1955). See also D.M. Smith, *Johannine Christianity: Essays on Its Setting, Sources, and Theology* (Columbus: University of South Carolina, 1984) 97-172.

Johannine writer's use of this alleged sign source.[11] Such a theory has many weaknesses. First, it is crucial to answer the following question: why should the admittedly creative fourth evangelist employ at length and in detail such an uncongenial source? Secondly, on the level of methodology, the linguistic and stylistic criteria used to isolate such a source are the most subject to criticism, for these are inadequate and lead to overly subjective reconstructions of the source. Instead linguistic study, originally formulated as a critique of Bultmann's proposals, convincingly demonstrates that there exists in John unity of style and argues strongly against much recent work done on the source.[12]

DEVELOPMENTAL THEORIES

Study of the Fourth Gospel has not been limited to source considerations. Some scholars have attended to the overall process which produced this text, among others, R.E. Brown and B. Lindars.[13] These scholars, along with source critics, recognize in John many incongruities of geography, plot, narrative sequence, style, and theology. Such puzzles lead them to seek the answer to the composition of the Fourth Gospel in complex but similar developmental processes:[14]

Brown	Lindars
1. Oral traditions	1. Traditions and sources
2. Traditions developed into Johannine patterns	2. Homilies
3. First edition of gospel	3. First edition of gospel

[11]Two names which figure prominently in this research are R.T. Fortna, *The Gospel of Signs: A Reconstruction of the Narrative Source Underlying the Fourth Gospel* (London: Cambridge University, 1970) and W. Nicol, *The Semeia in the Fourth Gospel: Tradition and Redaction* (Leiden: Brill, 1972), whose methodology, goals, and achievements are examined at length by R. Kysar, *The Fourth Evangelist and His Gospel: An Examination of Contemporary Scholarship* (Minneapolis: Augsburg, 1975) 17-37.

[12]See for example, E. Ruckstuhl, "Johannine Language and Style: The Question of Their Unity," 127-47 in M. De Jonge, ed., *L'évangile de Jean: sources, rédaction, théologie* (Gembloux: Duculot, 1977). On the sign source, see E. Richard, "Expressions of Double Meaning and Their Function in the Gospel of John," *NTS* 31 (1985) 105-7; *contra* Smith, *Johannine Christianity*, 62-93.

[13]R.E. Brown, *The Gospel According to John* (NY: Doubleday, 1966-70) and B. Lindars, *The Gospel of John* (Grand Rapids: Eerdmans, 1981).

[14]The comparative schema is given by Kysar, *The Fourth Evangelist and His Gospel*, 49.

4. Second edition of gospel   4. Second edition of gospel
5. Additions of "friendly   5. "Post-Johannine additions."
   redactor."

Each has discussed his theory at length and applied it in an extended commentary. Significantly, they agree on many points. They stress both the oral character of the Jesus tradition inherited by the Johannine community and its relation to Synoptic materials at the pre-literary level, stage one in both cases. Both also insist on successive editions and later additions to the gospel to explain many of its incongruities and its unique blend of traditional and highly Johannine material, stages 3, 4, and 5. Brown, however, insists upon the traditional association of John son of Zebedee with the developing tradition, stages 1 and 2, and ascribes the creative work of composition to the beloved disciple, stage 3. Prior to this level Brown sees the creative development of the tradition into Johannine patterns by what he describes as a "Johannine school" from which there emerged the principal writer and thinker who composed the gospel and later saw the need for another edition, stages 3 and 4.

Lindars, on the other hand, shies away from connecting the Johannine traditions with any apostolic figure, even the shadowy beloved disciple. His most original contribution to the understanding of Johannine composition relates to stages 2 and 3. An important figure of the community, according to Lindars, creatively employed the Jesus tradition, which existed in isolated oral, and perhaps short written, fragments to compose homilies or sermons for the community, stages 1 and 2.[15] These pastoral compositions, bearing the rhetorical marks of such productions (dramatic effect, emotional appeal, aggressive logic, and attempts at persuasion), were so successful that the preacher was persuaded to become an evangelist, stage 3. Here Lindars posits the influence of Mark as genre—the author knew about but was not influenced by the content of Mark—upon the fourth evangelist who in turn produced a gospel from homiletic notes. Later, because of changed circumstances within and outside the community, a new edition was required, an edition which occasioned the addition of several new

[15]See the seminal work of P. Borgen, *Bread from Heaven: An Exegetical Study of the Concept of Manna in the Gospel of John and the Writings of Philo* (Leiden: Brill, 1965), on the homiletic character of John 6.

narratives and the dislocation of others: prologue, cleansing of temple, bread of life discourse, Lazarus episode, anointing at Bethany, and sections of the supper discourse, stage 4. The special character of the Fourth Gospel, according to Lindars, is therefore owing to the preacher-evangelist of the Johannine community.

What can one say about such developmental approaches? At best, these assist the reader of the Johannine text to make sense of the gospel's incongruities and plausibly explain its problems and, at worst, such proposals remain hypothetical. Nonetheless, we should stress the following points of agreement.

1) Ultimately the gospel tradition employed by the Johannine community comes from apostolic times, however one explains the process of transmission. This material had its origin in the events of Jesus' life as communicated, preached, and preserved by early disciples, much as happened in other strands of the tradition. Additionally, owing to the state of our evidence attempts to identify the apostolic guarantor or tradents of this material are no more than conjecture.

2) The development of the tradition proceeded in two dynamic ways. On the one hand, there was a sense of fidelity to and a keen use of the tradition in support of Johannine theology. Stories about Jesus were preserved; his sayings were employed; and new situations and a developing theology generated new, and modified old, material to meet the community's needs. In fact, this tendency explains the choice which a member of this community made in writing a gospel or biography of Jesus rather than a christological tract. Interest in the Jesus tradition as the basis for the community's theology and existence was paramount for this group.[16] On the other hand, there developed active and original reflection on the meaning of the Christ-event in the divine plan, that is, Jesus as the revealer, Son of God, and source of union with the Father, as well as the community of believers as the intimates of the Father through faith in Jesus and love of the brethren.

3) Scholars see in this text evidence for proposing several crucial factors in the evolution of the Johannine community and its literature. It is agreed that the gospel has a very Jewish character but also exhibits a polemical attitude toward Judaism. Its Jewish origin and the expulsion

---

[16]This would agree with Neyrey's suggestion that the first stage in the community's development would have consisted of a "missionary christology" focused upon Jesus' saving activity and therefore upon his life and ministry, *Christ Is Community*, 144-51.

from the synagogue are credited for these characteristics. Additionally, the gospel exhibits an interesting mixture of Jewish and Greek ideas. These are often attributed to the influence of heterodox Judaism (akin to that of Qumran and other intertestamental literature), of Rabbinic thought, of wisdom speculation (Palestinian and Hellenistic Jewish as well as Hellenistic religio-philosophical currents of thought), and of mystery or salvation religions (Isis and other mystery cults, especially their sacramental and proto-Gnostic concepts).[17] This intricate constellation of ideas, as is often suggested, owes not only to the author's background but also to the mixed character of the community itself, for the gospel suggests that its membership included a variety of adherents: orthodox members of the synagogue, Hellenistic and other heterodox Jews, disciples of John (the Baptist), Samaritans, and probably some Gentiles.[18]

4) The Gospel of John, however, despite the aporias in its geography and organization, exhibits a unity of style, a consistency of thought, and a homiletic and dialectical character throughout. Whether this tradition was centered around John the apostle (rather improbable) or around a less defined disciple of importance (the beloved disciple?), a dominant mind lent its imprint to the Jesus tradition and as a consequence it was formed into theology and spirituality which attracted adherents who lived as a Spirit-inspired community under this charismatic leadership. Swayed by the philosophical and religious thought of the community's milieu and deeply affected by its checkered relationship with the synagogue, this Johannine theologian developed a unique perspective upon the Christ-event which dominated and directed the evolution of the community itself.

We believe that Lindars' work provides much insight for a challenging understanding of the Fourth Gospel, particularly his suggestion that John was first a preacher or homilist and then an evangelist. Thus, supplemented by structural considerations, theological sensitivity, religio-historical insight, persistent study of the Johannine community's make-up, and by other contributions of recent scholarship, such a homilist/evangelist theory of composition helps us appreciate the

---

[17]See particularly C.H. Dodd, *The Interpretation of the Fourth Gospel* (London: Cambridge University, 1953).

[18]Brown, *The Community of the Beloved Disciple.*

uniqueness, evolution, theology, and literature of one of early Christianity's most distinctive communities.[19]

SURFACE AND DYNAMIC STRUCTURAL COMPONENTS

The Fourth Gospel's surface structure consists of five fairly independent blocks of material.[20] The first extends through chapter 1 and consists of two sections: a poetic prologue (1-18) and a preparatory narrative concerning John and Jesus (19-51). The second block which encompasses chapters 2-12 is a section designated the book of signs[21] wherein the author by means of various acts and sayings brings the story's hero into confrontation with a large array of audiences in order to provoke commitment or opposition to Jesus on the part of the reader. The third block, called the book of glory, overlaps with chapter 12, is introduced by the foreboding episodes of the first half of chapter 13, and extends through the farewell discourses (13-17). Thus, after the public challenge to the audiences of Palestine (chaps. 2-12), Jesus directs his attention in this section to those who have followed him (see 1:11-12). A fourth block, whose content and character is similar to the Synoptic tradition, consists of the arrest, trial, passion, death, and resurrection (18-20). For John also the death and resurrection or kerygma remains central to an understanding of the Christ-event. The final block of material, chapter 21, is an addition to the original document and, though Johannine in style and theme, does not fit into the structure of the story.

Other indications of surface structure involve themes and literary conventions. In the first case, John makes extensive use of Jewish feasts to organize the life of the master. Reference has been made to John's threefold use of the Passover festival to structure the ministry and to make a theological point concerning Jesus' death. Within chapters 5-10 one finds the following Jewish references: Sabbath (5), Passover (6), Tabernacles (7), and Dedication (10). John also employs Christian

---

[19]Confer especially: Dodd, *The Interpretation of the Fourth Gospel*; R. Bultmann, *The Gospel of John* (Philadelphia: Westminster, 1971); R. Schnackenburg, *The Gospel According to St John* (NY: Crossroad, 1968-82); Barrett, *John*; J.L. Martyn, *History and Theology in the Fourth Gospel* (Nashville: Abingdon, 1979); Brown, *John*; and Lindars, *John*.

[20]More generally on plot development in John, see Culpepper, *Anatomy of the Fourth Gospel*, 86-98.

[21]Dodd, *The Interpretation of the Fourth Gospel*.

themes around which to organize the life of Jesus. From chapter 13 on, the structuring mechanism is the last supper and following this, chapters 18f, the kerygmatic themes of death and resurrection. As regards literary conventions, John employs the post-meal farewell discourse, well known from OT and intertestamental literature, to allow Jesus directly to address the concerns of the Johannine community. This series of discourses is concluded by a sublime prayer by Jesus, another convention related to farewell speeches in Jewish literature of the intertestamental period.

The dynamic structural indicators of John are equally complex and diverse. We begin by noting the homiletic method descerned by Lindars for chapter 5: "5:1 is an editorial note to maintain the narrative sequence, and the homily begins at verse 2. It consists of an opening sign (2-9a), a transitional dialogue (9b-18), the discourse (19-47), and a closing dialogue (7.15-24)."[22] A number of passages, whether homiletic in character or not, offer this organizational structure. An initial saying or episode from the Jesus tradition is connected to a discourse by a narrative link, usually in the form of a dialogue (see chap. 6). In some instances the author extends the dialogue at some length (Nicodemus story, chap. 3) or replaces the discourse by an extended dialogue (Samaritan episode, chap. 4) or by a dialogue in the form of a trial (the man born blind, chap. 9). The great Johannine theologian, therefore, is more than a homilist turned evangelist; this author was also one who, engaged in Christian-synagogue dialogue and eventual recrimination, composes exchanges between representatives of Judaism and Jesus, the voice of the Johannine community.

In other instances John alternates highly redacted blocks of Jesus tradition with extensive use of dialogue to review major christological titles (1:19-51), with saying and narrative material to underscore Jesus' relation to Judaism and to God (chaps. 7-8), or with judicial and plebeian dialogue within a dramatic two-stage setting to speak about his kingship (18:28-19:16). In composing both narratives and discourses the author makes frequent and compelling use of misunderstanding techniques (statement, misunderstanding, and clarification), expressions of double meaning, irony, "antithesis, verbal links through key-words, concatenation of ideas by means of recourse to earlier ones, *inclusio* whereby the thought is brought back to its starting-point, parallelism

[22]Lindars, *John*, 52.

and variation."[23] These techniques are put at the service of the author's revelatory purpose. One may not wish to conclude that "John is almost certainly a work which 'bursts the limits of rhetoric as known' previously"[24] or that it is a literary masterpiece, but one can appreciate the long-range influence which that composition had both on the Johannine community and on later theological development. Whether through effective use of climax, dialectical presentation of themes, or other rhetorical devices, the Gospel of John effectively brings into focus the dynamics of revelation and also brings about the development from a low to a high christology.

The Johannine Concept of Jesus

In trying to comprehend John's understanding of Jesus, it must be kept in mind that what he meant for the community was even more crucial. John, like the other evangelists, was committed not only to the meaning of the Christ-event but also to the story itself. John, in effect, wrote a gospel, a highly unusual one but a gospel nonetheless, to present a new portrait of the risen Lord, that is, a narrative of what that Lord said and did during his earthly sojourn. So we direct our attention to the two foci of John's composition: the earthly figure who dwells and acts in the world (a man who is nonetheless Lord and Messiah) and the heavenly figure who descends from and returns to God, leaving behind a special envoy, the Spirit. We deal then with the dialectical presentation which John makes of the low christology inherited from the tradition and the evolving high christology of the community. It was by writing about Jesus of Nazareth that John undertook to examine the meaning of that life, namely, that by believing that Jesus was both Messiah and unique Son of God all might experience eternal life with the Father (20:31).

THE HUMAN FIGURE

Of capital importance was John's decision to compose a life of Jesus. This fundamental option determined the work's content and method of

---

[23]Schnackenburg, *John,* 1:115-16; Culpepper, *Anatomy of the Fourth Gospel,* 152-98; Richard, "Expressions of Double Meaning," 96-112; and P.D. Duke, *Irony in the Fourth Gospel* (Atlanta: John Knox, 1985).

[24]Culpepper, *Anatomy of the Fourth Gospel,* 9.

procedure. While containing highly peculiar discourses of a non-Synoptic type, the Gospel of John is nonetheless organized along a recognizable time-line wherein Jesus acts and speaks on a human stage. He travels about Palestine, has human needs, and is affected by the vicissitudes of human existence. It is particularly his deeply human relationship to those about him (negative toward the Jewish authorities and eloquently positive toward his disciples and friends) and the stark events of the passion which stand out in this gospel.

In the same breath one must grant that Jesus is less human-like in John than in the Synoptics. If he has taken on human existence (1:14a), John's emphasis is upon his glory and not his human vicissitudes (1:14b; 2:11). Jesus possesses such intimacy with the Father that prayer is both unnecessary and, when considered in the story-line, a charade, since his prayer to the Father is not one of request or praise but for the benefit of the crowd (11:42). The same can be said of Jesus' knowledge and power since he knows the answer before he asks the question (6:6) and controls human events by his word (18:6 and 19:30). Further, one contrasts the moving, suppliant prayer of the Markan Jesus (14:36) to that of the Johannine character, who, brushing aside human considerations, is single-mindedly devoted to the Father's glorification (12:27).[25] Despite this attempt to compose a vita, the author has reduced in human verisimilitude the story's principal hero, and *dramatis personae* generally.[26] Jesus has become a transparent vehicle for christology and certain attributes mitigate against his appearing fully human.

One gets the impression, however, that the less than human treatment of Jesus in the Fourth Gospel owes more to the author's weakness as narrator, i.e., poor character portrayal and too great a concern for high christology, than to a docetic posture. For John the facts of Jesus' life and his sayings form the basis for Christian commitment, for they are either the signs which point to a greater reality or they are the source of heavenly wisdom. If the facts about Jesus, in the later stages of the evolution of Johannnie thought, are no more than prelude to the real drama of the Christ-event, they are nonetheless the foundation of that community's commitment and of its presentation of its beliefs. However, even within the Johannine community, there were some who did not

[25]See Brown, *The Community of the Beloved Disciple*, 114-16.

[26]Culpepper, *Anatomy of the Fourth Gospel*, 105-48, offers a good study of Johannine character portrayal.

view the situation in the same way, thereby compelling the evangelist to stress some human details of the ministry (e.g., 4:6-7; 20:27) in order to counter notions that Jesus was a purely spiritual being (early docetism) or that created reality was lacking in goodness (incipient Gnosticism). That such was the case is borne out both by the evolution of the Johannine community and its later history.

JESUS AS LORD AND MESSIAH

John inherited from the tradition a variety of christological concepts. Few of the titles familiar to us from the Synoptics are missing in this gospel,[27] since it makes generous use of these in its narratives and discourses. The concept of messiahship, expressed as Christ, prophet, king, Son of God, and the one sent, is taken over by John as a major theme. Messianic language pervades the story, for this writer speaks more frequently of the Messiah than do the other evangelists. Chapter 1 is directed to the theme of messiahship. The gospel story begins with a Jerusalem delegation to John (the Baptist). The burning question is: "who are you?" (vv. 19, 22). This theme, when applied to Jesus, is one of the principal concerns of the gospel. In solemn language (v. 20) John rejects for himself three messianic titles: Christ, Elijah, and prophet. He tells his questioners that he is a preparatory voice for the coming one (v. 23). John's role is represented by the fourth evangelist—as indeed by the other gospel writers—as pre-messianic. He is sent by God (messianic terminology) to witness to and prepare for a greater one (1:6, 15; 3:28). These three denials lead to two confessions about Jesus and a promise to the disciples later in the same chapter. From former disciples of John one hears that Jesus is the Messiah (41), the one promised by Moses and the prophets (45).

While some insist that allusions to Elijah have been eliminated by the evangelist,[28] it is best to view the issue raised about Elijah in verses 21 and 25 as corresponding to the promise made to Nathanael in v. 50: "you shall see greater things than these." The evangelist refers to the signs that are to follow and contrasts Jesus with the OT miracle worker, for in 7:31 the people remark: "When the Christ appears, will he do more signs than this man had done?" i.e., Jesus as Christ is a greater

---

[27]As for example: son of David, though see 7:42.

[28]J.L. Martyn, "We Have Found Elijah," 46-48 in *The Gospel of John in Christian History: Essays for Interpreters* (NY: Paulist, 1978).

wonder worker than Elijah. The episode, excluding v. 51, concludes with a messianic confession by Nathanael: "Rabbi, you are the Son of God! You are the King of Israel" (49). The expression, Son of God, is a messianic title here as it is partially in the Jesus tradition, i.e., it alludes to the royal messianic hope, as John indicates. Its use in the context of Jesus' baptism (1:32-34) as in the Synoptic tradition (Mark 1:11 and parallels) suggests an even wider application of the epithet. The other title, concerning Jesus' kingship, will be developed at length in the passion narrative. Chapter 1, therefore, in a manner reminiscent of Mark 6:14-15 and 8:27-29, is a developmental treatment of christology. The author employs John and his disciples to speak about the nature of Jesus' messiahship and, by means of the double meaning term "to follow" (1:37, 38, 40, 43) in a narrative context, to exemplify the concept of discipleship as acceptance of Jesus' messiahship.[29]

The theme of messiahship receives additional focus in the Samaritan episode where Jesus accepts the title as applied to himself (4:25-26, 29). As the messianic titles of chapter 1 are developed in a polemical context (negative treatment of John and his categorical rejection of any messianic claims) and treated dialectically, so this new episode, situated on the double stage of Jacob's well and the city of Sychar, sets up a situation where the author, through a complex dialogue replete with irony and misunderstanding techniques, leads the characters to confess Jesus progressively as "gift of God," "prophet," "Messiah and Christ," and finally "Savior of the world" (4:10, 19, 25, 42). Again, one notes the polemical thrust of the episode when Jesus states that both Jerusalem of the Jews and Gerizim of the Samaritans are being replaced as place of worship to the Father (4:21-24). It is precisely as Messiah that Jesus fulfils this new role (4:25-26; also 2:19-22).

For chapter 7 John reserves more material dealing with messianic speculation. In a complex section of the gospel stretching from 7:1 to 8:59 the author in the final edition of the document uses source materials either about messianic speculation and Jewish polemics or consisting of dialogue material and fragments of Jesus tradition in order to discourse about Jesus' relation to Judaism and to God. It is the source material concerning messianic speculation (probably developed at an

[29]Richard, "Expressions of Double Meaning," 100 and more generally F.F. Segovia, "'Peace I Leave You; My Peace I Give to You': Discipleship in the Fourth Gospel," 76-102 in Segovia, *Discipleship in the New Testament.*

earlier stage) which interests us here, namely, 7:11-13, 25-31, and 40-44. Structurally the three passages, after a typical Johannine opening with Jesus material (7:1-10), are introduced by teaching statements (6-8, 16-19, and 37-38) and form a progressive series of discussions among the people about Jesus' messiahship. Before his arrival in the city some in the crowd consider Jesus to be "a good man" while others view him as a trouble maker (7:12). After his arrival and dialogue with the Jews about the Sabbath and Moses' Law, there occurs further speculation about Jesus. Employing tongue-in-cheek irony John has some of the people ask "can it be that the authorities really know that this is the Christ?" (26). In Johannine fashion, the statement leads to discussion of Jesus' origin and further confession; Jesus is like the Christ "for when the Christ appears, will he do more signs than this man has done?" (31). Further into the discussion some confess Jesus to be the prophet or the Christ (40-41); but there is dissension as still others object once again to Jesus' (Galilean) origin (41-42). The discussion of the remainder of chapters 7-8 mounts to a higher christological level as John addresses Jesus' relation to the Father.

Several passages which refer to Jesus as Messiah deserve attention because of their polemical context and relation to the community's traumatic separation from the synagogue. The first two occur in discussions of Jesus' identity as Messiah (10:24) or about the nature of that messiahship, i.e., its relation to John's developing higher christology (12:34). The third, while appearing in a passage dealing with an emerging high christology, captures nonetheless the ideological dilemma of the early community, whose members, represented by the formerly-blind-man's parents, are confronted by the threat "that if any one should confess [Jesus] to be Christ, he was to be put out of the synagogue" (9:22). Two final passages, 11:27 (Martha's confession) and 20:31 (conclusion of the gospel) will be discussed below in relation to the title "Son of God" and in the final discussion of John's high christology.

The title of prophet is also retained by John to qualify Jesus' messiahship. As John is emphatically not to be identified as such (1:21 and 25) so Jesus is the prophet about whom Moses and the prophets wrote (1:45). Further, in dialectical passages Jesus, in a series of confessional statements, is given this title (4:19; 6:14; 7:40; 9:17) and in an additional discussion about his origin is denied this title by his Jewish enemies (7:52).

While the kingship motif is mentioned several times in the first half of the gospel (1:49; 6:15; 12:13, 15) it is extensively treated in the trial scene. Employing a two-stage technique with seven alternating outdoor and indoor scenes, John treats Jesus' kingship as a major messianic motif. Jesus, indeed, is king for that is his role and mission (18:37). But John insists in parallel scenes that both Jesus' kingship (18:36) and the royal power exercised by Pilate on Caesar's behalf are from heaven (19:11). In vignettes reminiscent of the Synoptic trial and mockery episodes, John emphasizes the royal nature of the messiahship since Jesus is frequently acknowledged and declared "king of the Jews" (18:39; 19:3, 19, 21) by all the characters of the story except, ironically, the Jewish crowd.[30] "It is the special use of the term 'king' which allows the evangelist to present Jesus' kingship both as mockery ('Behold your king'—and irony) and as fulfilment of the title announced in 1:49 by Nathanael and by the crowds of Jerusalem ('King of Israel' [12:13])."[31]

Also having a bearing upon Jesus' messiahship and requiring our attention are two participial constructions and a verbal expression: "the one coming/who is to come" (*ho erchomenos*), "the one who sent" (*ho pempsas*), and "to send" (*apostellō*). The first is employed with messianic titles such as prophet (6:14), Lord, Christ, and Son of God (11:27) and king of Israel (12:13; also 6:15), and in relation to John's role (1:15, 27) or even in a discussion of high christology (3:31). The second and third, drawn from traditional agency christology, shed light on the evolution of the community's thinking. The author favored an agency model for discussing Jesus' role in God's plan, since the verb *apostellō* ("send," see Mark 9:37) is used no fewer than 17 times to express God's action in sending the Son or Jesus into the world (e.g., 3:17; 5:36; 17:3). Jesus' soteriological role (3:17; 6:37), function as witness (5:36f), and relation to the Father (5:38; 8:42) are thereby stressed as the author dwells upon Jesus' significance for the community. John also employs a less common term, *pempō* ("to send"; see Rom. 8:3), to express this concept. While often used as a synonym of the former (e.g., 20:21), the participial use of this verb becomes for the Johannine author a theological title, for God is regularly referred to as "the one who sent me" (4:34f). Agency christology, with its pneumatic (14:26; 15:26; 16:7) and missionary (4:38;

---

[30]G.W. MacRae, "Theology and Irony in the Fourth Gospel," 91 in R.J. Clifford and G.W. MacRae, eds, *The Word in the World* (Cambridge: Weston, 1973).

[31]Richard, "Expressions of Double Meaning," 99.

13:20; 17:18; 20:21) implications,[32] therefore, figured prominently in the middle stages of the author's evolving thought.

While the sonship theme of John's Gospel is more complex and therefore difficult to understand, it seems that the expression "Son of God" often retains its early messianic sense. In the context of Jesus' baptism (as in Mark 1:11), John bears witness that Jesus is Son of God. Later in the chapter Nathanael confesses him Son of God and King of Israel, thereby associating the title with royal messianism. Several passages (5:25; 11:4, 27) retain the connotations of an exaltation christology where the title Son of God is related to the resurrection, although these and similar references to "Son," "only Son," and even "only Son of God" (3:18) are situated, in a later redaction of the material, within more advanced christological discussions. A similar observation can be made about the occurrence of the title at 10:36 and 19:7, where, in parallel passages, Jesus is accused of claiming the title for himself. The second, reminiscent of the trial of Mark 14:61-64, by dwelling upon the claim as blasphemy and deserving of death, retains the messianic overtones of the Jesus tradition; the first, however, forms part of a discussion of Jesus' equality with the Father and claim to be God (10:30 and 33).

The title "Lord" (*kyrios*) though frequently employed in the Fourth Gospel does not assume a prominent role in the author's portrait of the story's main character. Most occurrences simply substitute for the name of Jesus and thus stress reverence for the master as Lord of the community's faith.[33] On two occasions (13:13-16 and 15:15) John has recourse to the literal sense of the term to discuss the disciple's role as servant. In two instances, however, the title forms part of the author's higher christological discussions (9:38 and 20:28). The lordship of Jesus therefore is presumed throughout the gospel and greatly influences the author's redaction of the Jesus material.

We conclude that a major concern of the Johannine community and its evangelist was to establish the messiahship of Jesus. In all likelihood, as Jewish Christians the members of the Johannine community needed to demonstrate from the Hebrew scriptures (in midrashic fashion) and from the Jesus tradition that the long awaited Messiah was indeed Jesus

---

[32]Especially important for John's messianic thought are the traditional ideas of the role of the Spirit and the imagery of the harvest to describe the end-days.

[33]See especially John 6, 11, 13, 14, 20, and 21.

of Nazareth (1:45). The community presumes this in its everyday speech (use of "Lord"), attempts to demonstrate this in dialogue with fellow Jews, and eventually is "forced to leave" the synagogue because its members profess Jesus to be the Christ (9:22, 34; and 16:2).[34] Even the author's use of miracles as signs that lead to faith is an indication of the struggle that occurred between Jews who did or did not believe Jesus' messiahship. The increasingly harsh tones of the gospel resulted from growing debates, conflicts, and sharp polemics between opposing religious communities and their concern about the claims made in Jesus' name.

HIGH CHRISTOLOGY

Perusal of the Fourth Gospel reveals both a heightening of tension between Jesus and his opponents in succesive episodes and increasingly more elevated claims uttered by him or on his behalf. The author is not content to have characters in the drama accept Jesus' messianic claims; but in numerous episodes, in a dialectical fashion, John leads the *extra* and *intra* community discussions far beyond an exaltation or agency christology. The higher the level of the polemics between Jesus and the Jews or the more intense the discussion about Jesus' continuing presence, the more exalted are the christological claims made in Jesus' name. Since these affirmations cluster around four titles or themes: Son of Man, sonship, the "I am" formula, and "wisdom invitations," we will have to direct our attention to these.

1) In concluding a discussion of the christological titles of John 1 and after citing the Son of Man saying at the end of that chapter, R. Kysar makes the following comment: "Surely Jesus is the Messiah in the sense that all of these titles suggest. Surely he is greater than John the Baptist. But what he really is is tucked away in the meaning of this expression, Son of Man."[35] This statement captures well the tendency of scholars to see the Son of Man theme as a key element of John's high christology.[36]

---

[34]Martyn, *History and Theology in the Fourth Gospel*; see below for further discussion of this theme and also consider the reservations and caution of S.T. Katz, "Issues in the Separation of Judaism and Christianity after 70 C.E.: A Reconsideration," *JBL* 103 (1984) 43-76.

[35]*John the Maverick Gospel* (Atlanta: John Knox, 1976). 34.

[36]F.J. Moloney, *The Johannine Son of Man* (Rome: Libreria Ateneo Salesiano, 1978) and J.H. Neyrey, "The Jacob Allusions in John 1:51," *CBQ* 44 (1982) 586-605. The latter's conclusion might be cited as typical of recent scholarship: "The figure of the

In fact J.L. Martyn has graphically demonstrated how Christian-Jewish dialogue left its mark on at least four narratives where the christological movement by means of midrashic discussion involves passage from a messianic title to the identification of Jesus as Son of Man (John 3, 6, 7-8, 9).[37] The title, therefore, merits special study.

No fewer than thirteen times this title identifies the story's main character. In two cases it retains its apocalyptic connotation. In 9:35 it announces the culminating theme of chapter 9: "for judgment I came into this world" (v. 39). Nonetheless, the title is related to the community's profession of faith in Jesus ("believe" in vv. 35, 36) who receives divine honor ("worshiped," v. 38). The second occurrence involves the Son's being granted "authority to execute judgment, because he is the Son of Man" (5:27). The context is the Son's doing the Father's work (giving life and passing judgment, 5:19-22) and as a consequence also receiving divine honors (v. 23). We will return to the relationship of sonship to the title Son of Man. Two further occurrences from the bread-of-life discourse involve flesh or food. The first follows a discussion of the multiplication of the loaves (6:26) and the conclusion to be drawn, namely, that the crowd should seek heavenly bread (v. 33) or "the food which endures to eternal life, which the Son of Man will give" (v. 27). The second, about eating the flesh and drinking the blood of the Son of Man (v. 53), is also situated in the context of heavenly food (v. 58) which gives eternal life (53f). Both passages are interpreted by the author later in the discourse in relation to the ascending and descending Son of Man theme (v. 62). Two other texts speak of the Son of Man's glorification, (death and resurrection in Johannine usage), yet each serves a special function. The first (12:23) is reminiscent of the Synoptic tradition about the suffering/rising Son of Man (Mark 8:31, 34-35) and so stresses the imminent death of Jesus and its soteriological role (12:32: Jesus on the cross will draw all humanity to himself). The second (13:31) is more Johannine in its formulation and function since it stresses both

---

Son of Man in John undergoes a re-interpretation. There is one stream of traditional material in John which speaks of the rejected and vindicated Son of Man, which belongs to the low christology of the early Johannine community; but this is juxtaposed to and overlaid with another usage of the title which describes a pre-existent divine figure who descends from glory and returns to that glory. This usage reflects the high christology of the later community," 605.

[37] *History and Theology in the Fourth Gospel*, 130-35.

the mutual glorification of the Son of Man and God and the departure or absence of Jesus (v. 33).

The remaining seven occurrences are united thematically for they present the Son of Man either as ascending and descending or being lifted up (i.e., ascending).[38] The former theme derives from apocalyptic tradition, for apart from using this particular title, it emphasizes the relation between heaven and earth and the need for mediators. The first passage (1:51) stresses the concept of mediatorship for it envisions angels as going up and down between the Son of Man and heaven. The passage is inserted in the dual context of witness concerning Jesus' identity (John and then his former disciples confess Jesus to be Christ and prophet, 1:20-21, 41, 45) and of Jesus as worker of signs (one like Elijah who performs "greater things"). By means of a radical temporal shift, the author in 3:13 has Jesus speak of the Son of Man's coming from and returning to heaven and therefore constituting "the connecting link between the earthly and heavenly spheres."[39] Situated in the context of Jesus as revealer of heavenly things, the passage affirms the Johannine concept of Jesus, in the guise of the Son of Man, as a being whose origin and destiny are heavenly. A third ascending/descending passage (6:52), while presuming a divine origin for the Son of Man, is linked by the author to other thematic and narrative concerns. Since in the course of the bread-of-life discourse Jesus is described as "the bread of life" or "the bread come down from heaven" (6:35, 41, 48, 50-51, 58) or simply as having a heavenly origin (38, 42, 46, 57), the description of him in 6:62 as coming from a heavenly abode serves to strengthen the author's perception of Jesus as an extraterrestrial pilgrim. Yet it is from the narrative context that its function must be sought. After some disciples complain about Jesus' statement that obtaining eternal life depends on eating the flesh and drinking the blood of the Son of Man (53-54), the author places in Jesus' mouth a saying which stresses both the descending/ascending function of the Son of Man and his eschatological role as judge: "what if you were to see the Son of Man ascending where he was before?" (62). The remainder of the passage (vv. 64f) supports such an interpretation, for John emphasizes lack of belief, betrayal, and confession by the elect.

---

[38]See G.C. Nicholson, *Death as Departure: The Johannine Descent-Ascent Schema* (Chico: Scholars, 1983).

[39]Barrett, *John*, 212.

The remaining occurrences of the title speak of the Son of Man as being "lifted up," an acknowledged expression of double meaning.[40] The first of these (3:14) follows a statement about the descending/ ascending Son of Man and so suggests the meaning of glorification. Nonetheless, the author's contrast ("as . . . so") between Moses' raising of the serpent and the necessary lifting up of the Son of Man points to Jesus' death. This is borne out by the parallel passage in 12:32-34 and the contact with the Synoptic tradition about the necessity of the Son of Man's death and resurrection (Mark 8:31). The second occurrence (8:28) also implies more than it expresses for the author places the term within the context of Jesus' imminent departure in death (ironically expressed: "will he kill himself?" v. 22), eschatological judgment (24, 26), and "I am" sayings (24, 28). The final passage (12:31f) also offers a complex of Johannine themes to which the title Son of Man and the idea of "lifting up" are related. In this section John speaks of Jesus' hour of glorification, of judgment, and of his departure (in messianic and communal terms, 12:34-36). The author, after stating that Jesus' exaltation ("being lifted up from the earth") will result in universal salvation, insists in an aside that Jesus' being "lifted up" in glory is possible only through death (33), but a death which is both departure from the world and return to the Father.[41]

2) If the above discussion leads us to conclude that the theme of Son of Man, who descends from the heavenly realms and returns there, is a key to understanding John's portrait of Jesus, it also suggests that several other supplementary themes must be investigated. The first is the concept of sonship. Beyond the relatively rare use of the title Son of God, which sometimes retains its messianic connotation, the more general theme of sonship pervades the Johannine story where it often relates to more exalted claims for Jesus, who is often referred to as "Son," a relational concept which is further stressed by the ubiquitous title of Father for God. The Son was sent by the Father (3:16 and often) and so having come in God's Name (5:43; 10:25), works and speaks, not "on his own accord," but according to the will and command of the one who sent him into the world (8:42; 12:49; 14:10). The Father loves him and so has given all things into his hands (3:35; 13:3), whether executing judgment or granting eternal life to those who receive him (5:22; 6:40).

[40]Richard, "Expressions of Double Meaning," 101
[41]Nicholson, *Death as Departure*, 141-44.

As the Son has proceeded from the Father and so has been privy to the divine mysteries (1:18; 6:46; 14:7f), so now he does the works which the Father has shown him (5:20). He has become the revealer of the Father for he has come from the heavenly realm (5:37; 6:46). He knows and loves the Father. He does the Father's will by drinking the cup prepared for him (8:55; 14:31; 18:11). The relation between the Father and the Son, therefore, is one of mutual glorification, love, witness, and unity (8:18; 10:38; 14:10-11; 17:1, 21).

Johannine usage, however, requires further examination. While the title "Father" has become a virtual synonym for God,[42] that of Son often takes on some of the characteristics which Synoptic usage reserves for Son of Man. Jesus speaks of the Son (true also of Son of God and Son of Man) in the third person (5:19f; 6:40 14:13). Also, John, by relating similar concepts and sayings to the Son and to Jesus speaking in the first person (3:35 versus 10:17 or 5:19 and 5:30) and by making connections between the theme of sonship and the title Son of Man, implies that the community's exalted concept of Jesus involves these different themes and titles. So easily does John lapse from one title to another that some conclude that Son and Son of Man have virtually the same meaning in the Fourth Gospel.[43] While it is true that all the evangelists tend to extend the semantic range of christological titles, John nonetheless can exploit the connotations of specific titles as in 5:26-27 where the Son (also Son of God in v. 25) is granted divine powers (executing judgment) precisely "because he is the Son of Man." Though interrelated in John's perception of Jesus, these titles still retain some of their uniqueness.

3) We turn to the "I am" formula which is admittedly an important characteristic of John's Gospel. Estimates of this phenomenon, however, vary greatly. Some see in this usage a conscious attempt to defend a doctrine of equality, whereby Jesus, the movement's founder, would bear the sacred name. Others insist that the stress should fall on the pronoun ("I"), to emphasize the claims made on Jesus' behalf in contrast to those made in favor of other persons or deities. Still others see some of the uses of this formula as messianic (e.g., "I am the Christ or Messiah"). A brief discussion, therefore, is necessary to understand how

---

[42]See 8:54, however: "it is my Father who glorifies me, of whom you say that he is your God;" note also the frequent Johannine expression "my Father."

[43]Martyn, *History and Theology in the Fourth Gospel*, 134, n. 193 and Kysar, *John the Maverick Gospel*, 35.

this formula functions in Johannine christology. To achieve this objective we adopt the following categories (based on grammatical usage) as proposed by R.E. Brown: a. "the absolute use [of "I am"] with no predicate," b. "the use where a predicate may be understood even though it is not expressed," and c. "the use with a predicate nominative."[44]

Discussion of these formulaic statements centers on their origin, whether Jewish or Hellenistic, and on their relation to the first category. Many agree with Brown's estimate that the absolute usage is the determining factor in deciding its precise origin (Old Testament and Palestinian Judaism) and function (divine name).[45]

Under examination these proposals fail to convince. I doubt that the use of the ordinary Greek phrase "I am" (*ego eimi*) suffices to unite the texts where that expression occurs. Further, while one finds interesting examples of "I am" used as a Septuagintal rendering of the divine name (in Isaiah), I wonder if the Johannine reader would make such a connection. Besides, the distribution and narrative context of this expression argue against such proposals.

So we begin our discussion with the simplest group, namely, category b, where the predicate is not expressed and of which there exist two examples (6:20 and 18:5). Despite frequent disclaimers, the narrative contexts (walking on the water and arrest of Jesus) justify the interpretation of recent translators (RSV: "It is I" and "I am he") and on the narrative level require no further explanation. Category a, which occurs only in chapters 8 and 13, also calls for an examination of the narrative context. On the negative side one is led to concede that the contexts of both 8:24, 28 and 13:19 argue against the conclusion that Jesus is appropriating the divine name. In the first case, the formula leads to the following: "I do nothing on my own authority but speak thus as the Father taught me" (8:28b), while the second is explained by the statement: "he who receives me receives him who sent me" (13:20). In neither context does equality with the Father, functional or otherwise, make sense. Besides, chapter 8 leads to a last "I am" saying of the absolute category, a usage which must be explained in temporal and not onomastic terms. Since 8:58 stresses that Jesus existed before Abraham

---

[44]*John*, 1:523-38. For a convenient discussion of the various theories proposed in regard to the "I am" formula, see Brown, *John* ("Appendix IV: *EGO EIMI*—'I Am'"); Kysar, *John the Maverick Gospel*, 40-44; and Barrett, *John*, 341-42.

[45]*John*, 1:537.

did, we must conclude that John is here insisting that Jesus had "neither beginning nor end of existence" or simply that he "belongs to the eternal, heavenly world."[46] Thus John argues, in continuity with the messianic speculation of chapter 7, for a divine or heavenly origin for Jesus.

Finally, category c, the best known and more properly labeled group, provides much scope for discussing Johannine christology. The background and origin of this formula is probably related to OT symbolism and wisdom motifs, Hellenistic Isis "I am" sayings, and Christian parabolic language and imagery of the Jesus tradition.[47] Acquainted not only with the claims made in Isis' name by her devotees but also with the attractive theological medium employed in that goddess' cult and in the Old Testament in speaking of God's relation to humanity, of Wisdom's role vis-à-vis the human race and aware no doubt of the increasing tendency within many Christian communities to interpret the parabolic stories as means of christological revelation, the author settled on first-person sayings to reveal not Jesus' being or nature but his role in God's dealings with humanity. Nonetheless, the list of revelatory "I am" sayings is lengthy and their functions complex, for in some cases John wishes to stress Jesus' divine or heavenly origin (6:35f; 8:23), in others, his soteriological or ecclesiological (10:7, 9, 11, 14; 14:6; 15:1, 5), and eschatological (8:12; 11:25; 14:6) roles.

4) The above discussion of OT influence leads us to examine a final area for understanding John's treatment of Jesus, namely, the importance and development of the wisdom tradition within Hellenistic Judaism.

In the late biblical tradition, as well as in Jewish writings of the Hellenistic period, there is [a] figure . . . who is depicted as preexistent: Wisdom (Prov. 8:22-23; Sir. 24:9; Wisd. of Sol. 6:22). Wisdom not only preexists but has a role in the creation of the world (Prov. 8:23-31), since she serves as God's companion in the bringing of the world into existence (Wis. of Sol. 8:4-6; Sir. 1). As R.E. Brown has shown, Wisdom is portrayed in this literature as the effulgence of divine glory (Wis. of Sol. 7:25, 26), as the illuminator of mankind

---

[46]Barrett, *John*, 342; in general agreement with Barrett's treatment of John's use of the "I am" formula.

[47]See Brown, *John.*, 1:537-38 and Barrett, *John*, 292.

(Wis. of Sol. 7:10, 29), as descended from heaven (Prov. 8:31; Sir. 24:8 Wis. of Sol. 9:10), as returning to God (1 En. 42:2), as having the chief role in instructing mankind concerning heavenly things (Job 11:6-7; Wisd. of Sol. 9: 16-18), as taking the initiative to engage hearers of her message (Prov. 1:20-21; Bar. 3:12; 1 En. 42:2). All of these features and functions are also discernible in John's picture of Jesus.[48]

The example of Jesus as Wisdom incarnate is the image one finds in the edited christological hymn of chapter one. Influenced by current philosophical-religious speculation, whether of Hellenistic Judaism or of the popular Greek schools of thought, the author found appealing a Logos hymn which was then edited and appended as prologue to the gospel narrative during a later revision. The Word, being of divine origin and acting as agent of creation (1:1, 3-4), comes into the world of humans (1:14) as one who experiences reception and rejection (1:10-12). As one who comes from God, the Word radiates divine glory and fulness and functions as revealer of the Father (1:14, 16, 18). Wisdom speculation, however, is not limited to the prologue. Not only does the Son or Son of Man have a divine origin but he existed always (before Abraham, 8:58) and possessed divine glory since "before the world was made" (17:5). Jesus is the light of the world as illuminator of humanity (3:19; 8:12; 9:5), and light that exposes dark deeds (3:20). Jesus as the Son of Man is the one who comes down from heaven and returns (by being lifted up) to the Father (3:13-14; 16:28). Indeed, Jesus came to reveal the Father (1:18; 6:46; 14:7-9) or heavenly things (3:12; 5:20; 15:15). He came to cast a challenge to the world that is open to salvation. Thus, John's entire gospel is written against a backdrop of rejection (and judgment) and of reception (and "power to become children of God," 1:12).

Additionally, Wisdom offers humanity all manner of good things: gifts of knowledge and revelation under the guise of food and drink (Prov. 9:2-5; Sir. 24:19-21). It is characteristic of John to have Jesus issue a wisdom invitation (7:37) similar to that of Sirach 24:21; while Wisdom is made to say: "those who drink of me will thirst for more," Jesus is made to insist: "everyone who drinks of this water will thirst again, but whoever drinks of the water that I shall give him will never thirst; the water that I shall give him will become in him a spring of water

---

[48]Kee, *Jesus in History*, 243-44; the reference is to Brown, *John*, 1:cxxii-cxxv.

welling up to eternal life" (4:13-14). Jesus is a more sublime Wisdom, for not only does he give the water of life, but he is the beverage itself (water and wine, 7:37-38; 2:10) and the food (6:35f).[49] Jesus is Wisdom made flesh as Word, as salvation made available to humanity, and as a new and better Torah (a Law in the realm of "grace and truth," 1:17). Jesus, like the personified Wisdom or Law of Hellenistic Judaism,[50] becomes the Father's alter ego, for whoever sees and knows him has seen and known the Father (14:7). Indeed, the Father is with him (16:32) and the two are one (10:30). Wisdom, in the person of Jesus, came into the world to dwell among God's creatures (its effects are manifold), but it was destined to return to the heavenly realm (1 Enoch 42:2; John 16:28).

Having surveyed these four central components of John's christology, one cannot doubt that this document's portrait of Jesus is significantly different from that encountered in the Synoptics. Only in John does the narrator speak thus about the story's principal character: "Jesus, knowing that the Father had given all things into his hands, and that he had come from God and was going to God, rose from supper ... " (13:3). Clearly this view must be classified as high christology. Jesus, the pre-existent one, comes into the world of humans as flesh and blood, performs the works which the Father has shown him, calls those whom the one who sent him has given him, casts a light of illumination and condemnation, and, before returning to the Father to reclaim the glory that was his, confers upon his own another Paraclete or Counselor (14:15), thereby assuring his continued presence and that of his Father among his followers (14:23). Jesus then is the descending and ascending Son of Man, a heavenly figure whose relation to God is that of father and son or parent and child and whose kinship to the human world is that of Wisdom in flesh and blood, Wisdom whose invitation reaches to the core of the follower's being and commitment.

A final question, however, remains to be addressed: how and why did such a portrait of Jesus develop within the Johannine community? As a result of J.L. Martyn's work it has become clear that the community's evolution in social-structural and christological terms is associated with its peculiar relationship to the synagogue. Martyn, as a result of detailed study of three key passages which speak of exclusion from the synagogue (9:22; 16:2; 12:42), concludes that the author and community, first as a

---

[49]On the concept of wisdom invitation, see Lindars, *John*, 183-84, 254, 259-60.
[50]Hengel, *Judaism and Hellenism*, 1:169-75.

result of their profession of Jesus as the expected Jewish Messiah and secondly as the outcome of "the Jewish Benediction against heretics," were forced out of the synagogue.[51] He maintains that analysis of John's text permits the modern reader to trace that community's mental journey, that is, its passage from a christology that saw Jesus as the embodiment of "the prophet-messiah like Moses" to one which confessed him as the heavenly Son of Man present among his followers.[52]

It seems to me that there is no denying Martyn's contribution to our understanding of Johannine history. Nonetheless, I am led to question certain conclusions drawn from his analysis.[53] Is it not possible, contrary to his conclusion, that the exalted claims made in Jesus' name by the Johannine community were the cause (at least in part) and not the result (certainly not fully) of expulsion from the synagogue? Indeed, examination of the passages reviewed by Martyn supports such a conclusion. While each mentions excommunication from the synagogue (9:22; 12:42; 16:2), each also dwells upon christological themes. In all three the concept of agency is emphasized (9:4, 7; 12:44, 49-50; 15:21; 16:5); Jesus is the one sent by the Father. Further, each focuses on a particular facet of this agency christology. In the first case, while there is interest in the brevity of the Light's (Jesus) sojourn, the focus is on Jesus' origin. On two occasions the authorities question Jesus' heavenly provenance; i.e., he is "not from God" (9:16) or contrary to Moses, he is of unknown origin (29-30). John then stresses that, as a result of the man's confession ("if this man were not from God, he could do nothing"), he is cast out of the synagogue (vv. 33-34). In the second text, it is the continued presence of the Messiah that is of prime concern. If Jesus is the Christ sent by God, then why does he say that he must depart or be lifted up from the earth (12:32), since the Law claims "that the Christ remains forever" (34). There follows the statement about the Son of Man who must be lifted up (34b). One presumes that v. 42 maintains that the authorities sustained a hidden belief in Jesus as the departing/dying Son of Man. The third passage, no longer in an *extra* community context, focuses on Jesus' imminent departure to the Father (16:5, 10, 16, 22) and on his

---

[51] *History and Theology in the Fourth Gospel,* 37f; again see Katz, "Issues in the Separation of Judaism and Christianity after 70 C.E.," 71-74.

[52] *History and Theology in the Fourth Gospel,* 102f. and 129f.

[53] See also A.Y. Collins, "Crisis and Community in John's Gospel," *TD* 27 (1979) 313-21.

heavenly origin (v. 27). He has come into the world from the Father and returns to the Father (28). In response to the problem raised by this departure, Jesus promises to send the Paraclete (7) and in relation to the theme of Jesus' divine origin, the author constructs the chapter to terminate with the community's confession: "we believe that you came from God" (30). Again, one concludes that it is the claims made on Jesus' behalf that separate believing Christians (who are thereby thrown out of the synagogue) from these who do not accept Jesus as coming from and revealing the Father.

As a result we suggest that the expulsion from the synagogue was a consequence of the exalted claims made by Christian Jews on Jesus' behalf. Such claims are not unique to this community as the christological hymns of Col. 1:15-20 and Hebrews 1:2-4 testify. Besides, survey of Johannine texts expressing a high christology invariably finds an extension or development of a basic agency christology; i.e., they concern Jesus' origin, destiny, or relationship to God. A few examples will suffice. While at an earlier period of the community's development one understands the opposition Jesus (as representative of the community) encounters for his Sabbath healings (5:16), it is only at a later stage that vv. 17-18 serve as the expression of a developing higher christology, i.e., Jesus is said to share in the Father's creative power and to claim equality with God. The author is quick to modify, not to deny, the latter claim by stating in v. 19 that the Son is subordinate to the Father. On another occasion Jesus is accused of blasphemy (he does the works of the Father) because he as man makes himself God (10:33). Jesus' response is instructive: "do you say of him whom the Father consecrated and sent into the world, 'you are blaspheming,' because I said, 'I am the Son of God?'" (v. 36; see also 19:7). Ultimately, however, it is the claim of intimacy or union with the Father ("the Father is in me and I am in the Father") which provokes the Jewish crowd (10:38-39). In still another passage John proposes the reactions of three groups to Jesus' claim to have come down from heaven. First, the people cannot accept that Jesus is Wisdom personified in the guise of heavenly bread, for they think they know where he comes from; is he not the son of Joseph, the son of a well-known mother and father (6:42)? John then turns to *intra* community matters, namely, the reaction of would-be-disciples. They too take offense at Jesus' teaching; but this time the focus is on the theme of the ascending/descending Son of Man (6:62). It is the high christological claim which causes many of Jesus' disciples to turn away

(66). Finally, John addresses the twelve and obtains from them, in Simon Peter's words, the community's confession that Jesus is "the Holy One of God" (69).[54] What then was the catalyst which brought about this development from a pervasive agency to a higher christology? One suspects a combination of factors was operable. Impressed and intrigued by the sublime attributes ascribed to Wisdom and by the claims made on Isis' behalf, well acquainted with the Jesus tradition's presentation of his claim to unique sonship, and convinced that the Christ-event was the decisive eschatological action of God in the world (as Son of Man), the Johannine community and its evangelist by their exalted claims on their founder's behalf set in motion a process of ideological struggle, expulsion, and polemical dialogue which left its marks on the inward and outward dimensions of the community's development.[55]

If the charismatic character of the community, "communitas" in sociological terms,[56] allowed for the free scope of the great theologian's flights of speculation (note the striking inclusio: "the Word was God," 1:1 and "my Lord and my God," 20:28), that same undifferentiated structure had long-range consequences. On the one hand, one finds in the gospel a heightened sense of polemics against outsiders ("the Jews")[57] and an inward focus on the community's beliefs and loyalites. Love and hate became themes for categorizing and controlling membership.[58] The community adopted an us-versus-them perspective which took on many apocalyptic traits, not the least of which was to view the

[54]See Segovia, "'Peace I Leave You; My Peace I Give to You,'" 89-94, for a further delineation of the inner and outer conflicts of the Johannine community as they affected membership and discipleship.

[55]Collins, "Crisis and Community in John's Gospel," 317-21; see also Neyrey, *Christ is Community*, 151-65, for an understanding of this stage of Johannine development similar to that presented above.

[56]V. Turner, *The Ritual Process: Structure and Anti-Structure* (NY: Aldine, 1969), chapter 4: "Communitas: Model and Process," 131-65. See D.B. Woll, *Johannine Christianity in Conflict: Authority, Rank, and Succession in the First Farewell Discourse* (Chico: Scholars, 1981), for an analysis of the charismatic nature of the community.

[57]One should speak of polemics, for it is doubtful that, even in the later stages of the community's development, "dialogue has ended and mockery has begun," Duke, *Irony*, 150; instead see R.A. Whitacre, *Johannine Polemic: The Role of Tradition and Theology* (Chico: Scholars, 1982).

[58]F. Segovia, "The Love and Hatred of Jesus and Johannine Sectarianism," *CBQ* 43 (1981) 258-72.

"world" as meriting condemnation. On the other hand, the paucity of structures in the community had devastating consequences, if we are to judge from the data provided by the three Johannine documents which we study next.

Legacy of the Johannine Community

With the death of the evangelist, the community, its loyalities, and its theology underwent important modifications. If it is true, as current scholarship maintains, that this writer was also the charismatic leader of the community and that the group was of an undifferentiated or egalitarian type, then one expects major changes to have occurred.

1 JOHN: CHARACTER AND BACKGROUND

This document is best described as a theological tract or pastoral treatise written to denounce heretical tendencies among Johannine Christians and to establish a community code. Evidently, the author is polemicizing against a faction which once adhered to the same communities. In general terms, we accept R.E. Brown's description of the situation.

> In the decade after the main body of GJohn was written (*ca.* 90), the Johannine Community became increasingly divided over the implications and applications of Johannine thought. Before the writing of 1 John a schism had taken place. The resultant two groups, consisting of the epistolary author's adherents and his adversaries, both accepted the proclamation of Christianity known to us through GJohn, but they interpreted it differently ... almost surely the two groups justified their opposite positions on the basis of the Johannine tradition itself. One must be wary of arguing that GJohn led inevitably either to the position of the epistolary author or to that of his adversaries; nor is it clear that either position is a total distortion of GJohn. Rather the Johannine tradition enshrined in GJohn, as it came to both the author and to his adversaries, was relatively 'neutral' on some points that had now come into dispute. Either it did not contain direct answers for the divisive questions, or it contained texts that each side could draw upon for support.[59]

[59] *The Epistles of John* (NY: Doubleday, 1982), 69.

First John then is the statement of one faction's version of the events and doctrines involved, and that same side's characterization of the opposition as secessionists and even antichrists. While it is a genuine concern of the scholar to attempt a reconstruction of events which does justice to both sides of the conflict, it is not the focus of our inquiry. Instead we will focus on the document produced by one party to the debate and describe its portrait of Jesus. It will also be of interest to examine what the author thinks of the secessionists and their idea of Jesus.

One part of Brown's statement needs further comment at this point. That the position of either group did not "inevitably" derive from that of the Johannine evangelist does not require serious defense but that the later tradition's focus on Jesus' otherworldly origin and nature suggested docetic ideas or a disincarnated christology to some within the ambient of the Johannine group is probable and defensible. We turn therefore to the document itself.

Between a distinct Johannine introduction (1:1-4) and conclusion (5:13-21) the author has composed a series of alternating ethical and christological sections wherein these two central concerns of the community are explored and related in pastoral and polemical terms. Even the introduction's insistence on sensory witness to the meaning of the Christ-event (hear, see, look upon, touch) bolsters the author's claim that what follows in the document (v. 4), both the portrait of Jesus and its corollary ethical demands, is the only authentic teaching of the Johannine tradition. The document concludes on a similar note, namely, one should be on God's side in christological and ethical terms rather than succumb to the "idolatry" of those who have seceded from the group. Thus, we offer the following schema of the document's dynamics:

1:1-4   Introduction
1:5-2:17 Ethical Section: light and darkness—the world
   + 2:18-27 Christological Section—antichrist and threat to community
2:28-3:24 Ethical Section: children of God—love of brethren
   + 4:1-6   Christological Section—Jesus Christ in flesh
4:7-5:12   Combined Section: Ethical and Christological Concerns
   4:7-21   Love leads to faith
   5:1-12   Faith leads to love
5:13-21   Conclusion.

If in general terms 1 John is a pastoral application of and commentary on the Gospel of John, the concerns are no longer the same. In place of the gospel's polemical outreach to the estranged Jewish community, one finds a new situation where the older symbols are applied to *intra* community problems. Even the "love" terminology of the former is modified to address the group's new problems, namely, "a love of the disciples for one another, a love which demands a correct christological confession as well as the execution of definite ethical norms."[60] Correct conduct, true doctrine, and regard for the authority of the group's tradition are related by First John to proper christological views, the core problem of the later Johannine community. As some members pursued even further the high christological claims of their tradition, the community found itself in a quandry, since there existed few controlling mechanisms to moderate these views. Further, the social dynamics, which in earlier times had fostered inner unity and protection from outside opposition, contributed to the vehemence of the schism which took place within. As these members either went their own way as wandering missionaries[61] or were forced out by those opposed to their extreme views, they became a counter, successful group (4:5), but a group which, at the hands of its opponents, earned the names of "liar," "antichrist," and "false prophet" (2:22; 4:1, 3).

According to the writer of First John the secessionists professed a docetic christology, since they denied "that Jesus Christ had come in the flesh" (4:2). Additionally, the author charges that they rejected Jesus' messiahship (one presumes the author means a false concept of messiahship) and therefore denied both Father and Son (2:22). The critical issue then was the relative importance to be placed on Jesus' earthly sojourn. The secessionist so emphasized the claims made by the Johannine evangelist concerning Jesus' divine origin and nature that they had in effect negated the significance of the earthly ministry and the soteriological consequences of his death. Thus, the opponents had seized upon the tradition's tendency to underscore its high christology and to stress the Son's function as revealer of the Father, and, by so

[60]F.F. Segovia, *Love Relationships in the Johannine Tradition: Agape/Agapan in 1 John and the Fourth Gospel* (Chico: Scholars, 1982) 195.

[61]J. Bogart, *Orthodox and Heretical Perfectionism in the Johannine Community as Evident in the First Epistle of John* (Missoula: Scholars, 1977) 127-28.

doing, had minimized the importance of his life and death.[62] So it is not by accident that at every turn the writer emphasizes the "cleansing by blood" (1:7, 9; see also 5:6), "the expiation for or forgiveness of sins" (1:9; 2:2, 12; 4:10), Jesus' laying down of his life (3:16), and the Son's being sent by the Father (4:9, 10) as Savior of the world (4:14).

The author's favorite titles for Jesus are Son of God (16 times) and Christ (9), titles whose confessional usage (believe, confess, bear witness, know, or deny) stress their polemical use. True belief in Jesus as Son of God means confessing that God sent the Son to cleanse those who believe from sin by his blood, thereby providing them with the means of becoming one with him and his Father ("abiding" and "fellowship" terminology, 1:3; 2:6; and often). The author, even while attempting to avoid the docetic extremes of the secessionists by stressing Jesus' humanity and salvific death, does not fail to insist on his divine origin and nature (1:2; 4:9; 5:20).

What began as stress on the exalted status of the founder became, in some late formulations of the tradition, the virtual denial of his humanity. The author of First John resolved to correct this imbalance[63] by emphasizing the soteriological role of Jesus and therefore the necessity of his life and death for Christian belief. It is with this idea in mind that the author addresses the community's concerns about sin and perfection: "if anyone does sin, we have an advocate with the Father, Jesus Christ the righteous, and he is the expiation for our sins, and not for ours only but also for the sins of the whole world" (2:1-2). Finally, it is the middle position adapted by this author which later gained the approbation of canonical status.

1-2-3 JOHN: GENERAL CONSIDERATION OF AUTHORSHIP

When we turn to the remaining two Johannine documents we become painfully aware of the community's continued disintegration over the issues of authority, organization, and doctrine. These brief letters offer a tantalizing glimpse into the problems that were tearing the communities apart. Serious interpretation of these documents must address the issues of authorship, the relationship between these, and their plausible setting in life. To underscore the importance and tentative

---

[62]See Brown, *The Community of the Beloved Disciple*, 109-23 and *The Epistles of John*, 73-79.

[63]Brown, *The Community of the Beloved Disciple*, 107.

nature of this endeavor we cite R.E. Brown's honest assessment of the problem: "indeed, it is a *quess* that the three Epistles are all by the same person, based chiefly on the fact that I and II John seem to attack the same errors and use similar expressions."[64]

While it is frequently asserted that one author composed all three documents (position of Brown, among others), it is preferable to opt for separate authorship for each work, to see their relationship as owing to common adherence to the Johannine tradition, and to view their setting in relation to the community's ideological diarray and gradual social disintegration. The four documents under consideration bear common Johannine traits and themes, especially the gospel and 1 John. The interrelationship between the final three, however, is not easily understood. Analysis of stylistic features, of a non-conscious nature, leads us to view these as separate documents from independent authors. While John on two occasions speaks of "walking in the darkness" (8:12 and 12:35), verb followed by prepositional phrase, 1 John reverses the order (1:6 and 2:11) and adds the expression "walking in the light" (1:7) with the verb again following the remainder of the expression. Neither Second nor Third John knows either expression, but instead they employ the idiom "walk in the truth," the former with verb preceding prepositional phrase (2 John 4; see also v. 6 for "walk in the commandments") and the latter with the reverse (3 John 3, 4). A similar situation emerges when one examines these authors' use of the expression "abide in someone or thing." The evangelist employs both word orders; 1 John almost always situates the prepositional phrase before the verb (15 of 22 occurrences); 2 John in all three cases makes the verb precede the prepositional phrase (2, 9 twice); and 3 John offers no such usage. Such data which are unconsciously controlled elements of grammar suggest independent authorship. What makes these two sets of data even more significant is that they involve major Johannine themes, themes that would have been uppermost in their authors' consciousness.

Further evidence pointing to the separate authorship of 1 and 2 John is furnished by the texts employed to posit common authorship. 2 John 7 is obviously reminiscent of several passages from 1 John: 2:19, 22;

---

[64] *The Epistles of John*, x (emphasis added).

4:2-3. While both speak of "antichrist" and "confessing/acknowledging[65] Jesus Christ come in the flesh," there are differences. The former speaks of "deceiver," a term used only here in the Johannine corpus, while the latter employs "liar," a term which it utilizes five times and shares with the Gospel of John (twice). Even more telling is the word order found in two expressions used by both authors: "went out from us" or "have gone out into the world" (1 John 2:19; 2 John 7) and "Jesus Christ come in the flesh" (1 John 4:2; 2 John 7). In both cases, 1 John places the verb after the prepositional phrase while 2 John employs the opposite word order. Again, we conclude that the style of the passage in question indicates separate authorship for 1 and 2 John.[66]

EXTENDED COMPARISON OF 2 AND 3 JOHN

The problem is more complex for these two letters since they are obviously related in theme and style. The connection between them requires detailed analysis.

2 John	3 John
1 *The elder,*	1 *The elder,*
to the elect lady	*to* the beloved Gaius,
and to her children,	
whom I love in truth,	*whom I love in truth.*
and not I only	
but also all	
who know the truth,	
2 because of the truth,	
that abides in us and	
will be with us forever.	
3 There will be with us	2 Beloved,
grace, mercy, peace	in all things I wish you
from God the Father	to prosper and be healthy
and from Jesus Christ,	just as your soul prospers.
the Father's Son,	
in truth and love.	

[65]Same term in Greek: *homologeō*; this confessional expression is a favorite of 1 John (5 times), but is found only here in v. 7 of 2 John.

[66]We might also point out that "beloved," a favorite term of 1 John (6 times in the plural to address the readers) would be surprisingly absent in 2 John were it written by the same author.

4 *I rejoiced greatly*	3 For *I rejoiced greatly* when brothers arrived and testified to your truth as indeed you walk in truth.
that I have found some of *your children* *walking in the truth* as we received command- ment from the Father	4 No greater joy than these do I have *that I* hear *my children* *are walking in the truth.*

[Concerning commandment
  5-6 and deceivers 7-9
Non-reception of false
  missionaries 10-11
	Reception of missionaries,
	  esp. strangers 5-8
	Concerning Diotrephes 9-10
	  and Demetrius 11-12]

12 *Having many things* *to write to you,* *I did not desire to do* *so with* paper *and ink,*	13 *I had many things* *to write to you,* but I do not wish *with ink and* pen to write to you.
but hope to come to *you* and to *talk face* *to face* that our joy may be complete 13 The children of your elect sister *greet you.*	14 *But I hope* soon to see *you* and we will *talk face* *to face.* 15 Peace be to you. The friends *greet you.* Greet the friends, (each) by name.

Comparison of the parallels, indicated in italics, point to a significant relationship between the documents. There are, however, important variations, which one might explain as does Brown: "the differences reflect a letter writer who has a general pattern but who shifts details unconsciously and without significance within that pattern."[67]

---

[67] *The Epistles of John*, 724 (discussion of 2 John 12 and 3 John 13-14).

So many similar terms and phrases indicate a close connection between the two; either they are by the same author or one has imitated the other. While most scholars opt for the former, i.e., composition by one author, closer examination leads me to reject the former and to choose the latter as the more likely solution. Indeed, there are significant differences between the two in terms of style and vocabulary, of treatment of issues, of situation, and of concerns addressed.

The most telling area of difference is that of stylistic peculiarities. If both speak of "children walking in the truth," it should be noted that the order of prepositional phrase and verb in the two letters is different; besides, the expression occurs in the same pattern twice in 3 John 3 and 4. Also one "walks according to" and "in his/the commandment (s)" in 2 John 6. On the one hand, the author of 2 John favors two stylistic options. First, the document has a tendency to employ terms in clusters as it treats successive themes: "truth" 5 times (vv. 1-4), "commandment" 4 times (4-6), "from the beginning" twice (5-6), "deceiver" twice (7), union with the Father and the Son twice (9), and "doctrine" 3 times (9-10). Secondly, it relishes the use of doublets: "to the elect lady and her children" (v. 1), "not only I but also all who know the truth" (1), "from God the Father and Jesus Christ the Father's Son" (3), " in truth and love" (3), "the deceiver and the antichrist" (7), "you may not lose . . . but receive" (8), "both the Father and the Son" (9), "comes to you and does not bring this doctrine" (10), "do not receive him into the house or give him any greeting" (10), "with paper and ink" (10), and "hope to come to you and to talk face to face" (12). In one case it has recourse to a threefold list: "there will be with us: grace, mercy, peace" (3).

On the other hand, 3 John has a propensity for tautalogy, that is, the proximate use of the same or related terms and roots which often leads to repetition, redundancy or paronomasis. The author employs "beloved, love, beloved" (vv. 1-2), "prosper" twice (2), "rejoice" and "joy" (3-4), "walk in the truth" twice (3-4), "receive/support" twice (7-8), "receive/acknowledge" and "receive/welcome" (9-10), "evil/good" and "doing good/doing evil" (11), "testimony, testify, testimony" and "truth, true" (12), "to write to you" twice (13), and "the friends greet you" and "greet the friends" (15). Further, on two occasions the author builds an expresssion on an earlier phrase; v. 6 ("testified to your love") is patterned on v. 3 ("testified to your truth") and v. 10 ("the works which he does") on v. 5 ("a worthy thing you do whenever you perform a work"). These stylistic differences, therefore, argue strongly for separate authorship. This conclusion is reinforced by each authors' use of unique vocabulary and expressions.

The authors' treatment of issues also deserves attention. Scholars rarely fail to point out how differently the writers view traveling missionaries. In the case of 2 John outside preachers are suspect and are to be tested as to orthodoxy (10-11). In 3 John strangers are to be welcomed and assisted (5-8). The tone of the former is negative while that of the latter is more positive. Indeed, while 2 John is concerned about christological orthodoxy (note the triple use of "doctrine" in vv. 9-10 and the unique expression "abide in the doctrine," twice in v. 9), 3 John never mentions Christ nor employs "Father" in describing God. The former is preoccupied by the issues that caused the rift, i.e., christology and mutual distrust and recrimination; the latter focuses on ecclesiastical structures and authority. The terminology of "commandment" (4 times), "from the beginning" (2 times), and preoccupation with the secessionists' christological deviation (7-9) relates 2 John to a milieu similar to that of 1 John, but the insistence in 3 John on "church" (3 times, only here in Johannine literature), on authority (9-10), and on personal testimony for a new missionary (11-12) speaks of a different and later ecclesial situation within the Johannine churches.[68] Further indication of a later date for 3 John is the author's reference to community members as "my children" (4) as opposed to "children of the community" in 2 John 1, 4, 13.

2 John then is a document written by a member of the same group that produced 1 John. Its author is concerned about the issues raised in the first document, namely, the reality of Jesus' humanity (7), his being sent by the Father, and his relation to the Father (3, 4, 9). Also, the added threat of the secessionists' success even within the writer's own group (10-11) leads to distrust of their preachers. 3 John, however, has a different origin. The author claimed the authority of the community's leaders, precisely that of an elder whose earlier letter is imitated in detail. A careful study of 3 John suggests borrowing, rewriting, and editing of the basic features of 2 John. Finally, the author makes use of the elder's

---

[68] On the issues of outside preachers, traveling missionaries, and hospitality in regard to 2 and 3 John, see A.J. Malherbe, "Hospitality and Inhospitality in the Church," 92-112 in *Social Aspects of Early Christianity* (Philadelphia: Fortress, 1983); Brown, *The Epistles of John*, 728-39; and B.J. Malina, "The Received View and What It Cannot Do: III John and Hospitality," 171-99 in Elliott, *Social-Scientific Criticism of the New Testament*.

authority (see a similar situation in 2 Thessalonians) to introduce Demetrius, a more congenial missionary, in an attempt to regain control of the community.

The christology of 2 John is similar to that found in 1 John, namely, a high christology which nonetheless stresses the humanity of Jesus and anchors this belief within the community's tradition or doctrine. We see, however, a shift to "abiding in the doctrine" (9) rather than the Johannine "abiding in Christ." In the case of 3 John there is no hint of christology. Instead the problems of the community loom so large that other issues fade into the background.

The Johannine experiment in community living and christological speculation, therefore, had a long and tumultuous history. If the fate of these communities, like that of most NT groups, is unknown to us, their charismatic evangelist and literature had influence well beyond the disintegration of the communities. Indeed, this particular segment of the Jesus movement produced a sizeable portion of the New Testament and left its mark, in the guise of a particular, high christology, upon later theological speculation and controversy.

Part III
Jesus As Viewed By Paul
And the Paulinist Writers

8

The Letters of Paul

Paul holds a special place in the development of Christian thought. His is the first and possibly only NT author known by name.[1] He is responsible for a sizeable portion of that collection of books and has preserved much valuable information about the life and time of the communities of the 40s, 50s, and 60s. In Paul's letters one finds precious data concerning the beliefs of the first Christians and the spread of the Jesus movement. But more importantly in these same letters one encounters the ideas of one of Christianity's most original thinkers.[1]

The great missionary to the Gentiles had a large impact upon his contemporaries and captured the imagination of subsequent Christian writers. Paul left few indifferent to his thought and activity. In his lifetime he had enemies and opponents as well as devoted co-workers and faithful "children in the Lord." There developed after his death a large following and consequently frequent appeal to his authority. Writers of a later generation wrote in his name to resolve new problems (2 Thessalonians), to draw further conclusions from his original thought (Colossians and Ephesians), or to employ his prestige to consolidate new missionary fields (the Pastorals). So fascinating was this great figure that another author borrowed from the Pauline legends to teach in narrative form about the nature of discipleship (Luke in the Acts of the Apostles). In the following chapters, therefore, we direct our attention first to Paul and then to those who wrote in his name.

---

[1]See, however, our discussion on the Book of Revelation, chapter 11.

The Letter in the Hellenistic World

While the writing of letters for political, diplomatic, and commercial purposes was relatively common in antiquity, it was particularly during the Hellenistic period that the epistolary genre flourished. As Greek became the *lingua franca* of the newly conquered territories, replacing the Aramaic language favored by the Persian rulers, its culture became the basis for the cosmopolitan Hellenistic civilization of the five or six centuries following the death of Alexander the Great.

After the Macedonian conquest of the Persian empire numerous Greek-speaking colonies were founded in the new territories and Hellenistic dynasties established in Syria and Egypt. Along with commericial and political structures there developed a vast communication network. Royal chanceries used the letter for government business, whether land transactions, political benefactions, treaty or diplomatic proceedings. This vast correspondence was usually the product of well-trained royal secretaries whose style and terminology was generally stereotyped and formulaic. An example of this genre comes from the chancery of Ptolemy II Philadelphus (c. 262/1 B.C.):

> King Ptolemy to the council and the people of Miletus, greeting (*chairein*). I have in former times shown all zeal in behalf of your city both through a gift of land and through care in all other matters as was proper because I saw that our father was kindly disposed toward the city and was the author of many benefits for you and had relieved you of harsh and oppressive taxes and tolls which certain of the kings had imposed. Now also, as you guard steadfastly your city and our friendship and alliance—for my son and Callicrates and the other friends who are with you have written me what a demonstration you have made of goodwill toward us—we knowing these things praise you highly and shall try to requite your people through benefactions, and we summon you for the future to maintain the same policy of friendship toward us so that in view of your faithfulness we may exercise even more our care for the city. We have ordered Hegestratus to address you at greater length on these subjects and to give you our greeting. Farewell (*errōsthe*).[2]

---

[2]C.B. Wells, *Royal Correspondence in the Hellenistic Period* (New Haven: Yale, 1974) 72-73.

This letter, the first part of a stele which also contains a responding decree by the city-state of Miletus, presents the main features of Hellenistic letters. It opens with a salutation consisting of sender, addressee, and greeting and next, in lieu of the thanksgiving or prayer for good health found in personal letters, there follows a statement of past benefactions. This latter part leads into the body of the letter wherein the king seeks the continued loyalty of his Asian subjects. This goal is enhanced by the promise of future good will from the Ptolemaic dynasty. Prior to the farewell, a note indicates that the letter is but one means of communication since its bearer, Hegestratus, brings further and more personal greetings from the sender.[3] See Acts 15:23-29 for Luke's knowledge and use of these epistolary conventions.

If throughout the Hellenistic period the epistolary genre remained relatively stable and favored stereotyped and non-personal formulas, it displayed much variety as it took on different functions. The Hellenistic period offers official, public, business, non-real ("fictitious"), discursive ("letter-essay"), and personal letters.[4] The letter given above falls under the category of official letter, since it deals with government business and seeks to convey to the readers a sense of the writer's presence and authority. As Doty states. "It may be helpful to compare the epistolary situations of such letters with the primitive Christian epistolary situations, in which one strong leader sent information, directions, and the like, to the Christian communities, as one having the power and authority to do so."[5] Paul felt he had the authority to intervene in the affairs of communities he founded, though attention to his letters shows that he was reluctant to employ his authority as a means of persuasion (1 Thess. 2:6). The motivation of the Pastor in composing 1-2 Timothy and Titus, however, is illuminated by such comparison.

The Hellenistic letter was used for many purposes. Study of the numerous papyri discovered in Egypt at the turn of the century sheds light on the form, function, and vocabulary of NT letters. The Zenon archives offer a model letter of recommendation (255 B.C.):

---

[3]The issue of the letter carrier is discussed further below when considering the structure of 1 Corinthians.

[4]W.G. Doty, *Letters in Primitive Christianity* (Philadelphia: Fortress, 1973) 4-8 and J.L. White, "New Testament Epistolary Literature in the Framework of Ancient Epistolograhy," 2:25:2:1730-56 in Temporini and Haase, *Aufstieg und Niedergang der römischer Welt* (1984).

[5]*Ibid.*, 6.

Platon to Zenon greeting. The father of Demetrius the bearer of this letter happens, it seems, to be residing in the Arsinoite nome, and the lad therefore wishes to find employment there himself. On hearing of your kindly disposition some of his friends asked me to write to you about him, begging you to give him a post in your service. Please then do me a favour and provide some employment for him, whatever you may think suitable, and otherwise look after him, if you find him useful. As a token (of good will) I have sent you, from Sosus, 2 artabae of chickpeas bought at 5 drachmae each, and if there are any at Naucratis, I will try to buy you about two artabae more and bring them up to you myself. Good-bye. Year 31, Dius 12. (Addressed) to Zenon.[6]

The letter is a model of proper diction to "dispose kindly" the recipient of the letter and to induce him without undue pressure to grant the favor requested. Even a "token of inducement" is brought to bear upon the petition. As regard the New Testament, Paul is aware of the genre known as the letter of recommendation (2 Cor. 3:1-3) and even composes a short one for a fellow worker, "Phoebe, a deaconess of the church of Cenchreae" (Rom. 16:1-2).

For our study of Paul, however, it is the personal letter which is of concern. This type follows the standard conventions of opening (writer, addressee, greeting) and concluding farewell. After the opening a wish of good health or prayer to the gods follows and then the body of the letter with its principal message. Often the author concludes with exhortation and greetings or salutations to friends and members of the family. Paul in all his letters follows these epistolary conventions but regularly adapts these to his needs. While the openings tended to get longer and more complex as he progressed in his writing career, nonetheless, his letters retain the basic threefold structure of Hellenistic openings. It is the thanksgiving section, in lieu of wishes of good health, which call for Paul's greatest fervor as he thanks God for granting faith through Christ. In the body of the letters Paul addresses issues of concern to his young Christian communities. It is at the end of these compositions that Paul briefly exhorts his fellow-believers to live lives worthy of their calling. Finally, in place of the usual closing, Paul employs Christian formulas, doxologies, and benedictions to end his

[6]A.S. Hunt and C.C. Edgar, *Select Papyri I* (Cambridge: Harvard University, 1970) 274-75, # 92.

letters. Thus, Paul makes creative use of the epistolary conventions of his day to communicate with his dispersed communities.[7]

If, after Paul's death, Christians continued to compose letter-like documents, many of these have little resemblance to epistolary compositions. Some have only the barest similarity to the letter genre (James, 2 Peter, Jude), while others have no epistolary features at all (Hebrews, 1 John). A few, however, show a marked return to the conventional letter: 1 Peter, 2 and 3 John. The Paulinist writers of course modeled their compositions on the Pauline letter.

The Hellenistic letter, therefore, is important for comprehending the majority of NT compositions, for it is the immediate or distant model for these writings. NT authors, whether borrowing from contemporary Greek culture or imitating the apostle to the Gentile, composed epistolary, pastoral documents for the instruction, correction, and edification of their audiences. Their motives for writing, the vocabulary employed, and the relevance of their message are bound with their choice of the epistolary genre to express themselves. These texts, therefore, must be understood as "occasional" letters.

The Chronology and Background of Paul

There are three sources from which to draw data to reconstruct Paul's life. These are the seven authentic letters, later NT writings which speak of Paul, and post-NT sources. The last mentioned range from the anti-Pauline Pseudo-Clementines, to the fictitious compositions about Paul and Thecla and Paul and Seneca, and finally to Jerome's observations about Paul in his Lives of Illustrious Men (chapter 5). Only Jerome's Gischala traditions are seriously discussed and, as a result, all but the most conservative scholars dismiss these as 3rd or 4th century attempts, on the basis of NT data, to situate Paul or his family in a Palestinian milieu.[8]

[7]Doty, Letters, 43, presents a convenient chart of the epistolary components of the Pauline epistles.

[8]See D.J. Selby, Toward the Understanding of St. Paul (Englewood Cliffs: Prentice-Hall, 1962) and G. Bornkamm, Paul—Paulus (NY: Harper & Row, 1971). For excellent, popular introductions to Paul and the Pauline writings, see Keck, Paul and His Letters; C.J. Roetzel, The Letters of Paul: Conversations in Context (Atlanta: John Knox, 1982); Ziesler, Pauline Christianity; and J. Plevnik, What Are They Saying About Paul? (NY: Paulist, 1986).

Concerning the two other sources, the situation is far more complex. It is also at this point that discussion of Pauline chronology begins. Most scholars employ data both from the Acts of the Apostles and Paul's authentic letters to reconstruct this chronology. The pivotal data are drawn from Acts 18 and Gal. 1-2, Paul's encounter according to Luke with Gallio and Paul's own apologetic statement of his early years as a follower of Christ. These sets of data form the basis of most chronological schemas. From Acts 18:12-17 we learn that Paul was hailed before the proconsul of Achaia while staying in Corinth. Thanks to a Greek inscription discovered in 1905 at Delphi and to other historical information it is possible to date this event to the years 51/52 when Lucius Junius Gallio, brother of Seneca, was proconsul of the Achaian province.[9] Important for such reconstructions are two other statements from Acts 18. It is said in the verse preceding the Gallio episode that Paul "stayed a year and six months" in Corinth (v. 11). Prior to this Luke states that Paul encountered a husband and wife, "lately come from Italy . . . because Claudius had commanded all the Jews to leave Rome" (v. 2)—it is presumed by most scholars, on the authority of the 5th-century Christian writer Orosius, that the Claudian edict took place in 49 A.D.[10] Employing these data it is possible to date the Jerusalem council of Acts 15 to the years 48 or 49. In addition, scholars employ Paul's statements in Gal. 1-2 where he establishes the following chronological and geographical sequence: conversion and Arabian sojourn, first brief visit to Jerusalem 3 years later, sojourn in Syria and Cilicia, and finally another visit 14 years later to Jerusalem with Barnabas and Titus.

With these data scholars reconstruct the principal periods of Pauline chronology. There follows two such, frequently employed outlines[11]:

---

[9]See C.K. Barrett, ed., *The New Testament Background: Selected Documents* (NY: Harper & Row, 1961); H.C. Kee, ed., *The New Testament in Context: Sources and Documents* (Englewood Cliffs: Prentice-Hall , 1984); and J. Murphy-O'Connor, *St. Paul's Corinth: Texts and Archaeology* (Wilmington: Glazier, 1983).

[10]For easy access to the various ancient texts involved, see Murphy-O'Connor, *ibid.*, 129-50.

[11]J.A. Fitzmyer, "A Life of Paul," 2:215-22 in *JBC*; and Kümmel, *Introduction to the New Testament*, 252-55; see also Finegan, *Handbook of Biblical Chronology*, 315-25.

J.A. Fitzmyer	W.G. Kümmel
c 36 conversion	31/32 conversion
c 40 1st Jerusalem visit	34/35 lst visit to Jerusalem
c 46 famine visit	34/35-48 stay in Syria and Cilicia
46-49 1st journey	48 apostolic council
49 council	48-51/52 1st journey to Asia
49-52 2nd journey	Minor and Greece
(edict 49; Gallio 51/52)	51/52-55/56 2nd journey to Asia
54-57 3rd journey	Minor and Greece
58 imprisonment	c 55/56 arrival in Jerusalem
60 Rome	

The key to both outlines is the dating of the Gallio episode (51/52) and Claudian edict (49). Fitzmyer draws further from Acts to give chronological precision both to the missionary journeys and Paul's conversion. Since Luke in Acts 7 and 9 associates the death of Stephen and the conversion of Paul, Fitzmyer proposes 36 as the logical date for these since that year would explain the necessary sequence of events: removal of Pilate from office in Judaea, the death of Stephen and conversion of Paul in the interim, and the arrival of the new prefect. This requires further that the 14 years of Gal. 2:1 be read inclusive of the 3 years mentioned earlier in 1:18. Kümmel instead reads these two passages as consecutive and therefore places Paul's conversion 16 years prior to the Jerusalem council, 31/32.

Despite continued debate over the relation of Acts 15 (the Jerusalem council) to the Jerusalem visit mentioned in Gal. 2:1,[12] scholars generally follow the Lukan schema of Acts 13-21 as the basis for Paul's ministry and the framework for situating his letters. It was during the second missionary journey through Syria, east Cilicia, Asia Minor, Macedonia, and Achaia according to this schema that Paul founded the communities to which he later sent letters. It is also usually proposed that his first composition, 1 Thessalonians, was written during this journey, (c. the beginning of 51 from Corinth) and that the remainder of his correspondence belongs within the third ministerial journey, once again through Syria, Asia Minor, and the Greek mainland with special attention given to the Greek cities of the Achaian, Macedonian, and

[12]Richard, "The Divine Purpose: The Jews and the Gentile Mission," 188-209.

Asian Roman provinces. Thus, it is postulated that during his extended sojourns in Ephesus, Corinth, and in Macedonia generally he composed Galatians (c. 54 from Ephesus), Philippians (c. 56 also from Ephesus), probably Philemon (the last two are frequently situated during Paul's Roman imprisonment, c. 60), the Corinthian correspondence (c. 57 from Ephesus and Macedonia), and Romans (c. the beginning of 58 from Corinth).

The above synthesis and its apparent consensus may be short-lived for there are some fundamental problems. L.E. Keck's aptly formulated defense of this position will serve as starting point. "The closer the letters stand to one another in time [the 50s], the less persuasive are efforts to trace development in Paul's thought. Differences within the genuine letters must be accounted for on a basis other than development in Paul's thinking."[13] Following J.C. Hurd's important study of Pauline thought,[14] it has become commonplace to stress the important differences between the letters. Keck's observations highlight the problem which the consensus presents to the scholar. If one accepts the thesis that Paul's letters were composed during the 50s then it becomes very difficult to account for these differences. There then remains only one avenue to explain the varying positions which Paul adopts vis-à-vis the Law, the Jews, justification, etc., and that is the audience or context of individual letters.[15] Admittedly, this is a critical factor, but it is made to bear too great a burden, since other possibilities are excluded not because of incontrovertible evidence but on the assumption that Lukan chronology is a firm basis for dating Paul's literary activity. Were we to grant a longer time span for the letters, then "efforts to trace development in Paul's thought" might become more "persuasive."

Recently scholars have returned to the axiom, espoused by John Knox among others, that Paul's authentic letters should be given priority over Luke's chronological indications or, in a more radical vein, that Paul's letters not Acts should provide the temporal framework of the apostle's life and ministry.[16] Advances in Lukan studies have

---

[13]*Paul and His Letters*, 4.

[14]*The Origin of 1 Corinthians* (NY: Seabury, 1965).

[15]See for example K. Stendahl, *Paul Among Jews and Gentiles and Other Essays* (Philadelphia: Fortress, 1976) 1-77.

[16]For the former see R. Jowett, *A Chronology of Paul's Life* (Philadelphia: Fortress, 1979) and for the latter G. Lüdemann, *Paul, Apostle to the Gentiles: Studies in*

confirmed such conclusions.[17] As Luke is increasingly perceived as a historian of the Hellenistic period, Luke-Acts receives fairer judgment from scholars who neither seek the "critical historical accuracy" of modern history nor condemn Luke to the status of writer of fables or of edifying theology. Luke's purpose in composing Acts was to discourse upon the activity of the "absent Lord" whose words and influence were affecting the world of that time. To that purpose the writer employs the wealth of stories about the great missionary to the Gentiles to illustrate in narrative form how "the witness" concerning God's Christ, Son, and great prophet reached the center of the civilized world (Acts 1:8; 28:30). Luke's use of Pauline stories is schematic; the three missionary journeys with a final ministry in Rome are intentional parallels to the gospel's journey motif and final ministry in Jerusalem. Further, Luke's unhistorical (from our perspective), theological use of the census tradition (Luke 2:1-7) and tendency to "round out" stories about particular subjects (e.g., Mary, Luke 1:26-56; John the Baptist, 3:1-20; Peter, Acts 2-12; Jerusalem, Luke 9-Acts 7; Apollos, Acts 18:24-19:7) lead us to reevaluate Acts 18, the key passage for most reconstructions of Pauline chronology.

Since all the Athenian traditions of Acts are gathererd in chapter 17 around the Areopagus speech, we are not surprised to discover that those concerning Corinth are also assembled in one chapter: Aquila-Priscilla (18:1-4), Justus' house (5-11), Gallio (12-17), and Cenchreae (18f). While the reliability of each tradition needs to be tested, the chronology of chapter 18 is clearly artificial. As indicated in the chronological schemas given above, the dates (48/49-52) for the second journey (or first one through Greece) are determined by the data of Acts 18, namely, the references to the Claudian edict in v. 2, to the length of Paul's stay at Corinth in v. 11, and to the Gallio episode in vv. 12-17. But since Luke says in v. 2 that Priscilla and Aquila were "lately come to Italy" it seems inadvisable to press this chronological note. Further, the date usually given for the Claudian edict, 49 A.D., is now questioned and 41 is more likely for this event. Finally, in a recent study, J.

Chronology (Philadelphia: Fortress, 1984); for their overall chronological proposals see pp. 161f (foldout chart) and 262-63 respectively.

[17]Richard, "Luke—Writer, Theologian, Historian," 3-15.

Murphy-O'Connor,[18] while giving priority to the Pauline letters, has concluded that the sequence of events characterized as the "second missionary journey" should probably be situated before the Jerusalem council (51 A.D.) and dated to c. 45-51. I suspect that this new research will establish a longer ministerial and writing career for Paul which will provide greater temporal scope for understanding his developing notion of the Christ's special role and that of the Law within the Jesus movement.[19]

Paul gives ample information about his background and life.[20] On several occasions he underscores his Jewish culture; he belongs to the Jewish race, i.e., he is "of the people of Israel, of the tribe of Benjamin, a Hebrew of Hebrews" (Phil. 3:5; see also Rom. 11:1; 2 Cor. 11:22); he was circumcised on the eighth day, was an eager defender of the tradition of the Fathers, and was a zealous persecutor of the church (Phil. 3:5-6; Gal. 1:13-14; also 1 Cor. 15:9). Though we might expect Paul to be exaggerating when he says in Gal. 1:14, "I advanced in Judaism beyond many of my own age among my people,"[21] we conclude that he was as deeply attached to Jewish tradition as he was later to the Jesus movement. Paul proudly recalls these when he counters the claims of Jewish or Judaizing opponents (2 Corinthians, Galatians, Philippians) or defends the rights of non-Christian Jews (Romans). These are his credentials as far as race are concerned and are all found in passages of self-defense or intense pastoral argument. In one instance he even claims to have been a Pharisaic adherent of the Law and blameless under that same Law (Phil. 3:5-6). However, if he takes pride in his Jewish background; he is nonetheless true to his absolute

[18]"Pauline Missions before the Jerusalem Conference," *RB* 89 (1982) 71-91; see 84-86 for a discussion of the date of the Claudian edict and the acceptance, in agreement with Lüdemann, *Paul, Apostle to the Gentiles*, 164-71, of 41 as the probable date.

[19]See the convient overview of J.A. Darr, "Chronologies of Paul," 352-60 in D. Patte, *Paul's Faith and the Power of the Gospel: A Structural Introduction to the Pauline Letters* (Philadelphia: Fortress, 1983).

[20]On the proper interpretation and use of Pauline autobiographical statements, see G. Lyons, *Pauline Autobiography: Toward a New Understanding* (Atlanta: Scholars, 1985), especially 223-27. For Paul's background see Zeisler, *Pauline Christianity*, 8-27; Keck, *Paul and His Letters*, 1-29; Plevnik, *What Are They Saying about Paul?* 5-27; and Roetzel, *the Letters of Paul*, 6-28.

[21]Paul is alternately defending himself against Judaizers and expounding his gospel of freedom; thus he is doing no less than Josephus who, in *Against Apion*, describes himself in self-defense as a child prodigy; see also Luke 2:41-51 concerning Jesus.

commitment to Christ crucified, when he concludes "but whatever gain I had, I counted as loss for the sake of Christ" (Phil. 3:7). Thus, more than polemics is involved in Paul's autobiographical outbursts.

A major event turned Paul's world upside down; God revealed the Son to him (Gal. 1:16). This event Paul himself compares to the resurrection appearances of Christ to his early followers (1 Cor. 15:8). In other words, Paul transferred his single-minded alligiance from Pharisaic zeal for the Torah to an absolute faith in Christ crucified (we will return later to the meaning of the Christ-event for Paul). The successes and failures, the joys and sufferings, and feverish activity of the apostle to the Gentiles are glimpsed at various points throughout the Pauline correspondence, (e.g., 2 Cor. 11:23f; Gal. 1:16f; Phil. 3:7f).

Paul was proud of his Jewish culture and spent much effort developing the ramifications of the relationship between Israel and the Christ-event . When some (advocates of a Law-observant mission to Gentiles) attempted to relativize the role of Christ by subjugating his activity to Moses and the Law, Paul insisted that one "is justified by faith in Christ, and not by works of the Law" (Gal. 2:16); or when others (Jewish missionary opponents from Palestine)[22] tried to usurp Paul's place and undermine his gospel of freedom by boasting of their Jewish pedigree, Paul did not hesitate to claim as much for himself, noting that all such boasting was foolishness anyway (2 Cor. 11:21f). In less polemical situations, where Judaism is not at issue, Paul draws from his background and personal history to explore the richness of the Christ-event and to exemplify Christian behavior by using himself ("join in imitating me," Phil. 3:17) or Christ ("have this mind among yourselves which is yours in Christ Jesus," Phil. 2:5) as paradigm.[23] Finally, Paul theologizes by appealing to the Hebrew scriptures, from which he draws inspiration for his Christ-centered message. He quotes the Septuagint

---

[22]The characterization of Paul as a close ally of the Jerusalem church and as a Pharisaic Christian educated by Gamaliel should be credited to Lukan redaction of Pauline stories; see de Boer, "Images of Paul in the Post-Apostolic." 359-80 and Richard, "Luke—Writer, Theologian, Historian," 6-8.

[23]D.M. Stanley, " 'Become Imitators of Me': Apostolic Tradition in Paul," 197-211 in M.J. Taylor, ed., *A Companion to Paul: Readings in Pauline Theology* (NY: Alba House, 1975); Lyons, *Pauline Autobiography*, 223-27; W.S. Kurz, "Kenotic Imitation of Paul and of Christ in Philippians 2 and 3," 103-26 in Segovia, *Discipleship in the New Testament*; and V.P. Furnish, *Theology and Ethics in Paul* (Nashville: Abingdon, 1982) 218-23.

frequently and draws upon oral tradition to formulate his pastoral responses.[24]

Letters of Paul: A Brief Introduction

Paul, missionary to the Gentles, preached in Greater Syria (Syria-Palestine and Arabia) and founded churches in Asia Minor and the Greek peninsula. His letters reveal extensive pastoral activity in those areas, corroborated in large measure by Luke in Acts. Paul saw himself as entrusted with the Gentile mission (in this regard he claimed apostleship) and, in terms of service, as one who traveled about founding new communities. If initially he experienced uncomplicated success, his letters reveal that "planting and laying foundations" (1 Cor. 3:6, 10) became more involved as the process gained momentum. In some instances, Jewish Christian missionaries sought to transform his Gentile community into a Law-observant mission; in others, the fertile imaginations of new converts and the glory-seeking machinations of traveling preachers brought disunity and threatended chaos in the communities; in still other cases, new problems, projects (collection for the poor), and plans (visits, new mission fields) arose as Paul pursued his missionary activities. The Pauline mission, therefore, required more than initial contacts for preaching and founding of churches.[25]

If Paul did not realize at the beginning that authority and presence are related, he became convinced as the mission progressed, for all his letters deal in some way with this issue. There were several ways of being present (*parousia* in Greek) in a community: physical presence, written word, delegated authority, and live tradition.[26] The last mentioned, i.e., live tradition, alluded to in 1 Cor. 1:12 and the related theme of apostolic imitation (1 Thess. 1:6) will lead to pseudonymity in the post-Pauline letters. As regard delegated authority, Paul often employed emissaries to resolve problems, to send messages, or to convey his authority. By far the most important, however, were actual presence or, in lieu of this, a

---

[24]Richard, "Polemics, Old Testament, and Theology," 340-67.

[25]For an attempt to discern the patterns and degree of success of Paul's demonstrated leadership, see H. Doohan, *Leadership in Paul* (Wilmington: Glazier, 1984)

[26]See R.W. Funk on "apostolic presence," 81-102 in *Parables and Presence* (Philadelphia: Fortress, 1982).

letter which was considered an extension of that person. Hellenistic letters routinely mention the forthcoming presence of the writer; Paul's letters almost all contain travelogues where Paul announces his plans or imminent arrival. As a result of this Hellenistic convention and Paul's urgent, pastoral needs we have become heirs to several Pauline documents. As Paul traveled throughout the eastern part of the Roman empire, he found it helpful and necessary to write various communities to resolve problems or address pertinent issues since he could not or, in the case of the Corinthians, did not want to be among the addressees.

Scholars, therefore, rightly stress the "occasional" nature of the Pauline letters, for they are conversations of Paul with his communities. The letters were composed for specific groups with particular problems and backgrounds. Rather than being theological tracts addressed to abstract audiences, the letters are the result of a pastor's concern for his "children in the Lord." Thus, acquaintance with the context of each letter and with the social, religious, and political world of the time is essential for understanding the author's message.[27]

Several related issues need brief discussion before we treat the letters individually, namely, the order, chronology, and editing of the letters. Earlier in the chapter we discussed the standard dating and order of Paul's letters, i.e., based on the chronology of Acts and composed between 51 and 58. However, in view of new proposals for Pauline chronology, a wider span, beginning in the 40s rather than in the 50s, needs to be considered for the composition of the letters. Thus, owing to their eschatology, the Thessalonian correspondence and the letter to the Romans must be situated first and last in Paul's career.[28] Further, his increasing concern with Christ's atoning death in the Corinthian correspondence and Romans (note its absence in Thessalonians and Philippians and minor role in Galatians) offers an additional chronological indicator. Lastly, examination of the epistolary components of these texts, especially the opening, shows structural evolution as Paul

---

[27]W.A. Meeks, *The First Urban Christians: The Social World of the Apostle Paul* (New Haven: Yale University, 1983); Theissen, *The Social Setting of Pauline Christianity*; and Malina, *The New Testament World*.

[28]As an example of Paul's development in the use of eschatological concepts and terminology, see J. Gillman, "Signals of Transformation in 1 Thessalonians 4:13-18," *CBQ* 47 (1985) 263-81; though see the caution of J. Plevnik, "The Taking up of the Faithful and the Resurrection of the Dead in 1 Thessalonians 4:13-18," *CBQ* 46 (1984) 280-83.

develops as a letter writer. Based on these indicators and anticipating the discussion of the Pauline letters, we propose the following chronology:

early 40s: 1st Thessalonian missive (2:13-4:2)
later 40s: 2nd Thessalonian missive (1:1-2:12 + 4:3-5:28)
    1st Philippian letter (1:1-3:1a + 4:10-23)
    Philemon
end 40s/beg 50s: 2nd Philippian letter (3:1b-4:9)
after 51: Galatians (Jerusalem meeting)
mid 50s: Corinthian correspondence
c. 58: Romans.

Concerning the editing and publication of the Pauline letters, we are very much in the dark. It is clear from the letters that the author did not view them as showcases for posterity but as pastoral documents written to his communities. As Paul gained renown, various disciples imitated his writing style (Paulinists) or defended him against misinterpretation (James and 2 Peter). At the end of the first century or the beginning of the second Paul's letters became known to a wider audience. While little is known about the activity surrounding the dissemination of the Pauline letters, we can still detect the hand of an editor who combined letters and fragments to produce the composite documents of 1 Thessalonians, Philippians, and 2 Corinthians, and probably added chapter 16 to Romans. One thing clear about the publication of the Pauline letters is that these "occasional" documents, as a result of the interest stirred up by the Paulinist writers, were collected and edited in the first decades of the second century as the Pauline legend and his Christ-centered message gained increased prominence in the early churches.

Thessalonian Correspondence

If we are correct in seeing Paul's missionary activity as taking him first to Syria and Cilicia and, during the remainder of the fourteen years (Gal. 1:21; 2:1), to Asia Minor, and the Greek mainland, then we may conclude that, crossing the Aegean Sea from Troas, he picked up the Via Egnatia as he worked his way west. Prior to arriving at Thessalonica, he spent some time at Philippi, an important city on the Roman highway, where he preached the gospel but was also "shamefully treated" (1 Thess. 2:2). From there he traveled to Thessalonica, which received him warmly (1:9). The Thessalonian correspondence is a product of this missionary activity among the Gentile population. While not the first Pauline church either in Macedonia (Philippi, see above) or in Asia Minor (for Troas, see 2 Cor. 2:12 and for Galatia, Gal. 4:13 and Phil. 4:15),[29] the Thessalonian community, nonetheless, acquired the distinction of being the recipient of the first extant Pauline letter.

The structure of 1 Thessalonians presents several anomalies. While the document has a standard opening and closing, only it among the Pauline letters has two thanksgiving sections (1:2f and 2:13).[30] Further, 2:14-16 contains some very un-Pauline statements;[31] and 3:11-4:2 sounds like the conclusion of a letter. Also, there are several passages in the document which present tensions. In 2:17 Paul is writing shortly after having left Thessalonica, while in 1:8f he suggests that there has been a lapse of time since he first preached there. The central section (end of chap. 2 and all of chap. 3) deals with Paul's concern for the community and his desire to be among them, but the final two chapters dwell at length upon community problems which also presume a lapse of time. Taking the above indicators into consideration, we are led, in agreement with other scholars, to defend the composite character of 1 Thessalonians: first letter: 2:13-4:2 and second letter: 1:1-2:12 + 4:3-5:28.[32]

FIRST MISSIVE

2:13-4:2 represents the nearly-complete first missive of Paul to Thessalonica. The letter would have lost its opening and possibly part of its conclusion either during the process of transmission or of editing. Paul in this short letter thanks God for the faith of his beloved

[29]See the discussion of Murphy-O'Connor, "Pauline Missions," 82.

[30]See our discussion in the next chapter of the pseudonymous 2 Thessalonians, which also has two thanksgiving sections.

[31]One does not "imitate churches" in Paul; besides other such anti-Jewish statements are not to be found in the authentic letters. Further, the outburst against the Jews of Palestine is totally unmotivated in the document. We therefore conclude that 2:14-16 is an interpolation. For further discussion, see D. Schmidt, "1 Thess. 2:13-16: Linguistic Evidence for an Interpolation," *JBL* 102 (1983) 269-79 and Lyons, *Pauline Autobiography* 202-7.

[32]See also Murphy-O'Connor, "Pauline Missions," 82, including notes 15 and 16, both for the partition and relative dating of these two passages; *contra* Lyons, *Pauline Autobiography*, 177-82.

Thessalonians but manifests great concern in their regard. Apparently the community received the word of God in the midst of affliction (3:3-4) and though Paul does not say what these sufferings are, by using the terms "our lot" and "we told you beforehand" he suggests that social and religious separation of believers from their Roman neighbors would bring about difficulties. Why Paul had misgivings about the strength of his converts' faith is not immediately discernible, but that he was concerned can be read throughout the letter. While in the vicinity of Athens, he attempted unsuccessfully (Satan is said to be the obstacle; see 2 Cor. 12:7) to look in on them. Unable to go to them and to bear the uncertainty any longer, Paul sent Timothy to find out how the community was faring, hoping all the while that they had not reverted to pagan ways (3:1-5).

To Paul's relief, Timothy had only good news and reciprocal affection to report; things were as they should be at Thessalonica and Paul is thankful that they are "standing fast in the Lord" (3:8). He reiterates his desire to see them and prays that God will direct his way there (3:11). Satisfied that they have remained faithful, Paul wishes to strengthen their faith ("supply what is lacking") that love abound and they be presented in holiness before God at the parousia (3:10-13). At 4:1 we encounter what seems to be the beginning of an exhortation: "finally, brethren, we beseech and exhort you in the Lord Jesus."

What we have here, therefore, is a missive from a missionary who experiences anguish at being separated from a recently founded, struggling community. The composition focuses on the apostolic presence or parousia of the apostle who is "bereft" (literally: "made an orphan") of his beloved (2:17); since Paul could not be present, he reaches out to the Thessalonians first by sending an emissary, and then by writing a moving letter of concern and affection.

SECOND MISSIVE

1:1-2:12 + 4:3-5:28, in our estimation, is a later document which an editor used as a frame for the short missive discussed above. Further, it too bears the standard features of the Hellenistic letter. By the time Paul writes this letter the reputation of the Thessalonian believers has spread throughout the Roman provinces of Macedonia and Achaia (1:7-8; 4:10). Problems hinted at in the earlier letter now take center stage as Paul addresses the issues one expects in a maturing community. Previously he was concerned whether his "labor would be in vain" (3:5), now he knows that it was not (2:1). In the first letter there was merely an allusion to ministerial conflicts ("not as the word of men," 2:13), in the second the topic becomes more serious as accusations of greed and flattery are leveled against him and his associates (2:2-6a). For the first time we hear the familiar Pauline disclaimer that he "did not seek glory from men" as he defends himself solemnly (2:2): "you are witnesses, and God also, how holy and righteous and blameless was our behavior to you believers" (2:10; also 1:5). Here too one encounters what becomes a Pauline trademark, namely, his indirect and effective use of authority. Paul strives to persuade though he and his colleagues "might have made demands as apostles of Christ" (2:6b). This letter, therefore, represents a later stage in the Thessalonian community's development, a state of affairs paralleled in the letter to the Philippians. We would note that at Thessalonica some members are dying (4:13f) and that new ministers are laboring in the community (5:12).

Paul's relation to the community is an interesting feature of both letters. As the members experience the pains of growth and tests of their loyalty, they receive touching statements of Paul's dedication to them; he is "like a nurse taking care of her children" (2:7)[33] or "like a father with his children" (2:11) for they received him and his message with open arms (1:9) and continued to remember him with affection (first letter: 3:6). Like a father Paul is concerned about his children and they are solicitous of his advice, for the remainder of the letter (4:3f) reads like a series of responses made to questions addressed to Paul by the developing Thessalonian community. Thus, he comments on issues of concern to them: immorality (4:3-8), love of the brethren (4:9-12), believers who die before the parousia (4:13-18), and the time of the end-days (5:1-11). It should be noted that the last three are introduced by "now concerning" much as in 1 Cor. 7:1f. There is in both letters, therefore, praise and exhortation. Here also, at the beginning of Paul's writing career, one notices his acquintance with the philosophy and rhetoric popular in his day as he develops their favorite themes, employs their slogans, and puts to effective use their rhetorical devices to

[33]A.J. Malherbe, "'Gentle as a Nurse': The Cynic Background to 1 Thess. ii," *NovT* 12 (1970) 203-17.

communicate with and exhort to more sublime behavior his Thessalonian community.[34]

The letter ends with a paraenetic section (5:12-22) and a brief closing (5:23-28). In v. 27 already Paul is conscious of the pastoral role which his letters are to play in his ever-expanding mission. Finally, we note the kerygmatic fragment used by Paul in communicating and possibly preaching to Gentiles, 1:9-10.[35]

Philippian Correspondence

From Paul's correspondence we infer that he crossed from Asia Minor to Macedonia and proceeded west on the Via Egnatia where he made stops first at Philippi and then at Thessalonica to declare the good news to the inhabitants. In his second missive to the Thessalonians (2:2), while speaking of the adversity he encountered when proclaiming the good news to them, he states that he and his colleagues "had already suffered and been shamefully treated at Philippi." What Paul is referring to in this verse we can only conjecture; but, no doubt, this involved the treatment often received by the proponents of foreign cults. Later when defending his ministry to his Corinthian audience (2 Cor. 11:23f), he will speak of labors, imprisonments, countless beatings ("often near death"), lashes, stoning, and shipwreck in the service of Christ. Nonetheless, his work at Philippi was successful since we have inherited some of his correspondence with that community and have echoes of this in Luke's Acts and Polycarp. Furthermore, his relation to this community must have been cordial since they "entered into partnership with" him in contributing repeatedly to his support "even in Thessalonica" (Phil. 4:16).

Like the Thessalonian correspondence that to Philippi shows clear traces of editorial work.[36] Scholars point to abrupt transitions (3:2 and 4:10), to several "finally or rejoice" connectives (3:1; 4:4, 8, 10), to the

---

[34]See also Malherbe's analysis of 1 Thessalonians as a paraenetic letter in *Social Aspects of Early Christianity*, 22-28.

[35]Confer chapter 3 above for an analysis of these verses.

[36]The reference in Phil. 1:2 to "bishops/overseers and deacons" could be explained as terminology from Philippian trade or cult clubs to which some Christians would have belonged or else as a trace of a later editor who anachronistically read later church structures into Paul's letters.

independent character of 4:10-20 (on Paul's gratitude) and 2:19-30 (on the projected missions of Timothy and Epaphroditus), and finally to the unexpectedly severe tone of 3:2f against Judaizing opponents. It has become customary to speak of a principal document, called the "joyful letter" (1:1-3:1; 4:4-7, 21-23), to which were added several independent fragments.[37] After examining these literary and structural indicators, particularly the double conclusion of 3:1 and 4:8 ("finally": *to loipon*),[38] we conclude that Philippians is a composite document consisting of two letters: 1:1-3:1a + 4:10-23 and 3:1b-4:9.[39]

FIRST LETTER

The first of the two letters, 1:1-3:1a + 4:10-23, provides the frame of the present document for it furnishes its opening, thanksgiving, body, and developed but interrupted closing. Examination of Paul's attitude toward rival missionaries in these two segments indicates that the "joyful letter" is the earlier of the two. In it, while he castigates the envy and partisanship of some preachers to Philippi, he nonetheless in a conciliatory statement concludes that what is important is that Christ is proclaimed (1:18). His treatment of the Judaizers (3:2f) takes on a very different tone in the second letter. This first missive, however, is one of thanksgiving, partnership, joy, confidence, and attachment. Paul is overjoyed ("rejoice" and "joy" are used 10 times) at the behavior of this Macedonian community. Indeed the occasion for the letter is the arrival of Epaphroditus with "gifts" from Philippi (4:18). Further, the community's emissary, in performing his duty vis-à-vis Paul on behalf of the Philippians, has become homesick and ill while at the apostle's side and there is general concern about him. Paul decides to send him back (2:25-30), as bearer of this letter. He also expresses his hope both to send Timothy to them for further instruction (2:19-22) and to come himself in the near future (2:24); but all would depend on the outcome of his imprisonment (2:23).

---

[37]E. Lohse, *The Formation of the New Testament* (Nashville: Abingdon, 1981) 81-82; see also J.A. Fitzmyer, "The Letter to the Philippians," 2:248 in *JBC*, who adds that Polycarp in his correspondence to the Philippians speaks of Paul's letters (in the plural) to Philippi.

[38]This expression also indicates conclusions in 1 Thess. 4:1; Gal. 6:17; and 2 Cor. 13:11.

[39]For a slightly different assessment of the composite nature of Philippians, see J.-F. Collange, *The Epistle of Saint Paul to the Philippians* (London: Epworth, 1979) 3-15.

This letter was written some time after the original mission at Philippi for Paul speaks of a long period of partnership between him and the community ("from the first day until now," 1:5; also 4:14-18). At 4:10 he even hints at a period of separation and cooling off of relations between them, a relationship which is being renewed ("now at length you have revived your concern for me"). Besides, there are other preachers now at Philippi (1:15-18) and Epaphroditus and others have taken several trips to bring him news and assistance (2:26; 4:16).

Two themes, gift and imprisonment, are crucial for our understanding of the occasion and tone of the first Philippian letter. The two are related since it is Paul's predicament which evokes the renewed concern on the part of the Macedonian community. More fundamentally, these two themes provide us the key to Paul's pastoral situation vis-à-vis the Philippians. The arrival of Epaphroditus with the Philippian gift is only the immediate occasion for Paul's writing, for the theme of gift permeates the whole letter. Paul the imprisoned missionary is grateful for the gift and the concern of his children; the whole letter exudes gratitude. He is "thankful for [their] partnership in the gospel" (1:5; see also 4:15), for they partake (1:7), and share (1:14) in his ministry. Text after text hints at the gift which arrived from Philippi. He prays that their "love may abound more and more" (1:9), that they may be "filled with the fruits of righteousness" (1:11), and states that "God is at work in [them], both to will and to work for his good pleasure" (2:13). The thanksgiving section (1:3-12) and the two passages dealing with Epaphroditus (2:25-30; 4:10-20) stress Paul's gratitude for the Philippian gifts. In typical fashion Paul does not dwell on this personal theme; instead, the mention of gift leads him to speak of the Philippians' sharing in his ministry or God supplying their need (4:19). This tendency to avoid discussion of personal matters, therefore, makes the pervasive theme of gift the more significant. Why then does Paul insist on the action of the Philippians beyond the genuine expression of gratitude?

This leads to a discussion of Paul's imprisonment and its bearing on the situation of the first missive. The arrival of Epaphroditus with assistance is the catalyst for Paul's letter, for it persuades him that this Macedonian community understands the true nature of apostolic ministry and is not deceived by those who "preach Christ from envy and rivalry" (1:15). Paul's imprisonment is the cause of dissension at Philippi. Throughout the letter (1:7, 12f, 16, 19-26; 2:17f; 4:10f) reference is made to his situation. Apparently, some do not believe God is on

Paul's side; for them Paul and his chains are the problem. Paul, in an interesting passage, gives the clue to the problem:

1:15 a Some indeed preach Christ from envy and rivalry,
    b   but others from good will.
16 b'   The latter do it out of love,
        knowing that I am put here
        for the defense of the gospel;
17 a'   the former proclaim Christ out of partisanship,
        not sincerely
        but thinking to afflict me in my imprisonment.

The chiastic arrangement (neg/pos/pos/neg) gives clarity to the author's thought; some are on Paul's side; others are opposed to him. After qualifying these groups as motivated by good will and lack of sincerity, Paul dwells upon the key issue of his letter. Some ministers at Philippi see Paul's imprisonment as weakness and attempt to discredit him. Others, representing the community generally, see Paul's confinement as advancing the good news (1:16-17). Paul agrees, for not only does his imprisonment allow him to preach (1:12f), but he insists that Christian life and ministry (1:30) be patterned on the Christ-event itself, i.e., the death and resurrection (2:1-11). Only through obedient weakness (use of an early hymn for this purpose) was Christ able to conquer. By this pattern Paul's ministry, now confronted by imprisonment, must be judged. Paul rejoices not only that he is able to suffer for Christ (1:13), even perhaps in death (2:17), but also that the Philippians perceive his imprisonment as part of God's plan ("put here for the defense of the gospel," 1:16). Already in the thanksgiving section he had praised them for their knowledge and discernment and that they might continue "to approve what is excellent" (1:9-10). The gifts from Philippi, therefore, are for Paul a sign of the community's maturity, "a fragrant offering, a sacrifice acceptable and pleasing to God" (4:18). They, like Christ whom they are encouraged to imitate, recognize that only obedience to God's plan works "to the glory of God the Father" (2:11).

SECOND LETTER

3:1b-4:9 derives from a later document sent to Philippi. The tone, subject, and opponents of this section are different from what one encounters in the first letter. While there was opposition to Paul's continued influence at Philippi, the apostle concluded, in that first missive, that the disruptive activity of some preachers was not calamitous since Christ was still being proclaimed (1:18).[40] In Phil. 3:1b Paul addresses a new group of preachers. Far from conciliatory toward his Philippian opposition, he now, in a threefold indictment, labels them "dogs," "evil-workers," and "mutilators of the flesh" (3:2).[41] Further, he dwells on the themes of flesh and circumcision and on his own Jewish background. Finally, he is uncompromising toward these new preachers as he tearfully calls them "enemies of the cross of Christ" (3:18).

This new missive follows the concluding statement of 3:1a and itself contains an impressive paraenesis (4:1f) and conclusion (4:8-9). It is introduced by Paul's apologetic statement in 3:1b and is devoted to a different issue than was the first letter. In place of the joy and cordiality of a grateful Paul, we find here the theologian who senses a challenge to the Christ-event's primacy. So he confronts directly those who "oppose" the cross for, as he says, "to write the same things to you is not irksome to me, and is safe for you" (3:1b). From this statement and from 3:18 ("I have often told you") we conclude that the issue is not entirely new. The Philippians are put on their guard against Law-observant missionaries who insist upon circumcision for Gentile converts. Paul counters their claims of "confidence in the flesh" by insisting, that he once had a greater claim to confidence. Instead of clinging to such "gain" he counted it "as loss because of the surpassing worth of knowing Christ Jesus (the) Lord" (3:8; also 2:6f). He insists that righteousness depends on faith and is not based on the Law. Paul concludes with one of his most profound passages, 3:10-11; the power of Christ's resurrection is at work now in the one who shares in Christ's suffering and death while awaiting the resurrection from the dead. The past, present, and future of the Christ-event and its transforming power are at the center of Paul's Christ-centered anthropology.

In stream-of-consciousness fashion, the mention of what is yet to come recalls the opponents' claim that they have achieved perfection.

---

[40]The opponents of 1:28 have no relation to the Jewish preachers of chap. 3; they are to be identified as non-Christian opposition to the cross, much as one finds in 1 Cor. 1:18. See Phil. 3:19 where the Judaizers are also threatened with eschatological judgment.

[41]Since the term "dog" was sometimes used by Jews to designate Gentiles (Matt. 7:6) it is probable that Paul here uses the expression ironically of Judaizing Christians. For "evildoers" see 2 Cor. 11:13.

So, 3:12f attacks the notion that the resurrection has already occurred for the Christian and instead, relying on the popular image of the race, Paul challenges his Philippian audience to look ahead to "the goal for the prize of the upward call of God in Christ Jesus" (3:14). In this lies Christian maturity.[42] Paul mentions again the theme of apostolic imitation and its reverse in the lives of his Law-observant opponents (3:17f), who seek earthly things rather than strive for a heavenly prize. Paul, in opposition to these preachers' stress on the present nature of salvation, underscores the eschatological character and goal of the Christ-event and looks forward to the Lord's return (3:20-21).[43] Paul ends his letter by advising the community to stand firm in the Lord (4:1), to rejoice as they, relying upon God for every good thing (4:6), await the Lord's return.

The Epistle to the Philippians, as it now stands, presents two important "imitation" sections, having Christ as model in the first (chap. 2) and Paul as example in the second (chap. 3). Indeed, the two passages and their surrounding narratives offer interesting parallels of theme and language.[44] Nonetheless, close scrutiny shows that the passages have a different setting, focus, and function. In the first instance, owing to Paul's prison situation, there is a risk that his missionary project in Philippi will be jeopardised. Divine approval is paramount in the minds of many in the community (1:17). The apostle employs this argument by insisting that the Christ-event and therefore life in Christ are dependent on obedience to God's design, i.e., divine approval is based on obedient submission (2:8). Christ "poured out his life as libation" on the cross and even Paul might be called upon to do likewise (2:8, 17). The paradigm by which to judge success in Christian terms is the paradoxical example of Christ, the cross and resurrection. Paul is joyful that the Philippians have understood; the gift is proof and Paul promises to visit soon if the Lord permits. So in view of the eschatological hope, they are to "be glad and rejoice" (2:18).

---

[42]This theme involves a play on words, vv. 12 and 15, *teleioō* and *teleios*, with a range of meanings: "finish, run a course, or be fully developed, grown, or mature;" for a treatment of Paul's athletic imagery, see V.C. Pfitzner, *Paul and the Agon Motif: Traditional Athletic Imagery in the Pauline Literature* (Leiden: Brill, 1967), especially pp. 139-53 for a treatment of Phil. 3:12-14.

[43]Vv. 20-21 are clearly dependent upon early tradition as several non-Pauline terms attest.

[44]Kurz, "Kenotic Imitation of Paul and of Christ," 109-21.

In the second instance, new preachers in their far-ranging Judaizing, moralistic, and self-sufficient approach to Christian life are eliminating the realism of the Christ-event. By relegating the cross to a past event and claiming perfection in the present, they rely on rituals and self-determinations as the basis of Christian life ("confidence in the flesh," 3:3f) and present themselves as models for imitation. Paul utilizes the new preachers' argument and again focuses on a more critical issue. If the cross of Christ is a past reality in soteriological terms, it is a present reality as paradigm of Christian behavior in the world. Indeed, perfection is a goal still to be sought (3:13-14). The Philippians are advised to imitate the apostle, whose glory is the cross. He is not an "enemy of the cross of Christ" (3:18) since he looks to the future as he, and other believers, "await a Savior, the Lord Jesus Christ, who will change [their] lowly body to be like his glorious body, by the power which enables him even to subject all things to himself" (3:20-21). By employing the theme of a "future Savior" Paul insists that Christ's death is a past event but that its dynamism, efficacy, and promise continue into the present as discipleship, and into the future as realization of God's cosmic lordship.

Circumstances at Philippi called for different applications of Paul's Christ-centered, theological vision of the Christian reality. In the two imitation sections Paul employs the community's tradition, a Christ hymn in the former and a missionary formula in the latter, to dialogue with a maturing, beloved community of Macedonia. A later editor, therefore, has felicitously joined two letters into a major Pauline document for posterity.

Philemon

Paul's letter to Philemon is an enigma on several counts. Many are surprised that a personal letter was included in the NT canon, since it offers little of theological value and since what it proposes regarding slavery is looked on today with suspicion. While this may cause problems for the theologian, who must grapple with the role scripture plays in theology, for the scholar Philemon is a model of the "occasional" nature of NT documents. This document is written to three persons and a house-church though it is consistently addressed to a single person.[45]

---

[45]"You/yours" is singular in number in Philemon except in vv. 3, 22b, and 25. For a discussion of house churches in the early Christian community, see Malherbe, "House

Its personal character, however, must not be overstressed since it is stated that even so private a letter is to be read by the community (see also 1 Thess. 5:27).

Who are the people addressed; where do they reside; and when did Paul compose the letter? The three questions are interrelated. Two men and a woman are listed as recipients. The old suggestion that they were a family unit, a husband, wife, and son, remains a conjecture though the letter's message lends itself well to such a proposal (addressed to the paterfamilias and to his house-church about his slave). Further, one notes the prominence of family terminology: brother, sister, child, father, and slave. The names of Philemon (see the legend of Philemon and Baucis)[46] and Apphia are recognized as Phrygian in origin while that of Archippus is found in Asia Minor inscriptions. Finally, while some scholars see the relationship between this letter and Colossians, especially their common references to Archippus, Onesimus, Epaphras, Mark, Aristarchus, Demas, and Luke, as indicating Pauline authorship and a Colossian destination for both, we see this connection as supporting pseudonymity for Colossians and a possible Asia Minor locale for Philemon's home.[47]

The date for the composition of Philemon is more problematic. There is little evidence with which to operate since, as noted earlier, the Lukan framework for the chronology of Paul is not a reliable base. Old theories which situated the so-called captivity epistles to Paul's Caesarean or Roman imprisonments cannot be taken seriously. Colossians and Ephesians, we maintain, are deutero-Pauline and will be treated in the following chapter. We are left with Philippians and Philemon which both state that Paul is in prison. However, there are a few salient contacts between the first Philippian missive (1:1-3:1a + 4:10-23) and Philemon. Both mention Paul and Timothy as writers; in the first they are called "servants of Christ Jesus" and in the second Paul refers to himself as "prisoner for Christ Jesus." Only in these two letters does Paul refer to his imprisonment with the term "chains" (*desmos*, Phil.

Churches and Their Problems," 60-91 in *Social Aspects of Early Christianity* and R. Banks, *Paul's Idea of Community: The Early House Churches in Their Historical Setting* (Grand Rapids: Eerdmans, 1980).

[46]See Ovid, Metamorphoses 8:618f; the story is probably known and alluded to by Luke in Acts 14:8-18.

[47]See E. Lohse, *Colossians and Philemon* (Philadelphia: Fortress, 1975) 175-77 and 182.

1:7, 13, 14 and Phlm. 10, 13). In 2 Corinthians on two occasions he speaks of "imprisonments" but employs the term *phyakē* (6:5; 11:23). Further, the phrase "imprisonment for the gospel" (Phlm. 13) resembles several Philippian passages (1:7, 13, 16). One might also compare their final greetings. It is logical therefore to assume that both letters were composed during a critical imprisonment of Paul in the Greek mainland sometime before the Jerusalem meeting.

At this point an interesting contact between Philemon 23 and Romans 16:7 should be noted. In the former Paul includes greetings from his "fellow prisoner in Christ Jesus" while in the latter, employing the same term (*synaichmalōtos*), he sends greetings from two kinsmen and fellow prisoners. This I believe is an added reason for considering Romans 16 a separate fragment and to view its date and origin in conjunction with Philippians and Philemon.

The occasion for the composition of Philemon is Paul's appeal to the master to welcome with open arms his run-away slave, Onesimus, who has in the interim become a Christian. The letter is a rhetorical masterpiece. In the greeting Paul prepares the way for his request as he labels Philemon "our beloved fellow worker" (see also vv. 13 and 17 where Paul wishes that Onesimus be allowed to become a fellow worker and partner). The thanksgiving allows Paul the opportunity with much praise to prepare Philemon for what he will express in the body of the letter. He has heard of Philemon's benevolence (5-6) and is greatly refreshed on that account (7). As he did in earlier letters Paul mentions his authority (8) but refuses to employ it since he wishes to persuade rather than to command (9, 14). Because he is so committed to a gospel of freedom, he employs every rhetorical means to lead Philemon to do what is required (8).[48] Paul is so sure of the outcome that he says in v. 21,

---

[48]Paul is no less astute than Pliny the Younger in his appeal: "To Sabinianus. Your freeman, whom you lately mentioned as having displeased you, has been with me; he threw himself at my feet and clung there with as much submission as he could have done at yours. He earnestly requested me with many tears, and even with the eloquence of silent sorrow, to intercede for him; in short, he convinced me by his whole behavior, that he sincerely repents of his fault ... Allow something to his youth, to his tears, and to your own natural mildness of temper: do not make him uneasy any longer, and I will add too, do not make yourself so; for a man of your benevolence of heart cannot be angry without feeling great uneasiness. I am afraid, were I to join may entreaties with his, I should seem rather to compel, than request you to forgive him. Yet I will not scruple to do it; I may, perhaps, again have occasion to entreat you upon his account, and again obtain your forgiveness; supposing, I mean, his error should be such as

"confident of your obedience, I write to you, knowing that you will do even more than I say."

Paul makes his appeal under the three classical modes of persuasion. He exercises *ethos* in the way he dwells upon his own and Philemon's character; they are partners (17); Paul is a prisoner and ambassador (9); he is father to Onesimus and to Philemon (10, 19); and they are all brothers (16, 10). He makes excellent use of *pathos* as he plays upon Philemon's emotions; he appeals to free will (14), to fatherly, brotherly, and Christian motivation (10 and 16), to the reciprocity of partnership (17), and of course to his own paternal claim upon Philemon (19). Finally, Paul's language, *logos*, is masterfully calculated to achieve his goal. Beyond his attempts at persuasion, he respects the legal rights of the slaves's owner (12) and is so committed to his new son in Christ that he takes upon himself any debt which might have accrued (18). In his endeavor to win Philemon's good will Paul indulges in a pun on Onesimus' name (the *useless* slave now becomes a *useful* servant, 11) and on the master's benevolence (as he had refreshed the hearts of the saints, v. 7, thus Paul wishes that he treat him and refresh his heart in Christ, v. 20).

Some commentators insist that what Paul means by "even more than I say" is the manumission or freeing of Onesimus.[49] Nowhere in the letter, however, is this stated. One suspects that these students of Paul are reading him through 19th-century glasses to make him an emancipator of slaves. In fact, v. 16 suggests the opposite: Onesimus will not cease, on the social level, to be a slave, but on a higher plane he will be "more than a slave—a beloved brother." Paul pursues the theme of Onesimus' new status; he is a brother to Paul and will be so to Philemon both in the flesh (part of the household) and in the Lord (where there is no social distinction).

What, therefore, is Paul requesting of Philemon? What does "you will do more than I say" mean? Vv. 13-14 provide us with the key to that question. Paul wanted to keep Onesimus with him as a missionary associate (vv. 11, 13, 20) but did not presume to do even what he suspected Philemon would allow. He sends the slave/brother back and

become me to intercede for, and you to pardon. Farewell" (Letters 9.21) in Melmoth and Hutchinson, *Pliny: Letters.*

[49]See for example M.A. Getty, *Philippians and Philemon* (Wilmington: Glazier, 1980) 78-80.

"knows" that Philemon will dispatch him to the service for which he had become so useful. Employing the language of the household (father, child, brother, slave) as well as missionary (partnership, service, "fellow") and affective (love, sharing faith, heart, refreshing, usefulness, benefit) terminology, Paul seizes the opportune arrival and joyful conversion of the talented Onesimus to acquire an added member for his ministerial entourage. The Greco-Roman social and economic context and Paul's gospel of freedom required tact and persuasion to allow the transfer of Onesimus from Philemon's household to full partnership with Paul and his fellow workers. Thus the Letter to Philemon rates as a Pauline rhetorical masterpiece.

The letter, therefore, is about Christian fellowship in the real world, the world of Paul's time. Only gradually did it become clear to Christian thinkers that fellowship in the Lord would have consequences for social and economic structures. Rather than a reformer of Roman mores and legal system Paul was a missionary who, in seeking to share the riches of the Christ-event (6) with new audiences, did not hesitate to call in favors from fellow Christians (Philemon) to expand his service to the saints.

Galatians

The reader of Galatians is beset by problems, whether inquiring about the date of the community's founding and of the writing of the letter, the background of the audience intended, the opponents of Paul and their doctrine, or the nature and occasion of the composition. Furthermore, Paul's discussion of the role of Judaism and its Torah within the plan of God offers an interesting contrast to his views about these in his other letters. This letter particularly is open to a variety of interpretations depending on the positions taken vis-à-vis these issues.

GENERAL INTRODUCTION

From Paul's own account we learn that the foundation of the Galatian church was fortuitous; the apostle was traveling when he fell sick in Galatia ("it was because of a bodily ailment that I preached the gospel to you at first," 4:13). Once there he was graciously cared for by the local population, which eventually received him and the gospel with open arms and enthusiasm (vv. 14-15). When this occurred is debated by proponents of southern or northern Galatian theories. The former proposes, following Acts 13-14, that Paul founded the communities early during his missionary travels in the Roman province of Galatia. The latter finding discrepancies between the letters of Paul and the Lukan narrative and relying on Paul's presumed use of an ethnic designation for the Galatians (3:1), posits a later trip to the older, northern area which had in earlier centuries been the home of the Galatian people.[50] The problem with both theories is that they rely too greatly, positively or negatively, on Lukan chronology. The Pauline trips are artificially constructed in Acts and should not serve as points of reference for Pauline chronology. Instead, direct appeal should be made to the apostle's letters.[51]

While the data regarding Galatia in Paul are rather scarce (Gal. 1:2; 3:1; 1 Cor. 16:1), they nonetheless suggest the province rather than the Galatian territory as the locale of Paul's communities. In the first and last case the author speaks of "the churches of Galatia," so of a broad area. In the last citation one presumes that the Roman province is also meant. Since Paul is writing 1 Corinthians from the province of Asia, his statement in 1 Cor. 16:1 implies that he intended to make similar arrangements for churches he was about to visit in the surrounding territory, perhaps during his projected Ephesian sojourn (1 Cor. 16:8). Furthermore, Paul's travels usually suggest a route through Asia Minor and hence through the southern parts of the Roman province of Galatia. The Corinthian passage also indicates prior contacts between those churches and Paul and Gal. 4:16 ("have I then become your enemy by telling you the truth?") suggests an earlier confrontation or letter to the communities. Further, the letter is being written after the Jerusalem meeting (c. 51; Gal. 2:1). The earlier situation of the converts has greatly changed in terms of doctrine (1:6; 4:10-11) and of commitment to Paul (4:19). Also, we stress the fickleness rather than the brevity of the Galatians' adherence to Christ (1:6). We therefore date the founding of the Galatian communities in some temporal relation to the Pauline mission to the provinces of Asia, Macedonia, and Achaia,[52] or more precisely, during the period prior to the composition of the second Philippian missive (3:1b-4:9), i.e., in the mid-40's. The composition of the letter, on the other hand, occurred shortly (within a few years) after the Jerusalem meeting.

[50]See Kümmel, *Introduction to the New Testament*, 296-98.
[51]Lüdemann, *Paul, Apostle of the Gentiles*, 44f.
[52]Murphy-O'Connor, "Pauline Missions," 90.

Since discussion of the audience's background has been complicated in the past by adherence to one of the two theories mentioned earlier, we again note the fallacy of giving priority to Acts rather than to Paul's letters. Several passages in Galatians indicate clearly that the audience consists of Christians of Gentile origin. The most evident are 4:8 where Paul speaks of the audience's former adherence to idols and other verses (5:2-3; 6:12; also 3:3; 5:12-13) where he discusses circumcision as a new reality in the converts' lives. The Jewish themes, therefore, of circumcision and the Law (3:2f) were being introduced into the lives of the Galatians and did not form part of their religious background. In regard to the audience's religious milieu, one should at least mention Gal. 4:1-11 where Paul refers to the readers' subjugation to the "elemental spirits" (vv. 3, 9) and to their observance of "days, and months, and seasons, and years" (v. 10). A surface reading of vv. 8-10 suggests that "turning back again to the weak and beggarly elemental spirits, whose slave you want to be once more" (9) describes the audience's polytheistic background. Paul's use, however, of the same terminology in v. 3 to describe the Jew's situation prior to the Christ-event (child or slave to elemental spirits) disavows such an interpretation. Instead, employing Hellenistic Jewish terminology (*epistrephō*, "turn to or convert"),[53] he describes the acceptance of the Mosaic Law's requirements as a giving up of freedom and a return to the slavery of polytheism. Even the statement concerning the observance of liturgical seasons should be thus interpreted (v. 10).

We turn to the vexed problem of Paul's opponents. The issue of opposition does not relate to the community's founding but involves a later period of its development, the situation current at the time of Paul's writing. The apostle preached to the Galatian population with success and it had responded well to God's call (1:6; 3:3 4:9). In the meantime the situation in the churches changed. Paul's letter reveals that he is displeased with his communities because they have abandoned "his gospel," a betrayal which involved submission to the Mosaic Law. While scholars agree that this state of affairs was relatively recent within the communities' evolution, it should be noted that prior to Paul's

[53]This term is used only 3 times by Paul: 1 Thess. 1:9; Gal. 4:9; and 2 Cor. 3:16 and a solid case can be made that all three derive from the terminology of the Jewish mission to the Gentiles; see chapter 3 earlier for a discussion of the first and the writer's "Polemics, Old Testament, and Theology," 354-59, for a treatment of the last mentioned.

writing, he had warned the Galatians about such a situation ("testify again," 5:3). Paul has already encountered the problem both in Galatia and in Philippi (Phil. 3:1b), before he composed this letter.

But who were the opposing missionaries, the people who were introducing "a different gospel" or troubling the community by "perverting the gospel of Christ" (1:6-7)? The classic answer since the nineteenth century has been to call them Judaizers and to identify them as Jerusalem missionaries or to associate them with the circle of James or Peter. These were Jewish Christians who opposed Paul's Law-free mission to the Gentiles and who hounded the steps of the apostle. Many object to such a monolithic view of the opposition and of early Christian history and insist that the opponents were not outsiders but members of the Galatian communities who were either Judaeophiles or syncretists. The new converts in the first view became enamored by the Jewish character of the Jesus movement and in the second some attempted to fuse their diverse religious and social heritage to Paul's preaching about the Christ.

Serious objections have been raised against these proposals,[54] particularly that of the syncretistic or Gnostic solution. The Jewish character of the oppositon is too pervasive for serious consideration of the third hypothesis and allows little confidence in the second. The first proposal, while providing more satisfactory answers to the issues raised (stance on circumcision and the Law, frequent reference to the Jewish scriptures, and deference to the Jerusalem authorities), leaves many unresolved problems. Attention to Paul's text shows that the Jerusalem "pillars" are not the object of his displeasure. Instead, they give Paul "the right hand of fellowship" (2:9). There are "false brethren (who are) secretly brought in" during the Jerusalem meeting (2:4), individuals who must be distinguished from the pillars. One would have to agree with W.G. Kümmel: "Gal. 2:1ff precludes any disputing of the fact that the Jerusalem community, in addition to the 'pillars,' had a radical wing which rejected a Law-free Gentile mission—though it did not reject a Gentile mission as such."[55] The situation then presented some complexity.

---

[54]For an overall presentation of these and a balanced critique, see J.J. Gunther, *St. Paul's Opponents and Their Background* (Leiden: Brill, 1973); Kümmel, *Introduction to the New Testament*, 298-301; Roetzel, *Letters of Paul*, 64-68.

[55]*Introduction to the New Testament*, 301.

In trying to identify Paul's opponents at Galatia, therefore, one must understand the variety which existed within the early Christian movement,[56] for there were several groups, each with its own perspective vis-à-vis the Christian mission. J.L. Martyn has made a credible case for identifying Paul's adversaries as missionaries who advocated "a Law-observant mission to Gentiles."[57] If we qualify his presentation of their views as somewhat fanciful (as he himself does), we nonetheless accept his description of these "teachers" as outsiders who, parallel to "the gospel of Christ" (1:7) also preach "the law of Christ" (6:2) or the Messiah's Law as good news. These missionaries "necessarily view God's Christ in the light of God's Law, rather than the Law in the light of Christ, and this means that Christ is secondary to the Law."[58] This explains Paul's vehement oppositon to their theological views. Other issues are also explained. While one can see how Paul claimed the Pillars approved his Gentile mission (2:7-9) and entrusted Peter with a mission to the circumcised, one can also understand how others appealed to the Jerusalem authorities for support of their Law-observant mission to the Gentiles. We know from our study of the development of the Jesus tradition how positions vis-à-vis the essentials of Christian belief, particularly in christology, varied greatly. Fundamental differences and volatile personalities brought these differences to a crisis. Galatians is such a document; born in theological and personal conflict, the letter contains polemics, overstatement, self-defense, and preoccupation with justification by faith. The tone, the themes, and the message of Galatians are dependent on the occasion which led Paul to compose the epistle.

Attention has been directed to the occasion for and therefore the nature or genre of this document. It is the defensive or apologetic motif which has received most attention, and so we turn to that issue.

> The cause of the letter is the Galatians' readiness to accept a 'gospel' which includes circumcision; for the Galatians were about to turn to 'another gospel' (1:6). This is confirmed by the rest of the letter: Paul's single preoccupation is with the desire of the Christians in Galatia to

---

[56]See the introduction to the Lukan writings, chapter 6.

[57]"A Law-Observant Mission to Gentiles: The Background of Galatians," *MQR* 22 (1983) 221-36.

[58]*Ibid.*, 229.

live 'under the law' (4:21). In an effort to persuade the Galatians to give
up this desire, Paul wrote the letter.

The scholar cited defends his conclusion by citing H.D. Betz's thesis
"that Paul's letter to the Galatians is an example of the 'apologetic letter'
genre, and that it is a defense of Paul himself and his gospel without
circumcision."[59] Several of these conclusions need examination. That
the opposition preached a "'gospel' which includes circumcision" is
generally admitted. But there is debate about whether they also preached
"the cross." Betz, employing the enigmatic passage 5:11, insists that they
did not, though such might be Paul's own conclusion.[60] Nonetheless,
with halting grammar, Paul is careful not to deny that the opposition's
preaching is "gospel" (1:6-7).[61] Whether they preached the salvific
nature of the cross or not can be debated,[62] but it is probable that they
imposed circumcision beyond the cross; Paul's language is polemical in
this regard. He does not deny that the opponents preach the kerygma
but claims that, by insisting on circumcision, they rob the cross of its
effectiveness ("no advantage," 5:2) as a source of freedom (5:1, 13), life in
the Spirit (3:5; 4:6; 5:16), union with Christ (5:4, 24), and being made
righteous before God (3:14, 29).

We disagree, however, with the citation given above that the Galatians
"desire . . . to live 'under the law.'" Indeed 4:21 makes such a statement
but the verse is polemical. Paul is not saying that they wish to be under
the Law but that, by accepting one of the basic stipulations of that Law
(circumcision), they are "bound to keep the whole law" (5:3). Paul is
speaking about theological consistency, the logical consequence of
accepting the gospel of circumcision. We insist further that Paul's letter
is not a defense of his gospel, or much less of himself, but a plea for the
definitiveness of the Christ-event (1:1-5) which, of its very nature, has
brought about a new creation (6:15). In the process of doing this Paul

---

[59]D.J. Lull, *Spirit in Galatia* (Chico: Scholars, 1980) 29; see Betz, "The Literary
Composition and Function of Paul's Letter to the Galatians," *NTS* 21 (1975) 353-79 and
Galatians: A Commentary on Paul's Letter to the Churches in Galatia (Philadelphia:
Fortress, 1979). For a similar hypotheses see B.H. Brinsmead, *Galatians—Dialogical
Response to Opponents* (Chico: Scholars, 1982).

[60]*Galatians*, 315.

[61]See also Martyn, "Law-Observant Mission to Gentiles," 227-30.

[62]Betz, *Galatians*, 315;   Martyn, "Law-Observant Mission to Gentiles," 229, respectively.

comes to grips with the role which Judaism as a past phenomenon (as opposed to a contemporary one; see Romans 9-11) plays. It is the situation in Galatia which forces him to do this. This discussion, therefore, leads us to inquire about the nature and structure of the letter. Betz has proposed and developed a thesis that Galatians is an "apologetic letter" in which Paul the defendant defends himself before the Galatian jury against his accusers in what amounts to a "fictitious situation of the court of law."[63] He offers as divisions of the letter the structures of the "oration" of Greco-Roman times: the *exordium* (1:6-11), the *narratio* (1:12-2:14), the *propositio* (2:15-21), the *probatio* (3:1-4:31), the *exhortatio* (5:1-6:10), and the whole being introduced and concluded by epistolary *prescript* (1:1-5) and *postscript* (6:11-18). These same structures are those found in Cicero's *Rhetorica ad Herennium*, though Betz prefers to follow Quintilian in many particulars.[64]

Reception of Betz's study has been mixed because the letter is often forced to conform to the presumed rhetorical structures of the oration[65] and because it is hard to imagine Paul writing a full parody of a court trial to convince his Galatian readers, especially when he treats them so severely. While acknowledging that Betz's observations concerning rhetoric and structural issues are frequently enlightening, we see his apologetic thesis as not convincing. Themes of apology and polemics in Paul are the issue. Some scholars detect polemics in and opponents behind numerous Pauline statements, especially Paul's use of his enemies' slogans or texts, e.g., 2 Cor. 3 consists of the enemies' midrash on Exod. 34 or 2 Cor. 6:14-7:2 is an anti-Pauline fragment.[66] In the present case an entire letter consists of an apology. My own research shows that Paul is concerned with opposing missionaries but, while he

---

[63]*Galatians*, 24.

[64]*Ibid.*, 14-23; see his dependence upon A. Momigliano, *The Development of Greek Biography* (Cambridge: Harvard, 1971).

[65]W.A. Meeks in his review of *Galatians* in the *JBL* 100 (1981) 306, pointedly states: "He does not offer us a single instance of the apologetic letter with which we can compare Galatians. We are therefore asked to interpret Galatians as an example of a genre for which no other example can apparently be cited." See also the critique of Lyons, *Pauline Autobiography*, 113-19.

[66]For a discussion of the former see the present writer's "Polemics, Old Testament, and Theology," 340-44 and for a defense of the latter, confer H.D. Betz, "2 Cor. 6:14-7:1: An Anti-Pauline Fragment?" *JBL* 92 (1973) 88-108.

begins with polemical statements or references, he is quickly led to basic theological or christological issues. This is the way Paul thinks; he is impulsive and develops his ideas in a stream-of-consciousness way. On numerous occasions he delves into apologetic issues or indulges in polemics but, being so committed to the Christ-event and its ramifications, he quickly leaves personal concerns aside or, as in the case of Gal. 1-2, transforms these into rhetorical devices to support his gospel of Christian freedom or to offer his own conduct and advice as "paradigm of the gospel he preaches among the Gentiles."[67]

LETTER TO THE GALATIANS

We therefore direct our attention to the letter's structure and purpose. Two initial passages, both of which disrupt the standard features of Paul's epistolary opening, alert us to these concerns. As he introduces himself in the opening ("Paul an apostle"), in a parenthetical remark, Paul broaches the subject of apostolic authority. Further, even as he terminates the opening with his usual greeting, the name of "Christ" leads him, again in an aside, to stress the role of the Christ-event (vv. 4-5). The first tangent leads him into an autobiographical defense (chaps. 1-2) and the second into a lengthy discussion of the effects of the Christ-event, i.e., an exposé of the themes of Christ, faith, and Law (chaps. 3-4). In other words, in v. 1, the mention of the term "apostle," brings up a first reaction concerning a burning, personal issue (see v. 11); Paul, stung by personal accusations, charges in but quickly gets down to basic issues. The challenge to his apostleship, while deeply personal, is more importantly a denial of the Law-free mission to the Gentiles and will occupy him in a "historical" defense of the early years of that missionary thrust. In v. 4, the name of Jesus Christ brings about a second reaction, namely, a passionate defense of the fundamental concern of Paul's preaching: Christ crucified. If one does not preach Christ, then it is not "gospel" (he is hesitant to go that far in his accusation, 1:6-7). Or put another way: if the Law and circumcision are associated with the kerygmatic core of belief, then they displace Christ. What these outside preachers are proposing amounts to a denial of or impingement on the role of Christ. Jesus then becomes a hostage to the Law and circumcision and no longer God's definitive agent.

---

[67]Lyons, *Pauline Autobiography*, 171.

On the surface the first major part of Galatians, is a personal defense of the apostle's authority or an extended autobiograhical narrative by an offended missionary. However, careful reading and analysis of the apostle's train of thought, emphases, and focus show that it was not his apostleship which was at issue but the apostleship to the Gentiles whose impetus and nature, Paul insists, were of divine origin, so much so that the Jerusalem authorities were compelled to recognize its legitimacy and efficacy. In place of a standard thanksgiving Paul in 1:6-9 addresses in personal (v. 6), polemical (7), theological (8), and missionary terms (9) the key topic of the letter, "the gospel of Christ." He is hurt that the community is taken in by such preaching (v.6); he is unyielding toward those who dilute the basic core of the Christ-event ("pervert," v. 7); he insists that the gospel is of God's doing not, as in popular estimates of the Torah's origin (Gal. 3:19-20), the result of angelic action (8); and lastly, the Pauline mission, since it preaches the true gospel (2:5), is according to God's plan (9). With these ideas set forth Paul, in the remainder of chapters 1-2, defends the nature and origin of the Gentile mission.

After insisting that his gospel comes from a revelation of Jesus Christ (1:11-12), Paul devotes the remainder of chapters 1-2 to an extended narrative of the mission to the Gentiles, particularly his own activities, a procedure which is most unusual for him and which raises many questions. We approach this issue by citing similar problems elsewhere in his correspondence, e.g., his extensive use of Exod. 34 in 2 Cor. 3 or extended appeal to the Abraham narrative in Gal. 3-4. Granted that there is a variety of reasons for such unusual tactics, we suggest that these are due to extreme situations, the volatile Corinthian circumstances and the opponents' monopolizing of Jewish tradition respectively. In the Galatian context Paul sees the attacks against him as threatening the mission to the Gentiles. Paul views the situation in the Galatian churches as critical and therefore requiring extreme measures. Some Galatians are succumbing to a "false gospel" (1:6; 4:9, 20); Paul is anxious to pursuade them to remain true to the gospel of freedom (5:1); and so he fights fire with fire. It is in this critical context[68] that he decides

---

[68]An interesting parallel might be cited in this context. In his second Philippian missive, which we date to roughly the same period and attribute to a similar situation in another Pauline church, Paul encounters a problem with similarities to that of the Galatian churches. In Phil. 3:1bf he is severe with his Judaizing opponents and offers a lengthy autobiographical narrative (3:4-7) to counter their "Jewish gospel." The

to tell the "story of the Gentile mission" (1:13-2:14).

As a preliminary to his narrative Paul dwells on the themes of origin ("not man's gospel") and agency ("I did not receive it from man, nor was I taught it, but it came through a revelation of Jesus Christ," 1:11-12). When he reaches the point in the story where he describes, in prophetic terminology, his commission, he underscores the purpose of the autobiographical passage; he was chosen "in order that (he) might preach (the Son) among the Gentiles" (1:16b). The story, therefore, is told with the Gentile mission and its integrity in mind.[69] The attempt to distance himself from the Jerusalem authorities in the first part and the insistence on the approval of these same authorities in the second part (2:7f) demonstrates his dexterity and concerns—see already in 1:11-12. If Paul tells a straightforward, basically factual story, he nonetheless adds rhetorical and narrative elements either to highlight the fundamental issues or to tilt the argument in his favor. The noncircumcision of Titus (2:3) is included as a negative argument in his favor; "those ... of repute" did not insist on such action and so tacitly approved the Law-free mission to Gentiles. Paul reminds his readers that the mission was not won without a battle, for in 2:4 he recounts an episode which, on the one hand, reveals serious opposition and, on the other, attempts to distinguish between the opponents and the Jerusalem authorities. The "false brethren" not only try to enslave the Gentiles by insisting on the Mosaic Law but they do this underhandedly. Paul resists this maneuver and obtains the "right hand of fellowship" of the authorities (2:9). 2:8-9 must be understood as Paul's conflation of the results of his two Jerusalem meetings to stress the theme of unity between him and the "pillars" in Jerusalem,[70] lest he "should be running or had run in vain" (2:2).[71] Finally, Paul's history or autobiography goes only so far; in the middle of his speech to Peter, he breaks off his "Jew to Jew" reproach and, finding "his stride" again, offers a beautiful statement of what "faith in Jesus Christ" means (2:16-17).

---

difference in the two Pauline writings owes to the degree of success of the opponents and their threat to the Law-free mission to the Gentiles.

[69]Betz's analysis of this passage is particularly helpful in understanding Paul's rhetoric; see *Galatians.*

[70]Murphy-O'Connor, "Pauline Missions," 75-76 and, in agreement, Lüdemann, *Paul, Apostle to the Gentiles,* 292.

[71]Again see Pfitzner, *Paul and the Agon Motif,* 99-108, for a discussion of this particular athletic metaphor.

Lastly, we discuss briefly the relation of Paul's autobiographical narrative to Luke's treatment of his travels to Jerusalem. While Paul's text is heavily rhetorical in style and form it is by far the more trustworthy report of these meetings; Luke uses a later irenic version of Paul's role in the expansion of the Jesus movement. Attempts to conflate the two only result in deadends. Instead, a better understanding of Lukan redaction and purpose and of Pauline rhetoric lessens the tension scholars are wont to see between these two narratives.[72]

The next major section (chaps. 3-4) represents a second reaction on Paul's part to the Galatian situation. He focuses more directly on the Christ-event. While some stress the break between chapters 2 and 3, the continuity between 2:21 ("Christ died") and 3:1 ("Christ . . . portrayed as crucified") should not be overlooked. Nonetheless, Paul imposes a rhetorical break at this point as he addresses the communities more directly. The previous passage on "faith in Jesus Christ" permitted him to insist on the role of Christ's death and concluded on a very provocative note: "for if justification were through the law, then Christ died to no purpose" (2:21). Much of 2:15-21, therefore, has a negative tone and leads him naturally into chapters 3-4 to discuss the consequences of rejecting the Christ-event, of going backward to a state of spiritual slavery, of "nullifying the grace of God" (2:21), and of a mission that would have been pursued "in vain" (3:4). Thus there is a change in emphasis in this new section; Paul speaks of the role of Christ, of new life, of faith, and of the Spirit. This, however, is done in an unusual manner, i.e., by an extended appeal to the Jewish scriptures and a relatively negative assessment of the Law.

The rhetoric of the opening verses clearly demonstrates the crisis level of the situation in the Galatian churches. Although Paul speaks directly to his audience he nevertheless classifies them as "foolish" (3:1, 4), people who should "know" both what slavery and freedom mean (4:8-9). They had witnessed Christ crucified (rhetorical flourish: "before whose eyes Jesus Christ was publicly portrayed as crucified," 3:1) and were doing so well (5:7, "you were running well"). But now they are turning their backs on the Spirit to return to the flesh (3:3). The tour de force, however, is the rhetorical question he asks his audience: "let me ask you only this: did you receive the Spirit by works of the law, or by hearing with faith?" (3:2). Both author and reader know that the Spirit

[72]Richard, "The Divine Purpose: The Jews and the Gentile Mission," 188-209.

came upon them through his preaching before they heard of the Law. It would be a tragedy for them to begin with the Spirit (faith) and to end with the flesh (Law).

The Christ-event initiated the reign of faith which God foreordained and promised through Abraham (3:1-28), that is, "that in Christ Jesus the blessing of Abraham might come upon the Gentiles that (they) might receive the promise of the Spirit through faith" (3:14). To Abraham God made a promise concerning his descendant (i.e., the Christ) and the Law is unable to "annul (this) covenant previously ratified by God" (3:17). The Law then was added as a custodian until the Christ's coming that through him faith might reign in all who are constituted children of God ("because you are sons, God has sent the Spirit of his Son into our hearts, crying, 'Abba! Father'") by that same faith (3:24-25). Paul then directs his attention to the effects of the Christ-event: the Christ's followers have become heirs of Abraham's promise and no longer slaves of the elemental spirits of the flesh, or of the Law (3:29-4:1). The parallels between Romans (4 and 8) and Gal. 3-4 are striking and instructive for our understanding of Paul's thought, because in the latter, by force of circumstances, he is far more negative regarding Judaism than he is in the former. After a personal appeal, filled with concern and affection (warm reception of Paul, "my little children," mother imagery, 3:14, 19), Paul discusses at length the theme of freedom. He develops in detail the image of the free woman's children (4:21-31) and indulges in a brief polemical thrust when he reminds his audience that even in the patriarchal period the slave child persecuted the freeborn (4:29). He returns to the theme of freedom in the paraenetic section of the letter by advising his audience not to lose its newly acquired independence (5:1-12) and by insisting that they use it correctly (5:13-6:10).

Paul's extensive use of the Old Testament in the second part of the letter owes no doubt to the opponents' vigorous appeal to the scriptures to defend their own gospel.[73] Equally, however, it is probably due to the narrative character of Galatians generally,[74] for the first part of Paul's letter tells the story of the Gentile mission as explanation of Paul's

[73]Martyn, "Law-Observant Mission to Gentiles," 230-35.

[74]See R.B. Hays' interesting contention that the story of Jesus (faith and death) provides Gal. 3-4 with its substructural unity, *The Faith of Jesus Christ: An Investigation of the Narrative Substructure of Galatians 3:1-4:11* (Chico: Scholars, 1983).

apostleship (1:1), while the second part focuses on the drama of God's agent and that agent's self-gift in faith or fidelity to God's will (1:4) as promised or foreshadowed in the Jewish scriptures (chaps. 3-4), as accomplished and revealed in the cross (3:1, 10f), and as exemplified in Christian freedom (chap. 5). Thus, Paul is able to show that both the Law-free mission to the Gentiles (Gal. 1-2) and the scriptures (3-4) witness to the efficacy of the cross, by means of which "a new creation" emerged (6:15), a free people that lives and walks by the Spirit (5:25). Paul ends his letter confident that the cross has indeed won the victory both in ecclesial (6:15-16) and personal domains (6:17).

Corinthian Correspondence

Paul's relationship to the Corinthian community, his work in that church, and the correspondence which these generated continue to intrigue and challenge the modern reader. If the early mission to Corinth was successful, it also turned out to be troublesome for Paul and for others as well. In a city known for its commerce and for easy living, the Pauline gospel found fertile ground from which numerous hybrid forms of Christian thinking emerged.[75] Beyond this, Paul encountered adversaries there who further complicated the Corinthian situation.

OVERALL VIEW

Paul's ministry in the Roman province of Achaia, to which Corinth belonged, began at an early date. In his first missive to the Thessalonian community (2:13-4:2) he makes a unique but significant reference to Athens. Paul had recently founded the Macedonian community of Thessalonica and worried about his new converts (2:17). It is usually deduced from this passage that Paul was traveling south from Macedonia to the Achaian province and while on this journey was able to "bear it no longer" and decided to send Timothy north and himself "to be left behind at Athens alone" (3:1). An Achaian ministry is therefore postulated soon after that in the Macedonian area. Several issues, however, need discussion.

---

[75]For an excellent collection of ancient source material to complement the reader's understanding of the Corinthian correspondence, see Murphy-O'Connor, *St. Paul's Corinth.*

Many assume, on the basis of Acts 17-18 and with the presumed confirmation of 1 Thess. 3:1, that Paul first went to the Athenian area, where he converted a "few" people (Acts 17:34), and then moved on to Corinth in his missionary travels. Such a scenario, however, contradicts 1 Cor. 16:15, where Paul states "that the household of Stephanas were the first converts in Achaia" (lit.: "firstfruits of Achaia"). That household is from Corinth and some of its members are present as Paul writes (1:11, 16; 16:17). Scholars note the contradiction with Acts and suggest that "perhaps Paul was thinking of Corinth only" when he says Achaia.[76] Again Luke and not Paul himself dictates chronological assumptions. Closer analysis of 1 Thess. 2:17-3:5 suggests that there is another possibility. It is incorrect to maintain that Paul is going south after his Macedonian ministry, since he has tried repeatedly (*hapax kai dis*) to visit the Thessalonians but, for reasons unknown to us he was unable (2:18). We conclude that the trip which took him to Athens was not his first stop in the Achaian province. Paul's correspondence tells us, therefore, that Corinth was his first Achaian field of endeavor. There he also baptized Crispus and Gaius, among others (1 Cor. 1:14-16).[77]

What can be said about the date of this missionary activity, its length and nature, and the frequency of Pauline visits to Corinth? Again we refer to our discussion of Paul's activity during the latter part of the 14 years mentioned in Gal. 1:21-2:1, when he traveled north to Syria and Cilicia and presumably west to the Ionian coast and the Greek mainland. He arrived in the Achaian area sometime after his Macedonian preaching, which we dated roughly to the early 40s. How soon after this he arrived in the South is hard to determine.

Several factors should be taken into consideration. Paul's repeated attempts to visit his new Thessalonian community (1 Thess. 2:18) suggests a prolonged ministry to the south of Macedonia and perhaps even to the west of Thessalonica (see Acts 17:10, Beroea). Furthermore, Paul in his first Philippian missive thanks the community for financial

---

[76]C.K. Barrett, *The First Epistle to the Corinthians* (NY: Harper & Row, 1968) 393; see also J. Murphy-O'Connor, *1 Corinthians* (Wilmington: Glazier, 1982) 158.

[77]A short note on Lukan use of tradition is in order. Crispus is mentioned in Luke's version of Paul's Corinthian ministry (he is a ruler of the synagogue, Acts 18:8); however, Gaius is not. Instead a fellow traveler of Paul by that name, who is said to be Macedonian, appears, along with Aristarchus (see Philemon 24), in the following chapter (19:29; see 20:4 where it is said that he or another Gaius is from Derbe). Luke's use of Pauline tradition therefore indicates a considerable remove in time.

assistance. He is in jail somewhere in Achaia when writing (see our discussion earlier of the Philippian correspondence). Interestingly Paul states: "in the beginning of the gospel, when I left Macedonia, no church entered into partnership with me in giving and receiving except you only" (Phil. 4:15). Thus, Paul left one missionary field (Macedonia) and proceeded to another (Achaia). Also in the following verse he points out that the Philippians sent him help "once and again" even at Thessalonica. Clearly Paul spent time with his communities as he founded them. Additionally, the first Philippian missive indicates several trips by Epaphroditus (2:26; 4:18) and Timothy (2:19) to establish communication between the apostle and his community and to bring him assistance.

At this point we reconsider the data Luke offers in Acts 18 about Paul's Corinthian ministry. The Claudian edict, dated earlier to 41 A.D., is of value only for approximate dating since even Luke does not insist on a close chronological relation between Paul's arrival and that of the Roman couple. The 18-month stay need not be taken as any more than a rounded estimate of Paul's activity in the city. The Gallio episode, however, must be kept in mind as the overall chronological picture comes into focus.[78] At a minimum we conclude, if one takes Luke's two dates seriously, then Paul arrived in Corinth anywhere between c. 43 and 51;[79] more precision, however, is possible.

On the one hand, Roman chronology for the province of Achaia indicates that Paul arrived there, more precisely in Corinth, the capital, after 44 A.D. This is suggested by the fact that "temporarily, from A.D. 15 to 44, Achaea was again joined to Macedonia as an imperial province governed by the imperial legate of Moesia."[80] Paul's references to the two areas in his Thessalonian, Corinthian, and Roman correspondence suggest the post-44 political situation. On the other hand, analysis of the apostle's travel plans and companions and of his epistolary and preaching activity opens up new avenues. Because of the complexity of this

---

[78]Murphy-O'Connor, "Pauline Missions," 84-90.

[79]Lüdemann's date for the beginning of the Corinthian mission (c. 41) is too early and relies on a questionable reading of Acts 18:2, *Paul, Apostle to the Gentiles*, 164-71 and 262.

[80]H.H. Scullard, "Achaea," 3 in the *Oxford Classical Dictionary*, eds, N.G.L. Hammond & H.H. Scullard (Oxford: Clarendon, 1970); for further discussion see J. Wiseman, "Corinth and Rome I: 228 B.C.-A.D. 267," 2:7:1:502-3 in Temporini and Haase, *Aufstieg und Niedergang der römishche Welt* (1979).

part of the discussion I begin by stating my overall outline of Paul's Corinthian ministry, travel, and correspondence:

1. initial Corinthian letter (partly 2 Cor. 1:1-4 + 13:5-14)
2. Jerusalem council (collection mandate)
3. 1st Corinthians (written from Ephesus; Macedonian travel plans)
4. change of plans: double visit
5. bad scene in Corinth
6. letter "written with many tears" (2 Cor. 10-13)
7. note carried by Titus on his second visit (2 Cor. 8) and reconciliation
8. "apologetic" letter (2 Cor. 1:15-2:13 + 7:5-16)
9. later correspondence (2 Cor. 2:14-7:4; + ch. 9).

1. Paul wrote a letter prior to 1 Corinthians, for there (5:9, 11) he states: "I wrote you in my letter . . . but rather I wrote." While scholars routinely observe that it is now lost, it is proposed that part of it is preserved in 2 Corinthians, where it serves as a frame for several Pauline letter fragments (2 Cor. 1:1-14 and 13:5-14). There are several reasons for such a conclusion but the major one relies on a study of Paul's missionary colleagues and co-authors. Paul's letter openings are as follows:

1 Thess 1:1	Paul, Silvanus, and Timothy (2nd missive)
Phil. 1:1	Paul . . . and Timothy (1st missive)
Philemon 1	Paul and Timothy
Gal. 1:1-2	Paul . . . and all the brethren who are with me
1 Cor. 1:1	Paul . . . and Sosthenes
2 Cor. 1:1	Paul . . . and Timothy
Rom. 1:1	Paul.

Clearly, Timothy is co-author of all of Paul's early extant letters and co-missionary during that extended period, i.e., up to the Jerusalem meeting. Significantly, Titus then becomes Paul's companion both at the council (Gal. 2:1, 3) and during the Corinthian controversy recorded in 2 Cor. 2, 7, 8, and 12. Timothy disappears in the Pauline correspondence with the writing of 1 Corinthians, where Paul employs his services as letter carrier (4:17; 16:10). For that reason he does not appear as co-author of this letter. Instead a Corinthian co-worker (see Acts 18:17) replaces him at Paul's side. 2 Cor. 1:1f therefore comes from an earlier period when Timothy was Paul's junior assistant (see 1 Cor. 16:10 where Paul says "he is doing the work of the Lord, as I am"). Note also the reference to "Timothy, my fellow worker" in the independent Romans 16 (v. 21). Thus, a similar editorial process occurred in this case as did for the Thessalonian and Philippian correspondence. Finally, the content of the two sections which serve as a frame is what one expects of an early pastoral letter to a young, growing community.[81]

2. Sometime after the founding of the Corinthian community Paul encountered difficulties with Judaizing missionaries, a result of which we see in the second Philippian missive (3:1b-4:9). However, the trip to Jerusalem, after a 14-year hiatus, gave Paul a victory on the issue of the Law-free mission to Gentiles and an important mandate to assist the poor in Judaea (Gal. 2:1-10).

3. On his way west Paul stopped in Antioch where the well-known confrontation with Peter occurred (Gal. 2:11f).[82] Next he visited the Galatian churches, on which occasion he was apprized of the Galatian situation and gave instructions about the collections (Gal. 2:10; 1 Cor. 16:1). Upon arrival at Ephesus Paul is confronted by a host of issues. It is from this vantage point that he writes the angry, pleading letter to the Galatian churches. Since he is also greeted by a Corinthian party (1 Cor. 1:11; 16:17) bringing both oral reports about problems within the community and a list of questions from the Corinthian believers needing his attention, Paul composes the long pastoral letter which we now call 1 Corinthians. At the end of the letter Paul, in his response "concerning the contribution for the saints," discusses his immediate plans. He intends to go through Macedonia and then to have an extended sojourn in Corinth, where he might spend the winter (16:5-7). From there he hopes to have the contribution sent to Jerusalem (vv. 2-3). First, however, he expects to prolong his stay in Ephesus until Pentecost, since he has hopes of missionary success and opposition (v. 9).

---

[81] Both sections can be read within the context of Paul's early relation to his community to which he is already freely giving advice (1 Cor. 5:9-13).

[82] Lüdemann, *Paul, the Apostle to the Gentiles*, 75-77, places this incident prior to the Jerusalem meeting and conjectures that "the incident in Antioch was the direct occasion for Paul, Barnabas, Peter, and 'those from James' to travel to Jerusalem" (77).

4. In the meantime there is a change of plan. Instead of going first to Macedonia and then to Achaia as announced, Paul decides to pay his Corinthian community a double visit by sailing to Corinth, visiting the city, traveling by land north to Macedonia, and then returning for that community to see him off to Judaea (2 Cor. 1:16). Owing to the fragmentary nature of the material we can only guess at Paul's reasons for changing his mind, though in v. 15 he gives us a clue: "because I was sure of this, I wanted to come to you first, so that you might have a double pleasure." Paul misjudged the situation at Corinth as reported by Chloe's people, Stephanas, and the letter emanating from the city, for his reception was anything but a pleasure. Also contributing to the complexity of the situation is the probable activity of Titus in Corinth or in Achaia generally during the course of Paul's sojourn at Ephesus (2 Cor. 8:6). Titus gave Paul a favorable report concerning the Corinthian situation and their contribution in particular (7:14; 12:18).

5. Instead Paul is confronted by a less than happy situation. Rather than being the first part of a "double pleasure," the visit to Corinth was a disaster on a missionary as well as a personal level.

> Upon his visit to Corinth Paul found his opponents there; he also found among the members of the Corinthian community that some had decided for the opponents. Evidently Paul's visit precipitated a confrontation that resulted in Paul's departure back to Ephesus and his fear of the loss of the Corinthian community to the gospel he preached.[83]

Thus, upon arrival Paul encountered stinging accusations that he had employed bluster, craftiness, and greed to manipulate the community; he was also confronted by odious comparisons and verbal abuse (see 2 Cor. 10-13).

6. Paul cut short his visit, but I do not believe, as stated above, that he returned to Ephesus. Instead, he proceeded with his travel plans and went on to Macedonia (1 Cor. 16:5; 2 Cor. 1:16). During this northern ministerial visit he wrote what is referred to as the letter "written with many tears." Although some presume that this document is now lost, I propose, with many scholars, that 2 Cor. 10-13 is in fact the "painful

---

[83]F.T. Fallon, *2 Corinthians* (Wilmington: Glazier, 1980) 82.

letter" (2:2) which Paul composed and sent to his wayward community.[84] He decided to spare them a second visit, but he did not exempt them from an honest and heated expression of his views and feelings, thereby confirming to a certain extent the accusation that he was humble in person and bold in writing (2 Cor. 10:1-2). While defending himself against the accusations mentioned above he refers to Titus' first trip and asks if he or his envoy ever took advantage of them (12:17-18).

7. As he left Macedonia (use of past tenses: 2 Cor. 8:1-5) on his way back to Judaea but without the collection as originally planned (1:16), he decided to take an overland route through the province of Asia for we next find him arriving at Troas. While there he is so agitated by the absence of Titus, despite ministerial opportunities, that he decides to return to Macedonia (2:12-13). After some impatient waiting, Titus, who, along with two other emissaries,[85] had been dispatched with a missive about the collection for the saints (2 Cor. 8),[86] finally returns with the superb news that the community has recovered its senses (8:7f) and everything is as it should be in Corinth.

8. Titus' coming signals a heart-warming reconciliation between Paul and the rambunctious community. So Paul takes up his pen and composes an "apologetic letter" (2 Cor. 1:11-2:13; 7:5-16; 9), a missive which documents his affection for the community (2:4) and relief that his confidence had not been misplaced (7:16). He regrets the tone of the previous letter, since it hurt those he loved; but he insists that it was for their good.

---

[84]See the discussion of Kümmel, *Introduction to the New Testament*, 279-93; this is also the position of Fallon, *2 Corinthians*, 4-7 and 82f.

[85]The other envoys are probably Apollos ("the brother who is famous among all the churches for his preaching of the gospel," 2 Cor. 8:18; see also 1 Cor. 1-4; 16:12 and Acts 18:24f) and Timothy ("our brother whom we have often tested and found earnest in many matters, but who is now more earnest than ever because of his great confidence in you," 2 Cor. 8:22; see also 1 Thess. 3:2; Philemon 1; and 2 Cor. 1:1). While Titus is described as Paul's "partner and fellow worker," the other two are called "messengers [apostles] of the churches" (8:23). See also 2 Cor. 11:5, 9; 12:18.

[86]For a slightly different perspective on 2 Cor. 8 and 9, see G. Bornkamm, "The History of the Origin of the So-Called Second Letter to the Corinthians," *NTS* 8 (1962) 258-63 (also included in *The Authorship and Integrity of the New Testament* [London: SPCK, 1967]), who proposes that chapter 8 is a letter of recommendation for Titus and the brothers to the church of Corinth and that chapter 9 is a later composition sent to the churches of Achaia. The same theory is adopted by D. Georgi, "Second Letter to the Corinthians," 183-86 in *IDBSup* and H.D. Betz, *Corinthians 8 and 9* (Philadelphia: Fortress, 1985).

9. There remain within the confines of the document two blocks of material which require further attention: 2:14-7:4 and 9:1-15. The first begins with an elegant thanksgiving section (2:14-17) and defends Paul's ministry "in Christ" by stressing the themes of "commendation" (3:1f), sincerity ("renouncing disgraceful, underhanded ways," 4:2 and "preaching Jesus Christ as Lord," 4:5), reconciliation (5:16f), and confidence (7:4). The urgency of the situation described earlier is gone though some of its themes persist. Paul is now confident of the community's loyalty and reminds its members of the basis for Christian belief, reestablishes its total commitment to Christ crucified (5:14-15), and urges them to accept the ministry of reconciliation which God assigned to him (5:18-20). In a less polemical vein and with greater theological confidence Paul resumes his relationship to his community and again broaches the subject of the collection (with a certain rhetorical flourish, 9:1f), for he wishes to bring the project to a happy conclusion (9:11-13). The brief statement Paul makes at the end of Romans confirms the project's success (Rom. 15:25-27).

A final, brief note is called for regarding the Gallio episode and its bearing on Pauline chronology, particularly the Corinthian ministry. It needs repeating that this episode comes from Acts 18 and that its temporal setting cannot be used as a peg for organizing Paul's ministry. Even if the encounter is accepted as having occurred and as being firmly dated (both of which seem probable), the most one can say is that Paul was in Corinth in 51-52 and that he was emprisoned while in the city. It is clear from the above analysis that Paul made many visits to Corinth and so the Gallio episode finds a setting in Paul's ministry. Beyond this one is reduced to conjecture.

Paul's activity in Corinth, therefore, lasted a long time and his relationship to the community proved a challenge and source of frustration for him. The make-up of the community and the later arrival of outsiders combined to make the Corinthian situation a puzzling vignette of early Christian beginnings.

What in the Corinthian milieu led to such an unusual blend of ideas and emotions? And what exactly was the make-up of the Corinthian community? The point of departure for such a study is Paul himself. While discussing their call, he reminds them: "not many of you were wise according to worldly standards, not many were powerful, not many were of noble birth" (1 Cor. 1:26). From this one might conclude that the community consisted of poor, enslaved, and uneducated

Corinthians. However, Paul's rhetorical contrast in the following verse warns us against too literal an interpretation: "but God chose what is foolish in the world to shame the wise . . . " (v. 27). In fact a few verses later Paul maintains that he preached to them "in weakness and in much fear and trembling . . . not in plausible words of wisdom . . . not . . . in the wisdom of men but in the power of God" (2:3-5). Due consideration, therefore, must be given to Paul's rhetoric.

We conclude from an examination of the data that the Corinthian community was made up of individuals from a variety of social, economic, and cultural backgrounds. Some are financially able to bring matters to the public courts (6:1f); others participate in the religious and cultural events of the city, whether public banquets (8:1f), sacred prostitution (6:15), or new hair styles (11:2f). Analysis of the various strands of thought exhibited in the Corinthian correspondence leads us to recognize a blend of Hellenistic Jewish ideas, of social and civic concerns, and of popular Greek philosophy of a Cynic-Stoic type. There is a certain sophistication in the way the Corinthians manipulate Paul's utterances and tax his ingenuity. Clearly, there are poor and well-to-do in the community; see Paul's treatment of the Lord's supper (11:21f).

Even more important than the make-up of the community were the consequences these factors had for Paul's dealings with them. A recent scholar has described them as "conceited, stubborn, over-sensitive, argumentative, infantile, pushy . . . " with "a positive genius for mis-understanding" Paul, whose "every statement . . . took root in their minds in a slightly distorted form, and from (which) . . . came some of the most weird and wonderful ideas ever to dismay a preacher."[87] The community therefore included some socially mobile and educated people, many of whom had fertile minds and shallow loyalties. But in the long run Paul found in them a basis for "perfect confidence" (2 Cor. 7:16).

1 CORINTHIANS

Having offered my reconstruction of the sequence of events and order of the epistolary fragments which make up this correspondence, I turn now to an examination of the two documents as they exist in the NT canon. Not only does 1 Corinthians follow the standard epistolary

[87]Murphy-O'Connor, *1 Corinthians*, ix.

conventions, but its particular form and occasion cast added light on our understanding of epistolary practices. Its similarity to the following Hellenistic letter is striking.

Andro to Milo his brother, greeting.	Opening
If you are well and everything else is to your mind, it would be as I desire. I myself am in good health.	Good wishes/thanks-giving
On the arrival of Sanos I received your letter, and it was a pleasure to read it and hear your news. I inquired of Sanos whether he wanted anything in our district, but he merely thanked me and did not give any order.	Letter deliverer (1:11 and 16:17) with news (1:11 and 5:1)
About the twenty drachmae, Philo has not yet received them, for we have not found Pistocles.	Items of business (*peri tōn...*—7:1, 25; 8:1; 12:1; 16:1, 12)
About the wine, Praxiades has not yet come in from the country, but from what his mother tells me I do not think he has got it.	
Now you will do me a favor if you take care of yourself and do not hesitate to write and tell me what I could do to please you.	Requests, plans, visit (16:5f)
Goodby. Year 25, Mesore 18 (addressed) to Milo.[88]	Farewell.

Between opening and concluding sections the two letters deal with four topics. The first is a statement of good wishes or, in Paul's terms, of thanksgiving (1:4-9). There follow the two principal parts, one dealing with the letter bearer and the oral information transmitted, the other lending attention to the items of business discussed in the newly arrived letter. In the case of the Hellenistic letter, Sanos the bearer has no further message to convey, but in the case of the Pauline situation, Chloe's people and others (1:11; 16:17) have reserved the more scandalous items of information for oral transmission. So Paul devotes the first chapters to the issues of factions (1:10-4:21) and scandals (5:1-6:20), which the letter bearers have related to him firsthand (see 1:11 and 5:1). The second part is devoted to the business at hand, each item being introduced by "concerning the . . . ," (*peri tou/tōn* in the Greek of both

88Hunt and Edgar, *Select Papyri I.*

letters). The greater part of 1 Corinthians (7:1-16:4) therefore consists of short to lengthy responses to the questions sent Paul in writing from Corinth. After the business items, the authors mention future plans, good wishes, and requests.

Appreciation of the occasional, pastoral character of 1 Corinthians is crucial for understanding first the situation, crisis, or question being addressed and then grasping Paul's line of thought. Indeed, the reading of 1 Corinthians can be compared to the situation of a modern audience that overhears a telephone conversation and reconstructs the whole from the statements of one party. From Paul's text a modern reader first imagines what the questions or oral report was, what the situation was which generated these, and what personal conflicts brought these about. Then the reader is challenged to follow Paul's logic and advice as he resolves the issues. Paul then does not intend an eternally relevant answer to a perennial question or issue; it is not the answer which has significance for the reader but the motivation and process of the resolution. The moral relevance of Paul must be sought in the vision rather than in the concrete responses given to specific problems.[89]

At the outset Paul gives the reader several hints concerning the letter's content. He opens his epistle by describing himself as one "called by the will of God to be an apostle of Christ Jesus" (1:1); this was common knowledge in his churches. Nevertheless, owing to the Corinthian situation and the propensity of those Christians to question his authority and divisively to choose sides and boast of their gifts, Paul, as he often does in his correspondence, prepares the reader for the themes to be developed. Since they are so boastful about their achievements, Paul loses no opportunity to remind them that if they are "called to be saints" so are others "who in every place call on the name of our Lord Jesus Christ." Paul emphasizes further that Jesus is "both their Lord and ours" (1:2); i.e., he is not the exclusive Lord of the charismatic Corinthians. In the thanksgiving section Paul reminds them that the call is a "grace of God which was given . . . in Christ Jesus" (1:4). He stresses that God has in fact endowed the community with the gifts of speech and knowledge, so much that they "are not lacking in any spiritual gift" (v. 7). There is, however, a catch to this; the Corinthians boast of their present endowments while Paul reminds them first that these are gifts ·

---

[89]V.P. Furnish, *The Moral Teaching of Paul: Selected Issues* (Nashville: Abingdon, 1980); confer especially 11-29.

and require thanksgiving and not boasting and secondly that they are given in view of Jesus' return (vv. 7-8), and thirdly that they are meant to foster the fellowship of the Son (9). These gifts are a result of a past event (the Christ-event, v. 9), in view of the future return, and meant to have a bearing upon the present. There is something seriously wrong in the Corinthian situation.

Paul begins with the last item noted, the lack of fellowship. He wanted them to agree with one another but instead there is dissension and quarreling. The disunity had reached such proportions that there had developed loyalty parties; some claimed Paul, others Apollos, other Cephas, and still others Christ (1:12). True to his Christ-centered gospel, Paul tackles the problem at its core. How can Christ be divided? Paul knows that superficial issues can bring about fundamental differences. While he is their father in the faith and so they claim him as their own, Paul pointedly asks: "was Paul crucified for you? Or were you baptized in the name of Paul?" (1:13). Since no one can contest the first question, Paul in disgust turns to a second, but more tenuous issue, that of baptism. Since some claim the privilege of having been baptized by Paul—the context implies that some were doing just that—Paul transforms the whole ecclesiological fuss ("belonging to") into one of christology ("baptized in the name of" as a result of the crucifixion).

After derogatory remarks concerning baptism (done with a rhetorical goal in mind) Paul leads the discussion to the most fundamental issue of his preaching, "Christ crucified," the topic around which he develops his salvos against disunity, worldly standards, and boasting. Indeed 1:17 sets the tone for the first chapter of the letter: "for Christ did not send me to baptize but to preach the gospel, and not with eloquent wisdom, lest the cross of Christ be emptied of its power." Leaving aside the surface issue of baptism Paul directs his attention to the preaching of the gospel and the variety of ministries which the Corinthians witnessed and by which they were too easily impressed. They heard the preaching of Paul and Apollos, among others, and were greatly affected by the instruments of their religious transformation. Paul, however, was not pleased with the easy confusion which some made between the preachers and that which was preached. Since the Corinthians were so awed by eloquence, Paul denigrates cleverness, human wisdom, and eloquence generally, because they are the antitheses of God's chosen instrument, the cross. Broadening his argument to speak of more fundamental issues and noting that some want proofs or wise words, Paul insists: "we preach

Christ crucified, a stumbling block to Jews and folly to Gentiles, but to those who are called, both Jews and Greeks, Christ the power of God and the wisdom of God" (1:23-24).

Chapters 1-4, therefore, are a pointed discussion of the divisions that are splitting the community. Paul has been told of these and from his arguments one obtains a solid grasp of the underlying issues. After introducing the problem and its symptomatic slogans (1:10-17), Paul discusses "God's standards" (1:18-31). He insists, the weak are chosen, contrary to worldly standards, to establish God's power, i.e., "Christ Jesus, whom God made our wisdom, our righteousness and sanctification and redemption" (1:30). This topic leads him in turn to discuss true and false wisdom (2:1-3:4—role of the Spirit), and the role assigned by God to apostles. If the Corinthians possessed wisdom they would discern correctly the role God's instruments play and "not act like men" in their judgments (3:4). The apostles are servants of Christ (3:5-23) not earthly gurus. If each has been assigned a role (3:5-6), it is God who provides the growth (3:6). Furthermore, they are to refrain from judging their ministers (4:1-5); that will happen when the Lord comes. After his long and involved discussion of factions Paul applies directly his ideas to the Corinthian situation (4:6-13). His reproaches and biting sarcasm (4:7f) lead him finally to speak more lovingly as a father to his wayward children (4:14), but nonetheless one who does not spare the rod (4:21). Finally, the theme of boasting, a theme that permeates the entire Corinthian correspondence, is emphasized by Paul's celebrated statement of 4:7: "what have you that you did not receive ... why do you boast as if it were not a gift?"

With the beginning of chapter 5 Paul broaches in a systematic way the pressing problems the Corinthians made known to him via oral report (5:1f) or by letter (7:1f). In sequence Paul discusses a flagrant case of incest (5:1-5), the treatment of immoral members of the community (vv. 9-13, already discussed), and the embarrassing question of lawsuits among Christians (6:1-11). These pastoral vignettes make for difficult but interesting reading as one follows Paul's logic and concerns. On the one hand he delicately attempts to clarify the issues or suggest solutions but on the other he is adamant that the Christ-event and its consequences (particularly the good of the community) be at the core of behavioral decisions (e.g., 5:6-8, 11).

The next two issues discussed by Paul, immorality at Corinth (6:12-20) and sexual relations in marriage (7:1-7) receive added attention in our treatment since they offer the reader an opportunity to observe Paul at work and to appreciate his keen and subtle mind. In both passages one finds slogans from some Corinthians which either express cherished moral principles or which relate to Pauline preaching. The Corinthians had heard Paul speak of the Christ-event and the effects of this epochal happening on the lives of those who believe. In the first case, "all things are lawful for me" (6:12) represents Paul's insistence that the believer is free and therefore above the Law. From this some in the community, those who considered themselves "perfect," "mature," or "enlightened," concluded that physical action had no moral value and therefore all things were permissible. They concluded from Paul's preaching that there were no restrictions to a Christian's freedom. Thus, they reasoned: since bodily activities had no bearing upon one's spiritual status, and since sexual behavior, proper dress, the eating of meat offered to pagan gods, and the fate of the body after death were of no concern, one could then flout social conventions in these matters. In the second case, the slogan: "it is well for a man not to touch a woman," (7:1)[90] represents Paul's preaching, both as devoted celibate and one who expected the imminent return of the Lord, that one should be concerned about the anxious preparation for and devotion to the Lord (7:7, 29, 31, 35). From this some reasoned that certain physical actions were immoral and to be avoided. Thus, conjugal rights, marriage itself, and eating meat offered to idols are activities denied to Christians. As a recent scholar has said: "The Corinthian ideas were not all of them wrong, but they were badly out of proportion."[91]

Paul finds himself arguing both against antinomians who advocated libertinism and against ascetics who advocated the opposite. Both took from Paul what suited their philosophical or cultural tendencies and twisted the apostle's teaching out of shape. Paul delicately argues against the first that while certain things are "lawful," they may not be "helpful," conducive to freedom, or consistent with the Christian way of life. So sacred prostitution, while part of pagan religious rites, is not compatible with the new, Christian reality, since the believer's body becomes a temple of the Holy Spirit and therefore can have no part of such practices (6:15, 18-19). Paul insists: "the body is not meant for

[90]*Contra* RSV, the phrase should be in quotation marks as in 6:12.

[91]C.K. Barrett, *A Commentary on the Second Epistle to the Corinthians* (NY: Harper & Row, 1973) 38.

immorality, but for the Lord, and the Lord for the body" (6:13). In an even more delicate way Paul opposes the second position which holds that sexual relations within marriage are forbidden. In what may seem to a modern as a negative concession to human weakness, Paul insists that conjugal relations between married partners are not only permitted but are the normal state of affairs. He presumes that his audience agrees concerning the goodness of marriage and argues only against "an exaggerated idealism which led them to try and impose practical acceptance of the [celibate] ideal on all."[92] In both cases Paul's argument centers on the problem reported to him and in each he draws the consequences the Christ-event has on his audience. Paul's discussion is not an abstract consideration of the moral issues a Christian encounters in daily life, but rather the patient, caring advice of a pastor to his "gifted" community.

Chapter 7 deals with a host of social problems; Paul answers questions concerning marital relations (noted earlier), gives counsel to the unmarried, to widows, to the married, and to the whole community concerning marriage and divorce (vv. 8-16), and in a long discussion, whose objectives are good order within the community and being ready for the Lord's return, surveys social and marital changes, whether concerning the circumcised or slave or concerning the marriage or separation of men and women (17-40). Convinced that the end was imminent (26, 29-31) and that the believers' state in life at the time of conversion was divinely sanctioned (17-24), Paul, with the view that his children "promote good order" and direct their "undivided devotion to the Lord" (35), advises them to remain as they are, preferably celibate and attached only to the Lord, although he does concede that getting married (28, 36) and obtaining one's freedom (21) are permissible and good. Paramount in this confirmed celibate's mind (7:7, 8, 28, 32, 38, 40) is the community's "undivided devotion to the returning Lord." One's state in life, therefore, and one's social and marital choices are thus conditioned.

In the next major section of the letter (8:1-11:1) Paul addresses a social problem involving an inner community conflict regarding contact with pagan neighbors. The problem was twofold. On the one hand, some encountered difficulties in the marketplace when purchasing meat products and when dining with rich friends since most of this commodity

[92]Murphy-O'Connor, *1 Corinthians*, 59-60.

had been offered to the gods and was being sold on behalf of the priestly groups.[93] On the other hand, members of the community reacted to this state of affairs in one of two ways. Some (the weak) felt that anything associated with the cult of the gods was to be avoided. Others (the strong) were convinced that these so-called gods were idols and that the meat was not affected by false rituals. So Paul is forced to discuss a problem, which in the objective realm is easily resolved, i.e., the strong are correct (meats offered to idols are not an abomination), but one which in the subjective realm adds complexity. Paul must defend both the position of the weak (8:1-13) and the motivation of the strong (10:23-11:1), for the problem concerns the issues of conscience and motivation.[94] Ultimately, however, Paul's solution concerns not conscience but community. "A firmly held monotheism, which knew that an idol had no real existence [position of the strong], was, to Paul, less important than a loving regard for one's brother [concern for the weak and consequently the loving behavior of the strong]."[95] Community more than individualism is at the core of Pauline anthropology and ethics.[96]

The following block of material treats three abuses in the liturgical assembly. First, Paul addresses proper attire for community functions (11:2-16). A superficial reading often misconstrues the problem as dealing with women's attire or wearing the veil at prayer (v. 5). As Murphy-O'Connor has persuasively argued, both modern versions in their translations and subtitles[97] and interpreters in their discussion of these verses have obscured Paul's argument. The "new" attire of both men (long hair, vv. 4, 14) and women (uncovered heads, often in text) at Corinth is of concern to Paul, since it tends to blur male and female differences. Paul insists: "Women should be women, and men should be

[93]See Murphy-O'Connor, *St. Paul's Corinth*, 101, for a vivid example of such.

[94]R.A. Horsley, "Consciousness and Freedom among the Corinthians: 1 Corinthians 8-10," *CBQ* 40 (1978) 574-89 and J. Murphy-O'Connor, "Freedom or the Ghetto (1 Cor. 8:1-13; 10:23-11:1)," *RB* 85 (1978) 543-74.

[95]Barrett, *Second Epistle to the Corinthians*, 38.

[96]See Malina, *New Testament World*, especially his chapter on "the individual and the groups," 51-70.

[97]As for example, the RSV's poor rendering of v. 4 and its questionable use of "veil" and "covering" as well as subtitles of both the New American Bible and Jerusalem Bibles: "Headress of Women" and "Women's behaviour at services," respectively.

men, and the difference should be obvious."[98] In other words, new Corinthian dress styles notwithstanding, the good of the community and its devotion to the Lord demands that disruptive behavior, in this case unisexual tendencies, be outlawed (see 11:16); men and women should adopt the proper attire of their respective sexes in the liturgical assembly.

Secondly, Paul addresses the behavior of community members at the eucharistic celebration (11:17-34). In a manner characteristic of Pauline correspondence generally, we find here a threefold treatment of the topic: a) the Corinthian situation, b) the eucharist, and a') the Corinthian situation once more.[99] Paul begins by showing his displeasure at the evidence of non-Christian behavior ("divisions" and "factions," vv. 18-19) on the part of some during the commemoration of the Lord's supper. After giving examples of non-unitive behavior (vv. 21-22), Paul draws from the community's tradition (23) the earliest extant version of the Lord's supper,[100] a text bearing strong memorial and eschatological motifs (23-26). Paul then returns to the issue of proper behavior, i.e., receiving worthily and with discernment (29) the bread and the cup as one community (33). It is as concerned pastor that Paul approaches another behavioral problem at Corinth.[101]

Thirdly, the apostle discusses the volatile issue of spiritual gifts or *charismata* (12:1-14:40). To this topic he devotes three long chapters because the issue is an indication of deeper problems at Corinth and because it offers Paul an added opportunity to discuss the themes of gifts and boasting. Again in a threefold pattern (a-b-a') Paul discusses in turn the nature, kind, and interaction of gifts based on the analogy of the body and its members (12:1-31). After inquiring about the highest gifts, Paul launches into the well-known eulogy on "love" as the most excellent way (12:31b-13:13). This he reminds his boastful and not grateful Corinthians is the greatest gift of all, not the "angelic" or

---

[98]Murphy-O'Connor, *1 Corinthians*, 106; for a more detailed analysis see his article: "Sex and Logic in 1 Cor. 11:2-16," *CBQ* 42 (1980) 482-500.

[99]In 1 Corinthians alone this A-B-A' pattern is prominent in chapters 5-6; 7; 8:1-11:1; 11:17-34; and 12:1-14:40.

[100]Though see the discussion of Jeremias, *The Eucharistic Words*, 138-203.

[101]On the importance of architecture and custom in understanding Paul's letter, especially as they affected the foods served and the places assigned to rich and poor guests, see Murphy-O'Connor, *St. Paul's Corinth*, 158-61.

charismatic gift of language, and much less the ultimate sacrificial human act (13:1-3). In chapter 14 Paul discusses again the Corinthian situation, and there attempts both to be respectful of the community's gifts (including that of tongues) and insistent that they are on the one hand gifts and so not the object of boasting (13:4) and on the other that they are given for an ecclesial function, i.e., to build up the community (14:5, 12, 19, 26). Paul recognizes that his Corinthian readers in their "eagerness for manifestations of the Spirit" err in their boastful and divisive behavior, so he urges them, in the proper use of their gifts, to "strive to excel in building up the church" (14:12). Paul perceived in the activity of his Corinthian community a problem which would later be exacerbated by the arrival of new missionaries, namely the attempt on the part of many at Corinth "to keep divine, or spiritual, action under human control."[102] Paul's answer here, as later, is twofold: gifts are from God (12:3) and they are for the good of the community (14:40).

Next, the apostle directs his attention to the christological issue of the resurrection. The discussion is conditioned by its Corinthian formulation; those at Corinth who saw themselves as freed from the restraints of the body by the Christ-event (see 6:12f) also denied the resurrection of the body (15:12). So Paul gives his readers a complex treatment of a core element of the kerygma (chap. 15). He draws from the community's tradition the formulation of its fundamental beliefs (vv. 3-4) to show that the Christ's resurrection is both fact and promise. As Adam was the progenitor of death so the Christ as the second Adam is the author of life or the life-giving spirit (15:21-22; 45-50). The Christ has been raised by God (v. 4, fact), therefore, those who belong to him will be made alive (22) when all things are subject to the Son (27-28, promise). In the second half of the chapter Paul answers a remaining difficulty (raised as a rhetorical question, 35-36) regarding the nature of the resurrected body. After a highly conjectural discussion, which owes much to current Platonic thought (seeds, celestial, imperishable, and spiritual bodies, and the men of dust or of heaven), Paul, in a manner reminiscent of but slightly more advanced than his discussion in 1 Thess. 4:13-18, appeals to apocalyptic imagery to describe the resurrected body's fate as a metamorphosed entity that has put on immortality (51-54).[103]

Paul ends his letter with a note on the collection (16:1-4) and a series

---

[102]Barrett, *Second Epistle to the Corinthians*, 39.

[103]Gillman, "Signals of Transformation in 1 Thessalonians 4:13-18," 263-81.

of concluding items: a travelogue, projected plans, a note about Apollos (12), greetings, admonitions, and farewell.

2 CORINTHIANS: A COMPOSITE DOCUMENT

Discussion of the Second Corinthian Letter requires less length but far more ingenuity. In light of our earlier chronological discussion, we direct out attention to the following blocks of material: 2 Cor. 10-13; 1:15-2:13 and 7:5-16; and 2:14-7:4. Chapters 8 and 9 which deal with the collection will only be noted in passing.

Few doubt that 2 Cor. 10-13 forms an independent unit from the rest of the document owing both to its subject matter and tone. We identify it as the "letter written with many tears" and so conclude that it represents the anguished product of an angry, disappointed, yet concerned missionary who sees not only his person and work slandered and destroyed but the community itself abused and misled. These chapters represent Paul's heated reaction to the Corinthian situation encountered during his brief, disappointing visit. The arrival of new missionaries in the city made more complex an already involved situation. The boastful, grandiose claims of these newcomers appealed to many in a community that prided itself on its wisdom and spiritual gifts. Further, the tendency of some toward factionalism and extremes of various types found added impetus in the preaching of new missionaries.

Of late much has been made of these chapters' apologetic qualities, so it is to this topic that we turn our attention. Some scholars call this section of 2 Corinthians an apology or letter of defense. The newcomers, it is claimed, presented themselves as wonder-workers and men of wisdom, authority, and eloquence. They laid claim to ecstatic experience, to a unique relationship to Christ and his Spirit, to manifestations of power, and to commendatory prerogatives. As a consequence, in the speech of these missionaries and in the eyes of some Corinthians, Paul was portrayed as lacking the signs of true apostleship and was suspected and accused of being a religious fraud or charlatan. 2 Cor. 10-13 is an attempt by Paul to unmask the false apostles by employing "the arguments by which the true philosopher was distinguished from the charlatan ... By such means [sarcasm, irony, and parody] Paul presents this moving defense of his apostolate and gospel."[104] An

---

[104]Fallon, *2 Corinthians*, 83.

insightful, popular reading of chapters 10-13 as polemics and self-defense is offered by F.T. Fallon who interprets Paul's statements as irony, parody, or sarcasm. It is claimed that the apostle often cites or alludes to the accusations made in Corinth against him (10:1, 10 etc.) and counters their claims by employing a variety of strategies. 11:1-12:13, devoted to the theme of "foolishness," gains the most by this type of reading. Fallon summarizes Paul's strategy as follows:

> In the Hellenistic world the fool was not a jester but a person who had lost the correct measure of himself and the world around him. The true philosopher was often portrayed as a fool, especially by the sophists, because he was judged to have lost the measure. In fact, for the audience the philosopher had replaced the apparent measure of the sophists by the true measure. Thus in his foolishness the true philosopher ultimately and ironically spoke the truth.
>
> Since his opponents had charged Paul with being a false apostle Paul responds in the style of the philosopher responding to the sophist. He assumes the role of the fool in order to expose the weakness of his opponents' position and to bring the Corinthians to the truth. Paul can presume that the Corinthians, as participants in Hellenistic culture, will not fail to notice the style of his discussion and the force of his arguments.[105]

Thus Paul is able to appropriate the worthwhile claims of his opponents, even that of boasting, and still maintain, as he does in the Philippian correspondence, that "there is nothing to be gained by it" (12:1). By means of a complex, rhetorical letter Paul claims that he is, in human terms, at least the equal of these "superlative apostles" (11:5; 12:11),[106] but that he and they are "nothing" (12:11) if not servants of Christ crucified. Ultimately, only weakness allows God's power to be effective (12:10).

While we accept much of the above analysis, we suspect that Paul's statements in 12:19-21 are not taken seriously enough. Paul denies that he is defending himself before or to his Corinthian readers, as they

---

[105]*Ibid*, 92. One need not accept Fallon's "divine man" ideology (taken from D. Georgi; see Richard, "Polemics, Old Testament, and Theology," 364-67) to defend an apologetic thesis.

[106]*Contra* Barrett, *Second Epistle to the Corinthians*, 30-32 and 278, who distinguishes between the "false apostles" (11:13) and the "superlative apostles" (11:5; 12:11).

might think, and insists that it is before God, on the subject of the Christ-event, and for the community's benefit that he has struggled over his analysis of the Corinthian situation (v. 19). A rereading of chapters 10-13 shows that Paul is more concerned about the Corinthian audience than he is with the interlopers. Even when he addresses their accusations, claims, and alleged accomplishments, he has in mind the disastrous effects these have on the community. Earlier he combated the tendency of some in the community toward an exaggerated "realized eschatology" and now he saw in a more pronounced fashion, via these new missionaries' teachings, an attempt to manipulate God's action.[107] His apostleship, his gospel, and the community's well-being were affected by claims that robbed the Christ-event of its power, namely the weakness of Christ's servanthood. The nature of the Christ-event was in jeopardy and Paul reproaches his community for its lack of insight (10:1f, 7f) and loyalty (11:7f; 12:11f, 14f), and for its fickleness (11:3f).

It is not Paul's irony or sarcasm *per se* which qualifies these chapters as "a letter written with many tears" (*contra* Fallon). Rather, it is his repeated ironic and sarcastic reminders to his community that demonstrate Paul's profound love and deeper hurt. Every paragraph ends with a poignant statement about Paul's concern for the Corinthians, whether expressed sarcastically, out of desperation or unbelief, or even with a ray of hope (10:6, 13; 11:6, 11, 21, 29; 12:13, 17-18). True to his gospel that all be submitted to Christ, Paul reminds the community (12:19) that there was only one goal for his bitter words and stinging rebuke and that was the community's upbuilding that finally he might "destroy arguments and every proud obstacle to the knowledge of God, and take every thought captive to obey Christ" (10:5). Both weakness and strength find their meaning in the Christ-event; even Paul's final warning of punishment is intended as witness to God's power through Christ (13:1-4).

The letter of reconciliation or what remains of it (1:15-2:13 + 7:5-16) provides an interesting commentary on Paul's career at Corinth. What began as a hopeful reunion with his young but troubled community (2 Cor. 1:15-16) developed into a painful disruption of the relationship (2:1). Paul stresses the divine origin of his mission (1:21) and the terrible hurt which he imposed on himself by writing the disciplinary letter (2:4).

[107]See note 102 above.

This, however, was worthwhile because of the reconciliation to which Titus was witness; the letter grieved the community (7:8), but it provoked the desired effect and confirmed Paul in his boast about them (7:14).

The final segment of the Corinthian correspondence to be discussed is 2:14-7:4 along with chapter 9. This block of material represents a later stage in Paul's correspondence. The tone of the letter is more cordial and Paul is again the pastor who assists the community in its growing process; so the letter is a follow-up on the improved Corinthian situation. Paul raises lingering points of the earlier polemics: "peddlers of God's word" (2:17), "commendation" (2:17-3:1), "competence" (3:5), "underhanded ways" (4:2), etc., but in each case he focuses on more fundamental issues: the community as God's recommendation of Paul (3:2-3), the new covenant of the Spirit (3:6), of surpassing splendor (11), and of freedom (17), and the preaching of "Jesus Christ as Lord, with ourselves as your servants for Jesus' sake" (4:5).[108] In successive chapters Paul discusses the Christian experience as treasures in earthen vessels (chap. 4), the roles of Christ and the Spirit in God's plan for the believer (5), and his own relationship to the community (6-7)[109] before passing on to the subject finally of the collection (9). The last mentioned chapter is full of confidence from beginning to end. We conclude that, as the Corinthians' faith is increasing and as Paul's field has enlarged, he is again thinking of "preaching the gospel in lands beyond" the horizon of the Greek mainland (10:15-16).

Romans

Few contest that Romans is Paul's most important writing. It is the most ambitious and systematic presentation of his thought, and so represents the mature, non-polemical thinking of a seasoned missionary. Throughout the history of theological development no document has exerted such profound and far-reaching influence. If one agrees with J.A. Fitzmyer's estimate that "the contribution that Romans has made

[108]See Richard, "Polemics, Old Testament, and Theology," 340-67.

[109]With many recent scholars, we consider 6:14-7:1 to be both intrusive and non-Pauline; cf. J.A. Fitzmyer, "Qumran and the Interpolated Paragraph in 2 Cor. 6, 14-7, 1," *CBQ* 23 (1961) 271-80 and V.P. Furnish, *II Corinthians* (NY: Doubleday, 1985) 371-83.

to Western Christian thinking is inestimable,"[110] one also insists that the letter continues to be the center of lively theological and scholarly debate. While theologians of the past treated Paul's letter, in categories reminiscent of the Reformation, as a "compendium of Christian theology," modern scholarship created a new atmosphere for reading this important first-century document. Therefore, first we will examine current approaches to Romans, then discuss the reason for Paul's writing of this letter, and finally direct our attention to the epistle and its message.

ROMANS DEBATE

Scholarship now takes seriously the axiom that early Christian documents had specific settings within the community. As we have seen in our study thus far of the Pauline correspondence, it is hazardous to attempt a serious reading of Paul's letters without some understanding of the situation in his life and that of the document's audience. Since each of Paul's early letters corresponds to identifiable occasions and crisis within his churches, it is imperative to study Romans from this perspective. Along with the growing concern about the *Sitz im Leben* of the letter, scholars attend to Paul's statements in Romans, to his relationship to and make-up of this Italian audience, and to various textual, literary, historical, and theological issues relating to the epistle. The common motif of recent Romans scholarship has been: why did Paul write to the community of Rome?

In answering the question scholars have examined the clues offered by the letter, have assessed the data relating to its textual integrity, its literary character, and its many themes, and have opted for a particular factor or combination of factors as the key to the problem. The variety of answers given to the question has been disconcerting to those seeking a consensus but encouraging to those who delve into the intricacies of Pauline thought.

Recent studies can be classified into three groups in so far as they address certain issues or resolve the question of the *Sitz im Leben* of Romans in a given way. 1) Paul wrote either with his own concerns in mind or for the benefit of the Roman community. 2) Paul knew little about the Roman situation or else he was acquainted with Roman issues and wrote to address these. 3) Some focus on the integrity of the

---

[110]"The Letter to the Romans," 2:293 in *JBC*.

letter, particularly the status of chapter 16. These categories are not mutually exclusive; instead, they are an attempt to deal with Paul's letter by examining the insights offered by scholars as they address the issues involved.

In the first group are studies that see Paul expressing his basic theology in view of his projected Spanish mission (1:10f; 15:24, 28). Paul needs their assistance and therefore writes either to introduce himself or defend his gospel as he sets out for a new mission territory.[111] Many prefer to see Paul's reason for writing as owing to a more altruistic motive; he composes his document to assist the Roman community in resolving its problems in regard to the Law, Judaism generally, or the lack of unity between Christians of Gentile and Jewish origin. It is the conflict between the "weak" and the "strong" (chaps. 14-15) which receives the greatest attention. Some of these studies suggest a polemical motivation for Paul's treatment of the issues.[112]

The above discussion leads us to consider the second category of studies, namely, Paul's acquaintance with the Roman community and its problems. Some scholars, in defending Romans as a generalized statement of Paul's theology, insist both that Paul had little knowledge of the Roman situation and that the key to understanding the letter is to find a setting for it in the author's life (a mature theological document, possibly related to the collection being sent to Jerusalem).[113] Others, however, basing their views on a variety of factors (study of the genre, content, nature of the paraenetic sections, make-up of the Roman community, Rom. 16), claim that Paul was aware of some of the issues

[111]See Kümmel, *Introduction to the New Testament*, 311-14, for a presentation of this position.

[112]For this first category of studies, see G. Klein, "Paul's Purpose in Writing the Epistle to the Romans," 32-42 in K.P. Donfried, *The Romans Debate* (Minneapolis: Augsburg, 1977). See Kümmel, *Introduction to the New Testament*, 313, for a list of polemical theses.

[113]G. Bornkamm claims that Romans is Paul's "last will and testament" and must be situated in "the sphere of the eternally and universally valid," 31, "The Letter to the Romans as Paul's Last Will and Testament," in Donfried, *Romans Debate*. In the same volume R. Karris maintains that the paraenesis of the letter is of a general type and has little to do with the occasion for writing ("Romans 14:1-15:13 and the Occasion of Romans," 98), while J. Jervell insists that Paul was defending himself and the Gentile church vis-à-vis Jerusalem ("The Letter to Jerusalem," 74).

of concern to the audience and "that Romans addresses a concrete set of problems in the life of Christians in Rome."[114]

Some see further confirmation of Paul's acquaintance with the Roman community in the long list of names found in Rom. 16. Many discussions of the textual and theological problems of Rom. 16 attempt to show that Paul was familiar with many in the community.[115]

With these sharply opposing views in mind we now focus on the occasion for the writing of Romans. First, we attend briefly to chapter 16. Scholars increasingly reject this part of the document as belonging originally to Romans. There are strong textual and literary reasons for reaching such a conclusion. The present concluding verses, 16:25-27, are also found at the end of chapters 14 and 15 in some manuscripts of Romans; besides, a strong case can be made for its non-Pauline authorship.[116] These data lead scholars, in view of the apparent ending found at 15:30-33, to consider chaper 16 a later addition. Further, its nature and content suggest the same. The chapter is a letter of recommendation (in form and content) for Phoebe the deaconess (vv. 1f). The long list of names follows naturally in such a document and makes sense only if Paul is writing to a church he knows well. Despite attempts to show how so many "Pauline acquaintances" made their way to Rome, the most likely option is to see chapter 16 as a short Pauline letter, probably written from Corinth to Ephesus, which an editor appended to Romans when the Pauline corpus was compiled.[117] Further, the tone and content of 16:17-20 (about false teachers) presume an address to a church well-known to Paul rather than to Rome. Romans 16, therefore, should not be employed to demonstrate Pauline acquaintance with the Roman community.

---

[114]K.P. Donfried, "False Presuppositions in the Study of Romans," 122 in Donfried, *Romans Debate.*

[115]K.P. Donfried, "A Short Note on Romans 16," 50-60 in Donfried, *ibid.* T.W. Manson, in an earlier study of these textual data had concluded that Romans was a circular letter written first to the Romans and then sent also to Ephesus with the addition of chapter 16 ("St. Paul's Letter to the Romans—and Others," 1-16 in Donfried, *ibid*).

[116]E. Käsemann, *Commentary on Romans* (Grand Rapids: Eerdmans, 1980) 421-28 and C.K. Barrett, *A Commentary on the Epistle to the Romans* (NY: Harper and Row, 1957) 286-87.

[117]For a good survey of this problem, see Fitzmyer, "Romans," 2:292-93; *contra* Donfried, "A short Note on Romans 16," 50-60.

What then can be said about Paul's knowledge of the community and the problems it is experiencing? On the one hand, he has never been to Rome, though he hopes soon to arrive there (1:10-13; 15:22-24, 28-29). Thus, he is introducing himself and his gospel to the community. On the other hand, the theological and paraenetic content is such that scholars are divided over whether Paul is composing a summary of his thought and giving "universal" advice to the community or whether he is addressing concrete Roman problems. Those who hold that the epistle must be situated in Paul's life-setting rather than that of the audience detect little evidence for a Roman setting. R.J. Karris, on the basis of a comparative and exegetical study of 14:1-15:13, concluded that the section on the weak and the strong "is better explained as general Pauline paraenesis, which is adapted from his discussion in 1 Cor. 8-10 and is addressed to a problem that may arise in any community."[118] Karris insists that little is known about the Roman church and that attempts to discern individual communities to which Paul might bring unity is conjectural. He also maintains that the extensive use by Paul of rhetorical conventions, particularly the diatribe and circumstantial clauses, argues against a concrete Roman situation and for a generalized Pauline paraenesis.

Karris' study has not gone unanswered. Donfried has convincingly shown that since Paul's use of rhetorical devices in other letters does not indicate the absence of a concrete situation, so must it be for Romans.[119] We agree with recent trends that view the Roman situation as related to competing groups of Jewish and Gentile Christians. So we accept E. Käsemann's insistence that though Romans owes much to 1 Cor. 8-10, it is nevertheless specific enough to indicate concrete Roman problems:

> Paul obviously does not know the congregation. This does not mean, however, that he has no information about it. On the contrary, it would be quite incredible to want to contest that. From this center of communication reports must have reached Christians everywhere in the world at that time ... As a postulate we might venture the thesis that Paul presupposes or suspects the existence of contending groups at Rome and that this is important for his concerns in writing.[120]

---

[118]"Romans 14:1-15:13 and the Occasion of Romans," 99.

[119]"False Presuppositions in the Study of Romans," 127-43, especially 140.

[120]*Romans*, 364-65; see also Donfried, "False Presuppositions in the Study of Romans," 123-27.

Indeed, the situation of "the weak" and "the strong" has been clarified by W. Marxsen's suggestion that the context of the debate owes to the expulsion of Jews and of Jewish Christians from Rome by Claudius and the subsequent return of the latter as a minority within a predominantly Gentile-Christian church.[121] Paul addressed not only the paraenesis of chapters 14-15 to this situation but formulated the theological section (1-11) with this problem in mind. Paul then was interested in the unity of Gentile and Jewish Christians in view of his forthcoming missionary endeavor. To an extent Karris is right in seeing chapters 14-15 as a reapplication of the Pauline discussion of 1 Cor. 8-10. Nonetheless, this new text goes far beyond and in a different direction than did the Corinthian passage.

While it is not possible to discuss in detail the indications of Pauline acquaintance with the Roman situation, whether in the letter generally or in the paraenetic section, it is instructive to note a recent, convincing proposal concerning Rom. 13:1-7. Employing traditional ideas on "governing authorities" (*topos*) Paul gives his audience advice about the important, pending issue of taxation. Recent researchers[122] suggest that the debate over tax reform which occurred at the beginning of Nero's reign was about indirect taxation or abuses of the Knights and their *publicani* in the collection of these. Tacitus the Roman historian states that in the year 58 A.D. Nero considered the abolition of indirect taxation "as a consequence of repeated demands from the public, which complained of the exactions of the revenue-farmers" (Annals 13.50).[123] Thus, Paul advises the Christians of Rome, in view of the approaching end-time and their loyalty to a heavenly state, to abstain from this political and economic debate and to pay taxes of both kinds. Paul could afford to be optimistic for in his day

> there had not yet been any fundamental confrontation between Rome and the church; the Empire could still be hailed as the one political force capable of creating and maintaining political, economic, and

[121]*Introduction to the New Testament: An Approach to the Problems* (Philadelphia: Fortress, 1968) 96f.

[122]J. Friedrich, W. Pohlmann, and P. Stuhlmacher, "Zur historischen Situation und Intention von Rom. 13, 1-7," *ZTK* 73 (1976) 131-66. For a solid, popular presentation of these ideas, see Furnish, *The Moral Teaching of Paul*, 115-41.

[123]C.H. Moore and J. Jackson, eds., *Tacitus: The Histories, The Annals* (Cambridge: Harvard University, 1937).

social stability in the world, and the young Nero (only nineteen or twenty years of age when Paul wrote this letter) showed promise of being a just emperor.[124]

If we are correct in our analysis of 13:1-7 and in our assessment of chapters 14-15 as reflecting Roman problems, then it follows that Paul is acquainted with the issues of his readers. That he employs arguments he formulated in earlier discussions, especially in the Corinthian correspondence, does not detract from the specificity of his advice to the Roman community.

We now turn to a discussion of the occasion for the letter by considering several passages with a bearing on the issue. From the start Paul emphasizes his apostleship to the Gentiles, his commission to proclaim the gospel to them, and his desire to visit the Roman community (1:5, 10-11, 13-15). He also stresses the Gentile (the majority) origin of his readers (1:6, 13; see also 11:13). It is evident from his repeated statements that he was anxious to reach the West, Rome in particular, and also that he has been detained (1:10, 13, 15). The reason for this delay is not given until the last chapter when he returns to the reason for writing. Paul ends the thanksgiving section by stating that he is "eager to preach the gospel to you also who are in Rome" (1:15). This statement is intriguing since in 15:30 Paul claims as his "canon" or procedure the announcing of the good news only to areas that have not heard of the Christ.[125] These two statements help focus the problem and require added attention. The final section (15:14-29) develops further the topic of the initial thanksgiving and Paul is full of praise for this community (15:14). But he also stresses his commission as minister to the Gentiles (vv. 16, 18). Again he speaks of his plans to go west and for the first time mentions his projected mission to Spain (24, 28). Important are a number of items which Paul relates to his future visit and to his reason for writing. Before he broaches the subject of his projected visit, he defends his boldness in writing to the Romans (15) by recalling his commission to minister to the Gentiles. He expresses justified pride in his "work for God" (17) and describes the vastness of his labors (19)

---

[124]Furnish, *Moral Teaching.*, 136.

[125]Thus, Klein ("Paul's Purpose in Writing the Epistle to the Romans," 32-49) claims that since the Roman community had no apostolic foundation, Paul did not see his preaching there as violating his policy of non-interference in another's field of work.

which has resulted in the lack of "room for work" in the eastern part of the empire (23). Then he draws from Isaiah 52:15 a passage to justify his basic mission to announce the good news only "where Christ has (not) already been named" (20-21). Only at this point does he tell the reader that his visit will be brief as he passes on his way to Spain (24, 28). Paul adds a final element: he cannot come immediately to Rome since he must first make a trip "to Jerusalem with aid for the saints" (25).

In the recent Romans debate, however, scholars adopt or stress some elements to the detriment of others, such as the Spanish mission or the collection for Jerusalem. Others object to factors which they see as only superficially relevant (e.g., the Spanish mission is mentioned only at the end of chapter 15), and so describe Romans as a summary or testament of Paul's theology to a new community.

We believe that all the factors (Paul's statements as well as the content and shape of his letter) must be taken into consideration. We start by considering his desire to go to Rome, stated several times in chapter 1 and reiterated in chapter 15, but with the Spanish mission in view. This is a major factor in discovering the occasion for writing, since Paul has earlier told the Corinthians that he desired to "preach the gospel in lands beyond" them (2 Cor. 10:16). There he implies that problems within the community had kept him from carrying out his plan. Finally, in Romans we see him approaching the time (in his own mind) when the trip west will be possible. The writing of Romans is related to that project.

In Paul's perspective the crucial themes of canon, lack of room for work in the East, urgency of the mission, and of its focus on the Gentiles are related to other issues such as the nature and scope of Romans (its highly didactic character), his vaguely and awkwardly expressed request from the Roman community (chaps. 1 and 15), the completion and meaning of the collection, and the pervasive Jewish and Gentile problem. Thus, E. Käsemann makes these suggestions:

> When these questions are asked, and contrasted with the real yet concealed plans of the apostle and also with his tremendous claim in v. 5, we come face to face with the problem of Paul's apostolate which influences almost all his epistles and is often their crucial point. The authority which he asserts does not accord with what is conceded to him in fact. Even at the end of his course he stands in the twilight of unclear situations and in conflict with opposing opinions about him.

He has to reckon with the fact that doors which he passionately wishes to open are closed to him. The most important theological epistle in Christian history is undoubtedly also the record of an existence struggling for recognition and of an apostolicity called into question. Apart from this insight Romans cannot be interpreted correctly.[126]

Paul's apostolicity and his mission to the Gentiles are the key elements to understanding Romans. The epistle is a passionate plea to the premier western community and a subtle attempt to gain assistance (more in ideational than financial terms) for his new field of endeavor "beyond" the eastern Mediterranean. The background of this turn of events is correctly diagnosed by Käsemann. Paul encountered numerous difficulties; all his letters attest to this. In some cases competitive Jewish Christians with their own Gentile mission and in other cases syncretistic or spiritualistic opponents caused havoc in his communities. These situations were compounded by Paul's uncompromising theology and christology of lordship which many Jews and Gentiles found offensive. Attempts to control the spiritual realm or perceived threats to God's lordship and eschatological agent not only drew Paul into controversy and pointed pastoral advice but also helped him to formulate his enduring message.

The Epistle to the Romans shares in this evolutionary process and, since it comes toward the end of Paul's career, expresses in a more mature and far less polemical way some of the critical issues of the apostle's thought. Convinced of and confirmed in his apostolate to the Gentiles early in his ministry (Gal. 1:17; 2:7-9) and preoccupied by the approaching end-time,[127] Paul adopts a policy of non-interference in the labor of others. One might contrast 1 Cor. 16:8-9 with 2 Cor. 10:15-16 and Rom. 15:18-24 to see how matters evolved in his career. In the first we meet an apostle eager to stay in Ephesus "for a wide door for effective work has opened," but also aware that "there are many adversaries." In 2 Corinthians 10 we encounter a wish for rather than the reality of an

---

[126]*Romans*, 19-20; for a slightly different explanation see C.E.B. Cranfield, *The Epistle to the Romans* (Edinburgh: Clark, 1985) 814-23.

[127]Käsemann, *Romans* 395; also J.C. Becker, *Paul the Apostle: The Triumph of God in Life and Thought* (Philadelphia: Fortress, 1980) and C.K. Barrett, *The Signs of an Apostle* (Philadelphia: Fortress, 1972), 42, who, citing A. Friedrichsen, calls Paul an "eschatologic person."

"enlarged field," while in Romans we see that the apostle has taken the ultimate step toward the West.

At this point we need to consider the oft-repeated question: what did Paul hope to obtain from the Roman community? Chapter 1 (vv. 8-15) is vague and chapter 15 (23-24, 32) is only tantalizingly more specific. In the first we are confronted not only by a well-formulated Pauline thanksgiving but also by an awkwardly written diplomatic introduction. Paul is hesitant on the one hand to say that Rome will be a stop over on his way to Spain (he expresses this in a more diplomatic way in 15:24) lest he insult his audience and appear opportunistic. On the other hand, he finds himself in a quandary as to how he might present both apostolic mission and claims (already expressed in 1:5) as well as achieve his goal of winning the support of this important community.[128] In v. 10 he expresses his desire to come to Rome, that he might "impart . . . some spiritual gift" (1:11). Feeling at once that the expression lacks in diplomacy, Paul backs off and in an even more tentative sentence speaks of mutual encouragement (12). Paul then lessens his diplomatic effort as he insists that his visit is in view of reaping "some" (a bit tentative again) harvest among the Romans (13). All uncertainty disappears in vv. 14-15 when Paul relates his mission to all Gentiles (14) and concludes with the problematic v. 15: "I am eager to preach the gospel to you also who are in Rome."

At the end of the letter Paul returns to his stated goal. As he had insisted in 1:9 that he was at the service of "the gospel of [God's] Son" to all the nations, so again in 15:16 he claims "to be a minister of Christ Jesus to the Gentiles in the priestly service of the gospel of God." In this case, however, he focuses on the Spanish project rather than on his visit to Rome as he speaks of the completion of his eastern mission and expressses his reasons for moving west (15:19f). V. 24 is crucial for "Paul must avoid the suspicion that he wants to make the world capital his own domain and he does not want to say brusquely that he regards it merely as a bridgehead."[129] At the same time he writes: "I hope . . . to be sped [or given provisions or support] on my journey there by you" (24).

Why therefore does Paul write the Epistle to the Romans? He wishes to introduce himself to the community that can best assist him in his

---

[128]For an insightful reading of these verses see Barrett, *Romans*, 24-27 and Käsemann, *Romans*, 18-21.

[129]*Ibid.*, 397.

missionary endeavors in Spain. There is urgency in this commission ("the day is at hand," 13:12) and the need for recognition of his apostolicity and mission to all Gentiles. It is at this point that the collection for the poor of Jerusalem (15:25-33) takes on added importance. Paul longs for "the right hand of fellowship" extended earlier (Gal. 2:9) and strives to discuss the meaning of the gospel to win the support of the Roman community, both members of Jewish and Gentile origin. Thus, the expression "to preach the good news" in 1:15 stresses not the action of preaching but the exposition of the content of the good news, 1:1, 9.[130] Then in 1:16 Paul defends his concept of the gospel as it pertains to Jew and Gentile. The epistle itself focuses on one of the major themes of Paul's writings: God's power (in and through Christ) to save the ungodly. Paul needs the ideational support of the unified Jewish and Gentile Christian community, as he plans his next field of work. His relation to the Jewish Christian community in Rome and in Jerusalem remained problematic but nonetheless important for it was his wish that his service to the saints in Jerusalem be acceptable as a sign of unity (15:31) and that his gospel be heard in Rome (1:15-16).

Finally, one might dwell on the probably tragic non-realization of Paul's plans for Spain. Nevertheless, for our purposes it is the optimism, mixed with foreboding (15:31), with which Paul ends his letter that gives Romans an added degree of grandeur.

LETTER TO THE ROMANS

The document contains standard epistolary features: introduction or opening (1:1-7), thanksgiving (1:8-15), body consisting of doctrinal material (1:16-11:36), paraenetic section (12:1-15:13), and conclusion (15:14-33). Only the problem-solving 1 Corinthians compares with it in length and none of the other letters is as removed from controversy or pastoral issues. It is for this reason that many in the past have seen it as a theological tract. Of course such a perspective did not take into consideration the document's epistolary features. To account for its highly developed discursive or doctrinal and yet epistolary character some recent scholars have proposed the letter-essay or the demonstrative

---

[130]On the two meanings of "good news" in Paul, see H. Conzelmann, *1 Corinthians* (Philadelphia: Fortress, 1981) and G. Friedrich, "euaggelizomai," 2:729-34 in *TDNT*.

(epideictic) letter as the proper classification and model for Romans.[131] In either case the objective is to explain its unusual characteristics and to situate it within Paul's missionary career and theological development. The key to a proper understanding of the message of Romans and therefore of the central element of Paul's thought is in the proper analysis of 1:16f. Scholars readily see in these verses the thesis of the epistle,[132] for here Paul discourses on the nature and content of the good news. From the start Paul is preoccupied with this theme and at the mention of the term "gospel" (*euangelion*, 1:1) is led, in a manner similar to Gal. 1:1f, to digress from the standard opening and to dwell on the nature, content, and dynamics of the good news (vv. 2-6). Paul gives the theme its focus by relating it to the crucial motif of apostleship (vv. 1, 5). The latter becomes an underlying concern of the thanksgiving section and, with special attention to the Gentile mission (including Rome), provides the transition to the body of the letter. Because of his commission to the Gentiles (v. 14) Paul expounds the gospel to those who can assist him in his western mission as he strives for "the obedience of faith ... among all the nations" (1:5).

Special attention must be given to the form and content of the thesis statement, since it summarizes and structures the message Paul conveys to the Roman community. Rather than limiting ourselves to vv. 16-17, we propose to include v. 18 in this analysis. Paul begins v. 16 with a generalized parallel to v. 15 in the form of a *litotes*: "for I am not ashamed of the gospel." He then launches into a threefold statement which announces the basic structure of the epistle's doctrinal section.

16 for it is the power of God for salvation to every one who has *faith*, to the Jew first and also to the Greek.
17 for the righteousness of God *is revealed* in it through *faith* for faith, as it is written: 'the righteous shall live by faith.'
18 for the wrath of God *is revealed* from heaven against all the ungodliness and wickedness of men who by their wickedness suppress the truth (RSVmod).

---

[131]For the former see M.L. Stirewalt, "The Form and Function of the Greek Letter-Essay," 175-206 and for the latter W. Wuellner, "Paul's Rhetoric of Argumentation in Romans: An Alternative to the Donfried-Karris Debate over Romans," 152-74, both in Donfried, *The Romans Debate*.

[132]Barrett, *Romans*, 27-31; Käsemann, *Romans*, 21-32; Cranfield, *Romans*, 27-28.

Each phrase is introduced by postpositive "for" (*gar*) and presents a characteristic Pauline phrase: "the power of God," "the righteousness of God," and "the wrath of God." The first verse addresses the universal character of the Christ-event and therefore announces chapters 5-8; the second dwells on the period of the promise and so foreshadows the diatribe-like discussion Paul has with the Jew in 2:17-4:25; while the third introduces the theme of human depravity and then without pause gives way to an analysis of the situation of Gentiles prior to or apart from the Christ-event in 1:19-2:16. Thus, Paul announces the three groups of humanity: Jew and Gentile in Christ (16), Jew prior to the Christ-event (17), and Gentile apart from Christ (18), and then proceeds in reverse order, with much overlapping, to treat all three: the Gentile (1:19-2:16), the Jew (2:17-4:25), and the believing Jew and Gentile (5:1-8:39). At that point (chap. 9), influenced by the Jewish-Gentile problems of the Roman community, Paul returns to the second group, the "unbelieving" Jew. First Paul had discussed God's relation to Israel as promise and preparation for the Christ's coming and for the rule of faith, that is, the Jew "prior to" the coming of the Christ (2:17-4:25). In chapters 9-11 he returns to the subject but this time it is a question of the Jew "apart from" Christ, for Paul is painfully aware that so many of his "kinsmen by race" (9:3) have not embraced the Messiah. In these chapters he attempts to reconcile the eternally binding promise of God and the fate of Israel.

The letter to the Romans is Paul's most ambitious and latest composition and so one expects to find in it a more mature statement of his major ideas. The extensive doctrinal content, however, must be seen in light of the letter's purpose and Paul's missionary ambitions. Romans is argumentative, as Paul always is in his letters, but it is especially discursive since Paul delivers his message to the Christians of Rome as he prepares for his western project. He is interested and committed to "the obedience of faith among all the nations" and Rome is his gateway to the western Mediterranean.

Having presented his basic thesis (1:16-18) Paul focuses on the theme of divine judgment first of Gentiles and then of Jews, the first because of their arrogant refusal to acknowledge God's lordship and the second for their boastful self-reliance. Paul's thesis is that all human beings stand under God's judgment. Non-Jews have been exposed to the natural world and its visible manifestations of divinity, but have "suppressed the truth" by rebelling against the Lord. They have rejected their dependence on the Creator, "although they knew God they did not honor him as God or give thanks to him" (1:21). So due to their refusal to acknowledge this lordship they have been given over to all forms of licentiousness. Their minds have been darkened; they have become fools and have lapsed into idolatry (21-23). Proof of this is found in the depravity of the Gentile world. Employing Jewish notions of the degradation of the non-Jewish world (lists of evils in vv. 26f, 28f), Paul insists that "one is punished by the very things by which one sins" (Wis. 11:16). God's anger is at work as it is being poured out upon those who have rebelled against the divine lordship. Instead of being creatures of a loving God they have become slaves of other creatures.

Having passed judgment on the depraved, Paul focuses attention on the self-righteous, i.e., those who, while joining Paul in condemning moral wickedness, whether Jew or Gentile, assume they can escape God's judgment (2:3). All will be judged, "for God shows no partiality" (11). The simple preaching of virtue or the false reliance on God's goodness does not provide escape from God's judgment. Sin, under the Law or outside the Law, is subject to God's wrath (12). It is in this transitional section (2:1-16) that Paul begins to address the second group, the Jew apart from the Christ-event. Neither the Law nor moral indignation exempts one from judgment. On that score Jew and Gentile are equal before God.

Whereas in 2:1-16 Paul, in his diatribe, was addressing "the human race" (*o anthrōpe*, v. 3),[133] in vv. 17f he speaks to his fellow Jew, the one who, though he boasts of the Law, nonetheless, "dishonors God by breaking the Law" (23). Even circumcision does not justify in God's eyes for it is an external sign of one who is a Jew "inwardly" (29). Paul is aware that, in light of his preceding statements, his Jewish reader might conclude that there is no advantage in being a Jew (3:1). He forestalls that conclusion by pointing out that "the Jews are entrusted with the oracles of God" (3:2) but, after entertaining further objections, insists that since "all men, both Jews and Greeks, are under the power of sin" (9), they are subject to God's anger. So in the realm of justification there is no advantage for the Jew.[134]

---

[133]Käsemann, *Romans,* 54, is probably correct in viewing Rom. 2:1 as an early gloss on v. 3. For a general discussion of Paul's use of the diatribe in Romans, see S.K. Stowers, *The Diatribe and Paul's Letter to the Romans* (Chico: Scholars, 1981).

[134]S.K. Stowers, "Paul's Dialogue with a Fellow Jew in Romans 3:1-9," *CBQ* 46 (1984) 707-22.

At 3:21 Paul begins his treatment specifically of justification (the term appears 12 times in 3:21-4:25). Having proposed in 1:17 that the righteous lives by faith and insisted in the previous verse (3:20) that justification is not a result of "works of the Law," he begins a new part of his discussion with the Jew by declaring that at the present time "the righteousness of God has been manifested *apart from the law* ... *through faith* in Jesus Christ for all who believe" (21-22). The italicized terms emphasize the passage's dialectical character. It is in dialogue with Judaism that Paul develops his doctrine of justification by faith.[135] "The law and the prophets bear witness to it" but do not confer this justification or righteousness. Instead the believer is "justified by (God's) grace as a gift, through the redemption which is in Christ Jesus, whom God put forward as an expiation by his blood, to be received by faith" (24-25). As central as are the themes of "Christ crucified" and "justification as grace" to Paul's thought, in the present passage it is rather the inability of the Law to grant justification and its corollary the justification by faith which take center stage (vv. 21, 26; also 28). The human being, apart from Christ and left to human devices, is under the Law and can hear no other verdict but that of guilty, "since all have sinned and fall short of the glory of God" (23). The human being, in the person of Adam, lost all semblance of glory (Wis. 2:23f) but as a result of eschatological grace and in the realm of promise participates in the redemption brought about by the Christ's death. While Paul returns later to these themes, in the present context he is interested in the relationship between righteousness and the Law.

Having insisted that one is justified by faith not by works of the Law (27-30), Paul voices a pertinent Jewish question: "do we then overthrow the law by this faith?" To this he responds: "By no means! On the contrary, we uphold the law" (31). Chapter 4 then follows both as proof that the Law is not abolished and as scriptural support for the theme of justification by faith. In the first case, Genesis 15 and 17 (along with Psalm 32) provide Paul with the basis of his argument. Far from being overthrown, the Law provides the authority for such a doctrine. In the second case, we encounter Paul, in Rabbinic fashion, arguing for the priority of faith. Scripture states that Abraham was declared righteous by God before he was circumcised; i.e., chapter 15 precedes chapter 17

---

[135]Stendahl, *Paul among Jews and Gentiles*; see also Plevnik, *What Are They Saying about Paul?* 55-76.

in the Abraham story. Further, Abraham was not the first proselyte, as maintained by the Rabbis, but a Gentile when in view of his faith he was declared righteous and so was "made father of all who believe" (10-11). It was later (Gen. 17) that "he received circumcision as a sign or seal of the righteousness which he had by faith while he was still uncircumcised" (11). Abraham then is the ancestor of all who have faith, the uncircumcised believers as well as "the circumcised who are not merely circumcised but also follow the example of the faith our father Abraham had before he was circumcised" (12). In the remainder of the chapter Paul, in a more positive vein than previously in Gal. 3, treats the unwavering faith of Abraham, the promise of God to Abraham's descendants (both "the adherents of the law" and "those who share [his] faith," v. 16), and the importance of the Christ-event as death and resurrection (vv. 17, 19, 24-25).[136]

Before moving on to the next section, we examine the thrust of the author's logic thus far.

> Paul's whole argument is that no man can achieve the necessary righteousness, and so God has established a new possibility: a man will be justified by God,—i.e., declared "righteous" by him,—if he has faith in Jesus, and this is a possibility for Jew and Gentile alike. The Jew has failed to live up to the law and the Gentile to the conscience in his heart, but God nonetheless declares them righteous in his sight because of the righteousness of Jesus (who more than fulfilled all norms), which they appropriate to themselves by the act of faith.[137]

Paul ends his discussion of Gentile and Jew apart from Christ on the note of reparation and restoration, for the Christ-event has made a difference for humanity, since Jesus "was put to death for our trespasses and raised for our justification" (4:25).

The apostle next turns his attention to the effects of the Christ-event (5:1-8:39),[138] namely, God's power at work for the salvation of believing Jew and Gentile (1:16b). With hardly a transition Paul broaches the subject of the new Christian reality, the life of righteousness which

---

[136]On the compatibility of Rom. 3:31 and 10:4 as well as the defense of continuity between Law and faith in Paul see C.T. Rhyme, *Faith Establishes the Law* (Chico: Scholars, 1981).

[137]Perrin, *The New Testament*, 110.

[138]Cranfield, *Romans*, 253-54.

means freedom from death (chapter 5), sin (6), and also the Law (7), and entrance into the domain of the Spirit (8). Having discussed justification by faith in chapters 1-4, he now speaks of human reconciliation with God: "we have peace with God through our Lord Jesus Christ" (5:1). From the start Paul stresses both the theological and christological components of this new reality. The first consequence of justification concerns the believer's relationship to God. In place of the alienation of humanity's former state there is established a new affinity between Creator and creature, a state wherein the creature is no longer at odds with God but has been reestablished in a right relationship with the Lord of all reality. Peace becomes a characteristic of the believer's life since the state of rebellion has ceased for the one who acknowledges God's envoy. This new state has come about through the agency of the "Lord Jesus Christ," all three terms bearing significance in this context. Paul's use of the name "Jesus" lays stress on the death; use of the title "Christ" emphasizes the resurrection; while use of the term "Lord" expresses the believer's profession of faith in God's agent. The kerygma then is at the core of Paul's credo. The death and resurrection of Jesus provide the key to God's plan for humanity for they are the central elements of the Christ-event. Acknowledgement of these amounts to a recognition of God's lordship.

Indeed present and future results ("access to grace" and "hope of sharing God's glory," 5:2) are actualized as a result of God's action through Christ and the believer's acceptance of this fact (both objective and subjective soteriological reality). Now for the first time Jewish and Gentile believers have open to them (not yet a possession) the gracious gift (3:24) of God or that state which Paul defines as "grace in which one stands" (5:3). God's love is manifested as graced, present existence ("love poured into the heart," v. 5) and as eschatological hope. The glory that was once lost (3:23) has now become the object of a non-disappointing hope. These present and future realities are made possible by the Spirit's activity in the life of the believer (5:5; see 8:9-11; see also the Spirit as first installment in 2 Cor. 1:22; 5:5). So the Christian rejoices in the face of hardship for joy is the present manifestation of future reality (vv. 3-4).

Next Paul, as prelude to his discussion of death in light of the Christ-event (5:12f), focuses on the death which brought about the reconciliation between God and humanity (5:6-11). As a consequence of Christ's death, death itself takes on new meaning for the believer. If at this point 5:6-11 is of interest to us as an introduction to the subsequent discussion on death, its fuller meaning will be examined in our analysis of Pauline christology.

Christ's death and therefore his life have changed human relations vis-à-vis God so that the vicissitudes and enslaving realities of human existence have been deeply affected, whether death, sin, or the Law. In this context Paul renews his discussion of Christ as the new Adam. If in 1 Cor. 15:21f Paul draws upon this theme to emphasize the life-giving character of the Christ-event during his discourse on resurrection, in Romans he puts that theme to a slightly different use. In the former he contrasts Adam as the source of death and Christ as the guarantee of eternal life or resurrection. In Romans, however, while the theme of future life is reiterated (5:10), the stress falls on the believer's present state. Paul sets up a typology between Adam and Christ (12-14) and proceeds to discuss the legacy of each: sin and death in one case and in the other eternal life (vv. 18, 21) and the "free gift" of acquittal (18), righteousness (16-17), and grace (15). The section, which alludes to the role of the Law in this process (13, 20), comes to a climax in v. 21 which we paraphrase thus: "sin reigned in death for a time that grace might in its turn reign in the righteousness of the believer that eternal life might be obtained; all of this is made possible through the agency of Jesus Christ our Lord."[139] Sin, death, and Law played their part in God's plan, that "grace might abound all the more" (20). The legacy of Christ therefore is a graced existence (with God as center) for the believer with a view to eternal life.

In chapter 6 Paul addresses the subject of death to or liberation from sin. He is led to this subject by his previous discussion of death and sin as the antithesis of grace and especially by 5:20: "where sin increased, grace abounded all the more." His imaginary dialogue partner then might interject: if the believer is justified, then why be concerned about morality? Ever on his guard against moralism, Paul launches into a discussion of God's righteousness and power as it affects the believer. The Christian's life is not one of doing good deeds but of participation in the Christ-event. The believer was buried into the death of Christ through baptism and so death and its power (sin) have been ruptured. The domain of death or slavery to sin no longer reigns, since the Christian is freed from sin in and by the death of Christ (6:6-7). Paul's

---

[139]See Barrett, *Romans*, 118, for a similar reading of 5:21.

logic at this point is of particular interest. Some in his audience expected him to say, "as the Christ was crucified, buried, and 'raised from the dead by the glory of God' (v. 4), so is the believer 'baptized into (Jesus') death' (v. 3) and raised from the dead with him." Instead, Paul repeatedly insists that resurrection or eternal life is a future reality—one should note the future tenses Paul uses when speaking of the Christian's sharing in Christ's resurrection (e.g., vv. 5, 8). Nonetheless there is true parallelism between the Christ and his followers:

Christ: death ----------------➤ resurrection
                                            (alive to God)

Christian: death/ --➤walk ----------➤ future
               baptism   in newness of life   resurrection
                           (alive to God in
                           Christ Jesus)

The believer's life in the present means being "dead to sin and alive to God in Christ Jesus" (v. 11), for this new life is one of being under God's dominion in the present. The old self has been crucified and believers must yield themselves to God to become "instruments of righteousness" (v. 13). Essential to Paul's concept of morality therefore is that the believer's life be viewed in relation to God's gift of righteousness. As Christ Jesus through his death became obedient to God and lives for God (already in the resurrection), so too the believer through a baptismal death lives for God (in anticipation of the resurrection, 6:8) and is freed for obedience in the present (vv. 12f).

Paul continues his discussion of death by appealing to the images of slavery in 6:15-23 and of marriage in 7:1-6. As the themes of "God's dominion," "obedience," and being "not under law but under grace" brought to the fore the subject of freedom as the believer's status vis-à-vis sin, Paul stresses the nature of this freedom. The very notion of slavery requires allegiance to one master. Thus, the Christian is no longer a slave to sin, death, or the Law but of God (6:22). The same is true of the married woman who is bound to one husband; once freed of that bond, she is free indeed. So is the Christian, who, now dead to the

---

[140]J.A. Little, "Paul's Use of Analogy: A Structural Analysis of Romans 7:1-6," *CBQ* 46 (1984) 82-90.

Law, is free to "serve not under the old written code but in the new life of the Spirit" (7:6; see also 6:17).[140]

The next section (7:7f) presents numerous problems to the reader; the principal one is the meaning of "I" in Paul's text. By means of this pronoun is he discussing Christian experience generally, whether the psychological inner struggle of humanity, of the believer, or his own, or is he referring to pious Jews who strive to fulfil the Law?[141] Recent scholarship opts for an anthopological meaning and in this connection we find J. Murphy-O'Connor's interpretation of the chapter convincing.[142] The chapter then represents a history of salvation whose division, relation to Romans, and key terms are as follows:

1. Humanity before the fall (Rom. 7:7-13)
   7:9 "I was once *alive* apart from the law"
2. Humanity between the fall and Christ (7:14-24)
   7:24 "Wretched man that I am! Who will deliver
   me from this body of *death*?"
3. Humanity after the advent of Christ (7:25-8:4)
   8:2 "the law of the spirit of *life* in Christ
   Jesus has set me free."

The "I" of the passage refers then to humanity in its various stages of existence. While Murphy-O'Connor employs this schema to insist "that, for Paul, Christ was in fact what Adam was destined to be,"[143] we note that the concluding verses (8:3-4) suggest such an interpretation:

> for God has done what the law [second stage], weakened by the flesh [first stage], could not do: sending his own Son in the likeness of sinful flesh and for sin, he condemned sin in the flesh [Christ-event], in order that the just requirement of the law might be fulfilled in us, who walk not according to the flesh but according to the Spirit [third stage].

Humanity's relationship to the Law is seen in the context of the Christ-event and its meaning for believing Jew and Gentile. Death to the Law had been announced in introductory fashion in 6:15f and now its role in

---

[141]See Käsemann, *Romans*, 192-93, for a discussion of these options.

[142]*Becoming Human Together*, 42-43. The author's insistence that 7:7-13 is closely related in language and theme to Gen. 3 is convincing; see p. 42.

[143]*Ibid.*, 43.

God's plan, ultimately as "the law of sin and death" (8:2), is developed at greater length from a salvation historical perspective, allowing Paul finally to focus on the new Christian reality. The Law, being "holy and just and good" (7:12), nevertheless, served its purpose in the divine plan by provoking (7:5) and unmasking sin (7:13) and revealing humanity's need for God's gift of grace.

For our treatment of chapter 8 we appeal to Käsemann's structural observation and relate this to the above analysis of chapter 7.

> Chapter 8 is clearly structured. Verses 1-11 deal with the Christian life as being in the Spirit. Verses 12-17 expound this as the state of sonship. Verses 18-30 portray it as the hope of eschatological freedom. Verses 31-39 depict it as triumph. The reality of the dominion of the law is far transcended in all this.[144]

The contrast between chapters 7 and 8 is pronounced; the realm of the Law pales in comparison with that of the Spirit. Additionally, we need to stress the connections that exist between these two passages. Almost imperceptibly Paul moves in his discussion of the Law from a consideration of the human condition prior to the Christ-event (7:24) to an analysis of humanity after Christ's coming. His use of the term "law" (*nomos*) changes appreciably as he speaks of "the law of the Spirit of life in Christ Jesus" (8:2), "the just requirement of the law" (v. 4), and "God's law" (v. 7) in contrast to "the law of sin and death" (2), or "the law weakened by the flesh"(3). At this point the dominion of the Spirit and human freedom takes center stage.

In structural terms we should also stress that the end of chapter 7 (vv. 24-25) leads rhetorically into what Murphy-O'Connor classifies as the period following Christ's coming ("who will deliver me ... God through Jesus Christ our Lord"). In chapter 7 Paul establishes the salvation historical background of the new Christian reality; in the following chapter he addresses its apocalyptic nature and dynamic character.

The first part of Paul's discussion focuses on the concept of domain of power, namely, that of the Spirit as opposed to that of the flesh. It is in this context that the antithesis between flesh and spirit is developed. If Paul in chapter 7 mentioned in passing the themes of the flesh (7:5, 18,

[144]*Romans*, 212.

25; also 14, 23) and the Spirit (7:6), in 8:2-11 they become the principal images of the discussion. Those who are under the power of or walking according to the flesh "set their minds on the things of the flesh"(5) and so inherit death (16), since they are hopelessly rebellious against, hostile to, and "cannot please God" (7). On the contrary those who walk or live according to the Spirit "set their minds on the things of the Spirit" (5) and so are granted "life and peace" (6), for God's Spirit dwells in them (9) and their "spirits are alive because of righteousness" (10). The new Christian reality is one of life for the spirit now and one of promised life for the mortal body through God's indwelling Spirit, (the one "who raised Christ Jesus from the dead," 11). Paul reminds his readers that they are in the domain of the Spirit which dwells in them (9) and so must walk according to that Spirit with their minds attuned to the lordship and law of God (7).

Paul continues the discussion of life according to the flesh and the Spirit, first by summarizing in a loosely connected series of antithetical parallels the results of the previous analysis (vv. 12-13; see 5f) and then by introducing the major image of the believer's sonship. In vv. 14-17 he employs several terms to stress this theme: "sons of God," "sonship," and "children of God," all except the last of which he used in Gal. 3:23-4:7. There he contrasted the freedom of Christians with the slavery of those who were not children and heirs of God. While in Galatians the context of the discussion was the Jewish question raised by new missionaries and their Law-observant mission to Gentiles, in Romans Paul addresses more directly and less polemically the new Christian reality. The believer is one "led" or "driven" by the Spirit; only such a one is a child of God (14), who prays or allows the Spirit to pray the words of Jesus: "Abba Father" (15, 26; see also Gal. 4:6; Mark 1:12; 14:36). Only one who cooperates (the corollary of "gift") with the Spirit is a child of God in the way Jesus is and so is constituted heir with Christ (16-17). "Paul is interested in sons as heirs ... and in sonship as a relationship which guarantees future salvation, and is established in the present through the Holy Spirit, who anticipates the future (... v. 23)."[145] While Paul is aware that the activity of the Spirit is an eschatological anticipation of what is to come, he nonetheless, insists that believers are already in some measure children of God. So they are not "to fall back into fear" or "the spirit of slavery" (15), for they are

[145]Barrett, *Romans*, 163.

reestablished as children who can address or acclaim God as "Abba," the parent of children who acknowledge God's lordship over their lives and their destiny. Paul, therefore, is interested in the present character of the Christian's life, that of being daughters and sons and thus co-heirs with their brother the Christ, provided they "suffer with him in order that (they) also be glorified with him" (17). The present anticipation is based on the reality of the Christ-event, both its suffering and glory (see 1 Peter 1:11) as paradigm for Christian living and ground for hope of future actualization.

The content and tone of the remainder of chapter 8 justify the claim of recent scholarship that the thought of Paul cannot be properly understood without a recognition of its apocalyptic character.[146] So strong is Paul's sense of future fulfilment, revelation, and actualization of God's purpose as humanity and creation long to be conformed to the Son's image (19, 21f, 29), that the present and its vicissitudes pale in comparison to the glory that is coming (17, 18). As he reaches the climax of his discussion of Christian life, Paul shows how deeply committed he is to an apocalyptic view of reality both in his use of its imagery and acceptance of its cosmic, absolute, and urgent perspective on God's dominion. "The sufferings of the present time" (18) are indicative of the end-days; Paul speaks of the formidable human and cosmic restoration of the end as creation and humanity "eagerly long for" (19), "groan inwardly" or "in travail" (22-23) as they await the idylic conditions of God's dominion (incorruptibility, glorious freedom, and bodily redemption, 21, 23). Also prominent are the cosmic pessimism of apocalyptic thought (20-21) and its fondness for the theme of predestination (28-30). Even the designation of the righteous as "sons of God" (19) recalls the apocalyptic tradition reflected in Rev. 21:7 where God says of the victorious sufferer: "he shall be my son." Beyond this there is in the final section of chapter 8 the dramatic assurance of ultimate victory.

Balancing this stark apocalyptic imagery is the repeated insistence by Paul that these realities impinge in a profound and constitutive way on Christian life. So solidly based on belief in Christ's resurrection is Christian hope (6:8; see 1 Cor. 15) that Paul states simply: "in this hope we are saved" (24; RSV: "were saved"). In Käsemann's words: "hope is the situation in which [Christians] live as those who are saved" or "saved

---

[146]Käsemann, *Romans*, generally and Becker, *Paul the Apostle*; though see the caution most recently of V.P. Branik, "Apocalyptic Paul?" *CBQ* 47 (1985) 664-75.

because Christ brought salvation, they are so only in the hope that through the Spirit salvation will constantly be imported to them afresh from Christ."[147] Salvation, an eschatological reality and expressed in future terms in Paul, is a teleological constituent of Christian life which allows the believer to await the consummation "with patience" (25). Though beset by the travails of the end-time Christians, while yearning for the final revelation or establishment of God's children in the kingdom, "have the first fruits of the Spirit" (23, or "first installment" as in 2 Cor. 1:22; 5:5) as they live their lives in hope. Even the ecstatic utterances of the community give evidence of the Spirit's activity in view of the eschaton (26-27). Life in the present, appearances to the contrary, shows that "in everything God works for the good with those who love him, who are called according to his purpose" (28).

Finally, in a lyrical passage Paul concludes his lengthy discussion of Christian life in light of the Christ-event. It is on the note of assured victory that he brings his analysis to a close. This assurance is grounded on the only solid basis, namely, God's gracious gift to humanity. We paraphrase Paul as follows: "God is for us, and proof of this is that not even the Son was spared that he might become the instrument of our election, our intercession at God's right hand, and the personification of God's love for humanity" (31-35). God is on the believer's side or, put differently, the Christian now exists in God's domain of power, and, if led by the Spirit, becomes impervious to existence's extreme situations ("tribulation, or distress, or persecution, or famine, or nakedness, or peril, or sword," 35). For though the final battle is being waged in the lives of believers on the human stage (36) victory is already assured (37) over the warring powers of the cosmos (e.g., death, life, angels, principalities, things present, things to come, powers, height, depth, anything else in all creation, 38-39), forces whose spheres of power were assaulted by God's activity in the death and resurrection of the Son. So central is the Christ-event to the foundation of Christian existence and so absolute is its claim upon the community of believers that Paul states unflinchingly that nothing is "able to separate us from the love of God in Christ Jesus our Lord" (39).

Paul's stark conclusion concerning separation from the love of God in Christ (8:39) brings to his mind the painful subject of the fate of "unbelieving" Israel. He is brought back to the Jewish question, for not

[147] *Romans*, 238.

only does it involve the Jew prior to the Christ-event but the nagging issue of Israel apart from Christ. Despite frequent attempts of some either to detach Rom. 9-11 from the rest of the letter as interpolation or isolated fragment or to ignore its significance for Pauline thought, we begin our discussion by citing K. Stendhal:

> To me the climax of Romans is actually chapters 9-11, i.e., his reflections on the relation between church and synagogue, the church and the Jewish *people*—not 'Christianity' and 'Judaism,' not the attitudes of the gospel versus the attitudes of the law. The question is the relation between two communities and their coexistence.
>
> It should be noted that Paul does not say that when the time of God's kingdom, the consummation, comes Israel will accept Jesus as the Messiah. He says only that the time will come when 'all Israel will be saved' (11:26).[148]

While we do not agree that these chapters constitute the center and provide the key to understanding Paul's intention in writing Romans, we recognize the correctness of the remainder of the statement. In Rom. 9-11 Paul addresses the issue of the continued existence of Israel as a people apart from the messianic community. Basic to Paul's view of the Christian reality is its radical newness or discontinuity with the past. In Galatians as well as earlier in Romans he had either avoided or downplayed the role exercised by Moses and the Law in God's dealings with humanity. In other words, Paul subscribed only in a limited way to a salvation-history perspective; Christians are children of Abraham, not of Moses. However, he had to recognize that the Law played a part, though a limited one, in God's overall plan. In chapters 9-11 he returns to this subject with more passion than previously, with a more positive attitude toward his "kinsmen by race" and with a decidedly critical attitude toward Christians of Gentile origin.

If nothing can separate the believer from God's love, what about Israel, God's chosen people? Paul begins his discussion with solemnity (1) by expressing his anguish (2) and concern, to the extent of being willing to be "accursed and cut off from Christ" for the benefit of his kinsmen (3). From the start he brings their prerogatives into the discussion:

---

[148] *Paul among Jews and Gentiles*, 6.

they are Israelites, and to them belong the sonship, the glory, the covenants, the giving of the law, the worship, and the promises; to them belong the partriarchs, and of their race, according to the flesh, is the Christ (4-5).

As Käsemann insists: "the Jews are not just close to the apostle physically. They are and remain the people that God has chosen and set apart by his gifts."[149] If they were God's people what has happened; has God's word failed (6)? Paul attempts a first response: "not all are children of Abraham" (7); only those who are "children of the promise are reckoned as descendants" (8), for merit does not define lineage; only God's gracious call does (11).

The theme of "call or election" brings Paul back to the rhetorical device of the diatribe in vv. 14f, 19f, and 30f. In turn he gives attention to the nature of divine election (it is gratuitous, 15), to God's freedom and purpose as Creator (humans are made and called for glory, 22-24), and to the success of the Gentile mission (seeking works the Jews have stumbled, 32). In chapter 10 Paul expresses his desire that Israel be saved (1) but insists that they have not "submitted to God's righteousness" (3, 14f) by refusing to acknowledge God's agent with their lips and hearts (9). In chapter 11 Paul poses a fundamental question ("has God rejected his people?"), one which, after extended discussion of the Gentile situation of the church of his time (11f), he answers in v. 26: "all Israel will be saved." After reminding his Gentile Christian readers that in God's plan Israel's temporary fall was for their own benefit (11-12) and further that they are honorary Jews ("a wild olive shoot . . . grafted . . . to . . . the olive tree," 17f), he submits that Israel is still God's chosen people (28) and that God will see to their salvation (God will have mercy on all humanity, 32). The how and the why he leaves to "the depth of the riches and wisdom and knowledge of God" (33) and, significantly, does not mention the agency of Christ at this point.[150]

The final section of Romans (12-15), a passage which demonstrates "how powerful a preacher (Paul) must have been,"[151] is given to

---

[149]*Romans*, 258.

[150]Stendahl, *Paul among Jews and Gentiles*, 6; see also E.P. Sanders, *Paul, the Law, and the Jewish People* (Philadelphia: Fortress, 1983), especially 171-206 on "Paul as Apostle of Christ and Member of Israel."

[151]Perrin, *The New Testament*, 114.

paraenetic considerations or exhortation. The responsibilities of Christian living are addressed in a dramatic and fundamental way as the Christians of Rome are encouraged to offer their "bodies [as] a living sacrifice, holy and acceptable to God" (12:1) for it is in the flesh that the battle of Christ's lordship must be waged. Thus he pleads that faith, community concern, proper use of gifts, love of one another, zeal, prayer, hospitality, and forebearance be in evidence among them (12:3-21). In chapters 13-15 (already discussed at the beginning of our treatment of Romans) Paul addresses problems which had a more direct bearing on the Roman situation: taxes, relation to non-Christian neighbors, eschatological readiness, and the important issue of Judaeo-Gentile relations in their Roman setting (the weak and the strong). And, as mentioned earlier, Paul terminates his letter by addressing in a direct fashion his purpose for writing the Christians of Rome as he sets out for Judaea with a contribution from his churches which he hopes "may be acceptable to the saints [in Jerusalem], so that by God's will [he] may come to [them] with joy and be refreshed in [their] company" (15:31-32).

Paul's Creed: Christ Crucified

Having surveyed Paul's correspondence to discern the multiplicity of audiences, problems, and themes addressed, we now examine his conception of God's envoy. Not only does the shadow of Paul loom large in the early church and in the history of Christian thought, but his perception of the Jesus movement and its founder continues to fascinate and challenge reader and scholar. Paul, the second generation Christian, who claimed first generation status as apostle, but who refused to appeal to human legitimation as the basis of his mission (letters of recommendation, dependence upon Jerusalem authorities), was the early church's most original and profound thinker. The depth and focus of his thought owes no doubt to a highly developed sense of God's lordship, to a keen understanding both of the gratuity of divine favor and the function of the Christ-event as the realization of that divine gift, and to the importance of mission and the human response to that good news. Paul was

a Pharisee whose zeal led him to persecute a new faith among fellow Jews, and who then turned about and advocated what he had tried to destroy, and who regarded this transformation as God's act—such a person [could] scarcely develop any other kind of theology than one which emphasized the radicality of God's grace and power.[152]

In other words Paul's conversion to, membership in, and subsequent service to that movement's message did not owe to a sense of guilt on his part[153] but to an encounter with God's incomprehensible and unmerited choice, a choice he describes as God gratuitously revealing the Son to him (Gal. 1:16). As zealous adherence to the Law and its demands was at the core of Paul's religious consciousness earlier, so later the Christ-event took its place as the center-piece of God's dealings with humanity. This perception of radical choice, unrelenting sense of lordship, and the agency of the Christ defined Paul's commitment to the Jesus movement. In an effort to comprehend Paul's christology, we will devote this final section of our study to the three following areas: Paul's knowledge of and attitude toward the historical Jesus and the Jesus tradition, his presentation of the Christ-event, and finally the effects of this event in Paul's scheme of things.

JESUS TRADITION

From all indications Paul, a second generation believer, never met nor heard Jesus of Nazareth, even though he experienced a revelation or vision of the risen Lord, which he describes as "having seen Jesus our Lord" (1 Cor. 9:1). What, therefore, he knew about Jesus and the Jesus tradition was acquired indirectly. Though he sometimes speaks of having "received" tradition (1 Cor. 15:3; also 7:10; 11:23), most frequently he simply employs hymnic and confessional formulas and elements of the tradition in his discussions with his correspondents. Debate continues, however, concerning both his acquaintance with and attitude towards this tradition. The debate takes as its point of departure the relative infrequency of Paul's reference to this material, whether to the life and ministry of Jesus or to his teaching as attested in the gospel tradition. The status of the question has been conveniently summarized as representing two basic options:

---

[152]Keck, *Paul and His Letters*, 26.

[153]Stendahl, "The Apostle Paul and the Introspective Conscience of the West," *HTR* 56 (1963) 199-215 (also included in *Paul among Jews and Gentiles*).

the first regards the evidence of the letters as misleading and argues that Paul knew more, and valued what he knew, about Jesus than the letters show; the second regards the evidence of the letters as a quite accurate reflection of Paul's attitude.[154]

Beyond the tendency of the first to maximize contacts between Paul and the Jesus tradition and that of the second to minimize these, there lies a hermeneutical option at the basis of each. The first wishes to situate Paul more solidly within what is perceived to be the history of the Jesus movement and render him more compatible to the tradition represented in the gospels; the second divorces him from the historical Jesus and underscores his radical emphasis upon faith (Christ) over historical fact (Jesus of Nazareth).

Since the general issue of "the Jesus of history versus the Christ of faith" was examined in the three introductory chapters, we direct our attention here to Paul and his relation to the Jesus tradition. Recently Murphy-O'Connor has joined the debate by beginning his treatment of Paul's christology and anthropology by examining what he would have known of the historical Jesus. As he states:

> from data supplied by his own letters we can be certain that Paul had three sources of information concerning the historical Jesus: the Pharisaic tradition, his conversion experience, and the tradition of the Christian communities in which he spent the first years after his conversion.[155]

Essentially the same is true of most early Jewish Christians who were not eyewitnesses of Jesus' ministry. In Paul's case, however, one can venture beyond common-sensical observations on account of the data found in his letters. The three sources of knowledge noted above certainly deserve attention. In the first instance, Paul's Jewish and, more particularly, Pharisaic background provided him with knowledge of the young Jesus movement, sufficient at least for him to become a jealous opponent and persecutor of the movement (Gal. 1:13). How much contact he had with the Jewish authorities of Jerusalem (hinted at in

---

[154]Keck, *Paul and His Letters*, 40.

[155]*Becoming Human Together*, 19; on Paul's conversion exerience, see Plevnik, *What Are They Saying about Paul?* 5-27.

Acts)[156] is hard to determine and, in light of his own statement in Gal. 1:22 ("I was still not known by sight to the churches of Christ in Judaea"), should be decided in the negative. As regards his conversion experience, there is never any doubt that he is speaking of an appearance of the risen Lord, an experience which he compares to that of the early apostolic witnesses (1 Cor. 15:5-8). Nor of course is there any doubt that the risen one is Jesus the Lord (2 Cor. 4:14; Rom. 4:24).

It is the third source, Christian tradition, which is the most promising. Paul is acquainted with the basic facts of Jesus' life, death, and resurrection. While expressing surprise that he says so little about the historical Jesus, Murphy-O'Connor summarizes the facts known from Paul:

> Jesus was a Jew (Rom. 9:4-5) of the line of David (Rom. 1:3) who had a mother (Gal. 4:4). He was betrayed (1 Cor. 11:23) and crucified (1 Cor. 2:2 . . .), as a result of which he died and was buried (1 Cor. 15:3-5). Then God raised him from the dead (1 Cor. 15:5 . . .).[157]

One should add that Jesus participated in a memorial supper on the night of his betrayal (1 Cor. 11:23-26) and that this probably occurred at Passover (1 Cor. 5:7). Further, he was born "under the law" (Gal. 4:4), had brothers (1 Cor. 9:5; also Gal. 1:19), and ministered to and taught the Jewish nation (Rom. 15:8). Concerning Jesus' teaching there are clear but few references: sayings about divorce, support of ministers, and the Lord's return (1 Cor. 7:10-11; 9:14; and 1 Thess. 4:15-17 respectively). Nothing further is said about the many deeds of the ministry known from the gospels.

Beyond these explicit references to the Jesus tradition, one must inquire about the role it played in his preaching, though such an endeavor is highly conjectural. The Galatian churches are reminded that "Jesus Christ was publicly portrayed as crucified" before their eyes (Gal. 3:1); while the Corinthian audience is admonished for accepting "another Jesus than the one (Paul) preached" (2 Cor. 11:4). Further Paul tells the same audience that both the death and life of Jesus are to "be manifested in (their) bodies" (2 Cor. 4:10). These texts suggest that the life, ministry, and passion of the historical Jesus concerned Paul in

---

[156]*Ibid.*, 19-25.
[157]*Ibid.*, 29.

his preaching. Even his use of the Philippian hymn (2:5f), however schematic a presentation of these events, represents his tendency to presuppose the Jesus tradition. In effect these data served as the backdrop for his doctrine of Christ crucified. There is little reason to deny that Paul was well acquainted with the Jesus tradition. In fact, given that he composes not a gospel but "occasional" letters, we conclude that there exists a surprising amount of data about the historical Jesus in Paul's work.

We still need, however, to address his attitude toward and interest in these traditions. It has been maintained by R. Bultmann, especially on the basis of 2 Cor. 5:16, that Paul chose to ignore the historical Jesus and to "regard Christ from a human point of view [lit.: "according to the flesh"] . . . no longer." While it is now conceded that the passage refers not to knowledge of Jesus but to the believer's way of perceiving the Christ, one must examine what Paul says on this subject. Despite the polemical context and its negative assessment of human wisdom, Paul's statement in 1 Cor. 2:2 is instructive here. He tells his readers: "I decided to know nothing among you except Jesus Christ and him crucified." Beyond a stress upon the stark reality of the cross as opposed to preaching technique or eloquence, there is a clear statement of Paul's preferred themes. It is upon the man Jesus, the one acknowledged as Christ, that Paul chooses to direct his attention; and beyond that, it is the crucifixion which becomes the focus of his thought. It is that moment or that element of the Christ-event which, in a Corinthian context, allows Paul to counteract the audience's mistaken concept of the Christian reality. If Paul preaches "Jesus Christ as Lord" (2 Cor. 4:5), it is a Christ who has undergone crucifixion (2 Cor. 1:23). One must not, however, imagine that the stress on the cross is due to the Corinthian situation alone since the same is true in the other Pauline letters (e.g., Gal. 6:4). Paul's choice then is not one of ignoring or shunning the historical Jesus but rather an unrelenting focus upon the cross, i.e., the apex of Jesus' life. It is Jesus' death as a salvific event rather than his life and ministry which form the basis of Paul's vision, for Jesus' death and resurrection crystallized for him God's gratuitous act of reconciliation (Rom. 5:6-11).

CHRIST-EVENT

We turn our attention to Paul's presentation of the Christ-event. The reader of Paul's letters is never in doubt that Jesus is first and foremost the Lord of faith or the Christ. Paul sees the Christian reality from the perspective of the risen Lord, the one whom God raised from the dead. It is in this context that one examines his use of titles for God's agent. No other author employs the term "Christ" (*christos*) as frequently as Paul;[158] clearly "Christ" is Paul's preferred appellation. The term appears in a variety of constructs (according to their relative frequency): "Christ Jesus," "Lord Jesus Christ" (varying in word order), "Jesus Christ," and "Lord Christ Jesus." Scholars debate whether Paul uses the term "Christos" as a title or as a name, or even perhaps in the latter sense but with some awareness of its titular meaning. Since, when appearing alone, it is used regularly without an article, since as a single term it often replaces other appellations for God's agent, and since it so frequently follows the name "Jesus" ("Jesus Christ" or "the Lord Jesus Christ"), one must conclude that in Paul "Christ" usually functions as a second proper name. However, several considerations lead us to insist that it "may to some indeterminable degree bear also the suggestion of worth, function, and title."[159] In the first place, while the title "Lord" (*kyrios*) is often employed with "Jesus Christ," a few times with "Christ Jesus," and surprisingly often (19 times) with "Jesus," it is never used with "Christ" alone, because it still bore its titular sense. Secondly, Paul favors the order "Christ Jesus," a point which is greatly strengthened if one considers the abundant manuscript evidence which supports this reading. Thirdly, Roman usage of imperial titles offers interesting parallels (e.g., "Imperator Caesar Augustus" as contrasted to "Lord Jesus Christ") and confirms the close connection which existed between certain titles and proper names. Indeed, some titles, while retaining their titular force ("August Caesar, Son of the August God"), could also be used as surnames. Lastly, perusal of Paul indicates that the messianic or resurrection senses of the term are often at the fore of the apostle's discussion (see Rom. 5:1 and discussion earlier). We conclude, therefore, that while for Paul and others, at an early stage in the tradition's development, the term "Christ" was often employed as a proper name, for Paul it still retained its titular sense.

The reason for such usage in Paul is related to his focus on the death and resurrection, the central elements of his gospel. His use of the name

---

[158]For example, either Romans or 1 Corinthians, his two longest letters, surpasses in number the usage of any other NT document.

[159]W. Grundmann, "chriō," 9:542 in *TDNT*.

"Jesus" and the title "Christ" as well as the frequent interchange of these and their association with the *kyrios* title further emphasize the centrality and shape of the Christ-event in Paul's mind. While on occasion he employs the cross or the resurrection to symbolize the whole event, most often he combines various elements ("Christ crucified," "Lord Jesus," "the one/Son whom God raised from the dead," "Christ Jesus," "the Lord Jesus Christ") to capture the whole range of that crucial event in God's plan.[160]

Ultimately, Paul's thought focuses on a kyrios or lord christology. While he is not adverse to employing the traditional title "Son" or "Son of God" as he uses early credal or kerygmatic formulas (Rom. 1:3-4; 1 Thess. 1:10) to discuss his conversion (Gal. 1:16) or to stress the salvific nature of the Christ-event (Rom. 5:10; 8:3; Gal. 4:4), he is especially interested in the theme of lordship. Not only was Jesus "designated Son of God" at the resurrection but through that event acquired the title which Paul uses freely to speak of God's agent, for Jesus is the Lord of faith. His submission to God's will was, to Paul's mind, the ultimate acknowledgement of God's lordship and the means chosen by God to reconcile all humanity and the world itself to their Creator. The gospel becomes, in Paul, the preaching of this event and the goal of all missionary activity becomes the establishment of or obedience to Christ's lordship. Thus, "the characteristic linking of faith and obedience in Paul has a meaning which is not primarily ethical but ... eschatological: when the revelation of Christ is accepted, the rebellious world submits again to its Lord. This understanding of faith corresponds to the apostle's kyrios christology."[161] Submission to the Christ is the goal of Paul's preaching, for Jesus is the Lord of faith. For Paul, on the level of the special time of God's intended purpose (Rom. 5:6), the battle has already been won by Christ's action; but on another level, that of human and cosmic activity, it is an on-going, hard-fought battle, or in Paul's own words, "a worldly war" with "divine power to destroy strongholds ... and every proud obstacle to the knowledge of God ... (to) take every thought captive to obey Christ" (2 Cor. 10:3-5).[162] The ultimate

---

[160]See Plevnik, *What Are They Saying about Paul?* on the resurrection and cross, 28-58 and 77-90.

[161]Käsemann, *Romans*, 15.

[162]Another image for this struggle is that of childbirth as Paul strives "in travail until Christ be formed in" his Galatian audience, Gal. 4:19.

goal, after the subjection of all things to himself (Phil. 2:11; 3:21), is the Christ's final act of submission of all created reality to the Father. In Paul's own words:

> Then comes the end, when he delivers the kingdom to God the Father after destroying every rule and every authority and power. For he must reign until he has put all enemies under his feet ... When all thing are subjected to him, then the Son himself will also be subjected to him who put all things under him, that God may be everything to every one (1 Cor. 15:24-28).

Paul's christology, therefore, should be described as one of agency whereby the lordship of God finds its domain of power in the Christ's activity first on the cross and then, as a result and in conjunction with the Christ's resurrection, in the lives of believers who await the end of the ages. So "for Paul the kyrios is the representative of God who claims the world and who with the church brings the new creation into the midst of the old world that is perishing."[163] Jesus as the Christ then is the one who regains the Father's lordship.

Further, we propose that Paul has a low christology, one that focuses not upon a concept of pre-existence but upon the Christ as the perfect human agent or the new Adam. Several important themes are employed by Paul to articulate this highly developed kyrios christology.

> Son, Lord, and Wisdom are used in the Pauline letters, not to suggest a super-human dimension in Christ, but to highlight different facets of Christ's mediation between God and his creatures. Wisdom emphasizes that God has a plan for humanity. Son shows that plan to be inspired by love. And Lord guarantees the power necessary to bring it to completion. All three aspects are unified in him who displays the creativity of the New Adam.[164]

Even the hymn of Phil. 2:6-11, both in its pre-Pauline sense and Pauline usage, is seen in light of a new-Adam interpretation. The Christ, like Adam, was conformed to God's image, but unlike the other Adam who grasped at equality with God (Gen. 3:5), did not contest the lordship of

---

[163]*Ibid.*, 14.

[164]Murphy-O'Connor, *Becoming Human Together*, 67-68.

the Creator. What the old Adam was not, that the new Adam became, thereby reconciling Creator and creature (1 Cor. 15:20f; Rom. 5:12f) and setting up a pattern or paradigm for Christian existence (Phil. 2:1f).[165]

EFFECTS OF THE CHRIST-EVENT

Jesus, in the name of his Father and through his cross and resurrection, lays claim upon the world's dominion, a dominion which finds expression in consistent temporal and spatial imagery. In temporal terms Paul sees God's dealing with humanity as expressed in what was *formerly*, that is, before the Christ's coming, as expressed in *present* existence in submission to his lordship, and as the promise of what is yet *to come*. Both Jew and Gentile lived prior to and apart from faith in the Christ and so were "helpless," "weak," "sinners;" in effect they were "ungodly" and "enemies of God" (Rom. 1-4). Through acceptance of the Christ-event Jews and Gentiles have become "reconciled" and "have peace with God," have been made righteous or justified, live by faith, and have access to grace through Christ (Rom. 5f).[166] However, in true apocalyptic fashion they look forward to the Son's return and the actualization of salvation as they are taken up bodily in the cosmos' final submission and renewal (Rom. 8:18f; 1 Cor. 15) to share God's glory.

In spatial terms, Paul speaks of domains of power. Formerly, humans were slaves; i.e., they were under the dominion of Sin, Death, Flesh, and Law. Now they are under a new domain of power or force field; i.e., they are in Christ (*en Christ$\bar{\varrho}$*), subject to a new lord, and servants of a new master who bears God's power (1 Cor. 1:30). They have obtained the freedom of children, since they have received new life whose dynamism comes from the Lord's Spirit, so that, when they are finally revealed as God's children, they may be fully under God's domain.[167] The gospel, therefore, "is the power of God for salvation to every one who has faith, to the Jew first and also to the Greek" (Rom.

---

[165]*Ibid.*, passim; Kurz, "Kenotic Imitation of Paul and of Christ in Philippians 2 and 3," 103-26; Lyons, *Pauline Autobiography*, 119-21, 218-21, 223-27.

[166]See Plevnik, *What Are They Saying about Paul?* 55-76 and J.A. Fitzmyer, "Reconciliation in Pauline Theology," 155-77 in *No Famine in the Land: Studies in Honor of J.L. McKenzie*, eds J.W. Flanagan and A.W. Robinson (Missoula: Scholars, 1975).

[167]For an excellent, brief discussion of Christ as a "sphere of power and influence" see Ziesler, *Pauline Christianity*, 47-69.

1:16b). But Paul, seeking to follow the mysterious logic of God's plan, suggests that it is within the divine plan that "all Israel ... be saved" (Rom. 11:26).

Paul's terminology (see especially Rom. 5:1f) is therefore greatly clarified by the following schema:[168]

	Christ-event		
formerly	x *now*	*to come*	
prior to/apart from faith	believer/in faith	actualization of salvation	*schema*
helpless/weak sinners	reconciled justified/made righteous	shall be saved share glory of God	*terms*
enemies ungodly	faith access to grace (through X)	perfection of/ sight	
slavery Law/Sin/Death Flesh	in Christ domain of Spirit new life/freedom walk in Spirit children of God	[God's domain]	*domain*
Jew and Gentile	believing J/G	believing J/G (and Israel)	*people*

In the present, those who acknowledge the Christ's lordship, walk in the Spirit as children (8:14), as they work out their commitment in community and await the final revelation of the Son and the arrival of the Father's kingdom.

The Christ-event, therefore, looks to the ultimate lordship of God, the time (in an apocalyptic sense) when neither Jew nor Gentile will "fall short of the glory of God," for having been "justified by his grace as a gift, through the redemption which is in Christ Jesus" (Rom. 3:23-24), they will give honor and thanks to the Lord of creation (1:21) as the Spirit intercedes and prays to God on their behalf (8:15f, 26f). Formerly, the lordship of God had been challenged by the rebellious creation and now in a new state of reconciliation believers work and live for that day

---

[168]These observations owe much to extended discussions with a former colleague, Paul Sampley of Boston University.

"when God's righteous judgment will be revealed" (2:5) for then "there will be tribulation and distress for every human being who does evil, the Jew first and also the Greek, but glory and honor and peace for every one who does good, the Jew first and also the Greek" (2:9-10).

Beyond this, the Christ-event has long-range consequences, for relations to God and to others. As a result of the Christ's death and resurrection a reconciliation between Creator and creature occurred. The primordial disruption represented by the old Adam has been remedied and so there is now a state of peace or lack of enmity between God and those who acknowledge and emulate God's redemptive agent, the new Adam. There is union with Christ and thereby with the one who sent him. Believers are constituted children of the house and so no longer slaves of the household. There is justification or righteousness for the believer; it is not something earned but something given ("justified by God's grace as a gift," 3:24). The disrupted relationship between Creator and creature has been restored; the believer is declared righteous because God, through Christ, has made the believer so. There exists a new creation, i.e., a reconstitution of the realm of the flesh into a realm of the Spirit. Dead to or free from the enslaving domains of Sin, Death, the Flesh, and even the Law, believers submit to and are driven by the dynamism of the Spirit ("walk in the Spirit") as they address God as loving parent ("Abba Father"), as they have access to grace in which they stand (5:2), and as they acquire the status of membership in a new family.

This last point brings us to Paul's ethical stance. The believer has acquired a new status and thus new responsibilities. Being a child of God demands that one live according to that status; that is, *noblesse oblige*. For Paul, one must actualize what one has become. Through Christ believers have been constituted children of God. Thus the faith which acknowledges God's action in Christ must through its momentum or dynamism work itself out through love (Gal. 5:6), that is, honor and gratitude toward the Creator and building up of brothers and sisters in the faith. Ever distrustful of moralism which enslaves the spirit to a system of laws, which is inspired by merit rather than by gift, or which attempts to govern divine activity, Paul returns repeatedly to the Christ-event as constitutive of Christian living. Through it, through its preaching, and through its acceptance God has bestowed upon believers not the spirit of slavery but that of sonship, for as Paul tells his Roman audience:

> when we cry, "Abba! Father!" it is the Spirit himself bearing witness with our spirit that we are children of God, and if children, then heirs

of God and fellow heirs with Christ, provided we suffer with him in order that we may also be glorified with him (8:15-17).

The Christ-event and its paradigmatic structure, not a list of commands, is the basis of Christian life. Like Christ or like Paul himself (Phil. 2:6-11 and 3:2-11), believers must count as loss even advantages they have, so that like the Christ, they might be glorified by the God of glory as "fellow heirs." The key, therefore, to Pauline thought and praxis is "Christ Jesus the Lord" who assures the believer access to the love of God (Rom. 8:39). Believers are assured of Christ's love (8:25), a love that intercedes for them as they patiently strive with Christ for the final realization of God's lordship over all created reality. "Thus, Paul's ethic is radically and pervasively *theo*logical, *eschato*logical, and *christo*logical,"[169] for, while it presents the Christ-event as the paradigm of Christian living, it has as its goal the lordship of God and the establishment of the kingdom as it exhorts the believer to live in anxious anticipation of the Lord's return.

[169]Furnish, *Theology and Ethics in Paul*, 224.

9

The Paulinist Letters

Thirteen letters in the New Testament claim Pauline authorship. Seven of these were examined in the previous chapter, since they are the letters and composites thereof which scholarship attributes to Paul with virtual unanimity. The six remaining letters, however, have not gained such recognition. With the rise of critical methods, scholars have increasingly opted for non-Pauline authorship of all or most of these documents. Therefore, the objective of this chapter, after introductory considerations, is to examine each letter to discern its christological perspective.

Written in Paul's Name

An important objective of literary criticism is the quest for an understanding of a document's author. While we touched on this problem in earlier chapters, it is necessary to expand our discussion. Since the modern reader and scholar exhibit such fascination regarding authorship, a survey of our knowledge will be helpful. The names of most NT authors are unknown. Either the works are anonymous, i.e., by unknown authors, or they are pseudonymous, i.e., written in the name of some well-known figure. Only Paul and the author of Revelation (1:1, 4, 9; 22:8) are known to us by name. The list is as follows:

known authorship
Paul: 1 Thessalonians, Philippians, Philemon, Galatians, 1-2
        Corinthians, Romans
John: Book of Revelation

333

anonymous
    Mark, Matthew, Luke-Acts, John, 1-2-3 John, Hebrews
    (note that 2-3 John are said to be written by "the
    Elder")
pseudonymous
    "Paul": 2 Thessalonians, Colossians, Ephesians, 1-2
        Timothy, Titus
    James, 1-2 Peter, and Jude by "James," "Peter," and
    "Jude."

From the above one must conclude that the NT books were written in a society which did not emphasize authorship. Literary posterity was the farthest thing from the minds of those who took pen in hand to record the Jesus tradition or to send advice to various communities. Either these authors offered no signs of identification or these were lost or they appealed to the authority of well-known Christian figures to establish their ideas.[1] In the case of the former, as the communities became more diversified, appeal was made to early, venerable figures, as authors, to defend the authority or orthodoxy of traditions and documents, i.e., names were imposed on anonymous texts.[2]

In the case of the latter, it is the figure of Paul which caught the fancy of second and third generation Christians. As the legend grew and despite the fact that his letters remained unpublished, Paul became the center of controversy and admiration. As communities in the Mediterranean world kept alive the memory of the great apostle to the Gentiles, so did some of its members appeal to his authority and name to resolve new problems. Thus, members of Pauline and other churches had recourse to pseudonymity, a well-accepted convention of their day. As they spoke and wrote in the name of their venerable theological ancestors, schools of thought and centers of tradition reapplied the

[1]H.J. Rose, "Pseudepigraphic Literature," 894 in Hammond and Scullard, *Oxford Classical Dictionary*, gives an excellent, brief treatment of this common phenomenon of the Greco-Roman world. Confer also R.J. Karris, *The Pastoral Epistles* (Wilmington: Glazier, 1979) xi-xiii.

[2]For a discussion of the post-apostolic period, see R.E. Brown, *The Churches the Apostles Left Behind* (NY: Paulist, 1984), chapter 1; confer also chapters 12 and 13 below.

thinking inherited from the past (e.g., a Petrine circle).[3] It is particularly the figure of Paul which gained legendary prominence in NT times.[4]

Second Thessalonians

The term "Paulinist" is traditionally used to refer to letters of questionable Pauline authorship. L.E. Keck aptly describes the status of the question:

> "There is virtual unanimity that the following letters are authentic: Romans, 1, 2 Corinthians, Galatians, Philippians, 1 Thessalonians, Philemon; there is almost equal agreement that the Pastorals (1, 2 Timothy, Titus) are not genuine. The majority of students regard Ephesians to be non-genuine as well, but opinion is divided over Colossians and 2 Thessalonians."[5]

So we begin our study with the documents which bear the closest affinity to the authentic letters of Paul.

DEFENSE OF PSEUDONYMITY

The Pauline authenticity of 2 Thessalonians is defended by many. This letter in their view is a document sent by Paul to a favorite Macedonian community early in his writing career. It is asserted that the letter pursues the principal concerns of the first, especially the community's obsession with apocalyptic notions. Recognizing the difficulties posed by the eschatology of 1 Thess. 4:13-5:11 and 2 Thess. 2:1-12, champions of Pauline authorship choose various lines of defense.[6]

Typically scholars appeal to the flexibility and ambiguity of apocalyptic language to explain the differences between these. Paul, it is maintained, is beginning his writing career and is still experimenting

---

[3]For Peter in Acts, see Richard, "Luke-Writer Historian, Theologian," 7 and in 1 and 2 Peter, see D. Senior, *1 & 2 Peter* (Wilmington: Glazier, 1980) xii-xvi. More generally, confer R.E. Brown, et al. eds, *Peter in the New Testament* (NY: Paulist, 1973).

[4]De Boer, "Images of Paul in the Post-Apostolic Period," 359-80.

[5]Keck, *Paul and His Letters*, 3-4.

[6]See Kümmel, *Introduction to the New Testament*, 262-69, for an able presentation of the reasons for authenticity.

with language and idiom. A few have attempted to resolve these difficulties by proposing different audiences for the two documents or by insisting that the more explicitly apocalyptic 2 Thessalonian was written first. Still others have advanced partition theories to account for the ideology of 2 Thessalonians and for its peculiar literary composition.[7]

There are serious objections to these proposals. The literary, theological, and sociological problems raised by this letter are resolved if one subscribes to a theory of pseudonymity, namely, that someone in the Pauline churches wrote a letter in Paul's name to counter the highly dubious proposals made by apocalypticists in the communities. The new author chose as model a letter which the apostle had written early in his career to the Thessalonians.

The choice of 1 Thessalonians as model, a document probably known to both sides of the new apocalyptic controversy, explains the letter's peculiar character, highly un-Pauline on the one hand and closely related to 1 Thessalonians on the other. 2 Thessalonians, unlike other Pauline letters, has two thanksgiving sections as does 1 Thessalonians. This new letter treats problems in double cycles, each ending with benedictions (2:13-3:5). These anomalies are explained in relation to 1 Thessalonians which itself is a composite of two Pauline letters and other editorial activity. As the fate of the imitator would have it, a composite and therefore somewhat un-Pauline document was chosen as model.

One discerns the author's craft in the area of vocabulary and style. Phrases and terms are repeated from 1 Thessalonians (some see here the work of the same author) but usually the new usage has an un-Pauline character. While Paul often speaks of "the good news of Christ," 2 Thessalonians offers only one parallel expression: "the good news of our Lord Jesus Christ" (1:8). Also un-Pauline in their usage are a host of idioms ("inflicting vengeance," "love the truth," "belief in the truth," 1:8, 11; 2:10, 13) and of stylistic peculiarities (excessive use of parallelism, absence of typically Pauline vocabulary, and the choice of an authoritative rather than an argumentative approach to issues). The new author is more interested in divine retribution (as "comfort for believers," 1:9) than in Paul's fundamental concern for the cross and resurrection.

---

[7] *Ibid.*, 264-69; also Roetzel, *The Letters of Paul*, 106-10; and G. Krodel, "2 Thessalonians," 73-96 in G. Krodel, ed., *Ephesians, Colossians, 2 Thessalonians, the Pastoral Epistles* (Philadelphia: Fortress, 1978).

The tone and purpose of the letter are easily discerned in 2:1-3a. The issue is the Lord's imminent return and so the author's strategy in combating the notion that the Lord's day has arrived is an appeal to Pauline authority. Thus, the disavowal of misguided interpretations of the apostle in the teaching and writing of some opponent (2:2-3) amounts to a defense both of the author's point of view (2:5, 15) and composition (3:14, 17). The appeal to authority to reestablish order and the stress on authenticity to gain the allegiance of the readers further underscore the pseudonymity of 2 Thessalonians.

ESCHATOLOGY AND CHRISTOLOGY

Few scholars fail to note the difference between the eschatology of the two letters. The disagreement concerns the posture the respective authors take vis-à-vis the Lord's return. In the first case Paul states that like a thief in the night the Lord will return during his own lifetime (4:15). The author of 2 Thessalonians, in arguing against the notion that the parousia has already occurred, insists on the contrary that it has yet to come and that a series of events must take place before "the Lord Jesus slays the lawless one" (2:8).

A brief analysis of 2 Thess. 2:1-12 is required at this point. Apocalyptic fervor at Thessalonica has become so intense as a result of apocalypticist preaching that members of the community are assembled for the Lord's return (1-2). The author advises them not to be so easily "shaken in mind or excited" (2) and not to be "deceived" (3). Deception, they are reminded, has a part to play in the apocalyptic drama, but that time is yet to come. First, there is a time of oppression or persecution (7); lawlessness is at work even then and the community is being put to the test (1:4). This first period will come to an end when the "lawless one, the son of perdition is revealed" (2:3), but in the meantime God employs an agent, called "the one who restrains" (6-7), to hold the powers of evil in check before the final onslaught. This second period, the reign of evil (once the "one restraining" is out of the way),[8] will be marked by

---

[8]Most see in this enigmatic figure the role of the Roman empire and its emperor; others see Paul and his missionary activity as the "restraining" power—for discussion of these options see E. Best, *A Commentary on the First and Second Epistles to the Thessalonians* (NY: Harper & Row, 1970) 290-302. A third option is that the suffering of the church is a sure sign of divine retributive justice and that God is the "one who restrains," J.M. Bassler, "The Enigmatic Sign: 2 Thessalonians 1:5," *CBQ* 46 (1984) 486-510 and yet a fourth postulates that the figure is not "a 'restrainer' of the Antichrist" but another personification (of a pseudo-prophetic nature) of the "mystery of law-

deception of the faithful (vv. 3, 10-11) by the lawless one or rebel (3) who will attempt to usurp divine powers (4) and to deceive by working signs and wonders (9). In the midst of this satanic activity (9) the third phase will occur, when "the Lord Jesus will slay [the lawless one] with the breath of his mouth and destroy him by his appearing and his coming" (8; see also 1:7-10).

The author of 2 Thessalonians counters apocalyptic fervor (some would see the destruction of Jerusalem as the catalyst) by appealing to commonly-held views about the end-time.[9] The message is consistent with that of other NT writers who insist that the end is coming but that the time is unknown. There existed the constant temptation of interpreting the signs of the times as the beginning of the end-time. The author advises those who idly await the Lord to earn their own bread (3:6-12).

The principal image of Jesus presented in this document is an apocalyptic one. Jesus, as in the Book of Revelation, is the one who will slay the evil one. With his angelic host he will cast flaming fire upon the earth during the cataclysmic end-days (1:7). This is one of the clearest NT examples of a community situation producing an appropriate image of Jesus. We conclude our discussion, however, by noting that, contrary to the overly apocalyptic opponents, the author of this document stresses the present activity of the believer who is to glorify the name of Jesus (1:12) and to seek comfort now in Jesus and his Father (2:16-17). Beyond the apocalyptic image of Jesus, therefore, there is in 2 Thessalonians an added emphasis upon Jesus' earthly lordship (3:1f).

Colossians

Another letter over whose authenticity scholarship is seriously divided is the letter to the Colossians. Critical study must examine the close relationship which exists, on the one hand, between the undisputed Pauline letters and this document and, on the other, the literary and theological connection between Colossians and Ephesians. Since we

---

lessness," C.H. Giblin, *The Threat to Faith: An Exegetical and Theological Re-Examination of 2 Thessalonians 2* (Rome: Biblical Institute, 1967) 246.

[9]See the discussion below of Mark 13 and of the Book of Revelation in chapter 11.

address the latter below in our treatment of Ephesians, we begin the study of Colossians by considering the former.

NON-PAULINE AUTHORSHIP

Since the early 19th century, scholars increasingly accept the non-Pauline authorship of this document. Nonetheless, of the disputed Pauline letters this one attracts the most frequent defense. All scholars, pro or con, admit a close relationship between it and the undisputed letters in the major areas of comparison: style, vocabulary, and thought. Defenders of authenticity minimize the differences while those in favor of pseudonymity stress the diversity.

Since we will discuss below the major divergences between Paul and the author of Colossians, it suffices here to discuss briefly the reasons given to explain these differences. Commonly one hears that as Paul progressed in his theological and writing career he developed in style and thought. The differences then are due to a more mature Paul who, in theological and psychological terms, developed his ideas in christology, eschatology, and ecclesiology to a point beyond that found in the other letters, differences also reflected in style and vocabulary. Others point to the polemical nature of Colossians to explain the divergences, especially the author's use of the slogans, unique vocabulary, and concerns of the Colossian opponents. Still others underscore the author's use of liturgical or hymnic materials as contributing to the letter's hieratic or liturgical style. It is particularly a combination of the liturgical/hymnic and polemical explanations which has the greatest following.[10] Finally, a few propose that Paul makes freer use of a secretary to compose this letter.

None of the above explanations are convincing. There is little evidence of the "maturing or mellowing" Paul in the corpus and one would have to date the "less-developed" Roman epistle after the "more advanced" Colossians. Further, as most point out, the differences in style, vocabulary, and thought between Paul and Colossians are not limited nor concentrated within the polemical sections of the letter. Paul's use of opponents' slogans or vocabulary is well documented (e.g., in 1 Corinthians) and does not explain divergences such as found in Colossians. The hieratic style of this document bears little resemblance

---

[10]See Kümmel, *Introduction to the New Testament*, 340-46, for a lucid defense of authenticity in the terms described.

to Pauline methods of composition, even when he uses early formulaic or poetic fragments (1 Thess. 1:9-10; Phil. 2:6-11; Rom. 1:3-4). Finally, few today take seriously the once popular amanuensis theories, since appeal to the work of a secretary to explain these differences amounts virtually to the defense of non-Pauline authorship. Instead, we insist, along with more recent scholars, on the evidence against Pauline authorship and therefore for pseudonymity. A brief discussion then of the principal data follows.

A significant area of comparison concerns vocabulary. Colossians contains a large number of *hapax legomena* or unique expressions (34 terms used by no other NT writer), of non-Pauline vocabulary (28 words found in other NT writings but not in Paul), terms unique to it and Ephesians (10 in all) or used in these along with other NT documents (15 terms).[11] The statistics are only suggestive since this evidence is muted by other considerations, such as concentration of unique terms within the hymnic section of 1:15-20, the importance of polemics as a source of singular vocabulary, and the existence of similar though less persuasive data in the authentic letters. Other evidence, nonetheless, strengthen these statistical data. The absence of important Pauline terms and themes, such as "righteousness," "sin" (as a singular noun), "law," "promise," "revelation," "to believe," "salvation," or "brothers," would be surprising in a document such as Colossians whose subject matter would be enhanced by such vocabulary. Beyond the absence of favorite Pauline terms and themes, one encounters a number of uncharacteristic usages. Both "faith" and "hope" have a demonstrably different connotation. The former becomes "the faith," i.e., that which is believed (1:23; 2:7), while the latter constitutes the content of preaching as something already "laid up in heaven" (1:5, 23, 27). The author of Colossians employs non-Pauline expressions: "the blood of his cross" (1:20), "doing evil deeds" (1:21), "the forgivenes of sins" (1:14), Christ as "head of the body" which is the church (1:18, 24; 2:19), "being raised with Christ" (2:12 and 3:1), God "has transferred us to the kingdom of his beloved Son" (1:13), and "Christ is [already] all and in all" (3:11).

More persuasive in arguing for pseudonymity are the numerous stylistic differences. Paul's sense of rhetoric and his theology of freedom led him to adopt an argumentative style, to favor the diatribe and other

---

[11]Data listed and discussed in Lohse, *Colossians and Philemon*, 85-86.

persuasive devices, and to choose discussion over appeals to authority. In Colossians one encounters a different style.

> Col. . . . is marked by a liturgical-hymnic style. In its long sentences, in which parts are occasionally interlocked with each other, a seemingly endless chain of verbose expressions is arranged into a pleonastic unit. An example is the thanksgiving, starting at 1:3. . . Relative clauses, inserted causal phrases, participial phrases and secondary notes inflate the sentence to a degree that its form almost collapses . . . the style of Col. differs from the other letters by its liturgical-hymnic character, which results in a pleonastic manner of speaking, in long word-connections and in the stringing together of sentence after sentence.[12]

While one finds on occasion an unwieldy sentence in Paul, this type of construction is the rule in Colossians (1:3-8, 9-20, etc.). The author favors loosely connected genitives ("in the word of the truth of the gospel," 1:5 or "by the putting off of the body of flesh in the circumcision of Christ," 2:11), the tautologous use of synonyms ("to pray for you, asking that," 1:9; "anger, wrath, malice, slander, and foul talk from your mouth," 3:8; or "sing psalms and hymns and spiritual songs with thankfulness in your hearts," 3:16, or roots ("grows with a growth that is from God," 2:19), and the frequent and awkward addition of explanations by employing loosely appended relative clauses, participial phrases, and connectives (e.g., the ubiquitous "which is").

The theological differences between the undisputed letters and Colossians are equally impressive. While we could discuss these at length, it is necessary to limit our comments to three important areas: apostleship, eschatology, and christology. The issue of apostleship looms large in Colossians and its perception there differs significantly from Paul's. While Paul considers himself apostle to the Gentiles, nowhere does he claim universal or cosmic ministry (a non-Pauline term) as does the author of Colossians (1:23). In no way does Paul claim that his own suffering "adds to" or "completes" the suffering of Christ or certainly not that Christ's death was "lacking" in any way (1:24). On the one hand, Paul scoffs at those who hold that perfection is a possibility in this

---

[12]*Ibid.*, 89.

life, and on the other, he operates under the conviction that apostleship and discipleship are related to the imminent return of the Lord. The opposite is the case in Colossians where one "may stand mature and fully assured in all the will of God" (4:12; also 1:28) and where the cosmic victory of the Christ (2:15) has affected a shift from a temporal (end-time concern) to a spatial consideration of the Christian reality.

> So, while in some respects, the understanding of apostleship in Colossians resembles that of the undisputed letters . . . in its view of the suffering of the apostle, its understanding of the apostolic preaching as wisdom for the perfect, and its diminished sense of apostolic urgency, this epistle differs significantly from the letters we know to be genuine.[13]

The eschatological perspectives of Paul and Colossians present equally clear differences. Paul expects the end of the world to occur during his lifetime (evident from his earliest to his latest letters), and also employs generously the categories of apocalyptic thought to express his own. While past, present, and future dimensions receive proportional attention from Paul, in Colossians there is emphasis on the present almost to the exclusion of the future. For Paul hope and salvation are essentially future realities, which impinge upon the present, but in Colossians hope is a reality "laid up in heaven" (1:4) and salvation (a term not used) is realized in the present. The follower of Christ is already "delivered from the dominion of darkness and transferred . . . to the kingdom of his beloved Son" (1:13). Besides, for Colossians the Christian has already been raised with Christ (2:12-13; 3:1), an idea Paul would have repudiated (see Rom. 6:8; Phil. 3:11). The thought of Colossians, therefore, verges on realized eschatology even when it retains futuristic themes (see 3:1-4).

Finally, the difference between the christology of Colossians and Paul is equally significant. Since we will return below to a discussion of the author's perception of Jesus, it suffices here to note that Colossians goes well beyond Paul's thought in insisting that Christ is the head and the church his body and that Christ's cosmic rule has already been established (2:16) and begins its realization in the life and activity of the church (1:22; 2:19).

---

[13]Roetzel, *The Letters of Paul*, 95.

These differences were certainly affected by the liturgical, polemical, and thematic interests of the author. Nonetheless, the differences, especially of a stylistic and theological nature, permeate the entire letter and lead naturally to the conclusion that someone other than Paul composed Colossians.

OTHER INTRODUCTORY ISSUES

Whether this document reveals direct use or imitation of Paul's authentic letters is a disputed question. Study of the pertinent documents shows that the author of Colossians was familiar enough with Pauline thinking and tradition to have known the names of Paul's helpers as listed in Philemon (Timothy, Epaphras, Onesimus, Aristarchus, Mark, Luke, and Demas) and with the basic content and outline of his letters, especially Romans.[14] Further, the stress on ministry (1:7, 23, 25; 4:7, 17), apostolic (and even "divine," 1:25) authority (1:1, 23; 4:18), autobiographical detail (1:7-8, 23f; 2:1f; 4:3-4, 7f), associative vocabulary ("Timothy our brother," 1:1; "Epaphras our beloved fellow servant," 1:7; also 4:7, 9, 10, 11, 12, 14), and the command to exchange letters (4:16) further suggest pseudepigraphy. The author, therefore, employed features of the Pauline tradition as strategy to bolster a claim to apostolic authority and to ensure that the letter be received in that spirit.

The structure of the letter is relatively easy to discern and we offer the following outline:

> Opening 1:1-2
> Thanksgiving and plea 1:3-6 and 9-11
> Lordship of Christ 1:12-23 (use of early hymn: 15-20)
> Ministry to the lordship 1:24-2:5
> Lordship of Christ threatened by submission to the
>   powers 2:6-23
> Ethical application: live what you are in Christ
>   3:1-4:6 (use of household codes: 3:18-4:1)
> Conclusion 4:7-18.

Clearly the central theme of the letter is Christ's lordship and associated to it are the ethical ramifications of "living in Christ."

As regards the date of writing, locale of audience, or opponents

[14]Lohse, *Colossians and Philemon*, 175-77 and 182.

addressed, there exist only educated guesses. In light of the conclusion reached earlier in favor of pseudonymity, one should opt for a generation or two (c. 20 years or so) after the death of Paul as the logical date for this composition (c. 70-80). Further, since the choice of Colossae as designated audience is due probably to the pseudonymic strategy of the author, one can not expect precision in locating the author and intended readers. At best, the choice of Colossae and the related use of Philemon suggests a diverse Gentile Christian audience in southern Asia Minor. As to the opponents addressed in the letter, we will treat of this subject in the following section.

THE LETTER'S PURPOSE AND CHRISTOLOGY

The occasional nature of Colossians is evident even from a casual reading. After a few hints about the subject matter of the letter (1:9 concerning "spiritual wisdom and understanding" and 1:13 about "deliverance from the dominion of darkness and transference to the kingdom of the beloved Son"), the author, employing an early hymn extolling the cosmic significance of the Christ-event, focuses on the central issue of Christ's lordship (1:15-20). So all encompassing is that event that it "has been preached to every creature under heaven" (1:23, a non-Pauline expression) and is actualized in Christ's body, the church (1:18, 24) and enfleshed within the community (1:27, "the riches of the glory of this mystery, which is Christ in you"). In 2:4, after having reiterated the themes of understanding, wisdom, and mystery, the author broaches the problem of the Colossian church more directly;[15] the readers are being "deluded with beguiling speech." The remainder of the chapter is then devoted to the objectionable doctrine which the cosmic christology of chapter 1 is meant to rectify.

From the polemical statements of 2:8-23 we can appreciate the Colossian situation. The community is put on its guard lest it become the victim of "philosophy and empty deceit" (2:8). It seems that the term "philosophy" forms part of the opposition's jargon and, in light of the author's insistence on the Christian's possession of true wisdom and understanding, should be interpreted as proto-Gnostic. This is especially true when seen in relation to 2:23 where it is claimed that the opposition's many regulations have only the "appearance of wisdom," since they "are

---

[15]The term "Colossians" will be used henceforth simply to refer to the readers of the letter.

of no value in checking the indulgence of the flesh." The false teachers claimed special knowledge (*gnosis*) which they translated into supplicating devotion to the elemental spirits (2:8, 18), into supplementary festivals and rites, and into ritual observance of an ascetic nature. Also, the author describes the opponents' alleged wisdom as "promoting rigor of devotion and self-abasement and severity to the body" (2:23).

The new doctrine consisted of an appeal to the protection of and the submission to the elemental spirits (2:8, 20), that is, the angelic or divine powers which many in the Greek world believed had control over the world and so decided cosmic order and individual human destiny. As a result Christians of Gentile origin were urged to worship (2:18) and to placate the powers through magic-like observances: festivals, new moons, sabbaths (16), visions, sensual indulgence (18?), and abstinence from certain foods and drink (16, 21-22). Interestingly, on three occasions the author introduces elements of the opponents' views (2:8f, 16f, 20f), discusses these in relation to Christian tradition, and terminates the explanation by insisting on the primacy of Christ (2:15, 19; 3:1-4).

As Lohse rightly points out "Col. develops its *Christology* on the basis of the Christ-hymn"[16] and it is precisely the position of the Christ vis-à-vis all creation, particularly the cosmic powers, which attracts the author's attention. The christology of the hymn, which the author has inherited or redacted from traditional fragments, has provided the antidote for the Colossian problem. Christ is lord of the cosmos in virtue of his relation to and function vis-à-vis God ("image of the invisible God" and "in him all the fulness of God was pleased to dwell," vv. 15 and 19), as agent and basis of creation (vv. 15-17), and in his role as ruler of things on earth ("head of the body, the church," 18; also 13, 24) and in heaven (v. 16), and as reconciler of all things to himself (20). But, more to the point, it is as "the beginning, the first-born from the dead" that he is "pre-eminent in everything" (18b); that is, he has first place in the cosmos, so that all "powers" are subject to him (1:16; 2:10, 15). He, not the cosmic powers, has the fulness of deity dwelling in him (1:15, 19; 2:9); he, not the elemental spirits, is called "beloved Son" (1:13; also 1:3) or Lord (1:3; 2:6f). It is through the death and resurrection of Christ (1:18, 20f) that God "disarmed the principalities and powers and made a public example of them, triumphing over them in him" (2:15).

The author of Colossians develops this cosmic christology as an

[16]*Ibid.*, 178.

antidote to the new doctrine propounded in the community. "Christ is all and in all" (3:11); he is "seated at the right hand of God" (3:1) from whence he "will appear in glory," believers with him(3:3). Since Christ is head of the church, lord of humanity and of the cosmos, the Christian must look to the cosmic Christ not to earth and its spirits. It is not by "self-abasement and worship of angels," not by visions, and other ritual and moral observances that the follower of the Christ must live. Instead, as one who has died and been raised with Christ (*contra* Paul), the believer must put to death the things of the earth (3:5f) and put on the new nature of "God's chosen ones" (3:10, 12f).

The author's high, pre-existent christology has left profound traces on the eschatology, ecclesiology, and paraenesis of the letter. In the first place, the immediacy of final judgment has diminished. Christ will return at the end-time (3:4) but the author is more concerned about "making the most of the time" (4:5) than about its urgency. The emphasis is on the present, the actualization of hope, resurrection, and maturity (1:5; 3:1; 1:28). This stress is more developed in the author's ecclesiological concerns, wherein the Christ's lordship is most fully exercised within his body, the church. Christians are told to hold "fast to the Head, from whom the whole body, nourished and knit together through its joints and ligaments, grows with a growth that is from God" (2:19). The eschatological realities, for the most part then are focused on the present where God has "transferred us to the kingdom of his beloved Son" (1:13). The author adds in the next verse, that the believer already "has redemption" in Christ, and as a result is advised to "let the word of Christ dwell in [them] richly, as [they] teach and admonish one another in all wisdom . . ." (3:16). The paraenesis consists especially of household codes whose advise is conditioned by its relation to Christ's lordship (3:18, 20f).[17]

The portrait of Jesus found in Colossians is the product of a definite situation in the early church. What we find here is the development of a cosmic christology to combat a false appeal to god-like "powers" for protection. The author borrows a Pauline concept (the eschatological

---

[17]For a discussion of the household codes (*Haustafeln*) in the New Testament (Colossians, Ephesians, the Pastorals, and 1 Peter) and more generally its use by Hellenistic authors, see J.E. Crouch, *The Origin and Intention of the Colossian Haustafel* (Göttingen: Vandenhoeck & Ruprecht, 1972); D.C. Verner, *The Household of God: The Social World of the Pastoral Epistles* (Chico: Scholars, 1983); and D.L. Balch, *Let Wives Be Submissive: The Domestic Code in 1 Peter* (Chico: Scholars, 1981).

subjection of all creation to Christ, Rom. 8:19f) which is then put at the service of the christological crisis taking place in the local Christian community. To this end the author employed the community's traditional christological images and the authority and spirit of Paul to construct a new and far-reaching image of the Lord Jesus Christ.[18]

Ephesians

Further removed from Paul in stylistic, theological, and chronological terms is the letter to the Ephesians, whose Pauline authorship nonetheless has adamant defenders.[19] The increasing attention and careful work of recent scholarship, however, has tended to support pseudonymity and to seek a better understanding of the document's contributions to the developing Jesus movement.

> In recent years, studies in Ephesians have begun to enter into a new phase. Previous investigations of the epistle were dominated by questions of authenticity, relation to Colossians and the homologoumena and by dogmatic inquiries into themes that by historical accident occur in Ephesians. The newer approach to the study of Ephesians is dominated primarily by the hypothesis that the document is a unique, syncretistic collection of a variety of traditions extant in the early church.[20]

This study, therefore, after a discussion of the document's dependence on Colossians, will focus more specifically on the text, its message, and particularly its christology. This NT work, as part of the Pauline school of thought (homologoumena) and as a reformulation of early tradition in a new and later environment, offers a real challenge to the educated reader in search of a better understanding of the Jesus movement at the end of the first century.

---

[18]See E. Schweizer, *The Letter to the Colossians: A Commentary* (Minneapolis: Augsburg, 1982) 245-302.

[19]Kümmel, *Introduction to the New Testament*, 357.

[20]J.P. Sampley, *'And the Two Shall Become One Flesh': A Study of Traditions in Ephesians 5:21-23* (London: Cambridge University, 1971) 1.

A REWRITING OF COLOSSIANS

Many of the claims made earlier in defending the pseudonymity of Colossians could be repeated. Nonetheless Ephesians differs in language and style from the undisputed letters to a greater degree than does Colossians. Its sentences in Greek, though not regularly indicated in translations, are even more involved and unwieldy than those of Colossians (1:3-10, 15:23; 3:1-7, 14-19; 4:11-16), for they are rambling structures composed of numerous relative clauses, appositional phrases, and other modifying constructions built around a principal verb or two. Another characteristic of this author's style is the frequent, redundant use of synonyms (e.g., 1:19-20, "and what is the immeasurable greatness of his *power* in us who believe according to the *working* of the *might* of his *strength* which he *worked out* in Christ," RSVmod). Equally significant is the large number of terms (c. 40) which do not appear in the undisputed letters and yet are found in the late writings of the New Testament and in the works of the early Church Fathers, e.g., "freely bestow . . . the Beloved" (1:6), "commonwealth" (2:12), "holiness" (4:24), "tenderhearted" (4:32), "debauchery" (5:18), etc. On the whole one finds in Ephesians a unique non-Pauline vocabulary used with much redundancy.

Beyond a singular style and vocabulary, Ephesians exhibits a number of distinctly non-Pauline ideas. The end is no longer imminent nor central for this author. In its place one finds an interest in the fulness of God's plan or dispensation (1:10; 3:9), a fascination for "the heavenly places" (1:3, 20f—in lieu of the noun "heaven"), and a strongly realized eschatology (chosen or destined from the beginning and blessed with every spiritual blessing: love, grace, redemption, wisdom, and insight; see for example 1:3-10). In the author's statements about Christ as cosmic ruler (1:21), about the Gentiles as already incorporated into the community of salvation (2:13), and about the believer's gift of wisdom to understand the mysteries of God's plan (3:18-19), "space rather than time is the controlling category."[21] Further , salvation is no longer an eschatological entity as it was for Paul but a present reality (2:5, 8). In fact Phil. 3:20 and Eph. 5:23, which exhibit the only two occurrences of the term "Savior" in the Pauline tradition (apart from the Pastorals), are very instructive here. In the former, Paul says "our commonwealth is in

[21]Retzel, *The Letters of Paul*, 101.

heaven, and from it we await a Savior, the Lord Jesus Christ," but in the latter Ephesians insists that "Christ is the head of the church, his body, and is himself its Savior."[22] Other issues which receive different treatment in Ephesians than they do in the undisputed letters are the subject of marriage, the exalted status and role attributed to the apostles and Paul himself, the focus on the church as universal reality and sphere of the cosmic Christ's activity, and, finally, a christology whose function is conditioned by ecclesiology.[23]

Ephesians, we conclude, was written at a later date (contemporary with 1 Peter, the Pastorals, and Acts), by an author who invoked Pauline thought and authority to present a new synthesis of Christian tradition in ecclesiology, christology, and ethics. To do this the author relied greatly on the Paulinist letter to the Colossians, a subject to which we now direct our attention.

The consensus of scholars, save for those who defend Pauline authorship, is that Ephesians is literarily dependent upon the Colossian letter. In overall terms the former reproduces about a third of the content and vocabulary of the latter and about half of its sentences contain terms from that source. In fact, the following simplified structural outline of the two letters highlights this literary dependence:[24]

	Colossians	Ephesians
Greeting	1:1-2	1:1-2
Thanksgiving	1:3f	1:3-14
God's plan and the ministry	1:21f	2:1f
Vices and Virtues	3:1-17	4:17f
Household code	3:18-4:1	5:21-6:9
Prayer	4:2-6	6:18-20
Arrival of Tychicus	4:7-8 (+ 9)	6:21-22
Final Blessing	4:18	6:24

[22]The Greek terms for "commonwealth" in Phil. 3:20 and Eph. 2:12 are different though from the same root and represent future and present realities, respectively.

[23]For further treatment see J.P. Sampley, "The Letter to the Ephesians," 9-39 in Krodel, *Ephesians, Colossians, 2 Thessalonians, the Pastoral Epistles*, and Roetzel, *The Letters of Paul*, 95-100.

[24]See I. Havener, "The Epistle to the Ephesians," 86-87 in *First Thessalonians, Philippians, Philemon, Second Thessalonians, Colossians, Ephesians* (Collegeville: Liturgical, 1983).

The blocks of material, sequence of ideas, and overall structure are based on those of Colossians. Significantly, these parallels go well beyond the features one expects in the epistolary genre.

The clearest case of verbatim borrowing is the following (RSVmod):

Colossians 4		Ephesians 6
	21	Now that you also may be aware of
7 My affairs		my affairs, how I am doing,
all		all
will be made known to you		will be made known to you
by Tychicus		by Tychicus
the beloved brother		the beloved brother
and faithful minister		and faithful minister
and fellow servant		
in the Lord,		in the Lord,
8 whom I have sent to you	22	whom I have sent to you
for this very purpose,		for this very purpose,
that you may know about		that you may know about
our affairs		our affairs
and that he may encourage		and that he may encourage
your hearts,		your hearts.
9 ...all the things		
happening here		

The author lifted the passage from Colossians, omitting only "and fellow servant" and expanding the introductory section with the help of Col. 4:9b. A comparative study could also be made between the two letters' domestic codes (Col. 3:18-4:1 and Eph. 5:21-6:9), showing that Ephesians has expanded and modified its source, while following closely its sequence, themes, and vocabulary. Other parallel verses could be examined, e.g., Eph. 1:7; 2:5; 4:2; 5:15-16 compared to Col. 1:14; 2:13; 3:12; 4:5, where the author borrowed vocabulary, extended phrases, or thematic sequences. Often Ephesians combines disparate units from Colossians to express its own thought (2:1-5 = Col. 2:13; 3:6; or 5:20 = Col. 3:17) or significantly modifies the meaning of Colossian terms, e.g., "mystery" or "oikonomia," and "rooted and built upon him" (Col. 2:6 vs Eph. 2:20; 3:17).[25]

GENERAL CONSIDERATIONS

In light of the above discussion we conclude that this letter was composed by a later admirer of Paul, a third generation disciple who employed Pauline ideas and also generously borrowed from and radically rethought the earlier Paulinist document Colossians to express a new, unique blend of Christian tradition. Who the intended audience was is a mystery to us, since the traditional designation "the saints who are at Ephesus" (1:1) must be rejected as a weakly attested reading (see RSV footnote). Despite extended discussion by past scholars regarding the situation which called forth this document or about the author's purpose, we cite two brief statements of a contemporary Ephesian scholar. On the one hand, he states that the letter "lacks clues concerning a concrete crisis or occasion," despite hints about disunity and even "a Jewish-gentile split." On the other, that same scholar proposes the following general purpose, namely, that the author "wrote a letter to some gentile Christians needing assurance and instruction in the faith."[26]

The surface structure which only superfically bears the form of a letter is readily discernible. Between opening and concluding paragraphs, the author offers a doctrinal section concerning God's call to humanity and a paraenetic segment on proper conduct. Its major divisions, therefore, are as follows:

Opening 1:1-2
Mystery of God's call through Christ 1:3-3:21

1:3-14	hymnic doxology
1:15-24	worldwide redemption in Christ
2:1-10	made alive through Christ
2:11-22	reconciliation of Jew and Gentile (fellow citizens with the saints)
3:1-13	summons of pagans to faith
3:14-21	mystery of Christ (+ doxology)

Admonitions (paraenesis): "proper walk" 4:1-6:20

4:1-16	summons to unity, love, and faith as community

---

[25]See C.L. Mitton, *Ephesians* (Grand Rapids: Eerdmans, 1981) 11-13.

[26]Sampley, "The Letter to the Ephesians," 9 and 12 respectively.

4:17-24   turn away from pagan way of life
4:25-5:21 demonstrate Christian way of life in all areas
5:22-6:9   and in all social strata
6:10-20   eschatological struggle and the power of God
Conclusion 6:21-24.[27]

This outline assists the reader in perceiving the author's principal concerns, namely, the cosmic dimension of Christ's work within the universal Christian community (*ekklēsia* is used 9 times) and the ethical ramifications of God's call.

Below the surface outline one sees an even greater stress on proper conduct, for the entire letter prepares for the final instructions to the members of the community. It has been pointed out recently that the document begins by discoursing on God's cosmic design (chaps. 1-2), focuses more specifically on the universal church (3:1-5:21), then on the larger family unit or household (5:22-6:9), and concludes by addressing those who, sharing "in the strength of [God's] might" (6:10, i.e., divine armor, 6:13f), must persevere in their fight against the spiritual powers through prayer and supplication (6:18).[28] Through an understanding of and a submission to God's eternal design "which he set forth in Christ as a plan for the fulness of time" (1:9-10), the believer, "sealed with the Holy Spirit", awaits the full possession of that inheritance of which the Spirit is the guarantor (1:13-14). Nonetheless, already there has been created, by union with Christ the head, a oneness between heaven and earth, a oneness that calls for "imitation of God" in the present.[29]

ETHICAL MESSAGE OF THE DOCUMENT

The fundamental dimension of the author's message is broached at the beginning. From the start there is discussion of God's plan and choice of the believer "before the foundation of the world" (1:4). The latter theme is expressed with the terms: "mystery," "purpose," "council," or "plan" (1:5, 9, 10), its temporal nature defined as once hidden but now revealed or climaxed in Jesus Christ (1:4-5, 9-10, 11), and its goal for the most part as already realized. Believers are secure in God's plan, for they

[27]Adaptation of Kümmel, *Introduction to the New Testament*, 351-52.
[28]Sampley, "The Letter to the Ephesians," 34-38.
[29]R.A. Wild, "'Be Imitators of God': Discipleship in the Letter to the Ephesians," 127-43 in Segovia, *Discipleship in the New Testament*.

were chosen or destined and not only died with Christ but were saved by grace and raised up with Christ (1:4, 5; 2:5-6; *contra* Paul). The focus is on the present ("no longer" as contrasted to "now," 4:17), the new work or creation in Christ Jesus (2:10), and the guarantee or first installment, i.e., the Spirit (1:13-14).

This divine plan, however, finds its locus within the church, no longer a house church as in Paul, but the universal community of believers as the sphere of the cosmic Christ's activity. The community becomes, following the lead of Colossians, the body of Christ, i.e., Christ understood as the head of the cosmos (1:22) and of the church (4:15; 5:23). It is also the bride of Christ (5:22f), household of God (2:19), holy temple (2:21), and its members are "no longer strangers and sojourners, but ... fellow citizens with the saints" (2:19).

This last statement leads us to speak of the author's fascinating perspective on the relationship between the heavenly and earthly spheres. Taking a cue from Colossians (that God had subjugated the cosmic powers through Christ, 2:15), the author insists that God's plan, made known to believers, was "set forth in Christ" as the apex of reality, "to unite all things in him, things in heaven and things on earth" (1:10). As a result of the Christ-event there exists an unbreakable bond between heaven and earth. In Christ believers have been blessed "with every spiritual blessing in the heavenly places" (1:3), the locus of the reign of Christ (1:20) and of believers (2:6). Interestingly, the community becomes both the source of revelation for the heavenly powers (3:10) and the eschatological battlefield (6:12). So the church is the Christ's sphere of activity par excellence and its members already dwell in the earthly and heavenly spheres (2:19).

If the community or universal church is the milieu of the Christ's work, it is on the human stage, involving the family unit and personal choice, that this activity finds its raison d'être. The letter, after its initial doctrinal and ecclesiological sections, directs its attention to the practical consequences of the call that God sent out through the Christ-event and put into effect through the ministrations of the Son (4:11-13). Christians must "walk" or behave according to God's plan (4:1). The letter then becomes a call to responsible action on personal, household, and ecclesial levels.

Ultimately the letter's purpose is an ethical one. The term "to walk" (7 times *vs.* 4 in Colossians) takes on a significant role. Borrowed from the Pauline tradition, and more specifically from Colossians, the expression receives further development and becomes a central motif of the letter. One must "walk worthily of the call to which [one is] called" (4:1, RSVmod; Col. 1:10), that is, "walk in love as Christ loved us" (5:2; Col. 2:6; "walk in Christ") or as "children of light" (5:8). To do this one must no longer walk according to past evil deeds (2:2; 4:17; 5:15; see Col. 3:7; 4:5) but in "good works," "created in Christ" (2:10). Christian behavior or "proper walk" is the believer's part vis-à-vis the Christ-event. Formerly the audience "walked as Gentiles" in darkness, ignorance, and uncleanness (4:17-19) but now they are admonished to be renewed, to "put on the new nature, created after the likeness of God in true righteousness and holiness" (4:23-24).

Beginning in chapter 4, the author appeals to the reader to "walk worthily" of God's call (4:1), to seek love, unity, and peace (4:2-3), in effect, to acknowledge "one Lord, one faith, one baptism, one God and Father of us all, who is above all and through all and in all" (4:5). The remainder of the letter is a series of imperatives ("put off your old nature . . . put on the new nature," "let everyone speak the truth," "be imitators of God," 4:23-24, 25; 5:1) or moral suggestions ("we are to grow up," "you must no longer walk as the Gentiles," 4:15, 17). Having put aside their pagan ways (4:17), believers are to walk in honesty, love, good works, and be full of the Spirit (4:25f; 5:2, 18; also 2:10). Thus, "together with Christ" (2:5), they have received a heavenly or new-nature status from God (2:6; 4:24) and so are required to live accordingly.

> This status is existentially achieved in very 'earthly' activity: speaking the truth (4:25), controlling anger (4:26), working with one's hands (4:28), loving one's wife (5:25), obeying parents (6:1), etc. These ordinary tasks are given the highest ontological significance. Human marriage, for example, serves as the best image of ultimate heavenly realities (5:22-23). For the author of Ephesians, that is, "imitation of God" is achieved and made manifest in living response in this world and not by a flight from this world.[30]

Two final points should be made regarding the ethical character of Ephesians. First, the author retains from Colossians (4:15-16 = Col. 4:5) and underscores the eschatological nature of the believers' action in the world. If the time is short and the days are evil (5:16), the personal and

[30]*Ibid.*, 138.

community struggle will be a battle not only in the world but also against the cosmic powers, requiring the "armor of God" and the assistance of the good news and of the Spirit (6:12-13, 17). Secondly, the author employs and greatly develops the traditional household code to address the believer's daily activity (5:21-6:9). Wives, husbands, children, parents, slaves, and masters are all addressed in turn, being reminded at the start that they are to "be subject to one another out of reverence for Christ" (5:21). It is this verse which sets the tone for the entire household code (5:22-6:9)[31] and provides a key to understand the author's christological stance.

CHRIST AND THE CHURCH

5:21, terminating a long section on the Christian way of life and on the relationship between members, states emphatically that the bonds that exist between Christians derive from the body's association with the head. "The theme of the *una sancta ecclesia* is dealt with in such a way that ecclesiology is developed on the basis of Christology. Christ, the head, is in heaven, and the church is his body embracing the whole world."[32] Believers are bound to one another and are to be subject to one another because of their unity in Christ. The first part of the code (5:22-33) becomes the focus of a discussion of marital relations and of Christ's relation to his church. The theme of mutual love (verb used 5 times in this passage) becomes the paradigm of familial and community behavior, for thus Christ loves his own body the church of which "we are members" (vv. 23, 25, 29-30). The letter concludes on the same theme: "grace be with all who love our Lord Jesus Christ with love undying" (6:24). Christians are to imitate God (who loves humanity with great love, 2:4) by "walking in love as Christ loved [them] and gave himself up..., a fragrant offering and sacrifice to God" (5:1-2). Unity and mutual love (4:15-16; see also 2:14f) are the criteria for incorporation and growth into the body of Christ.

The author's christology nevertheless incorporates familiar themes from the Jesus tradition. Jesus is God's Son (1:3; 4:13), the one chosen to achieve God's great designs (1:19). He is the one whom God raised from the dead, established at the right hand and over all powers, and "made the head over all things for the church, which is his body"

---

[31]Sampley, *'And the Two shall Become One Flesh'*, 148; see also p. 10.
[32]Lohse, *The Formation of the New Testament*, 95.

(1:20-23). In this same Christ believers were chosen, blessed, and foreordained to be God's children (1:3-5) for that is the mystery, set forth and revealed in Christ (1:9-10; 3:9-11). Christ, through his death and resurrection, was constituted giver of spiritual blessings (1:3, 7) and savior of the church (5:23; also 2:13, 16).

But more importantly for this author, the Christ is the head of the church which repeatedly is called his body (8 times), a body which is cosmic in extension and fulness (1:10, 22-23), but also one which needs to be built up (4:12, 16) and cherished (5:30). Related to the theme of "building up" is the author's reference to the "members of the household of God" as "growing into a holy temple of the Lord" and even as "a dwelling place of God in the Spirit" (2:19-21); and connected to the imagery of "nourishing and cherishing" (5:29) is the theme of Christ's love for his church and the author's use of the language of bride and groom or wife and husband to describe that concern (5:22f).

Rather than highlighting the high christology of Colossians, Ephesians dwells on the Christ's function in the working out of God's plan. Christ is the savior and head of the community of believers, for it was the eternal design that human beings (those divided and far off, 2:14, 17) become imitators and children of God (1:5; 5:1) through and in Christ and that they walk in love as Christ did, this Christ who, in the perspective of this author, is now head and lover of his own body the church.

The Pastorals

Of the letters classified as deutero-Pauline or Paulinist the farthest removed from Paul in time and thought are the documents referred to as the Pastorals. This last term, inherited from 19th-century scholarship and used throughout this study, designates 1-2 Timothy and Titus—the author will be called the Pastor.[33]

ORDER AND COMPOSITION

Within the NT canon the thirteen letters attributed to Paul are found in one group beginning with Romans and terminating with Philemon.

---

[33]For a brief, balanced introduction, see Karris, *The Pastoral Epistles* and R.H. Fuller, "The Pastoral Epistles," 97-121 in Krodel, *Ephesians, Colossians, 2 Thessalonians, the Pastoral Epistles*.

The Pastoral letters are situated just before the last mentioned and in the following order: 1 Timothy, 2 Timothy, and Titus. Since it is universally recognized that the works of the Pauline corpus were artificially organized according to two principles: names of places followed by those of persons and within these two categories from longest to shortest, it is no surprise to learn that the three letters are not listed in their order of composition. In effect, 2 Timothy was the first composed, followed by Titus and then 1 Timothy.

The author's progressive treatment of heretics, a major theme of the Pastorals, is a clue to the order of composition. In 2 Tim. 2:17 and 20 heretics are singled out but remain within the community, while in Titus 3:10 the advice is given that the obdurate brother must be excommunicated, and finally in 1 Tim. 1:20 Hymenaeus (see 2 Tim. 2:17) has now been delivered to Satan. A similar examination of the three letters in terms of church structures reveals the same sequence. In 2 Tim. 2:1-2 Timothy must appoint "faithful men" who will be ordained by the apostle (1:6). The ministers, therefore, consist of the apostle/writer and "faithful" helpers. When we take up Titus we note that Timothy is to appoint elders in every city (1:5) and, while nothing specific is said about ordination, we suppose that the ministers consist of a committee of elder/bishops that rules over the community in each city. Finally in 1 Timothy, the existence of elder/bishops is taken for granted and their qualifications, briefly examined in Titus 1:5f, are discussed at length in chapters 3 and 5. Ordination is conferred by elders or a committee of prophets (4:14). There is further development of the ministerial character of the community which now includes the apostle, presbyter/bishops, and deacons (3:8-12). The Pastor takes considerable care to discuss the duties of the various ministers (4:13; 5:9, 17), duties intimately related to the social structures of the traditional Hellenistic Household Codes.[34]

Another indicator of order involves the pseudonymic character and composition of these documents. Employing the rich legend about Paul's life and activity as the framework and justification for this treatment of and response to the false teaching rampant within the community, the Pastor borrows one of the many stories which arose concerning the late activity of Paul in the Mediterranean world. In Clement of Rome we hear of Pauline travel in the West (Spain) and so in the Pastorals we encounter Pauline activity to the east of Rome (Crete).

[34]Verner, *The Household of God*, 127f.

Presumably Paul's statements in Rom. 15:24, 28 about his plans to go to Spain and the story behind Luke's inconclusive ending of Paul's work in Rome (Acts 28:30-31) provided impetus to such creativity. 2 Timothy is by far the most detailed in its use of biographical material; see especially 4:9-22. As authority is established over the audience, the Pastor finds less need defensively to employ biographical materials; see Titus 3:12-15 and 1 Tim. 1:1.

PURPOSE, DOCTRINE, AND PORTRAIT OF JESUS

In the three letters one finds repeated hints to the author's purpose for writing. Perhaps the most telling statement is found in Titus 1:5; the recipient of the letter was left in Crete, the Pastor says, that he "might amend what was defective." The Pastorals, therefore, were composed as polemical responses to the widespread heretical tendencies of some members of the community. Each letter inveighs against false doctrines being preached. This ever-present danger leads the writer to dwell at length on several related issues: church order and ministry, ethics or proper Christian behavior, and sound doctrine.[35]

It comes as no surprise that, as the Jesus movement acquired a greater and more diversified membership, its traditions were affected by contemporary culture.[36] Already during the lifetime of Paul there had been great intellectual, if not always orthodox, ferment among the newly baptized. At a further remove from the apostolic age, the audience of the Pastor found itself involved in speculative and moral turmoil. Based on the author's various statements, 2 Tim. 2:16-3:17; Titus 1:10-16; and 1 Tim. 1:3-20; 4:1-11, we accept the following description of the heresies as a "combination of speculative mythology with a rigid legalism and asceticism" including possible contacts with Rabbinic and Gnostic-like tendencies.[37] While there is controversy concerning the nature of the unorthodox thinking attacked in the Pastorals, it is at least clear that the heretics were world-negating (1 Tim. 4:1-5) and exhibited a love for speculative (Jewish, Titus 1:16) mythologies and endless genealogies. The various proto-Gnostic tendencies (denial of the resurrection, stress on knowledge rather than salvation,

---

[35]Karris, *The Pastoral Epistles*, xi-xvi.

[36]For an overall assessment of the social world of the Pastorals, see Verner, *The Household of God*, 180-86.

[37]Fuller, "The Pastoral Epistles," 105.

negative view of marriage, the avoidance of various foods) as well as the explicit references to Jewish influences (in Titus) leads us to date the letters late in the first or early in the second centuries A.D. and at the same time to appreciate the Pastor's world-affirming theology.

The theologian-writer sees the issue of church order and ministries as the means to combat heretical tendencies (Titus 1:5b) and the lack of order as their underlying cause (1:10 the heretics are labeled "insubordinate men"). To that end the author dwells at length on the various ministries, their duties, and the qualifications of those to be appointed. Their duties include the teaching of sound doctrine and the charge to "certain persons not to teach any different doctrine" (1 Tim. 1:3). The author intends to set up a chain of command (2 Tim. 2:1-7) whose ministers are upright in behavior and faithful to the deposit of faith.

Not only are those who aspire to the noble ministries advised on proper behavior, but all members of the community are instructed on the believer's role in the world. Since the church is a society that is here to stay, its members are shown how to live as citizens of this world (see 1 Tim. 5; Titus 2). Further, the author subscribes to the ideals of Stoic ethics: reverence for the deity, concern for others, and self-discipline.[38] Finally, the believer must be world-affirming, for God made the world good (1 Tim. 4:4) and through Jesus sent his grace for the salvation of all "in this world" (Titus 2:11-14).[39]

What unites the above themes is sound doctrine; that is what the heretics have betrayed; that is what proper Christian behavior must be based on; and finally that is what the minister and the community must safeguard (1 Tim. 6:20; Titus 2:1). The stress is on orthodoxy—the term "correct/sound" appears only in the Pastorals within the New Testament. Further, "doctrine" (*didaskalia*) is used 15 times in these letters. Thus, the Pastor's main concern is to safeguard what has been inherited, to protect the doctrine of the community, and to reaffirm its saving power.

To understand fully the christology of the Pastorals, we must examine their theology, appreciate their treatment of morality, and recall the author's purpose for writing (polemics against proto-Gnostic tendencies). In many respects the Pastor's thought is theologically

---

[38]M. Dibelius and H. Conzelmann, *The Pastoral Epistles* (Philadephia: Fortress, 1972) 8-10 and 39-41.

[39]Karris, *The Pastoral Epistles*, 105-19.

centered; the plan, the choice, and the goal of eternal life are centered in God (Titus 1:1-3) who is the Sovereign One (1 Tim. 1:17; 6:15-16), the Savior, and Creator. The author stresses the goodness of creation (1 Tim. 4:4) and God's will that all be saved (4:10). These themes are a countermeasure to the thinking of members of the community who look down on created reality and preach the salvation of the initiated few. So God and Christ Jesus (the author's preferred usage) are given the title of Savior. It is especially in Titus that this double usage occurs: 1:3; 2:10; 3:4 about God and 1:4; 2:13; 3:6 about Jesus.[40] In this way the author draws a close link between the divine realm (God's will and action) and the earthly activity of Jesus. It is in the final letter that one finds the clearest description of the theological and christological underpining of the Pastor's thought. Thus, while only God is referred to as Savior in 1 Timothy (1:1; 2:3; 4:10), the author is insistent that Jesus is the Christian's hope and lord (1:1, 3), and that he "came into the world to save sinners" (1:15).

The author, therefore, presents a low christology[41] whose principal function is soteriological. Perhaps the clearest statement of this idea is in 1 Tim. 2:3b-6:

> ...God our Savior, who desires all men to be saved and to come to the knowledge of the truth. For there is one God, and there is one mediator between God and men, the man Christ Jesus, who gave himself as a ransom for all, the testimony to which was borne at the proper time.

The author lays stress on divine, universal salvation, on the humanity of Jesus, and on his soteriological mission, proposals counter to the tenets of the proto-Gnostic teachers. In 1 Tim. 3:16 the author further stresses the humanity of the Savior by citing an early christological hymn which emphasizes both the earthly and heavenly aspects of the Christ-event.

This last text brings us to consider another crucial factor in our attempt to understand the christology of the Pastorals, namely, their treatment of morality. The author is impressed by models or examples (a frequent term in the Pastorals), whether the standards of con-

---

[40]See also Luke 1:47 and 2:11.

[41]Titus 2:13 should read "the appearing of the glory of the great God and our Savior Jesus Christ" as in the RSV note.

temporary Greek culture, the Old Testament, Jesus, or Paul. The last mentioned and his suffering are presented as model for ministers and believers to follow. Interestingly these comparisons are usually related to christological passages, e.g., 2 Tim. 1:9-12; 2:8-13. It is in this light that Jesus appears as a model of perfect patience for the Christian (1 Tim. 2:5-6), as a true confessor (6:13), or as one zealous for good deeds (Titus 2:14).

This picture of Jesus, therefore, is intimately related to the Pastor's purpose in writing. Jesus, as God's mediator, performs a soteriological function as he brings God's salvation to a world that needs it and profits from it. Through Christ Jesus the mercy and grace of God have been poured out abundantly upon those who believe that they might in turn, in the hope of eternal life, apply themselves to good and profitable deeds (Titus 3:5-8).

Part IV
Jesus In The General Letters
And The Book of Revelation

10

The General Letters

In this chapter we consider five independent documents: Hebrews, James, First Peter, Jude, and Second Peter. All except the first are pseudonymous, that is, written in the name of an early Christian figure: James and Jude the brothers of Jesus, and Peter the apostle. Hebrews makes no claim of authorship. These documents are treated together, not because they bear a relationship to one another but because they are late pastoral works which bear witness to the variety of early Christian thinking and activity. In this group are often included the three Johannine letters which are thus situated in the NT canon. However, since scholarship has clearly established a relationship between these three documents and the community that produced the Fourth Gospel, they are discussed with that gospel.

Hebrews

The long, well-written NT document referred to as the Epistle to the Hebrews is an enigmatic work which taxes the ingenuity of reader and scholar. From the beginning it caused controversy within Christian communities, particularly in the Latin church where exception was taken to its denial of a second repentance for apostates. During the fourth century, under the influence of the Greek and Syrian churches, the document was accepted by the western church as part of the Pauline canon. After consideration of general issues, we will examine the document's composition and purpose, and will conclude with a synthesis of its peculiar christology.

GENERAL CONSIDERATIONS

Despite Greek and Syriac tradition and eventual acceptance in the Latin church, Pauline authorship of and influence on Hebrews have not been corroborated by modern research. While earlier scholars pointed to similarities between this document and works of the Pauline corpus (treatment of the Law, role of Christ in creation, importance of the covenant), it is now held that these few similarities derive from general Christian tradition. The reference to Timothy in 13:23 (if indeed the person of apostolic time is intended) led early Christians to posit Pauline influence or authorship for this work. There is little connection between it and the Pauline corpus, whether in style or vocabulary, use of the Old Testament, form and structure, or especially in terms of christology and eschatology. One must seek the background of Hebrews in an entirely different milieu.

Who then was the author of this document? From the second century various names have been proposed: Paul, a secretary of his or a translator (Luke), Clement of Rome, Barnabas, Apollos, or even the teachers of the last mentioned, Aquila and Priscilla. These suggestions, however, are no more than conjecture. The unknown author was a Jewish Christian of Hellenistic background. The Greek of this document is perhaps the finest in the New Testament and its thought shows signs of the Platonism favored by Alexandrian Judaism. The author's typological method of interpreting the Old Testament and its great personalities finds parallels in the slightly earlier contemporary, Philo of Alexandria.[1]

The identity of the addressees has attracted some attention. Many point to data within the document (extensive use of OT texts, a profound interest in Jewish institutions and traditions as the basis for its christology: covenant, Levitical priesthood, sacrifice and Day of Atonement) to maintain that the audience and author of Hebrews were converts from Hellenistic Judaism. Indeed, second-century tradition which gave the document its name ("to the Hebrew") supports this conclusion. A major concern of the author was the possible apostasy of

---

[1] See the discussion of J.W. Thompson, "The Riddle of Hebrews," 1-16 in *The Beginnings of Christian Philosophy: The Epistle to the Hebrews* (Washington: Catholic Biblical Association, 1982).

these Christians "back to their former allegiance."[2] More generally scholarship insists that the addressees were either Gentile converts or Christians simply. The use of the Old Testament to theologize was a general Christian phenomenon and besides one would hardly speak of Jewish Christians returning to their former communities as "falling away from the living God" (3:12).[3] Where was the document's audience residing? Since at the end of the work we read: "Those who come from Italy send you greetings" (13:24b), some see Hebrews as destined for Italy generally or for Rome. The text, however, is unclear since "those who come from Italy" could refer either to people formerly from Italy now in exile or to the original addressees of the homily.

The issue of genre must also be discussed. While it is usually called a letter and is either situated after the Pauline corpus or classified as a general epistle, it has few epistolary characteristics. The standard epistolary opening is lacking and its tone is not that of a letter. Only the ending, which is probably a later addition, suggests the letter tradition. The verdict of scholars is that Hebrews was a homily delivered to a specific audience but later sent to a more general audience by its author who added chapter 13 as an accompanying "word of exhortation" (13:22) and provided the document with an epistolary ending (22-25). We conclude, contrary to traditional claims, that "the work is not a letter, it is not by St. Paul, and it is not addressed to 'Hebrews'" but that "this is a magnificent work, treasured for centuries in the life of the church and well worth our effort to read and study it carefully."[4]

COMPOSITION AND PURPOSE

"In the New Testament [Hebrews] has neither antecedents nor descendants and is not part of any movement; it is simply a text of such excellence that it forced its way into the canon of the New Testament, and ascribing it to Paul was only an excuse to include it in the New Testament."[5] Indeed, Hebrews is unique and few have denied its excellence. Even Luther in his 1522 preface to the Bible, while objecting

---

[2] J. Casey, *Hebrews* (Wilmington: Glazier, 1980) xiv and D. Peterson, *Hebrew and Perfection: An Examination of the Concept of Perfection in the Epistle to the Hebrews* (London: Cambridge University, 1982) 186.

[3] See Kümmel, *Introduction to the New Testament,* 399-400, for further arguments.

[4] G.W. MacRae, *Hebrews* (Collegeville: Liturgical, 1983) 7.

[5] Perrin, *The New Testament,* 137.

to the document's "rejection of a second repentance as contrary to all the Gospels and the Letters of Paul, ...in other respects thought that Hebrews was an uncommonly fine letter which speaks masterfully of the priesthood of Christ from a solid scriptural basis."[6] Hebrews, therefore, merits a careful study of its thought, structure, and purpose in order to understand its unique portrait of Jesus.

Hebrews is a moral document whose purpose ultimately lies in its frequent advice and warnings, i.e., the paraenesis which permeates the work. This is another reason for distinguishing Hebrews from real NT letters; moral advice becomes a central concern. One scholar has suggested that the work consists of alternating proclamations about Jesus (1:1-3:6; 4:15-5:10; etc) and paraenetic sections (3:7 -4:13; 5:11-6:20; etc).[7] Such a proposal is too simple to do justice to the intricacy of the author's thought but it captures one of the dynamic features of the work's structure.

However, the document is not simply a moral sermon. If it frequently has recourse to paraenesis in its effort to influence the behavior of the audience, it repeatedly engages in doctrinal discourse to establish a solid christology and eschatology. Whether Son of God (1:2; 3:6), eternal High Priest (4:14; 9:11) or Perfector of faith (12:2), Jesus is the heavenly one through whose sacrificial death God has established in heaven the eternal city (13:14) whose entrance is gained by faith. Jesus is the one whose activity has joined heaven and earth, that is, the world and its Christian community as copy of the heavenly sanctuary (9:24). As God's pilgrim people the community awaits Christ's salvific return (9:28). With these truths in mind the author encourages the audience to live a life of faith in the midst of adversity.

In relation to the principal titles given to Christ: Son of God, High Priest, and Pioneer and Perfector of faith, we suggest a threefold division for the document.[8] The first (1:1-4:13) proclaims Jesus as Son who is superior to the angels and to Moses. After a hymnic prologue (1:1-4) where it is stated that God speaks in the last days through the Son, the author insists that Jesus was superior to the angels (1:5-14) and so obedience is owed him (2:1-4) and that he was made lower than the

[6]Lohse, *The Formation of the New Testament*, 202.

[7]Perrin, *The New Testament*, 138.

[8]Basically these structural observations agree with the proposals of Kümmel, *Introduction to the New Testament*, 389-92.

angels to save his brothers (2:5-18)—already in 2:17 the central theme of Jesus as High Priest is introduced. Next the author addresses Jesus' relation to Moses; as Son he is superior to Moses, God's servant (3:1-6).[9] So the audience is advised to hear Jesus' voice (3:7-19) concerning the promised rest (4:1-10) and "to strive to enter that rest" (4:11-13).

The document's second division (4:14-10:31) focuses on the author's principal christological theme, Jesus as High Priest. Believers are advised to approach him, i.e., to cling to their confession and to remain true to Jesus the eternal, heavenly High Priest (4:14-16). Being obedient in suffering, he is gentle with the ignorant and wayward (5:1-10). In light of this the document inveighs against dullness of hearing, immaturity, apostasy and fosters hope in God's promises (5:11-6:20). The author dwells at length on Jesus' priesthood as deriving from the mysterious figure of the Abraham story, Melchizedek, the one called the priest of righteousness and peace (7:2, already introduced in 5:6, 9).[10] Jesus like Melchizedek, is superior to the legal, finite priests descended from Levi. He is an eternal priest, made perfect as Son forever (7:28). Thus, his ministry is superior to that of the old covenant which itself is vanishing (8:13). In its place and substituting for its ineffectual ritual, holy place, and sacred personnel "there appeared the Christ as a high priest of the good things that have come" (9:11), namely a new sacrifice, "not the blood of goats and calves but his own blood" (9:12).[11] He has become the mediator of the new covenant (9:15), purifying all by the sprinkling of the blood shed in his once-for-all sacrifice (9:26-27). This sacrifice has conferred perfection for all time (10:14), a forgiveness which demands confession or merits judgment (10:19-31).[12]

In the third division the author appeals to the audience's perseverance in the midst of past afflictions as motivation for its continued fidelity

---

[9]On the document's Moses-Jesus typology, see M.R. D'Angelo, *Moses in the Letter to the Hebrews* (Missoula: Scholars, 1979).

[10]For a discussion of the recently discovered "texts from Qumran that deal with the heavenly Melchizdek and Melchiresha" (p.1) and the light they shed on Hebrews, see P.J. Kobelski, *Melchizedek and Melchiresha* (Washington: Catholic Biblical Association, 1981).

[11]Underlying the pervasive theme of superiority is "a constant metaphysical dualism" whereby "the Christian experience is identified with abiding, unshakable, and firm realities" and "the historical Israel is identified with tangible and transitory realities," Thompson, *The Beginnings of Christian Philosophy*, 13.

[12]Peterson, *Hebrews and Perfection*, 168-87.

(10:32-39). There was a danger that some in the community might "shrink back" from their commitment. They are reminded that the "righteous live by faith" and thereby "keep their souls" (10:38-39). The author then focuses on the subject of faith by presenting "a great cloud of witnesses" to Jesus as "pioneer and perfector of faith" (12:1-2). The examples of Abel, Enoch, Noah, Abraham, Sarah, Moses, etc., show that theirs was a faith of promise not the "something better" of the Christ-event (11:39-40).[13] For the believer this "involves living as a stranger on earth and 'seeing' a better reality"[14] (11:13; 13:4).

The audience's situation is addressed and, after being contrasted to that of Jesus who shed his blood (12:4), is subsumed under the theme of discipline, for God "disciplines us for our good, that we may share his holiness"(12:10). As a consequence the readers are admonished through the example of Esau not to refuse God's grace (12:12-17) and, rather than fostering the fearful distance of the Mosaic covenant, to approach the heavenly Jerusalem and its perfect mediator (12:22, 24). The author concludes the document with a traditional paraenetic section on love of brothers, hospitality to strangers, modest way of life, patient endurance, and obedience to rulers and with an epistolary note of personal greetings and benediction (chap. 13).

If it is the christological perspective (Son, High Priest, and Perfector of faith) which gives the document structural unity, it is the author's use of the Old Testament which provides its building blocks. As Lohse has observed: "The sermon is closely related to OT texts: Psalm 8 in chapter 2; Psalm 95 in chapters 3-4; Psalm 110 in chapter 5 (taken up in chapter 7); Jeremiah 31 in chapter 8; Psalm 40 in chapter 10."[15] Beyond this list we point to the critical role played by other important citations. While the principle governing the selection of citations in chapter 1 is the theme of angels, it is important to note that Ps. 2:7 (along with 2 Sam 7:14, both cited at 1:5) emphasizes the theme of sonship which dominates the first section of the document, especially 3:1-6, and reappears at 5:5 in

---

[13]Thompson, *The Beginnings of Christian Philosophy,* 80.

[14]See J. Swetnam, *Jesus and Isaac: A Study of the Epistle to the Hebrews in the Light of the Agedah* (Rome: Biblical Institute, 1981) 119-23, on "Hebrews 11:19 as an allusion to Christ."

[15]*The Formation of the New Testament,* 197; see also R.H. Fuller, "The Letter to the Hebrews," 6-8 in G. Krodel, ed., *Hebrews, James, 1 and 2 Peter, Jude, Revelation* (Philadelphia: Fortress, 1981).

relation to the high-priest motif. At the end of the first chapter (v. 13) one encounters for the first time the recurring importance of Ps 110. Significant also are Gen. 14 for the document's Melchizedek theme (chap. 7), various parts of the Torah for the Levitical motifs of chapter 9, and the long survey of biblical heroes for the composition of chapter 11. The OT text plays a major role in the composition of Hebrews.

Analysis of the document's content and of its composition stresses its paraenetic character and holds the key to its purpose. The author states that some in the community had been ostracized by the general populace and been treated to public abuse and confiscation of personal property (10:32-34; also 13:3, 13). It is implied that this continues and so they are not to lose their confidence but rather to persevere and consider these tribulations as discipline from a loving Father (10:35-36; 12:9).

We need to consider the document's denial of a second repentance for apostates, a doctrine which caused embarassment to the church during the Donatist controversy and generated negative criticism of the work. At the beginning of chapter 6, it is stated that, having committed apostasy, "it is impossible to restore again to repentance those who have once been enlightened" (v. 4). Related ideas are also expressed at 10:26-31 and 12:16-17. One wonders whether the absoluteness of the denial owed to the seriousness of the situation within the community, and therefore should be interpreted rhetorically as negative inducement for those who are tempted to apostasize[16] or whether the author might have had the Synoptic saying about "blasphemy against the Holy Spirit" in mind (Mark 3:29). In defense of the latter we note that those who apostasize not only "have been enlightened," but also "have tasted the goodness of the word of God and the powers of the age to come" (6:4-5). Their action is tantamount to "crucifying the Son of God ... and holding him up to contempt" (v. 6). The author envisions a similar situation where the sin is a deliberate rejection of the covenant and "the Spirit of grace" (10:26, 29), much like the absolute, irremediable trivializing of birthright by Esau (12:16-17). While not incompatible with the first option, this second one stresses the author's eschatological doctrine, namely, that commitment is an either/or fundamental option. In what follows, the author, by way of strategy, expresses confidence in

---

[16]Fuller, "The Letter to the Hebrews," 24.

the readers: "yet in your case, beloved, we feel sure of better things that belong to salvation."[17]

CHRISTOLOGY OF HEBREWS

To bolster the community's commitment the author establishes a christological framework which participates in a pre-existence and exaltation scheme. For the author Jesus is both one who has been enthroned at God's right hand (1:3, 13f), after having "endured the cross" (12:2) and one who "bears the very stamp of God's nature" (1:3), even before creation since it was through him that God made the world (1:2). These are the two poles of the author's structural perspective, a Son who existed before creation and who was enthroned as high priest (5:5-6). It is within that perspective that the author situates Jesus' salvific role as a historical event (his body, blood, cross) with once-and-for-all effectiveness (10:10) and eternal consequences (7:25) and as a heavenly mediation or intercession (7:25; 9:24) for his house (3:6; 10:21) or pilgrim community (11:13f; 13:14).

From the start the document focuses on the two poles of this structure, for in the first four verses it treats both Jesus' pre-existent relation to God and his "sitting down at the right hand of the Majesty on high" (1:3). Employing an early hymnic fragment,[18] the author constructs a solemn preface for the ensuing theological treatise. In terms reminiscent of the Colossian hymn (1:15f), the author says of Jesus (here called Son) that God "appointed (him) the heir of all things" and "created the world" through him (1:2). These lofty attributes (agent of creation and lord of created reality; see also 2:10: "for whom and by whom all things exist") establish Jesus' relation to the cosmos and to the earth for whose sins he was to make purification (1:3). The range of Jesus' lordship extends from one end of creation to the other. If it is his exaltation at the right hand or his obtaining that excellent name (1:4) which constitutes him superior to the angelic host, it is his relationship to God as Son which receives the author's attention in the remainder of the chapter. Jesus is said to "reflect the glory of God and bear the very stamp of his nature" (1:3). The terminology which derives from wisdom literature advances the discussion of Jesus' divinity, for the mirror ("reflect") and signet ("stamp") images show that the Son is no ordinary

[17]Peterson, *Hebrews and Perfection,* 178-83.
[18]See chapter 3 for discussion of this hymn.

creature but shares the attributes of God, whether "glory" or "authority." Of further interest is the author's deliberate association of pre-existence with the title "Son" (1:2-3), which in the tradition refers to resurrection and enthronement (see Rom. 1:4).

The document, however, does not dwell long on the pre-existent character of the Christ for it situates the discussion in a soteriological and eschatological framework. Recalling God's activity on Israel's behalf, it directs its attention both to the "last days" when God intervened in a definitive way through the Son (1:2) and to the Son's "purification for sins" (1:3).

This last theme leads to a discussion of the second pole of the author's structural schema, namely, Jesus as the exalted one. At the end of the preface Hebrews introduces the theme of the Christ's superiority to the angels (1:4), a topic which occupies the remainder of the chapter. Jesus while superior to these angelic creatures was made lower than they to save humanity (2:9), i.e., his brothers "sharing in flesh and blood," descendants of Abraham, and children of God (2:13, 14, 16).

But not content with insisting on Jesus' superiority to the angels, the author claims that he also is greater than Moses. Moses was a faithful servant in God's house, but "Christ was faithful over God's house as a son" (3:6). As High Priest of the new covenant he is declared the perfect mediator (9:15) who replaces the priesthood of the Mosaic dispensation. "In the days of his flesh" (5:2) when he pleaded for humanity before God (5:1, 7), he was weak like all humans, yet sinless (4:14; 5:2). Through suffering he was made perfect (2:10) and thereby "became the source of eternal salvation to all who obey him, being designated by God a high priest after the order of Melchizedek" (5:9-10; also 7:1-3). The story of the mysterious priest of Salem furnishes the author with a prototype for the eternal non-legal priesthood of Jesus (7:16). He is an eternal priest made so by divine oath, related to Melchizedek, and so the guarantor of a better and definitive covenant (7:21-22), saving "all who draw near to God through him" and always making "intercession for them" (7:25).[19]

In lyrical prose, Hebrews expresses its favorite christological theme:

> For it was fitting that we should have such a high priest, holy, blameless, unstained, separated from sinners, exalted above the heavens. He has no need, like those high priests, to offer sacrifices

[19]Peterson, *Hebrews and Perfection,* 124-25.

daily, first for his own sins then for those of the people, he did this once for all when he offered up himself. Indeed, the law appoints men in their weakness as high priests, but the word of the oath . . . appoints a Son who has been made perfect for ever (7:26-28).

The sacrifice, superior to the earthly or material offering (8:1f), was made once as a perfect gift by an obedient Son, whose eternal entrance into heaven was accomplished willfully by his own blood (9:12), for "he has appeared once for all at the end of the age to put away sin by the sacrifice of himself" (9:26; also 10:10, 14).[20]

By insisting that Jesus is the pre-existent Son and the exalted High Priest, the author sets the stage for the description of Jesus' soteriological role, since he is both an earthly and heavenly being who connects the heavenly and earthly realms. Employing traditional apocalyptic categories and applying current Platonic ideal categories, the author sees Jesus as the only real link between the world of shadows or copies (9:1-10) and the heavenly reality (8:5). His earthly existence (his sacrifice) established an eternal bond between earth and heaven and provided an entrance for all who would draw near. By the use of philosophical and liturgical language the author is able "to impress upon believers the nearness of the invisible world without insisting upon the nearness of the *parousia*."[21] Jesus, particularly as High Priest, participates in both worlds; as enthroned High Priest or minister in the sanctuary and the true tent (8:2) he is the perfect mediator on behalf of his earthly brothers and sisters (9:24). He became "the pioneer of their salvation" (2:10), "the pioneer and perfector of [their] faith" (12:2), their eternal intercessor (7:25), "the great shepherd of the sheep" (13:20) and still the one who is to save those who await his "second" coming (9:28; also 10:12-13).

A final moral note is in order. The document's high, but nonetheless functional, christology serves to undergird the author's urgent plea that the heavenly mediator is close. Being human in every respect, with a body (10:5) and weaknesses and loud cries and tears, he is able "to sympathize and to provide assistance in time of need" (4:14-16; 5:7). This moral tract concludes on an interesting christological note: "So

---

[20]Thompson, *The Beginning of Christian Philosophy,* 115 and 126-27.

[21]C.K. Barrett, "The Eschatology of the Epistle to the Hebrews," 391 in W.D. Davies and D. Daube, eds, *The Background of the New Testament and Its Eschatology* (London: Cambridge University, 1956).

Jesus also suffered outside the gate in order to sanctify the people through his own blood. Therefore let us go forth to him outside the camp, bearing abuse for him" (13:12-13). The community must live in an alien world while "seeking the city which is to come" (13:14). Since the earthly and the heavenly have been joined in the exalted High Priest, the author advises: "through him [the heavenly] then let us [the earthly] continually offer up a sacrifice of praise to God, that is, the fruit of lips that acknowledge his name" (13:15). In Christ reality finds its perfection, so the believer too in anticipation is able through him to participate in the reality of the heavenly city.

James

The letter of James is strange by any account; it entered the canon only with difficulty; it has generated controversy throughout the history of interpretation; and, even today, it rarely attracts an enthusiastic audience. Perhaps it was the judgment of Martin Luther in 1522 (he called James "a straw epistle"), which has most influenced modern attitudes toward this document. Popular opinion, caricatured as Lutheran versus Catholic approach, has opted either for the Pauline "justification by faith alone" or for "the merit of good works" of James. Beyond a discussion of these basic issues, it will be our goal to examine its author's perception of Jesus and early Christianity.

INTRODUCTORY ISSUES

James is usually referred to as a "catholic or universal" letter and, in a sense, insistence on its universal character is correct and equally applicable to most post-Pauline epistolary documents. James and other late pastoral works were written for general audiences and rarely address identifiable problems or issues as do the vibrant letters of Paul. As regards the genre of James, however, there is need for some discussion. Besides the minimal greeting which follows the standard Hellenistic pattern, there is little that resembles the form of the Greco-Roman letter. There is no final greeting nor any doctrinal section; the entire document consists of exhortation and its style is certainly not that of the Hellenistic letter. James resembles most the letter essay or moral tract that utilizes superficially the letter form to express its moral doctrine or message. It is in this sense that we call it a letter.

To understand the nature of this work several facets of its background require attention: its Jewish character and, in relation to this, its appeal to prophetic and wisdom literature to formulate its moral exhortation, its Stoic style and thought, and its Christian character. The letter is deeply influenced by all four elements.[22]

Even a cursory reading of James shows that it is centered on God and not on Jesus. So prominent is this feature that scholars at the end of the 19th century proposed that James was a slightly Christianized Jewish document. While few have been convinced by this proposal, it has led recent scholars to take seriously its Jewish character. One asks God for wisdom (1:50); it is also God who gives the crown of life (1:12) and heavenly gifts (1:17). The document is Jewish in style and character. It begins with a Jewish greeting: "to the twelve tribes in the Dispersion"— see also its use of the term "synagogue" for the assembly, 2:2). It represents the concrete mentality of the Old Testament rather than the Greek love for abstraction; examples rather than moral principles fill the pages of James (e.g., Abraham, 2:20f, Rahab, 2:25, the prophets, 5:10, Job, 5:11, Elijah, 5:17). While the text quotes explicitly only three OT passages, nearly every verse has reminiscences of the Jewish scriptures or intertestamental literature, e.g., "wind tossed waves," 1:6, "withering flower of grass," 1:10, or duty to orphan and widow, 1:27. Typical Jewish terms appear in every verse, particularly as related to the ethical maxims of Israel's moral literature; the author provides frequent echoes of Jewish thought and style. Thus, both the content and style of the letter of James are Jewish in character.

In attempting to explain further the Jewish quality of James, we note that this document has most in common with the literature of the late Old Testament, intertestamental moral works, and Hellenistic synagogue homilies. James shows a marked interest in the moral maxims of the sages and prophets of Israel; it draws from their ethical wisdom the insights it communicates to its readers; in its assessment of current problems it imitates the prophetic oracles of the past. The document's concerns are those one finds in the social prophets, Ben Sirach, the Testaments of the Twelve Patriarchs, Enoch literature, Fourth Mac-

---

[22]L.T. Johnson, "Friendship with the World/Friendship with God: A Study of Discipleship in James," 166-83 in Segovia, *Discipleship in the New Testament* and S. Laws, *A Commentary on the Epistle of James* (San Francisco: Harper & Row, 1980) 1-43, give a good overview of recent approaches to the study of James.

cabees, and some Qumran texts.[23] The author transposes these themes into exhortations to the widespread Christian communities. Thus, James is equally a book of Jewish wisdom (1:5; 3:17) and a prophetic call to action and righteousness (2:14f; 3:18).

This letter was also deeply influenced by the culture of its day, particularly Stoicism and Hellenistic moral philosophy. The author employs the Stoic diatribe, imaginary dialogue, and question and answer technique (e.g., 2:18-20). Love of memorable images ("doubt" is a wind tossed wave or a double mind, 1:6-8; lack of action is compared to seeing one's image in a mirror, 1:23; see also light and shadow, 1:17 and mist, 4:14), fondness for comparisons (usually introduced by "so will," "so also," "is like," "in like manner"), skill in the use of vocabulary, and elevated Greek style argue for a writer who had a considerable degree of education and training in Stoic thought. A good example of the author's use of moral stereotypes (*topoi*) can be found in 3:1-5, a passage similar to a text from Philo (Laws 3:223ff) where the bridle of a horse, the rudder of a ship, and a fire are employed to great effect. For the author of James they serve as excellent examples of the power of the tongue (the overpowering effect of so small an element).[24] The author's Stoic training is also evident in the style of the letter. In 1:19-25 James introduces the themes of words ("quick to hear, slow to speak," 1:19) and deeds ("doers of the word, and not hearers only," 1:22), themes developed at length in 2:14f (on faith and works) and 3:1f (on guarding the tongue). With considerable finesse the author repeats major themes at strategic points in the composition, e.g., 1:2 ("save your souls") and 5:20 ("save your soul from death") and interjects traditional sayings and subjects by the frequent use of "catchwords."[25]

Finally, we consider the Christian character of James. We have already alluded to its infrequent reference to Jesus Christ (1:1 and 2:1), although the title "Lord" is often used in speaking of Jesus (e.g., chap. 5). The Christian character of the text, however, is not to be sought primarily in its christological context but in its moral doctrine. While parallels to OT and other Jewish literature are numerous, the contacts

---

[23]M. Dibelius and H. Greeven, *James* (Philadelphia: Fortress, 1976) 26-28 and Laws, *James,* 11-12.

[24]For further examples of *topoi,* see Johnson, "Friendship with the World/ Friendship with God," 168.

[25]Dibelius and Greeven, *James,* 6-11.

with early Christian tradition are just as plentiful. Many of the author's maxims are echoes of sayings of Jesus found in the sermons of Matthew (especially 5-7) and Luke (6). It is possible that the author was acquainted with the Q-Source employed by Matthew and Luke since James shows many contacts with that material. There are also parallels to the letters of Paul and First Peter; Christian moral themes abound in this document.[26] The author is a moralist, a Jew for whom trust in God, knowledge of divine wisdom, and obedience to the Law and performance of its works are consonant with the teachings of Jesus. This author is also a Christian whose Jewish piety provides the basis for Christian living. Thus we agree with G.S. Sloyan: "James is 'Jewish Christian' in that it reflects much that we know about Hellenist Judaism, with acceptance of Jesus as the Christ added."[27]

MAJOR CONCERNS: THEOLOGY, ETHICS, CHRISTOLOGY

James is a Hellenistic Jewish text which consists of loosely connected moral maxims and exhortation. It begins with the human quest for completeness (1:4) and adopts as the basis of its ethics the Jewish principle that the human being must be holy because God is holy. S. Laws has made a convincing case for viewing the ethical principle of James as being "the imitation of God." Human inconsistency, disunity, and double-mindedness (conflicting desires, 4:1f, partiality, 2:1f, failure to guard the tongue, 3:1, hearer and not doer of the word, 2:14f) are confronted at every level of behavior and action. The human being is made according to God's image (3:9) and must strive for wisdom, for "wisdom from above is first pure, then peaceable, gentle, open to reason, full of mercy and good fruits" (3:17). As God is one (2:19), so should the human being strive to be one.[28]

It is within this context that one views the concern for rich and poor treated at the beginning (1:9f) and at the end of the letter (5:1f) and frequently illustrated by telling examples: treatment of orphans and widows (1:27), partiality to the rich (2:1-7), love of every neighbor (2:8), need for mercy (2:13), necessity of works (2:15, food and clothes). The

[26]Laws, *James*, 12-20 and Dibelius and Greeven, *James*, 28-31.

[27]"The Letter of James," 48 in Krodel, *Hebrews, James, 1 and 2 Peter, Jude, Revelation.*

[28]*James*, 29-32. See the previous chapter for a similar suggestion regarding Ephesians by Wild, "'Be Imitators of God.'"

author borrows from the prophetic writings the terminology of censure against the rich for it is a truism of Jewish wisdom that "God has chosen those who are poor in the world to be rich in faith and heirs of the Kingdom which he has promised to those who love him" (2:5). The author is concerned not for rich or poor but for the good works of faith which overcome human divisiveness.[29]

The author's treatment of speech or use and abuse of the tongue requires attention. Employing powerful images from Stoic philosophy to emphasize the power of the tongue (3:1-5), James pessimistically dissuades others from becoming teachers (3:1-2) since the tongue cannot be controlled (3:8). The author almost despairs from the knowledge that the tongue is "a restless evil, full of deadly poison" (3:8b) that can bless God and curse fellow human beings (3:9). But the tongue can also be the means of prayer, a major theme of James (see especially the power of prayer and the example of Elijah, 5:13-18).[30]

Next, we consider the theme of faith and works. It is particularly this issue which has attracted attention in the history of interpretation. Since James is combatting an abstract type of Christianity whose practice left much to be desired, 2:14-26 should be seen as part of the author's overall approach to Christian morality. This type of Jewish Christian piety laid stress on practice and deeds. So it is probable that James is, in part, a correction of abuses regarding the Pauline teaching of justification by faith (see also 2 Peter 3:15b-16). There are too many contacts between James and Paul's arguments and use of the Abraham traditions of Genesis in Romans to deny that the former is responding to abuses of Pauline teaching. Paul is combatting a work ethic which tends to deny that faith is a gift, while James, who is embued with a piety of good works, is opposing a religion of empty words and pledges. Both Paul and James, therefore, would subscribe to this formula: "Faith alone justifies, but not faith which is alone."[31]

Finally, as might be expected, theology rather than christology is central in this Jewish Christian text; but one should remember that Jesus' teaching was also focused on the kingdom of God (see particularly

---

[29]Johnson, "Friendship with the World/Friendship with God," 175-77, develops at length the theme of divisiveness or double-mindedness. More generally on the theme of "poor and rich," see Dibelius and Greeven, *James,* 39-45.

[30]Laws, *James,* 27.

[31]L.E. Elliott-Binns, "James," 1024 in *PCB.*

the "Lord's Prayer," Matt. 6:9-13 and Luke 11:2-4). The christology of James is submerged. Because the author is dealing with ethics and is a devotee of good-works Jewish piety and Stoic natural-law morality , soteriology and christology are not of primary concern in the document; one hears very little about Jesus' role in the history of salvation. Instead the author presumes these traditions and refers to Jesus as the Lord who is to return at the end-time (5:7-9).

> Christianity for James and his community is not then a matter of paticipation in a charismatic movement, of initiation into esoteric knowledge, or of sacramental participation in the mystery of salvation. Primarily, it is a way of life before God, a moral code (cf. the definition of "true religion" in i.27). Precepts for behaviour are backed by a notion of salvation associated with conversion and baptism (i.18, 21), and with reclamation from sin (v. 19f.), and also by an expectation of judgment.... [32]

Even if allowance is made for the author's lack of concern for the Jesus tradition as due probably to ethical preoccupations, many will regret the moralism of the letter, the defining of religion as good works (1:27) rather than life in Christ, and the far-reaching influence the type of Christianity represented by James had on later generations.

First Peter

This document is receiving considerable scholarly attention of late. It is no longer considered a pious fabrication of second-century Christianity whose goal was to establish the traditions and structures of the "Great Church." Instead, 1 Peter is seen as an important document for the study of early christianity at the end of the first century.[33] Also, it offers a fascinating christology to foster perseverance among the Christians of Asia Minor.[34]

[32]Laws, *James*, 33-34.

[33]For two excellent surveys of recent scholarship on 1 Peter, see J.H. Elliott, "The Rehabilitation of an Exegetical Step-Child: 1 Peter in Recent Research," *JBL* 95 (1976) 243-54 and D. Sylva, "1 Peter Studies: The State of the Discipline," *BTB* 10 (1980) 155-63.

[34]For a more extensive treatment of this topic, see E. Richard, "The Functional Christology of First Peter," 121-39 in C.H. Talbert, *Perspectives on First Peter* (Macon: Mercer University, 1986).

INTRODUCTION TO 1 PETER

Already in the 40s and 50s, during Paul's ministry, Christian communities are attested throughout Syria, Asia Minor, Greece, and Rome. 1 Peter states that it is being written from Rome (i.e., Babylon, 5:13) to the provinces of Asia Minor (1:1). The Christian movement has undergone important transformations since the time of Paul; so the author calls it a "brotherhood" (2:17; 5:9), refers to its leadership as "elders" (5:1), takes seriously the believers' relationship to the state (2:13f), and acknowledges that suffering as a Christian has become a common phenomenon (4:16; 5:9).

There is virtual unanimity that the letter is pseudonymous; it was the author's strategy to invoke the name of Peter to add authority to the document's exhortations and to insure a positive response from the audience. It is unnecessary to review the numerous indications of non-Petrine authorship or to restate once-popular amanuensis theories, namely, that Peter employed a secretary; see 5:12. We propose that the author employed a Petrine legend when composing 1 Peter. In fact, there are many hints in NT and post-NT writers that lend credence to the hypothesis of "a Petrine group at Rome" to which this author, and that of the later writer of 2 Peter, belonged.[35] Appeal is made to the venerable figures of this group (Peter, Silvanus, and Mark) to obtain a better hearing from the churches of Asia Minor.

Though the addressees are called "exiles of the Dispersion" (1:1; see also James 1:1) and though there are frequent allusions to the Hebrew scriptures as well as repeated use of Jewish images, there are good indications that they are Gentile Christians (1:14, 18, etc) and not Jewish converts. Furthermore, there is little concern for typically Jewish issues such as kosher food laws, circumcision, and the Law generally. The term, diaspora, must therefore represent Christians living in the midst of non-Christians, who are in fact called Gentiles (2:12; 4:3). Lastly, the extensive use of the Old Testament and its images points both to a church that is in close contact with its Jewish heritage, though of a limited scope, and to an author who may be a Hellenistic Jewish Christian.

If in some post-Pauline texts the epistolary characteristics have

---

[35]Brown, *Peter in the New Testament,* 149-56; Senior, *1 & 2 Peter,* xii-xvi; R.J. Bauckham, *Jude, 2 Peter* (Waco: Word Books, 1983) 146-47, 161.

diminished, this is not the case for 1 Peter.[36] The letter begins and ends with a standard epistolary opening and closing. Though it starts with a thanksgiving and a doctrinal statement, it adopts the form and tone of the later paraenetic epistles (1:13f). The letter, without fail, consists of alternation between imperative and indicative, that is, advice followed by examples or statements of theological justification.

Earlier composite theories (a liturgical tract or baptismal homily followed by a paraenetic text about persecution) once common in introductions are now rejected or greatly undermined by redaction and structural analyses.[37] Recent studies are convincing which see 1 Peter as a unified composition whose epistolary features are integral to the document. Vocabulary and stylistic studies as well as structural and theological examination show that there exist no notable differences between the two sections and that the letter provides many links between the two. Further, the break at 4:11-12 is real but no greater than the one at 2:11. Scholars admit that between the opening (1:1-2) and closing (5:12-14), the author has inserted three major sections: 1) 1:3-2:10 on God's chosen people (birth, baptism); 2) 2:11-4:11 on ethics for exiles or interim ethics; and 3) 4:12-5:11 consisting of renewed exhortation. Admittedly, there are many links between these sections and certain ones are strategically developed throughout the letter.

A final introductory item for consideration is the occasion for the writing of First Peter and the related issue of the date of composition. Both of these revolve around the theme of suffering. From the beginning the author is concerned with this theme. Reference is made to "the sprinkling of (Christ's) blood" in 1:2 (also 1:19), to the "various trials" which the audience "may have to suffer for a little while" in 1:6 and a repetition of this last statement at the end of the letter (5:9-10). Further, the reference in 1:7 to purification by fire immediately calls 4:12 to mind: "the fiery ordeal which comes upon you to prove you." 1 Peter then is focused on a theology of suffering.[38] What is of concern to us, however, is the nature of the suffering alluded to in the text, since 4:14-16

---

[36]Doty, *Letters,* 65-81.

[37]Balch, *Let Wives Be Submissive: The Domestic Code in 1 Peter,* 123-31; J.H. Elliott, *A Home for the Homeless: A Sociological Exegesis of 1 Peter, Its Situation and Strategy* (Philadelphia: Fortress, 1981) 234-36; and W.J. Dalton, *Christ's Proclamation to the Spirits: A Study of 1 Peter 3:18-4:6* (Rome: Biblical Institute, 1965) 62-71.

[38]Most recently see T.P. Osborne, "Guide Lines for Christian Suffering: A Source-Critical and Theological Study of 1 Peter 2, 21-25," *Bib* 64 (1983) 381-408.

maintains that Christians are being persecuted or harassed because they are Christians.

Earlier scholars interpreted these data as referring to persecution and proposed three dates: the time of the Trajan-Pliny correspondence (c. 112), that of Domitian's reign (81-96), or that of Nero's administration (54-68). There are, serious objections to all three. First, Nero's persecution is too early and was limited to Rome; secondly, there is no reference to the emperor cult in 1 Peter as there is in the Book of Revelation (on the contrary see 1 Pet. 2:17); and lastly, the late, legal prosecution during Trajan's reign is ruled out. Besides, if 1 Peter were dated to the second century, one would expect a more developed structure for the Christian communities, some indication of the delay of the parousia, and a different reaction vis-à-vis Roman society.

Because 1 Peter manifests a positive attitude towards Roman culture and society, we suggest that it was written earlier than the Book of Revelation (negative reference to Babylon and the theme of emperor cult), probably earlier than Hebrews (where "public abuse and affliction" are an accepted fact of Christian existence), and about the time of Luke-Acts (c. 80-90). The correlation between 1 Peter and Luke-Acts has many facets: similar positive attitudes toward Roman culture, optimism vis-à-vis secular culture, many common motifs, fondness for the Greek Old Testament, and appeal to the Jesus tradition as an "imitatio Christi." The years of persecution have arrived neither for Luke nor for 1 Peter who both believe that some *modus vivendi* can be worked out with the Roman populace. The two authors opt for different solutions to the problems which their communities or audiences face. Thus, 1 Peter focuses on Christian suffering, not as a result of persecution but because of hostility, harassment, and social unofficial ostracism on the part of the general public.[39]

USE OF THE CHRISTOLOGICAL HYMN TRADITION

It is clear that the author employed early hymnic material in composing the letter. Relying on past attempts to isolate this material, employing literary criteria, and conscious of hymnic motifs we detect fragments in 1:20 and 3:18, for both passages are anaphoric in style, that

---

[39]See D.J. Harrington's interesting essay, "The Church as a Minority Group," 81-94 in *God's People in Christ,* which treats 1 Peter, Hebrews, and Revelation from such a vantage point.

is, each consists of two participial phrases which have Jesus as antecedent.

1:20	destined from the foundation of the world manifested at the end of the times
3:18	put to death in the flesh made alive in the spirit.

While it would be tempting to see a continuation of the hymn in 1:21 (we find there two participial phrases), it is obvious that the pattern is broken, since the phrases no longer modify Christ but God as agent. Besides, the content of 1:21 is similar to that of 3:18, following which we find several likely hymnic candidates:

3:19*	having gone to the spirits in prison
3:22	who is at the right hand of God having gone to heaven where angels and authorities and powers are subject to him.

V. 19, while betraying the author's literary activity, nonetheless with slight modification (indicated by an asterisk) falls into the hymnic pattern. After discussing the theme of the imprisoned spirits, the author in v. 22, as a commentary on the phrase "through the resurrection of Jesus Christ," develops the post-resurrection activity of Christ. The whole verse deals with the hymnic themes of enthronement, ascension to the heavenly realm, and subjection of the cosmic powers and even retains the original anaphoric style in 22b. We conclude that there is a significant amount of hymnic material in 1 Peter but owing to the author's extensive redaction there is little hope of reconstructing the original hymn(s).

Having isolated these liturgical fragments, we must inquire about the hymnic pattern presumed by 1 Peter, since both the pattern of its christological vision and the basis of its soteriological exposition are taken from this tradition. Six elements are discernible from the fragments discussed: 1) destined, 2) manifested, 3) suffering/death, 4) resurrection/alive in the spirit, 5) cosmic domination, and 6) glory/right hand. Some have proposed in the past that the pattern indicated by these elements corresponds to a pre-existence christology with "destined" and "manifested" signifying pre-existence and incarnation. Instead, the hymnic material and the author's own thinking reflect a lower, exaltation christology. The terms "destined" and "manifested" express an apocalyptic rather than an incarnational perspective. The author shows no interest in pre-existence but much preoccupation with the divine plan. "Destined or foreknowledge" marks the beginning (pretemporal) and "manifested" the final period of God's plan.[40] These two terms are employed by 1 Peter to set up the eschatological framework both of the Christ-event and of the believer's life in the world.

CHRISTOLOGY-RANSOM
AND IMAGE OF SUFFERING AND GLORY

All six elements noted above play a part in the composition of 1 Peter, though some are more central. Acquainted with the binary kerygmatic pattern of death and resurrection (3:18b), the author nonetheless chooses, as the basis for the document's overall structural schema, to emphasize two moments within the traditional christological pattern: suffering/death and glory/right hand.

In 1 Peter Jesus is the image of suffering and glory. The author opts for the term "suffering" for the first part of the pattern because of the situation of the audience and associates with that theme several related concepts: blood of Christ, ransom, passion, death. The Christ-event is put at the service of the author's needs. Wishing to discuss suffering, not death or the life of Jesus, the author focuses on that element of the Jesus tradition.

The second element of the pattern is also chosen with theological intent. The author could have stressed the theme of resurrection, as does Paul in 1 Cor. 15 to establish a foundation for Christian hope, but instead chooses to develop the theme of glory (*doxa*). A review of the texts where this term appears shows that it refers either to the glory which God has given Jesus or that which the believer will share when Jesus returns at the final revelation. The term glory then is chosen to emphasize the heavenly or post-resurrection life of Jesus and its bearing on the Christian's life as a sojourner.

We offer, therefore, the following schematic analysis of 1 Peter's christology:

---

[40]Dunn, *Christology in the Making,* 237-38.

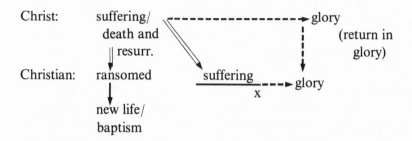

It is the kerygmatic formula which serves as the basis of 1 Peter's christology. The first part of the document (1:3-2:10) emphasizes the death and resurrection as the basis of new life ("born anew," "obedient children," and "newborn babes," 1:3, 14; 2:2). Humanity has been ransomed by Jesus' blood (1:18-19; the author returns often to the soteriological function of Jesus' death) and has been given hope through the resurrection (1:21). Jesus' death and resurrection establish the Christian community as God's chosen people (2:4-5, 9).

Having established a doctrinal basis for exhortation the author develops the letter's major thesis: Jesus is the Christian's model of suffering and glory, for between these two poles, the suffering which has ransomed the Christian and the establishment in glory which is a future reality for the believer, lies an interim period of crucial importance to author and audience. The patient suffering of believers has God's approval, for "to this you have been called, because Christ also suffered for you, leaving you an example [hypogrammos], that you might follow in his steps" (2:21).[41] Through Christ we have been ransomed (1:18); we are dead to sin (2:24), healed by his wounds (2:24), under his guardianship (2:25), have been constituted a house, priesthood, people of God, all realities which have a direct bearing on the present Christian situation.

Christ's passage in time has not simply achieved a series of given results (soteriological data) but has constituted a framework (see diagram) for the believer's vision of life: suffering which is teleologically conditioned by glory or salvation (3:18). In view of the audience's situation and as compositional strategy, the author employs the term

---

[41]For extended commentaries on 2:21 consult Osborne, "Guide Lines for Christian Suffering," 389-93 and J.H. Elliott, "Backward and Forward 'In His Steps': Following Jesus from Rome to Raymond and Beyond. The Tradition, Redaction, and Reception of 1 Peter 2:18-25," 184-209 in Segovia, *Discipleship in the New Testament*.

"suffering" (rather than "death"), a term which characterizes the pain, abuse, and ostracization that Christians as a minority group suffer in a pagan society. This suffering makes sense in light of the author's christological model, for imitation of Christ means obedience to the plan of God (1:2, 14, 22), the testing of one's faith (fire terminology), love of friend/brother and foe (1:22; 3:8 and 2:12; 3:6), responsible living within a society that must be subjected to God on the day of visitation (2:12),[42] and gentle, rational, and evangelistic confrontation with non-Christian neighbors (2:9; 3:15, 19, 22).

While the term glory (*doxa*) in the majority of cases refers to Christ's heavenly enthronement or the future participation in this by the believer, it is important to emphasize that for 1 Peter the future reality of glory is so crucial and dynamic that it impinges on the interim period. Thus, the spirit of glory rests now upon the believer (4:14) who in anticipation is to rejoice with unutterable and glorious joy (1:8) that God may be glorified through Jesus Christ (4:11). This is the reason for the author's emphasis on Christ's glory, for not only is it a goal which gives hope (the resurrection theme would have sufficed) but it is the goal of all beings to be glorified at the final revelation. When the period of exile is terminated the inheritance of the obedient will be revealed as the Chief Shepherd returns with the crown of glory (5:4) to which God has called the believer (5:10).

The Jesus tradition, drawn especially from early hymnic materials, has here been put at the service of an early Christian community's situation within Roman society. Fully aware of the challenge which confronted the Christians of Asia Minor the author of 1 Peter drew on the Christian community's treasured wisdom about Jesus to present them a model or example that they "might follow in his steps."

Jude

The short letter of Jude is treated before 2 Peter because the latter has borrowed heavily from it in composing its second chapter (see below). This document has been a controversial one from the beginning for

---

[42]See First Peter's use of the domestic code (2:11-3:12) to discuss the believer's life in the world and especially its judicious use of the "servants" section as context for discussing the Christ-event as pattern for Christian life (2:18-25).

several reasons. First, it is an extremely polemical document whose method of presentation is one of condemnation rather than argumentation. Secondly, it makes undisguised use of apocryphal books as though they form part of the Jewish scriptural canon, and thirdly, Jude, as Martin Luther noted five centuries ago, is not particularly concerned about the Jesus tradition. Modern scholarship, however, requires us to take a closer look at this forgotten book. Therefore, after a brief introduction to the document, we will examine the author's presentation of Jesus.

COMPOSITION AND CONTENT

Jude is another pseudonymous work. Its style and language are those of a Hellenist and its appeal to the Old Testament and to Jewish apocryphal works in their Greek form point to a Jewish writer of the Diaspora. A clear distinction is made between the author and audience on the one hand and the first generation of Christians on the other (v. 17). Besides, the letter addresses heretical tendencies of a later period. We propose then that Jude, in the greeting of the document, appeals to the successful pseudonymous letter of James to muster authority in a critical battle against errant teachers within the communities. "Faith," for this author as for several other late NT writers, refers to content or true doctrine, a deposit which requires defense (v. 3).

Jude has only the outward appearance of a letter: a standard greeting, a body, and a liturgical conclusion. Its audience is rather general and its treatment of the false teachers lacks specifics. Thus, many describe it as a polemical tract to which the author has given epistolarly features. Its contents, found within vv. 4-23, present an interesting alternating pattern. V. 4 introduces the false teachers and their heresy, while vv. 5-7 give three groups which, owing to their evil deeds, underwent divine punishment: the desert generation of Israelites, the fallen angels, and the cities Sodom and Gomorrah. The author then addresses the teachings of the opponents (8), but again focuses on the example of the fallen angels to stress the divine nature of the condemnation (9). A third time the author treats the opponents' activity (10) and concludes with three examples of evildoers: Cain, Balaam, and Korah (11). In vv. 12-13 the activity of the teachers is again discussed, only to be excoriated by means of a citation from the book of Enoch (14-15). V. 16 dwells again on the evil teachers who are condemned by the words of the apostles (17-18). In v. 19, after speaking a last time about the opponents in the community, the author in vv. 20-23 advises the audience on proper conduct vis-à-vis the intruders.[43] These teachers are usually described as proto-Gnostic outsiders, for "even if an exact description of [them] is not possible, still the basic outline of their views is clear: Christological heresy and libertine ethics."[44]

THEOLOGY, CHRISTOLOGY, AND THE APOCALYPTIC CHARACTER OF JUDE

The author's theology and christology merit closer attention. The letter centers on divine activity, for it is God who judges and punishes. All the examples given by the author of the punishment which is to befall the false teachers have God as subject. The same one who saved the people from Egypt[45] also punished the unbelievers of the desert generation (5). It is God who keeps the fallen angels in chains (6). It is also the Lord God not Michael the agent who punishes (9). In the citation from the book of Enoch, it is clearly God ("the Lord") who "executes judgment on all" (15). The author uses the divine passive (use of the passive with God understood as agent) in vv. 10 ("they are destroyed") and 13 ("for whom ... darkness has been reserved"). Even impersonal constructions in vv. 7 and 11 indicate divine activity in meting out punishment. Further, the author is concerned with the divine plan: God is the one who calls and has once and for all "delivered" faith to the saints (1, 3; both divine passives) and guards the elect for the return of the "Son" (1, 24).

The author's treatment of Jesus is of interest, for he is presented as the returning Lord at the end-time. The beloved are kept by God for Jesus (1); the beloved, while abiding in the love of God, are to "wait for the mercy of our Lord Jesus Christ unto eternal life" (21). While the document insists on the lordship of Jesus (7, 21, 25) and notes his soteriological role (25), it is his apocalyptic function which is central to the author's purpose.

[43]Bauckham, *Jude, 2 Peter,* 4, considers the entire letter "as background to the appeal (vv 20-23), which is Jude's main purpose in writing."

[44]Lohse, *The Formation of the New Testament,* 215; see also Bauckham, *Jude, 2 Peter,* 11-13.

[45]Internal logic and textual considerations point to a theological rather than a christological solution to the textual problem of v. 5. The conjecture of F.J. A. Hart of an original *ho* as subject for v. 5 makes the most sense here; see B.M. Metzger, *A Textual Commentary on the Greek New Testament* (London: United Bible Society, 1971) 726.

This last point leads us to inquire about the literary character of Jude and, in this context, to discuss its image of Jesus. In an effort to combat the false teachers in the community the author borrows from apocalyptic tradition. The community is seen as a self-contained entity that is being secretly invaded from the outside (4) and whose unity is being disrupted by the intruders (19). The treatment of the false teachers is situated in an eschatological context, for they are said to be the scoffers of the end-days predicted by the apostles of Jesus (17-18). The author draws upon apocalyptic texts, Enoch and the Assumption of Moses (4, 6, 7, 9, 12, 14-15), to present suitable models for the impending judgment of the opponents. The fallen angels, the devil, Michael the archangel, the people of Sodom and Gomorrah are familiar characters in apocalyptic stories. The punishment meted out to them involves eternal fire and chains. The teachers rebel against the laws of God, like Cain, Balaam, and Korah (11). They are accused of denying the lordship of God (4), of rejecting divine authority as well as that of the heavenly powers (8b).[46] Their activity is compared to all manner of apocalyptic abomination: perversion, licentiousness (4, 12, 16), rebellion against God and divine agents (4c, 8), animalistic behavior (10, 16), and ecological and cosmic phenomena (12-13).[47] Jude, therefore, has employed an apocalyptic schema to present the activity of the heretical opponents as the satanic activity of the end-days. God the Father, who has chosen a people, keeps them and protects them until the coming of Jesus in glory. In the meantime, "the beloved of God" (1:1) must build upon the deposit of faith, pray in the Spirit, abide in the love of God, and await the mercy of the returning Lord Jesus (20-21). They must also extend a "discerning," helping hand to the errant (22-23).

Jude, if read as strict polemics, may rank as the most negative book of the New Testament, but, if understood in light of the author's apocalyptic strategem (as a last resort),[48] may offer a stern rebuke of atheistic doctrine and immoral behavior within the community as it attempts to

---

[46]V. 4 refers to the lordship of God not of Jesus (see RSV footnote), while v. 8 probably alludes to divine authority and the heavenly powers. More generally, it should be noted that Jude has a low christology; see verses 1, 4, 21, and especially 25 and contrast these with 2 Pet 1:1; 2:1; 3:18. Also see n. 59 below.

[47]These are frequent themes in intertestamental apocalyptic texts; see G. Krodel, "The Letter of Jude," 96-98 in *Hebrews, James, 1 and 2 Peter, Jude, Revelation.*

[48]*Ibid.*, 95.

remain faithful to its tradition, that is, as it "contend[s] for the faith which was once for all delivered to the saints" (3).

Second Peter

The last book of the New Testament to have been written was 2 Peter, a document whose tone and content are similar to the Letter of Jude. These two documents vie for the honor of having the worst reception among Christian readers. In the light of modern scholarship, however, 2 Peter deserves a more serious and sympathetic reading. Thus, we will study its relation to Jude, seek its raison d'être, and then examine its portrait of Jesus.

JUDE AND SECOND PETER

Even a cursory reading of these two documents reveals that there is a literary relation between the two. It is generally agreed that 2 Peter borrowed from Jude and not the other way around; the editorial process strongly supports such a conclusion. It is estimated that 18 or 19 of the 25 verses of Jude have either been appropriated by the author of 2 Peter or have offered significant terms or ideas to that writer. While 2 Peter chapters 1 and 3 reveal some dependence on Jude, it is especially the relation of chapter 2 to Jude 4f which is the clearest. In effect, 2 Peter 2:1-18 is an undisguised rewriting of Jude 4-16. The order of the material is unmistakenly dependent on the latter:

Jude		2 Peter 2		Jude		2 Peter 2	
4	=	1-2		11a	=	13a	
5	=	3	edited/Egypt	11b	=	14-16	Balaam
6	=	4		12a	=	13b	
–	=	5	Noah	12b	=	17a	
7	=	6		12c		–	
–	=	7-9	Lot	13a		–	
8	=	10		13b	=	17b	
9	=	11	edited/Michael	14-15		–	Enoch citation
10	=	12		16	=	18	

It is obvious from the above that the author of 2 Peter found Jude congenial, borrowed heavily, and, in a manner reminiscent of Matthew and Luke's use of Mark, reordered, added to, omitted from, and freely rewrote the main part of Jude to compose chapter 2 of this new document. Like Jude, the author of 2 Peter was interested in combatting heretical teachers within the Christian communities and found that text amenable to such a goal.

Finding the apocryphal material of the source embarrassing or distasteful, the author modifies greatly the text of Jude. Verses such as Jude 14-15 containing a citation from Enoch and phrases in vv. 4 and 13 (about an extraterrestrial book of destiny[49] or "wandering stars") are omitted. Terminology is toned down; for example an account about sexual relations with angels in Jude 6 and 7 is rendered rather vaguely in 2 Pet. 2:4 and 6 (see also Jude 12 and 16 for other examples). In other instances the source undergoes major changes as in v. 9 concerning Michael the archangel and the devil fighting over Moses' body or in v. 11 regarding Cain, Balaam, and Korah. Only the example of Balaam is retained and expanded in 2 Pet. 2:15-16. In this editorial process the author of 2 Peter manifests a love for abstract terminology (Jude 7: "acted immorally and indulged in unnatural lust"[50] becomes "were . . . ungodly" in 2 Pet. 2:6 or Jude 8: "defile the flesh" becomes "the lust of defiling passion" in 2:10) and a fondness for OT examples not only to condemn the false teachers but also to defend the activity of true teachers (Noah, Lot, and Balaam in 2:5, 7-9, and 15-16). Finally, in relation to the editorial process, it should be noted that the author of 2 Peter, while omitting the example of the desert generation of Jude 5, nonetheless retains the idea of the destruction of unbelievers and sets up the program for the entire chapter: "false prophets also arose among the *people,* just as there will be false teachers among you . . . bringing upon themselves swift *destruction*" (2:1, *italicized* terms are borrowed from Jude 5). The author proceeds in the rest of the chapter to draw parallels between past examples and the present heretics.

PURPOSE, COMPOSITION, AND CHRISTOLOGY OF SECOND PETER

The author of this document, possibly influenced by the group

---

[49]The RSV translates as "long ago . . . designated."

[50]Literally: "having given themselves to fornication and having sought after other flesh"(angels); more generally on the language of 2 Peter, see Bauckham, *Jude, 2 Peter,* 135-38.

responsible for 1 Peter, draws on the reputation of the apostle to establish a new message to troubled Christian communities. While the first document had simply appealed to the apostleship of Peter (1 Pet 1:1) and made brief reference to venerable members of the group (5:12-13), the second takes pains to underscore the Petrine tradition out of which its author writes or pretends to write. The author claims the titles of "servant" and "apostle," titles borrowed from Jude and 1 Peter. The document also stresses the Petrine tradition and strives for authenticity by employing both the apostle's Semitic and Hellenistic names: "Simon Peter" (1:1). Later in the chapter two scenes from the Jesus tradition in which the apostle Peter participated are evoked, namely, the foretelling of his death (1:13-15; see John 21:18-19) and the transfiguration (1:16-18; see Mark 9:2-8). In 3:1 the author makes explicit reference to 1 Peter: "this is now the second letter that I have written to you." And finally, at the end of the letter the author refers to "our beloved brother Paul" (3:15; post-NT traditions also associate Peter and Paul).

> "Unlike 1 Peter, the author of this letter will repeatedly stress the unique authority of Peter as a privileged and authentic witness to Jesus. One reason for this emphasis on authority is the very purpose of 2 Peter which is to oppose false teachers in the community."[51]

Study of 2 Peter's genre and structure also help to clarify its purpose. The farewell-discourse genre serves as the setting for the author's message.[52] This genre has a rather long history in the biblical world, since it was customary for stories of great figures to terminate with such a discourse: Jacob (Gen 48-49), Moses (Deut 32-33), Joshua (Josh 22-24), and David (1 Chron 28-29). Tobit is also given such a discourse (Tob 14), as are Rebecca and Isaac in the intertestamental book of Jubilees (35-36). The Testaments of the Twelve Patriarchs are full-blown farewell discourses. The New Testament provides several examples; Jesus is given a farewell discourse in Mark 13 and parallels and several such discourses in John 13-17, while Paul makes a farewell speech in Acts 20. The genre offers several important features: imminent death or departure of the speaker, sorrowful reaction and consequent

---

[51]Senior, *1 & 2 Peter*, 105.
[52]Bauckham, *Jude, 2 Peter*, 131-35.

reassurance of audience, recitation of personal or national history and deeds, the warning against deception, and the giving of advice. When in the first chapter the impending death of Peter, the alleged author, is stressed (1:13-14), reassurance is immediately provided: "and I will see to it that after my departure you may be able at any time to recall these things" (v. 15).[53] 2 Peter more than any other pseudonymous NT writing, except perhaps 2 Timothy, takes pains to tell the story of its alleged writer. The author stresses God's benevolence for those destined to "become partakers of the divine nature" (1:3-4; see also 3:5f, 9), yet warnings against deception and false teachers permeate the letter (1:4, 16; 2:1f; 3:3f, 16). In fact the document ends with such a warning: "beware lest you be carried away with the error of lawless men and lose your own stability" (3:17). Finally, the letter gives advice to its audience as regards false teachings and has recourse to the standard farewell advice of loving one another (1:7) and of keeping God's commandments (2:21; 3:2).

Also important for our purpose is appreciating the use which the author makes of that genre, in attempting to defend true Christian prophecy against the proliferation of false teachings. Peter's name and credentials are put forward to anchor the author's teaching, for Peter was an eyewitness that Jesus is the beloved Son and therefore the guarantor of the prophetic word (1:19). Thus, the term "remember or remind" (1:12, 13, 15; 3:1, 2) is frequently employed as the author insists on the content of true Christian prophecy (1:10, 19-21; 2:16; 3:2) or knowledge and wisdom. In fact this deposit of belief (1:1) is classified as scripture which results from the guidance of the Holy Spirit (1:21). This too, along with the apologetic use of the transfiguration story (1:16-18) "as a prophecy of the parousia,"[54] forms part of the author's strategy.

In chapter 2 the author, in apocalyptic terms borrowed from Jude, terms very much in keeping with some farewell discourses (see especially Mark 13), takes the community's opponents to task. Apocalyptic judgment will be their reward as it was for figures of the past who violated God's prophecy. There is hope, however, for even Balaam was ineffective when God employed "a dumb ass ... [to] restrain the

[53]A.B. Kolenkow, "The Genre Testament and Forecasts of the Future in the Hellenistic Jewish Milieu," *JSJ* 6 (1975) 57-71.

[54]J.H. Neyrey, "The Apologetic Use of the Transfiguration in 2 Peter 1:16-21," *CBQ* 42 (1980) 504-19; citation from p. 519.

prophet's madness" (2:16). The false teachers' mocking denial of the parousia merits the Lord's condemnation (1:16-19), for according to his promise there will be "new heavens and a new earth in which righteousness dwells" (3:13). Christian prophecy, therefore, is not the object of one's whims (1:20) but must be subject to authentic community tradition which is under the guidance of the Holy Spirit (1:21). The letter and its strategy, therefore, reveal an acute episode in the quest for authority in the midst of structural and doctrinal strife. If the author of 2 Peter shows considerable knowledge of biblical traditions (both Jewish and Christian)[55] and is at home in pagan culture,[56] it is nonetheless the letter's strategy which dominates the composition and gains the reader's attention. Additionally, it is this perspective which dictates the role christology plays in the document.

Thus, we are led to inquire about the nature of the heresy under scrutiny. We would have to agree that

> the central theme of their teaching was eschatological skepticism. The Parousia of Jesus Christ had been expected during the lifetime of the apostles, but the first Christian generation had now passed away, and in the view of the false teachers this proved the primitive Christian eschatological expectation to have been wholly mistaken (3:4, 9a). There would be no eschatological judgment (2:3b), no divine intervention to eliminate evil and establish a world of righteousness.[57]

The author borrowed from biblical tradition and Stoic philosophy to defend early Christian eschatology against disillusionment ("delayed parousia and denied judgment") and Epicurean pessimism (denial of providence).[58]

---

[55]On the one hand, the author borrows many Jewish references from Jude but goes far beyond in modifying, developing, and adding to these. On the other, 2 Peter seems to presuppose 1 Peter (3:1), James, some form of Jesus traditions (perhaps Mark), and certainly Jude; for both confer Bauckham, *Jude, 2 Peter,* 138-51.

[56]Even the Jewish stories of Noah, the fallen angels, and creation seem to be related to the Classical narratives of Deucalion and the flood story and the casting of the Titans into the underworld (Tartarus, 2:4) or Stoic cosmology and its version of the destruction and re-creation of the cosmos (3:10-13).

[57]Bauckham, *Jude, 2 Peter,* 154.

[58]J.H. Neyrey, "The Form and Background of the Polemic in 2 Peter," *JBL* 99 (1980) 407-31.

Finally, in examining further this author's presentation of Jesus, it is necessary to remember that polemics against the false teachers' denial of the parousia not christology is the principal objective of the letter. The author is acquainted with various elements of the Jesus tradition, e.g., the transfiguration story, the foretelling of Peter's death, the coming of the Lord's day like a thief, the saying about the last state being worse than the first. The letter also refers to Jesus' soteriological role, for the title "Savior" is frequently used. One should note the expression: "the Master who bought them" (2:1) and consider Jesus' relationship to the believer (i.e., "knowledge of," 1:2, 8; 2:20; 3:18). 2 Peter inherited Jesus' apocalyptic role from Jude (e.g., 1:11 about the kingdom of Jesus and 1:16 about his "power and coming") but modifies this to underscore the theological base of the apocalyptic schema.

A strong case can be made that 2 Peter has a high christology. Jesus on four occasions is given the title of "Savior." In 2:1 the author intentionally modifies the text of Jude 4 where the opponents are accused of "denying the only Master and our Lord Jesus Christ"[59] to "even denying the Master who bought them" (2:1). Only in 2 Peter is the divine title "Master" used unambiguously of Jesus. Further, the author's use of the transfiguration story (1:17) seems, in this Hellenistic setting, to insist on the special sonship of Jesus; only here, in 2 Peter, is God called "Father." Also, one must read 1:1 as "our God and Savior Jesus Christ" (as does the RSV) rather than the possible, alternate translation "our God and the Savior Jesus Christ." This is supported by the author's love for double titles for Jesus (1:11; 2:20; 3:18). Only 2 Peter has the phrase "the eternal kingdom of our Lord and Savior Jesus Christ" (1:11).[60] The portrait which 2 Peter gives of Jesus, therefore, shows clear signs of development toward a higher christology wherein the role of Christ rather than that of God receives increasing emphasis[61] and divine titles and attributes are freely conferred upon God's Son (1:17).

---

[59]The low christology of Jude seems to rule out the "possible" reading "our Master and Lord, Jesus Christ" (see RSV).

[60]Two other NT usages are considerably different: Eph 5:5 ("the kingdom of Christ and of God") and Rev 11:15 ("the kingdom of our Lord and of his Christ").

[61]Despite Neyrey's insistence ("Form and Background of the Polemic in 2 Peter," 430) that the argument of 2 Peter is "*theo*logical" rather than christological.

11

Christian Apocalyptic Thought and the Book of Revelation

This survey of NT literature has revealed much variety of literary genre and theological perspective. Both factors are due to the great diversity of early Christian communities and the Greco-Roman environments in which they thrived. The apparently unique community which produced the Book of Revelation was far from singular in its outlook. Long before the advent of the Jesus movement within Judaism a strand of thought had developed which is best described as apocalyptic. This theological perspective is the subject of this chapter since it is one of the major components for our understanding of Christian beginnings, since it permeates all facets of the New Testament, and since it is central to our analysis of the final book of this Christian anthology. We begin by delving into the origins and Jewish background of apocalyptic, for this is one more instance of the great debt which the Jesus movement owes to Judaism.

Origins and Jewish Character of Apocalypticism

In sections of the Old Testament and often in the New one encounters a distinctive cluster of themes and theological characteristics: dualism (good and evil, light and darkness, heaven and earth), historical pessimism or transcendentalism, personal and universal eschatology, claims of revelation (through visions, heavenly visitation, or disclosure of mysteries), cosmic and supernatural conflicts and battles, judgment, day of the Lord, prominence of the Son of Man, frequent reference to the two ages or aeons, speculation concerning the origin of evil, reward and punishment, and hope in the future. These ideas are common in passages of the exilic and post-exilic prophets, in the Book of Daniel, in intertestamental literature, in the Synoptic tradition (especially Mark 13 and parallels), and in other NT works, particularly the Book of Revelation. Even the thought of Paul is virtually incomprehensible without some understanding of the basic themes of apocalyptic. Further, the teaching of Jesus and of most early Christian missionaries was couched in eschatological imagery and inspired by apocalyptic considerations.

To comprehend the apocalyptic mentality which produced the Book of Revelation it is necessary to situate this theological perspective within its Jewish milieu.[1] From the beginning it is necessary to distinguish between an apocalyptic mentality or worldview and a literary genre often produced by people who held such views. The first had its origins in the exilic period and the latter first appears during the Hellenistic age (1 Enoch).

Traditionally, apocalyptic thought is explained as a development of prophetic themes and concerns. Indeed the relation of the former to the latter confirms this, even if as recent scholarship insists, the prophetic component was not the only one. In pre-exilic Israelite society the role of the prophet was enhanced as it evolved in relation to royal and priestly ideologies. While these three components of Israelite society had parallels in neighboring Near Eastern cultures, it was the prophetic which developed the eschatological component endemic to the mythology of the fertile crescent. The prophet reminded the believer that God intervened in human history and that the divine plan for humanity was to be worked out in history. Increasingly as Israelite policy turned to political intrigue and as Canaanite beliefs and cult competed with covenantal Yahweh worship, prophetic eschatology came to the fore. Oracles of doom and judgment, the day of the Lord, and the call to repentance were the hallmark of the pre-exilic prophets as they sensed

---

[1]For a short but incisive introduction to the ideas which follow, see P.D. Hanson, "Apocalypse, Genre," and "Apocalypticism," 27-34 in *IDBSup;* J.J. Collins, "Excursus on the Apocalyptic Genre," 130-45 in *Daniel, 1-2 Maccabees* (Wilmington: Glazier, 1981); and P. Vielhauer, "Apocalypses and Related Subjects: Introduction," 2:581-607 in E. Hennecke and W. Schneemelcher, *New Testament Apocrypha* (Philadelphia: Westminster, 1963-65).

the approaching disaster from the North.

Not once but three times the Mesopotamian armies struck devastating blows to the Hebrew kingdoms of Palestine, first with the annihilation of the northern kingdom of Israel and then, in successive campaigns of destruction and deportation, the leveling of the Judaean countryside and capital. The trauma of the fall of Judah and of the exilic experience, however, was a creative period in Jewish thought and literature. The years in the Babylonian environs saw a ferment of activity as Jewish historians (the Deuteronomic school), priests (initial compilation of Pentateuchal traditions), and prophetic schools (collections of prophetic oracles and lore) preserved Jewish traditions by applying them to the new and uncertain status of the exiled people of Judah. It is particularly in the writings of Ezekiel, of the anonymous prophet called second Isaiah (chaps. 40-55), and, to a lesser extent, those of Jeremiah that we perceive a shift in eschatological perspective. The imagery becomes more mythological and the outlook more cosmic, as a result of historical and institutional disruption.

> The full force of the alienation resulting from the disintegration of the pre-exilic social system and its supporting symbolic universe was experienced by Second Isaiah, in whose writings we witness an early, vivid expression of apocalyptic eschatology (*passim*). The bold application of myth (e.g., 51:9-11) led to a full description of the cosmic drama of salvation and introduced the heaven/earth and the past aeon/future aeon dichotomies (43:18-19) which became central to later apocalyptic subuniverses. Nevertheless, the integration of the cosmic vision into historical realities was kept alive by Second Isaiah's optimistic sense of nationhood (45:1-7).[2]

The last sentence underscores one of the major differences between apocalyptic eschatology and fully developed apocalypticism. Second Isaiah, despite political and social upheaval, did not succumb to historical pessimism. So, many passages of this author are described as proto-apocalyptic. Similar observations can be made about Ezekiel, particularly concerning his reform and restoration program (chaps.

[2]Hanson, "Apocalypticism," 32.

40-48).[3] The peculiar trait of these exilic prophets was the stress on newness: new exodus, new temple, new life, new covenant, new creation. These new emphases were a reinterpretation of old Israelite themes now projected into the future and seen from a more universal perspective.

The period following the exile, referred to as the restoration, saw the continued flowering of apocalypse-like literature. Though in the form of prophetic oracles the writings of this period took on many of the major characteristics of full-blown apocalyptic literature: cosmic disruption and victory, universal salvation, new heaven and earth, and heavenly banquets. With J.J. Collins, we insist first that "all these writings [Zechariah, Joel, Ezekiel 38-39, Isaiah 24-27, and Trito-Isaiah] must still be categorized formally as prophetic oracles, not as apocalypses, since they lack the apocalyptic manner of revelation, i.e., with an otherworldly mediator" and secondly that we have in these "the reflection of an early form of Jewish apocalypticism."[4]

While one might venture into the intricacies of post-exilic politics and social alienation to elucidate the apocalyptic movements of the late sixth and fifth centuries which produced these writings,[5] it is to those of the early Hellenistic era, which led to the composition of the oldest apocalypses, and to those of the Maccabean period, which generated the Book of Daniel and other documents, that we now turn our attention. Several pre-Maccabean apocalypses have been isolated in the important Jewish composition 1 Enoch, namely the Book of Watchers (1-36), the Book of the Heavenly Luminaries (72-82), and the Apocalypse of Weeks (91 and 93). For the first time all the requisite elements of the genre "apocalypse" are found:

> revelatory literature with a narrative framework, in which a revelation is mediated by an otherworldly being to a human recipient, disclosing a transcendent reality which is both temporal, insofar as it envisages

---

[3]J.D. Levenson, *Theology of the Program of Restoration of Ezekiel 40-48* (Missoula; Scholars, 1976) and S. Nidtch, "Ezekiel 40-48 in a Visionary Context," *CBQ* 48 (1986) 208-24.

[4]"The Jewish Apocalypses," 29 in J.J. Collins, ed., *Apocalypse: The Morphology of a Genre* (Missoula: Scholars, 1979).

[5]Hanson, "Apocalypticism," 32-33, posits two apocalyptic movements, one involving the prophets Haggai and Zechariah and a later one opposing the Zadokite leaders, to account for the popularity of apocalyptic writings during the late sixth and fifth centuries when the Persians were in power in Palestine.

eschatological salvation, and spatial insofar as it involves another, supernatural world.[6]

These compositions established a flexible pattern for revelatory literature which persisted for the next four or five centuries. In this genre the seer or human recipient receives the revelation in visions or during a heavenly journey. The content of the revelation expresses a pessimistic view of earthly reality and looks to a future existence in an idealized, otherworldly realm. The early part of 1 Enoch (1-36) makes for interesting but intriguing reading, since its portrayal of widespread violence, introduction of weapons of war, and general corruption of humanity by the fallen angels are variously interpreted. The Watchers are identified either as the divinized kings of the Hellenistic era or as the Hellenizing priesthood of the pre-Maccabean period. Unfortunately for us, the texts nowhere provide unambiguous clues to the historical and social milieu which resulted in these novel writings.[7]

A clearer picture of historical and social conditions begins to emerge about the time of the Maccabean revolt. As a result of the intense Hellenization program of the Seleucid ruler Antiochus IV Epiphanes, the stage was set for an equally intense resistance on the part of Jewish traditionalists. The catalyst for the Jewish victory and independence was the family of Mattathias, whose exploits and ideals received different degrees of support from writings such as First and Second Maccabees, the section of 1 Enoch called the Animal Apocalypse (85-90), and the Book of Daniel, the last of which requires further attention. After a long narrative section, consisting of older court-tales

---

[6]J.J. Collins, "Introduction: Towards the Morphology of a Genre," 9 in Collins, *Apocalypse.*

[7]Collins, "Excursus on the Apocalyptic Genre," 132-39, concludes his analysis of 1 Enoch 1-36: ". . . unlike Daniel, the Book of Watchers provides no hint of the historical events underlying the text. We may safely say that the story presupposes some kind of crisis. The violence and general disruption of the story was, at least most readily applicable to a situation where there was some disturbance. 1 Enoch, however, does not describe that disturbance with any specific detail. As it now stands the story of the Watchers could have been applied to any of a wide range of historical incidents. Moreover, because of its lack of explicit references, the story could be applied over and over again long after the original situation passed" (134). More generally see M. Stone, "New Light on the Third Century" and "Enoch and Apocalyptic Origins" in *Scriptures, Sects, and Visions: A Profile of Judaism from Ezra to the Jewish Revolt* (Philadelphia; Fortress, 1980), 27-35 and 37-47.

(1-6), we find in Daniel 7-12 a series of eschatological visions where historical and cosmological revelation is mediated by angels. The author employs older narrative materials and borrows from the Enoch traditions to calm the anxieties of those less than sanguine about the Jewish armed resistance to Antiochus. In apocalyptic fashion the author constructs a symbolic world peopled by heavenly hosts to help the audience cope with the hopelessness of current events. Perseverance and hope are possible because the heavenly powers are on the side of the elect (Dan 10:10-21).

What results from a study of Daniel and its milieu is a clearer picture of an apocalyptic movement from the ranks of the early Hasidic supporters of the revolt, whose pessimistic vision of the world and its institutions necessitated a transcendental world of power and images, from which they derived hope and meaning. Subsequently, as a result of the roller-coaster history of the post-Maccabean period and the ensuing occurrences of political, social, and religious alienation (abundantly documented by Josephus), numerous apocalyptic movements emerged whose existence and enigmatic ideologies left traces in the pseudepigrapha (e.g., the Testaments of the Twelve Patriarchs, the Apocalypse of Zephaniah, the Book of Jubilees).[8]

The best known of these movements is that of the Essenes, whose library was recently discovered in caves at Khirbet Qumran on the NW shore of the Dead Sea. While they did not produce any apocalypses as such, their library was stocked with such literature and their own compositions exhibit a sectarian form of apocalypticism. The members had withdrawn into the desert as a pure remnant awaiting the final victory (note their composition "the Battle of the Children of Light against the Children of Darkness").

Finally, we note that Jewish apocalypses were written and apocalyptic movements existed well into the Christian era, as the social and political conditions of the Roman occupation of Palestine and other eastern areas grew worse. A critical event in the evolution of late apocalyptic thought was the fall of Jerusalem and the destruction of its temple (e.g., see Fourth Ezra, Second Baruch, the Apocalypse of Abraham).[9]

[8]See Charlesworth, *The Old Testament Pseudepigrapha* and Sparks, *The Apocryphal Old Testament* for translations of Jewish apocalyptic literature.

[9]See Collins, "Jewish Apocalypses," 21-59; A.J. Saldarini, "Apocalypses and 'Apocalyptic,' in Rabbinic Literature and Mysticism," 187-205 in Collins, *Apocalypse;*

Apocalyptic thought and ideology, therefore, were common, for throughout NT times within the spectrum of Jewish thinking a very pronounced liking for eschatology and even a tendency toward apocalypticism existed. Indeed when social and political circumstances became unduly oppressive, many looked to God for a mediator or for life in another world, thus eschatological tendencies frequently developed into an apocalyptic frame of mind.

This liking for eschatology was broader still, as frequent references to messianic claimants (Josephus, Acts 5, Mark 13) [10] and certain Pharisaic doctrine demonstrate. As is known, the latter defended a doctrine of angels, resurrection and afterlife, and a belief in a messiah. Since the Hasmonean period the concept of a Davidic or even a priestly messiah or both (as at Qumran) had become popular. While most pseudepigraphic writings do not contain specific references to a messianic figure, the first-century B.C. Psalms of Solomon (chap. 17) and three first-century A.D. apocalypses (Fourth Ezra, Second Baruch, and Similitudes of Enoch [1 Enoch 37-71]) describe the function of such a figure. [11] The Pharisees, because of their defense of an oral law along side the written Torah, were able to incorporate popular eschatological trends into their thinking. From the time of Hillel (30 B.C.-10 A.D.) when the Pharisees relinquished political activism for pastoral concerns, eschatological issues of the day became theirs as well. Besides the themes mentioned above, one increasingly hears about the coming kingdom of God and the two ages (the present evil age and the messianic era). [12]

M.E. Stone, "Reactions to Destructions of the Second Temple," *JSJ* 12 (1981) 195-204; and G.W.E. Nickelsburg, *Jewish Literature Between the Bible and the Mishnah* (Philadelphia: Fortress, 1981) 277-309.

[10] See P.A. Horsley, "Popular Messianic Movements around the Time of Jesus," *CBQ* 46 (1984) 471-95 and Horsley and Hanson, *Bandits, Prophets, and Messiahs.*

[11] Charlesworth, *Pseudepigrapha,* xxxi-xxxiii. On the dating of the "Similitudes," Collins, in "Jewish Apocalypses," 39, states: "Despite the recent attempt of Milik (1971, 1976) to attribute the Similtudes (1 Enoch 37-71) to a Christian of the second or third century CE, there can be little doubt that they are Jewish and early... It is very highly improbable that a Christian author would have identified Enoch with the Son of Man (71:14). The most reliable indications of date are still the references to the invasion of Palestine by the Parthians in 40 BCE (56:5-7) and to Herod's attempt to heal himself in the waters of Callirhoe (67:7-9). Since there is no reference to any event later than Herod, the Similitudes should be dated some time about the turn of the era;" see also D. Suter, *Tradition and Composition in the Parables of Enoch* (Missoula: Scholars, 1979).

[12] Neusner, *From Politics to Piety;* Rivkin, *A Hidden Revolution* (see chap. 2 above for further discussion); in more general terms see also Hengel, *Judaism and Hellenism.*

It is in such a climate, the period before the fall of Jerusalem, after which the direction of Judaism was radically altered, that the life of Jesus and the beginning of the Christian movement must be placed. It was a time of political and social turmoil as indigenous factions and exterior political, economic, and military forces strived to control the ancient Near East. Below the surface of the seemingly tranquil *pax romana*, there existed within Judaism a social and religious ferment conducive to eschatological hopes and apocalyptic ideology.[13]

Apocalyptic Thought
and the Early Christian Movement

Scholarly interest in apocalyptic thought and literature can be traced to the turn of the century when two noted German scholars published their conclusions concerning the nature of Jesus' teachings and ministry. Both Johannes Weiss and Albert Schweitzer, though in different ways and perspectives, insisted that Jesus' life, ministry, and preaching were permeated by apocalyptic imagery and themes, by its sense of imminent fulfilment, and by the dominant concept of the reign or kingdom of God.[14] Since that time and following the sensational discovery of the Dead Sea Scrolls, an increased awareness among NT scholars "that apocalyptic Judaism provided the framework for the message and ministry of Jesus" has developed.[15] Despite the suggestion of E. Käsemann, that the apocalyptic perspective of the early traditions within the New Testament, including that of the gospels, stems from Jesus' followers rather than from the master himself, current scholars agree that the eschatological perspective, apocalyptic imagery and urgency, and the very concept of the approaching kingdom are too deeply embedded within the Jesus traditions to be of a late date.[16] It is

[13]For graphic examples of life in the Hellenistic and Roman cities of the period, see Frost, *Greek Society*, 139-207 and H.C. Boren, *Roman Society: A Social, Economic, and Cultural History* (Lexington: Heath, 1977) 127-277 and for an equally vivid description of life in Palestine, confer Rhoads, *Israel in Revolution*.

[14]Weiss, *Die Predigt Jesus vom Reich Gottes* (Göttingen: Vandenhoeck & Ruprecht, 1892/1964) and Schweitzer, *The Quest of the Historical Jesus: A Critical Study of Its Progress from Reimarus to Wrede* (orig. 1906; NY: Macmillan, 1964).

[15]Kee, *Jesus in History*, 27.

[16]See E. Käsemann's major article "The Beginnings of Christian Theology," 82-107 as well as "On the Subject of Primitive Christian Apocalyptic," 108-37, both in *New

reasonable to hold that Jesus and John the Baptist before him endorsed the messianism and apocalyptic eschatology of that period and shared many of the concerns of the Essenes and Pharisees of first-century Palestine.[17]

The story of Jesus in the earliest strands of the gospel tradition (see Mark 1:2f; Matt. 3:7f–Luke 3:7f [=Q-Source]; and John 1:19f) and Luke's kerygmatic summaries (Acts 10:37; 13:25; also 1:22) begins with the preaching of John. There is no mistaking the prophetic and apocalyptic setting and character of his preaching. The first verses of Mark (1:2-3), drawn from a combination of Mal. 3:1 (concerning the forerunner) and Isa. 40:3 ("the voice of one crying in the wilderness"), set the stage for John's career. The latter citation is also used by the Essenes of Qumran to describe their withdrawal to the Dead Sea wilderness (Manual of Discipline: 1QS 8:14), while the former is another indication of the tradition's acquaintance with the ending of Malachi where the precursor is said to be Elijah redivivus (see Mark 8:28; 9:12; Matt. 17:11; Luke 1:17). John is described as a messianic figure in his preaching ("baptism of repentance") and dress (like Elijah, Mark 1:4, 6). Matthew (3:7f) and Luke (7:7f) add the themes of judgment and fire to John's eschatological teaching.

Jesus' preaching was immersed in the apocalyptic tradition, for the major theme of his teaching is the kingdom of God. The first words which Mark places on his lips merit citation here: "The time is fulfilled, and the kingdom is at hand; repent, and believe in the gospel" (1:15). All the themes of this verse find their home in apocalyptic thinking as do the temptations by Satan, the ministry of angels (Mark 1:12-13 and parallels), the opening of the sky, the descending dove, the heavenly voice at the baptism (Mark 1:9-11), and the prophetic and apocalyptic figures at the transfiguration (Mark 9:2-8). Also from this tradition is the title Son of Man which is given to Jesus in the gospels, Acts 7:56, and the Book of Revelation. It is not the usage of the Psalms or of Ezekiel, where the phrase connotes human frailty, which we find here but that of Daniel, 1 Enoch 37-71, and Fourth Ezra, all well-known Jewish

Testament Questions of Today (Philadelphia: Fortress, 1969) and more recently P.J. Achtemeier, "An Apocalyptic Shift in Early Christian Tradition: Reflections on Some Canonical Evidence," *CBQ* 45 (1983) 231-48.

[17]For a summary of apocalyptic materials found in the New Testament, see P. Vielhauer, "Apocalyptic in Early Christianity: Introduction," 2:608-42 in Hennecke and Schneemelcher, *New Testament Apocrypha.*

apocalypses.[18] Further, Jesus is presented as one demanding eschato-logical commitment, immediate and total. This is emphasized in the call scenes and in the parables; invariably, the latter offer an eschatological perspective on reality. Jesus is seen as one who exercises the power or authority of God through miracles and new teaching.

What is described above is said about Jesus and so might reflect the apocalyptic mentality of the early community or gospel writers rather than that of Jesus. This is true and we should recall what was said earlier about the quest for the historical Jesus. Nonetheless, it should be noted that Jesus' teaching, which is the most conservatively preserved part of the tradition, is prophetic and eschatological in character and content. The best hypothesis is that Jesus used the title Son of Man to refer to himself (only he in the gospels employs the expression).[19] His parables heighten the immediacy of the response demanded in his preaching. There is a constant tension in his teaching between the present (prophetic) and future (apocalyptic) reality of the kingdom, for it is near, is coming, and already is present (Mark 1:15 and Luke 17:21). The themes of resurrection and parousia also fit into the apocalyptic eschatology of the period.

This brings us to a discussion of the problem of imminent parousia in early Christian thinking. One might wonder whether Jesus believed the end was near and, on the basis of a text such as Mark 9:1, conclude that he did: "Truly, I say to you, there are some standing here who will not taste death before they see the kingdom of God come with power"—one should note that both Matt. 16:28 and Luke 9:27 modify this difficult saying. While it is not possible to offer an extended discussion of this problematic text, it should be noted that the saying of Mark 9:1, stressing the present reality of the kingdom, counterbalances that of the previous verse which emphasized the future return of the Son of Man. Besides, the establishment of the kingdom "in power," on the level of Markan redaction, points to the following episode (the transfiguration: 9:2-8) and, in pre-Markan terms, recalls the early tradition used by Paul in Rom. 1:4 that Jesus "was designated Son of God in power according to the Spirit of holiness by his resurrection from the dead."[20]

[18]For a discussion of the Son of Man in the gospel tradition, see chapters 4-7.

[19]Confer Lindars, *Jesus Son of Man* and Donahue, "Recent Studies on the Origin of 'Son of Man' in the Gospels," 484-85, for a survey of the issues.

[20]E. Nardoni, "A Redactional Interpretation of Mark 9:1," *CBQ* 43 (1981) 365-84.

Hence, it is not clear from our texts whether Jesus thought the end was near, but it is evident from this tradition that he did not claim to know when the final hour would be (Mark 13:32; Matt. 24:36; Acts 1:7). It is impossible for us today, due to the nature of our sources, to get back to Jesus' mind; our images of him are mediated images and the sayings we have from him were rendered complex and ambiguous by the process of transmission.

Another conclusion one draws from an analysis of the NT books is that the members of the early community and its writers believed that the end was near, within their own lifetime. Paul, the first Christian writer, subscribed to this idea from his earliest to his latest correspondence; this was the general belief of the early communities. None of the NT writers gave up the idea of an imminent parousia though some, employing eschatological terminology, laid more stress on the theme of urgency and moral readiness. Writers such as Luke, 1 Peter, and the Pastor increasingly directed their attention to the believer's life in the world though without denying the possibility that the end was near. It was left to post–NT writers to grapple with the question of the delay of the parousia.[21]

We return, in more general terms to the subject of apocalyptic thought in the early community. It is recognized among scholars that Matthew and Luke's non-Markan source (Q) was embued with apocalyptic eschatology. Its particular emphasis was upon the present and future Son of Man. Special stress was also placed on the themes of judgment and repentance, on Jesus' combat with the devil (only Matthew and Luke describe the three temptations), and on the parousia. Employing recent sociological studies of apocalyptic movements, some propose groups of socially marginal and charismatic Christians as the community responsible for developing the traditions of the Q-Source.

The gospel writers employ apocalyptic imagery and are concerned with eschatological issues because the Jesus material was thus formulated and because the writers themselves and their communities were fervently committed to such a view. A major factor in the development of Christian eschatological thought was the early followers' treatment of the resurrection experience. The fragment used by Paul in 1 Thess

---

[21]For a recent attempt, employing sociological models, to clarify this process, see J.G. Gager, *Kingdom and Community: The Social World of Early Christianity* (Englewood Cliffs: Prentice-Hall, 1975).

1:9-10 emphasizes the relationship of eschatology to Jesus' resurrection in the minds of early believers;[22] the new converts "await God's Son from the heavens, this Jesus whom God raised from the dead, who delivers believers from the approaching wrath"(RSVmod). One should also note the relation of sonship to resurrection in pre-Pauline tradition of Rom. 1:4. Eschatology and christology then coalesced in explaining God's plan. The theme of the first coming prepared for a doctrine of realized eschatology or fulfilment of OT prophecy, while that of the parousia or second coming took on the temporal and spatial categories of apocalyptic thought. The return of the Son of Man would be accompanied by cosmic signs and other end-time phenomena (Mark 13). Note also that Paul speaks of the Lord's descent from heaven, 1 Thess. 4:15-17.

An important text for our investigation of early Christian apocalyptic thought is the passage called the Synoptic or little apocalypse, Mark 13 and parallels. The text, as it now stands in Mark, functions as a farewell discourse. Situated before the arrest and passion of Jesus, this speech, dependent on the Book of Daniel for its imagery, is a revision of earlier apocalyptic tradition. In it Mark reviews the destruction of Jerusalem (seen as a sign of the end-time) and other apocalyptic signs: messianic pretenders (5-6, 21-23), civil and natural disturbances (17f, 21-23), cosmic disruptions (24-25), and the Son of Man and the end-time (26-27). The passage ends with two parables about the end and the readiness required (28-37). Structurally the passage is not an apocalypse but a farewell discourse. The principal concern is anti-apocalyptic for, while admitting that the time of the end is unknown and fast approaching, the author wishes to warn the audience that though the signs listed are expected the community must go about its business (9-13). The passage as structured has three points of emphasis: a) despite apocalyptic signs, the community, even in the midst of persecution, must bear testimony and preach the gospel (9-13), b) the only sure and indisputable sign is the final one, "the Son of Man coming in clouds with great power and glory" (26); and c) the interpretation given in chapter 13 about apocalyptic expectation rests on the Lord's own words (31). Mark was concerned about exaggerated apocalypticism in the commu-

[22]See the discussion of this passage in chapter 3.

nity,[23] possibly in light of the Roman invasion and destruction of Palestine in 66 A.D. and following.

While Matthew (24-25) and Luke (21) borrowed heavily from their Markan source, they modified, and Matthew added to the farewell discourse. Interestingly Matthew, on the basis of Dan. 12:1-2, enhances the apocalyptic atmosphere around Jesus' death by recording the occurrence of earthquakes and the opening of the tombs of the dead, 27:51-54. Luke also employs apocalyptic imagery to describe the disciples' power over Satan (10:17-19) and calls the time of Christian beginnings "the last days" (Acts 2:17). Apocalyptic imagery and mentality, therefore, are fundamental to the gospel writers' presentation of the Christ-event. Even John, who is the farthest removed from such a mentality, makes extensive use of apocalyptic concepts and transforms them into a present reality, although without eliminating the tension between present and future soteriological realities.[24]

E. Käsemann has demonstrated at length that Paul's thought and concerns, the schema of his theology, and his presentation of the Christ-event are governed by the apocalyptic ideas then current: the two ages, messianic tribulations in the present, the final submission of all creation under God's lordship, and the agency of Christ for the salvation of all believers.[25] Some authors (those of Acts, Hebrews, and 1 Peter) reinterpret eschatological categories to dwell upon the lot of Christian communities in their Greco-Roman world, while others (Colossians, Jude, and 2 Peter) employ apocalyptic imagery to address problems current within their communities.

Also significant for an understanding of the apocalyptic character of early Christian thought is the importance and frequent resurgence of apocalypticism in the NT period. Paul's community at Thessalonica is obsessed by questions of the end-time, namely, the fate of those who die before the parousia and the time of the end (1 Thess. 4:13f). Some in the community to which 2 Thessalonians is sent believe that the day of the Lord has arrived and have resorted to idle waiting (chaps. 2-3). We hear

---

[23]See chapter 4, note 9.

[24]For a discussion of eschatology in each of the evangelists see the following: Achtemeier, *Mark;* Kingsbury, *Matthew;* Richard, "Luke–Writer, Theologian;" and C.K. Barrett, "The Dialectical Theology of St. John," 49-69 in *New Testament Essays* (London: SPCK, 1972).

[25]*Romans.*

of the antichrist in the Johannine communities (1 John 2:18, 22; 4:3 and 2 John 7), of false messiahs and prophets in Mark (13:21f) and Matthew (24:23f), of messianic deception in all the Synoptics and 2 Thess. 2, and of the great deceiver in the book of Revelation (13:11-18). Finally, the authors of Jude and 2 Peter offer us a glimpse of communities which had intimate knowledge of apocalypticism. It is no surprise that the late work, 2 Peter, should be so immersed in apocalyptic thought since the second and third centuries A.D. saw the flourishing of Christian apocalypses as a result of the vicissitudes of the Bar Cochba rebellion (Apocalypse of Peter) and other instances of social and political alienation as Christian communities arose throughout the Roman empire.[26]

Introduction to the Book of Revelation

No NT book has received worse press whether in antiquity, during the Reformation, or in recent times than Revelation. We recall the judgment of Dionysius, a third-century bishop of Alexandria, who objected to the millennial teaching of the Book of Revelation, as interpreted by Nepos, his contemporary Egyptian bishop. Dionysius deplored its faulty style and barbarous syntax and idiom and, along with the Alexandrian school, was hesitant to accept it into the church's canon of recognized scriptures.[27] While this book eventually obtained a place in the canon, its acceptance has not been enthusiastic. Martin Luther for one found it alien to his perception of Christianity and explained his low esteem for the book as follows: "in it Christ is neither proclaimed nor acknowledged." Recently, some scholars have deplored the book's negative attitude toward the world and its desire for revenge and R. Bultmann concluded that "the Christianity of Revelation has to be termed a weakly Christianized Judaism."[28] Renewed study of the apocrypha and of apocalyptic literature in particular, however, has cast new light on the understanding of this NT work.

[26]A.Y. Collins, "The Early Christian Apocalypses," 61-121 in Collins, *Apocalypse;* see also Achtemeier, "Apocalyptic Shift;" Vielhauer, "Apocalyptic in Early Christianity: Introduction," 2:626-42 (on the Didache and the Shepherd of Hermas); and Nickelsburg, *Jewish Literature,* 311-17.

[27]His views are reported by Eusebius, Eccles. History 7:25-26.

[28]*Theology of the New Testament* (NY: Scribner's, 1951-55) 2:175.

GENERAL CONSIDERATIONS

The author calls himself John (1:1, 4, 9; 22:8); since there is no serious reason to question this and since the writer nowhere attempts to associate himself with apostolic figures, we refer to him simply as John.[29] Besides, as Dionysius of Alexandria insisted, there is no basis for associating this writer with the author(s) of the Johannine corpus. Indeed, the differences in grammar, style, and perception are vast. John the author of Revelation is the worst writer in the New Testament. While his language, alone with that of Mark, is comparable to the colloquial or idiom reflected in contemporary papyrus letters, his command of Greek grammar leaves much to be desired. Among NT writers he has a virtual monopoly on solecisms or lack of grammatical agreement; frequent cases of pleonasm and anacolutha (incomplete sentences), carelessness with or disregard for gender and number of nouns, and stylistic misuse of participles are found.

In spite of these "frequent violations of the rules of concord in Greek grammar and syntax,"[30] John gives color, vigor, and a certain poetic character to his composition. The author loves symbolism; and so the animal world is well represented: horses of various colors, wild animals (lion, leopard, bear), creatures of the wilderness, sea, and air (locust, scorpion, frog, fish, eagle, vulture, and other birds), monsters (red dragon, sea, land, and scarlet beasts). Imagery is taken from agriculture, commerce, and the military (the reaper, the builder, the merchant, the king—with their sickles, measuring rods, ships and merchandise, princely robes and double-edged swords). Cosmic and mythological symbolism is abundant: the heavenly bodies, the rivers, and the land. Thunder and lightning, flash floods, a sea of glass, falling stars, and the four winds are all found. One also encounters a mother, a harlot, and a bride.

Much of the symbolism is borrowed from the Jewish scriptures. The dragon or serpent of Rev. 12 comes from Isa. 27:1, the four beasts of 13:1-2 from Dan. 7:3-8, the four horses of 6:1-8 from Zech. 1 and 6, the

[29]A.Y. Collins, "Who Wrote the Book of Revelation?" 25-53 in *Crisis and Catharsis: The Power of the Apocalypse* (Philadelphia: Westminster, 1984).

[30]B.M. Metzger, "The Language of the New Testament," 7:49 in *IB*. Dionysius of Alexandria is no less severe: "I observe his style and that his use of the Greek language is not accurate, but that he employs barbarous idioms, in some places committing downright solecisms" (in Eusebius, *Eccles. History* 7:25:26-27).

plagues of 8:6f from Exod. 7f, Gog and Magog of 20:7-10 from Ezek. 38-39. From the same source and contemporary Jewish literature come the names of locales (the Euphrates, Rome, Jerusalem, Sodom, Egypt, Armageddon, Babylon, Hades) and of human and superhuman figures (Satan, Balaam, Jezebel, Michael, David, Moses, names of the twelve tribes). From the Jewish scriptures are such themes as the day of the Lord, manna, heavenly liturgy, the temple, its furnishings and architecture, priestly vestments, musical instruments, and the Son of Man. Even such metaphors as water, tree, book of life, root of David, and new heavens and earth are borrowed from the Old Testament. In fact it has been estimated that of the book's 404 verses, about 278 contain OT allusions or citations, the most frequent being from Daniel, Ezekiel, Isaiah, Zechariah, the Psalms, and Exodus.

The author is also fond of colors and numbers, most of which bear some symbolic meaning. For example, black stands for death, purple for kingship or luxury, seven for fullness; 3½ and 6 therefore represent imperfection or transitoriness, and four signifies the totality of the cosmos. The number of the beast (666 in 13:18 and the 1000-year reign of Christ (20:6) are clearly symbolic.[31] Love of imagery leads the author to draw material from many sources: from mythology (dragons in cosmic combat with the angelic host), from numerous OT authors, intertestamental literature (particularly apocalyptic traditions), contemporary culture, and the community's Jesus tradition (especially the eschatological strand: the Son of Man theme and the tradition behind Mark 13).

Not only does the author draw his imagery from a variety of sources but he also employs an assortment of compositional techniques.[32] Owing to this dexterity it is customary for introductions to give special attention to the threefold literary character of Revelation, namely, its

---

[31]For discussion of the latter, see below and for the traditional interpretation of the former as the granting of numerical value to the letters of a name (*gematria:* Nerôn Qaesar or *nrwn qsr* = 50 + 200 + 6 + 50 and 100 + 60 + 200 = 666) and for the discussion of Domitian as Nero come back to life, see G.R. Beasley-Murray, *The Book of Revelation* (Grand Rapids: Eerdmans, 1981) 215-21; Vielhauer, "Apocalyptic in Early Christianity: Introduction," 2:620-26; and A.Y. Collins, "Numerical Symbolism in Jewish and Early Christian Literature," 2:21:2:1222-87 U270-72 gematria) in Temporini and Haase, *Aufstieg und Niedergang der römischer Welt* (1984).

[32]On the author's linquistic background i.e., probable bilingualism, see Collins, "Who Wrote the Book of Revelation?" 46-49.

epistolary, prophetic, and apocalyptic features, since it has connections with all three genres.

The author's acquaintance with the epistolary form is clear, for chapters 2 and 3 consist of seven messages, in the form of letters, addressed to seven Asian churches. These are not strictly epistolary since they are dictated by the heavenly voice of "the one like a son of man" (1:13) and written down in a book (1:11) which is to be sent to the seven churches. The epistolary element therefore is a compositional device of the finished work. A further indication of this is the author's use of customary letter formulas to begin and end the book; thus 1:4-6 employs the usual opening (writer, addressee, greeting) and 22:21 ends with a standard blessing. This, however, is as far as the epistolary genre has influenced the composition of the work.

The author begins the composition with a blessing (1:3), one of seven found throughout, and not only closes with an almost identical beatitude (22:7b) but counterbalances this with an extended warning against modification of the narrative's prophecies. If its author borrowed this convention from public inscriptions which often called upon the gods to bless or to curse the reader thereof,[33] he would also have been acquainted with the Mosaic tradition of Deut. 4:2 forbidding anyone to add to or take away from the prophetic utterances of Moses.

This last point calls for a consideration of the book's prophetic character. The author, at the beginning (1:3) and end of the work (22:7, 10, 18 19), calls the whole a prophecy and is conscious of belonging to a guild of prophets (22:9).[34] He uses phrases such as "saints and prophets" or "saints, apostles, and prophets" to describe those who are faithful (11:18; 16:6; 18:20, 24) and the verb *propheteuō* to represent his own activity (10:13; see also 11:3, 10). There are false prophets in the community (the people of Thyatira are condemned for "tolerating the woman Jezebel who calls herself a prophetess," 2:20; see Acts 21:8-9 for

---

[33]C.F.D. Moule, "A Reconsideration of the Context of Maranatha," *NTS* 8 (1962) 307-10.

[34]Various individuals in the early communities spoke inspired utterances in God's name; see Acts 11:27-28; 13:1; 21:8f; 1 Cor 14:3; and 1 Tim 4:13-14; confer E. Käsemann, "Sentences of Holy Law in the New Testament," 66-81 in *New Testament Questions;* E.S. Fiorenza, "Apokalypsis and Propheteia: Revelation in the Context of Early Christian Prophecy," 133-56 in *The Book of Revelation: Justice and Judgment* (Philadelphia: Fortress, 1985); and Collins, "Who Wrote the Book of Revelation" and "Social Radicalism in the Apocalypse," both in *Crisis and Catharsis,* 25-53 and 111-40.

a positive reference to women prophets). The term "pseudoprophet" is reserved for the communities' external enemy, the second beast: 16:13; 19:20; 20:10.

The prophetic character of the Book of Revelation extends beyond the author's use of terminology; actually this feature of the book distinguishes it from Jewish apocalypses. Prophetic visions introduce the two major sections of the book; 1:9-20 prepares for the messages to the seven churches and chapters 4 and 5 are a prelude to the five septets of the work. The first vision is reminiscent of the classic commissioning visions of Jer. 1:1f and Isa 6:1f where biographical elements are incorporated into the prophet's description of the initial divine encounter, when he becomes privy to the plans of God and is commissioned as prophet. Rather than the well-known prophetic oracles, we find in the Book of Revelation the apocalyptic concern for writing (eleven times). The second prophetic vision, chapters 4 and 5, draws on the beginning of Ezekiel for its imagery and inspiration. The whole, however, is placed within an apocalyptic setting, for John is allowed a glimpse of the heavenly throne through heaven's open door (4:1). There is no doubt that an important characteristic of the Book of Revelation is its close relationship to OT prophecy (note also the dependence of 10:8-11 on Ezek. 3:1-3).

GENRE AND CHARACTER

While some relate the Book of Revelation to the prophetic tradition in whole or in part,[35] recent genre studies confirm the majority opinion that it is best classified as an apocalypse. The author's choice of title has provided later generations with appropriate terminology for the genre and general character of the literature (*apocalypsis*) and has offered, in the very first verse, the clues for categorizing an apocalypse: "the revelation of Jesus Christ, which God gave him to show to his servants what must soon take place; and he made it known by sending his angel to his servant John. . ." (1:1). The entire work is perceived as a divine revelation mediated to the author by an otherworldly figure. The revelation relates to the near end ("what must soon take place") and its contents consist of what John has seen before the divine throne: God's

---

[35]e.g., D. Hill, "Prophecy and Prophets in the Revelation of St. John," *NTS* 18 (1971-72) 401-18 and E.S. Fiorenza, "Composition and Structure of Revelation," 158-80 in *The Book of Revelation*.

plan for the world and Jesus' role therein (i.e., "the word of God" and "the testimony of Jesus Christ," 1:2). After a series of eschatological exhortations to the seven churches (chaps. 2-3) and a prophetic introduction (chaps. 4-5), the author offers five cycles of visions which present the reader with a foretaste of the end-time (6-22). The work, therefore, fulfils the requirements of the definition given earlier of the genre "apocalypse;" it is revelatory literature couched in a narrative framework, a story whose heavenly knowledge is communicated by angels to the prophet John, and whose concerns are imminent divine intervention in and salvation from a corrupt, hostile world.[36]

Not only did early Christian believers expect an imminent end to the world, they also subscribed to a familiar scenario for the end-time; the last day would be ushered in by eschatological signs and plagues, by the blast of the angelic trumpet, by the defeat of the last enemy (death, Satan, evil), by the resurrection of the dead and final judgment (involving heavenly records), by cosmic signs, and by the coming of the Son of Man on the clouds of heaven.[37] The stress on judgment, urgency of moral decision, and personal eschatology were common themes of the period, as were the premonitions of international and cosmic upheaval. To the east of the Roman empire, of which Palestine, Syria, and parts of Asia Minor were boundaries (*limes*), there was the constant Parthian menace. In Palestine itself there was the growing unrest of the population owing to Roman misrule which led finally to the devastation of the country in 70 A.D.[38] Furthermore, for the Christian communities in the frontier areas stretching from the Roman province of Asia as far as those of Pontus, Galatia, and Cappadocia (see 1 Peter 1:1 and Rev. 1:11), there existed the danger that nonconformist sects should be suspected of collaboration with anti-Roman factions or of being a threat to Roman consolidation of the buffer zones. In the case of 1 Peter we see that peaceful coexistence with and Christian participation in the activities of Roman life are offered as the ideal, while for Revelation the opposite obtains. John and his community even express the treacherous

[36]See earlier at the beginning of this chapter; confer also Collins, "The Early Christian Apocalypses," 70-72.

[37]For these see 1 Cor 15; Mark 13; 2 Thess 2; and contemporary Jewish texts: Apocalypse of Zephaniah, Fourth Ezra, Second Baruch.

[38]See the earlier discussion in chapter 2 of the historical context for the NT period and A.Y. Collins, "The Social Situation—Perceived Crisis," 84-110 in *Crisis and Catharsis*.

wish that Parthia, the archenemy, be victorious over the Roman empire.

SOCIO-RELIGIOUS SETTING

In the Book of Revelation there are numerous clues for an appreciation of the cultural and religious context of both author and audience. We are told at the outset that John is a religious prisoner on the island of Patmos (1:9) and that he shares the difficulties or tribulation of his audience. The conflict with Rome involves not only the author but also his general audience (see also 2:10), the cities of the province of Asia. Indeed the seven letters to the Asian churches are a veritable panorama of the problems encountered by the Jesus movement in this part of the empire. Repeatedly one hears of the tribulations, toil, and works of the communities which are praised and encouraged in their "patient endurance" (1:9; 2:2f). While there existed a number of critical issues within the churches of Asia Minor, such as false apostles at Ephesus (2:2), the beguiling, Jezebel-like prophetess at Thyatira (2:20), those who called themselves Jews but belonged to the synagogue of Satan at Smyrna and Philadelphia (2:9; 3:9), and a plethora of false teachings associated with Balaam, the Nicolaitans, and false teachers (invariably related to eating food sacrificed to idols and the practice of immorality, 2:14-15), one concern appears to emerge as the key element for understanding the context of the Book of Revelation: the imperial cult.

In the message to the seven churches (chaps. 2-3) the author mentions Satan or the devil no fewer than six times. He is concerned, negatively and positively, about the fidelity of his audience to its Christian commitment: soiled or white garments, nakedness, "abandonment of first love," concern for idols, and "patient endurance." He provides an added clue in 2:13 where he speaks to the community of Pergamum: "I know where you dwell, where Satan's throne is." This city along with others in the province in Asia took pride in fostering the emperor or imperial cult.

> From the time of Augustus (30 B.C.-A.D. 14), the cities of Asia Minor vied with one another for the favor of the Roman rulers by fostering the cult of Rome and the divinized emperor. The divinity of the king had been an accepted politico-religious concept in the eastern Mediterranean since ancient times, but it had been promoted by the

successors of Alexander the Great. Now the fundamental issue for the Christians of the area, many of whom were from the wealthy merchant classes, was whether they should participate in the ceremonies of divine honors to the emperor. To do so even in a perfunctory way, would contribute to social acceptance and freedom from governmental hostility. To refuse to do so might mean death. Should Christians go along with what they knew to be an empty show in order to survive? On this issue John could not allow any compromise.[39]

The same scholar later concludes that "it is not likely that John expected to persuade all the members of all the seven churches about the truth of his revelation,"[40] for he is rather pessimistic about how many will hold fast against Satan and his agents (2:24; 3:4; 3:15). What we encounter here is John the apocalypticist in a pastoral endeavor where he addresses the Christian churches of the province of Asia. While there is an appeal to each church and a warning against infidelity, the author's main concern is to commend the faithful and strengthen those who are hard-pressed. In the seven messages the reader is introduced to the urgency of the situation by the appeal to "patient endurance," to the imminent coming of the Son of Man (2:5, 16, 25; 3:3, 10, 20), and to the promise of a short duration to the tribulation, i.e., ten days (2:10). Clearly, the author and some of his audience are apocalypticists.

The central chapters especially assist us in appreciating the work's *Sitz im Leben* or social setting. Chapter 13 in its description of the two bestial assistants of the great red dragon provides ample evidence that the emperor cult and its popularity in Asia was the crucial issue which provoked the apocalyptic response of the author. The first beast rising out of the sea is the Roman empire and its personification the emperor, for it has been given the power, throne, and great authority of the dragon (13:2). All inhabitants are made to worship this first beast (13:4, 8), and it is the function of the second, indigenous beast ("arising out of the land," 13:11), through its ministrations and its great signs, to foster the cult of the first (13:12-14). The author describes in surprising detail the construction of images to the beast, its "humanization" (granting of

[39]Kee, *Understanding the New Testament,* 342-43.
[40]*Ibid,* 344.

breath and voice), and the coercion of worship under pain of death (vv. 14-15).[41]

Thus far one does not have sufficient cause for an apocalyptic ideology for, as the message of Smyrna indicates, the threat is that of martyrdom for some Christians (2:10). It is in the next two verses that one finds the clue to the church's apocalypticism:

> Also it causes all, both small and great, both rich and poor, both free and slave, to be marked on the right hand or the forehead, so that no one can buy or sell unless he has the mark, that is, the name of the beast or the number of its name (13:16-17).

The author views the zealous enforcement of the imperial cult by the local religious and political authorities (the second beast) as a diabolic scheme against God's people. What began as a litmus test of one's allegiance to Rome and its emperor became the undoing of the young movement in that part of the empire. Not only were those publicly apprehended either killed or imprisoned (if they were Roman citizens), but many in the community viewed themselves as disenfranchised. Their movement would be unable, publicly, to exist within the Roman community, for without authenticated documents (the mark of the beast) they would be reduced to a marginal or underground existence with no means of subsistence. Cut off from Roman society in such a radical way, many members of the Christian community withdrew from that menacing society and longed for an end to its tribulation. Acquainted with current Jewish and Christian apocalyptic thinking, the author directed his attention to the signs of the times: persecution of the elect, a concerted effort to deceive and entice God's people, and blasphemy against God. The last mentioned sign seems to be born out by the claim that toward the end of his reign Domitian, believed by scholars to be the emperor in question, allowed himself to be addressed as "our Lord and God" ("Dominus et Deus noster," Suetonius, Domitiani Vita 13:4).[42]

---

[41]On the emperor cult, see D.L. Jones, "Christianity and the Imperial Cult," 2:23:2:810-98 in Temporini and Haase, *Aufstieg und Niedergang der römischer Welt* (1980) and S.J. Scherrer, "Signs and Wonders in the Imperial Cult," *JBL* 103 (1984) 599-610.

[42]J.C. Rolfe, ed., *Suetonius* (Cambridge: Harvard University, 1964-65).

This interpretation, involving the ideological crisis brought about by emperor cult, the likelihood of political and economic disenfranchisement, and the seriously frustrated hope of the establishment of the messianic kingdom, is plausible in light of the author's apocalyptic treatment of various themes. The righteous and, therefore, those who are saved are the ones who have the Lamb's "name and his Father's name written on their foreheads" (14:1), while the ungodly, i.e., the one destined for condemnation, is anyone who "worships the beast and its image, and receives a mark on his forehead or on his hand" (14:9). The mark of the beast or its antitype, the name or mark of the Lamb, become the refrain of the remainder of the book. The appendix concerning the fall of Babylon/Rome (17:1-19:10) dwells at length and with glee on the economic disaster which awaits the Roman empire; anti-Roman sentiments are evident throughout. The economic, commercial, and political advantages which are denied to the Christians of Asia, the author assures his readers, will be summarily withdrawn from mighty Rome (see particularly the dirge for fallen Babylon—chap. 18). The Book of Revelation, therefore, is written and circulated to the churches to encourage the audience to bear patiently with its ever-worsening situation and impossible conditions, for the time of reckoning, the time of the end, so they believed, was near (1:3), a time when finally the kingdom (new heaven and new earth) would be established around the "throne of God and of the Lamb" (22:3).[43]

Content and Structural Analysis

In light of what was said concerning its genre and its epistolary, prophetic, and visionary characteristics, it is possible to isolate several sections of the Book of Revelation without much effort. Chapters 2-3 are an epistolary unit. Furthermore, one easily discerns an introductory section or prologue (1:1-8) and a concluding part or epilogue (22:6-21), both of which could be related to virtually any genre of writing. One also discerns two prophetic visions, one to introduce the letters (1:9-20) and the other to open the series of visions (4:1-5:15). This leaves only the long narrative given to the author's multiple cycles of visions.

---

[43]In general agreement with Collins' perhaps overly cautious evaluation of the situation, "The Social Situation—Perceived Crisis."

Even a cursory reading of the book's principal section indicates that there are three numbered cycles of visions: 7 seals, 7 trumpets, and 7 bowls. A.Y. Collins has also shown that there are two other septets: 12:1f concering the woman and the dragon and 19:11f regarding the final, cosmic battle. We offer, therefore, the following outline:

1:1-8	Prologue	
1:9-20	Prophetic Vision	
2:1-3:22	Letters to Seven Churches	
4:1-5:14	Prophetic Vision	I Sealed Scroll
6:1-8:1	Seven Seals	
	+ interludes on salvation	
	7:1-8 four angels	
	7:9-17 multitude	
8:2-11:19	Seven Trumpets	
	+ interludes	
	10:1-11 commission	
	11:1-13 witnesses	
12:1-15:4	Seven Unnumbered Visions	II Open Scroll
15:5-16:21	Seven Bowls	
	+ Babylon Appendix—17:1-19:10	
19:11-21:8	Seven Unnumbered Visions	
	+ Jerusalem Appendix—21:9-22:5	
22:6-21	Epilogue	

Collins has demonstrated both that while three of the cycles are distinctly numbered, the other two are linguistically indicated by the repetition of "I saw" (*eidon*) to introduce the seven visions of each cycle, and that each septet offers an internal pattern of: persecution, judgment, and triumph.[44]

Some of the contents of the prologue were discussed earlier, especially the topics of revelation, mediation, and blessing. In 1:4 John has recourse to the epistolary form when he says: "John to the seven churches that are in Asia; Grace to you and peace from him...." The

---

[44]*The Apocalypse* (Wilmington: Glazier, 1979) ix-xiv and 3. For a more detailed treatment see her other work, *The Combat Myth in the Book of Revelation* (Missoula: Scholars, 1976). See Fiorenza, "The Composition and Structure of Revelation," 159-80, for a somewhat different perspective.

remainder of the prologue is an extension of the thanksgiving section of the standard letter. The first and second prophetic visions have already been discussed as have the seven messages to the churches. The first vision emphasizes the seer's encounter with the Son of Man and his commission to write to the seven churches. The seven messages that follow in chapters 2-3 are stylized exhortations to the principal cities of the province of Asia, messages that extend encouragement to the persecuted, hope to the righteous, warnings to the less than perfect, and condemnation to idolaters and followers of Satan. The second prophetic vision provides a glimpse of the divine throne and its liturgy: the well-known "holy, holy, holy" passage from Isa. 6:2-3 and two beautiful hymns, one theological and one christological, both beginning "worthy art thou;" it also introduces the theme of the sealed scroll. By means of this last motif the author develops Jesus' role as mediator of revelation, for he emphasizes that only the Lamb is worthy to open the seals of the scroll.

In chapter 6 the author begins a series of five septets of visions, the first one of which concerns the breaking of the seals. Employing traditions similar to those of Mark 13, the author offers a glimpse of the end-time as a progression of evil on earth, from international crisis through the devastating effects of war (famine and death), represented by the four colored horses of Zech. 6:1-8, to the persecution of the righteous, and the judgment of the wicked. The first six seals present a series of evils which confront the world and build to the climactic fifth and sixth, the latter of which represents the traditional day of wrath. Only after the opening of the seventh seal does the reader hear about the divine victory and heavenly liturgy. Prior to this seal, however, the author has wisely (as artistic and psychological convention) inserted an interlude to the barrage of evils that confronts the elect (chap. 7). This interlude offers two visions; the first concerning the sealing of God's servants and the second about the white robed followers of the Lamb. The whole terminates with a poetic description of afterlife before the throne under the guidance of the Lamb (7:15-17).

In chapter 8, after the final seal, the author begins a series of seven trumpets, each introducing a progressively worse situation on earth and throughout the cosmos. OT imagery is employed to construct a macabre picture of the end-time. The first six trumpet scenes are drawn from the plagues of Exodus (chap. 7f) and their effect heightened with the eschatological-battle imagery of Joel 2. As was the case for the seven seals, the victorious trumpet scene is preceded by an equally interesting interlude. Chapter 10, as a parallel to chapters 1 and 5, is a commissioning scene which introduces the central part of the book (chaps. 12-15) and chapter 11 prepares for the two appendices: the heavenly Jerusalem and the fall of Babylon.

For the center of the work, the author has reserved the messianic cycle of unnumbered visions, namely, the vision of the struggle between the mysterious woman with a crown of twelve stars and the red dragon with its bestial helpers (12:1f). This part, however, will be discussed in the next section on Revelation's christology.

In chapter 15 the author again numbers the components of the visions and, employing temple imagery, introduces a series of seven bowls which are poured out on the earth. In successively worsening sketches he describes the judgment of those who "bear the mark of the beast and who worship his image." As in the series of trumpets so here the author employs the imagery of the plagues to describe the divine judgment which will come upon the community's enemies. In this series the author identifies Armageddon as the now well-known location of the final battle (16:16). The focus of this series of scenes, especially that of the Babylon appendix (17:1-19:10), is universal and historical judgment placed in the current political situation. The author dwells on the recurrent imagery of the great final earthly battle as a contest between Parthia (East; see the white horse of 6:2, the forces gathering at the Euphrates in 9:13f, and the final onslaught from the East in 16:12f) and Rome and its allies (West). He makes no secret of his desire to see the fall of Rome, the source of persecution and satanic activity, even if this destruction comes at the hands of the eastern powers.

The final unnumbered septet of visions (19:11-21:1-8) is probably as well-known as that of the woman and the dragon because here one finds the promise of the 1000-year reign with Christ (20:4-6). The focus is the great final battle described in cosmic, heavenly terms; the forces of good and evil are gathered for the final encounter. Employing the banquet imagery of heavenly triumph, the author draws a grisly description of its antitype, namely, the feasting of the vultures on the dead bodies of those who have taken pleasure in devouring the righteous. Since one of the community's anxieties is that its members are being beheaded, the author gives this issue special attention. Just as in the Book of Daniel, the martyrdom of the wise members of the community generated a doctrine of resurrection for those faithful even to death (Dan. 11:32-34;

12:1-3), so here in the Book of Revelation, the death of the righteous has led to a promise of a special reward.[45] Those who have been beheaded rather than receive the mark of the beast will participate in a first resurrection and 1000-year reign with Christ. The other righteous will share only in the final resurrection (20:4-6).[46] The reward for special valor, therefore, is a foretaste of a heavenly reward, for as the proverbial saying has it, "a day with the Lord is like a thousand years."[47]

The book concludes with an account of the heavenly Jerusalem, described as the bride of the Lamb. Employing current imagery (paradise, the zodiac, and the temple) John dwells on final union between God and the faithful, those who have worshiped God instead of the beast and those who have the Lamb's rather than the beast's mark on their forehead (22:4). An epilogue of blessings, warnings, and final instruction brings the work to a close.

Apocalyptic Christology

Analysis of John's presentation of Jesus is not an easy task owing to several factors. In the first place the name "Jesus" (also "Jesus Christ," "Christ Jesus," or "Christ" alone) does not appear frequently in the Book of Revelation. While the name "Jesus" occurs only 14 times in the book, more than half of which appear in the epistolary introduction and conclusion, the title "Christ" is found only seven times, three of these in the prologue. Earlier scholars used such statistics to support a wide range of editorial theories, usually the Christian updating of an original Jewish work.[48] Other factors rendering analysis difficult are the apocalyptic character of the work and the apocalyptic role which it assigns to Jesus. Many of the standard elements of the Jesus tradition which readers have become accustomed to find in NT texts are lacking or modified in this book. The Jesus of history virtually does not appear,

---

[45]J.J. Collins, "Apocalyptic Eschatology as the Transcendence of Death," *CBQ* 36 (1974) 21-43.

[46]M. Gourgues, "The Thousand-year Reign (Rev 20:1-6): Terrestrial or Celestial?" *CBQ* 47 (1985) 676-81.

[47]See 2 Pet 3:8; Ps 90:4. John employs the traditional promise of an earthly messianic kingdom (1 En 91-104; Ps of Solomon 11:17; 1 Cor 15:23-28) to encourage perseverance among those hard-pressed in the community.

[48]See note 28 above.

while his soteriological function is not stressed. Also, theological rather than christological themes are emphasized throughout. Finally, the orthodoxy of John's vision, whether of the Christ-event, of salvation history, or of the Christian's role in the world, is ambiguous for modern readers who, as members of mainstream churches, have little appreciation for apocalyptic ideology or imagery or, as devotees of millennial communities, interpret literally the images of the book and see its message as "prophetic foretelling" of the end-time (biblical prophecy). The former avoid the book like the plague and the latter mistakenly employ it as the measuring rod for authentic Christian thinking.

First we should insist that no part of Revelation is devoid of christological concerns or themes. Contrary to earlier attempts to isolate a primitive Jewish apocalypse, recent scholars see its multifaceted christology as deeply embedded both in the work and in the author's thought. John is acquainted with numerous elements of the Jesus tradition and with Jesus' soteriological role. While the author seemingly is not interested in relating the events of Jesus' life—the same is true of the most NT writers except the evangelists—he offers clear evidence of knowing and appreciating the tradition. He often refers to the suffering, death ("piercing," "slaying"), and resurrection (1:5, 7, 9; 5:6f) and even has Jesus say: "I am . . . the living one; I died, and behold I am alive for evermore" (1:18; also 2:8). Jesus will return on the clouds whereupon all will recognize him (1:7; see Mark 13:26; 14:62). Reference is made to the twelve apostles (21:14), the Davidic lineage of Jesus (5:5; 22:16), Jesus' love for humanity (1:6f; 3:9), to the themes of kingship (1:5; 17:14), kingdom (1:6, 9), fatherhood of God (1:6; 2:29), the marriage supper (19:7, 9), source of living water (7:17; 21:6), and the holding fast to the name (12:3, 13). There are several allusions to Jesus' sayings: coming like a thief (3:3; 16:15), confessing before the heavenly Father (3:5), knocking at the door (3:20), and the frequent "he who has an ear, let him hear" (2:7, 11f).

Careful reading of the work shows that Jesus' soteriological role is frequently mentioned. On four occasions the Lamb is described as having been slain (5:6, 9, 12; 13:8) and in fact the hymn to the Lamb describes eloquently Jesus' soteriological role: "thou wast slain and by thy blood didst ransom men for God" (5:9; see also 14:3-4). The author refers also to the blood of Jesus or of the Lamb (1:5; 17:14; 12:11). The first reference sets the tone for the entire work: "To him who loves us and has freed us from our sins by his blood and made us a kingdom, priests to his God and Father, to him be glory and dominion forever and ever. Amen. Behold, he is coming with the clouds . . . " (1:5b-7b). While John is primarily interested in Jesus' imminent return, he is not unmindful of the implications of the Christ-event.

Chapter 11:3-14 merits special attention for its contribution to the christology of Revelation. This passage, along with chap. 10, constitutes an interlude between the sixth and seventh trumpets and provides an interesting story about two end-time witnesses. "The basic pattern of the witnesses' destiny very clearly repeats that of Jesus' ministry: a prophetic ministry including mighty deeds, violent death in Jerusalem, resurrection after three days and ascension."[49] Without concern for detail the author presents two ideal witnesses, patterned on the work of Moses and Elijah and on that of "their Lord [who] was crucified" (11:8) as a model for his community to follow. So like most elements from the Jesus tradition, the master's life is put at the service of the author's purpose. From the beginning of the story we are told the witnesses "are the two olive trees and the two lampstands which stand before the Lord of the earth" (11:4), that they have eschatological powers, that they will be crushed, like Jesus before them, by the power from the bottomless pit (v. 7), and that their fate, after cataclysmic events, will involve universal salvation (v. 13). The author employs christology to convey his apocalyptic message.

Another passage, the central septet of the book (chaps. 12-15), offers crucial data for the analysis of the author's christology. The seven unnumbered visions concerning the woman, the dragon, and the Lamb are structurally and thematically central to the Apocalypse. While the first and fifth septets, the seals (6:1-8:10) and the final unnumbered visions (19:11-21:8), treat of the end-time in military terms, i.e., the devastation of war and the final, cosmic battle, and the second and fourth, the trumpets (8:2-11:19) and the bowls (15:5-16:21), make use of the plagues of Exodus, the middle septet, the unnumbered visions of chapters 12f, employs diverse traditions to present the author's central, messianic cycle. Indeed, this is the only cycle which makes structural use of the messianic savior. Employing the well-known tale of the mythic serpent's attempt to destroy the world's savior by attacking mother and child, by combining this with the Jewish story about the rebellion and

---

[49]Collins, *Apocalypse,* 72.

fall of Satan, and finally by superimposing the Christian messianic traditions, John has constructed a fantastic cosmic narrative to explain to his audience the reason why evil was running rampant and the elect were in such distress.[50]

It is in this context that one must understand the multifaceted symbols of the cycle. The woman with the crown of twelve stars is variously Israel, Mary, and, most basically, the community of the elect as personified in the bride, the new Jerusalem (19:7; 21:2, 9). At one level the story is that of Jesus the male child who will usher in the golden age, as Apollo or other savior figures were wont to do. One might be tempted to see in 12:1-6 a stylized version of Jesus' birth, but if one wishes to make sense out of the narrative sequence which John has given to the story, one must envision the taking up of the child into heaven (v. 5), the woman's "protected" exile in the wilderness (6), and the subsequent angelic battle in heaven (7f) as related to Jesus' soteriological and apocalyptic roles, that is, death/resurrection and return. The casting of the devil and its host of angels out of heaven is a result of the child's enthronement for as a heavenly voice states: "now the salvation and the power and the kingdom of our God and the authority of his Christ have come" (10). The heavenly battle is over; there will be an interim of evil on the earth (the time and situation of the embattled audience)[51] but, since the Lamb has conquered (v.11), there is assurance that the "time is short" (12). Chapter 12, therefore, is deeply christological in character for the cosmic victory has been won by the Lamb which was slain, i.e., "Jesus Christ the faithful witness, the first-born of the dead, and the ruler of kings on earth" (1:5). Patience is enjoined for the final establishment of his rule is soon to come (see 12:5; 19:15).

Beyond the author's use of the Jesus tradition there is also evidence of

---

[50]For a discussion of the mythic background of chapters 12f, see Collins, *The Combat Myth in the Book of Revelation.* See also her short but instructive summary of the Apollo version of the myth: "It is the story of the dragon Python's attempt to prevent the coming to power of Apollo, the son of Zeus by Leto. Python pursues Leto, while she is pregnant with Apollo, in order to kill her. By order of Zeus, the north wind rescues Leto by carrying her off to an island. Then Poseidon, god of the sea, hides her by covering the island with waves. Python cannot find her and so gives up his search," *Apocalypse,* 85.

[51]Satan's stay on earth is devoted to enlisting fellow monsters to persecute God's elect, i.e., the rest of the woman's offspring (12:17), until the cataclysmic battle of the end-days.

a richly developing christology. At first glance the plethora of titles given to Jesus is disconcerting, for he is called a "faithful witness," "ruler of kings," "the Amen," "the holy one," "the first and the last," "the Lord of lords," "the Lamb who was slain," "the one who bears the sharp sickle." It is clear from systematic reading that the author is immersed in the community's cultic life since a large number and variety of the titles employed are derived from hymnic resources. The first series of titles is an indication of this for Jesus is called: "the faithful witness, the first-born, and the ruler of kings on earth" (1:5a). The three titles represent the death, resurrection, and enthronement of Jesus, much as one finds in early christological hymns: Phil. 2:6-11 and Col. 1:15-20. In this case the verse and its surrounding themes are related to Ps 89:19-37, especially v. 27,[52] and has much in common with the Colossian hymn. Indeed, the phrase "the first-born of the dead" is found in Col. 1:18[53] and both passages refer to the blood of Jesus (Rev. 1:5 and Col. 1:20). Further, the title "the beginning of God's creation" (3:14) is reminiscent of "the first-born of all creation" (Col. 1:15).

The introductions to the seven messages to the churches present a large variety of titles, titles which emphasize the author's heavenly source of revelation, his authority to admonish and exhort, and the basis of the promises made to the churches. Other passages stress the apocalyptic role of Jesus, for he is the one who wields the double-edged sword, the sharp sickle, the one who treads the wine press, and the one who sits on the white horse and "judges and makes war" (1:16; 14:18; 19:11, 15). Also, he is the bridegroom of the end-days, the king of kings, God's Christ, the shepherd of the elect, the heavenly lamp, and the bright morning star (19:7, 16; 11:15; 7:17; 21:23; 22:16).

The most important, and indeed the central, christological title is that of "Lamb." The term (*arnion*) appears 29 times in Revelation, where it is first employed to introduce the apocalyptic cycles. The theme is greatly developed in the prophetic vision of chapter 5, in which it is stressed that

---

[52]"I will make him the first-born, the highest of the kings of the earth." In more general terms see E.S. Fiorenza, "Revelation as Liberation: Apoc 1:5f and 5:9f," *CBQ* 36 (1974) 220-32.

[53]One might be tempted to interpret this phrase as indicating a low christology for the Book of Revelation, that is, Christ as first creature; however, the meaning of the phrase is similar to that of Col. 1:15 and indicates "not a temporal advantage but rather the superiority which is due to him as the agent of creation who is before all creation," Lohse, *Colossians and Philemon*, 49.

only "the Lamb that was slain" is worthy or able to open the seals. The author then uses this title six times in the section on the seals and its interlude (chaps. 6-7). He returns to this title in the central, messianic cycle (chaps. 12-15: 8 times), and the two appendices: that on Babylon (17-19: 4 times) and that on Jerusalem (21-22: 7 times). The author employs the title to stress the relationship between the soteriological (the Lamb that was slain for the redemption of humanity) and the apocalyptic, as both judgment and lordship (the Lamb who judges, makes war, and reigns as "Lord of lords and King of kings").

In view, therefore, of the diversity of titles and the generous use which John makes of the Jesus tradition, it is important to summarize the major functions which he assigns to Jesus. The soteriological role is crucial but its function is presupposed rather than emphasized. Thus, there are three principal christological roles which John wishes to stress: the revelatory, the messianic (as judge and warrior), and the hortatory.

John begins his book by noting that the work is a "revelation of Jesus Christ," though one "which God gave him to show to his servants" (1:1). Throughout the work Jesus or an angel is the otherworldly figure who communicates the secrets of God's plan. Rather than being superficially Christian, the work underscores one of the principal functions of Jesus Christ as that of revealer (see the Q saying of Matt. 13:16-17 and Luke 10:23-24; also John 1:18). Chapter 5, the beautiful, intriguing narrative about the opening of the seals, is particularly important in this regard. The one who sits on the throne has a scroll (the symbol of the divine plan) which no heavenly or earthly creature can open or read. Central to the author's perspective is that only one is worthy, the Jewish messiah (5:5, "Lion of the tribe of Judah, the Root of David"), for only he has conquered. By his blood he has become worthy to take the scroll and break its seals (5:9). Importantly, this apocalypticist situates the Christ-event at the very center of his vision. It is the Lamb only who has access to the secrets of the divine throne. Through Jesus, as the Lamb which was slain, the revelation of God becomes available to the elect and serves as guide, standard of judgment, and source of promise.

The second principal function is that of Jesus as the end-time Savior who will return to bestow justice, to mete out punishment, wage war against the ungodly, and to lead the elect as shepherd or bridegroom. This function is related to the author's conviction that the end is near (1:3, 7; 2:10) and that the messiah will "rule all the nations with a rod of iron" upon his return (12:5). Three times the term "conquer" is used of

Christ. In one occurrence it is said that he is worthy to open the scroll because he has conquered by his blood (5:5, 9) and in another it is promised that, although the powers of evil will gather against the Lamb and its host in the war at Armageddon, "the Lamb will conquer them, for he is Lord of lords and King of kings" (17:14). The Lamb will bring about the fall of Babylon, the ungodly enemy of the elect which will feel his wrath, and it will be united to its followers as a groom to its bride. Further, the image of the Son of Man is twice employed, first (1:13f) to establish the heavenly authority of the revelation of the book, to confirm the promise of salvation ("I have the keys of Death and Hades," 1:18), and to encourage or warn the audience and second to portray the return of the Messiah "with a golden crown on his head and a sharp sickle in his hand" (14:14). It is the sixth vision about the coming of the "one like a son of man" and the final cycle of unnumbered visions (19:11f) about the role of the one on the white horse in the final, cosmic battle, which stresses the military role of Christ in the finest apocalyptic fashion. Those who die a martyr's death rather than receive the mark of the beast will receive a special reward, a first resurrection and a priestly reign with Christ on earth (20:4,6). When he returns he will wield the sword and the sickle, but will also bear the crown and lead to fountains of living water. It is he who bears the book of life wherein are recorded the deeds of the righteous (13:8).

This brings us to the third function which the author stresses, namely, Jesus as one who warns and encourages. The first part of the work is given to warnings and exhortations. Each message to the churches bears the ominous "he who has an ear, let him hear" (2:7f). The theme of "patient endurance" is repeatedly stressed. In each message the risen Lord is made to say: "to him who conquers I will grant . . . " (2:7, 11, 17, 26, etc.) and there follows a promise of an eschatological nature: taste of the tree of life or the hidden manna, freedom from the second death. Readers are encouraged to resist the beast and its enticement and to follow the Lamb and worship God (22:9) and if necessary to wash their garments in the blood of the Lamb (7:14). Since Jesus is coming soon, they are encouraged to be faithful and to pray: "Come, Lord Jesus" (22:20).

The christology of the Book of Revelation is a complex one on the one hand, for it betrays much variety and considerable knowlege of the developments one finds in other NT books, and it is a unified one on the other hand for its various elements focus on the apocalyptic character of the book's perspective and message. The christology of the Apocalypse has a distinct functional character for it serves to communicate the author's principal message. One would have to agree:

> The major theological motifs of Revelation are those of power and justice. The central theological symbol of the book is the throne signifying divine or demonic power. While the Christians are the representatives and agents of the power and empire of God and Christ here on earth, the universal Roman empire and its imperial powers are the agents of the demonic and destructive power of Satan.[54]

The term "throne" appears 46 times in Revelation where it becomes a name for or a symbol of God's lordship. The book is about power and the lack of power which the Christians of Asia Minor experienced during the reign of Domitian, a disenfranchisement and consequent alienation which made many lose hope for a better world. Both author and audience looked to the near-end of the world and the return of their Lord to establish justice and a new earth.

The christology of the book serves the purpose for which the author wrote. He stresses theology rather than christology. Power is the principal issue, the absolute power of God. It is God who is worshiped and is sovereign Lord and Creator. The Lamb has ransomed humanity for God (5:9), has become God's Christ (12:10), and leads the sheep to the divine throne (7:15-17). While the author frequently associates God and the Lamb—they share titles, functions, and even worship—it is the reign of God (11:17) and, in association, that of the Lamb and its followers which is of concern to him: "he who conquers, I will grant him to sit with me on my throne" (3:21). It is in this way that one must understand the stress on the lordship of God rather than on that of Christ. In true apocalyptic fashion, based on elements of the Jesus tradition, only in the heavenly realm is there victory, for the victorious Lamb is absent for the time being (12:5) while the evil powers have sway upon the earth for a brief time (42 months, 1260 days) for "he knows that his time is short" (12:12).

John, for the benefit of his fellow-sufferers throughout the province of Asia, gathered his apocalyptic "homilies" and organized them into a narrative of warning, encouragement, and instruction. Employing the

---

[54]E.S. Fiorenza, *Invitation to the Book of Revelation* (NY: Doubleday, 1981) 27-28.

Jesus tradition and current mythological lore the author reassured the audience that though they were now deprived of power they would receive real power in the heavenly Jerusalem, and that while justice was sorely lacking in this life, there would be a time of reckoning for Rome and its ministers and a time of reward for the elect. The very nature of God (lordship) demanded this and the Christ-event made salvation a reality. He had conquered once and would conquer again, but in the meantime his followers had to conquer by resisting the beast even if it meant death. The Lamb has his book in hand so the author advises: "here is a call for the endurance and faith of the saints" (13:10).

Apocalyptic Legacy

The Book of Revelation is but one of many apocalypses that were written in the first few centuries of Christian history. One presupposes that often when social and political conditions in various parts of the Roman Empire provided adverse conditions for Christian minorities apocalyptic movements sometimes developed. As metropolitan centers developed and populations became dislocated and alienated, as old worldviews were replaced by competing mystery cults, and as official and unofficial ostracization and persecution increased, many had recourse to heavenly solutions for their earthly problems. The post-NT period is poorly known and its literary works not well studied. Nonetheless, there are a number of literary texts which are classified as apocalypses. Christians either composed new works (e.g., the Testament of Isaac or the Bartholomew literature) or Christianized older Jewish apocalyptic texts (e.g., the Sybillene Oracles or the Testament of the Twelve Patriarchs). We conclude that apocalypticism continued to flourish for some time after the close of the NT canon.[55]

Eventually, as major political, social, and religious changes occurred within the Roman Empire and as Christianity became the official state religion, apocalypses ceased to be written. The need, however, for consolation for the oppressed did not cease. Later generations of Christians often found tantalizing solace in the apocalyptic strand of both the Old and New Testaments. There is ample evidence of Christian

---

[55]Collins, "Early Christian Apocalypses," 61-121 and Vielhauer et al, "Apocalypses and Related Subjects," 2:579-803 in Hennecke and Schneemelcher, *New Testament Apocrypha.*

fascination with the millennial doctrine of Rev. 20:1-6 throughout the centuries of Christian history.[56] During the Middle Ages one hears of messianic figures attracting large followings among the poor classes. During the 16th century the well-known Münster apocalyptic episode occurred where an Anabaptist community under the guidance of its Dutch charismatic leaders, especially Jan Brockelson, declared itself the millennial kingdom.[57] A few centuries later, as a consequence of the monumental dislocations resulting from the industrial revolution and the political and social upheavals of the period, there developed a climate out of which grew the numerous apocalyptic movements which have survived into the twentieth century. The 1830-60s saw the beginnings of the Millerites and other Adventist groups, the Mormons, the Shakers, and, slightly later, the Jehovah's Witnesses. Beyond these tightly knit groups there also developed in the English-speaking world, along with a general fundamentalist and literalist mood, a fascination for apocalyptic speculation of an Adventist type (e.g., *The Late, Great Planet Earth* by Hal Lindsay). Frequently, evangelical and charismatic groups find such thinking rather appealing,[58] while smaller churches of the dispossessed opt for such a stance, e.g., the Peoples' Temple of Jonestown.[59]

Apocalyptic thought, therefore, persists into the present century and, one suspects, will continue to do so as long as there are threats to human existence such as war, famine, and nuclear weapons, and as long as there is alienation and despair. Some will choose to become survivalists, apocalypticists, or "doomsday sayers" and will seek in apocalyptic texts the clues for a heavenly solution to the impossible situations sometimes encountered in life. The Book of Revelation is the product of such a community and, when properly understood, has much to offer the attentive reader, for it is a powerful testimonial of one Christian response, whether destructive or cathartic, to the realities that often confront the righteous. Christ is many things to his followers; this author offers the reader his own, unique presentation of Jesus.

[56]For an excellent, brief introduction to this subject, see M. Rist, "Millennium," 3:381-82 in *IDB*.

[57]N. Cohn, *The Pursuit of the Millennium* (NY: Oxford University, 1980).

[58]R.D. Brinsmead, "The Apocalyptic Spirit," *Verdict* 4 (1981).

[59]J.R. Hall, "The Apocalypse at Jonestown," 171-90 in T. Robbins and D. Anthony, eds, *In Gods We Trust: New Patterns of Religious Pluralism in America* (New Brunswick: Transaction Books, 1981).

Part V
Jesus In Post-New Testament Times

12

The Early Church Fathers and the Great Councils: The Emergence of Classical Christology

Author's Note:
This chapter is the contribution of
my colleague, Stephen H. Duffy.

Introduction

Christianity entered the human drama bearing a message of salvation and reconciliation with God. Its proclamation grew out of and focused on the life, death, and resurrection of Jesus of Nazareth. Christian preaching sprang from the belief that Jesus' own proclamation of a new age had been verified and realized by his resurrection. Through his dying and rising God's promised transformation had become reality. Jesus himself was the embodiment of the new order and the door through which others could enter. Through him the Spirit of God came to life in all who took him as the revealer and shaper of their destiny. For Christians he was indeed Messiah, Christ, and Son of God.

And so christology was born, i.e., reflection on what is presupposed and implicit in the affirmation that Jesus is Messiah and unique Son of God, the agent in and through whom God acts to carry out his designs for humanity. From the start a certain logic inevitably grips christology. It must articulate Jesus' relationship to God. But equally it must search for ways to articulate the representative character of his humanness, his role as the figure who normatively reveals and exemplifies our human destiny.

The earliest Christian literature contains a plurality of christologies. One of the earliest was content to announce Jesus as the man marked by the resurrection as the awaited Messiah. In this primitive christology the title "Son of God" would signify not possession of any divine quality but election as an agent of God's plan. This deceptively simple christology would yield to other more complex ways of understanding Jesus as Christianity moved more and more into the Hellenic culture of the Mediterranean world. This development already begins to appear in Pauline and Paulinist depictions of Jesus. Not only is he the coming Messiah, but he is even now the active "Lord" of both church and cosmos. Through his resurrection a new creation is already breaking in. A heavenly figure, according to some NT writers, he is the embodiment and universal agent of God's saving purposes for humankind. Moreover, everything Jesus was and did reflects God's will and derives from God's initiative. The presence of Jesus in our midst derives from God's "sending" (Gal. 4:4). In Christ God was reconciling the whole to Godself (2 Cor. 5:19). Elsewhere in the New Testament, the earthly Jesus is the human presence of the heavenly Son of God who is the very expression of God's own self. The author of Colossians clarifies the identity of this heavenly figure: "He is the image of the invisible God, the firstborn of all creation; in him all things were created.... He is before all things and in him all things hold together" (Col. 1:15-17). Personified divine wisdom, the dynamic expression of all God is and wills, that is the Christ. In him the divine power that sustains all things is redemptively present.

This development reaches in John's Gospel a form that would become a powerful and dominating force shaping christology for centuries. Jesus is God's creative Logos or Word who "became flesh" (John 1:1-14). The same theme appears in Hebrews which affirms the Son of God as the one through whom God created all things. He "reflects the glory of God and bears the stamp of his nature" (Heb. 1:2-3). In a word, Jesus is the historical enfleshment of the divine creative power first revealed in the cosmic creation. Implied in all this is the universal significance of his life and death and even more, the normative and definitive quality of the salvation wrought through him.

Early Non-Biblical Christian Writing

Early non-biblical Christian writing continues in this vein. The First Epistle of Clement (c. 96), coming out of the Roman Church, refers to Jesus as Son of the Father God and "radiance of his majesty," therefore true revealer (1 Clem. 36 and 59:1). The Jewish-Christian Shepherd of Hermas (c. 150), another product of the Roman community, in his relatively popular religion, asserts that "the Holy Spirit . . . which created the whole creation, God settled in the flesh which he willed" (Similitudes 9:1:1; 5:6:5). For Hermas, later often regarded as scripture, the Spirit and the Son are the same. He is "older than all his creation . . . he was the counselor of his creation to the Father" (ibid. 9:12:2). Hermas is on a direct line of belief running from Hellenistic Judaism to many of the Fathers. It is interesting that he never mentions Jesus or Christ.

Ignatius, bishop of Antioch, who penned seven letters c. 110 as he marched under guard to a Roman martyrdom, provides the most "advanced" christology of the early second century.[1] He takes some of the ideas of Paul and the Paulinist authors of Colossians and Ephesians and combines them with some of the language of John. In his christology of exaltation Ignatius felt free to speak repeatedly of "Jesus Christ my God." His impassioned devotion and penchant for rhetorical paradox override all theological difficulties. In his letter to the Magnesians twice he refers to the preexistent life of the divine Son Jesus Christ. "Before the ages he was with (*para*) the Father and was manifested at the end." He "proceeded from (*apo*) the one Father and is with him and departed to the one" (Magnesians 6:1; 7:2). Not much taken with the Johannine Logos, he speaks but once of "the one true God, who manifested himself through Jesus Christ his Son, who is his word proceeding from silence." His usual preference is for the relational terms "Father" and "Son." So high is his christology that he used traditional God language in regard to the Son. The Son as divine was "above seasons, timeless, invisible, intangible, passionless." Yet he knows much of the life of the Son: "truly born . . . baptized by John . . . truly nailed in the flesh." The incarnation is paradoxical for Ignatius, for Jesus is flesh and spirit, born and not born, God in flesh, life in death, and so on (see Smyrneans 1:2; Polycarp 3:2; Ephesians 7:2). Ignatius' language reflects the florid rhetoric common to the second century.

Areas of christological speculation, e.g., the role of the Logos in creation, are avoided by Ignatius, perhaps because they might verge on the Gnostic speculations (Trallians 5). What stands out is Ignatius' unsophisticated insistence that Jesus Christ is God. It is emphasized in

---

[1]Cf. W. Schoedel, *Ignatius of Antioch* (Philadelphia: Fortress, 1985).

his letters to the Romans, Ephesians, and Smyrneans, all churches which by the end of the second century were tolerant of Patripassianism, the teaching that the Father suffered or even died. Ignatius, however, nowhere confused the Son with the Father, nor held that the Father suffered on the cross. Nevertheless, his is a high christology whose roots may reside in apocryphal traditions about the risen Christ as well as in NT teaching. We do not know how much support Ignatius found in Antioch for his high christology, since we know of no letters of his to or from the church there. We do find hints of the low, "Jewish" christologies which probably were in vogue at Magnesia and Philadelphia. Ignatius, who hated the Jews, denounces his opposition there so roundly that it is difficult to detect their precise position. Perhaps they were adoptionists. It is not without significance that some of his most important avowals of the Son's preexistence turn up in his letter to the Magnesians.

Finally, from the Ignatian flair for paradox emerges a rudimentary christological pattern of duality in unity. "There is one physician, fleshly and spiritual, born and unborn, God become man, true life in death, sprung both from Mary and from God, first subject to suffering and then incapable of it, Jesus Christ our Lord" (Ephesians 7:2). This binary pattern will become recurrent and paradigmatic for all future christological reflection. Unabashedly and without concern for theological niceties the devout bishop can say "Our God Jesus Christ was carried in the womb by Mary" (ibid., 18). As he makes his way to Rome, the death of Christ is linked by Ignatius with his own approaching martyrdom and his thought is consumed in linking himself to Christ in his suffering. The hope is for life through the "blood of God" (Smyrneans 6).

Second- and Third-Century Christologies East and West

Reflection on this early christological pattern of duality in unity led Christian thinkers in the second, third, and fourth centuries into a thicket of questions that they were forced to cut through with a more critical christology. The process is set in motion in the second century. First there was the felt need to somehow find a place for Jesus within the life of God. How identify and define the heavenly power experienced in Jesus? The answer would eventually lead to a dialectic of divine "persons" within the life of God. It would also occasion the problem of reconciling this plurality with divine unity. Prior to that, however, there was also the problem created by denials of Jesus' humanness. How could he belong to the divine space while being in our flesh? Is he human or divine? Must we choose? These problems of unity and diversity were to preoccupy the Church, especially in the East, in the first seven centuries. And since they were to be worked through in a Hellenistic culture, it is crucial for understanding the settlements that ensued to know something of the tendencies of the Hellenic mind.[2] Early Christian thinkers and pastors were not Christians who had to learn to think as Hellenists, but Hellenists who had to learn, with some difficulty, to think as Christians. Something more was involved than simply adopting an already existing Christian thought pattern. In a sense, theirs was the difficult task of creating that thought pattern.

THE HELLENIC MINDSET

In the first place, in the Greek cast of mind to be is to be stable, enduring, immutable. Change is imperfection and the failure to be fully real. Of concern to the Greek mind is what underlies change and stands constant. Change is possible only in a being that is an unfortunate mixture of actuality and purely potential being, or that which is not. In this perspective a God who is eternal and living, acting in new, unpredictable ways can only appear strange and challenging. In addition, such high regard for changelessness throws a pall over the human world of time, space, matter, and the stream of events. We are exiled souls in a foreign world, souls housed in the prisons of our bodies. The implications for thinking about a God who becomes enfleshed are obvious.

Secondly, Greek thought was not completely at ease with the idea of human freedom. The ideal is the divine self-love, which is not free because it is determined by its object. But human freedom as indeterminacy before imperfect earthly goods is difficult to esteem. As a corollary there is a disvaluing of the experiential and the unique, which could never be of ultimate significance. In history, which is cyclical, one might discern the operation of eternal laws in politics or ethics, but history could not be seen as the area where one might form oneself

[2]Cf. C. Cochrane, *Christianity and Classical Culture* (NY: Oxford University, 1940); J. Dillon, *The Middle Platonists* (Ithica: Cornell University, 1977); J. Dwyer, *Son of Man and Son of God* (NY: Paulist 1983), especially C.2.

through uniquely free decisions. Necessity and fate cast a shadow over self-determination. As a linear, historical faith irreducible to a cyclical, dualistic scheme or to a set of ideas, Christianity could only be enigmatic to the Hellenic mind. How could the immutable God decisively manifest Godself in a unique event of human history? Neo-Platonic Christian thinkers will affirm the reality of Jesus' humanity, but they will have difficulty in assigning to it a soteriological significance. There will be a marked tendency to absorb his humanity into the divine sphere. In a word, Jesus will become for many a divine man, or God in human dress.

Thirdly, there is the Hellenistic tendency to think of the changeless God as distanced from the world by an unbridgeable gulf. The unmoved mover resides alone in heaven. God is not a creator. Indeed, God does not, according to Aristotle, even know the world. At all costs God must be quarantined lest God be contaminated by contact with worldly multiplicity. Transcendence is remoteness, immanence sheer impossibility. Consequently, the religion of late antiquity is marked by a frenzied search for mediators and the pursuit of mystery cults in an attempt to commune with the divine. The Jewish-Christian God shatters this view, though it will not be without its influence, especially in intensifying the mediatorial role of Jesus Christ. A fourth trait of the Hellenistic mentality is an insensitivity to paradox and dialectical language. A deity who is transcendent and immanent and takes a flawed and wounded world to itself is absurd. How could divine power be revealed in human powerlessness or wisdom in the foolishness of the cross? How could an ascetic anthropology with its stress on acquired virtue be squared with the Pauline doctrine of gratuitous justification? Finally, in the Hellenist world the basic human problem is how to overcome finitude, escape from this inconstant material world into a realm of immortality. The situation is desperate, for humans are locked in time and God is in eternity. Again, the anxious need for mediators, beings of a third ontological kind, bridges ranging between time and the timeless, who might reveal the way to escape finitude. Thus the word "God" was adjectival and applied to a pantheon of demi-gods and saviors spanning the forbidding chasm between the One and the multiplicity of the world.

Even before Plotinus (205-270) and the neo-Platonists fixed upon a middle-range being to cope with the problem of the separation of the transcendent One from the world, there already was such an intermediary standing in the wings. From before the Christian era it was termed Logos, or Nous, the mind, reason, or thought of the One and the principle of order and rationality in the universe. The Logos stood waiting and ready as Christian thinkers began to articulate the relations of Jesus to the Father God and they could not help but see its similarity to the Jewish personification of divine Wisdom. The tortuous journey from John's prologue to the Nicene resolution (325) will erupt into conflict over the ambiguous status of this Logos with regard to God. But in the end Christianity will have traversed from son of the carpenter to Son of God and on to God the Son. More functional christologies will yield to ontological christologies, and more concrete, symbolic, and descriptive modes of discourse to abstract, conceptual, and definitive modes. While the two modes of thought are inseparable, nonetheless attention will be less on the life and work of Jesus and his relation to humans and more on his person and being and his relation to God. It would be a transcultural shift fraught with far-reaching consequences for Christian life for centuries after. The rich diversity of the New Testament will recede in an unrelenting search for unity and orthodoxy.

THE APOLOGISTS:
JUSTIN, IRENAEUS, AND TERTULLIAN

Between 125-190 a group of Greek apologists attempted to defend Christianity against charges of atheism and black magic and to make a philosophical defense of the religion on more orthodox lines than those drawn by the Gnostics. With the Apologists a Logos christology emerged. In Justin Martyr, (c. 100-165),[3] a Samarian of Greek parentage, who had made a long odyssey to Christianity through a variety of philosophical schools, the Logos is God's Son, an entity distinct from God, generated before all creatures and begotten to be the agent of creation and revelation. It is this Logos that is enfleshed in Jesus, the same Logos who revealed God to Israel's prophets and to the Greek philosophers and poets (1 Apol. 10:1). Dependent upon Platonic and Stoic thinking, Justin's Logos is the immanent, formative principle of cosmic order. The Logos, however, while the self-expression of God's being and purpose, is a subordinate deity and not the ultimate deity, a fire lit from the fire that is God. It is an intermediate god through whom the invisible, unoriginated God has contact with the mutable world. By

---

[3]Cf. L.W. Barnard, *Justin Martyr: His Life and Thought* (Cambridge: Cambridge University, 1967).

giving humans a share in God's reason the Logos brings knowledge of God to all. Following the Stoics, Justin terms it the seminal Logos, planting the seed of reason in all, and becoming incarnate in Jesus to conquer demonic reason.

The crucial role of Justin's Logos is appreciated only when one understands how Justin conceives God. God is "the eternal, immovable, unchanging Cause and Ruler of the universe, nameless and unutterable, unbegotten, residing far above the heavens, and is incapable of coming into immediate contact with any of his creatures, yet is observant of them although removed from them and unapproachable by them."[4] The titles God bears such as Father, Creator, Lord, refer to his activities, not to his essence (Apol. 2:6:1-2).

In his effort to harmonize Christianity and the Hellenic culture, Justin catholicized Christianity as the true philosophy and sounded its universal significance. All that had been good and valuable in the past among the poets, philosophers, and prophets was implicitly Christian. "Those who live in accordance with Reason (Logos) are Christians, even though they were called godless" (I Apol. 46). Abraham and Socrates were Christians before Christ. Through Jesus Christ, however, the Word had become fully revealed, hence his followers share in his revelation more completely than had Jews and Greeks before them. This would not please all. Despite Justin's hierarchic view of the cosmos with its subordinationism whereby the Logos is a second, inferior god and a buffer between the transcendent God and the world, some, called Monarchians, saw the Logos christology jeopardizing monotheism through the introduction of plurality and diversity into the godhead. The paradox of immanent transcendence was too much to hold. Justin, a Platonist before becoming a Christian, and not a consistent thinker, never saw the incompatibilities between the two modes of thought. Indeed, there is no evidence he was influenced by any of the NT writers. Yet he is the first orthodox thinker to critically evaluate the role of philosophy in Christian thought. Justin had shown it possible to combine middle Platonism and Christianity without becoming Gnostic.

The Logos christology, then, generated hard questions. In what sense is Jesus mediator? Simply as Logos? Or as the being in whom God and humanity have somehow become one? Is Justin's view that the impassible God cannot enter into direct commerce with "flesh" authentically

[4]*Ibid.*, 79.

Christian? Why cannot the incarnate Logos be taken as God present in person? On the other hand, some second-century thinkers, the Docetists, found it unthinkable that any divine being could become subject to the indignities of flesh. The humanity of Jesus was purely "appearance." The opposition between God and material creation was absolute. Indeed creation was the unfortunate work of a second inferior and evil god. Hence, salvation for these dualists and Gnostic thinkers was the escape of exiled human souls from the prison house of the material world by following the way revealed by the Christ, the Logos, whose flesh was a phantasm.

The life and ministry of Jesus had little place in such thinking. Christ was the "divine messenger," the "bringer of knowledge" sent by God to enable his hearers to "know themselves," to light the hidden spark within them, to rouse them from slumber and fit them for salvation. Christ's earthly sojourn was the stay of a heavenly being temporarily and illusorily united to mortal flesh.[5]

Unsurprisingly, then, Marcion of Pontus (c. 140) rejected the evil Jewish creator God of Genesis who spawned this evil universe and the outrageous belief in the incarnation of God's Logos. The God of whom the Law and the prophets spoke was not the Father of Jesus; the former is known, the latter unknown. There were two Gods therefore; the OT God, the Demiurge who is the creator and judge, and the good God, the Father of the Christ (Heresies 1:27:1 and 4:17:11). True Christianity contrasts the judicial God and the God of goodness, law and gospel. That was its newness and its glory. The Father of Jesus is the unknown God recognized by Paul (Acts 17:23). Jesus represented the boundless grace of God against the base justice of the Law. He himself was "revealed as a man but not a man." His was a body in appearance only and not subject to birth or passion, except in appearance.[6] But despite the problems concerning a mediating Logos and the very possibility of incarnation raised by Justin and Marcion, Logos theology slowly edged early Christianity away from the static unity of the Greek God. In continuity with its scriptures, it could conceive only of a God who, while

[5]Irenaeus, *Against Heresies* 1:24:4.

[6]Tertullian, *Against Marcion* 3:8; 4:8. Information about the life and teaching of Marcion is derived from opponents, chiefly Irenaeus, Tertullian, and Hippolytus. On Marcion's use of scripture to ground his teaching, see W.C.H. Frend, *The Rise of Christianity* (Philadelphia: Fortress, 1984), 213 f.

wholly transcendent, did not choose to remain in isolation, but freely engaged God's own self and power on behalf of humankind and somehow became a "God with us."

In Irenaeus of Lyons Catholic orthodoxy found a champion who combined a long life with a determined character and a fine turn of phrase. In his enormously influential book "Against Heresies," the classic statement of emerging orthodoxy in the early Greek-speaking church, Irenaeus, (c. 135-200), the bishop of Lyons, both pioneer and traditionalist, launched a frontal attack on the dualism and docetism of Marcion and other Gnostic thinkers.[7] Irenaeus, more biblical than philosophical, with little time for that "ancient Athenian, Plato,"[8] insists on the continuity of creation and redemption. There was no contrast between "natural man" made by the "creator God" and "spiritual man" made by the "unknown God" (Heresies 5:16:1-2). "The two testaments were ordained by one and the same God." The one and same ultimate God is creator and savior and is directly involved with material creation through "two hands," the Son and the Spirit, who were always with God and are God's way of being present in the world (ibid. 4:20:3). Both were active even in the Old Testament. There were distinctions in their functions but the non-philosophical bishop would not speculate on these. He is slow to identify the Son with the mediatorial Reason or Mind of God emanated by God for fear it would make of God a composite being (ibid. 2:28:5). Irenaeus simply retreats to biblical formulas: "Who shall describe his generation?" (Isa. 53:8). He will not be pushed into "foolish, rash, blasphemous explanations" (ibid. 2:28:3).

Irenaeus has learned from Justin but repudiates the latter's subordinationism and insists on the true divinity of the Son, who through his coming into real flesh can play the mediator. He is not mediator because he is a halfway house between God and humankind; his divinity is true and full. Moreover, in Irenaeus' panoramic linear view of history the incarnation of the Logos is the climax of the human story. It sums up or recapitulates what God has been up to through the Word and the Spirit since the dawn of creation, drawing humanity to a saving and trans-

---

[7]Cf. J. Lawson, *The Biblical Theology of St. Irenaeus* (London: Epworth, 1949); G. Wingren, *Man and the Incarnation: A Study of the Biblical Theology of Irenaeus* (Edinburgh: Oliver and Boyd, 1959).

[8]For Irenaeus' limitation of the range of reason, see his indignant response to the Gnostic query, "What was God doing before he created the world?" (*Heresies* 2:41:4).

forming knowledge of and assimilation to Godself. The whole history of humankind told in the two testaments is a story of education (*paideia*) and restoration of a likeness (*homoiosis*) obscured by Adam's sin (ibid. 5:6:1). The story of humankind told in the two testaments was the story of the gradual recovery of that "likeness." Each stage on the long way home is marked by a covenant; that of Noah, Abraham, and Moses, and thence through the prophets to the revelation of God in Christ (ibid. 3:11:8). God became what we are that we might become what God is. While God's self-communication in Jesus is in continuity with God's self-communication everywhere, the incarnate Logos is its highest realization and Christ is the exemplar of all that humans are meant to be (ibid. 3:11:8). The bishop of Lyons scans reality through Hellenist lenses: God's plan for the world will achieve completion only with the divinization of all flesh. Christ does not suddenly erupt upon the scene at Capernaum as an alien from nowhere. Rather the incarnation marks the climax in the ordered regularity of humanity's development. In it all previous progress toward salvation was summed up. The second Adam reversed step-by-step the errors of the first (ibid. 5:19:1). Irenaeus has welded basically Pauline themes into a coherent theological vision which embraced a christology and anthropology, the unity of scripture, the authority of the gospel-tradition, and the emergent power of the clergy. The cornerstone was his theory of recapitulation.

Gnostic dualism and docetism, however, died a slow death. A generation after Irenaeus we find Tertullian of Carthage (c. 165-240), a Latin-speaking North African, and possibly a lawyer, doing battle with them in his writings *Against Praxeas* and *On the Flesh of Christ* with its companion piece *On the Resurrection of the Flesh*.[9] But it was not only Gnosticism that triggered Tertullian's reflection on the Christ but the nagging problematic inherited from Justin's Logos-theology as well.

Tertullian's trenchant polemic is hurled against the Gnostic denial that salvation, a code word for which is resurrection, is inclusive of flesh as well as spirit along with its consequent denial of Christ's fleshly reality. For Tertullian, to reduce the incarnation to illusion is to undermine the worth and redeemability of physical reality. For all its squalor and feebleness flesh is capable of being the vehicle of God's

---

[9]Cf. T. Barnes, *Tertullian* (NY: Oxford, 1971).

presence and activity. "*Caro cardo salutis*;" flesh is the hinge of salvation. The other side of Tertullian's christology mounts a defense of the Logos doctrine against the Carthagian Monarchians, those who were so taken with the absolute oneness, the undifferentiated unity of God that they could not abide the diversity and distinctions which the novel Logos theology had smuggled into Christian monotheism. To their way of thinking it came dangerously close to Gnostic dualism. Consequently, while holding to the incarnation and the absolute unity of God, the Monarchians had to contend that it was God the Father who was incarnate in Christ. Noetus of Smyrna, teaching in Rome (c. 200), held that "Christ was the Father himself, and the Father himself was born, suffered, and died."[10] Noetus voiced what many Christians felt, that God truly suffered for humans on the cross. Most important of all Monarchians was Sabellius, the Libyan (c. 220). He argued that the Trinity consisted of modes or aspects of the one God: God as Father in creation, as Son in redemption, and as Spirit in sanctification. There was one substance (*hypostasis*) but three activities (*energeiai*). Another branch of Monarchianism was less well received. These dynamic Monarchians, like the Modalists, or Sabellians, stressed the biblical oneness of God. Focusing on the Synoptic accounts, they viewed Jesus as a man in whom the Godhead as divine power (*dynamis*) had descended at baptism, only to adopt him into the Godhead after his resurrection. Here is a position that embodies elements of primitive christology linked to Jewish angelology. Both types of Monarchianism ran the risk of leading back to Judaism. The Sabellian or Modalist view allowed little difference between Jesus' ministry and the theophanies of Genesis and Exodus. With the Adoptionists the legacy from the Hebrew prophets was at work.

The Modalist Monarchians had wed the Christian idea of God as Father to the Greek idea of God as one and immutable. But for them the Father is not one who is in dialogue with another, with a Son, but is rather the source and origin of all things. They had depersonalized fatherhood and rendered it a qualitative description. Moreover, their focus was on the One, the deity; they were little concerned with Jesus. The Monarchians, however, could not carry the day, for they could not account for the growing cult of Christ, his acknowledged soteriological

---

[10]This we learn from Hippolytus, *Against Noetus* 1.

role, and the alterity between him and the Father that the New Testament witnesses to (Against Praxeas 20:11:10). Tertullian charged them with subjecting the Creator himself to suffering and death and coined the term Patripassian to label his Modalist opponents. Deity is one in the nature that constitutes it, said the Carthaginian, but threefold in the articulation of that nature. Only fools, said Tertullian in reference to John 10:30, could not see that "I and the Father" meant two persons, but in unity, likeness, and mutual love. Father and Son were one (John 22:10). To explain the Father-Son difference Tertullian resorts to images of the fountain and its stream, the sun and its radiance (Apol. 21:12), all images that have led some to detect a subordinationism in his thought. God's Word or Son was projected; his inner Word (*ratio*) became his spoken Word (*sermo*) for purposes of creating and ordering the world. This same Word revealed God in the old dispensation and finally appeared incarnate in the Nazarene.

To explain Christ's relation to the Father, Tertullian also says that the two are of one substance, which for Tertullian is not, though it may seem so, an assertion of their equality. By substance he meant "stuff," the perceptible, fine material God is composed of. Christ, as Son, is an extrusion of this divine stuff. "The Father is the whole substance, whereas the Son is something derived from it, and a part of it" (ibid. 9). Tertullian, in his picture thinking did assert the Son is divine, but he was inconsistent in holding also that the Son is not the whole divine substance. Nor is he eternal. For Tertullian, as for Arius later, there was a time when "there was no Son to make God a Father" (Against Hermogenes 3).

In his Against Praxeas, Tertullian minted a christological terminology that has shaped Christian thinking to the present. He did so as he struggled to describe the person of the incarnate Logos. The Monarchians were maintaining that "Father" refers to the deity of Jesus, "Son" to his humanity. Tertullian in response cut a clear distinction between Father and Logos within the divine realm. Yet Jesus Christ could not be two separate entities, or *personae*; he is one, or more precisely, he is duality in unity according to Tertullian. He is one "person" (*persona*) constituted of two "substances" (*substantiae*), flesh and spirit. The human and the divine properties comingle in him without alteration and ground both divine and human actions. We recognize in this newly coined formula of the two substances in one person an anticipation of the classical resolution to the christological problem that will be hammered out more than two centuries later. In it we also see again Tertullian's love of paradox and contrast.

ORIGEN OF ALEXANDRIA

By far the greatest Christian thinker between Paul and Augustine was Origen (185-253), younger contemporary of Tertullian and head of the great catechetical school at cosmopolitan Alexandria.[11] With Origen, Alexandria assumed intellectual leadership of the Christian world. He spent his final years in exile in Caesarea following a falling out with his bishop, Demetrius. Steeped in knowledge of the Jewish and Christian scriptures and immensely learned in Greek philosophy, Origen was a skilled Christian apologist whose mental horizon was an eclectic middle-Platonism. For this seminal thinker Christianity was the highest form of philosophy, the only religion worthy of a rational being's belief. Its superiority could be demonstrated triumphantly. Immersion in Greek literature and philosophy was a *paideia* preparing the mind to grasp this greatest of philosophies, Christianity. While still young he crafted his famous work On First Principles (c. 225), an exposition of Christian doctrine and a response to the questions it raised for the contemporary mind. In this tract he lays the groundwork for a Logos doctrine and an understanding of the person and work of Jesus.

Origen is the first Christian thinker to clearly maintain that God, who alone is ungenerated (*agennētos*) and immutable, eternally begets Logos or Wisdom. There never was when the Logos did not exist (*ouk estin hote ouk ēn*—Principles 1:2:9). He even notes the words "when" and "never" have a temporal meaning that is not applicable in this case (ibid. 4:4:1). Though forever with the Father and sharing divinity, the fact of eternal generation distinguished the Logos from and subordinated it to the Father, who alone was unbegotten and the source of divinity (Jer. 9:4; Principles 1:2:4). The complete expression of God's being, wisdom, is distinct from the Father God; it is God's image (*eikon*), a "second God" (*deuteros theos*), and subordinate. It was less than God, but superior to all created beings, as it alone knew God and

---

[11]Cf. J. Daniélou, *Origen* (NY: Sheed & Ward, 1955); P. Nautin *Origène: sa vie et son oeuvre* (Paris: Beauchesne, 1977). Origen was prolific but only a fragment of his 6000 tracts and volumes remain. He lived in the bible, which he read as a Platonist, and wrote commentaries on practically all of its books. His *Hexapla* was an effort to establish a critical text of the Hebrew Scriptures. For an intimation of the scope of this giant see J. Trigg, "A Decade of Origen Studies," *RSR* 7 (1981) 21-27.

God's will (Principles 1:2:4). To Origen's mind, one must in one sense affirm the existence of two gods, in another sense, only one. He insists on the importance of holding there are two; their unity is comparable to the unity of marriage. "We must not fall into the opinion of those who, fearful of asserting two Gods, have separated from the church for the fantasy of the Monarchians, withdrawing the Son from the Father and thus practically suppressing the Father, nor, on the other side, fall into another impious doctrine, that which denies the deity of Christ" (Commentary on the Gospel of John 2:2). Origen thinks his position finds a warrant in the Eucharist where "the offering is always to be made to God through Jesus Christ (because) the offering is made to God through God" (Dialogue with Heracleides, 438). Origen cannot agree with Tertullian "that a part of God's substance was changed into the Son, or that the Son was begotten by the Father out of no substance at all ... so that there was a time when the Son did not exist." Rather "setting aside all thought of a material body," he argues that God's Word and Wisdom "was begotten of the invisible and incorporeal God apart from any bodily feeling, like an act of will proceeding from the mind" (Principles 4:4:1). Yet even though for Origen the Son is God, there is more than a hint of subordinationism in his teaching. For him the Father alone is "the God" pure and simple (*ho theos*) while the Son-Logos is *theos,* God only by participation and he uses terms with the prefix *autō* (in himself) of the Father, not of the Son.

Through the Word God created a world of intelligent spirits destined for contemplation of the Godhead. But defectible as they were, they rebelliously fell away from God, from unity into multiplicity, from eternity into time, from the immaterial into the material (ibid. 1:8:1). Hence through the Logos God created for them a material universe, a second-best cosmos. The physical world is a kind of purifying prison, a place of redemption by a schooling that begins a laborious education back to the contemplation of God. Education and remediation replace retribution and vindictive divine justice, for all; even Satan will be saved (ibid. 1:8:3). All creation moves to the goal of ultimate restoration of the harmony lost in the pre-cosmic fall, for evil is not a positive force and so it can hold no lasting reality (ibid. 1:6:3). All this necessitates the mediation of wisdom to the fallen, benighted spirits. Herein for Origen is the meaning of the incarnation. Mediation commences with the union of the Logos with the sole pure, undefiled intelligent spirit that did not defect from God, the rational soul that was to belong to Jesus (ibid.

2:6:3). Intense contemplative love is the modality of this communion. The faithful spirit's love of Wisdom draws it to identification with God's eternal Word. Thus it becomes the expression and mediation of divine Wisdom. Origen understands the union in terms of the blending of two substances, e.g., iron thrown into fire. Never ceasing to be what it is, the iron is penetrated and transformed, taking on all the attributes of fire. Similarly, the human soul of Jesus is assimilated to the divine Logos and transformed into the conveyor of wisdom.

Further, this soul suffused with the Wisdom that is God's self-expression becomes enfleshed. For Origen, as for the Alexandrians generally, this body by virtue of its union with the Logos, is as it were, divinized. The gospel story of the transfiguration catches a glimpse of that. Nevertheless, it is true corporeality and it is the medium in and through which the Logos reveals itself to sense-entrapped intelligences. Thus it becomes the means whereby exiled souls make their painful spiritual ascent which transcends space, time, and body to return to the spirit world of the Logos and their glorification. Certainly we are right in detecting here the hierarchical world of Justin and even the Gnostics where the divine does not soil itself by dealing directly with the physical order but makes use of mediation. The Logos mediates the deity to the soul, the soul mediates God's Logos-Son to the body, the body mediates wisdom to souls exiled from and forgetful of their homeland. For Origen, Jesus is the unique human being, perfectly one through his mind with the divine Wisdom. One cannot but note the continuity between the Gnostics and a Christian Platonist like Origen. He is able to say, "By nature Christ is divine (*theoteta*), but we being able to grasp truths concerning him only in material terms, regard him as man, although to know Christ crucified thus is the knowledge of babes" (Commentary on the Gospel of John 1:18 and 20). Belief in Christ as Redeemer also belongs to the lower life. "Blessed is he who wants the Savior no longer as Physician, Shepherd, or Redemption, but as Wisdom, Word, and Righteousness" (ibid. 1:22). It is inferior intellects that are preoccupied with the humanity of Jesus.

In any overview of Origen's christology, attention must also be given to his theology, his view of God.[12] In the work On First Principles, Origen asserts that God is incorporeal and incomprehensible, a commonplace of Judaism, Christianity, Gnosticism, and Middle Platonism.

[12]See R. Grant, *Gods and the One God* (Philadelphia: Westminster, 1986), 91-94.

God transcends creatures. A simple intellectual nature without admixture, God is a Monad, the source from which proceeds the beginning of mind or intellectual nature. God needs no place, just as our intelligence needs none. As intelligence, God is invisible. The anger or repentance of God spoken of in the scriptures are not to be taken literally, nor eliminated; rather they are to be interpreted properly, by which he means allegorized. Twenty-five years later in his treatise Against Celsus, Origen referred to "the doctrine of Jews and Christians which preserves the unchangeable and unalterable nature of God" (1:21). However, Origen seems to have been reconsidering his position on divine immutability. In his late Commentary on the Gospel of Matthew he affirms of the divine Logos that "as loving humankind the impassible one suffered with compassion" (10:23). And in his Homilies on Ezekiel (6:6) he ascribes emotion to God the Father caused by the Son's suffering. The change is striking and may be due to Origen's discovery of the letters of Ignatius of Antioch. In his earlier writings he never mentions Ignatius or his letters; later Origen approves the letters of the martyr and defends Ignatius' statement in his letter to the Romans that "My Eros has been crucified," which he takes as referring to Christ (Homilies on the Gospel of Luke 6; Exposition of the Song of Solomon, Prologue). In the same letter Ignatius makes reference to "the passion of my God," not likely to have pleased a younger Origen, though now he apparently accepts it.

Origen is asserting divine passibility. The Savior "came down to earth, taking pity on the human race, and experienced our passions before he suffered the cross and condescended to assume our flesh. For if he had not suffered he would not have entered into human life." (Exposition of the Song of Solomon, Prologue).

The point Origen is making is that the Savior experienced suffering in his divine, preincarnate condition, not just during his terrestrial life. Origen adds: "First he suffered, then he came down and was seen." This may derive from Ignatius (Ephesians 7:2) who states that Christ was "first passible and then impassible," referring to the incarnate and risen Lord. Origen, however, speaks of a state prior to the incarnation. "What is that passion he experienced for us?" Origen asks. Citing Psalm 103:8 he tells us it is the passion of love. This may tie in with his contention that *Eros* in Ignatius (Romans 7:2) means Christ. "Don't you know that when God deals with human affairs he experiences human passions?" This, Origen thinks, is borne out by Deuteronomy 1:31: "In the wilderness . . . you have seen how the Lord your God put up with you as a man puts up with his son." Taking this literally, he concludes that God puts up with our ways just as the Son of God puts up with our passions. "The Father himself is not impassible. If he is asked, he takes pity and commiserates, he suffers something of love and enters into circumstances in which by the greatness of his nature he cannot enter, and for us human beings endures passions."

Origen appears unfearful of Patripassianism. In his work On First Principles he was not rigid concerning divine impassibility. He encouraged exegetes to search for a spiritual understanding of texts attributing emotions to God "in order to think worthily of God" (First Principles 2:4:4; 4:2:9). Origen seems to have believed there are in God realities corresponding to these emotions. It is worth noting that even in the third century Christian doctrine was still in a fluid condition and open to contradiction by theologians. The battle did not merely pit the orthodox against the heretics. Orthodoxy was itself being shaped. What we have here is a struggle between Origen and Origen over a problem that occupies theologians even today.

The Arian Crisis

ARIUS OF ALEXANDRIA

The next step in the emergence of classical christology was necessitated during the Constantinian era by the Arian crisis in which the issues of the status and nature of the Logos, whom Origen had identified with the Son, came clearly to a head and threatened to tear a burgeoning Christianity asunder.[13] It was the inevitable question whether the Logos is a creature. While Christians generally took the Logos to be divine, the adjective divine was riddled with ambiguity. For many it signified a quality susceptible to gradations. On that reading the Logos is divine but not God in the same sense as the Father. We have detected this subordinationist tendency in Justin, Tertullian, and Origen. Indeed, theology was at this time almost universally subordinationist. A presupposition of some subordinationist views was a hierarchical world-

---

[13]On Arianism see R. Gregg and D. Groh, *Early Arianism: A View of Salvation* (Philadelphia: Fortress, 1981).

picture with a sovereign God who neither does nor can traffic with creatures. Some were drawn to subordinationism because through it the twin fears of Adoptionism and Monarchian Modalism were skirted.

Arius (c. 250-336), an Alexandrian presbyter, and an heir of the traditional doctrine that the Son was subordinate to the Father, boldly asserted the unity and transcendence of this deity who can not mix with the messy flux of the created world. The Logos, said Arius, cannot be God in any proper sense; rather the Logos, a demi-god, performs a mediating function between the true God and the world. Arius thought of the Logos as a creature, the greatest of creatures, not unoriginated but brought into existence out of nothing by God before the ages to serve as God's demiurge or artificer in creation. Though the Logos made all else, the Logos itself was made by the Father. The Son had a beginning but God is without beginning. "There was when he was not," said Arius (*ēn hote ouk ēn*). This became the slogan of Arius and his followers, the direct opposite of Origen's statement that "there is not when he was not" (First Principles 1:2:9). At best the Logos is God's son by adoption. For "how can the Logos, who sleeps like a man and weeps and suffers, be God?"[14] Arius found a warrant for his radical subordinationism in the scriptures (e.g., Prov. 8:22; Rom. 8:29; Col. 1:15; Mark 13:32; Acts 2:36; Phil. 2:4-11; John 14:24).[15] In addition, this Logos made flesh in Jesus performed all the functions of the human soul, which it rendered superfluous in this case. In this Arius voices the *Logos-sarx* or Word-flesh christology so typical of Alexandrian thinkers who, even when they affirmed a human spirit in Jesus tended not to give it full play. Arius accepted the idea of Christ's ethical development, the harmonization of his will with the Father's but he attributed this to the Word employing the body of Jesus.[16] Jesus *became* the Son of God by obediently holding to the will of God. He grew into Sonship as a reward for his fidelity. Only a difference of degree distinguishes him from God's other adopted children. Godly and godlike he may be—but not God.

In the end Arius, having moved further along the subordinationist road and negated the human soul of Jesus, offered a Christ who is neither fully God nor fully human. The problems for his contemporaries

[14]See Athanasius, *Orations Against the Arians,* 3:27.
[15]*Ibid.,* 3:26.
[16]Athanasius, *Apology Against the Arians* 1:5.

are obvious. The Arian Christ could neither create nor redeem and he could hardly be an object of worship.

THE SETTLEMENT OF THE COUNCIL OF NICAEA

In 318 Arius was condemned and deposed by Alexander the bishop of Alexandria. A schism ensued. The wily emperor Constantine,[17] who, like all great conquerors dreamed of world unity, and who hoped Christianity would be the cement of his empire, in 325 called a council at Nicaea to restore unity to a fragmented church. Some 318 bishops, mostly Eastern and Origenist, attended. The emperor exerted all his influence to create a unanimous consensus. In the end only two bishops demurred. In its famous creed the Council of Nicaea repudiated the Arian position and declared the Son is "true God of true God, begotten, not made, one in being with the Father" (*homoousion tō Patri*). The Nicene contention that the Logos was not a creature, but divine (and presumably eternal, as Origen had worked out the doctrine) in the same sense as the Father has ever since been codified in the non-biblical term imposed by the emperor, *homoousios,* which denotes a substantial identity between the Father and the Son. Creation language about *Sophia* in Prov. 8:22 yields to generation language required by the metaphor "Son." "True God from true God" indicates rejection of the philosophical distinction between the perfect God and the subordinate Demiurge. It is interesting that the term Logos does not occur in the creed. Nicaea preferred metaphors of personal relation (Son-Father) to those of linguistic analysis (Word-Thought). Moreover, whatever it means to be God must be affirmed of the Logos or Son as well as the Father, except that the Son is not the Father. Yet there is a certain incompleteness, if not ambiguity, in the Nicene formula. A new and technical term smacking of pagan philosophy and patient of Sabellian and adoptionist interpretations, "homoousios" raised as many questions as it solved. Nothing is said concerning the nature of the Father/Son distinction. If there is a numerical identity of nature between the two, how avoid the charge of Modalism? Many, even anti-Arians, distrusted the non-scriptural cipher homoousios precisely because of its modalist ring. But if, on the other hand, the identity is generic, how avoid

---

[17]Studies on Constantine are numerous. See e.g., N. Baynes, *Constantine the Great and the Christian Church,* (NY: Oxford University, 1972); R. MacMullen, *Constantine* (NY: Dial, 1969); T. Barnes, *Constantine and Eusebius* (Cambridge: Harvard University, 1981).

suspicion of ditheism, or perhaps another subordinationist interpretation. Finally, the council said nothing concerning the nature of the union of the Logos with the humanity of Jesus. Nor did it say how he is homoousios with us.

Creed of the Council of Nicaea 19 June 325

We believe in one God,
    the Father, the Almighty,
    maker of all things visible and invisible.
We believe in one Lord, Jesus Christ,
    the Son of God,
    begotten of the Father as only-begotten,
    that is, from the substance of the Father,
    God from God, Light from Light,
    true God from true God,
    begotten, not made,
    of one being (*homoousion*) with the Father,
    through whom all things were made,
    all things in heaven and on earth.

For us and for our salvation he came down;
he became incarnate and was made man and suffered.
On the third day he rose again;
he ascended into heaven.
He will come again to judge the living and the dead.

And we believe in the Holy Spirit.

But as for those who say, "There was when he was not,"
    or "Before he was begotten he was not,"
    or "He was made out of nothing,"
    or who affirm that the Son of God
        is of a different subsistence (*hypostaseōs*)
        or substance (ousias), or a creature, or mutable,
        or subject to change,
    these the catholic and apostolic church denounces
    and cuts off.

Unsurprisingly, the word selected to end the Arian controversy only complicated it; it would take the church another half century to exorcise the spirit of Arianism, which won the support of Constantine's successors, increasingly important players as the church-empire entanglement develops. Meanwhile, in 335 Constantine recalled Arius, who had been exiled in Illyria, and ordered a grand reconciliation at Constantinople. As fate would have it, Arius died the day before his reconciliation, poisoned according to some.[18] It is difficult to overestimate the impact of the *homoousios* on all the centuries to follow. In a sense it marked a Christianization of Hellenism. The rigid logic of Arius is rejected in favor of a more flexible logic employed since Paul onward through Ignatius, Tertullian, and Origen. God's relation to the world of humans is now affirmed as internal to God's being. There is no need for semi-divine bridge-builders; God is with humanity. The middle realm is eliminated; God is not distant, for God's presence is experienced in space and time. There is no hiatus between being and becoming, God and nature. And a God who is incarnate and related revalues time, history, corporeality, and the individual. Nicaea is, therefore, less about who Jesus is than about who and what God is. In a word, Nicaea is more theological than directly christological, treating as it does the being and nature of God more than the incarnation, though there are obvious christological implications. From Nicaea to the present the Greek and Christian Gods have been juxtaposed and the tension between the two never resolved. Moreover, the Nicene confession, reduced in folk-piety to "Jesus is God," will contribute to centuries of christocentrism and the recession of theocentrism, to ecclesiological triumphalism, and exclusivism, to a eucharistic liturgy that becomes increasingly removed from the people, to a cult of Marian mediation, and to a tendency to nudge the humanity of Jesus into oblivion.

For christology Nicaea's creed became the touchstone of orthodox christology and would impose a controlling structure that would perdure well into the 20th century. High christologies, christologies from above will be the order of the day.[19] These abstract, essentialist

---

[18]For Athanasius' account of Arius' death, see his *On the Death of Arius*, 3:3.

[19]Reference to high and low or to descending and ascending christologies, or to christologies from above and from below are not without ambiguity, for the meaning of the terms seems to shift with the context of their usage. In NT studies "pre-existence

christologies will focus on the incarnation as the central redemptive event with little attention to the soteriological value of the life, ministry, cross, and resurrection of Jesus. And the dialogue portrayed in the gospels between Jesus and his Father will be projected inside the Godhead to become a dialogue between the Father and the Logos, in which the humanity of Jesus recedes.[20] In sum, the Alexandrian school of thought would dominate the field. Nicaea with its homoousios very rightfully eschewed biblicism, the mere parroting of biblical formulas, and condoned the enterprises of intellect and the use of philosophy in the Christian search for understanding. But the transcultural shift in modes of thought and discourse from narrative and descriptive to discursive and philosophical was a large one seeded with unforeseen positive and negative consequences that would flower in due time. Meanwhile Nicaea would be held in great esteem, having given the community its first "dogma." Later councils would refer to it as "the holy and great synod."

ATHANASIUS

In 328 the great churchman Athanasius (295-373), the arch-opponent of Arius, succeeded Alexander as bishop of Alexandria. At times he was almost alone, championing the Nicene decree as the whole world seemed to turn Arian. Throughout his forty-five year episcopate the shrewd ecclesiastic reveled in controversy and seldom spared an opponent.[21]

Athanasius admitted "homoousios" was new and it would have been desirable to stick to the words of scripture. He saw, however, this route was no longer viable, blocked as it was by the skill of the Arians in construing scripture to suit their views. There was no choice but to go outside the scriptures for an unequivocal formula. Whether homoousios makes the issue as clear as Athanasius believes depends on how one understands "substance." If it means material stuff, or some mysterious

christologies" are high and "agency" and "exaltation" christologies are low. Liberal theology of the nineteenth century is said to have a low christology insofar as it views Jesus as little more than an outstanding human being in his relationship to God, or as merely a great teacher. Many who speak of low christology in the New Testament seem to intend more. In the context of this chapter high christology is a christology that heavily emphasizes the divine dimension of Jesus' being, while low christology emphasizes his full humanity. In neither case is there a denial of the unemphasized dimension, though there may well be a tendency to neglect it.

[20]Dwyer, *Son of Man*, 143 f.

[21]Cf. E. Meijering, *Orthodoxy and Platonism in Athanasius* (Leiden: Brill, 1968).

ectoplasm, all of Tertullian's problems resurrect; the problems of Patripassianism or ditheism would then accompany the avowal Father and Son are "of one substance." Athanasius, however, chose not stuff but sunlight as his metaphor, a common image for the Father-Son relation. The sun and its radiance are distinct. Yet the radiance does not come after the sun as an addition. Neither is it a different light. Nor does it become light by participating in the light that is the sun. Rather the sun generates brightness as its offspring. And the two, unlike children and parents, are one and inseparable. So Father and Son are two though the Deity is but one. This image provides a preliminary idea of what homoousios might mean. But all images pale when applied to God. Origen was right; God is not imaginable. Athanasius knew this. "Just as we have no human thoughts when we say 'offspring,' and just as we entertain no material ideas about God though we know he is a Father, so in like manner, when we hear 'consubstantial' (*homoousios*) we ought pass beyond our senses" (On the Councils of Ariminum and Seleucia 52; 42; 49). What is left of the sunlight image, then, is this. As one light belongs equally to the sun and its light, so there is one divinity and it is as much the Son's as the Father's "All that you find said of the Father, you will find equally said of the Son, all except his being Father." To support this Athanasius marshalls thirty scripture quotations and sets them in pairs to show how attributes of God are predicated of Christ. For example, both are said to be Lord, almighty, everlasting and to both are ascribed remission of sin and the raising of the dead.

Having started with a familiar image to suggest what homoousios means, Athanasius proceeded to qualify it by distilling out any hint of materiality or visuality. In a sense, we are left without an image. For consubstantiality is not a sensible quality such as pinkness or sweetness. As Athanasius explains it, the homoousios doctrine means no more and no less than a rule of speech: whatever is said of the Father is likewise said of the Son, except the name "Father."

In keeping with the rule, Athanasius thought Christ as Lord was to be worshiped because of what he did and still was doing. According to the Arians he had only done what everyone can, in principle, do. He holds his sonship in the same way other creatures do, hence what is predicated of the redeemer can and must be predicated of the redeemed. To the contrary Athanasius insisted Christ's saving work was a work that only God can do, hence what is predicated of God can and must be predicated of the redeemer. Again, this is his rule for interpreting "homoousios." According to Athanasius, the bishops at Nicaea culled a series of scriptural assertions about Christ "and finally they wrote, more plainly and concisely, that the Son is consubstantial with the Father, for that is what all these passages mean" (Synodical Letter to the Bishops of Africa 6). Homoousios is, then, for the council a kind of code word or shorthand for a statement about statements. It stands for a second-order proposition: all the predicates of God, except the name "Father," are also predicates of the Son. The Athanasian rule is a logical rule and thus open-ended; as such it concerns the form, not the content of propositions. It does not dictate which attributes are to be predicated of the Father, and so of the Son as well. The believer is free to conceive the Father in scriptural, patristic, medieval or modern terms. The discovery of logical techniques was a major human achievement. The introduction of one such technique into Christian discourse marks a major shift in context. The moving and colorful language of scripture is not jettisoned, any more than a youngster ceases to talk after learning to talk *about* talk.[22] However, the Christian message had now come to be reflected on as well as preached. The community continued to proclaim Christ; but it had also begun to probe and systematize its teaching. Nicaea and its champion, Athanasius, mark an important turning point.

We cannot leave Athanasius without noting that in his treatise On the Incarnation of the Logos of God he essays to state the "why?" of the incarnation: to restore humanity to the condition God originally intended for it. According to Athanasius, influenced by Hellenist thought, the Creator had intended humans to be conformed to God's own divine way of being through union with Godself by knowledge. Sin meant aversion from the knowledge of God and entailed forfeiture of the gift of immortality with the incurrence of physical and spiritual death which consists in the obliteration of the image of God in humans. Restoration is thus a re-creation which cancels liablity to death and reestablishes the image of God in humanity. The death of the incarnate Logos pays the debt whereby humans are liable to physical death and the presence of the Logos in the world empowers people to participate in the divine life. Restoration therefore involves retrieval of the gift of

[22]See C. Hefling, Jr., *Why Doctrines?* (Boston: Crowley, 1984) and G. Lindbeck, *The Nature of Doctrine: Religion and Theology in a Postliberal Age* (Philadelphia: Westminster, 1984). Both authors develop well the notion of dogma as a rule of speech and use the "homoousios" to exemplify this viewpoint.

immortality and the rediscovery of the true self in the one perfect image of God, the Logos.

Since salvation or the realization of true selfhood is found in divinization (*theopoiēsis*) or assimiliation to God's way of being, an idea typical of the Christian Gnostics of Alexandria, it can be effected only through God's active presence. The Savior must be God; the incarnation must be the enfleshment of God. "The word would never have made us divine if he were merely divine by participation and not himself the essential Godhead, the Father's veritable image" (De Synodis 51). Athanasius stands squarely opposed to Arianism, which conceived of salvation as a superior sort of formation. For Athanasius it was nothing short of transformation, being drawn into the very life of God. "For he became human so that we might become divine" (On the Incarnation 54). Salvation as re-creation of fallen humanity could be the work of God alone, not of a Logos interposed between the divine and the human. Like Irenaeus before him, Athanasius holds to a direct union of God with humanity in Jesus. In championing Nicaea Athanasius was not just squabbling over a word. He saw Arian teaching was at odds with the church's cultic life. "We do not worship a creature. Far be it. Such an error belongs to pagans and Arians" (Letter to Adelphius 3). To many, however, Athanasius appeared Sabellian. And what of the Arian objection that much that is said of Jesus in the gospels cannot be predicated of the Logos if the latter is true God? The hunger and thirst of Jesus, his anger and sadness, his ignorance and growth, do these not indicate his creatureliness? As a Logos-sarx or Word-Flesh christology, Arianism assumes that the Logos is the sole real subject or self in Jesus and is affected by all Jesus does or suffers. The analogy of the embodied soul is the key to understanding the incarnated Logos. Jesus is the divine Logos joined to a body with no human soul. Arianism had posited an irreconcilable difference between divine and human ways of being. The transcendent God could not be affected by physical realities, feel emotion, or experience ignorance as the Logos was and did.

Exiled five times in seventeen years during the post-Nicene Arian ascendancy, Athanasius, in the third of his Orations Against the Arians, written in the Egyptian desert (c. 360), strives to counter the Arian objection by distinguishing the Logos in itself and the Logos in flesh. Emotion and ignorance cannot be attributed to the former, but only to the latter. Human qualities may be truly predicated of the Logos as incarnate, though only indirectly.

While disavowing the Arian's denial of the Logos' divinity because of his view of soteriology as continuing the divine work of creation, Athanasius otherwise agrees with them on the constitution of Jesus and shares their Logos-sarx approach. For the champion of Nicaea, as for the Arians, incarnation does not mean that the Logos indwells in a complete human being. Incarnation is not mere inspiration. Rather, the Logos assumed as his own a human body, flesh (*sarx*) and became the sole real self or subject in Jesus. Though he never explicitly denies a rational soul in Jesus, Athanasius does not affirm a conscious human subjectivity in him. As for the Arians, so for Athanasius; Jesus is the divine Logos united to flesh as its passive instrument. Indeed, he even speaks of Jesus feigning weakness and ignorance, masking his omnipotence and omniscience, acting "as if" he were human (Against the Arians 3:43).[23] To check the Arian attack on the divinity of Jesus because of his fear, suffering, etc. we would expect Athanasius to appeal to Jesus' human mind and subjectivity. But he never does. Obviously, this approaches Docetism, for it impoverishes the full humanity of the Galilean. We are far from the gospel story and far too from the community's early days. "The old creeds were creeds for catechumens, the new creed was a creed for bishops."[24] It tested the orthodoxy of clerics, not of baptismal candidates.

[23]Note that the term "incarnation" began as the Latin translation of the assertion made in John 1:14: *Logos sarx egeneto*. Sarx in John connotes the created realm in all its weakness and vulnerability, not that which is posed over against the soul. The Johannine prologue seems less concerned with the coexistence of the Word with God than with the fact that "God was (the) Word" (John 1:1). Though often invoked as a proof text of the divinity of Christ, the assertion seems to be not so much about the Word but about God. God is a God who goes outside Godself to be with creatures. Because eternally God is Word there can be a human in whom God may take to Godself the weakness of the sarx condition. The Alexandrians not only tend away from the biblical notion of sarx; they also render incarnation problematic, as do many today, because for them incarnation means a divine being takes on a truncated humanity. This literalizes the myth and fails to see the Christ as an event in which God's commitment to history becomes real in a human person. In fact, such a view isolates God from history in its attempt to protect God from the *becoming* that is intrinsic to history and to satisfy an imperative of Greek thought to the neglect of an imperative of Christian thought. Dwyer, *Son of Man*, 150 f.

[24]J.N.D. Kelly, *Early Christian Creeds* (London: Longmans, Green, 1950), 205 and 209 f.

APOLLINARIS OF LAODICEA

Perhaps Athanasius never openly addresses the question whether Jesus was or was not endowed with a human consiousness, though he does tend to suggest he was not. His scholarly and ascetic friend, Apollinaris (310-390), the bishop of Laodicea in Syria, did raise the question of Christ's relationship to humanity and his human personality and converted Athanasius' suggestions into a strongly argued position.[25] A respected champion of Nicene orthodoxy in Antioch, Apollinaris defended the Alexandrian Logos-sarx christology in opposition to those who taught the incarnation to be the special indwelling of the Logos in a human being. He accents the unity of Christ's being and person with the formula "one incarnate nature of the Word of God" (*mia physis tou Theou Logou sesarkōmenē*). Concerned with the Arian argument that if the Word is joined to a mutable human body, it in turn becomes mutable, Apollinaris needed to show how the divine Logos could enter such a union while remaining immutable. Apollinaris thought the two natures could not be united unless they were complementary; some element must be missing in one that the other will provide. Moreover, he feared the presence of two conflicting centers of consciousness in Jesus, one human, one divine (Fragment 81). Further, how could a fallible, depraved human spirit be the source of our salvation? Here were the issues shaping Apollinaris' christology. Humanity was saved by the incarnation (*sarkōsis*) of the divine Word, not by the Word's being liable to human weakness and failings.[26]

Seizing wrongly upon the Pauline spirit/flesh contrast (e.g., 1 Thess. 5:23), Apollinaris wove it into his own tripartite neo-Platonic anthropology. "Spirit" (*pneuma*) refers to the intellect, the rational soul; "flesh" (*sarx*) to the body; and "soul" (*psychē*) simply to the irrational, animal principle. The incarnation of the divine Logos was comparable to the enfleshment of a rational soul. The Logos became human insofar as it was embodied. There could be no created intellect in the Christ; such

[25]For texts of Apollinaris, see H. Lietzmann, *Apollinaris von Laodicea und seine Schule: Texte und Untersuchungen* (NY: G. Olms, 1970). On Apollinarianism, cf. C. Raven, *Apollinarianism: An Essay on the Christology of the Early Church* (NY: MacMillan, 1923).

[26]Barsumas (d. 459), a Syrian monk, summed it up well: "If the nature of the blood of the crucified only Son had been the same nature as the blood of the sons of Adam, how could it have expiated the sins of the sons of Adam?" Cited in Frend, *The Rise of Christianity*, 779.

could only be superfluous in the presence of its divine original. The Logos, the divine spirit of God the Son, substituted in Christ for a human mind. Had the Logos taken to itself a rational soul as well as encasement in flesh, there would have been a clash of wills, a schizoid disunity, or the divine Logos would have simply dominated the human subjectivity. If there are two Sons, one by nature, the other by adoption, into which is the Christian baptized? "There cannot co-exist two minds with opposing wills in one and the same subject" (Fragment 1509). Thus a man-God was an impossibility (Fragment 91). Moreover, the Word is changeless. "A human mind is subject to vain imaginings; but he was a divine mind, changless and heavenly" (Letter to Bishops of Diocaesarea). God could not redeem and be impure or even liable to impurity. At any rate, the Word can be only the active, never the passive agent in Christ. It is the sole center of consciousness, governing and informing the body of Jesus. "The flesh of Christ united itself to the heavenly governing principle, the Word, and was fused with it. So out of the moved and the mover was composed a single living entity" (Fragment 107). Hence to the divine Logos alone do we attribute the conquest of sin and the assimilation of humanity to a divine quality of life. Thus Apollinaris, eliminating any partnership of two sons, greatly tightened the unity of the two elements constitutive of the Christ. The truly human body of Jesus is somehow divine flesh, for Word and flesh are one composite reality. Apollinaris followed a course pursued by Athanasius. But he went farther and in his clarity pressed to its full logical consequences the Alexandrian Logos-sarx model. It is not simply that he did not give sufficient play to the human consciousness of Jesus. He eliminated it. The Logos wore humanity like a cloak.

Apollinaris was condemned by the bishop of Rome in 374 and again by the Council of Constantinople in 381. It is interesting that while the council considered Apollinaris wrong, and implied two centers of consciousness in Jesus, it did not say how unity was to be safeguarded. Even more interesting, however, is the refutation of Apollinaris by the Cappadocians.[27] Their argument is grounded in the Hellenist tradition that salvation is deification. Specifically, if the Christ had no human

---

[27]The Cappadocian fathers are Basil the Great, Gregory of Nazianzus, and Gregory of Nyssa. Cf. the three essays on them in H. von Campenhausen, *The Fathers of the Greek Church* (London: Black, 1963). See also G. Prestige, *St. Basil the Great and Apollinaris of Laodicea* (London: SPCK, 1956).

mind, the Logos does not touch and heal humanity at its point of greatest need. True enough, salvation must have God as its author, but also full humanity as its recipient. "What he did not assume he could not redeem," said Gregory of Nazianzus (Letter 101:7). There must be a commonality between savior and saved. In the Cappadocians' minds Christ does not merely pay a debt or provide an example; he changes, divinizes the very being of humanity in all its dimensions. Therein lies the meaning of the incarnation of the Logos. In their typically Greek thinking, for the Logos to have transformed one instance of human nature is to have transformed all, for there is but one human nature. Nonetheless, the Cappadocian argument is not completely consistent. For them too the divine is the center of Christ's being; his humanity is divinized if not absorbed. The stars may have their own light, but when the sun shines, says Gregory of Nazianzus, their light fades away (Letter 101). And Gregory of Nyssa found the humanity of Jesus absorbed by the divinity of the Logos as a drop of vinegar in the sea (Against Eunomius 5:5). What seems crucial to the Cappadocians is that in Christ the Logos took on humanity, not that it remained like our own. This was perilously close to Arian and Docetist views of Jesus' humanity. And it suggests a hybrid from the mingling of the human and the divine which is not, perhaps, too far removed from the view of Apollinaris. Yet it gave voice to the soteriological foundation of Alexandrian theology. This was the principle that only the divine can deify and therefore not only is the Logos divine, but the flesh of Christ must be divine flesh, the flesh of God.

The School of Antioch

A WORD-MAN CHRISTOLOGY

It is important to note, however, that the Logos-sarx pattern of the Alexandrian school met its opposition in a cluster of thinkers who came to be tagged "the Antiochene School" because it was centered in the catechetical school of Antioch in Syria.[28] These thinkers countered the

---

[28]On the two schools of thought see H. Chadwick, *Early Christian Thought: Studies in Justin, Clement, and Origen* (NY: Oxford University, 1966); R. Sellers, *Two Ancient Christologies* (London: SPCK, 1954) and C. Gibbs, *The Christian Platonists of Alexandria* (NY: Oxford University, 1913).

Apollinarian stress on one nature with a focus on the duality in Christ, the divine Logos and the complete man, Jesus. The controlling model for the Antiochene understanding of the incarnation is indwelling. In time, their way of thinking came to be designated as a *Logos-anthropos* or Word-man christology. In the first place, the Antiochenes were fearful that Logos-sarx christology rendered the Logos mutable, subject to human limitations and passions. Rather than saying with Athanasius that the Logos wept, hungered, and suffered "according to the flesh," the Antiochenes would contend it was the human being Jesus who did all these things, not the Logos. Thus there were in Christ two subjects of predication. Apollinaris might erroneously speak of one hypostasis, one reality, or one nature in Christ, but the truth is that Christ is constituted of two hypostases and two complete natures. Secondly, the Antiochenes knew that the identity of Jesus with the Logos was crucial for the Alexandrians because they viewed the Logos as the prototype of humanity, the divine image in which it was created. Assimilation to the Logos was the vocation of the human being. The Antiochenes, however, assume a more modest starting point, the very human life of Jesus. The destiny of humans is imitation of the human Jesus in his struggle with iniquity and his effort to live a moral life according to God's law. Antiochene christology was everything its Alexandrian rival was not. Focusing on the life, ministry, and death of the Jesus of the Synoptics rather than on incarnation, it was a low christology rather than a high christology, for it began from below with the Nazarene, not from above with the pre-existent Johannine Logos. It was ascending rather than descending, for it focused on the laborious ascent of Jesus to the Father above rather than on the descent of the glorious Logos to flesh. Finally, the Antiochenes took the scriptures more literally and did not allegorize them as the Alexandrians did.

The school of Antioch had no difficulty uniting the human and the divine in Jesus. The humanity of Jesus, and his humanity alone, is God's own. But the Antiochenes did not express this unity in ontological terms. The unity is not located at the level of being, for two different realms of being are involved. Rather unity is expressed in the moral terms of intention and action. If the humanity of Jesus is to be assumed by the Word a human response is needed. The Word summons; the humanity responds. The Word elects; the humanity accepts. The union is one of wills and minds.

THEODORE OF MOPSUESTIA

The Antiochene traits are best exemplified in the school's leading thinker, Theodore (†428), the bishop of backwater Mopsuestia.[29] Theodore voices the Antiochene soteriology and it is different from that of the Alexandrians: salvation is through participation in the humanity of Christ, which is the same as ours and not therefore passively controlled and motivated by the Logos. It was not merely a human body that was assumed but a complete man, body and soul, and it is the latter which brings about the experiences of human weakness. According to the Apollinarian understanding, the flesh of God could not suffer weakness or defects. Theodore thus had to face the problem of the natural liability of Christ's soul to sin. Apollinaris had secured the sinlessness and immutability of Christ's will by postulating as the seat of his will the Logos in place of a rational soul. For Theodore, however, Christ was sinless because of God's grace acting on his human soul (Catechetical Homilies 5:19).

Central to the great exegete's christology is the divine presence by indwelling. Theodore has more in mind than the divine omnipresence, more even than the presence of God in the inspiration of the prophets and holy persons; certainly a circumscribed local presence is not even a consideration. The incarnation entails a unique kind of indwelling presence. The human Jesus can identify with the Sonship of the Logos as no saint could. God abides in Jesus "as in a son." United with the Logos in the instant of conception, and growing and maturing through his combat with evil, Jesus progresses in his union with the Logos until finally, in the resurrection, there is the manifestation of what has been all along, the functional identification of the man Jesus with the Logos. The two are one *prosōpon*, (On the Incarnation 7), or as is misleadingly put in English, one "person." This permanent, indestructible union of the whole assumed man with the Logos is, according to Theodore, a prosopic union grounded in God's gracious initiative. The human Jesus in all his willing and acting is completely one with the Logos. But this union, it must be emphasized, is not an indwelling according to good pleasure (*eudokia*), if that means merely a divine reward for a life well

[29]Cf. R. Norris, *Manhood and Christ: A Study in the Christology of Theodore of Mopsuestia* (Oxford: Clarendon, 1963); R. Greer, *Theodore of Mopsuestia: Exegete and Theologian* (Philadelphia: Westminster, 1961).

lived by Jesus, even though a genuinely human victory is central to Theodore's christology. It is wholly God's doing, the initiative of God's gracious will. It must also be noted that Theodore, in sharp contrast to the Alexandrians, understands the bonding between divinity and humanity in the incarnation in terms of total harmony of will or a moral union of mutual love and not in terms of a substantial or physical union. God, thinks Theodore, is present to chosen ones by the "disposition" of his will. Consequently, all of this implies for Theodore two conscious subjects in Christ. He can distinguish the true Son by nature from the one who shares Sonship by union. Yet he disallows talk of two sons. Distinction of natures and unity of prosōpon must be safeguarded (ibid. 12 and 5). The Antiochenes speak indifferently of two hypostases (two entities) or two unconfused natures, not in any abstract sense but in the concrete sense of two very different realities, the Logos and the man assumed to whom it is united. Each nature has in itself its own concrete subsistence and is a hypostasis, an entity in its own right with its own external individual presentation (prosōpon); but there is one external presentation (prosōpon) of the two conjoined (ibid. 8).

Though Theodore provides an advance towards a more satisfactory christology by ascribing soteriological significance to Christ's humanity and avoiding the Alexandrian necessity to explain away much in the gospel narratives, the Antiochene employment of indwelling would lead to the charge that it allowed only a difference of degree, not the required difference in kind, between Jesus and other humans. And the Antiochene insistence on duality would be considered by the Alexandrians as a threat to the unity of Christ. The two subjects in Christ merely appear to be one; they are said to be one prosōpon, a word well chosen because it denotes a mask, a role, an external appearance. Hence the charge that Theodore and the Antiochenes end with a conjunction, not a union. And where then was the uniqueness of the incarnation? How differentiate Jesus from the saints and prophets? In fairness, if Theodore liked to speak of a "conjunction" (*synapheia*), Apollinaris also used the term and it can signify any degree of unity from mere association to fusion.

The Nestorian Controversy

NESTORIUS AND CYRIL OF ALEXANDRIA

The two schools of thought, on a collision course, met head on in the second quarter of the fifth century. The bitterness was aggravated by the intense political rivalry between Constantinople and Alexandria. The first blow was struck when the loquacious and tactless Nestorius (†451), an Antiochene presbyter and disciple of Theodore, became in 428 patriarch of Constantinople.[30] His views, which did not differ significantly from Theodore's, were to put him in conflict with the able scholar Cyril (†444), bishop of Alexandria and an unscrupulous ecclesiastic. Nestorius riled popular piety by attacking the use of the term "theotokos" (God-bearing) for Mary as unscriptural, blasphemous, and a confusion of the two natures in Christ, and suggested "christotokos" or "theodochos" (God-receiving) as more suitable.[31] Not only was the attack offensive to folk piety, but also to the Alexandrians who saw the theotokos as a guarantee of the unity of Christ. For the Alexandrians, since the Logos is the ultimate subject of the human predications of Jesus, it was proper to say the Logos was born of Mary. Nestorius felt theotokos, which is not found in the creed, implied the Logos underwent suffering and became mutable. No mother can, moreover, bear what is not consubstantial with herself. Theotokos was preserved for the Father in the generation of the Logos. Yet Nestorius concedes use of theotokos if it does not signify that deity was born of Mary but that the union of Jesus with deity begins with the moment of conception.

Nestorius also wished to maintain the full reality of Christ's humanity with its own separate prosōpon, or concrete presentation. For Nestorius prosōpon seems to connote a psychological entity, a center of consciousness, personhood as many would say today, a unique set of psychological traits and activities, not merely the ontological or metaphysical entity or the independently subsisting individual. Taking prosōpon or person in this psychological-existential sense, he asserted there were two prosōpa in Christ, the prosōpon of the logos and the prosōpon of the man Jesus because each nature is real, distinct, and complete in its own individuality. Hence one could distinguish in Christ the Son of God from the son of David. The Nicene Creed, said

---

[30]Cf. J. Bethune-Baker, *Nestorius and His Teaching* (NY: MacMillan, 1908); F. Loofs, *Nestorius and His Place in the History of Christian Doctrine* (NY: MacMillan, 1914); Nestorian texts can be found in Loofs, *Die Fraqmente des Nestorius* (Halle: Max Niemeyer, 1905).

[31]The contemporary historian Socrates described Nestorius as "disgracefully illiterate," and causing needless alarm by his "extreme ignorance" (*Ecclesiastical History* 7:32:10).

Nestorius, indicates this duality of natures in its profession of belief in Jesus Christ, "Christ" signifying both natures. Any failure to hold to the duality led to the mutable Logos of the Arians, or to the incompletely human Christ of Apollinaris. It is also an attack upon the truth of redemption through its refusal to recognize that it was as an authentic human that Christ experienced evil and suffering and won the victory (Heraclides 132ff.).[32] But duality is not all. In addition, by reason of the union there is in Christ a distinct overarching prosōpon of union which is designated by the name, "Christ," for there is but one concrete external presentation of the natures (212; 219). He also calls it the common prosōpon or voluntary prosōpon. What kind of union is this? A union of will (Kath'eudochian), a union of good pleasure, a voluntary or personal union. Within the prosōpon of union there is an interchange of properties (*communicatio idiomatum*). The properties of either nature can equally be predicated of Christ, who is the single external presentation of the two. It implies no actual exchange of properties between diety and humanity (ibid. 289; 331; 343).

Note the Antiochene accent on the ethical character of the union; Jesus is a man who does God's will. But when Nestorius used terms such as "cojoined," "linked," "juxtaposed," etc., his opponents charged him with denying a true ontological, substantial union of two natures. The prosōpon of union only muddied the waters for it seemed to connote simply the outward appearance of unity and individualness. In a word, Nestorious would appear to his opponents to have negated the oneness of the Christ with his talk of two sons, which could not be smoothed over by more talk of a common prosōpon.

Nestorius' opposition to the theotokos fired angry opposition among the people but especially among the Alexandrians led by Cyril, the tough champion of Alexandrian christology and a crafty ecclesiastical politician.[33] Cyril's refusal to make the least concession to Nestorius' christology or even to try to grasp his view seems motivated more by inter-patriarchal rivalry than by theological concern. His later success in coming to terms with the Antiochenes at the price of Nestorius' removal

---

[32]*The Bazaar of Heraclides* is Nestorius' personal Apologia, written toward the end of his life, English ed. G. Driver and L. Hodgson (NY: Oxford University, 1926).

[33]Cf. Sellers, *Two Ancient Christologies*; J. Liebaert, *La doctrine christologique de Saint Cyrille d'Alexandrie avant la querelle nestorienne* (Lille: N.P., 1951). The enigmatic Cyril awaits his biographer.

is evidence of this. Between 429 and 431 Cyril, the bishop of Alexandria, urged the patriarch of Constantinople in three letters to jettison his views, denounced him to the bishop of Rome, Celestine, and in writings sent to some Egyptian monks and the Eastern Emperor put forth what he thought to be orthodoxy: the Christ is "one incarnate nature of the Word of God." Cyril found the formula in a work spuriously attributed to Athanasius but actually an Apollinarian forgery. Intensely loyal to Athanasius (Letter 39), Cyril affirmed the completeness of Jesus' humanity, mind and body, and the Nicene roots of the Apollinarian phrase. The Nicene creed confesses the Logos is the very one who was born, suffered, died, and raised up. Jesus, contended Cyril, is the Logos incarnate, existing within the conditions of humanity. "Man" for Cyril meant representative of humanity, second Adam, not a pre-constituted particular individual, not even the man Jesus of Nazareth. And he grounds the contention in John 1:14 and Phil. 2:5-11. Nestorius notwithstanding, this was not to imply mutability in the Logos, nor the loss of divinity. Without ceasing to be what God always is, God became what we are (Letter 4). Cyril encapsulated his views in the formula "union in hypostasis" (*kath'hypostasin*) or "hypostatic union." "We confess the essential (*kath'hypostasin*) union of word with flesh, we worship one Son and Lord, neither sundering man and God" (Letter 17:5). Only the most fundamental union between Godhead and humanity could endow human flesh with invincibility against death. Humanity's salvation, to become divine, called for a savior whose divinity cannot be doubted. "To one hypostasis must be attributed all the expressions used in the Gospels, the one incarnate individuality (*hypostasis*) of the Word" (Letter 17:8).

Cyril means that the Logos is the subject of human experience; the eternal Logos is born, suffers, and knows human weakness. In line with the Alexandrian tradition, he maintains that the union of divinity and humanity in Christ is a union in the hypostasis of the Logos, and not in Nestorius' "Christ." Nestorius reduces Christ to an inspired man who has been awarded divine status (Against the Blasphemies of Nestorius, Pref.). As Cyril sees it, the Logos is united hypostatically to flesh "ensouled with a rational soul" (ibid.); the case against Apollinaris had settled that much. Cyril, nonetheless, affirms Apollinaris' belief that the subject of Christ's human experience is none other than the eternal Logos. Holding to Christ's complete humanness, yet closing the door on the Antiochene idea of indwelling, Cyril denies Christ's humanity any independent existence. It is a true Platonic universal. Christ is "man" but not "a man"; his humanity has no hypostasis of its own, that is, no concrete subsistence in its own right. It is hypostatized in the hypostasis of the Logos, who is now by nature man (Letter 3). Cyril thinks the name "Emmanuel" significant and uses it constantly in his christology. The historical figure of the gospels is "God with us." And Mary is "theotokos" because the humanity born of her belongs hypostatically to the deity. Moreover there is a real and not merely a conceptual interchange of properties with the humanity possessing the glory of the Logos and the latter taking the experiences of flesh its own. This has its soteriological importance. The work of Christ must be the work of God incarnate (Against the Blasphemies of Nestorius 3:2; 4:4). The flesh of Christ is God's very own and to it life-giving divine energy has been imparted, as coals are energized by fire. If not, says Cyril, the eucharistic body would be a man's, not God's, and, reversing Nestorius' assertion that Christ spoke of eating the flesh of the Son of Man, not of God, those who take Christ to be talking of a literal, cannibalistic eating of a man's flesh would be right (ibid. 4:5).

In summary, Cyril asserts a duality in Christ, who is "from two," the divine and the human, which are neither confused nor changed. The union of the two, far from being a conjunction "according to good pleasure," is like the union of soul and body in a human being or fire and coal in a red hot lump (ibid. Pref.). The distinction of natures remains theoretical since the two are indivisible. At times Cyril appears to go back on all this. The Logos "was impassible in the suffering body," he says (ibid. 5:4; Letter 45). On the analogy of the fiery coal one could say the fire is not affected if the red coal is poked; or on the soul/body analogy that the former is unaffected by a physical blow. Here the weakness of the Alexandrian tradition reappears in Cyril. The presuppositions that the subject of the gospel narratives is the Logos and that deity is immutable and impassible are reconcilable only by predicating suffering of Christ's humanity alone.

In Nestorius' view, Cyril made the union so tight that it became a kind of chemical fusion of two substances into one nature, a blending or confusion wherein the divinity of Christ underwent change. And here for want of space we can only allude to the severe terminological problem that bedeviled the entire christological development.[34] Nestorius found grist for his mill in Cyril's use of the phrase "one nature" (*mia physis*) as an equivalent for "one hypostasis." This seemed a negation of the completeness of either the divinity or, more likely, the humanity in Christ. To redeem humanity the Word assumed *a* man, not "man" or "humanity" as Cyril claimed. Despite the murkiness of the terms, in fairness, Cyril appears not to be guilty of such a negation. The interchangeable phrases (*mia physis* and *mia hypostasis*) meant for him simply that the full humanity of Jesus belonged so completely to the Logos that there could be in the Christ only one subject of predication, for he was one subsistent reality. The one hypostasis, or one nature, is the Logos incarnate making its own full human existence. Cyril cannot be tarred with the same brush as Apollinaris. Cyril, moreover, knew how to articulate the belief of Greek-speaking Christians and as a clever tactician won fervent popular support. With Origen and the Cappadocians, Cyril molded a whole tradition of Greek Christianity.

THE COUNCIL OF EPHESUS

A council was convoked at Ephesus by the emperor Theodosius II to meet in 431 to settle the controversy lest it result in schism. The powerful and ruthless Cyril, who would stop at nothing to procure his ends, refused to await the arrival of all the bishops, many of whom were sympathetic to Nestorius, and on June 22 gathered a group of more than 200 bishops unfavorable to the patriarch. This group unanimously

---

[34]Up to the time of the Cappadocians, and even after, *physis, ousia,* and *hypostasis* were used interchangeably to denote "nature," that which makes a thing what it is, a distinctive set of properties or qualities. In the West this was generally termed *substantia.* After the Cappadocians *ousia* came gradually to refer to "nature" while *hypostasis* denoted a concrete, individual reality subsisting in its own right, a logical subject of which actions and properties are predicated. In other words, a *hypostasis* was a concrete realization and externalization of a universal, abstract essence. *Hypostasis* did not connote "person" in our modern sense. All too frequently *hypostasis* is translated as "person" in the study of christology, with the result that Jesus is denied a human personality. But the translation confuses ontological and psychological categories. For that reason we have avoided translating *hypostasis* as "person." The Latin West's use of *persona* comes closer to our own "person" but is still closer to *hypostasis* and not the full equivalent of what we understand by "person," a center of consciousness, transcendence, and freedom endowed with a distinctive set of psychological characteristics. Using *person* in the modern sense and restricting ourselves to the classical christology, there are two persons in Christ. What we mean by "person" is closer to what they meant by "nature."

condemned and deposed Nestorius as the "new Judas" and approved Cyril's views exposed in a letter written in 430, his third and strongest to Nestorius.[35] When the other bishops arrived four days later led by John of Antioch, they met separately, condemned and deposed Cyril, and rejected the twelve anathemas he had hurled at Nestorius with his third letter. These anathemas, which he demanded Nestorius to accept, expressed Cyril's doctrine in its boldest polemical form. On July 10, legates from the bishop of Rome recognized the decision of Cyril's meeting. The emperor concurred and Nestorius was exiled. Cyril, having reduced to a cipher the emperor's representative and council president, was in control from start to finish. Ephesus would be awarded canonical status as the third ecumenical council. The teaching of Ephesus, which formally recognized Cyril's second letter to Nestorius while the twelve anathemas were not so blessed, crystallizes in six points. First, in the incarnation of the Logos no already existing hypostasis or prosōpon is assumed; the humanity of Christ never existed independently (*oude hōs en proslēpsei prosōpoumonon*). Second, the union of the Son of God and man is not only a union of wills in good pleasure (*ou kata thelesin monēn ē eudokian*) on the part of either. Third, the union is hypostatic (*hath'hypostasin*) or physical, substantial. Hypostasis here means "reality," not the modern notion of person; thus Cyril asserts that the humanity of Jesus and the Logos are so intimately bound as to form one concrete reality. This echoes Cyril's third anathema. Soteriologically, it was crucial to the Alexandrians that the Logos not merely associate with a human being, but that it take on human nature as its own thereby deifying it. Fourth, though the natures are distinct, they come together in such a way that in Christ there is one and the same subject of predication for the two sets of attributes (*diaphoro men hai . . . physeis; heis de ex amphoin Christos kai Huios*). Fifth, Mary who gave birth to this one subject, according to its human nature, is therefore truly theotokos. Finally, Christ has a rational soul animating his human body (*sarka epsychōmenēn psychei logikē; tou hagiou sōmatos psychothentos logikos*). Cyril had emerged victorious.

---

[35]Small wonder that Cyril's Antiochene opponents wished that a heavy stone be placed on his grave lest he return to earth. See Theodoret of Cyrus, Letter 180. Cyril wielded formidable wealth and power. See Frend, *The Rise of Christianity*, 758 ff. On Cyril's massive bribes at the imperial court, see J. Bury, *History of the Later Roman Empire*, (NY: Dover, 1958), 1:354 n. 2.

His deliberately provocative twelve anathemas, while never officially approved at Ephesus, came to be taken in the years following as the orthodox teaching, though they are extreme and treacherously close to Apollinarianism. They tended to make of Christ an abstraction and to deprive his life and teaching of any historical meaning. Alexandria and its high christology were now stronger than ever.

The Council of Ephesus
(From the Second Letter of Cyril to Nestorius) 22 July 431

We do not say the Word became flesh by having his nature
    changed, nor that he was transformed into a complete
    human being composed of soul and body.
Rather, we say that in an unspeakable and incomprehensible
    way the Word united to himself, in his hypostasis *(kath'*
    hypostasin), flesh enlivened by a rational soul,
    and in this way became a human being
    and has been designated Son of man.
He did not become a human being simply by an act of will
    or "good pleasure" *(eudokian)*
    any more than he did so by merely taking on a prosōpon.
We also say that the natures that are brought together
    into true unity are different.
Nevertheless, from both there is one Christ and Son;
    not as though the difference between the natures
    were taken away by their union,
    but rather both divinity and humanity
    produce the perfection of our one Lord, Christ and Son,
    by their unutterable and mysterious joining into unity...
It is not the case that first of all
    an ordinary human being was born of the holy Virgin
    and that the Word descended upon him subsequently.
Rather in virtue of the union,
    he is said to have undergone birth according to the
    flesh from his mother's womb,
    since he claims as his own birth,
    the generation of his own flesh....

Thus (the holy fathers of the church) have not hesitated
to call the holy Virgin Mother of God (*theotokon*).

THE FORMULA OF REUNION

Ephesus expressed "the belief of the whole world," said Cyril's
bishops. Though it had been Cyril's council, the end was not yet. The
imperial court of Theodosius II maneuvered to cut through the Alex-
andrian-Antiochene bitterness to reach a point where Antioch could
live with the deposition of Nestorius and the use of theotokos while
Alexandria could drop the twelve anathemas and consent to a common
statement of faith. Neither pope nor bishop could hope to repudiate the
expressed wish of the emperor.

A peace was made between Cyril's party and the Antiochenes
through the Formula of Reunion in 433. The Antiochenes, led by John
of Antioch, generally allowed the theotokos. However they objected to
Cyril's behavior at Ephesus and even more to certain of his formulations
which speak of the union as "physical" or "natural" (*hath'henōsin
physikēn*) or which appear to obliterate the distinction of natures (*mia
physis tou theou Logou sesarkōmenē*). Actually Cyril employed "physical" or "natural" to indicate the reality in *being* of the union, which he
thought tighter and greater than a moral union of love. But *physis* also
means "nature," hence the unhappy "mia physis" left the impression that
the duality fused into unity in Christ, though this was not Cyril's mind.
Extending the olive branch, Cyril agreed to drop these ambiguous
formulas, to explain his anathemas less offensively, and to accept the
Antiochene language which spoke of a unity of prosōpon and a duality
of natures (*physeis*) so long as a real union of natures was maintained
and Christ was confessed to be one. In return the Antiochene party
agreed to the sacrificial exile of Nestorius to Southern Egypt, where he
remained until his death in 451. It was agreed too that the creed of
Nicaea was a sufficient declaration of faith, but a supplementary
formula might "bar the way against those who wish to attack us" (Letter
39). Here was a considerable achievement. For two centuries Alexandria
and Antioch had been fashioning divergent christologies, if not in
isolation, then in mutual suspicion. "Hatchers of serpent's eggs" was
what Theodoret called Cyril and his supporters (Mansi 4:81409B).
Now, as urged by the imperial court, an agreed statement was drafted
that would, with its double homoousion, be the basis of the Chalcedonian formula eighteen years later (DS 271-73). The main tenets of

Antioch, duality and distinctness of natures, and of Alexandria, the Logos as the subject of human experiences, were alike enshrined. The settlement cost Cyril the favor of extreme Alexandrians who read the compromise as too costly, indeed a sell-out. Yet Cyril held to it until his death in 444. But an Alexandrian backlash there would be due to the differences between schools.

The Way to Chalcedon

THE MONOPHYSITISM OF EUTYCHES

The embers of conflict were fanned to flame after Cyril's death by those extremists who clung to the "one nature" formula. They urged that while the union is "from two natures," *after* the union there is only one nature. They would not admit a union in two distinct natures. Because they held to one nature, they came to be labeled monophysites (monē + physis).[36] One of their leaders, Eutyches, an aged and wily archimandrite ruling a monastery of three hundred monks in Constantinople, insisted the Lord's body was not consubstantial with that of other humans. The Godhead so assimilated the humanity that the two natures seem to fuse into a third reality. Eutyches appeared to hold that the Word had been made flesh, not merely "assumed" flesh, hence Christ's flesh was not derived from Mary but had a heavenly source. His humanity was thus not humanity in any ordinary sense.

Eutyches was accused of heresy and condemned at a synod in Constantinople in 448. Flavian, the bishop of Constantinople, and a Word-flesh theologian, though anti-Apollinarian, in a profession of faith echoing the Formula of Reunion and sent to Theodosius II, stated: "we confess that Christ is of two natures after the incarnation, and we confess one Christ, one Son, one Lord, in one hypostasis and in one prosōpon." Like many Word-flesh thinkers, Flavian found himself awkwardly sitting between Antioch and the extreme Cyrillists of Alexandria. The credal statement of Flavian's council is interesting because the unity of Christ is now articulated in terms of one hypostasis

---

[36]T. Camelot, "De Nestorius à Eutyches: l'opposition de deux christologies," in H. Grillmeier , ed., *Das Konzil von Chalkedon*, (Wurzburg: Echter, 1953), 1:213-42; W.C.H. Frend, *The Rise of the Monophysite Movement* (London: Cambridge University, 1979).

or prosōpon. The two are synonymous and mean one concrete individual being. Hypostasis ceased to be used for the natures. Cyril himself had spoken of two hypostases, meaning natures. This usage with all its confusion is now ruled out.

Dioscorus, ambitious successor of Cyril in Alexandria, and anxious for Alexandria's political ascendancy over Constantinople and its theological triumph over Antioch, entered the lists in defense of the monk. With imperial backing, Dioscorus in 449 presided over a council called at Ephesus by Theodosius II, where the Antiochenes were shut out, Eutyches restored and declared unjustly condemned, Cyril's twelve anathemas approved, the Formula of Reunion set aside, and Flavian physically assaulted and deposed. A year later Flavian would die as a result of these injuries. Moreover, legates bearing a letter in reply to Flavian from Leo, bishop of Rome, were not permitted to read it. The letter, now known as the Tome of Leo, a fine prose piece with its rhythms and balanced cadences, endorses the synod of 448 and reflects the traditional western understanding of the incarnation in formulas tracing peacefully back to Ambrose of Milan and Tertullian. Leo insists Christ is one yet has two natures, each unimpaired and the principle of a distinctive activity of its own. The human nature wept for Lazarus, the divine raised him from the dead. The former can say "The Father is greater than I," the latter "I and the Father are one." Yet he also asserts the ontological identity of Christ as the eternal Son and subject of the duality. His recognition of the two natures is combined with the idea of their interchange of properties (*communicatio idiomatum*), so crucial to the oneness of Christ and to the western idea of atonement. "Humility was assumed by majesty, weakness by power, mortality by eternity." The Tome could be reconciled with the Formula of Reunion, but not with Cyril's 12 anathemas. Leo's restatement and his heavy emphasis on duality, if it does not divide the one Christ, can be criticized for splitting the personality. His contention, derived from Tertullian, that each nature operates in its own domain, though in concurrence with the other, suggests the throwing of a switch and the turning on of one nature and the turning off of the other.

Leo refused to recognize the actions of Dioscorus' council, denouncing it as "a synod of robbers" (Letter 95), and pleading in vain with Emperor Theodosius II for a new council in Italy to restore the truth. The wedding of politics and theology ignited explosive passions. The emergence of the christological doctrine was not without its tragic toll on individual lives and Church unity. Nor was it without its ironies. From his exile in an Egyptian oasis, an aging Nestorius, in his personal apologia, the Bazaar of Heraclides, welcomed Leo's Tome as orthodox, irreproachable, and a vindication.

THE COUNCIL OF CHALCEDON

With the passing of Theodosius II in 450 and the coming of Pulcheria and Marcian to the Eastern imperial throne Leo's call for a new council was heard. The imperial shift in policy was designed to restore harmony between Rome and new Rome, Constantinople. The Council assembled at Chalcedon, near Constantinople, in October of 451, with about 520 bishops in attendance along with representatives of the Roman bishop.[37] The Council deposed Dioscorus and condemned Eutyches. The step beyond that was more difficult. The Roman delegates considered Leo's Tome authoritative; most Eastern bishops, loyal to Cyril, closed ranks behind the christology of Ephesus, which also affirmed the sufficiency of Nicaea for the resolution of christological problems. The emperor for his part felt the need for a new pronouncement that would quiet the debates fragmenting his empire. Despite the eruption of fist fights, the assembly produced a document that attempted to cater to the divergent concerns. It was a balancing act of the first rank. The Chalcedonian definition begins by affirming that the true doctrine about Christ is found in the Nicene Creed of 325 as confirmed and expanded by the Council of Constantinople and the teaching of Ephesus. It continues with condemnations of Appollinarianism, Nestorianism, and Eutychianism, all considered distortions of the traditions of Antioch and Alexandria. To redress the balance the bishops put forward three documents as authoritative: the Tome of Leo, greeted with shouts that "this is the faith of the fathers, the faith of the apostles," Cyril's second letter to Nestorius, approved with loud applause, and Cyril's letter accepting the Formula of Reunion. Here were the norms of orthodoxy. Finally, as the Emperor wished, the Council issued its own statement signed by 452 bishops and read by "the new Constantine," Marcian himself, on October 25. This definition closely resembled the formula of 433, Flavian's statement of 448, and, in substance, Leo's Tome of 449.

With Chalcedon the classical christology, today a powerful force in

[37]Cf. R. Sellers, *The Council of Chalcedon* (London: SPCK, 1954); Grillmeier, ed., *Das Konzil von Chalkedon.*

Christian thinking, reached its high water mark. Chalcedon maintains, first, that Jesus Christ is one prosōpon and one subsistent reality (*eis en prosōpon kai mian hypostasin*), though the adjective "divine," it should be noted, was not added. This focus on unity is Cyrillian. Eight times the Council refers to Christ as "the same." Secondly, with the Formula of Reunion, Chalcedon affirms, with some ambiguity, that this one subsistent reality exists in two natures (*en dyo physesin*), each of which is integral (*teleion ton auton en Theotēti kai teleion ton auton en anthrōpotēti*), so that the Christ is consubstantial with the Father and consubstantial with us (*homoousion tō Patri ... kai homoousion hēmin*). Obviously *physis* or *ousia* cannot mean the same thing when applied to God and humans. This is not a union of equals; moreover, humanity is generic, but not divinity. Thirdly, the Son is united to human nature not accidentally nor by a moral union but substantially; the two natures are united in one hypostasis (*eis en prosōpon kai mian hypostasin*—note, the council made *prosōpon* and *hypostasis* interchangeable). Henceforth, theologians will speak of a hypostatic union. Fourthly, though the two natures are distinct and are united, they abide unconfusedly, unchangeably, indivisibly, and inseparably, four boldly negative terms (*asynchutōs, atreptōs, adiairetōs, achōristōs*). The first two counter Eutyches while the second pair check the possibility of dividing the two natures so as to make two Christs. The substantial union does not result in a third, new essence or nature as the monophysites insisted. Lastly, because the two natures are joined in one hypostasis, the properties and qualities peculiar to each nature may be predicated of that one hypostasis. Thus it is possible to say "Jesus Christ is the creator of all" as well as "Jesus Christ suffered and died." In certain ways the properties of each nature may even be predicated of the other by what had come to be termed the "communion of the properties" or exchange of predicates (*communicatio idiomatum*). Thus, "God died on the cross"; "Mary is the mother of God." This dramatic language would leave its mark on the Christian psyche and on folk-piety.

The Council of Chalcedon Definition of Faith
22 October 451

Following the holy fathers, we are united in teaching all to acknowledge:

one and the same Son, our Lord Jesus Christ,
the same complete in divinity, and the same complete
    in humanity,
truly God and truly man,
    consisting of a rational soul and body,
the same of one substance (*homoousion*) with the Father
    in his divinity,
and the same, of one substance (*homoousion*) with us
    in humanity;
like us in every way except for sin;
as regards his divinity,
    begotten of the Father before all worlds,
but as regards his humanity,
    begotten for us and for our salvation of Mary the
    Virgin, the God-bearer (*theotokon*),
one and the selfsame Christ, Son, Lord, Only-begotten,
recognized in two natures,
    without confusion, without change, without division,
    without separation;
    the distinction of natures being in no way nullified
    by the union but rather the specific characteristics
    of each nature being preserved and both coming together
    to form one prosōpon and hypostasis (subsistence),
not as split or separated into two prosōpa,
but one and the same Son and Only begotten God the Word,
    the Lord Jesus Christ,
even as the prophets from earlier times spoke of him,
and even as our Lord Jesus Christ himself taught us,
and the creed of the fathers handed down to us.

The above having been considered with all and every care and diligence, this holy ecumenical Synod has defined that no one may advance, put in writing, construct, hold or teach to others any other faith.

For Rome, Chalcedon was an unalterable definition of faith. For much of the East, especially in Egypt, Palestine, and Syria, Chalcedon, the end product of the classical christological development, established a common ground between Antioch and Alexandria at the cost of repudiating Cyril and his achievement at Ephesus in 431.[38] It was a compromise acceptable to the emperor but close to a vindication of Nestorius. In reality it is more a statement of the problem than its solution, for it brought together two different christologies without harmonizing them. Its true value resides in providing a rule of language for speaking properly of Christ, just as Nicaea before it had. Orthodox Christ-talk within the Chalcedonian parameters must acknowledge a duality in unity. Jesus is one subject who is properly spoken of as a man and as more than a man, the divine Logos. One can speak of all he is and does only by recognizing him as somehow God's Word in our midst. In his human life God is at work. Chalcedon, then, gave authoritative guidelines for christological discourse and not, strictly speaking, a christology. To accept the doctrine was to agree to speak in a certain way. It is an authoritative paradigm for cult and theology, not a formula to be slavishly repeated. It says nothing of the dynamic interrelationship between the humanity and divinity in the Christ or of the inner being of God and Jesus. At the end of this long and winding road we have reached a Christ who has been analyzed into properties, natures (*ousiai, physeis*), prosōpon and hypostasis, all post-biblical novelities. We are far from the Christ who excited the fervor that impelled Ignatius to seek him in the beasts of the Roman arena. But this abstract, static chris- tology, which crystallizes from two centuries of conflict and at a great cost in human wreckage, is not without its own power. All that was said earlier of the influence of Nicaea's high christology in shaping all later christologies and ecclesiologies and serving as their center of gravity applies even more to Chalcedon. And regulative second-order language

[38]The theological issues were complicated by the question of precedence which divided Rome and Constantinople. The latter's 3rd canon and Chalcedon's 28th canon stipulated over the opposition of Rome that New Rome (Constantinople) should be honored equally with old Rome as an imperial city. That honor and precedence be accorded on grounds other than apostolic foundation took Rome aback. But Marcian insisted and Chalcedon granted Constantinople precedence over the other eastern sees. Thus no Byzantine emperor could renounce Chalcedon. For Leo's position cf. his Letters 104-106 and 110. See W. Lindsey, "Christology and the Roman Primacy at Chalcedon," *Toronto Journal of Theology* (1985) 36-51.

though it is, propositions about propositions, it was to mold and form the Christian self, its identity, and its world in all dimensions of its existence, just as any language molds a people's experience.

An Ongoing Community of Interpretation

This movement over five centuries from son of the carpenter to Son of God and God the Son is perhaps not one of complete discontinuity. Paul insisted that what he was handing down was the same message handed down to him (Gal. 1:8-9; 1 Cor. 15:3). The bishops at Chalcedon asserted that they were endorsing what had been handed down to them, nothing else, and they anathematized those who taught the contrary. Between Paul and Chalcedon there is an obvious difference of manner. Is there also a difference of matter? This complicated question cannot be adequately answered here. Let us be content to say this much. However low some NT christologies might first apear when compared with the high christologies of Nicaea and Chalcedon, it would be simplistic to say the movement begins by thinking and speaking of the Christ as a mere man and in the end comes to represent him as God. Whenever Jesus' designation as Christ or Son of God is said to occur, whether at his resurrection (Rom. 1:4; see also Acts 2:32 and 36; 5:31; 13:22f) or at his baptism (Mark 1:11), he is in any case claimed to be the one in and through whom God is definitively revealed. The same can be said of the "conception christology" of the infancy narratives (Matt. 1-2; Luke 1-2) and of the high "pre-existence christology" (John 1:1-18). Diverse as these christologies are they proclaim the same christological assertion that Jesus is the decisive, unsurpassible representative of God and of normative significance for human existence. And although early christologies may have spoken of Jesus in terms furnished by Jewish tradition and therefore as in all ways human and in no way divine, the thrust, nevertheless, was to situate Jesus somehow on the divine side of the relationship between God and humankind, not on the human side. He was the one through whom God spoke and acted as in no other to judge and save. Hence the claims made for Jesus in the earliest Jewish-Christian christology are somehow maximal, not minimal, and at least to that extent the conciliar development is in continuity with it. Biblical and conciliar language alike illustrate the maximalism which John Knox contends runs through the entire sweep of the history of chris-

The Dialectical Movement of the Christological Development

UNITY Alexandria Logos-Sarx	UNITY IN DUALITY Church Councils	DUALITY Antioch Logos-Anthropos

300   Arians
    –Logos a creature.
    –Christ has no
    rational soul.

325   Athanasius
    –Logos is divine.
    –Ambiguity con-
    cerning soul of
    Christ.

Nicaea 325
–Logos is one in
being with the
Father.
–Homoousios.

375   Apollinaris
    –Logos is divine.
    –Christ has no
    rational soul.

Constantinople
381
–Christ has a
rational soul.

Theodore of
Mopsuestia
    –Word dwells in
    Jesus as in a son.
    –Union according to
    good pleasure.

420   Cyril
    –One nature of
    the Word of God
    incarnate.

    –Union is hypo-
    static.

Nestorius
–Two natures and
two prósopa united
in a prosópon of
union.
–Union is a moral
union of wills.

Ephesus
431
–Ensorsement of
Cyril's hypostatic
union.

(Formula of Reunion)
433

440   Eutyches
    –Monophysitism.
    –Two natures be-
    fore the union,
    one after.

Chalcedon
451
–Two natures in
one hypostasis or
prosópon.

tology: " . . . where a greater or lesser name is proposed for Christ, it is always the greater that is adopted,"[39] as long as it does not conflict with the criteria of monotheism and the stories of Jesus which refer to a real human being who lived and died in a particular time and place.

As for the end product of this dialectical development, the conciliar creeds are second-order rules for Christian discourse and not first-order assertions concerning the inner being of God or Jesus. They are the distillation of long reflection on the jumble of presystematic symbols, predicates, and titles applied to God and Jesus. The champion of Nicaea, Athanasius, reflecting on the data of scripture, tradition, and the homoousion, could interpret consubstantiality as the rule of speech that whatever is said of the Father is said of the Son, except that the Son is not the Father. The ancient conciliar teaching is simply the instantiation, therefore, of three regulative principles. First there is the principle of monotheism; God is one, the God of Abraham, Isaac, Jacob, and Jesus. Second, there is the principle of historical specificity; the gospels refer to a real human being who was born, lived, and died within the bounds of a particular place and time. Third, there is the principle of christological maximalism; every importance possible must be attributed to Jesus so long as it is not in conflict with the first two principles. Already in the NT era these principles were at work. The five centuries of christological development we have examined are the result of their pressure on Christian thought and speech. Docetism and Arianism, among other positions, were rejected because they were considered in violation of these criteria.[40]

The conciliar doctrines, then, regulate what the Christian community says about Christ by means of propositions about what it says.[41] With Nicaea the church turned a corner and entered the domain of logic. However, the church did not abandon the appealing imagery and

---

[39]J. Knox, *The Early Church and the Coming Great Church* (Nashville: Abingdon, 1955) 80. Helpful on this whole issue is S. Ogden, *The Point of Christology* (NY: Harper & Row, 1982), especially chap. 4. The definitive normativeness of Jesus is under attack today. See e.g., P. Knitter, *No Other Name: A Critical Survey of Christian Attitudes toward the World Religions* (NY: Orbis, 1985).

[40]On all this see Lindbeck, *The Nature of Doctrine*.

[41]For an elaboration of what follows see Hefling, *Why Doctrines?* especially 130-133 and 170-172.

colorful symbolic language of its scriptures. On the other hand, it did preclude the Humpty Dumpty approach to language. The Christian message does not mean just what anyone wants it to mean. There are definite parameters that control acceptable speech about the Christ of the New Testament. This had to be the case if the church was to present a unified front to outsiders and maintain harmony within. Just as the early church accepted the logical techniques that were the discovery of the Greek mind in the ancient world, so too the church today accepts the modern discovery of human historicity. Once again the community finds itself at a momentous turning point, one more difficult to cope with than the homoousios. To enter this new horizon is not to forsake the logical context of the councils, any more than the latter forsook the imaginative context of the bible. But it is to ask questions that could not be framed prior to the rise of modern scholarship. In grappling with answers to these questions the church comes to awareness of itself as an ongoing community of interpretation. In this continuing hermeneutical process the community can no more set aside all previous interpretations and start anew than one can erase all previous phases of one's life to start afresh. Such a feat would be the erasure of oneself since the self is self only because of its past. One is what one has become. So too the Christian community is what it is because it has shaped and defined itself through a specific historical set of interpretive decisions. But acknowledgment of a past need not be uncritical. Not all interpretive decisions have been intelligent and reasonable. Yet they too are part of what the church has come to be. The way to undo the mischief is to change course. To do that one must know the course steered so far.

Therein lies the importance of NT scholarship. It charts the starting point of the trajectory created by the church in interpreting the message it lives by. What the message *meant*, how the NT writers understood it, did not predetermine all it would mean forever. The message is not frozen in the canon. Nonetheless, knowing what it did mean provides a landmark by which the church can take its bearings. But even that is inadequate. For there is still the question of the link between what the NT writers meant and what the message has come to mean today. Has the trajectory been the correct one? What course is to be taken now? These are questions that may be met by the sensitivity of faith but they must be met also by the acumen of scholarship and reflective discernment.

Conciliar teaching then provides permanently authoritative guidelines for discourse. However, they are not meant to be slavishly parroted but to be used as grammatical paradigms in the creation of fresh christological language. The language of "one substance and three hypostases" or "two natures" may fall into disuse, but if the same principles that guided the formation of these conciliar paradigms are at work in the making of new formulations that speak to our time, they will faithfully articulate one and the same doctrine. The classical christology would perdure even though the historically conditioned language and imagery of Nicaea and Chalcedon were to recede from worship, preaching, and theology into the mists of memory. It is possible to speak of Jesus and his relationship with God using a conceptual framework very different from the world of late antiquity.[42] The substance of christology is that the man Jesus is considered by Christians to be in a unique sense of and from God, the healing Word and presence of the Father in the world, the central clue to existence. Unfortunately, Greek ways of articulating this have over the centuries given birth to problems and solutions which made it difficult to encounter this Jesus and so a new christological language is needed always. Christian faith is never faith in creeds or statements but in the reality Christians all too clumsily struggle to express, the reality they stumble after in their theologies and pieties.[43]

[42]Chalcedon's teaching was a means to an indispensable (for the Christian) end. It is not an end in itself. The authority of conciliar teaching is in a sense derived, binding to the extent it protects the scriptural vision. It may do that within one horizon yet fail to do so within another.

[43]"Actus credentis non terminatur ad enuntiable sed ad rem." This dictum of Aquinas merits constant recall.

13

Images of Jesus in Popular Post-New Testament Literature

Neither our survey of NT writings and their variety of portraits of Jesus (chaps. 4-11) nor the examination of the christological evolution which took place within theological and ecclesiastical circles (chap. 12) exhausts the wide range of literature produced during the first centuries of this era. For alongside these more formal or official works there emerged an assortment of popular Christian writings. Initially there was little to distinguish works which eventually were admitted into the scriptural canon from other writings produced contemporaneously. For example, the letters of recommendation of Paul's opponents in Corinth (2 Cor. 3:1-3) would hardly have differed from Paul's own on behalf of Phoebe (Rom. 16:1-2) or of Onesimus (letter to Philemon), or the pseudonymous Second Thessalonians from the letter of the alleged forgerer (2 Thess. 2:2). However, as the Jesus movement gained in numbers, increased in complexity, and gained in historical awareness, a considerable differentiation of power/interest, cultural, ethnic/regional groups occurred. The NT canon itself owes much of its variety to such factors. Few NT books were free of ideological, societal, or religious controversy. Indeed most were the product of personal or community struggles. The post-NT period, however, underwent an even greater differentiation of structures, interest groups, and ideologies. Thus, while most of this book studied the canonical works of the early community, and while the prior chapter directed its attention to the literature and thinking of the official church and its theologians and councils, the present chapter will concern itself with the literature of the popular culture of that same church.

Before addressing that literature, however, it is necessary to discuss the history of those early years. This will be done from two different but complementary perspectives. First, we consider the views which non-Christians, both Jewish and Roman, had of the new movement and, secondly, we examine the Christian data for understanding the emergence of popular Christian culture.

The Jesus Movement as Seen by Outsiders

It is easy to forget that the Christian movement began inauspiciously and was subject to the usual pressures of growth, differentiation, and survival. The movement took root within the Roman society of the first and second centuries and at the beginning must not have seemed any different from other mystery cults or fraternal societies. So it must have appeared as an innovative, intrusive, and increasingly troublesome social and religious menace to the established populations of various Roman communities.

It is easy to simplify Christian beginnings, on the basis of uncritical use of the polemical and idealizing histories of the Church Fathers, and to view these years as the triumphal progression of a divinely instituted church within a human context as it was cleansed inwardly (orthodoxy versus heresy) and was preserved outwardly (in the midst of cruel, ungodly persecution). R.L. Wilken characterized this perspective as "the myths of Christian beginnings," for indeed it has tended to ignore the historical process to which all institutions are subject. Scholarship has directed its critical eye to the sources at our disposal for the reconstruction of this history and has forced the modern reader to take more seriously the axiom that the Jesus movement is a historical phenomenon.[1] It is clear from the previous chapter that the process of doctrinal evolution was not one of progress from truth to an ever more clearly defined expression of that truth nor the persistent extirpation of heresy from the body of the faithful. It was a slow, dialectical process with much ideological diversity, some of whose doctrinal tendencies eventually led to the classical definitions of the great councils as the

---

[1]R.L. Wilken, *The Myth of Christian Beginnings* (Notre Dame: University of Notre Dame, 1980).

church established itself more deeply within the cultural structures of the Greco-Roman world.

In various NT texts we are aware of the Jesus movement's relations with the outside world. Beyond its missionary thrust into the Jewish synagogue and the Gentile world, and perhaps as a result of it, the Jesus movement was soon required to resolve the problems caused by this interaction and further to define itself over against the various movements of its time.[2] It is clear that the Matthean and Johannine communities, among others, were affected adversely by their separation or expulsion from the synagogue. Paul and other missionaries defined their gospel, at least in part, in relation to the Jewish community. Hence, one is forced to take seriously the fact that the Jesus movement emerged from early Judaism.

By the same token one must consider seriously the latter's reaction to what it considered a questionable tendency within its ranks. Whether one envisions this reaction as active persecution of co-religionists (Gal. 1:13; Acts 8:1; Mark 13:9), excommunication of heretics from the synagogue (John 9; Matt. 10:17), or the violent opposition merited by a renegade movement (mutual recrimination between rival groups, reciprocal attempts at discrediting the other's doctrines: stolen body, virginal conception, etc.), it is hardly reasonable to expect the break between Judaism and the young Jesus movement to have been a pacific one. At the same time far too much, on too little evidence, has been said about official Jewish persecution of Jewish Christians, whether through official documents, decrees of excommunication, or liturgical maledictions against heretics.[3] The antagonistic relationship between the emerging Jesus movement and the severely disrupted Jewish community of Palestine was the result of a gradual, worsening relationship that involved a quest, on the part of both, for self-protection and self-definition.[4] In fact the gospels are a testimony to early Christianity's tense relations with its parent body. Late Mishnaic stories deprecating

[2]E. Urbach, "Self-Isolation or Self-Affirmation in the First Three Centuries: Theory and Practice," 2:269-98 in E.P. Sanders, ed., *Jewish and Christian Self-Definition* (Philadelphia: Fortress, 1980-81).

[3]Katz, "Issues in the Separation of Judaism and Christianity after 70 C.E.," 43-76.

[4]Several articles in Sanders, *Jewish and Christian Self-Definition*, are especially pertinent to this issue.

Jesus and his mother[5] and equally severe anti-Jewish statements in various Patristic sources[6] emphasize the fact that these feelings were mutual.

We now turn our attention to the pagan reaction to and view of this new religious movement. R.L. Wilken has addressed this topic at some length in studying the views of Pliny the Younger, who was Roman governor of Bithynia in 112 A.D., of Galen the philosophical and medical writer of the end of the second century, of the Greek philosopher Celsus whose work True Doctrine of 170 merited an extended response by Origen in Contra Celsum (c. 248), of the third-century Neo-Platonist philosopher Porphyry, and of the former Christian turned pagan, the fourth-century emperor, Julian the Apostate. In separate chapters Wilken also discusses two early descriptions of the Jesus movement as "political club or associations" (*hetaeria*) and as "superstition" (*superstitio*).[7] A cursory reading of these sources convinces the modern reader that the perception, toleration, and acceptance of the Jesus movement by the Roman populace had a long and complex history. On the Christian side an urgent need for apologetical response emerged, especially in view of the works of Celsus, Porphyry, and Julian. Some of the popular works we will examine below have as a primary goal the apologetic presentation of Jesus to Roman readers. On the Roman side one recognizes the constant refrain that Christianity is a threat to the "old" Roman religion and to the empire's Greco-Roman culture and way of life.

We begin with and use as the basis of our survey a discussion of Tacitus' well-known description of the Jesus movement, while describing Nero's role in the fire of Rome. To divert suspicion from himself, Tacitus tells us

> Nero substituted as culprits and punished with the utmost refinement of cruelty, a class of men, loathed for their vices, whom the crowd

---

[5]M. Goldstein, *Jesus in Jewish Tradition* (NY: Macmillan, 1950); E. Bammel, "Christian Origins in Jewish Tradition," *NTS* 13 (1967) 317-35; and Kee, *Jesus in History*, 48-54.

[6]R. Wilde, *The Treatment of the Jews in the Greek Christian Writers* (Washington: Catholic University, 1949); N. DeLange, *Origen and the Jews* (London: Cambridge University, 1976); and A.F.J. Klijn and G.J. Reinink, *Patristic Evidence for Jewish-Christian Sects* (Leiden: Brill, 1973).

[7]*The Christians as the Romans Saw Them* (New Haven: Yale University, 1984).

styled Christians. Christus, the founder of the name, had undergone the death penalty in the reign of Tiberius, by sentence of the procurator Pontius Pilate, and the pernicious superstition was checked for a moment, only to break out once more, not merely in Judea, the home of the disease, but in the capital itself, where all things horrible or shameful in the world collect and find a vogue. First, then, the confessed members of the sect were arrested; next, on their disclosures, vast numbers were convicted, not so much on the count of arson as for the hatred of the human race. And derision accompanied their end ... (Annals 15:44).[8]

Tacitus then describes Nero's disgraceful behavior and the sympathetic backlash which resulted. These unfortunate Christians, while innocent of the charge of arson in the eyes of this Roman historian, were nonetheless worthy of his scorn. His incidental statement is ideal for our discussion of Roman attitudes and judgments in regard to the Jesus movement for it raises and foreshadows the basic items of that pagan critique. We therefore address four crucial areas suggested by Tacitus' statement.

1) The first issue is a negative one, namely, the role played by persecution in the early years of the movement's development. In the case described by Tacitus, persecution was clearly a reality. While the historian proceeds, immediately after the passage cited, to describe in gory detail the savage punishment undergone by those hapless Christians, it is evident from a reading of Roman sources that this was an isolated incident of official persecution by the less-than-stable Nero. N.M. Bailkey, in his discussion of "Trajan's enlightened policy" insists:

there is no evidence of an official state pronouncement regarding Christianity before the early second century A.D. Persecutions were sporadic and local, being the product of popular hostility and action. They were handled by provincial governors (with the exception of Nero's persecution at Rome), who based their action on the laws against secret societies and the refusal of the Christians to demonstrate their loyalty to the state by the purely political gesture of sacrificing to the emperor ... This policy, which placed the label of traitor upon convicted Christians but also protected them against both sporadic

[8]Moore and Jackson, *Tacitus: Annals*; for a brief interpretation of this text, see R. Syme, *Tacitus* (Oxford: Clarendon, 1958) 2:531-32.

and systematic persecution, continued until the Empire began to disintegrate in the last half of the third century. Measures to wipe out Christianity as a danger to the unity and security of a troubled state culminated in the Great Persecution (303-311 A.D.) under Diocletian. When this failed, Constantine's proclamation of toleration in 313 A.D. became the established policy.[9]

Contrary to older estimates of the movement's early years and former generations' fascination with the theme of persecution and veneration of martyrs, recent Classical and biblical scholars discover little evidence for such a perspective.[10] It was the work of later generations of polemical, pious, and idealizing writers which placed upon these early years an apocalyptic interpretation wherein the ungodly forces of the pagan Roman empire were overcome not by the final eschatological struggle of the end-days nor even by the Christ-event, but, in the spirit of the Maccabean martyrs, by the pious, virtuous, and self-effacing struggles of believers who witnessed to the divinely instituted and soon-to-triumph Christian community. Eusebius, the well-known church historian of the fourth century, for one, begins his Ecclesiastical History by underscoring this attitude. He proposes to discuss apostolic succession, the menace of heresies, the misfortunes of the Jewish race, the bitter persecutions directed at the church, and the heroism of the martyrs. In the words of Wilken, "Eusebius intends to present a history of the divine truth as it met resistance, conflict, and persecution by its foes."[11] This is ideology rather than history. Tacitus, while disliking Christianity which he classifies as one more disruptive secret society,[12] is nonetheless representative of the general Roman attitude of prosecution rather than persecution of movements foreign to Roman interests and policy.

2) Tacitus' description of the Christians as "a class of men, loathed for their vices" may sound curious to the modern reader, unless it is

---

[9]*Readings in Ancient History from Gilgamesh to Diocletian* (Lexington: Heath, 1976), 446.

[10]See for example P. Keresztes, "The Imperial Roman Government and the Christian Church. 1: From Nero to the Severi," 2:23:1:247-315 and "2: From Gallienus to the Great Persecution," 375-86 in Temporini and Haase, *Aufstieg und Niedergang der Römischer Welt* (1979).

[11]*The Myth of Christian Beginnings,* 63.

[12]For Tacitus, "alien religions presented a double danger—the aristocracy weakened, the lower classes a prey to fanatics and false prophets," Syme, *Tacitus,* 2:532.

remembered that the historian here reflects the common Roman view, that the Christians were shirking their religious and civic duties. The following statement by H. Chadwick of Celsus' opinion helps to explain Tacitus' accusation:

> Christianity is a dangerous innovation, and if it is not checked it will be a disaster for the Roman Empire. The Christians are not pulling their weight; they ought to take their share of civic responsibility, hold public office, fight in the army, and support the Emperor in his struggle to maintain the peace of the Empire.[13]

Such a criticism by Celsus, a common accusation in later writers, forces us to look more closely at Tacitus' statement. The term for vice (*flagitium*) means "shameful action or crime." The stress is on shame and lack of gratitude and this interpretation accords with Porphyry's reproach that Christians are ungrateful to the gods:

> How can men not be in every way impious and atheistic who have apostasized from the customs of our fathers, through which every nation and city is sustained? What good can reasonably be hoped for from those who stand as enemies and warriors against their bene-factors? What else are they than fighters against God?[14]

Indeed, it is a frequent accusation that the Christians are lacking in gratitude both to the gods and to the Roman system on which civilization depends. The Roman empire was based on toleration, and "as the Roman state saw it, the Christians failed to satisfy the terms on which toleration could be granted in that they appeared to be subversive of the moral, political, and social order and refused to tolerate other religions."[15] For that reason, in Tacitus' opinion, they were despised by the populace.

In a similar manner Tacitus' claim is explained that the Christians

---

[13]*Origen: Contra Celsum, Translated with an Introduction and Notes* (London: Cambridge University, 1980) xxi-xxii; see also Keresztes, "The Imperial Roman Government and the Christian Church," 2:23:1:252.

[14]Fragment cited in R. Wilken, "Pagan Criticism of Christianity: Greek Religion and Christianity," 119 in W.R. Schoedel and R.L. Wilken, eds, *Early Christian Literature and the Classical Intellectual Tradition*) Paris: Editions Beauchesne, 1979). See Acts 5:39 for an interesting parallel.

[15]Bailkey, *Readings in Ancient History*, 445.

were "convicted . . . for the hatred of the human race." On the one hand they have rejected both the gods and the customs which Greeks and barbarians had accepted from the earliest times (accusations made by Celsus and Porphyry) and so had acted shamefully and arrogantly. On the other, as a religious and social minority within Roman communities, early Christians were isolated and ostracized by Roman neighbors who resented or were suspicious of their new customs and on their own count as they chose the powerful bonds of Christian fellowship or association (Ag. Celsus 1:1) and tended to shun polytheistic practices. One will remember Paul's discussion of lawsuits in the public courts and meats offered to idols in 1 Cor. 6 and 8f. 1 Peter, however, is an excellent example of a Christian writer's attempt to reverse this exclusivistic attitude of the early Christian movement. Tacitus' statement that Christians were disliked by the Roman populace finds its raison d'être in their rejection of what Celsus will call "the true doctrine" of the ancients. According to Tacitus and other Romans critics, they have shown disdain or hatred (*odium*) for human and divine wisdom (critique especially of Galen) and have acted shamefully.

3) There is an acknowledgement both in Tacitus' statement and in subsequent critiques of the centrality of christology. Already at this early date it is clear that the term "christ" is used as a proper name and that the adherents of the movement are known by the name of "Christians." There is also the recognition that Christ or "that fellow from Palestine" (as Julian disdainfuly calls him) was the central figure of the new movement. The historical facts, presumed by later critics, are pared to a minimum in Tacitus' statement and it is the ignominious death sentence which draws his attention, as though he wishes to justify his qualification of the movement as a "contagious disease" that has invaded the Roman organism. Even Lucian of Samosata, the second century writer, acknowledges in his parody of Christian gullibility, that they "worship the man who was crucified in Palestine because he introduced this new cult into the world" (Peregrinus 11).

Not only is Christ's centrality acknowledged in these critiques, but his life, deeds, teaching, and the claims made in his name receive increasing attention from Roman writers. His life and ministry become the object of Roman critiques, particularly his miracles and teachings. Sensing that miracles were a key element in Christian apologetics, Roman authors zeroed in on these elements of Jesus' activity. Celsus admits that Jesus might have performed certain miracles (1:6, 68), but insists that it was through magic that they were accomplished. To that effect he presents the well-known story of Jesus' Egyptian sojourn: "because he was poor he hired himself out as a workman in Egypt, and there tried his hand at certain magical powers on which the Egyptians pride themselves; he returned full of conceit because of these powers, and on account of them gave himself the title of God" (1:28; also 38).[16] Magic then becomes for Celsus a means of dismissing the high christological claims made in Jesus' name by his followers. Porphyry, while also willing to admit the reality of the miracles rejects the accusation of magic and insists that "Jesus was not a 'sorcerer but pious and wise and has access to the heavens.' "[17] He, like Celsus and Julian later, maintains that the claim that Jesus was not only wise but also divine was made by Jesus' disciples who transformed the religion of Jesus, so to speak, into a religion about him as God. Julian, at a later remove, attempts to minimize these accomplishments, sensing their weakness as an apologetic tool:

> Yet Jesus, who won over the least worthy of you, has been known by name for but little more than three hundred years: and during his lifetime he accomplished nothing worth hearing of, unless anyone thinks that to heal crooked and blind men and to exorcise those who were possessed by evil demons in the villages of Bethsaida and Bethany can be classed as a mighty achievement (Ag. Galilaeans 191 D-E).[18]

The object of such critiques, therefore, was to discredit Christianity's claims about its founder.[19]

Jesus' teachings are also the object of criticism. Either it is claimed that these bear little originality in relation to Classical or barbarian culture or else, in an effort to drive a wedge between Judaism and its ungrateful offspring, that there exist irreconcilable differences between the writings of Moses and the teachings of Jesus; for example, Celsus points out that Moses promises riches and power to his descendants,

---

[16]Chadwick, *Origen: Contra Celsum*, 28.

[17]Wilken, *The Christians as the Romans Saw Them*, 159.

[18]W.C. Wright, ed., *The Works of the Emperor Julian* (Cambridge: Harvard University, 1959-69).

[19]H. Remus, *Pagan-Christian Conflict over Miracle in the Second Century* (Cambridge: Philadelphia Patristic Foundation, 1983).

while Jesus warns that riches and reputation are irreconcilable with the acquisition of the kingdom by the true descendants of Moses. Celsus then asks: "Who is wrong? Moses or Jesus? Or when the Father sent Jesus had he forgotten what commands he gave to Moses? Or did he condemn his own laws and change his mind, and send his messenger for quite the opposite purpose?" (7:18). In Julian's case we cite the discussion on circumcision, among many conflicts between Christian practice and the Mosaic Law. The emperor notes that Paul and Peter in dispensing from circumcision find themselves in opposition first to Moses who says that Abraham's circumcision of the flesh was enjoined as a "token of ... covenant" between God and him and between God and his descendants and secondly in opposition to Jesus who came not to destroy but to fulfil the Law (reference to Matt. 5:17, 19). Julian addresses his Christian audience: "either Jesus will be found to speak falsely, or rather you will be found in all respects and in every way to have failed to preserve the law" (Ag. Galilaeans 351). It was Julian, whose knowledge of both the Jewish and Christian scriptures was quite advanced, who paid much attention to the contradictions between what Christians saw as prophecy in the Old Testament, e.g., a prophet like Moses, a descendant of Judah, or the virginal conception, Deut. 18:18; Gen. 49:10; and Isa. 7:14, and its fulfilment in the New Testament. Julian concludes about the first: "Moses says that the prophet will be like him and not like God, a prophet like himself and born of men, not a god," about the second: "how could he be [i.e., from Judah] when according to you he was not born of Joseph but of the Holy Spirit?" (he notes the disagreements between the Matthean and Lukan genealogies), and of the third: "does Isaiah anywhere say that a god will be born of a virgin? But why do you not cease to call Mary the mother of God, if Isaiah nowhere says that he that is born of the virgin is the 'only begotten Son of God' and 'the firstborn of all creation?'" (Ag. Galilaeans 253 C-E, 262 C-D).

Three final areas of Greco-Roman critique concerning Christian teaching require attention, namely, the doctrine of the resurrection, Christ's divinity, and the Christian (and Jewish) concept of God. a) The doctrine of resurrection drew severe criticism from both Celsus and Porphyry, particularly the former who calls into question the historical trustworthiness of the resurrection narratives and witnesses (Ag. Celsus 2:55) and the very concept of restoration of the body, an idea repugnant to Greeks (5:14; see also Acts 17:32 and 1 Cor. 15:35f).

b) Few Roman critiques fail to note, following Pliny's early observation that believers "sang in alternate verses a hymn to Christ, as to a god" (Letters 10:96),[20] that Christians made exalted claims on behalf of their founder. Celsus states that Christians betray monotheism since they worship extravagantly the newcomer Jesus, i.e., God's servant rather than God (8:12). As noted earlier, Porphyry insists that Jesus was a wise man, not an object of worship as his disciples shamefully claim. It is from Julian, however, that the most severe criticisms of high christology emanate. He tells his readers: "if it is God's will that none other should be worshiped, why do you worship this spurious son of his whom he has never yet recognized or considered as his own? . . . You . . . foist on him a counterfeit son" (159 E). He reproaches Christians for not being true to apostolic tradition since "neither Paul nor Matthew nor Luke nor Mark ventured to call Jesus God. But the worthy John . . . was the first to venture [and "not . . . clearly or distinctly," 213 B] to call Jesus God" (327 A-B). There is even a hint in Celsus (8:14) that Jesus might replace God in the scheme of things, an idea which Origen, by citing John 14:28, counters by insisting that the Son is subordinate to the Father.[21]

c) Finally, the concept of God held by Jews and Christians is basic to all attacks against the young Christian movement. The sublime role attributed to Jesus offended the increasingly strong sense of monotheism or of henotheism which was gaining an audience in the Greco-Roman period. Further, Jewish anthropomorphic stories about God and the exclusivistic claims of this God (choice of one people, sending of prophets to a limited portion of humanity, and the Christian assertion that God had sent the Son on their behalf) greatly offended Romans versed in the Classical tradition and its notion of divinity. We end our discussion of this point by citing both Celsus and Julian, who poignantly ask why God waited so long to care for the whole of humanity, the first: "is it only now after such a long age that God has remembered to judge the life of men? Did he not care before?" (4:7) and the second: "from the

---

[20]Melmoth and Hutchinson, *Pliny.*

[21]Significantly, Tertullian who is writing about 85 years later, borrows generously from Pliny's letter to formulate his defense of Christianity and reports not that Christians sang "a hymn to Christ, as to a god," but that they sang "to Christ and to God," Apology 2:6; see T.R. Glover, ed., *Tertullian: Apology; De Spectaculis* (Cambridge: Harvard University, 1960).

beginning God cared only for the Jews . . . finally God sent unto them [Jew and Gentile according to Paul] Jesus also . . . to announce his love for man which should one day, though late, reach even unto us also. Nay he even looked on for myriads . . . of years . . . For if he is the God of all of us alike, and the creator of all, why did he neglect us?" (106 AD).

4) Finally, we address Tacitus' claim that the Jesus movement is a "pernicious [or deadly] superstition," indeed a "disease," or the latest in vogue of "horrible or shameful things." The charge especially of "superstition" is significant since Tacitus' contemporary Pliny makes the same claim concerning the Christians,[22] who are brought before him for judgment in the province of Bithynia. In a letter to the emperor Trajan where he asks for advice concerning his treatment of those accused of belonging to this secret, outlawed society—i.e., whether age, repentance, or proof of accompanying crimes or vices should be taken into consideration— he provides the modern reader with a mine of information, fragmentary and suggestive though it may be, of the growth of the Jesus movement in the early part of the second century and of Roman law vis-à-vis that movement. One gets a tantalizing glimpse of a variety of historical, sociological, and religious data. The Christian movement is growing, so much so that it "is not confined to the cities only, but has spread through the villages and rural districts" (Letters 10:96). We learn that there are people of all ages who belong to the movement, some for as many as 25 years; some are even Roman citizens (and therefore require special treatment). There are many adherents to this movement. Thus, Pliny is concerned about indiscriminate accusations: "especially considering the numbers endangered. Persons of all ranks and ages, and of both sexes are, and will be, involved in the persecution." But there are signs of problems; many are falling away, whether through lack of conviction or in the face of political and legal pressure; some pagan, Roman neighbors are growing suspicious of and others are taking advantage of denunciation procedures against their Christian neighbors; and the two ideologies seem on a collision course as emperor cult becomes a test of civic loyalty.

The accusation of "superstition" and its explanation are major concerns. Pliny's letter gives important clues to this understanding. He

---

[22]Another contemporary, Suetonius, in his Lives of the Caesars, calls Christians "a class of men given to a new and mischievous superstition" (Nero 16:2); see Rolfe, *Suetonius.*

is concerned "whether the mere profession of Christianity, albeit without crimes, or only the crimes associated therewith are punishable." While he calls not only belonging to but the movement itself "a crime,"[23] indeed one to be punished, he seems surprised at the alleged crime of these Christians. He cites former Christians as maintaining that

> the whole of their guilt, or their error, was, that they were in the habit of meeting on a certain fixed day before it was light, when they sang in alternate verses a hymn to Christ, as to a god, and bound themselves by a solemn oath, not to any wicked deeds, but never to commit any fraud, theft or adultery, never to falsify their word, nor deny a trust when they should be called upon to deliver it up; after which it was their custom to separate, and then reassemble to partake of food—but food of an ordinary and innocent kind.

As a result he pursues his examination of two deaconesses and concludes with the statement: "I could discover nothing more than depraved and excessive superstition." As in the case of Tacitus, two elements are central: Christianity is called not only an "unenlightened and meaningless worship" (*superstitio*), which of itself might be innocuous,[24] but also a dangerous ("depraved" or "pernicious") force within Roman society. It is begrudgingly recognized, and, in the case of Pliny, vindicated as a religious movement with laudable ideals; but it is a threat to Roman society. Pliny expresses his confidence that it will be "checked" and the disease "cured":

> 'Tis certain at least that the temples, which had been almost deserted, begin now to be frequented; and the sacred festivals, after a long intermission, are again revived; while there is a general demand for sacrificial animals, which for some time past have met with few purchasers.

---

[23]Interestingly, when asked by Pliny whether he should punish "the name itself" or "the crimes associated with the name," Trajan simply "brushed . . . aside" the issue and agreed with the punishment; see Syme, *Tacitus*, 2:468, n. 4. More generally on the Pliny correspondence, see Keresztes, "The Imperial Roman Government and the Christian Church," 2:23:1:274-87.

[24]H.J. Rose, "Superstition," 1023 in Hammond and Scullard, *Oxford Classical Dictionary*.

The Christian movement, therefore, is one more extravagant, if well-meaning, cult which is contributing to the disintegration of the old Roman order.

Early Roman writers seem then to have viewed Christianity as a popular, pious movement, like others within the general culture, which appealed to the lower classes, but one which was also becoming a threat to the Roman way of life.[25] Some early writers, like Pliny, Galen, and Porphyry, saw the movement as not lacking in moral or religious merit. Most nonetheless, when comparing the Jesus movement to Classical culture, found the former inferior in intellectual, moral, and social content. Further, they never failed to perceive in this new movement a threat both to Greco-Roman civilization and the good of the empire. If Tacitus saw Christianity as a spreading disease, Julian with considerable perception viewed it as the death knell of Classical civilization.

Development of Popular Christian Culture and Literature

When one looks back on the early years of the Christian movement one is struck by the dialectical and yet complementary themes of diversity and unity. The NT canon is witness to the enormous diversity and the basic unity which existed from the outset of the Jesus movement.[26] However, while the kerymatic focus on the Christ-event and its soteriological consequences united the vision of the early missionaries and provided coherence to NT literature, it is the diversity of concerns, perspectives, and historical situations which predominate in the books of the NT canon. It has been one of the major objectives of this project to examine, particularly in relation to christology, the surprising diversity of these early documents. Each work or author witnesses to diverse situations, audiences, and perspectives within the expanding Jesus movement.

When, however, one pays close attention to the literature of the Church Fathers and the definitions of the councils in the lengthy period

[25]Seemingly the former (lower classes) constituted the majority and, when persistent in their faith, were summarily executed for the good of the state, while the latter, "being citizens of Rome" but nonetheless "possessed with the same infatuation," were sent to Rome for judgment (Pliny, Letters 10:96).

[26]Dunn, *Unity and Diversity in the New Testament.*

following the writing of the New Testament, one finds a greatly changed situation. In Clement of Rome one finds a greater stress on morality and martyrdom, in Ignatius of Antioch more interest in structures, and in Irenaeus greater insistence on succession and true doctrine than one encounters in the earlier literature. There develops within the communities an unrelenting quest for unity and orthodoxy. The christological evolution presented in chapter 12 above is testimony of this fact. Even the views of Christianity's pagan critics and the responses of its own apologists confirm this view. Both the Church Fathers and the church's pagan critics either forgot or overlooked the multiplicity of views within the New Testament and treated them as a monolithic Christian book of scriptures. While Julian (for example: Ag. Galilaeans 237 B) is able to play one NT author against the others, he joins post-NT authors in viewing the New Testament as an undifferentiated book of Christian scripture. Concomitant with this quest for unity within the general church and the perception of such by the movement's critics is a startling abundance and bewildering variety of compositions written by and used within the lower ranks of the movement. The remainder of this chapter examines a sampling from this literature to enable the reader to discern the major images of Jesus which have in the past and continue in the present to fascinate Christian believers.

QUEST FOR UNITY AND ORTHODOXY

While it was a common characteristic of 1960's scholarship to detect numerous indications of "early catholicism" in post-Pauline writings of the New Testament and while it has become equally common to contest these earlier observations in the late '70s and '80s, it cannot be denied that what E. Käsemann and others characterized as "early catholic" (stress on morality, ecclesiology, hierarchy, and history) is found in an ever-increasing concentration in early Patristic literature. It is clearer presently that the relationship between these two bodies of literature must be sought in the gradual evolution of the Christian community from a small missionary movement (with the specter of apocalyptic urgency ever at the fore) into an empire-wide social, political, and theological reality, first in conflict with and then in consort with the Roman empire. Already in the various NT communities there are traces of some of the themes often described as "early catholic," e.g., Johannine, Matthean, and Pauline quarrels about authority, increasing concern for paraenesis and morality generally in the later epistolary literature, a consuming interest in true doctrine and structures in the Pastorals, and a greater concern for history and universalism in Luke-Acts.

Due to fragmentation and disunity internally and ostracization and opposition externally, the Christian community underwent drastic changes as its membership increased and changed in geographical, cultural, and linguistic terms. Loosely structured communities needed more highly organized social mechanisms; and increasingly greater diversity in philosophical and cultural terms often compromised and threatened the role to be played by the Christ-event. As the Jesus movement gained in numbers and its ideas grew complex the process of institutionalization changed both the structures and the thought of the young movement. The local communities adopted the structures of the Greco-Roman world (an increasingly imperial and bureaucratic system) and the theologies of the young movement adjusted to the cultural and ethnic communities in which they existed. The latter contributed both to greater diversity in religious thought and practice and to an increasing urgency for standards, canon, and authority.

It was in such an atmosphere that later generations appealed to the figures of the past to substantiate policy and theology. As new problems arose within and outside the communities, as social and political pressures were brought to bear on the young movement, and as the memories of its Jewish origins and of its early days receded into the past, its intellectuals directed their attention more and more to self-defense and apologetics and to polemical thrusts against threatening forces within the movement itself. The best-known early Christian writer who fits most of these charcteristics was the second-century bishop of Lyons, Irenaeus. In his famous work Against Heresies Irenaeus took pains to trace the church's apostolic lineage or succession, to combat at length the heretical tendencies he saw within the theological currents of his day (particularly Gnostic writers), and to discuss proper interpretation of the scriptures. The author is interested in the criteria of truth, particularly apostolic origins and uninterrupted tradition as the guarantee of the truthfulness of Christian teaching. One of his strongest arguments in attacking some of the leading Gnostic teachers runs as follows:

> prior to Valentinus, those who follow Valentinus had no existence; nor did those from Marcion exist before Marcion; nor, in short, had any of those malignant-minded people, whom I have above enumer-

ated, any being previous to the initiators and inventors of their perversity (3:4:3).[27]

Clearly, innovation and novelty were the first signs of heresy. Lack of continuity between a teacher's work and apostolic witness, either via continuous tradition back to apostolic sources or in conformity to the apostolic writings or scriptures, was a sure indication of a lack of orthodoxy. Besides, Irenaeus ascribed both the church's structures and doctrine to divine origin.

Communion or continuity with the source of truth, the Lord Jesus Christ, was essential in this quest for orthodoxy. Book 3 of Against Heresies is instructive in this regard. Irenaeus begins his discussion with his well-known statement concerning the authorship of the gospels. After establishing the apostolic origin of "the gospel," Irenaeus insists that all four gospels find their authority within the apostolic circle: the apostles Matthew and John, Mark the interpreter of Peter, and Luke the companion of Paul (3:1:1). He proceeds to show how the heretics have followed neither scripture nor tradition and are not in communion with the successors of the apostles. Even when they appeal to the gospels they choose the author they like and proceed to mutilate that text to justify their errors. The Ebionites or Judaizers chose Matthew; Marcion the anti-Judaizer opted for his own version of Luke; the Docetists ("those who separate Jesus from Christ, alleging that Christ remained impassible but that it was Jesus who suffered") preferred Mark; while Valentinus the Gnostic made profuse use of John (3:11:7). It was owing to the divisive forces within the Christian community, therefore, that Irenaeus and others had recourse to such a strategy, a strategy which not only fostered unity from above but also tended to downplay the differences within the tradition[28] and to foster polemics. In this way there developed further differences not only within the developing theology of the official church (chapter 12) but also in relation to those labeled heretics (especially the extensive and diverse Gnostic movement) and those who continued to find fascination in the particularities of the gospel narratives.

[27]A.R. Roberts and J. Donaldson, eds, *The Anti-Nicene Fathers*, vol.: *The Apostolic Fathers—Justin Martyr—Irenaeus* (Grand Rapids: Eerdams, 1979).

[28]Another example of this would be the second-century Syrian attempt (Tatian in the Diatesseron) to bring unity to the fourfold gospels by combining them into an overall harmony.

EMERGENCE OF POPULAR CULTURE AND LITERATURE

If pagan critics, as outsiders, tended to see Christianity as a monolithic association of devotees of the God-man from Nazareth, the church's theologians also fostered a monolithic view by their attempts to achieve a more unified christological and ecclesiological doctrine. The consequences were, on the one hand, greater conflict between theological schools and polemical confrontation between polarized concepts of orthodoxy and heresy,[29] attitudes which, in part, characterized the great christological controversies of the following centuries, and, on the other hand and more germane to our study, the freeing of the creative energies of popular pietistic and folkloric movements. As happened in the Middle Ages when folk-piety became fascinated with gospel and hagiographic lore, so in the period following the creation of the New Testament there was a keen interest in the large variety of stories told about the master and other related personalities. When Christians confronted the miracle stories of the Hellenistic world's great heroes and healers, there developed a parallel lore concerning the master who was bound, in the popular as well as intellectual mind, to compete against and to defeat these demi-gods on their own territory. As there developed in the Classical world of the second and third centuries A.D. a fascination for the romance or fictionalized wonder stories of interesting personalities,[30] so there grew up within Christian communities fictionalized episodes and lives of the child Jesus, stories which served didactic and dramatic purposes in the popular mind.

Populations in different parts of the Roman empire and beyond possessed their own cultural and intellectual traditions and drew from these a variety of genres, literary and folkloric conventions, and cultural perspectives which they applied to the developing Jesus lore. As these communities emerged, whether as ostracized sects, ascetical or pietistic movements, or as competing intellectual traditions (particularly Gnosticism), there also appeared a rich literature of a self-serving, polemicizing, and legendary nature. As the fascinating stories about the master were withdrawn from popular access by the increasing stress on the

---

[29]W. Bauer, *Orthodoxy and Heresy in Earliest Christianity* (Philadelphia: Fortress, 1971).

[30]For a brief introduction to the "ancient novel," see S.M. Praeder, "Luke-Acts and the Ancient Novel," 278-83 in K.H. Richards, ed, *Society of Biblical Literature 1981 Seminar Papers* (Chico: Scholars, 1981).

written word and as a shroud of apostolicity and sanctity began to form around the NT writings during the canonizing process,[31] the popular imagination seized on the loose ends and lacunae of the tradition to nurture its love for fantasy. Out of these tantalizing hints and open-ended episodes (e.g., Jesus' hidden years, the wonder-child of the temple scene, the sympathetic Pilate, or the risen Lord) there grew folk-tales in the form of apocryphal gospels, acts, letters, and revelations.

This literature is commonly labeled NT apocrypha, by analogy with OT apocrypha or works rejected by the Hebrew canon. Such a comparison, however, is false since none of these works were ever considered for canonical status. Instead, this body of literature consists of an amorphous collection of works produced at the end of the NT period.

> Different motives were operative, motives which emerged at different times and led to the production of this literature. The form-historical study of this literature shows that in the earliest times it underwent a development parallel to that of the canonical scriptures and that in later times there was a further development of the New Testament forms and types. To this must be added differences in doctrine and belief, which in the earlier period obtained expression in different renderings of the gospel and also of the acts of the apostles and other works. This, however, had as its consequence that the form of Christian proclamation which was not accepted, which was eliminated by the early Catholic Church as heretical, created for itself an independent means of expression in a "tendency literature."[32]

But alongside this heretical literature there also developed a popular lore to supplement the received stories of the scriptures, to legitimate local traditions and practices, to provide scope for folkloric creativity of a romantic and legendary type, and to allow for new ideas and conventions of expression. The emergence of the NT apocrypha was a long and complex process. There exists in this collection a large variety of forms: gospels, acts, other types of narratives, revelatory discourses, apocalypses, and letters. Some are modeled on scriptural genres, while

---

[31]Kelber, *The Oral and the Written Gospel* and P.J. Achtemeier, "Epilogue: The New Testament Becomes Normative," 367-86 in Kee, *Understanding the New Testament*.

[32]W. Schneemelcher, "General Introduction," 1:64 in Hennecke and Schneemelcher, *New Testament Apocrypha*.

others owe more to the contemporary Classical romance or Gnostic revelatory literature. Many attempt to fill the gaps left by the canonical gospels in the life of Jesus; e.g., the Protevangelium of James on the early life of Mary, including Jesus' birth or the Infancy Gospel of Thomas on Jesus' early years up to and including the temple scene of his twelfth year. Some expand various facets of the master's life, ministry, or role after the resurrection, e.g., the Acts of Pilate on the procurator's role and value as a witness for Jesus' passion, death, and resurrection, the Coptic Gospel of Thomas which offers a long series of sayings and parables of Jesus, the Teaching of Addai on Jesus' commissioning of a disciple for Syrian Odessa, or the Gospel of Bartholomew on Jesus' descent into hell. Still others appropriate the gospel tradition for their own purposes: the Gospel of the Egyptians to offer its perspective on sexual asceticism, the Secret Gospel of Mark to serve as a foundation document for the Carpocratians, the Gospel of the Hebrews to meet the needs of a Judaeo-Christian community, the Gospel of Peter (in its later form) by radically altering the gospel stories to underscore the guilt of the Jewish authorities and the innocence of the Roman governor, the Coptic Gospel of Thomas and other revelatory gospels to foster the teachings of Gnostic groups or the Epistula Apostolorum to defend the orthodox doctrine of the official church ("the catholics") against the Gnostic teachings of Simon and Cerinthus.

Portraits of Jesus: Study of Representative Texts

In typological terms the NT apocrypha owe much both to the genres represented in the NT canon and to contemporary narrative, epistolary, and revelatory conventions. Apocryphal gospels, at least in the early stages of their development, e.g., the Gospel of the Hebrews and the Coptic Gospel of Thomas, existed alongside the canonical texts. The former forms part of the same genre classification as the Synoptic gospels, while the latter would be close in structure to the lost Q-Source employed by Matthew and Luke. As the canon began to take shape through the process whereby some texts grew in popularity and reputation while others were forgotten, more and more attention was lent to the reproduction, expansion, and appropriation of the received texts. In the second stage greater creativity was exercised as older forms and content were incorporated into and fused with new Jesus lore[33] and an even larger variety of oral and literary conventions.

While each text to be examined below requires both literary and content analysis, it will be the latter which claims our maximum attention. The choice of the works to be studied, therefore, and the order in which to review them will be determined by their relation to the life story of Jesus, since it is the portrait of the master which is the focus of our concern. The remainder of this chapter then will be governed by the following schema:

birth	baptism		trial		
childhood	ministry/teaching		death		resurrection
1)	2)	3) 4)	5) 6)		7)

1) The Protevangelium of James
2) The Infancy Gospel of Thomas
3) The Teaching of Addai
4) The (Coptic) Gospel of Thomas
5) The Acts of Pilate (Gospel of Nicodemus)
6) The Questions of Bartholomew
7) The Apocryphon of James

Our study of these works, then, is determined by each document's relationship to the canonical storyline.

THE PROTEVANGELIUM OF JAMES

This infancy gospel, which was very popular in the early church, expands the story of Jesus by dwelling on the years before his birth.[34] In a conscious imitation of the infancy narratives, particularly of Luke, and of passages from the Greek version of the Old Testament, for example, the song of Anna, the author tells the story of Mary's birth and

---

[33]For a convenient summary of lore concerning Jesus' life, appearance, lifestyle, character, and chronology, see W. Bauer, "Jesus' Earthly Appearance and Character," 433-36 in Hennecke and Schneemelcher, *New Testament Apocrypha*.

[34]For an easily accessible English translation and brief introduction to this work see O. Cullmann, "Infancy Gospels," 1:370-88 in Hennecke and Schneemelcher, *New Testament Apocrypha* and R. Cameron, *The Other Gospels: Non-Canonical Gospel Texts* (Philadelphia: Westminster, 1982) 105-21, who reproduces the translation of the former.

youth, then of her relationship with Joseph, and finally in 17:1-20:4 rewrites the birth story of Jesus with considerable modification. This work, which seems to have been written in the late second century by a non-Jewish writer, exhibits tendencies characteristic of this later literature. On the one hand there is reverence for what will become the canonical gospels. Indeed they are the author's principal source. On the other hand the writer displays much freedom in the use and modification of this source. It is clear that the Christian community is evolving from one that depends on oral tradition to one that relies on texts. The Gospels of Luke and Matthew enjoy official status within the church, but not to the extent that storytellers would have felt hindered from modifying and expanding them in their own creations.

There is also a tendency to fill gaps in the story and to explain what later generations considered puzzling or embarassing details in the gospel narratives. For example, to explain the fact that in the gospel tradition James is called the brother of Jesus and that Jesus is said to have brothers and sisters, the author speaks of Joseph's sons (9:2; 17:1, 2; 18:1) and explicitly describes him as a widower before his marriage to Mary (8:3f). Thus the author resolves the problem by making these individuals sons of Joseph by a former marriage. Also related to this issue is the graphic defense of Mary's virginity. Employing the Johannine theme of "touching" (John 20:25), the author crudely offers gynecological proof of Mary's perpetual virginity (19:3-20:1). A final characteristic should be noted, namely, the writer's free use of the biblical tradition and its narratives to build new episodes. Mary's mother Anna is modeled on the Marian discriptions of Luke while Mary's youthful activities are patterned on those of Jesus as found in the gospel narratives. Also characteristic of this literature is the interweaving of folkloric (story of the midwife, 18:1f; see also 5:2) and other mythological and biblical themes (frequent angelic messengers, food from heaven, 8:1, signs from God, 9:1, or the idyllic cave of the birth scene, 18:1-19:2).

What image of Jesus emerges from this composition? We agree with O. Cullman that "the whole work is written for the glorification of Mary"[35] and, therefore, seek the clues for the author's christology in that direction. The key to the writer's perspective is found in the battle cries of fifth-century christological controversy that Mary is "bearer of God" (*theotokos*). The work finds its inspiration in the concept that whoever

[35]"Infancy Gospels," 373.

or whatever comes in contact with the child Jesus must be pure—whether virginal, fed by the angels, or raised either in "a sanctuary in her bed-chamber," 6:1 or in the temple of God, 8:1—must be divinely approved (theme of childlessness, consultation of the priests, testing of Mary and Joseph, 16:1-2, and the role of the Holy Spirit), and must of necessity be affected by the child's presence. This final theme deserves more attention. It is clear that by merely touching the child, the "doubting" Salome is healed (20:3-4) and that the universe is affected by his birth (18:1-2; 19:1-2). In particular, Mary is transformed by her relation to the child. Building on gospel themes and extending these, the author transforms Mary into a temple that must be prepared to receive God's Son. Her parents are righteous people who depend totally on God; her upbringing offers a mixture of otherworldly, ascetic, and heroic elements which prepare her for her role as bearer of the heavenly child; her genealogical and moral worthiness are underscored (e.g., "the priest remembered the child Mary, that she was of the tribe of David and was pure before God," 10:1); and, of course, the themes presented by Luke are reiterated in the new birth narratives.

Finally, we attend to several other factors which focus on Mary's relation to the temple and therefore on the author's special perspective on Jesus. Mary is repeatedly associated with the temple. Not only does the author state that she was presented and reared there (8:2), but stresses her relation to the temple; she was received from the temple by Joseph as a virgin (19:2; see also 13:1, 2; 15:2f); it was the duty of the temple priests (8:2) and of Joseph to see that she remained pure (13:1f and 15:1f); and, lastly, it fell to Mary's lot to spin and weave the cloth for the temple veil (10:1-2). This last theme appears again during the annunciation scene (11:1) and before Mary leaves to visit Elizabeth (12:1). In all three cases the author relates this theme to Mary's role in the coming salvific events. Without explicitly connecting the veil theme to the crucifixion episode when the veil is split in two, the author ends the narrative[36] on the note that the whole story finds its meaning in the child's going to Jerusalem (20:4). Mary's role as mother was that of preparing for the Christ-event.

The author chose the pre-gospel years for many reasons, not the least being popular interest in Mariology and folklore generally. Beyond the telling of an interesting narrative, one perceives an emerging high

---

[36]Cullmann, *ibid.*, 373, suggests that chapters 21-24 would have been a later addition.

christology and, in relation to it, a fascination for hagiography (in this case Mariology), which had far-ranging consequences in later Christian theology, spirituality, and art.

THE INFANCY GOSPEL OF THOMAS

This collection of childhood miracles dates back to the second century in some form and was known to Irenaeus. It recounts a series of miracles performed by Jesus between the ages of five and twelve.[37] The author dwells on what is often referred to as "the hidden years" of Jesus and ends with the temple episode from Luke. The author wishes to present Jesus as a child prodigy and in this way to foreshadow or anticipate the miraculous power displayed in the canonical gospels. Further, there are in these narratives signs of legendary and folkloric motifs, parallels of which can be found in stories about the heroes of the Classical world and the religious figures of eastern religions. The reason for gathering these stories into one collection seems to be twofold. In the first place the author believes that "the first public words and deeds of the hero were thought to be indicative of his status and future career."[38] The Christian's hero was in no way inferior to the great figures of the Greco-Roman world and could compete in the same arena. Secondly, the author relishes telling miracle stories; "the cruder and more startling the miracle, the more the compiler is pleased with it."[39] For this author it is in Jesus' miracles and, to a lesser degree, in his wisdom that his greatness and importance resided.[40]

Our discussion of this short narrative will consider three basic topics. 1) The author's fascination for the miracle story is certainly the dominant feature of this gospel. In fact the whole is introduced as a narrative of "all the works of the childhood of our Lord Jesus Christ and his mighty deeds, which he did when he was born in our land" (1:1). There follows an uninterrupted series of wonders performed by the boy

---

[37]*Ibid.*, 388-401; Cameron, *The Other Gospels*, 122-30.

[38]Cameron, *The Other Gospels*, 123.

[39]Cullmann, "Infancy Gospels," 391.

[40]Cameron, *The Other Gospels*, 123, correctly observes, "these stories adumbrate the tyranny of the miracle tradition"; more generally on miracles in the apocryphal literature and the prevalence of magic in that period, see P.J. Achtemeier, "Jesus and the Disciples as Miracle Workers in the Apocryphal New Testament," 149-86 in E.S. Fiorenza, ed., *Aspects of Religious Propaganda in Judaism and Early Christianity* (South Bend: University of Notre Dame, 1976).

Jesus. In a manner reminiscent of the creation account the child fashions twelve sparrows from soft clay and, in anticipation of the adult Jesus, not only accomplishes this on the Sabbath, but is accused by a Jewish neighbor and reproached by Joseph his father for thus violating the holy day. As if to spite them, Jesus is made to clap his hands and order the sparrows to fly away (2:1-4). A young boy is made to wither (3:2), a careless child is struck dead for having bumped against Jesus' shoulder (4:1), and another, after having fallen from an upper story, is raised from the dead by Jesus that he might defend him against the charge that he pushed the lad down (9:3). In a slightly less exhibitionist fashion Jesus is made to heal a young man who has split the sole of his foot (10:1-2), to raise a dead carpenter (18:1-2) and a little child (17:1-2), in a manner reminiscent of the widow of Nain story (Luke 7:11f). Other miracles reveal a more complex origin; the seed miracle of 12:1-2, for example, depends on the parable tradition; while those concerning the snake bite (16:1-2), the lengthening of a wooden beam (13:1-2), and the broken water jug (11:1-2) also relate to the Jesus tradition. Throughout these miraculous episodes the child Jesus might be described as temperamental, mischievous, vengeful, and uncontrollable. He is a child-wonder in whom divine power operates, usually at everyone's peril (3:3; 4:2; 5:1f; and 14:3). The author tells and the audience hears these miraculous narratives with naive abandon, since each story allows both for the vicarious expression of human emotions and sentiments, no matter how homely or crude, and for the exercise of their faith in the Lord Jesus Christ at the conclusion of each miracle story.

2) Perhaps not as dominant but certainly obvious is the theme of Jesus' wisdom and authority as teacher. Four lengthy passages focus on this issue. The first, most extensive treatment of Jesus' knowledge is introduced in 6:1-8:2 when a teacher named Zacchaeus offers to educate the young child. On two other occasions teachers are again provided for the young child, always with disastrous consequences. Zacchaeus, the first teacher, is humiliated and overcome by the child's Gnostic-like knowledge of the alphabet (7-8); the second teacher is intimidated by Jesus' knowledge and is smitten for having struck the child (14:2); and the third fares no better, though he does recognize that Jesus "is full of great grace and wisdom" and thus obtains the healing of the second teacher (15:3-4).

The fourth passage, conclusion of the gospel, consists of an intricate rewriting of Luke's temple scene (2:41-52). The author copies most of the Lukan text but imposes numerous minor (stylistic) and major changes. The pathos of the passage, as one expects in folklore, is heightened and the focus in this episode, as opposed to the rest of the gospel, is on Mary. In fact, the gospel ends on a Marian note, even to the extent of adding a significant passage (drawn partly from Luke 1) in the mother's praise (19:4). Other changes, however, are significant and invariably reflect the author's christology: Jesus did not simply "stay behind in Jerusalem" but "went back;" nor does he merely "listen and ask questions" but more specifically becomes an expert in the Law and the prophets; and lastly, the author, through the addition of 19:4 along with other modifications underscores Jesus' superior wisdom.

3) The picture of Jesus which emerges from the Infancy Gospel of Thomas is therefore related to two important themes, namely, the miracle-worker and wise-teacher motifs of the earlier gospels. This particular text "lays stress on what it understood to be Jesus' self-awareness, wisdom, divine identity, and destiny."[41] For this author Jesus is a divine being in human clothing. Convinced that Jesus possessed to the fullest the divine power to affect the created world, the author employs and revels in the opportunities which the tradition offers in portraying numerous manifestations or epiphanies of the divine. Most episodes, after presenting some miraculous display of power or show of wisdom, terminate with some christological query, statement, or profession of faith: At the beginning the Jews are amazed at (2:5) or question Jesus' power (3:3) and inquire about his origin (4:1). But as the text progresses, Zacchaeus is heard to say "this child is not earth born ... perhaps he was begotten even before the creation of the world" (7:2) or later "he is something great, a god or an angel or what I should say I do not know" (7:4; see also 7:2; 18:2). In keeping with the gospel tradition, the author presents the characters in the story not only as amazed and as glorifying God for the miracle but also as worshiping Jesus (9:3; 10:2; 18:1; in the second case the crowd proclaims: "truly the spirit of God dwells in this child"). In some instances the author seems to have in mind no more than naive fascination for miracles (8:2; 12:2; 13:2; 16:2; 18:2) or their dubious effects (4:2; 5:1; 14:3; 15:4)—in relation to the former one might note the author's preferred expression: "his every word is an accomplished deed" (4:1; also 5:2; 17:2). For this author, therefore, Jesus is a divine dynamo whose power and wisdom

---

[41]Cameron, *The Other Gospels*, 123.

seek every opportunity to manifest themselves. At the same time, owing to the author's "excessively crude emphasis on the miraculous [and exhibitionist displays of knowledge on Jesus' part], often quite devoid of ethical feeling,"[42] one must classify this author's portrait of Jesus as a caricature, which, though appealing to some, would be offensive and suspicious even to popular taste.

THE TEACHING OF ADDAI

The next work to be examined is a Syriac document, probably composed about 400 in Edessa, a text which is described as the teaching and acts of Addai, the apostle sent to the city of Odessa. The author of this highly "catholic" work used the earlier Abgar legend about the alleged correspondence between Jesus and the Edessan king, Abgar Ukkama. The legend is documented in the Ecclesiastical History of Eusebius (325 at the latest), which states that he took from the archives of the city of Edessa and translated literally the correspondence mentioned earlier as well as a short narrative about the arrival of Taddaeus (Addai) in Edessa. The text under consideration, therefore, is an expansion of the earlier material. The final document consists of the following:

> 1) A narrative introduction to the correspondence: the king sends emissaries to the governor of the Syrian province. There they encounter Jesus and report all they have seen to King Abgar who concludes: "these powers are not of men but of God. For there is none who can restore life to the dead except God alone." He sends a letter to Jesus and receives a response via Hanan the archivist (1-4a)
>
> 2) The mission of Addai: after Jesus' ascension Addai is sent to Edessa and there heals the king, at whose request he recounts to the royal entourage the miraculous events accomplished in the risen Lord's name, especially the finding of the true cross by Protonice, Claudius Caesar's wife and the raising from the dead of her virgin daughter (4a-11a)
>
> 3) Addai's long speech to the assembled city and the subsequent conversions to Christianity (11a-22a)
>
> 4) The establishment of the Edessan church: Addai gathers disciples, builds a church, and establishes a community (22a-23b)
>
> 5) Christian foreign policy: Abgar corresponds with the Assyrian king

[42]Cullmann, "Infancy Gospels," 392.

about the Christian disciple Addai and exchanges letters with Tiberius Caesar concerning the punishment of the Palestinian Jews (23b-25a) 6) Establishment of a hierarchical structure and Addai's long farewell discourse (25a-30b)
7) The death of Addai, succession, and the beginning of persecution (30b-33).[43]

Our discussion focuses on two topics: the reason for the composition of the work and the popular piety reflected in this post-Nicene writing, especially its christology. 1) A casual reading of this lengthy narrative shows that the author from the start is interested in establishing a connection between Jesus and the city of Edessa. The alleged correspondence between the king and Jesus had this precisely as its goal. The king requests that Jesus come to Edessa to heal him. Jesus responds that the Father's will dictates otherwise, but promises after his ascension to send a disciple to heal him and to establish a Christian community there (3b)—this promise is alluded to in the subsequent narrative (4a-b, 5a, 6a and following). Addai is described as Jesus' "true and faithful disciple" (11b, 12a-b), the one who confirms Jesus' promise. The author proceeds to describe in an anachronistic and idyllic fashion the beginnings of the Jesus movement in the region of Edessa. The mass conversions and the succumbing of pagan religion to the Christian movement are reminiscent of the period following Constantine's conversion, especially the idealistic cooperation between religious and civil leaders and the exalted piety of members of the royal entourage (the finding of the true cross by the Caesar's wife, 7b-11a). This work expresses the author's desire to establish an apostolic link for the Edessan church. For though the Abgar legend, plausibly attributed to the time of Kune, the orthodox bishop and founder of the Edessan church (c. 313),[44] had defended such a claim, the author of this narrative endeavored to bolster these claims further by describing, in a manner similar to Luke's Acts, the teachings and deeds of the legendary apostle of Edessa. Thus, the ending of the narrative deserves comment. On the one hand, the final note on Edessa's reversion to paganism demonstrates that the author is not

---

[43]The Eusebian text of the legend is found in W. Bauer, "The Abgar Legend," 1:437-44 in Hennecke and Schneemelcher, *New Testament Apocrypha* and the longer Syriac work in G. Howard, *The Teaching of Addai* (Chico: Scholars, 1981)—the folio numbers are given in the latter.

[44]Bauer, "The Abgar Legend," 1:440.

devoid of historical realism. On the other, the concluding episode stresses the author's concern for apostolic connections and for episcopal continuity with Rome. The story ends with Addai's successor Aggai dying too suddenly to permit the laying on of hands on Palut. The latter must therefore seek priestly ordination from the bishop of Antioch, whose episcopal succession is carefully traced back to "Simon Peter who received [the ordination to the priesthood] from our Lord, and who had been Bishop there in Rome twenty-five years" (32b-33a).

2) The final note on apostolic succession brings us to our second topic, namely, the post-Nicene context of this narrative. The author's theology and ecclesiology clearly reflect centuries of evolution. If the author is speaking of the years following Jesus' ascension, the ministerial and organizational structures are those of the Constantinian era, and the theology and apologetics those of the post-Nicene period (see 19-21). The author speaks of the ordination of priests, or episcopal succession, of scriptural canon, and of a formalized trinitarian theology. This text is a good example of popular and uncritical expression of high christology. While frequently speaking of the three persons of the trinity, the author virtually fuses the Son with God. The writer is able to say "he is the adorable Son and glorious God" (18b) and even that "he is the God of the Jews who crucified him" (19a; see also 18a). Related directly and indirectly to this high, aberrant christology was a growing sense of anti-Judaism which tended to obliterate all things Jewish within the tradition which did not foster Christianity. Also evident in such a popular theology was the fascination for the miracle: those related to Jesus, his disciples, or even relics. The Teaching of Addai was therefore the product of a spirituality whose theology had developed into an all-encompassing christological perspective which was first at odds with and then antagonistic toward both Judaism and Greco-Roman culture (8a). The Jews meet just judgment at the hands of a "Christian" state;[45] Greco-Roman culture, as one sees in narrative sequence, is viable only when it adopts Christianity (Abgar versus his rebellious son, 32). Finally, the story of Jesus serves first the Abgar legend and then the Teaching of Addai with an anchor for their claims of apostolic succes-

---

[45]At King Abgar's instigation, "when [Tiberius] had respite from war he sent and killed some of the rulers of the Jews who were in Palestine. Upon hearing this King Abgar rejoiced greatly over the fact that the Jews had received just punishment" (25a).

sion. The story of Jesus is told once more, to help undergird a later generation's perspective upon the world.

THE (COPTIC) GOSPEL OF THOMAS

At the turn of the century with the discovery of numerous Greek fragments at Oxyrhynchus, Egypt,[46] and then in 1945 with the finding of a Coptic monastery library at Nag Hammadi, also in Egypt, the Gospel of Thomas emerged as more than a vague title known through Patristic references and has almost acquired cult status in the popular mind. The text which has its written roots in the late NT period or the beginning of the second century is a relatively long collection of parabolic, prophetic, and other didactic sayings of Jesus.[47] Some of these have close parallels to Synoptic sayings, while others have few or any contacts with the Jesus tradition. Initially, this text caused surprise since it contained virtually no narrative element. Scholars were quick to point to the lost non-Markan source of Matthew and Luke (Q) as a close parallel to this sayings gospel. The debate, however, persists concerning the text's relationship to the Synoptic gospels and the Jesus tradition generally. One side of the controversy might be stated as follows:

> Could it be that (1) the Coptic Gospel of Thomas represents a tradition of Jesus sayings which is independent of the New Testament Gospels, and (2) this Gospel has some sayings which are older in form than their parallels in the synoptic gospels? Many scholars tend to answer yes to both questions.[48]

[46]J.A. Fitzmyer, "The Oxyrhynchus *Logoi* of Jesus and the Coptic Gospel according to Thomas," 355-433 in *Essays on the Semitic Background of the New Testament* (Missoula: Scholars, 1974).

[47]A variety of translations and editions of this text are available: T.O. Lambdin, "The Gospel of Thomas (II, 2)," 117-30 in J.M. Robinson, ed., *The Nag Hammadi Library* (San Francisco: Harper & Row, 1981); Cameron, *The Other Gospels*, 23-37 (reproduces Lambdin's translation); D.R. Cartlidge and D.L. Dungan, *Documents for the Study of the Gospels* (Philadelphia: Fortress, 1980) 25-35; B.M. Metzger, "The Gospel of Thomas," 517-30 in K. Aland, ed., *Synopsis Quatuor Evangeliorum* (Stuttgart: Württembergische Biblanstalt, 1967); and A. Guillaumont, et al, *The Gospel According to Thomas* (Leiden: Brill, 1959).

[48]Cartlidge and Dungan, *Documents for the Study of the Gospels*, 25; similar conclusions are drawn by Cameron, *The Other Gospels*, 24, and by H. Koester, the mentor of these several scholars, in his introduction to the Lambdin translation in Robinson, *The Nag Hammadi Library*, 117.

The other side insists that the Gospel of Thomas is a Gnostic appropriation of the Synoptic gospels or tradition. Unfortunately too many presume that both questions must be answered in a similar fashion. It is one thing to admit (or deny) that the Gospel of Thomas offers some sayings that are "older in form" than the Synoptics but it is quite another thing to make a case for a sayings tradition "which is independent of the New Testament Gospels." More and more scholars recognize some truth in the first option but not very many are convinced by the second. In fact, the evidence is overwhelmingly against such a possibility. Careful analysis of the data reveals a complex situation. Sayings that are virtually identical with Synoptic texts are juxtaposed with others that have significant editorial differences (with or without Gnostic characteristics) or little resemblance to other forms of the Jesus tradition.

Considering these factors, I conclude that the Gospel of Thomas is the end product of a long evolutionary process. Initially the gospel was a sayings collection similar to the Q-Source though dependent more directly on the Synoptic tradition or texts either as primary or as secondary source. It should be emphasized that even borrowing from the Synoptic gospels does not rule out the concomitant use of oral tradition, a fact which would account for some of the older and less allegorized forms of some of the parables (e.g., the parables of the weeds, Thomas 57; Matt. 13:24-30, of the great supper, Thomas 64; Luke 14:16-24; also Matt. 22:2-10; or of the wicked tenants, Thomas 65; Mark 12:1-9 and parallels). Originally written in Greek (witness the Oxyrhynchus fragments) for a Jewish Christian community (emphasis on James the Just, the Sabbath [12 and 27], and use of early Jesus tradition of a Synoptic type), the text made its way from Asia Minor or Syria and became popular in Egypt where it underwent a substantial Gnostic editing during the late 3rd or early 4th centuries, the approximate date of the extant Coptic manuscript.

It is not our purpose here to attempt an analysis of the stages through which this writing passed, but rather to describe the portrait of Jesus which emerges from the end product, the Gospel of Thomas as it now stands. From the start one is confronted by the themes of Jesus as teacher (sayings material), of secrecy or esoteric knowledge, and of knowledge or interpretation as the source of salvation. Indeed, the work is called "the secret sayings which the living Jesus spoke" (title) and Jesus is made to say: "whoever finds the interpretation of these sayings will not experience death" (1). Jesus and his sayings are made to bear a revelatory or Gnostic message. Jesus promises them otherworldly knowledge (17), knowledge both of the inner kingdom (3) and of the heavenly place(s) (4, 19, 64, etc.). But most particularly he teaches about the disunity of reality and promises knowledge and therefore mastery "over the All" (3). In response to the disciples' query about whether they must be like "suckling infants" to enter the kingdom Jesus says:

> when you make the two one, and when you make the inside like the outside and the outside like the inside, and the above like the below, and when you make the male and the female one and the same, so that the male not be male nor the female female; and when you fashion eyes in place of an eye, and a hand in place of a hand, and a foot in place of a foot, and a likeness in place of a likeness; then will you enter [the kingdom] (22).

Basic to such an outlook, traceable to Platonic, Encratitic, and Gnostic influences, is the claim that reality is dual by nature, particularly the human creature, and that it yearns to be restored to its original wholeness, whether by overcoming plurality (passim), returning to a primordial androgynous state (see 114), or discovering the unity of the self and of the non-material realm (3).

The knowledge which Jesus brings, reveals, or teachers his disciples permits "the sons of men" to see that "for the moment they are intoxicated" (28) and that they must "become passers-by" (42) as they seek to return to or discover their primordial home, the kingdom (49). They are a spark from the heavenly Light, a spark that needs to be recognized (51), purified, and released. Jesus' role in this is that of teacher of the primordial unity who seeks what is lost, concealed, or immered in the lower realm of matter. He comes with and teaches the knowledge (*gnosis*) which will liberate or save. The christological presuppositions of the Gospel of Thomas might, as does J.E. Ménard, be expressed by reference to another ancient story.

> In one of the most beautiful poems of the Syriac literature, the "Song of the Pearl" (Acts of Thomas 108-13), the individual soul is the pearl which has been lost in Egypt, the realm of matter. The coming of the young prince from his Parthian kingdom to look after the pearl and to save it is interpreted as the fall of a universal soul into the world. In the

end the prince saves himself when he discovers the pearl which is part of himself and carries it back to its homeland.[49]

In such an allegory there is a role for the agent of the Christian tradition, Jesus the teacher and merchant-seeker of pearls (76). Such an anthropological framework allows for the use of numerous christological themes and for a liberal Gnosticizing of the Jesus tradition.[50] Eschatology has given way to the present, but unrecognized kingdom (113); Jesus' coming in the end-time has disappeared and instead his role as dispenser of wisdom or secret knowledge to the initiate (13) has gained center stage; and his salvific death has been replaced by that wisdom to which the Gnostic ascribed liberating power. Interestingly, Jesus, who is never called Christ (nor Savior or Lord), is the incarnation of pre-existent Wisdom, come into the world of intoxicated humans, to bring water to the thirsty, light to the blind, in short, salvific knowledge (*gnosis*) to the unwittingly alienated sons of men (28). Finally, the author views the revelations presented in the composition as the words "which the living Jesus spoke" (title), that is, it is suggested that it is the risen Lord who has given believers the sayings of the gospel, sayings whose interpretation gives eternal life (1).

THE ACTS OF PILATE

We begin our discussion of this work with the following description. The Acts of Pilate is

> a somewhat elaborate account of Jesus' trial before Pilate, his crucifixion and burial, reports of the empty tomb, and an alleged discussion of his resurrection by a council of the leaders of the Jews. This document was incorporated into the *Gospel of Nicodemus*, with which it was transmitted in the Middle Ages. The prologue of the *Acts of Pilate* states that it was written in Hebrew by Nicodemus shortly after Jesus' death, and translated into Greek ca. 425 C.E. by one Ananias. In fact, this prologue is almost certainly a secondary

---

[49]"Gospel of Thomas," 904 in *IDBSup*.

[50]In agreement with H.C. Kee, "'Becoming a Child' in the Gospel of Thomas," *JBL* 86 (1963) 307-14 ("the synoptic themes have been placed by the Gospel of Thomas in service of a viewpoint that is anthropologically, eschatologically, and theologically alien to the NT"), 313 and Fitzmyer, "Oxyrhynchus *Logoi*," 416.

addition to a more original work, which undoubtedly was written in Greek.[51]

From this statement the reader gets an immediate sense of the complexity of the literary problems and a fair statement of the scholarly opinion regarding this work. It forms part of the extensive Pilate literature of antiquity and offers clear evidence of having existed independently of the Gospel of Nicodemus to which it is now joined. The prologue was added when the Gospel of Nicodemus was assembled and so one must identify as pure strategy Ananias' claims that he is employing an eyewitness account of Jesus' last days, namely, the Hebrew records of Jesus' secret disciple, who with Joseph of Arimathaea, was so involved in the resurrection stories. The work was composed in Greek and depends on the Johannine and Matthean Gospels.

How and why this document and more generally the Pilate literature came into existence is a debated issue. Earlier it was customary to explain the creation of this material as the Christian response to the active persecution under the emperor Maximin at the beginning of the fourth century, since it is well known from Eusebius (Eccles. History 9:5:1) that the Roman administration attempted to use alleged Acts of Pilate in its anti-Christian strategy. This Christian text then would have been an antidote calculated to counter Roman propaganda. More recently scholars have taken seriously the references in Justin Martyr and Tertullian (mid and late second century) to various elements of this literature. In the case of the former, on two occasions in his First Apology he appeals to Acts of Pontius Pilate to authenticate the prophecies both concerning Jesus' passion and crucifixion (35) and about his many miraculous deeds (48). In the second case we find a report assigned to Pilate which allegedly confirms in detail Jesus' miraculous powers, a fact which leads Tertullian to speak of "Pilate, himself in his secret heart ["deeper self," *conscientia*] already a Christian" (Apology 21:24; see also 5:2). Two centuries later Eusebius cites and discusses at length Tertullian's story concerning Pilate's report (Eccles. History 2:2:1-6), thereby adding greater impetus to the development of

---

[51]Cameron, *The Other Gospels*, 163. See F. Scheidweiler's translation of the Gospel of Nicodemus including the Acts of Pilate in Hennecke and Schneemelcher, *New Testament Apocrypha*, 1:444-84; Cameron, *The Other Gospels*, 163-82, reproduces Scheidweiler's translation of the Acts.

such lore.[52] There is in various strands of the Pilate literature a letter allegedly sent by Pilate to Tiberius (or Claudius). The letter describes Jesus as one who "restored sight to the blind, cleansed lepers, healed paralytics, expelled evil spirits from men, and even raised the dead, and commanded the winds, and walked dry-shod upon the waves of the sea, and did many other miracles, and all the people of the Jews acknowledged him to be the Son of God."[53] The document exonerates Rome at the expense of the Jerusalem authorities. Associated with this letter (called the "Anaphora") is another short document, the "Paradosis" or "Handing Over of Pilate." While it is speculative to insist that these last two documents explain the origin of the Acts of Pilate, it is reasonable to conclude that Pilate literature clustered around a well-known actor in the Jesus story and drew from his role as eyewitness and sympathetic judge much apologetic value.

The story told by the Acts of Pilate, therefore, is a retelling of the central elements of the Jesus story, namely, the death and resurrection. Beginning the story with the trial before Pilate and ending the narrative with resurrection appearances the author employs the role of two potential eyewitnesses to bolster the credibility of the new tale. From the Roman and Jewish sides two sympathetic characters are chosen as the focus of the story, Pilate and Nicodemus. Both act as defenders of Jesus—this is foreshadowed in the canonical gospels. In the first episode, when Jesus is accused of sorcery and therefore casting out demons by the power of Beelzebub, he is defended by Pilate who observes: "this is not to cast out demons by an unclean spirit, but by the god Asclepius" (1:1). The Roman governor delivers, at his first appearance in the narrative, a short speech defending Jesus, a speech modeled on Gamaliel's statement in Acts (5:1). The work takes its structure from the passion narratives of the canonical gospels, from which it borrows freely both episodes and sayings. The work is built around three thematic episodes: the trial before Pilate (1:1-9:5), Jesus' death on the cross (10:1-12:2), and the resurrection (13:1-16:8).

In the first instance the author employs the trial episode to pass in review before Pilate an impressive series of witnesses. Beginning the scene with the accusation discussed above, the author sets the scene by

---

[52]Scheidweiler, "The Gospel of Nicodemus," 444-45. The letter sounds like a digest of Tertullian's text (21:17-18).

[53]*Ibid.*, 477.

having "the Jews" ask Pilate: "we beseech your excellency to place him before your judgment-seat and to try him" (1:2). All except the Jews treat Jesus with reverence (Pilate even commands: "let Jesus be brought with gentleness," 1:2), and witness to his miraculous powers (even the standards of Caesar do him reverence, 1:6). Jesus is defended against the charge of having been "born of fornication" (2:3-5), of claiming to be king and Son of God (3:2; 5:1), and of blasphemy (4:1-3). More important is the repeated accusation (1:1; 2:5; 4:2) that Jesus performed miracles on the Sabbath. The author never denies nor attempts to cast doubt on the fact (see 6:1-7:1), instead, the logic of the story is to focus upon the unreasonableness and even perversity of such an accusation. When discussing the unreasonableness of the Jewish leaders, Pilate can only ask in disbelief: "for a good work do they wish to kill him?" (2:5). Repeatedly Jesus is declared either innocent (8:1, see also 3:1; 4:1, 2, 4; 5:1) or righteous (2:1; 4:1; 9:4, in the last two instances the author copies Matt. 27:24 and in both cases adds the term "righteous" to the Matthean text; see also 12:1) by Pilate and Nicodemus. Faced with the list of miracles, the Jewish leaders blindly reiterate their charges (even to the point of dismissing female witnesses' testimony on strictly legal grounds, 7:1), while the crowds of men and women cry out: "this man is a prophet, and the demons are subject to him"—ironically only the Jewish teachers are not subject to him (8:1).

The second and third sections concerning the death and resurrection again allow the author to expand the themes of righteousness and innocence. For the death scene the author employs the Lukan narrative which offers opportunity for development of these themes: the "good malefactor" declares that Jesus "has done nothing wrong" (10:2), while the centurion proclaims Jesus "righteous" (11:1; see also 12:1). The Lukan narrative also offers the author the opportunity to introduce Joseph of Arimathaea (11:3), who along with Nicodemus, is a central character in the third part of the narrative, as Pilate fades into the background. The final part focuses on the marvelous events that surround the resurrection and displays a list of witnesses either to the actual episode (the guards at the tomb: 13:1-3) or to the risen Jesus (seen by a priest, a teacher, and a Levite, 14:1f and by Joseph of Arimathaea, 15:6). The third section, in a manner similar to part one, functions as a trial with the unwilling Jewish leaders playing the role of judges as they cross-examine the various witnesses to the resurrection (13:2f; 15:5f; 16:5). Clearly the author's purpose is to establish the historicity of the resurrection, of Jesus' unusual death, and of his miracles.

In the popular spirituality represented by this work, christology, which in earlier tradition focused either on Jesus' salvific death or the kerygmatic themes of death and resurrection, has shifted to a historicist apologetics where the characters in the Jesus story become key witnesses who provide authentic reports (prologue) about Jesus' miraculous powers (2:5; 5:1; 12:1) and resurrection. For this author, then, Pilate, Nicodemus, the good thief, the centurion, Jewish teachers, Joseph of Arimathaea, and finally Annas and Caiaphas provide irrefutable proof (16:7) for the accuracy and authenticity of the Christian movement. The work ends[54] with the last mentioned declaring:

> we saw how he received blows and spitting on his face, that the soldiers put a crown of thorns upon him, that he was scourged and condemned by Pilate and then was crucified at the place of a skull; he was given vinegar and gall to drink, and Longinus the soldier pierced his side with a spear. Our honourable father Joseph asked for his body; and, he says, he rose again, and the three teachers declare: "we saw him taken up into heaven." (16:7).

For this author, therefore, Jesus was, as God's Son, the great miracle worker whose activity, past and present, was confirmed by an authenticated resurrection, i.e., by "two or three witnesses" (16:5) as required by Jewish law.

THE QUESTIONS OF BARTHOLOMEW

There is evidence today for two separate works associated with the apostle Bartholomew: the document under consideration and a fragmentary Coptic composition titled "the Book of the Resurrection of Jesus Christ by Bartholomew the Apostle." The work which is here given the title of "Questions of Bartholomew" probably is the same text which Jerome called "the Gospel according to Bartholomew" in the prologue to his Commentary on Matthew. The text is extant in Greek, Latin, and Slavonic and consists of five uneven sections:

i. The descent into Hell: the number of souls saved and lost
ii. The Virgin's account of the Annunciation
iii. The apostles see the bottomless pit

---

[54]*Ibid.*, 469, for a discussion of the manuscript evidence.

    iv.   The devil is summoned and gives an account of his doings

    v.   Questions about the deadly sins. Commission of the apostles to preach. Departure of Christ.[55]

From a quick glance at this description and in light of recent research on apocalyptic literature,[56] one can see that parts 1, 3, and 4 deal with eschatological subjects, while sections 2 and 5 do not. The last section sounds like a later moralistic addition with only a slight relationship to the rest of the document; Mary does not appear in this chapter and there is a distinct trinitarian concern—note, however, the references to Jesus' command to preach, his sending of the Holy Spirit in his place, and the continuation of the question-answer format. The second section focuses upon Mary, who, despite the male-centered, Petrine ecclesial structures of the author's time (2:7; also 4:2-5), is considered the most worthy to address God since she was the one who "contained" the uncontainable, the "highly favoured tabernacle of the Most High," and "the mother of the heavenly king" (2:2, 4, 10, 12, 13). This section too makes use of a question-answer format to introduce both a long prayer and a story by Mary. The former betrays the weakness of popular spirituality wherein theology and christology are conflated (Father and Son tend to become indistinguishable—this, however, is true throughout the document; see 1:3), and the latter shows a liking for the lore favored by the infancy gospel tradition (Mary is fed in the temple by an angel—2:15f). Chapter 2 though different in genre from the rest of the document is the work of the same author.

    The other three sections are rightly described as an apocalypse or series of revelatory scenes. By means of extensive dialogue between the risen Christ and his disciples the author is able to communicate to the audience "the secrets of the heaven(s)" (1:1). Narratively, the author situates the promise of Jesus to reveal these secrets at a time prior to the death and resurrection (1:1-2) and focuses on the risen Lord as an otherworldly messenger or revealer (1:3). The rest of the work consists of questions (usually by Bartholomew) addressed to the risen Christ and his answers to these. The first question of Bartholomew establishes the

[55]M.R. James, *The Apocryphal New Testament* (Oxford: Clarendon, 1955) 166; see also F. Scheidweiler and W. Schneemelcher, "The Gospel of Bartholomew," 1:484-508 in Hennecke and Schneemelcher, *New Testament Aprocrypha.*

[56]See particularly A.Y. Collins, "The Early Christian Apocalypses," 61-121 in Collins, *Apocalypse.*

theme of the document. The apostle, contrary to the Synoptic tradition, claims to have witnessed from a distance Jesus' crucifixion and, while there, to have seen angels worshiping Jesus, to have noted his vanishing from the cross, and to have heard voices or Jesus' voice[57] emanating from the underworld. He then asks: "tell me, Lord, where you went from the cross?" (1:7c). There follows the story about Jesus' "descent into hell" to release Adam and others, a description of the dialogue that occurred between Hades and Beliar (devil) who are troubled at Jesus' (or God's) coming, and the exposition of several eschatological themes: Adam's relation to Christ, the avenging angel, sacrifice in paradise, and the fate and number of souls departing from the world. On another occasion, in the third part of the work, when the disciples ask to see the abyss, Jesus reluctantly allows them to do so , but the author provides no description of the underworld (3:9).[58] After this, following another exchange between Mary and Peter on the question of who will approach Jesus, the lot again falls on Bartholomew who asks Jesus that "the adversary of men" (4:7) be shown to them. Again with reluctance Jesus grants the apostles' request by having Michael call Beliar up from the underworld (12). Bartholomew pursues a dialogue with Beliar. In their conversation the two discuss the identity of Beliar (originally Satanael, 25), the creation of the various angels, the chastisement of souls (in graphic detail, 37f), the cause of the devil's rebellion (refusal to "worship" God's human image, i.e., Adam, 54-55), and Satan's attempts to deceive humanity (58-59). The work ends with the dismissal of Beliar back into the underworld, a prayer by Bartholomew (an addition stressing the virginal conception, the passions, and the trinity), and Jesus' command to reveal the mysteries to the faithful and to keep them from those who do the devil's work.

From this document emerges an image of Jesus as the revealer of the divine mysteries of the underworld. The author's obsession with the fate of departed souls (personal eschatology, 1:28-29) has transformed the story of Jesus into a drama of demonic conflict and conquest, wherein Jesus acts as the spoiler of the demonic, earthly kingdom and thus as the revealer of the secrets needed on the day of judgment (4:68). The theme

---

[57]There is considerable textual variation between the versions of the story.

[58]Tours of the underworld seem to have fascinated both Jews and Christians: see M. Himmelfarb, *Tours of Hell: An Apocalyptic Form in Jewish and Christian Literature* (Philadelphia: University of Pennsylvania, 1983).

of the decent into hell[59] becomes for this author the key to Christ's salvific role as opponent of the demonic forces that beset those who are faithful.

THE APOCRYPHON OF JAMES

The last text to be studied is also taken from the Nag Hammadi codices.[60] It is a Coptic document allegedly written in Hebrew by James recounting a revelation from the risen Lord which he and Peter received. The main part of the work consists of dialogue which, in chapter 9, becomes a monologue. While the work employs sayings, parables, prophecies, and paraenesis of the Jesus tradition to construct a secret revelation (*apocryphon*, 1:10, 30), the whole is couched in an epistolary format:

1:1-2:18	Epistolary introduction and scribal setting
2:19-15:5	Appearance of and dialogue with the Risen Lord
15:6-16:30	Ascension of the Lord, comission, and paraenesis.

The introductory and concluding sections provide narrative context and highlight the revelation given Peter and James.

> In this revelation the seers are exhorted to be filled with the Spirit; to endure persecution; to believe in the cross; to have faith, love, and works (8.11-14); to receive the kingdom of Heaven through knowledge (8.24-27) and to be awake (9.33-35). After James and Peter witness the ascent of the Savior, the other disciples are informed, believe and are sent off to other places.[61]

There is debate concerning several features of this document. It is not clear whether it can or should be classified as Gnostic, since many of the major concerns of fully developed Gnostic systems are lacking in this work. Nonetheless, "the emphasis is upon knowledge, and the use of such typically Gnostic themes as sleep, drunkenness, and sickness, suggest that the tractate would be at home within Christian Gnosti-

---

[59]This motif functions in a rather different way in the other apocryphal texts; see Scheidweiler, "The Gospel of Nicodemus," 470-76.

[60]F.E. Williams, "The Apocryphon of James (I, 2)," 29-36 in Robinson, *The Nag Hammadi Library*.

[61]F.T. Fallon, "The Gnostic Apocalypses," 145 in Collins, *Apocalypse*.

cism."[62] Additionally, its inclusion in the Nag Hammadi Gnostic library points to its acceptance and compatibility with Gnostic thought. Another point of controversy centers on the Apocryphon's relationship to the canonical gospels and Jesus tradition generally. Some argue for use of an independent sayings collection rather than dependence on the gospels. One scholar argues further that this work can "be profitably compared with the Gospel of John which also uses individual sayings to compose Jesus' dialogues in the first half of the gospel as well as his 'farewell discourse' in the second half."[63] The last statement goes a long way in explaining the data, namely, that the author, in a manner analogous to the situation of the fourth evangelist, uses the developing oral tradition and popular lore as well as the Egyptian community's literary heritage (knowledge and use of at least some of the canonical gospels; see 8:5-10) to articulate that community's particular perspective. In dialogue with proto-Gnostic ideas the author has refashioned the sayings of Jesus in terms of "diminution and fullness, persecution and death, prophecy and parables . . . [and has the Savior tell] the apostles that he wishes them to know themselves and to live as sons of God, filled with the kingdom."[64] Lastly, this tractate is dated to a period after the composition and diffusion of the canonical gospels and prior to the third-century flourishing of the major Gnostic systems.

The portrait of Jesus which emerges from a reading of the Apocryphon of James is that of a heavenly Savior that has come down to dwell in receptive human houses (9:2-8), that by his cross has overcome ("carried off my crown") the power of the archons or rulers (8:37-39), has delayed his departure (2:17-21; 7:35-8:4) to reveal the secrets by which one might be saved (1:26-28), and finally one who ascends to the Father to show his followers the way (10:22-29). The author's favorite christological title is that of Savior. While one would expect this title to indicate Christ's salvific death, for this author the cross is clearly related to the theme of persecution (that of Christ and of the believer, 4:31f) and the title Savior focuses on Christ's role as the revealer of saving knowledge (1:25-28; 6:7-10). The risen Jesus becomes the one who communicates secret knowledge to the initiate (his children) that they might be enlightened (16:16) and "be filled with the kingdom" (12:30).

---

[62]D. Mueller, in the "Introduction" to Williams, "The Apocryphon of James," 29.

[63]Cameron, *The Other Gospels*, 56.

[64]Mueller, "Introduction" to Williams, "The Apocryphon of James," 29.

Suggested Readings

Chapter 1: Jesus in the New Testament

G. Bornkamm, *Jesus of Nazareth* (NY: Harper , 1960)

B.D. Chilton, ed., *The Kingdom of God in the Teaching of Jesus* (Philadelphia: Fortress, 1984).

C.H. Dodd, *The Founder of Christianity* (NY: Macmillan, 1970).

J.A. Fitzmyer, *A Christological Catechism: New Testament Answers* (NY: Paulist, 1982).

A.E. Harvey, *Jesus and the Constraints of History* (Philadelphia: Westminster, 1982).

J.H. Hayes, *Son of God to Super Star: Twentieth-Century Interpretations of Jesus* (Nashville: Abingdon, 1976).

M. Hengel, *The Charismatic Leader and His Followers* (NY: Crossroad, 1981).

L.E. Keck, *A Future for the Historical Jesus: The Place of Jesus in Preaching and Theology* (Philadelphia: Fortress, 1981).

E. Rivkin, *What Crucified Jesus? The Political Execution of a Charismatic* (Nashville: Abingdon, 1984).

E.P. Sanders, *Jesus and Judaism* (Philadelphia: Fortress, 1986).

R.H. Stein, *The Method and Message of Jesus' Teaching* (Philadelphia: Westminster, 1978).

G. Vermes, *Jesus the Jew: A Historian's Reading of the Gospels* (NY: Macmillan, 1974).

Chapter 2: Brief Introduction to the New Testament

A. HISTORICAL-CULTURAL

S. Freyne, *The World of the New Testament* (Wilmington: Glazier, 1979).

M. Grant, *From Alexander to Cleopatra: The Hellenistic World* (NY: Scribner's, 1982).

A.R.C. Leaney, *The Jewish and Christian World 200 BC to AD 200* (London: Cambridge University, 1984).

E. Lohse, *The New Testament Environment* (Nashville: Abingdon, 1974).

E.M. Meyers and J.F. Strange, *Archaeology: The Rabbis and Early Christianity* (Nashville: Abingdon, 1981).

C.J. Roetzel, *The World That Shaped the New Testament* (Atlanta: John Knox, 1985).

M.E. Stone, *Scriptures, Sects and Visions: A Profile of Judaism from Ezra to the Jewish Revolts* (Philadelphia: Fortress, 1980).

G. Vermes, *The Dead Sea Scrolls: Qumran in Perspective* (Philadelphia: Fortress, 1981).

B. LITERARY—CRITICAL

R.E. Brown, *The Critical Meaning of the Bible* (NY: Paulist, 1981).

D.J. Harrington, *Interpreting the New Testament: A Practical Guide* (Wilmington: Glazier, 1979).

_____ *The New Testament: A Bibliography* (Wilmington: Glazier, 1985).

H.C. Kee, *Understanding the New Testament* (Englewood Cliffs: Prentice-Hall, 1983).

_____ ed., *The New Testament in Context: Sources and Documents* (Englewood Cliffs: Prentice-Hall, 1984).

T.J. Keegan, *Interpreting the Bible: A Popular Introduction to Biblical Hermeneutics* (NY: Paulist, 1985).

W.G. Kümmel, *Introduction to the New Testament* (Nashville: Abingdon, 1975).

C. Osiek, *What Are They Saying about the Social Setting of the New Testament?* (NY: Paulist, 1984).

R.N. Soulen, *Handbook of Biblical Criticism* (Atlanta: John Knox, 1981).

Chapter 3: Development of the Jesus Tradition

R. Bultmann, *History of the Synoptic Tradition* (NY: Harper & Row, 1963).

M. Dibelius, *From Tradition to Gospel* (NY: Scribner's, 1965).

J.D.G. Dunn, *Christology in the Making: A New Testament Inquiry into the Origins of the Doctrine of the Incarnation* (Philadelphia: Westminster, 1980).

R.A. Edwards, *A Theology of Q: Eschatology, Prophecy, and Wisdom* (Philadelphia: Fortress, 1975).

R.H. Fuller, *The Foundations of New Testament Christology* (NY: Scribner's, 1965).

_____ and P. Perkins, *Who Is This Christ? Gospel Christology and Contemporary Faith* (Philadelphia: Fortress, 1983).

R.G. Hamerton-Kelly, *Pre-Existence, Wisdom, and the Son of Man: A Study of the Idea of Pre-Existence in the New Testament* (NY: Cambridge University, 1973).

I. Havener, *Q: The Sayings of Jesus* (Wilmington: Glazier, 1987).

M. Hengel, *The Son of God: The Origin of Christology and the History of Jewish-Hellenistic Religion* (Philadelphia: Fortress, 1976).

H.C. Kee, *Jesus in History: An Approach to the Study of the Gospels* (NY: Harcourt Brace Jovanovich, 1977).

J.D. Kingsbury, *Jesus Christ in Matthew, Mark, and Luke* (Philadelphia: Fortress, 1981).

W. Kramer, *Christ, Lord, Son of God* (London: SCM, 1966).

B. Lindars, *New Testament Apologetics: The Doctrinal Significance of Old Testament Quotations* (London: SCM, 1961).

J.I.H. McDonald, *Kerygma and Didache: The Articulation and Structure of the Earliest Christian Message* (NY: Cambridge University, 1980).

J.T. Sanders, *The New Testament Christological Hymns: Their Historical Religious Background* (NY: Cambridge University, 1971).

Chapter 4: The Gospel of Mark

P.J. Achtemeier, *Mark* (Philadelphia: Fortress, 1975).

E. Best, *Mark: The Gospel as Story* (Edinburgh: Clark, 1983).

S.P. Kealy, *Mark's Gospel: A History of Its Interpretation* (NY: Paulist, 1982).

H.C. Kee, *Community of the New Age: Studies in Mark's Gospel* (Philadelphia: Westminster, 1977).

_____ "Mark's Gospel in Recent Research," *Int* 32 (1978) 323-68.

W.H. Kelber, *The Oral and the Written Gospel: The Hermeneutics of Speaking and Writing in the Synoptic Tradition, Mark, Paul and Q* (Philadelphia: Fortress, 1983).

J.D. Kingsbury, *The Christology of Mark's Gospel* (Philadelphia: Fortress, 1983).

W. Marxsen, *Mark the Evangelist: Studies on the Redaction History of the Gospel* (Nashville: Abingdon, 1969).

D.E. Nineham, *Saint Mark* (Philadelphia: Westminster, 1977).

D. Rhoads and D. Michie, *Mark as Story: An Introduction to the Narrative of a Gospel* (Philadelphia: Fortress, 1982).

V.K. Robbins, *Jesus the Teacher* (Philadelphia: Fortress, 1984).

E. Schweizer, *The Good News according to Mark* (Atlanta: John Knox, 1977).

A. Stock, *Call to Discipleship: A Literary Study of Mark's Gospel* (Wilmington: Glazier, 1982).

C.H. Talbert, *What Is a Gospel? The Genre of the Canonical Gospels* (Philadelphia: Fortress, 1977).

V. Taylor, *The Gospel according to St. Mark* (NY: Macmillan, 1963).

Chapter 5: The Gospel of Matthew

F.W. Beare, *The Gospel according to Matthew* (San Francisco: Harper & Row, 1981).

G. Bornkamm, G. Barth, H.J. Held, *Tradition and Interpretation in Matthew* (Philadelphia: Westminster, 1963).

J.C. Fenton, *St. Matthew* (Philadelphia: Westminster, 1978).

D.J. Harrington, "Matthean Studies since Joachim Rhode," *HeyJ* 16 (1975) 375-88 and in *Light of All Nations* (Wilmington: Glazier, 1982).

J.D. Kingsbury, *Matthew: Structure, Christology, Kingdom* (Philadelphia: Fortress, 1975).

―――――― *Matthew* (Philadelphia: Fortress, 1977).

J.P. Meier, *The Vision of Matthew: Christ, Church and Morality in the First Gospel* (NY: Paulist, 1979).

―――――― *Matthew* (Wilmington: Glazier, 1980).

E. Schweizer, *The Good News according to Matthew* (Atlanta: John Knox, 1975).

D.P. Senior, *What Are They Saying About Matthew?* (NY: Paulist, 1983).

P.L. Shuler, *A Genre for the Gospels: the Biographical Character of Matthew* (Philadelphia: Fortress, 1982).

G. Stanton, ed., *The Interpretation of Matthew* (Philadelphia: Fortress, 1983).

Chapter 6: The Gospel of Luke and the Acts of the Apostles

H.J. Cadbury, *The Making of Luke-Acts* (London: SPCK, 1961).

R.J. Cassidy and P.J. Scharper, eds, *Political Issues in Luke-Acts* (Maryknoll: Orbis, 1983).

H. Conzelmann, *The Theology of St. Luke* (NY: Harper & Row, 1961).

J. Crowe, *The Acts* (Wilmington: Glazier, 1979).

M. Dibelius, *Studies in the Acts of the Apostles* (London: SCM, 1966).

J. Dupont, *The Salvation of Gentiles: Essays on the Acts of the Apostles* (NY: Paulist, 1979).

J.A. Fitzmyer, *The Gospel according to Luke* (NY: Doubleday, 1981-85).

E. Franklin, *Christ the Lord: A Study in the Purpose and Theology of Luke-Acts* (Philadelphia: Westminster, 1975).

E. Haenchen, *The Acts of the Apostles* (Philadelphia: Westminster, 1971).

J. Jervell, *Luke and the People of God: A New Look at Luke-Acts* (Minneapolis: Augsburg, 1972).

L.E. Keck and J.L. Martyn, eds, *Studies in Luke-Acts* (Philadelphia: Fortress, 1980).

I.H. Marshall, *The Gospel of Luke* (Grand Rapids: Eerdmans, 1978).

_____ *The Acts of the Apostles: An Introduction and Commentary* (Grand Rapids: Eerdmans, 1980).

R.F. O'Toole, *The Unity of Luke's Theology: An Analysis of Luke-Acts* (Wilmington: Glazier, 1984).

E. Richard, "Luke—Writer, Theologian, Historian: Research and Orientation of the 1970's," *BTB* 13 (1983) 3-15.

E. Schweizer, *The Good News according to Luke* (Atlanta: John Knox, 1984).

C.H. Talbert, *Reading Luke: A Literary and Theological Commentary on the Third Gospel* (NY: Crossroad, 1982).

_____ ed., *Perspectives on Luke-Acts* (Danville: Association of Baptist Professors of Religion, 1978).

_____ ed., *Luke-Acts: New Perspectives from the Society of Biblical Literature Seminar* (NY: Crossroad, 1984).

S.G. Wilson, *The Gentiles and the Gentile Mission in Luke-Acts* (NY: Cambridge, 1973).

Chapter 7: The Johannine Writings

C.K. Barrett, *The Gospel according to St. John* (Philadelphia: Westminster, 1978).

R.E. Brown, *The Gospel according to John* (NY: Doubleday, 1966-70).

_____*The Community of the Beloved Disciple: The Life, Loves, and Hates of an Individual Church of New Testament Times* (NY: Paulist, 1979).

_____ *The Epistles of John* (NY: Doubleday, 1982).

R.A. Culpepper, *Anatomy of the Fourth Gospel: A Study in Literary Design* (Philadelphia: Fortress, 1983).

C.H. Dodd, *The Interpretation of the Fourth Gospel* (London: Cambridge University, 1954).

E. Haenchen, *John: A Commentary on the Gospel of John* (Philadelphia: Fortress, 1984).

J.L. Houlden, *A Commentary on the Johannine Epistles* (NY: Harper & Row, 1973).

R. Kysar, *The Fourth Evangelist and His Gospel: An Examination of Contemporary Scholarship* (Minneapolis: Augsburg, 1975).

_____ *John: The Maverick Gospel* (Atlanta: John Knox, 1976).

B. Lindars, *Behind the Fourth Gospel* (London: SPCK, 1971).

_____ *The Gospel of John* (Grand Rapids: Eerdmans, 1981).

F.J. Maloney, *The Johannine Son of Man* (Rome: Libreria Ateneo Salesiano, 1978).

I.H. Marshall, *The Epistles of John* (Grand Rapids: Eerdmans, 1978).

J.L. Martyn, *History and Theology in the Fourth Gospel* (Nashville: Abingdon, 1979).

P. Perkins, *The Johannine Epistles* (Wilmington: Glazier, 1979).

R. Schnackenburg, *The Gospel according to St. John* (NY: Crossroad, 1968-82).

D.M. Smith, *John* (Philadelphia: Fortress, 1976).

Chapter 8: The Letters of Paul

C.K. Barrett, *The First Epistle to the Corinthians* (NY: Harper & Row, 1968).

_____ *The Second Epistle to the Corinthians* (NY: Harper & Row, 1973).

J.C. Beker, *Paul's Apocalyptic Gospel: The Coming Triumph of God* (Philadelphia: Fortress, 1982).

H.D. Betz, *Galatians: A Commentary on Paul's Letter to the Churches in Galatia* (Philadelphia: Fortress, 1979).

G. Bornkamm, *Paul* (NY: Harper & Row, 1969).

R.F. Collins, *Studies on the First Letter to the Thessalonians* (Leuven: Leuven University, 1984).

H. Conzelmann, *1 Corinthians: A Commentary on the First Epistle to the Corinthians* (Philadelphia: Fortress, 1975).

C.E.B. Cranfield, *Romans: A Shorter Commentary* (Grand Rapids: Eerdmans, 1985).

K.P. Donfried, ed., *The Romans Debate: Essays on the Origin and Purpose of the Epistle* (Minneapolis: Augsburg, 1977).

W.G. Doty, *Letters in Primitive Christianity* (Philadephia: Fortress, 1973).

F.T. Fallon, *2 Corinthians* (Wilmington: Glazier, 1980).

J.A. Fitzmyer, *Pauline Theology: A Brief Sketch* (Englewood Cliffs: Prentice-Hall, 1967).

V.P. Furnish, *The Moral Teaching of Paul: Selected Issues* (Nashville: Abingdon, 1979).

_____ *II Corinthians* (NY: Doubleday, 1985).

M.A. Getty, *Philippians and Philemon* (Wilmington: Glazier, 1980).

G.F. Hawthorne, *Philippians* (Waco: Word Books, 1983).

E. Käsemann, *Perspectives on Paul* (Philadelphia: Fortress, 1971).

_____ *Commentary on Romans* (Grand Rapids: Eerdmans, 1980).

L.E. Keck, *Paul and His Letters* (Philadelphia: Fortress, 1979).

E. Lohse, *Colossians and Philemon: A Commentary on the Epistles to the Colossians and to Philemon* (Philadelphia: Fortress, 1971).

G. Lüdemann, *Paul, Apostle to the Gentiles: Studies in Chronology* (Philadelphia: Fortress, 1984).

I.H. Marshall, *1 and 2 Thessalonians* (Grand Rapids: Eerdmans, 1983).

W.A. Meeks, *The First Urban Christians: The Social World of the Apostle Paul* (New Haven: Yale University, 1983).

J. Murphy-O'Connor, *Becoming Human Together: The Pastoral Anthropology of St. Paul* (Wilmington: Glazier, 1982).

_____ *1 Corinthians* (Wilmington: Glazier, 1979).

C. Osiek, *Galatians* (Wilmington: Glazier, 1980).

J. Plevnik, *What Are they Saying About Paul?* (NY: Paulist, 1986).

J.M. Reese, *1 and 2 Thessalonians* (Wilmington: Glazier, 1979).

C.J. Roetzel, *The Letters of Paul: Conversations in Context* (Atlanta: John Knox, 1982).

E.P. Sanders, *Paul and Palestinian Judaism: A Comparison of Patterns of Religion* (Philadelphia: Fortress, 1977).

K. Stendahl, *Paul Among Jews and Gentiles and Other Essays* (Philadelphia: Fortress, 1976).

G. Theissen, *The Social Setting of Pauline Christianity: Essay on Corinth* (Philadelphia: Fortress, 1982).

J.A. Ziesler, *Pauline Christianity* (NY: Oxford University, 1983).

Chapter 9: The Paulinist Letters

C.K. Barrett, "Pauline Controversies in the Post-Pauline Period," *NTS* 20 (1974) 229-45.

M.C. de Boer, "Images of Paul in the Post-Apostolic Period," *CBQ* 42 (1980) 359-80.

M. Dibelius and H. Conzelmann, *The Pastoral Epistles: A Commentary on the Pastoral Epistles* (Philadelphia: Fortress, 1972).

I. Havener, *First Thessalonians, Philippians, Philemon, Second Thessalonians, Colossians, Ephesians* (Collegeville: Liturgical, 1983).

R.J. Karris, *The Pastoral Epistles* (Wilmington: Glazier, 1979).

G. Krodel, ed., *Ephesians, Colossians, 2 Thessalonians, the Pastoral Epistles* (Philadelphia: Fortress, 1978).

E. Lohse, *Colossians and Philemon: A Commentary on the Epistles to the Colossians and to Philemon* (Philadelphia: Fortress, 1971).

C.L. Mitton, *The Epistle to the Ephesians* (Grand Rapids: Eerdmans, 1973).

P.V. Roger, *Colossians* (Wilmington: Glazier, 1980).

J.P. Sampley, *"And the Two Shall Become One Flesh": A Study of Traditions in Ephesians 5:21-33* (London: Cambridge University, 1971).

E. Schweizer, *The Letter to the Colossians: A Commentary* (Minneapolis: Augsburg, 1982).

L. Swain, *Ephesians* (Wilmington: Glazier, 1980).

Chapter 10: The General Letters

D.L. Balch, *Let Wives Be Submissive: The Domestic Code in 1 Peter* (Chico: Scholars, 1981).

R.J. Bauckham, *Jude, 2 Peter* (Waco: Word Books, 1983).

J. Casey, *Hebrews* (Wilmington: Glazier, 1980).

M. Dibelius and H. Greeven, *Epistle of James: A Commentary on the Epistle of James* (Philadelphia: Fortress, 1981).

J.H. Elliott, *A Home for the Homeless: A Sociological Exegesis of 1 Peter: Its Situation and Strategy* (Philadelphia: Fortress, 1981).

D.A. Hagner, *Hebrews* (San Francisco: Harper & Row, 1983).

G. Krodel, ed., *Hebrews, James, 1 and 2 Peter, Jude, Revelation* (Philadelphia: Fortress, 1977).

R. Kugelman, *James & Jude* (Wilmington: Glazier, 1980).

S. Laws, *A Commentary on the Epistle of James* (San Francisco: Harper & Row, 1980).

D. Senior, *1 & 2 Peter* (Wilmington: Glazier, 1980).

C.H. Talbert, ed., *Perspectives on First Peter* (Macon: Mercer University, 1986).

J.W. Thompson, *The Beginnings of Christian Philosophy: The Epistle to the Hebrews* (Washington: Catholic Biblical Association, 1982).

Chapter 11: Christian Apocalyptic Thought and the Book of Revelation

G. Beasley-Murray, *The Book of Revelation* (Grand Rapids: Eerdmans, 1981).

N. Cohn, *The Pursuit of the Milennium* (NY: Oxford University, 1980).

A.Y. Collins, *The Apocalypse* (Wilmington: Glazier, 1979).

_____ *Crisis and Catharsis: The Power of the Apocalypse* (Philadelphia: Westminster, 1984).

J.J. Collins, *Daniel, 1-2 Maccabees with an Excursus on the Apocalyptic Genre* (Wilmington: Glazier, 1981).

_____ *The Apocalyptic Imagination: An Introduction to The Jewish Matrix of Christianity* (NY: Crossroad, 1984).

_____ ed., *Apocalypse: The Morphology of a Genre* (Semeia 14; Missoula: Scholars, 1979).

E.S. Fiorenza, *The Book of Revelation: Justice and Judgment* (Philadelphia: Fortress, 1985).

P.D. Hanson, ed., *Visionaries and Their Apocalypses* (Philadelphia: Fortress, 1983).

J.J. Pilch, *What Are They Saying About the Book of Revelation?* (NY: Paulist, 1978).

D.S. Russell, *Apocalyptic: Ancient and Modern* (Philadelphia: Fortress, 1978).

J.P.M. Sweet, *Revelation* (Philadelphia: Westminster, 1979).

Chapter 12: Early Church Fathers and Great Councils: The Emergence of Classical Christology

W. Bauer, *Orthodoxy and Heresy in Earliest Christianity* (Philadelphia: Fortress, 1971).

H. Chadwick, *Early Christian Thought and the Classical Tradition* (NY: Oxford University, 1966).

C. Cochrane, *Christianity and Classical Culture* (NY: Oxford University, 1940).

J. Daniélou, *The Development of Christian Doctrine Before the Council of Nicaea* (London: Longman, 1964).

R. Deferrari et al, eds., *The Fathers of the Church* (Washington: Catholic University 1946-   ).

J. Dillon, *The Middle Platonists* (Ithaca: Cornell University, 1977).

J. Dwyer, *Son of Man and Son of God: A New Language for Faith* (NY: Paulist, 1983).

W.H.C. Frend, *The Rise of Christianity* (Philadelphia: Fortress, 1984).

M. Goulder, ed., *Incarnation and Myth: the Debate Continued* (Grand Rapids: Eerdmans, 1979).

R. Gregg and D. Groh, *Early Arianism: A View of Salvation* (Philadelphia: Fortress, 1981).

A. Grillmeier, *Christ in Christian Tradition*, vol. 1: *From the Apostolic Age to Chalcedon* (Atlanta: John Knox, 1975).

C. Hefling, Jr., *Why Doctrines?* (Boston: Crowley, 1984).

J. Hick, ed., *The Myth of God Incarnate* (London: SCM, 1977).

W. Jaeger, *The Theology of the Early Greek Philosophers* (NY: Oxford University, 1947).

J.N.D. Kelly, *Early Christian Doctrines*, (NY: Harper & Row, 1978).

G.W. Lampe, "Christian Theology in the Patristic Period," 21-180 in H. Cunliff-Jones, ed., *History of Christian Doctrine* (Philadelphia: Fortress, 1980).

B. Lonergan, *The Way to Nicea: The Dialectical Development of Trinitarian Theology* (Philadelphia: Westminster, 1976).

J. Meyendorff, *Christ in Eastern Christian Thought* (Washington: Corpus, 1969).

R. Norris, *The Christological Controversy* (Philadelphia: Fortress, 1980).

J. Pelikan, *The Christian Tradition*, vol. 1: *The Emergence of the Catholic Tradition (100-600)* (Chicago: University of Chicago, 1971).

G. Prestige, *God in Patristic Thought* (London: SPCK, 1959).

J. Quasten et al, eds, *Ancient Christian Writers* (Westminster: Newman, 1949-   ).

A. Roberts and J. Donaldson, eds., *The Ante-Nicene Fathers* (Grand Rapids: Eerdmans, 1979).

P. Schaff and H. Wace, eds., *The Nicene and Post-Nicene Fathers* (Grand Rapids: Eerdmans, 1979).

R. Sellers, *The Council of Chalcedon* (London: SPCK, 1953).

_____ *Two Ancient Christologies* (London: SPCK, 1954).

F. Young, *From Nicea to Chalcedon: A Guide to the Literature and Its Background* (Philadelphia: Fortress, 1983).

Chapter 13: Images of Jesus in Popular Post-New Testament Literature

W. Bauer, *Orthodoxy and Heresy in Earliest Christianity* (Philadelphia: Fortress, 1971).

S. Benko, *Pagan Rome and the Early Christians* (Bloomington: Indiana University, 1984).

R.E. Brown and J.P. Meier, *Antioch and Rome: New Testament Cradles of Catholic Christianity* (NY: Paulist, 1983).

R. Cameron, *The Other Gospels: Non-Canonical Gospel Texts* (Philadelphia: Westminster, 1982).

W.H.C. Frend, *The Early Church* (Philadelphia: Fortress, 1982).

J.G. Gager, *The Origins of Anti-Semitism: Attitudes toward Judaism in Pagan and Christian Antiquity* (NY: Oxford University, 1983).

E. Hennecke and W. Schneemelcher, eds., *New Testament Apocrypha* (Philadelphia: Westminster, 1963-65).

R. MacMullen, *Christianizing the Roman Empire (A.D. 100-400)* (New Haven: Yale University, 1984).

J.M. Robinson, ed., *The Nag Hammadi Library* (San Francisco: Harper & Row, 1981).

E.P. Sanders, ed., *Jewish and Christian Self-Definition* (Philadelphia: Fortress, 1980-82).

R.L. Wilken, *The Myth of Christian Beginnings* (Notre Dame: University of Notre Dame, 1980).

_____ *The Christians as the Romans Saw Them* (New Haven: Yale University, 1984).

Index